# Ubuntu® Server Administration

### MICHAEL JANG

New York   Chicago   San Francisco
Lisbon   London   Madrid   Mexico City   Milan
New Delhi   San Juan   Seoul   Singapore   Sydney   Toronto

*The McGraw·Hill Companies*

**Cataloging-in-Publication Data is on file with the Library of Congress**

McGraw-Hill books are available at special quantity discounts to use as premiums and sales promotions, or for use in corporate training programs. To contact a special sales representative, please visit the Contact Us page at www.mhprofessional.com.

**Ubuntu® Server Administration**

1234567890   FGR FGR   0198

ISBN    978-0-07-159892-7
MHID   0-07-159892-8

| | | |
|---|---|---|
| **Sponsoring Editor**<br>Jane K. Brownlow | **Technical Editor**<br>Elizabeth Zinkann | **Composition**<br>International Typesetting and Composition |
| **Editorial Supervisor**<br>Janet Walden | **Copy Editor**<br>Lisa Theobald | **Illustration**<br>International Typesetting and Composition |
| **Project Manager**<br>Aparna Shukla,<br>International Typesetting and Composition | **Proofreader**<br>Jean Butterfield | **Art Director, Cover**<br>Jeff Weeks |
| | **Indexer**<br>Claire Splan | |
| **Acquisitions Coordinator**<br>Jennifer Housh | **Production Supervisor**<br>James Kussow | |

*Ubuntu: humanity towards others.*

# ABOUT THE AUTHOR

**Michael Jang** (RHCE, UCP, LPIC-2, LCP, Linux+, MCP) is currently a full-time writer who specializes in operating systems and networks. His experience with computers goes back to the days of jumbled punch cards. He has written other books on Linux certification, including *RHCE Red Hat Certified Engineer Linux Study Guide*, *Ubuntu Certified Professional Study Guide*, *Linux+ Certification Passport*, and *Sair GNU/Linux Installation and Configuration Exam Cram*. His other Linux books include *Linux Annoyances for Geeks*, *Linux Patch Management*, and *Mastering Fedora Core Linux 5*. He has also written or contributed to books on Microsoft operating systems, including *MCSE Guide to Microsoft Windows 98* and *Mastering Windows XP Professional, Second Edition*.

## About the Technical Editor

**Elizabeth Zinkann** is a logical Linux catalyst, a freelance technical editor, and an independent computer consultant. She was a contributing editor and review columnist for *Sys Admin Magazine* for 10 years. Some of her editing projects have included *RHCE Red Hat Certified Engineer Linux Study Guide*, *Linux+ Certification Passport*, *Mastering Fedora Core Linux 5*, *Linux Patch Management*, and *Write Portable Code*. She owns an iBook that thinks it's an "UbuntuBook" and is an avid digital photographer. In a former life, she also programmed communications features, including ISDN, at AT&T Network Systems.

# CONTENTS

# PREFACE

The market for Linux servers has been growing steadily over the past decade. Based on server revenues, in the year 2000, the market for Linux servers was around US $1.5 billion. In 2007, International Data Corporation (IDC) confirmed that the market for Linux servers was US $21 billion. IDC projects that the Linux server market will grow at more than 35 percent per year through 2011. What company would not love that kind of growth?

Despite these numbers, Unix and Microsoft Windows are still the dominant players in server software. At the time of this writing, IDC's quarterly server tracker estimates that these proprietary options each have about one-third of the server market. But as Linux can be downloaded and installed for free, these IDC numbers might understate Linux's real market share.

Linux is everywhere: Amazon runs on Linux. DreamWorks movies are built on Linux. Yahoo! systems run on Linux. The New York Stock Exchange is moving to Linux. And that's just the United States of America.

Linux is popular worldwide with people, companies, and governments that do not want to depend on a specific company for important server requirements. Governments that encourage local development are moving their systems to Linux. And Ubuntu (an African word that roughly translates to "humanity toward others") is becoming the brand name in Linux.

Yes, Microsoft is afraid of Google. But as suggested by Microsoft's chief software architect, the open source movement spearheaded by Linux is "much more potentially disruptive." Even Oracle has joined the movement, repackaging open source code into its own "Unbreakable Linux" distribution.

Linux is not the only open source player on the server. The Apache web server and Samba file server have also become dominant players, as they can be installed on Microsoft and Unix operating systems. The overall server market is growing despite the furious adaptation of virtualization.

With the Hardy Heron (8.04) release of the Ubuntu Server Edition, Canonical is making its push into the server market. It remains to be seen whether Ubuntu can duplicate its success as a desktop operating system. As Canonical has committed to support Ubuntu Server 8.04 for five years, it is stable. This book is written based on the 8.04 release, as well as the June 2008 update, known as 8.04.1.

Ubuntu is now well known for its success as a Linux operating system. As Red Hat has explicitly moved away from supporting the desktop, Ubuntu now has the mind share among Linux experts. Can Ubuntu Server Edition take advantage of its newly found mind share to take the Linux server market from leaders such as Red Hat and Novell/SUSE? Only time will tell.

## Acknowledgments

I personally would like to thank the following people:

**My beautiful wife, Donna**—I love everything about you. I love your eyes, I love your smile, I love your heart. After the sadness we've shared, I'm thankful for every day I have with you. You give me hope, you give me love, you give me happiness. You show incredible patience as I write these books. Marrying you was the best decision I could ever have made. This book is also dedicated to your Randy and my Nancy, who brought us together from the hereafter.

**The Ubuntu community**—With your efforts, Linux is now gaining market share and mind share with the eventual goal of overtaking Microsoft's market share in the server and the desktop operating system environments.

**The technical editor**—Elizabeth Zinkann is a magnificent editor and friend, someone who has taught me much about Linux in the real world, someone who has gently prodded me when my writing goes wrong.

**All the incredibly hard-working folks on the McGraw-Hill team**—Jane Brownlow, Jennifer Housh, Aparna Shukla, James Kussow, Janet Walden, Lisa Theobald, and Jean Butterfield, for their help in creating the book you now hold in your hands.

# INTRODUCTION

This book focuses on the Hardy Heron (8.04) release of Ubuntu Server Edition. When Hardy Heron was released in April 2008, Canonical committed to support through 2013. In this book, I describe the Ubuntu community, as well as the installation process for Ubuntu Server Edition. I describe the innards of the operating system and basic configuration and administration tools. I show you how to install and configure a variety of services for basic operation, including CUPS, NIS, LDAP, DHCP, DNS, Apache, NFS, Samba/CIFS, Postfix, sendmail, vsFTP, and NTP. Finally, I illustrate how you can reconfigure the Linux kernel and set up various types of virtual machine managers.

Chapter 1 describes the Ubuntu community. It is arguably now the most active Linux community, serving the needs of developers, administrators, and newbies with equal fervor. Ubuntu's commitment to regular releases of an operating system that "just works" has broad appeal. With their bug #1, "Microsoft has a Majority Market Share," Ubuntu is demonstrating its commitment to the marketplace.

Chapter 2 includes a step-by-step description of the installation of Ubuntu Server Edition and shows its roots in Debian Linux. The installation is enhanced with the easy selection of servers, none of which are installed unless specifically requested during the installation process.

Chapter 3 details the efforts toward automated installations using the Kickstart system. Administrators will appreciate these efforts that can supplement the ghosting that is now commonly used to create so many server systems.

Chapter 4 describes the boot process with the new Upstart system. It emphasizes the skills needed to get around the problems that seem inevitable in any enterprise—both from the GRUB prompt and using available rescue media.

Chapter 5 specifies the popular ways to configure Linux filesystems—as regular partitions, in RAID arrays, and with logical volumes. The chapter starts with a description of the Linux filesystem hierarchy standard.

Chapter 6 serves as somewhat of a command-line primer for administrators who are more comfortable with GUI tools. It describes an array of commands, shell tools, and a variety of permissions as well as the Linux implementation of access control lists.

Chapter 7 continues with a variety of administrative tools, from the secure shell commands that can help administer remote systems. It continues with a description of the standard and one-time job schedulers cron and at, service scripts in the /etc/init.d directory, and a basic description of logging in Linux.

As Chapter 8 provides a basic description of update management, it starts with a discussion of the fundamental update commands: **dpkg** and **apt-\***. If you administer a substantial number of Ubuntu systems, consider the tools described in this chapter, which can help you create a local repository mirror. It includes a description of Canonical's web-based management tool, Landscape, which can help you remotely administer groups of Ubuntu systems.

Chapter 9 describes the Ubuntu implementation of CUPS as a print server. It includes a discussion of key CUPS configuration files as well as the associated Ubuntu and web-based configuration tools.

Chapter 10 introduces various methods of managing users and groups. It describes the Shadow Password Suite in detail and shows how user resources can be managed with quotas. Administrative authority can be regulated with the sudo system, Pluggable Authentication Modules, and the newly implemented PolicyKit.

Chapter 11 describes the basics of configuring a network on Ubuntu, from the basic configuration of a network interface card to the configuration of an Ubuntu system as a gateway. It also describes basic troubleshooting tools for networks as well as TCP/IP service ports.

Chapter 12 introduces two services that can help you create a central authentication database for a network. The Network Information Service is the traditional service cloned from Unix. The Lightweight Directory Access Protocol appears to be the emerging standard for network authentication.

While many administrators have no need for a graphical environment for their Ubuntu servers, some administrators do prefer the GUI. Chapter 13 describes the basic process for installing the Canonical-supported desktop environments, with focus on the lightest of the desktops, Xfce.

Chapter 14 describes the basic installation and configuration of the most common DNS and DHCP servers on Ubuntu. It includes detail on DNS that describes how it can be configured as a forwarding, caching, secondary master (slave), and primary master server.

Chapter 15 focuses on one of the strengths of Ubuntu Server Edition—its implementation of the LAMP stack. It describes how the components of LAMP (Linux, Apache, MySQL, and PHP) can be configured to set up Ubuntu as a web server with regular and secure virtual hosts.

Chapter 16 describes how you can configure two of the more popular file servers: NFS and Samba. NFS is the traditional file sharing service on Linux and Unix systems. Samba enables communication in a mixed network with Microsoft Windows systems.

Chapter 17 goes into a variety of services. It covers the configuration of two SMTP e-mail services: sendmail and Postfix. It also describes how you can configure the very secure FTP service, as well as a network time protocol (NTP) server.

Chapter 18 discusses various methods for securing data, from regular backups to security systems such as AppArmor, **iptables**-based firewalls, and TCP Wrappers. AppArmor is based on the mandatory access control system developed by Novell for SUSE Linux.

Chapter 19 details the process of Linux kernel management. It describes when and how kernels can be upgraded to one built by Ubuntu. It also describes in detail the configuration and compilation process for a custom kernel.

Finally, Chapter 20 covers various solutions for virtualization. Two virtual machine managers available for Ubuntu are VMware Server and VirtualBox Open Source Edition. The native solution that requires components capable of hardware virtualization is the Kernel-based Virtual Machine (KVM). The chapter closes with a discussion of a different kind of virtual terminal, based on the work of the Linux Terminal Server Project.

While I'd love to go into additional detail on each of the services described in this book, a full description of services such as Apache, Samba, Postfix, DNS, and more would each require book-length works. In fact, I include notes on several excellent books that provide more detail on many of the services described in this book.

# CHAPTER 1

# The Ubuntu Community

Y es, the key part of the operating system popularly known as Linux was first developed by Linus Torvalds. But the kernel developed by Torvalds is just one part of this operating system. Linux has advanced to a leading position in the server environment through the community of developers and users who have shared their contributions. The Ubuntu distribution provides an excellent expression of this community's vision: *Ubuntu* is a word from the Zulu language that roughly translates as *humanity toward others*. Ubuntu has come a long way since its initial release in 2004. It has clearly become the most popular Linux distribution in the community. While it is probably not the current leader in revenue, it is beginning to push its way into the enterprise.

Part of the appeal of Ubuntu is its leadership. As expressed by *Ubuntu's Bug #1*, "Microsoft has a majority market share," Ubuntu's ultimate goal is to topple Microsoft from its perch atop the world of operating systems, and that goal is inspiring the Linux community to get behind Ubuntu.

**NOTE**    The Ubuntu project for Linux distributions is not affiliated with the Ubuntu Project dedicated to helping the children of a province in South Africa.

This book is designed to help less committed Linux users understand the advantages of Ubuntu Server; this chapter starts with a brief history of Linux and Ubuntu and highlights the latest Ubuntu Long Term Support (LTS) release, code named Hardy Heron. It continues with a history of Ubuntu releases, including variants associated with other markets and desktop environments. As Hardy Heron is the latest LTS stable release as of this writing, you'll probably want to install it on the systems you administer. This chapter also provides an overview of the different channels associated with the Ubuntu community, as well as how you can watch and participate in making Ubuntu work for your organization and enterprise.

Some of you will find the content of this chapter helpful in alleviating any doubts of key decision makers. At the least, the information presented here will give you a place to start when encountering nontechnical concerns about the value of Linux. Some might choose to use Ubuntu's commercial support options; others might find cost-effective options in community-based support.

**NOTE**    Do expect changes to what you see in this chapter. The Ubuntu project is constantly evolving and improving.

# A SHORT HISTORY OF UBUNTU AND LINUX

As an operating system, Linux was developed as a clone of Unix; in other words, the original developers built Linux with the same basic functionality. To avoid conflicts with Unix licenses, Linux commands and services were developed independently of Unix programming instructions, also known as the source code. Despite this development process, you can run most of the same operations from the command line on both Unix and Linux.

If you understand the history of Linux development, you can better understand how Linux works as a community effort. The following sections offer an interpretation of the history of Linux development and how these efforts contributed to the work done by the Debian Foundation.

# Background on Unix

Computers were once rare and expensive, available only to large corporations and universities. Administrators used *time-sharing* to allocate resources from each computer to individual users. The time-sharing concept survives today in Linux servers, as they are most commonly configured as multiuser servers.

Unix was developed by the old American Telegraph and Telephone (AT&T) company in the late 1960s and early 1970s. During that time, AT&T was a regulated US telephone monopoly. The regulations associated with the monopoly effectively prohibited AT&T from selling Unix for a profit, but did not prevent AT&T from sharing Unix to gain goodwill. To that end, in 1974, AT&T distributed Unix to the University of California at Berkeley for a nominal fee. The distribution agreement meant that AT&T was not liable for a warranty and did not provide support, other than the academic cooperation that was common at the time between scientists at its Bell Labs subsidiary and various universities.

In many ways, the timing was excellent for Unix. Various universities adapted Unix for use on mainframes, minicomputers, and microcomputers. The Defense Advance Research Project Agency of the US Department of Defense was starting to work on a redundant nationwide communications network that eventually evolved into the Internet. In other words, Unix has been integral in the development of the Internet. As a Unix clone, Linux shares the functional advantages of Unix in cyberspace.

# Linux Is Not Unix

While Linux is not Unix, that's not the whole story. Strictly speaking, Linux is just the kernel, the part of the operating system that enables communication between software and hardware. When Torvalds released the first Linux kernel in 1991, he designed it to work with the software cloned from Unix, as developed by the Free Software Foundation (FSF), also known as the GNU Project. (GNU is a recursive acronym, short for *GNU's Not Unix*. Recursive acronyms are a common jab against conformity in the open source community. For more information, see www.fsf.org.)

Richard Stallman, founder of the GNU Project, and the FSF firmly believe that the Linux operating system is more correctly known as GNU/Linux, as it combines the large number of commands and libraries cloned by the GNU project from Unix, with a Linux kernel.

**NOTE**   Some of you may face questions about a legal action associated with Linux, namely that from The SCO Group, Inc., formerly a developer of the Caldera Linux distribution. The premise behind the lawsuit is that SCO owns the source code to Unix and wants payment because it believes that IBM incorporated Unix code in Linux. Based solely on press reports, SCO has not shown any offending code in Linux. Furthermore, a presiding court declared in August 2007, in a summary judgment, that Novell, the owner of SUSE Linux, is the rightful owner of the Unix source code.

# A Linux Distribution

The Linux that you see, download, and install from CDs/DVDs is more than just a kernel, commands, and libraries. A Linux distribution often includes an X Window System server with a graphical user interface (GUI) desktop environment. Distributions often include substantial applications such as the OpenOffice.org suite and Evolution personal information manager. They also usually offer specialized services, such as Domain Name Services (DNS) based on the Berkeley Internet Name Domain (BIND), web services such as Apache, file sharing services such as the Network File System (NFS), and much more.

The software included with a Linux distribution can be customized. For example, while the Ubuntu Server variant does not include an X Window System server or associated GUI applications, they can be installed as needed. Or Ubuntu user groups in every country could create custom distributions that install the appropriate human languages and dialects by default.

The first distribution released by the Ubuntu project is Ubuntu. This release includes the GNOME desktop environment by default. Officially, other releases from the Ubuntu community are known as *variants*; for example, Kubuntu includes the K Desktop Environment (KDE) by default and is officially listed as a variant on www.kubuntu.org. Kubuntu is called a *derivative* of Linux on Wikipedia and is commonly referred to as a distribution. Each of these references is technically correct: The key point is that all (well, almost all) distribution releases from the Ubuntu community use the same code base.

**NOTE**    GNOME isn't quite another recursive acronym; it's short for the *GNU Network Object Model Environment* and is the backbone behind the GNOME desktop environment. KDE is another variant, sometimes also known as the *KDE Desktop Environment*. There's also Xfce, and even though it's another desktop environment, its developers say that the acronym doesn't stand for anything.

# Linux and Open Source Licenses

Software included in Linux distributions, including Ubuntu, are organized in *packages*, logical bundles of files, libraries, devices, and data required for a specific program. For example, dedicated packages are associated with NFS, passwords, and applications. Every Linux package is usually released under one or more open source licenses. In general, open source software can be copied and used in other open source systems, so long as credit is given to the original author. The source code is included in the open source release, and it can be modified as long as the modified package is also released under the same open source license.

Some developers of software packages are unable or unwilling to release their source code. Some companies such as Microsoft do not adhere to open source principles. These packages are known in the Linux world as *closed source* packages.

**CAUTION**    I am not a lawyer, and am not making any legal analysis of open source licenses. For more information on a wide variety of available open source licenses, see Eric Raymond's Open Source Initiative website at www.opensource.org. Raymond is the author of *The Cathedral and the Bazaar*, which addresses many questions associated with the open source model.

Possibly the most important open source license was developed by the FSF, known as the GNU General Public License (GPL). Two versions of this license are in common use today: GPL version 2 (GPLv2) and GPL version 3 (GPLv3). Both versions purport to follow the principle of the open source "golden rule." In Stallman's words, "I consider that the golden rule requires that if I like a program I must share it with other people who like it" (www.gnu.org/gnu/initial-announcement.html).

**NOTE**   There are a number of controversies associated with the release of GPLv3 in mid-2007. The opinions of the open source community vary. Torvalds declared that the Linux kernel will retain its GPLv2 license. Future releases of some open source software, such as that released by the Samba project, will be licensed under GPLv3.

Open source licenses might not be interchangeable; in fact, people such as Raymond and Stallman get into heated arguments on what is the best open source license. And some open source activists do not favor the approach of Ubuntu, which incorporates a number of closed source packages in default installations.

# The Debian Project and Ubuntu

The Linux distribution that might most closely follow the open source model is Debian GNU/Linux. First released in 1993, it included the software cloned by FSF developrs and the kernel developed by Torvalds. Debian is just about the oldest continuously running Linux distribution, and the Debian Project consists entirely of volunteers. The Debian Social Contract includes the following features, as paraphrased from www.debian .org/social_contract:

▼   Debian GNU/Linux is 100 percent free—in other words, while non-free software is available, it's never required for proper system operation.

■   Packages developed for Debian GNU/Linux are always released under free software licenses.

■   Bug reports are publicly available. (Contrast this approach with those at closed source companies such as Microsoft.)

■   Users come first and are allowed to use non-free packages on Debian GNU/ Linux. Others, including Ubuntu developers, are allowed to create their own distributions based on Debian GNU/Linux and other non-Debian packages.

▲   Packages that do not meet Debian GNU/Linux open source guidelines are grouped into *non-free* and *contrib* repositories.

The Debian GNU/Linux distribution organizes software into *repositories*. As suggested in part by the Debian Social Contract, open source packages can be part of the *main* repository. Other packages released under closed source licenses are considered part of the *contrib* or *non-free* repository.

Debian repositories are further classified by their release status. Packages in the *stable* repository are associated with the current stable release of Debian GNU/Linux.

Packages in the Debian *testing* repository are known in Ubuntu as *developmental packages*. In effect, the testing repository is the beta version of Debian GNU/Linux. Packages in the Debian *unstable* repository are packages in true development.

Each Debian repository can be further subdivided by CPU architecture—and Debian currently covers at least 13 architectures. For more information, see www.debian.org/doc/manuals/repository-howto/repository-howto.

The Debian Project also has a fairly rigorous definition of *free software*. Some Debian developers have been dismayed at the compromises made by Ubuntu developers. Nevertheless, Mark Shuttleworth, the man behind Canonical Ltd., has stated that "every Debian developer is also an Ubuntu developer." Given Debian's adherence to open source licenses and Ubuntu's reliance on the developmental packages of Debian GNU/Linux, that is a true statement, even if it does not please many Debian developers.

On the other hand, Debian releases are relatively infrequent—the last three releases have been made approximately every other year. The slow release cycle has led many Debian users to run the beta version of the distribution. Because Debian relies solely on volunteers and has committed to build and test software to 13 different architectures, infrequent Debian releases are probably inevitable.

Every release of Ubuntu incorporates the latest developmental packages from the Debian GNU/Linux testing repository. New developmental packages from the testing repository are added during each Ubuntu development cycle. This is made possible courtesy of the copyright licenses associated with Linux. Their work has culminated in the Ubuntu release known as Hardy Heron, which will be supported for three years on the desktop and five years on the server.

**NOTE** Canonical sponsors Ubuntu development. This private company was founded by Shuttleworth to promote free software projects. Canonical also provides commercial support.

## Ubuntu Just Works

One reason for the popularity of Ubuntu is that it "just works." That ability is based on a compromise. Packages that do not conform to open source licenses are included in default installations of Ubuntu as needed. For example, the full multimedia features of some laptops are not available without closed source packages, sometimes as provided by the manufacturer. The same is true of some wireless cards. When such hardware is detected, Ubuntu installs the closed source packages *by default*, for optimal operation.

Ubuntu developers organize standard packages into four basic repositories:

▼ **main** Includes packages that conform to open source licenses and are supported by the Ubuntu project.

■ **restricted** Collects closed source packages that are supported by the Ubuntu project.

■ **universe** Includes packages that conform to open source licenses but are not supported by the Ubuntu project.

▲ **multiverse** Incorporates closed source packages that are not supported by the Ubuntu project.

More categories of repositories are available, similar to those previously described for Debian GNU/Linux. Other Ubuntu repositories support security updates, backports, and packages from Ubuntu partners. Chapter 8 provides a detailed discussion of Ubuntu repositories and how you can take advantage of them on your systems.

One more decision by Ubuntu developers that helps them maintain a regular release schedule is their limits on architecture support. Current Ubuntu desktop distributions support only i386 and AMD64–based CPUs. That's a much less daunting task than the 13 architectures associated with Debian GNU/Linux.

## Hardy Heron Highlights

Ubuntu 8.04, code named Hardy Heron and released in April 2008, is the second Ubuntu release for which Canonical and the Ubuntu project provides long term support. Canonical and the Ubuntu project have committed to support the server release through April 2013.

To facilitate this level of support, Hardy Heron is designed as a stable distribution. In many ways, it is a stable version of the previous release, Gutsy Gibbon. Nevertheless, as with all Ubuntu releases, Hardy Heron includes new features, several of which are listed in Table 1-1.

| Feature | Description |
| --- | --- |
| X.org 7.3 | Adds improved hotplug, rendering, and backlight support |
| Kernel 2.6.24 | Incorporates power savings, new wireless drivers, better Kernel-based Virtual Machine (KVM) support, and more |
| PulseAudio | Enables the PulseAudio sound server |
| PolicyKit | Adds a tool for finer grained control of administrative tools; based on Red Hat development work |
| Virtualization | Supports KVM, with libvirt and virt-manager tools originally developed by Red Hat |
| Virtualization client | Incorporates improvements in the JeOS (Just enough Operating System) specification, for virtual clients |
| Firewall | Includes the Uncomplicated Firewall application |
| Third-party repository files | Allows easier incorporation of third-party repositories |
| Microsoft domain support | Incorporates a simplified method for joining Microsoft domains |
| Bootloader | Adds improved Grand Unified Bootloader (GRUB) support to maintain manual edits |
| Graphical installer | Includes fault-tolerant features to Ubiquity, the Ubuntu graphical installer |

**Table 1-1.** Hardy Heron Highlights

# THE UBUNTU RELEASE CONFIGURATION

The Ubuntu project is responsible for a number of releases. Some are focused on specific desktop environments, such as GNOME, KDE, and Xfce. Others are dedicated to certain interests, such as servers, multimedia, and limits on free software. Each Ubuntu distribution is released on a regular six-month cycle.

None of the releases is mutually exclusive; for example, I've installed the GNOME desktop environment on my Kubuntu system, which includes the KDE desktop environment by default. This is the same GNOME desktop environment available for the default Ubuntu release. The Ubuntu project makes this possible by making the same package libraries available for all releases.

This section chronicles the history of Ubuntu releases, the Ubuntu development cycle, commercial support options, and the variety of custom distributions created for desktop and server environments.

## Past Releases

As this book goes to print, the Ubuntu team has just made its ninth release, code named Intrepid Ibex. The developers behind the Ubuntu project try to release new versions of its distribution on a six-month cycle, every April and October. The releases of Ubuntu to this date are described in Table 1-2. As of this printing, the asterisked releases are no longer supported by Canonical or the Ubuntu project.

As shown in Table 1-2, Ubuntu has followed a regular release schedule. A couple of these releases have LTS. Ubuntu missed its intended release date only once: Dapper Drake was originally scheduled for an April 2006 release. Incidentally, the version number is based on the release year and month: for example, Ubuntu Hardy Heron is designated as version 8.04, as it was released in the year 2008, during the *4th* month (April).

| | | |
|---|---|---|
| Warty Warthog* | 4.10 | The first Ubuntu release, October 2004 |
| Hoary Hedgehog* | 5.04 | Released April 2005 |
| Breezy Badger* | 5.10 | Released October 2005 |
| Dapper Drake | 6.06 | First LTS release, June 2006 |
| Edgy Eft* | 6.10 | Released October 2006 |
| Feisty Fawn* | 7.04 | Released April 2007 |
| Gutsy Gibbon | 7.10 | Released October 2007 |
| Hardy Heron | 8.04 | Second LTS release, April 2008 |
| Intrepid Ibex | 8.10 | Released October 2008 |
| Jaunty Jackalope | 9.04 | Project release, April 2009 |

**Table 1-2.**    Ubuntu Releases

Not all variants were included in the release schedule. For example, the first Kubuntu release was made under the Hoary Hedgehog code name in April 2005, and the first Xubuntu release was made under the Dapper Drake code name in June 2006.

Regular releases (other than those designated as LTS) are supported for 18 months.

# The Ubuntu Development Cycle

The Ubuntu team is continuously at work. Timely development depends on a certain sequence of events, including some that are outside of the team's control. Like other Linux distributions, Ubuntu depends on the work of other open source projects, such as GNOME. In fact, the Ubuntu release cycle is designed to incorporate the latest GNOME release.

**NOTE** If you're interested in the latest Linux software, you should follow the Ubuntu development cycle. Even if you're using a LTS release such as Hardy Heron, the backports repository, discussed in Chapter 8, allows you to incorporate the latest features when you're satisfied with their level of development.

Early in the first month of the release cycle, specifications are developed at an "all-hands" summit and finalized by the end of that month. Then the first experimental alpha release is made public. You can choose to monitor and install an alpha release on a test system to preview upcoming features. If you're interested in the day-by-day progress of Ubuntu development, daily builds are often available as downloadable ISO files.

**NOTE** *Alpha* and *beta* are terms associated with developmental software. For most software, the distribution of an alpha release is limited to testers and developers within the company or organization. Beta releases come later and are intended for testing by advanced outside users. For Ubuntu and variants, alpha and beta releases (along with their schedules) are publicly available. In fact, most developmental Ubuntu releases are alpha releases; in general, only one beta release occurs in each cycle. In any case, alpha and beta release software should never be used on production computer systems.

Other major Ubuntu project development milestones include the following:

▼ **Debian import freeze**   Prior to this milestone, new packages are frequently imported from the Debian GNU/Linux unstable (development) repository.

■ **Feature freeze**   At this point, developers stop introducing new features and focus on bug fixes.

■ **User interface freeze**   Changes to the look, feel, and functionality of the GUI and related applications are frozen.

■ **Beta freeze**   After this point, package changes are limited to minimize the risk of package dependency issues.

■ **Beta release**   At this point, real-world testing is encouraged.

■ **Documentation string freeze**   Basic documentation is no longer changed after this time; this occurs concurrently with beta freeze to allow time for translations.

- ■ **Non–language pack translation freeze**   Certain items, especially those related to GUI icons and menus, are translated and input to packages manually.
- ■ **Kernel freeze**   Final date for new kernel updates.
- ■ **Release candidate**   A production quality prerelease.
- ▲ **Final release**

Exceptions can be made at each milestone when the Ubuntu teams think they are justified. Ubuntu delayed its first LTS release (Dapper Drake) by a couple of months, for example, to ensure stability of that release.

Ubuntu development work for LTS releases can vary. For example, the Hardy Heron development plan assumed fewer new features relative to the standard development cycle. Most of the development work for that release was focused on creating a more stable distribution.

## Support Levels

Regular Ubuntu releases are supported for 18 months, and LTS releases are supported for three years on the desktop and five years on the server. Security and feature updates for packages are available as well, as described in Chapter 8.

Commercial support is also available from Canonical for the specified support periods. For more information, see www.ubuntu.com/support/paid. As of this writing, enterprise level support is available on a work day or 24/7 basis, for desktops, servers, and thin clients.

## Desktop Environments

To summarize, the Ubuntu, Kubuntu, and Xubuntu releases are associated with the GNOME, KDE, and Xfce desktop environments, respectively. GNOME is also the default desktop environment for Gobuntu, a variant limited to open source software. It is also the default desktop environment for the education-focused Edubuntu and multimedia-focused Ubuntu Studio releases. These releases are listed in Table 1-3.

Most Ubuntu project distributions and variants include more than just open source software, such as non-free software—drivers for graphics cards for which reliable open source alternatives are not available, for example. These packages are often included because they provide the means by which the distribution can interface with some video cards, wireless devices, and other devices. The exception is Gobuntu, whose developers have made a commitment to limit releases to open source packages.

As most Ubuntu packages are released under the GPL, others allow developers to use the source code to create their own Linux distributions under the GPL—and a number of organizations have done so. At the time of this writing, 20 such Ubuntu-based derivatives, several of which are listed in Table 1-4, have been released. Just as the Debian Foundation has no control over Ubuntu, these distributions are released by companies or organizations other than Canonical or the Ubuntu project.

| Name | Default GUI Desktop | Comments |
|------|---------------------|----------|
| Ubuntu | GNOME | Baseline Ubuntu desktop distribution, available from www.ubuntu.com/getubuntu/download |
| Kubuntu | KDE | Ubuntu desktop distribution with KDE, available from www.kubuntu.org/download.php |
| Xubuntu | Xfce | Ubuntu desktop distribution with the Xfce desktop environment, available from www.xubuntu.org/get |
| Gobuntu | GNOME | Limited to open source software, available from http://cdimage.ubuntu.com/gobuntu/releases/ |

**Table 1-3.**   Ubuntu Distributions Associated with Canonical and the Ubuntu Project

## The Ubuntu Server

Because this book is designed for administrators, the focus is on the Ubuntu Server Edition. Built for security, it has a minimal number of open ports; the default installation specifies only that software considered essential for smooth server operation. It includes a preconfigured option to install a "stack" of packages known as LAMP (Linux, Apache, MySQL, and PHP), which is designed to speed configuration of the Ubuntu Server as a web server.

| Ubuntu Derivative | Comments |
|-------------------|----------|
| Fluxbuntu | Lightweight, uses Fluxbox window manager, uses only free software; http://fluxbuntu.org |
| Freespire | Released by Linspire, formerly known as Lindows, once based on Debian Linux; www.freespire.org |
| gNewSense | Uses only free software, endorsed by the Free Software Foundation; www.gnewsense.org |
| gOS | Developed by Good OS LLC, installed on the Everex Green PC sold by Walmart; www.thinkgos.com |
| Impi Linux | Released by a separate company (also owned by Mark Shuttleworth), subtitled Ubuntu for Africa; www.impi.org.za |
| Linux Mint | Focuses on a more elegant desktop environment, was originally a derivative of Ubuntu; www.linuxmint.com |
| Mythbuntu | Incorporates the MythTV application for digital multimedia; www.mythbuntu.org |

**Table 1-4.**   Ubuntu Derivatives

*NOTE*    LAMP is the acronym for a stack of packages used to host dynamic web servers: Linux is the operating system, Apache is the web server, MySQL is the database server, and PHP is a computer scripting language. (Incidentally, PHP is a recursive acronym for PHP: Hypertext Processor.) The combination of packages selected by Ubuntu for the so-called LAMP stack is arbitrary; some administrators substitute the Perl or Python programming languages in the LAMP stack.

While the default installation for Ubuntu Server does not include a default GUI desktop environment, it does add thin client support using the work of the Linux Terminal Server Project (LTSP). All files and information for remote LTSP terminals are stored on the Ubuntu Server system, which facilitates administration and maintenance.

As Ubuntu Server uses the same repositories used for the other Ubuntu variants, it is possible to install a GUI desktop on Ubuntu Server. (In fact, that's what you'll do in Chapter 13. Xfce is featured in that chapter because it's the most "lightweight" of the three major GUI desktop environments available for the Ubuntu project.)

Ubuntu Server is built and supported for only two CPU architectures: 32-bit x86 and 64-bit AMD64. Support for the UltraSPARC CPU, the Sun Microsystems processor, has been discontinued as of the Hardy Heron release. However, unsupported ports for other architectures are available at http://ports.ubuntu.com.

# PARTICIPATE IN THE UBUNTU COMMUNITY

The Ubuntu project is backed by Canonical and its 200 paid employees. In contrast, Red Hat employs more than 2000 and Microsoft employs more than 80,000 people. For a small company, Canonical targeting Microsoft's market share with its Bug #1 seems like brave talk, until you understand the power of the Ubuntu community.

The community is organized in part through Launchpad, Canonical's platform for hosting open source projects, bug tracking, and more. Bug reports include feature requests and problems that are fixed by the community of developers. Documentation is constantly evolving through the Ubuntu Wiki. The power of the community is harnessed through channels such as mailing lists, IRC (Internet Relay Chat) chat rooms, and message boards.

## Sponsored by Canonical

Canonical's mission statement includes commitments to deliver "the world's best free software platform" and to facilitate "the continued growth and development of the free software community." Through the ShipIt program, described shortly, Canonical mails CDs of the various Ubuntu releases free to anyone who asks for them. (Yes, that does sound like a lot of freebies from a private company.)

Canonical does get revenue from the distributions and derivatives released by the Ubuntu project by selling support for those releases. As noted on www.canonical.com/ services, Canonical sells custom engineering, support, hardware certification, training, and packaging services for Ubuntu project distributions. However, since Canonical is a private company, little is known about its balance sheet. All that is known for sure is that Shuttleworth was the founder of Thawte and sold this digital certificate company in 1999 to VeriSign for more than $500 million. So it is reasonable to assume that Shuttleworth has the means to fund Canonical for some time, if it isn't already profitable.

## Request a "Hard Copy" Release with ShipIt

ShipIt (https://shipit.ubuntu.com) is Ubuntu's free CD distribution and shipping service that allows anyone to request and receive physical copies of the Ubuntu distribution CD by postal mail. The CDs are currently shipped from Europe, so delivery to North America and other continents can take several weeks or more. The ShipIt option is currently available only for Ubuntu, Kubuntu, and Edubuntu variants and Ubuntu server. While Canonical does sell DVDs for a nominal fee, it plans to include DVDs as a ShipIt option in the future.

Of course, ISO files for all Ubuntu releases are available for download, and this is a practical option for anyone with a high-speed Internet connection. ISO files can be used by standard Linux and Microsoft Windows software to burn bootable CDs and DVDs. Virtualization systems such as KVM, Virtualbox, and VMware can read ISO files directly as virtual CD/DVD drives.

Unfortunately, not everyone has a high-speed Internet connection. As of this writing, nearly 50 percent of US Internet users still connect from their home computers via telephone modem. High-speed connections are also less common in some of Ubuntu's target markets, such as South Africa.

**NOTE**  I once tried to download the CD for a different Linux distribution via telephone modem. Not only did it tie up my home telephone line, but after three days, the download was corrupt and unusable.

## The Ubuntu Launchpad

Launchpad is a platform for developing free software. Ironically, it is also a proprietary platform—one of the ways Canonical makes money. Launchpad provides services to people and companies who develop their own Linux distributions based on Ubuntu. There are over 800 Launchpad projects, all of which use the tools described in Table 1-5.

Any user with a valid e-mail address can sign up for a Launchpad account. Launchpad is constantly changing, and as of this writing, a new release is issued every four weeks. The last major release was made at the end of July 2008.

Sign up for a Launchpad account at www.launchpad.net. It'll help you keep up to speed on bug reports and much more. Click the Register link in the upper-right corner of the Launchpad site and follow the instructions to create a display name and password. Be aware that participation is subject to terms of use, as noted at https://help.launchpad .net/Legal.

| Component | Comments |
|---|---|
| Code | Source code management using the Bazaar version control system, intended as an alternative to two other version control systems: CVS (Concurrent Versions System) and Subversion (SVN) |
| Bugs | A bug tracker, also known as Malone |
| Blueprints | A specifications tracker for documenting new software features |
| Translation | A community development tool for human language translation, also known as Rosetta |
| Answers | A community-developed knowledge base |

**Table 1-5.** Launchpad Components

## Bug Reports

The Ubuntu bug tracker is a key part of the Launchpad platform. Formerly known as Bugsy Malone, it is now simply known as Bugs. It goes beyond standard user reports to collect information from the system with the bug. First implemented for Gutsy Gibbon (7.10), Bugs includes a GUI-based tool to assist in bug reporting.

*TIP* Before reporting a bug, use available tools to search for existing bug reports. If you add credible new information to an existing bug report, it's more likely Ubuntu developers will pay attention to the report and address it quickly.

**Searching the Existing Bug List** Before reporting a problem as a bug (or perhaps a feature request), you should check the list of existing bugs in one of two ways. One method is with the **reportbug-ng** command, installed from the package of the same name, which opens a GUI tool. A sample list of current bugs for the samba package is shown in Figure 1-1.

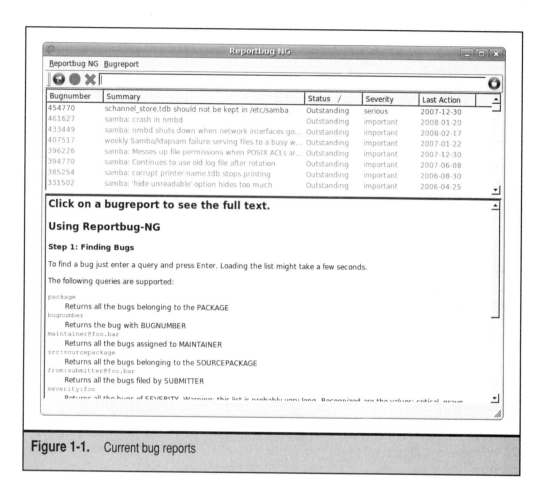

**Figure 1-1.**  Current bug reports

**NOTE**  For more information on installing new packages, see Chapter 8. If you just want to install a specific package, such as reportbug-ng, one method is with the **sudo aptitude reportbug-ng** command.

You can also search bug reports online from a Web browser. Navigate to https://bugs .launchpad.net. Use the Search Bug Reports text box to search for bugs based on the name of the package or other key words. While the bugs created from the reportbug-ng tool and those listed online appear different, they actually depict the same bugs, organized in a different format.

**Reporting a New Bug**    Bug reports can be made in one of two ways. First, you can use the **ubuntu-bug** script to report the bug directly from the operating system. Normally, the script is run against a specific package; for example, the following command files a bug against the samba package:

```
$ ubuntu-bug -p samba
```

The **ubuntu-bug** command requires the GUI and Internet access, as it next opens a browser to access Bugs via Launchpad. (If you don't have the **ubuntu-bug** script, install the apport package.)

A bug report is immediately added to the appropriate bug list. A developer then must take the time to evaluate the bug.

**NOTE**   Please don't report unnecessary bugs. The volunteers who have to read them don't have the time to waste.

Of course, it's also possible to file a bug report online at https://bugs.launchpad.net. If you haven't logged in already, you're prompted to use your Launchpad account. Find and click the Report A Bug option.

You'll see the Launchpad Bug Tracker, where you should be able to specify the distribution, package, and project. After you've entered the appropriate information, Launchpad compares your report to existing bug reports, to help you determine if your problem has already been reported. Note the variety of distributions that can be reported—even Linux distributions associated with other companies, such as Fedora, SUSE, and Mandriva, are also covered.

If you decide that the bug report is unique, you can then describe the problem in more detail and specify whether you believe the problem presents a security issue.

## Blueprints

The development work associated with new Ubuntu releases are chronicled under the Blueprints section of the Launchpad platform. Each blueprint is associated with a problem to be fixed or a feature to be added. Current Ubuntu blueprints are available at https://blueprints.launchpad.net/ubuntu; you can review blueprints for the latest distribution using the first word of the code name. For example, you can review current work and goals on Intrepid Ibex at https://blueprints.launchpad.net/ubuntu/intrepid.

Each blueprint item is given a priority, status, series goal, and other information. The example shown in Figure 1-2 lists the blueprint associated with the KVM for Hardy Heron. The full specification typically links to a wiki page that details what is being or has been done for the blueprint.

# Ubuntu Community Resources

In addition to Launchpad, five categories of community help are associated with the Ubuntu project: mailing lists, IRC-based chat rooms, message boards, community-contributed documentation, and LoCo groups. Be aware that traffic on the main Ubuntu mailing lists can seem overwhelming, but this is a positive indicator of a large and active community. Chat rooms and message boards dedicated to various Ubuntu topics are also available for those who prefer that mode of communication.

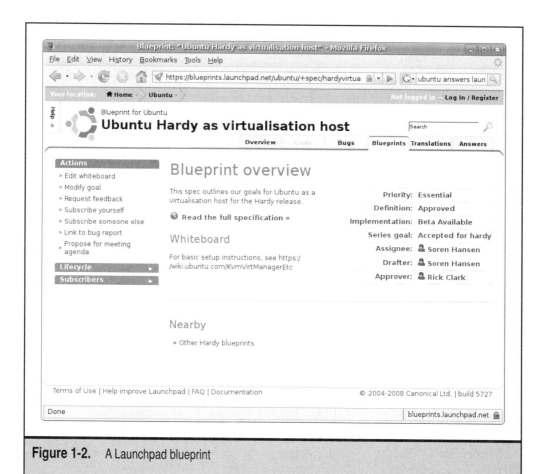

**Figure 1-2.** A Launchpad blueprint

*NOTE*   The broad variety of third-party message boards, blogs, user groups, and other forums that have sprung up to discuss and help others understand and use Ubuntu are not discussed here. This section is limited to Ubuntu-based community resources, as those forums are more likely to be noticed by Ubuntu developers.

## Mailing Lists

To subscribe to an Ubuntu mailing list, navigate to https://lists.ubuntu.com/, select a list, and sign up using your e-mail address. Some Ubuntu mailing lists require moderator approval. As described in Table 1-6, mailing lists are available in 12 different categories. As of this writing, nearly 300 different Ubuntu mailing lists are available.

| Mailing List Category | Comments |
|---|---|
| Ubuntu Announcements | Limited to distribution release announcements |
| Community Support | Basic community support mailing lists, divided by derivative (Ubuntu, Kubuntu, Edubuntu, Ubuntu Studio, Xubuntu, and Launchpad) |
| Announcement Lists | Announcements associated with specific projects |
| Development Lists | Discussion forums for software development in a wide range of areas |
| Quality Assurance and Related Lists | Specialized groups which work with bugs, laptop systems, and more. |
| Bug Lists | Groups for bugs in different categories, including kernels, desktops, and accessibility |
| Package Upload and Automatic Notification Lists | Notification groups for changes, organized primarily by distribution release |
| Ubuntu Worldwide LoCo Teams | Geographic-specific Ubuntu user groups |
| Localization Lists | Groups primarily for translators |
| Other Ubuntu Projects and Groups | Miscellaneous Lists |
| Bazaar-related Lists | Discussions related to Ubuntu and related source code |
| Storm Lists | A single list associated with the Storm Object Relational Mapper (STORM) |

**Table 1-6.** Ubuntu Mailing List Categories

**NOTE** I subscribe to several Ubuntu lists in digest mode, which groups messages together before sending them to my e-mail client. Otherwise, I'd be overwhelmed by the amount of traffic.

## IRC Chat Rooms

One venue that can sometimes connect users who provide real-time help is the IRC-based discussion area. The Ubuntu chat rooms are often crowded with dozens of users and more, so be focused and polite with your questions. If you don't get the response you need, it's possible that the problem is more suited to a mailing list or message board–type discussion.

For more information on using IRC in the Ubuntu community, refer to https://help
.ubuntu.com/community/InternetRelayChat. You'll find more information on current
Linux-based IRC clients and lists of available subject, team, and geographic-based IRC
channels for Ubuntu support (and more).

If you choose to look for help via IRC, the Ubuntu IRC Council has created a code of
conduct, available as part of the Ubuntu Wiki at https://wiki.ubuntu.com/IrcGuidelines.
Follow the code to make a positive impression on those with the knowledge to help you.

## Ubuntu Message Boards

The main Ubuntu message boards of the Ubuntu Forum Community are available
at http://ubuntuforums.org/. They're organized into a number of categories, from
"Absolute Beginner Talk" to functionally based discussions on everything from games
to virtualization.

As of this writing, Launchpad accounts aren't recognized on Ubuntu message boards,
so before posting, you'll have to register separately at http://ubuntuforums.org/register
.php. Whether you use a message board or a mailing list is often a matter of personal
taste—or where you get the best answer.

## Ubuntu Community Documentation

Members of the Ubuntu community can and do contribute to many pages at http://help
.ubuntu.com/community. Pages in this area can be modified, wiki-style, by users with a
Launchpad account. Just be aware that the quality of this documentation is subject to the
same positives and negatives associated with any Wikipedia documentation on technical
subjects.

## Ubuntu LoCo Teams

It's remarkable that a distribution originally based out of South Africa can have such a
worldwide impact. Ubuntu recognizes the importance of local community (LoCo) support,
volunteers who understand the language and local conditions, who in the words of the
Ubuntu LoCo Teams Wiki (https://wiki.ubuntu.com/LoCoTeams), "help groups of
Ubuntu fans and enthusiasts work together in regional teams to help advocate, promote,
translate, develop and otherwise improve Ubuntu."

LoCo teams are available in a substantial number of countries and in most US states.
The web page at https://wiki.ubuntu.com/LoCoTeamList displays currently approved
LoCo teams, mailing lists, IRC channels, message boards (forums), and websites. Some
have declared that they also provide local support.

# Launchpad Answers

Launchpad Answers is intended to provide another community support network. While
the main focus is the distributions and derivatives released by the Ubuntu project,
Launchpad Answers also provides a forum for other projects such as HP Linux Imaging
and Printing (HPLIP).

To access the Launchpad Answers page, navigate to https://answers.launchpad.net/. It includes a text box where you can enter key words associated with related questions and allows you to browse the list of active questions.

> **NOTE**   If you have experience with Ubuntu, I encourage you to take some time to answer some of the questions presented through this forum (as well as the other community forums). It can add to the positive karma so valued in the Linux community. A few enterprising gurus who have provided many consistent and excellent answers have reportedly been hired by Canonical.

## The Ubuntu Wiki

Strictly speaking, the Ubuntu Wiki is another community resource. However, many Ubuntu wikis are maintained by key developers, which provides credibility to the documentation found on these web pages.

The main Ubuntu Team Wiki page at http://wiki.ubuntu.com is one way development and documentation is organized. The current version of this wiki illustrates how resources and teams are organized, lists community councils and boards, cites current Ubuntu events, and notes a list of releases.

If you're interested in future directions for Ubuntu Server, read the roadmap of the Ubuntu Server Team. It lists tasks by triaged bugs, packages to be updated, systems that require testing, services to be documented, and perhaps, most important, development work in progress. The current roadmap is available at https://wiki.ubuntu.com/ServerTeam/Roadmap.

> **NOTE**   Anyone with a Launchpad account has permission to edit much of the Ubuntu Wiki. Just be aware that any edits you make will be associated with your account (and perhaps IP address), so poor or malicious edits can be tracked back to you.

## Ubuntu News and Security Notices

Ubuntu has its own news site with the latest information on Ubuntu developments. Known as The Fridge, the weekly newsletter provides "news, grassroots marketing, advocacy, team collaboration, and great original content." Available at http://fridge.ubuntu.com, the community news site details release announcements, conference events, hot new features, project reports, and other information.

Closely related to The Fridge are Ubuntu Security Notices (USNs). As an administrator, you may want to monitor this site (www.ubuntu.com/usn) for the latest security notices. Linux administrators don't always automatically install updates, even those listed as security issues. Updates can break custom solutions to hardware issues, specialty database systems, and more. After reading a USN, you may conclude that the issue does not apply to your systems. You can also subscribe to the RSS (Really Simple Syndication) feed for both the Fridge and USN websites. It provides headlines associated with each new item.

# SUMMARY

This chapter provided a brief history of Unix and discussed how it evolved through the work of the FSF and the Debian Project into Ubuntu. It emphasized the importance of open source licenses, especially the GPL, and included some basic definitions. Canonical is the commercial backer of the Ubuntu project, which releases distributions or variants including Ubuntu, Kubuntu, Ubuntu Server Edition, and others. The chapter highlighted features associated with the Hardy Heron release.

The chapter continued with a history of Ubuntu releases and described key milestones in the Ubuntu development cycle. Commercial and community support is available for basic releases for 18 months and available for five years on the LTS Ubuntu Server Edition releases.

The chapter described the success associated with the Ubuntu community, including Launchpad features such as Bugsy Malone, Blueprints, and Answers. Also important to Ubuntu's success are the community support provided by mailing lists, IRC channels, message boards, and the Ubuntu Wiki.

# CHAPTER 2

# Installing Ubuntu Server

I n this chapter, you'll learn how to install Ubuntu Server Edition from the CD and set up the same installation over a network. One way the Ubuntu Server Edition is different is that it does not have a graphical installation option or LiveCD boot method. As described in this chapter, server installation is based on the use of Expert Mode to help you learn more about the installation process.

The Ubuntu installation program is based on and closely related to the program used for Debian Linux. This chapter does not cover the more popular installations of the Ubuntu desktop releases; however, the desktop installation process in Text Mode is similar to the one demonstrated here.

This chapter starts with a description of how to download or otherwise acquire Ubuntu media, followed by a step-by-step Ubuntu Server Edition installation process. You'll see how to set up TFTP (Trivial File Transfer Protocol) and DHCP (Dynamic Host Configuration Protocol) services to configure a network installation, which takes advantage of the Preboot Execution Environment (PXE) capabilities of modern BIOSs (Basic Input/ Output Systems) and network cards.

Be aware that as Ubuntu releases evolve, these steps can change, but, historically, the changes have been small between releases. The steps described in this chapter were tested on a virtual machine with 256MB and 10GB of hard drive space. If you have more RAM and less hard drive space, you'll need to allocate space appropriately. Fortunately, this amount of RAM and hard drive space is simple to configure on an appropriate virtual machine such as VMware Server, Virtualbox Open Source Edition, or the Linux native Kernel-based Virtual Machine (KVM).

***CAUTION*** The steps described in this chapter will delete data. Use a test/nonproduction system such as a virtual machine if you intend to follow along in this chapter.

# ACQUIRE THE MEDIA

Users with a high-speed Internet connection may choose to download the installation media for Ubuntu Server Edition. This section describes a basic method for downloading the ISO file and burning it to appropriate CD/DVD media. If you do not have the requisite high-speed Internet connection or media burning tools, other options are available. Ubuntu Server Edition is available for a nominal fee from several third parties as well as the ShipIt program described in Chapter 1.

If you want more than just the Ubuntu Server Edition, the DVD supports both desktop and server installations. The DVD can be downloaded or purchased from many of the same sources as the Ubuntu Server Edition CD.

## Download the ISO File Online

Many Linux administrators download the installation program for the latest version of several Linux distributions, including Ubuntu Server Edition. These downloads correspond to the contents of the appropriate CD or DVD. In this context, an ISO file is a standard format for downloads that can be recorded to appropriate media. Downloadable ISO files are typically quite large and correspond to the size of the CD/DVD media.

**NOTE** In the context of CD/DVD downloads, an ISO file is short for an ISO image file, associated with the ISO 9660 filesystem standard. ISO is an acronym for the International Organization for Standardization, and ISO 9660 is its standard for such files.

To download Ubuntu Server Edition from the Ubuntu website or an authorized mirror site take the following steps:

1.  Navigate to the Get Ubuntu website at www.ubuntu.com/getubuntu/download.

2.  As of this writing, the options show Ubuntu 8.04 LTS – Supported to 2013 and Ubuntu 8.10 – Supported to 2011. These options correspond to the Hardy Heron and Intrepid Ibex releases, respectively.

3.  Under What Type Of Computer Do You Have?, select an architecture. The options also specify the associated CPUs.

4.  Under the "Choose a location near you" option, click the Please Choose A Location drop-down box. Scroll to a server mirror location geographically close to you. There are locations available on six continents.

5.  Click the Start Download link. The Ubuntu website should take you to another page, with a message suggesting that the download will begin shortly. The URL for that page is a long one that starts with www.ubuntu.com/getubuntu/downloading.

6.  When the download is ready, accept the option to save the noted ISO file to disk.

If the download fails for some reason, the second Ubuntu website page noted in step 5 should include a download URL for the ISO file and server. For example, it lists the following site for Ubuntu downloads at the main Linux kernel servers: http://mirrors .us.kernel.org/ubuntu-releases/.

The second Ubuntu download site noted also include links for help and suggestions to help if you encounter trouble during or before the download. Two of the suggestions are relevant to this section:

▼ *Try choosing a different download location.* Depending on traffic and the connection from the target mirror, the geographically closest location might not be the fastest option.

▲ *Try waiting for just a little while.* Many download servers have limits on the number of connections.

Incidentally, these tips also apply when selecting a mirror for package updates, as discussed in Chapter 8.

Be aware that downloads of large files sometimes don't work. A power surge, a mistake on a router, or even a running microwave oven too close to a wireless network can interrupt and even corrupt a downloaded large file. Every downloaded ISO file can be verified with an MD5 message digest. For example, to find the MD5 message digest of the Hardy Heron Ubuntu Server Edition, 32-bit CPU ISO file, run the following command:

```
$ md5sum ubuntu-8.04.1-server-i386.iso
```

The output can be verified against the MD5 hash listed at https://help.ubuntu.com/community/UbuntuHashes. The MD5 hash is often also available in the same server directories as the ISO files.

## Download the ISO File from the Command Line

The advantage of downloading a large ISO file with certain commands is that such commands can handle interruptions in the download process. Specifically, the **wget** and **curl** commands can restart a download from the point of an interruption. If these commands don't already exist on a local Ubuntu system, they can be installed from packages of the same name using the following command:

```
$ sudo apt-get install wget curl
```

These commands can then be used to download any file, based on a known URL. For example, if to download the first Ubuntu Server Edition LTS release (6.06), Dapper Drake, from the Kernel.org server, navigate to http://mirrors.kernel.org/ubuntu-releases/6.06/.

Alternatively, in the Firefox web browser, right-click the desired link, and then click Copy Link Location from the pop-up menu that appears. Then activate a GUI-based command line interface and start the command with **wget -c** and a single quote:

```
$ wget -c '
```

Then press CTRL-INSERT to add the copied link to the command, and end the command with a second single quote, which leads to a result similar to that shown in Figure 2-1.

```
michael@ubuntuserver:~$ wget -c 'http://mirrors.kernel.org/ubuntu-releases/6.06/
ubuntu-6.06.2-server-amd64.iso'
--11:40:49--  http://mirrors.kernel.org/ubuntu-releases/6.06/ubuntu-6.06.2-serve
r-amd64.iso
           => 'ubuntu-6.06.2-server-amd64.iso'
Resolving mirrors.kernel.org... 204.152.191.39, 204.152.191.7
Connecting to mirrors.kernel.org|204.152.191.39|:80... connected.
HTTP request sent, awaiting response... 200 OK
Length: 451,426,304 (431M) [application/x-iso9660-image]

 4% [>                                    ] 19,205,949    563.35K/s    ETA 12:47
```

**Figure 2-1.**   Download an Ubuntu ISO with **wget**

If an interruption occurs, repeat the command; the download continues from the point of the interruption. If you want to test this feature, press CTRL-C and run the same command again. If you're familiar with the history feature of the command line, all you need to do to repeat the same command is press the UP ARROW key once to replay the previous command. If you would rather use the **curl** command, start the download with the following command:

```
$ curl -C - -O '
```

Then repeat the same process described for the **wget** command. Don't forget to end the command with a second single quote.

**NOTE**  While writing this book, I worked with Ubuntu Server during its development process. The Ubuntu developers make a daily build available from http://cdimage.ubuntu.com/ubuntu-server/daily/current/. Of course, you should almost never use such a download on a production system.

## Downloading the ISO File Cooperatively

Many Ubuntu mirror sites support the use of peer-to-peer (P2P) file sharing, using BitTorrent- and Jigdo-based P2P tools. If you see files like these,

```
ubuntu-8.04-server-i386.iso.torrent
ubuntu-8.04-server-i386.iso.jigdo
```

you can use the contents of these files to download Ubuntu ISO files using the afore-mentioned P2P tools. For more information, see www.bittorrent.com and www.debian.org/CD/jigdo-cd/.

**NOTE**  Some high-speed Internet service providers (ISPs) reportedly block or otherwise regulate the TCP/IP ports associated with P2P file sharing. That might prevent downloads using the P2P applications described in this section.

## Write the ISO File to Disc

Many excellent tools are available for writing ISO files to CD/DVD media. Some Linux distributions use the **cdrecord** command; Ubuntu uses the **cdrdao** command. Excellent GUI front ends to these commands are available through the Nautilus file browser and the K3b writer. Microsoft based CD/DVD write applications can burn ISO files to CD/DVD media equally well.

**NOTE**  As the variations are large, and GUI options are common, I do not detail these options here. For more information, see https://help.ubuntu.com/community/BurningIsoHowto, which provides detailed instructions for burning to appropriate media in Microsoft Windows, Mac OS X, Ubuntu, Kubuntu, and Xubuntu Linux.

It's often not necessary to burn the ISO file to CD/DVD media, based on the options described in the following sections.

## Mount the ISO File on a Virtual Machine

If you're testing Ubuntu Server Edition, you can connect the ISO file directly to a virtual machine. For this book, I installed Hardy Heron in a number of different configurations on VMware Server Edition. While VMware Server is freely available from www.vmware .com/download/server/, the source code is not included and therefore is not associated with an open source license.

For more information on downloading and installing VMware server, see Chapter 20.

For the purpose of this chapter, I assume you have some virtualization system installed. For those virtualization systems described in Chapter 20, there is some way to mount the ISO image directly, as if it were a physical CD/DVD. Once configured, the virtual machine automatically boots the noted ISO file as if it were a CD inserted in the appropriate drive. For the purpose of this chapter, Figure 2-2 specifies one example of how an ISO image is configured as a CD on VMware 1.0.x server.

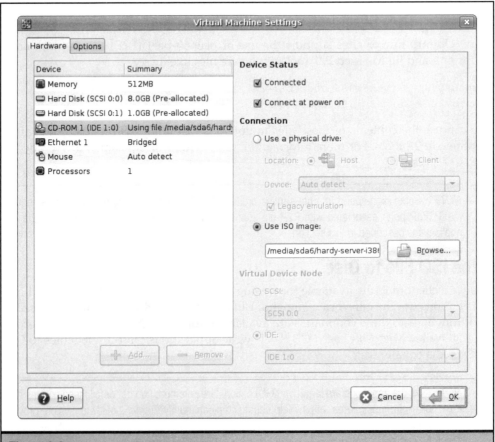

**Figure 2-2.**    Using an ISO Image in VMware Server

The native option for virtual machines on Ubuntu distributions and variants is KVM.

## Mount the ISO File

Another way to use a downloaded ISO file is to mount it. You don't have to burn the ISO file to CD/DVD media and then insert the media into a drive. For example, if you've downloaded the Hardy Heron DVD, it might be in a file such as ubuntu-8.04-dvd-i386 .iso, which can be mounted with the following command:

```
$ sudo mount -o loop -t iso9660 ubuntu-8.04-dvd-i386.iso /mnt
```

The **sudo** in this command supports administrative privileges. The **mount** command in this line mounts the noted ISO file on the /mnt directory. The **-o loop** switch uses the loop device, which is necessary when mounting from a file. The **-t iso9660** specifies the ISO standard for files described earlier. As the **mount** command automatically detects the file type being mounted, the **-t iso9660** switch is not even required.

Once the ISO file is mounted, it can be shared as any other directory can be shared from a Linux server. In fact, in the "Network Installations" section later in this chapter, you'll learn how this command can be used to help set up a network installation of Ubuntu Server Edition.

## Alternatives to Downloads

Of course, if you don't have a high-speed connection, you might prefer to acquire the actual Ubuntu Server Edition CD. It is also available from the ShipIt site described in Chapter 1.

Ubuntu Server Edition CDs can also be purchased for a nominal fee from third parties such as Amazon or CheapBytes (www.cheapbytes.com). It's also available in packs of 20 (handy for Linux user groups) from the Canonical store at https://shop .canonical.com.

Remember, you can also install Ubuntu Server Edition from the DVD available from the aforementioned sources.

## INSTALL FROM THE CD

Now that you have the CD, it's time to install it on your system—well, almost. Before installing Ubuntu Server Edition, a couple of basic decisions are required. While this book assumes readers will prefer to install the latest LTS release, that won't always be true. And users who want to install Ubuntu Server Edition in a production environment will want to make sure that it works with the hardware available to them.

*NOTE*    Especially if you're installing Ubuntu for the first time, I strongly recommend that you use a test environment such as a VMware, Virtualbox, or KVM as described in Chapter 20. Alternatively, you could use a test computer on a system with a new hard drive—or at least with hard drives where the data is not important. You'll learn how to delete partitions and more in this chapter, which means that any data on existing drives will be lost. As you follow along with this chapter, you'll try out a number of options that might or might not work for you.

## Stability or Features

The choice of Ubuntu Server Edition releases boils down to whether you want a stable release or the latest features. As noted in Chapter 1, the LTS Ubuntu Server Edition release is supported for five years. Stability is required to make this level of support feasible. That means Ubuntu developers can't incorporate every desirable new feature. If you choose a LTS release, chances are good that you won't get new kernel-related features (other than security updates) until you upgrade to the next regular or LTS release.

Regular releases of Ubuntu Server Edition are supported for 18 months, The choice you make depends on the requirements of your organization.

## Hardware Configuration

Be careful when purchasing a new computer to use with Linux. Although Linux has come a long way, and you should have little problem installing it on most modern PCs, you shouldn't assume Linux will install or run flawlessly on *any* PC, especially if the PC is a state-of-the-art computer (although many, perhaps most, manufacturers seem determined to maintain good relationships with the Linux community). Laptops especially are often designed with proprietary configurations that work with Linux only after some reverse-engineering. Perhaps the best way to test a laptop is with a LiveCD. If a retailer wants your business, they'll let you boot Ubuntu on their computers.

Linux runs very well on lower-end computers. This is one of Linux's strong points over other operating systems, especially Microsoft Windows Vista. The Ubuntu installer can even run fine on 32MB of RAM, although more is always better, especially if you want to run any graphical applications. And the latest versions of Linux do have limits: modern distributions, including Ubuntu, don't run on anything less than a Pentium-class system.

For most hardware, the question is not one of compatibility, as the great majority of hardware is already compatible in some fashion, especially with Ubuntu. The question is one of licensing. Drivers included with the Linux kernel, whether they're embedded or loaded as modules, are open source drivers. But Ubuntu includes restricted drivers, which are proprietary drivers for which source code is not publicly available. Security updates for these drivers depend on the hardware manufacturer.

# Linux Hardware Documentation

Many resources are available to help you select the best hardware for Linux. Thousands of Linux gurus who *might* be willing to help are available online via mailing lists, IRC rooms, and message boards. They document their experiences on wikis and blogs. Perhaps the most authoritative source for hardware is still the Linux Documentation Project (LDP), a global effort to produce reliable documentation for all aspects of the Linux operating system, including hardware compatibility.

## Linux Hardware Compatibility HOWTO

The Linux Hardware Compatibility HOWTO is a document listing most of the hardware components supported by Linux. It's updated frequently with the latest in newly supported hardware. To read this document, search for the Hardware-HOWTO at www.tldp.org. Where appropriate, this HOWTO includes links to existing individual hardware projects, such as the Linux USB project at www.linux-usb.org.

## Ubuntu Hardware Compatibility Lists

The Ubuntu project is building the infrastructure associated with a fully supported distribution. The hardware compatibility lists (HCLs) associated with Ubuntu are far from complete and currently rely on community input and support. As of this writing, two of the most promising sites for an Ubuntu HCLs are http://ubuntuhcl.org and https://wiki .ubuntu.com/HardwareSupport. While both sites use Ubuntu logos, they appear to be run by users and rely on reports from people like yourself.

# The Ubuntu Server Installation Screen

Before we start the installation process, you should have an Ubuntu Server Edition CD available and know how to boot from the CD on your system. Insert the CD (or Ubuntu DVD) into the appropriate drive. Alternatively, use a virtual machine such as VMware Server, Virtualbox, or KVM as discussed in Chapter 20. Press a key (other than a function key or ENTER) within 30 seconds of loading the software to follow along with this section. You'll see a screen similar to that shown in Figure 2-3, with subtle differences if you're booting from the Ubuntu DVD (and I do not detail every one those differences in this chapter).

Two sets of options are available from the menu that appears from the Ubuntu Server Edition CD. Direct options are available in the middle of the screen, starting with Install Ubuntu Server. And function keys are briefly labeled at the bottom of the screen.

## Installation CD Boot Options

There are several options available in the middle of the installation CD boot screen. From the Ubuntu Server CD, the first option starts the Ubuntu Server Edition installation process. Alternatively, from the Ubuntu DVD, select Install Ubuntu In Text Mode, and then press F4 once. From the pop-up menu that appears, select Install Ubuntu Server.

**Figure 2-3.** The Ubuntu Server installation boot screen

**Install Ubuntu Server**   The Install Ubuntu Server option starts the installation process in Standard mode. You'll learn how to install in Expert mode shortly. On older releases, this was shown as the Install From Hard Disk option.

**Check CD for Defects**   The Check CD For Defects option does not install anything on your system; it loads a minimal amount of software required to check the integrity of the CD or DVD. It does take a few minutes; if successful, it displays the following message in a blue screen:

```
The CD-ROM integrity test was successful. The CD-ROM is valid
```

If you see an error message, you could try the check again. But in most cases, you'll have to try different media—or even download the associated ISO file again. Errors based on this option normally indicate corruption either in the ISO file or CD/DVD media.

**Rescue A Broken System**   Many administrators don't use the Rescue A Broken System option, as booting the LiveCD starts a fully functional copy of Ubuntu, without mounting any partitions on local hard drives. For more information on rescuing a system in this mode and from a LiveCD, see Chapter 4.

**Test Memory**   The Test Memory option runs a local memtest86 program to check the status of current RAM. This program can take an hour or more to complete. Some version of this program is also available from many modern BIOS menus.

**Boot From First Hard Disk**   If you already have an operating system installed on the first local hard disk, this option bypasses the Ubuntu Server Edition installation program and searches for whatever program currently resides in that hard disk's master boot record (MBR).

## Installation CD Function Keys

I describe the several function keys shown at the bottom of the Ubuntu boot screen in Table 2-1. Here's a hint: To review the command options associated with the menu choices just described, press the F6 key, *once*. Command line boot options appear.

| Function Key | Description |
| --- | --- |
| F1 | Opens a menu of help screens, with options associated with F1 through F10. |
| F2 | Accesses available installation languages; installation proceeds with that language by default. Almost 60 human languages are available for Ubuntu. |
| F3 | Allows selection of a keyboard keymap, mostly associated with country-specific keyboards. |
| F4 | Starting with the Hardy Heron release of Ubuntu Server, only Normal installation mode is available. |
| F5 | Provides accessibility options for specialized situations such as Braille terminals and on-screen keyboards. |
| F6 | Opens a command line screen that lists options for the installation. The administrator can add or remove options as desired. If pressed twice, allows you to set Normal, Expert, no Advanced Configuration and Power Interface (ACPI), no Advanced Programmable Interrupt Controller (APIC), enable the BIOS Enhanced Disk Driver (EDD), or configure a "free-software only" installation. |
| ESC | An undocumented option that accesses the **boot:** prompt. See the installation options described in the next section for available options. |

**Table 2-1.**   Ubuntu Boot CD Function Key Options

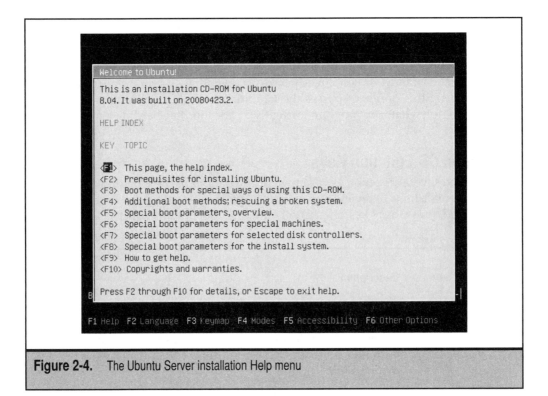

**Figure 2-4.**   The Ubuntu Server installation Help menu

As noted in Table 2-1, the F1 key opens a submenu of help screens, also accessible via function key, as shown in Figure 2-4. Don't confuse these function key *help* options in Table 2-2 with the function key options described in Table 2-1.

# INSTALL UBUNTU SERVER, STEP BY STEP

Finally, you get to see how Ubuntu Server Edition is installed, step by step, in Expert mode. I assume you know how to boot from the CD on your system. The same steps are required if you've set up an ISO file as a CD/DVD on a virtual machine.

1. When you boot from the Ubuntu Server CD, you'll see a list of languages obscuring the screen. Select a language and press ENTER.

2. Once you see the menu shown in Figure 2-3, press F6 twice. In the pop-up menu that appears, highlight Expert Mode and press ENTER. An X should appear next to the Expert Mode option.

3. Press the ESC key to return to the main CD menu.

4. Press ENTER to start the installation process.

5. The installer menu that appears in Figure 2-5 illustrates the basic steps associated with the Ubuntu installation process. What happens in each of these menu options is described in the dedicated sections that follow.

If you're installing from the Ubuntu DVD, press TAB to highlight Go Back and press ENTER to get to the menu shown in Figure 2-5. Be aware that you'll have to run this same step again and again to return to the First Ubuntu Server Installer Main Menu. Other steps described in this chapter will vary if you're installing from the Ubuntu DVD. As installation would proceed in regular (not Expert) mode, you'd miss several options.

The following sections are based on installation options from the Main Menu shown in Figure 2-5, and the Expert mode Main Menu that follows after the Load Installer Components From CD subsection in Figure 2-6.

| Function Key | Description |
|---|---|
| F1 | Returns to the help index |
| F2 | Lists basic prerequisites: 32MB of RAM is required to use the installer. More is necessary even in most text-mode installations, but those requirements would go beyond the installer. Also lists a requirement for at least 2GB for a desktop or 400MB for a minimal server installation. |
| F3 | Describes different boot methods, associated with the **boot:** prompt accessible earlier with the ESC key. |
| F4 | Notes the rescue mode, available by typing **rescue** at the **boot:** prompt. |
| F5 | Provides an overview of other boot parameters that you might include in the installation process. |
| F6 | Suggests basic hardware boot parameters. |
| F7 | Suggests boot parameters associated with SCSI drives. |
| F8 | Includes more suggested hardware-related boot parameters. |
| F9 | Lists generic help suggestions at www.ubuntu.com. |
| F10 | Lists the basic Ubuntu copyrights and warranties. |

**Table 2-2.**    Ubuntu Boot CD Help Options

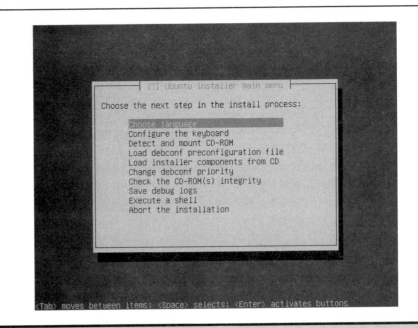

**Figure 2-5.** The Ubuntu Server Installer Main Menu

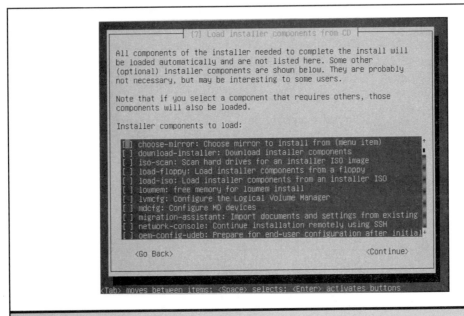

**Figure 2-6.** Additional installer components

## Installation Consoles

There are four consoles available during the Ubuntu text mode installation process: The first console (ALT-F1) is the blue screen you normally see. Two provide command line consoles (ALT-F2 and ALT-F3); and the other lists system messages (ALT-F4).

| Console | Key Combination | Description |
|---|---|---|
| 1 | ALT-F1 | Installation messages |
| 2 | ALT-F2 | Command line access (ash shell) |
| 3 | ALT-F3 | Command line access (ash shell) |
| 4 | ALT-F4 | System messages |

To access a command line console, press ALT-F2 or ALT-F3. The first time you enter one of these consoles, you'll see the following message:

```
Please press Enter to activate this console.
```

After ENTER is pressed, you're taken to a command line screen, where most bash shell commands can be used to help monitor the progress of the installation. If something goes wrong, the shell can facilitate modification of key configuration files. (For example, during one installation, a DNS server went down, and I was able to replace its entry in /etc/resolv.conf to keep the installation going.)

System messages in the fourth virtual console are available when you press ALT-F4. They can help diagnose problems during the installation process. When you're ready to return to the actual installation, press ALT-F1.

The menu screens are all low-resolution blue screens. None of the options are clickable; to navigate between options, you can use the TAB and arrow keys. Selections can be made with the ENTER key and sometimes the SPACEBAR.

# Choose a Language

Select the Choose Language option from the Main Menu shown in Figure 2-5, and then take the following steps:

1. Select a language for the installation process, which will also be used for the default language for the installed system. Other languages can be added after installation is complete. For the purpose of this chapter, select English and press ENTER to continue.

2. Based on the language, you might see choices of different countries; for example, the English language is associated with nations from Australia to Zimbabwe. If you're not located in one of these countries, select Other at the bottom of the list. The country you select determines options such as the dictionary, keyboard, and time zone. Make a selection and press ENTER to continue.

3. Select a Locale, which specifies parameters such as fonts and other symbols. Unless you have good reason for doing otherwise, accept the default and press ENTER to continue.

4. Choose additional locales as desired; this loads appropriate language packages. Make a selection as needed (I did not choose any additional locales). Press TAB to highlight the Continue option and press ENTER to continue.

When these steps are successful, you're returned to the Ubuntu installer Main Menu.

## Configure the Keyboard

Select the Configure The Keyboard option from the Main Menu shown in Figure 2-5. The following steps are based on a standard US keyboard. Other keyboards might lead to different steps:

1. Select a keyboard from available models; approximately 100 are available. Click Enter to continue.

2. You can have the Ubuntu Installer detect your keyboard layout. If you choose to do so, you'll be asked to type in one of several characters. For the purpose of this chapter, I select no. If you select yes, you'll be taken through several options before reaching step 3.

3. Select the national Origin of the keyboard, and press ENTER to continue.

4. If more than one keyboard layout is associated with the selected national origin, you'll be allowed to select from associated layouts. Make a selection and press ENTER to continue.

5. Some keyboards support special keys such as ALTGR key, which activates access to a third option on a key. Make a selection (I select No AltGr Key) and press ENTER to continue.

6. Some keyboards support key combinations, which are activated by a compose key or key combination. Make a selection (I select No Compose Key) and press ENTER to continue.

7. Select an encoding for the command line console; unless you know what you're doing, the default is usually best. Make a selection (I select UTF-8) and press ENTER to continue.

8. Select an appropriate font for the console. Again, unless you have a specific reason for doing otherwise, the default is usually best. Make a selection (I select Latin1 and Latin5) and press ENTER to continue.

9. Select from available console fonts. Options are explained on the screen; the default is usually best. Make a selection (I select VGA) and press ENTER to continue.

10. Select from available font sizes. Make a selection (I selected the largest available size) and press ENTER to continue.

11. Configure a list of virtual consoles. By default, the /dev/tty[1-6] option is entered, which configures six virtual consoles, accessible with the ALT-F1 through ALT-F6 key combinations. Up to twelve virtual command line consoles can be configured. Make any changes if desired, and press ENTER to continue.

When these steps are successful, you're returned to the Main Menu.

## Detect and Mount the CD-ROM

Select the Detect And Mount The CD-ROM option from the Main Menu. It should detect any available CD/DVD drive and provide options as needed for modules to load. At that point, take the following steps:

1. Accept any options for loadable modules, as they are normally required for full functionality. Press ENTER to continue.

2. You'll see the option, Start PC Card Services? If the CD/DVD drive is connected via a PC card or a PCMCIA (Personal Computer Memory Card International Association) interface, select Yes. Make a selection and press ENTER.

3. You'll see a line where you can enter PCMCIA memory resource addresses. Any entries are included in the /etc/pcmcia/config.opts configuration file. Make any specialized memory resource entries (I do not enter anything, as suggested) and press ENTER to continue.

4. Tune access parameters to the CD/DVD drive as desired. Options entered here are associated with the **hdparm** command. Make any desired entries (I do not enter anything) and press ENTER to continue.

5. After a few moments, you should see a message associated with successful detection of the CD/DVD drive. Read the note, and press ENTER to continue.

When these steps are successful, you're returned to the Main Menu.

## Load the Debconf Preconfiguration File

Select the Load The Debconf Preconfiguration File option from the Main Menu. It installs the default Preseed configuration file and then returns to the Main Menu.

## Load Installer Components from the CD

Select the Load Installer Components From The CD option from the Main Menu. It opens a menu with additional installer components—all but four are as shown in Figure 2-6.

These components are described in Table 2-3. For the purposes of this chapter, I selected the asterisked components to customize the mirror, download the latest version of the installer, and configure logical volumes, RAID devices, and remote access during the installation process.

Be warned that the selections you make can change the installation options you see. Make desired selections using the arrow keys and SPACEBAR. Press TAB to highlight the Continue option, and press ENTER to continue.

| Installer Component | Description |
|---|---|
| choose-mirror* | Supports custom selection of a custom repository mirror |
| download-installer* | Allows downloads of Ubuntu installer components |
| iso-scan | Scans for an installer ISO image on the local hard drive |
| load-floppy | Accesses a local floppy drive for installer components |
| load-iso | Accesses a local ISO image for installer components |
| lowmem | Frees memory; suitable for systems with less than 256MB of RAM |
| lvmcfg* | Supports configuration of logical volumes during the installation process |
| mdcfg* | Supports configuration of RAID volumes during the installation process |
| migration-assistant | Allows import of settings from existing systems |
| network-console* | Supports remote access of the installation process |
| oem-config-udeb | Incorporates tools for manufacturer customization |
| open-iscsi-udeb | Supports configuration of iSCSI devices |
| openssh-client-udeb* | Adds the secure shell client; related to network console |
| ppp-udeb | Supports access by telephone modem; in some cases required for direct access via digital subscriber line (DSL) |
| rescue-mode | Diverts the installation to mount specified partitions with rescue tools |

**Table 2-3.**  Ubuntu Installer Additional Components

*NOTE*  The iSCSI standard is associated with storage access networks (SAN). The iSCSI acronym stands for an initiator client, which sends Small Computer Systems Interface (SCSI) commands over a network.

The installer continues by adding the desired components from Ubuntu's debian-installer repository, which is not normally available after installation is complete. Once complete, you'll see a new larger menu, as shown in Figure 2-7.

## Detect Network Hardware

Select the Detect Network Hardware option from the expanded Ubuntu Installer Main Menu shown in Figure 2-7. In many cases, it'll detect configured network hardware automatically, without any additional steps. However, if you did not activate PC Card services during the CD-ROM detection process, you'll be prompted with the following steps:

1. If the network card is a PCMCIA or PC Card, accept the option to Start PC Card Services; otherwise select No and press ENTER to continue.

2. If you selected Yes (or even if you selected No) to Start PC Card Services, you get a chance to enter PCMCIA Resource Range Options, which specify memory addresses. Normally, no special memory addresses are needed; if entered, they're included in the /etc/pcmcia/config.opts configuration file. Make any desired entries and press ENTER to continue.

When these steps are successful (and the network card is installed), you're returned to the expanded Ubuntu Installer Main Menu.

## Configure the Network

Select the Configure The Network option from the expanded Installer Main Menu shown in Figure 2-7. It should allow you to configure dynamic or static networking. If there's more than one network card on the local system, you're prompted to choose. After selecting the noted option (and if needed, the network card), take the following steps:

1. Select whether to configure the local network card using a DHCP (Dynamic Host Configuration Protocol) server. I select No for illustration purposes; if you select Yes, skip to step 7. Highlight the desired selection using the TAB key, and press ENTER to continue.

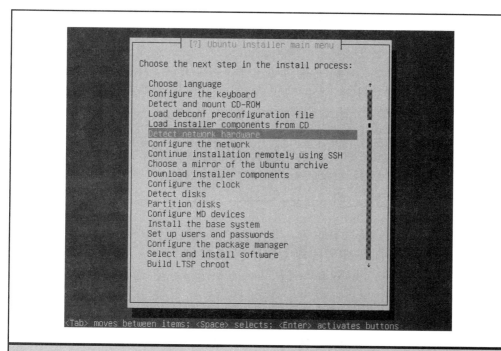

**Figure 2-7.**   Expanded Ubuntu Installer menu

2. Enter an IPv4 address. IPv6 addresses are not yet enabled for the Ubuntu installation program. I enter an IPv4 address consistent with my private IP address network. Press TAB to highlight Continue, and press ENTER to continue.

3. Enter an appropriate network mask. A default network mask is normally suggested by the installer program, depending on the IPv4 address entered in step 2. Make any needed changes and press ENTER to continue.

4. Enter an appropriate gateway IP address. A default gateway address is normally suggested by the installer program, depending on the IPv4 address entered in step 2. The gateway address should be the address that supports routing to an external network such as the Internet. Make any needed changes and press ENTER to continue.

5. Enter an appropriate name server IP address. A default name server address is normally suggested by the installer program, depending on the IPv4 address entered in step 2.

   The name server address should correspond to the system(s) with a Domain Name Services (DNS) server. I normally enter two IP addresses for two DNS servers, separated by a space. The DNS servers you choose can correspond to those on your local network or, if so allowed, those provided by your ISP. Make any needed changes and press ENTER to continue.

6. You'll now see the settings entered in steps 2 through 5. If those settings are correct, select Yes; otherwise select No to repeat steps 2 through 5. Make the desired choice and press ENTER to continue.

7. Enter a hostname for the local system. The default is ubuntu; make a change if needed to make this hostname unique on your network, and press ENTER to continue.

8. Enter a domain name for the local system. If you're working on a private network, you could use one of the domain names reserved for documentation—example .com, example.net, or example.org. Type in the desired domain name (none is required) and press ENTER to continue.

When these steps are successful, you're returned to the expanded Ubuntu Installer Main Menu.

## Continue Installation Remotely Using SSH

You don't have to select the Continue Installation Remotely Using SSH option from the expanded Main Menu. If you do (and I do so to demonstrate the capability), it should allow you to continue the installation process from another client on your local network. One of the problems with SSH-based installation is that it becomes more difficult to access to the console and system-related messages. If a break in the network connection occurs, you might even need to restart the installation.

After selecting the noted option, take the following steps:

1. Enter a password for remote access, and press ENTER to continue. This becomes the password entered from a remote system.

2. Enter the same password and press ENTER for verification.

3. Note the instructions similar to those shown in Figure 2-8.

4. Move to a remote system if desired.

5. Log into the system being installed, using the IP address assigned or entered in the previous section. For example, if the IP address is 192.168.0.102, the command from the remote client would be

   ```
   $ ssh installer@192.168.0.102
   ```

6. You'll see a message associated with the "key fingerprint," which should correspond to the same setting shown in your version of Figure 2-8. Assuming the key fingerprint entries match, type **yes** and press ENTER to continue.

7. Enter the password created in steps 1 and 2, and press ENTER to continue.

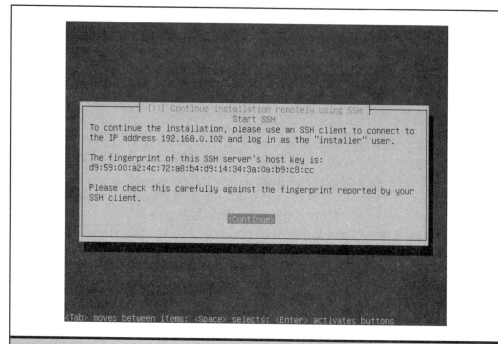

**Figure 2-8.**    Instructions to continue the installation remotely

8. Review the three network console options: Start Installer, Start Installer (Expert Mode), and Start Shell. While I proceed with the Start Installer (Expert Mode) option, keep this menu in mind. If you need to access the installation shell, you can open up a second console and repeat step 5 to create another connection to the remote installation screen. Select one of the Start Installer options and press ENTER to continue.

When these steps are successful, you're returned to the expanded Main Menu. But there's one difference—the option to Continue Installation Remotely Using SSH is no longer part of the menu.

## Choose a Mirror of the Ubuntu Archive

Select the Choose A Mirror Of The Ubuntu Archive option from the expanded Main Menu. It should allow you to set up a connection to the mirror of your choice. Before you continue, review the list of available mirrors at https://wiki.ubuntu.com/Mirrors. Generally, a mirror geographically close to you is best, but the wiki does not include other relevant information such as the connection speed between the mirror and the Internet. (For my own system, since I'm geographically close to the kernel.org mirrors, and they're pretty fast, I often select http://mirrors.kernel.org/ubuntu/.)

**NOTE** The standard mirror associated with each nation might not be best for everyone in that country; for example, when I tried to trace the route to the supposedly US-based Ubuntu mirror (us.archive.ubuntu.com), it connected me to a mirror in the UK. For more information on selecting a repository, see Chapter 8.

After selecting the noted option, take the following steps:

1. Select a protocol for file downloads; the Ubuntu installer supports access to mirrors via HTTP or FTP. Make a selection and press ENTER to continue.

2. A default mirror is associated with each country on the list. However, if you have a custom mirror, scroll to the top of the list and select Enter Information Manually. Make your choice and press ENTER to continue.

3. If you've selected Enter Information Manually, specify the URL to the hostname of the desired Ubuntu Archive Mirror. (Since the protocol was selected in step 1, I just enter the plain URL, without any directories–that's mirrors.kernel.org.) Type in the desired mirror and press TAB to highlight Continue. Press ENTER to continue.

4. Enter the directory of the desired mirror with the Ubuntu repository files. In most cases, it's /ubuntu/, and that directory is normally entered by default. If in doubt, check the URL for yourself in an appropriate browser. Type in the desired entry, and press ENTER to continue.

5. Enter any required proxy server information—if a proxy this server regulates access from your network, enter the required information in the format *(http://[[user][:pass]@]host[:pass]/)*, where *pass* = password, *host* = hostname of proxy server, and *port* is the port number of the proxy server, if it's something other than the default, *3128:*.

If no proxy server regulates access from your network to the Internet, leave this entry blank. Make any required proxy server access information and press ENTER to continue.

When these steps are successful, information is downloaded from the selected mirror. Be aware, this process may take several minutes and depends on the speed of the Internet connection. You're then returned to the expanded Main Menu.

## Download Installer Components

Select the Download Installer Components option from the expanded Main Menu. It should automatically take the mirror and proxy server information described earlier to support access to the screen shown in Figure 2-9. Just about all of these components are described earlier in Table 2-3, except crypto-modules, used for decrypting certain installation package.

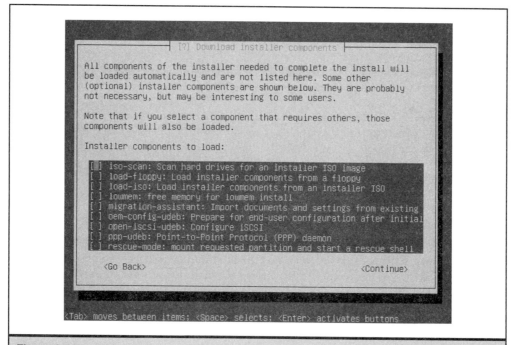

**Figure 2-9.** Additional installer components that can be downloaded

Add any desired additional installer components, press TAB to highlight Continue, and press ENTER to continue. For the purpose of this chapter, I do not choose any additional components.

When successful, you're returned to the expanded Main Menu.

## Configure the Clock

Select the Configure The Clock option from the expanded Main Menu. Then take the following steps:

1. If you're confident in the stability of your network connection, accept the option to Set The Clock Using NTP, associated with the Network Time Protocol. It's especially important to synchronize actions between different servers in geographically distant locations. However, this can lead to delays during the boot process. Use the TAB key to choose Yes or No and press ENTER to continue. (I select Yes for the purpose of this chapter.)

2. Select an NTP server to use. A default may be presented to you, such as ntp .ubuntu.com. If you don't know much about NTP, the default is acceptable for now. Better options are available, as discussed in Chapter 17. Generally, the best option for NTP services is an "official" server physically close to you.

3. Select a Time Zone. The zones presented to you depend on the country specified earlier in the installation process, specifically in the Choose Language section. In a few cases, an appropriate time zone is not available, such as at most foreign embassies. Make a selection and press ENTER to continue.

When these steps are successful, you're returned to the expanded Main Menu.

## Detect Disks

Select the Detect Disks option from the expanded Main Menu. The installer takes a few seconds to detect available storage devices. Then take the following steps:

1. If a storage device is connected via a PCMCIA or PC Card, and if it wasn't started in previous steps, accept the option to Start PC Card Services; otherwise select No and press ENTER to continue.

2. If you selected Yes (or even if you selected No) to Start PC Card Services, you may get a chance to enter PCMCIA Resource Range Options, which specify memory addresses. Normally, no special memory addresses are needed; if entered during this step, such addresses are included in the /etc/pcmcia/config .opts configuration file. Make any desired entries and press ENTER to continue.

When these steps are successful, you're returned to the expanded Main Menu.

# Partition Disks

Select the Partition Disks option from the expanded Main Menu. I've run this exercise on a virtual machine with 256MB of RAM. Make a note of the amount of RAM configured for your system. If the space configured doesn't match the steps shown, please feel free to deviate as needed. Be aware, there are more options under Partition Disks than I can clearly cover in a single section. Take the following steps:

1. As shown in Figure 2-10, several options are available for partitioning method. If free space is available, additional options might be shown. The LVM shown in the figure is short for Logical Volume Management. Briefly, it supports the creation of volumes over multiple partitions. For more information, see Chapter 5.

   Briefly, the Guided options configure partitions with some default configuration for directories on specific volumes. For this chapter, I want to show you how to customize the partition scheme, so select Manual and press ENTER to continue.

2. If a partition configuration already exists, it's presented for your review. Depending on any preexisting configuration, it could look similar to the Partition Disks menu shown in Figure 2-11. You can avoid changing partitions, potentially saving existing data. To continue, you may select Guided Partitioning or Undo Changes To Partitions. The right step depends on the current state of the hard drive.

   Otherwise, select a hard drive to partition and press ENTER to continue.

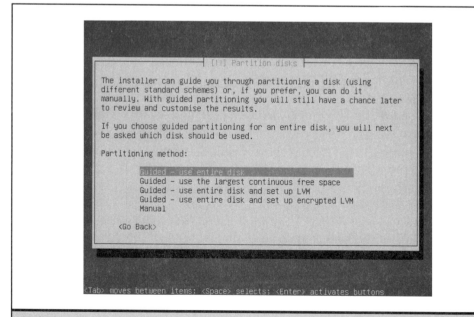

**Figure 2-10.**    Options for partitioning disks

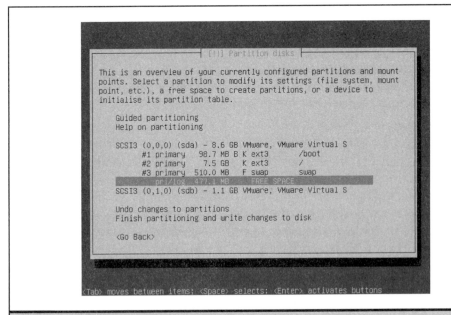

**Figure 2-11.**  Partition Disks menu

3. Assuming you accept the idea to delete all data on the current disk, confirm the suggestion to Create New Empty Partition Table On This Device. If you do, press TAB to highlight Yes, and press ENTER to continue.

4. Select a Partition Table type. Believe it or not, the default partition table type for Linux partitions is *msdos*. (Those of you who understand the parted tool may recognize this idiosyncrasy.) Make the desired selection and press ENTER to continue.

5. You're returned to the Partition Disks menu. Select the Free Space on one hard disk and press ENTER.

6. You're asked How To Use This Free Space. As shown in Figure 2-12, there are three options: Create A New Partition, Automatically Partition The Free Space, and Show Cylinder/Head/Sector Information. You could select Automatically Partition The Free Space, but you wouldn't learn much about this part of the installation process. Therefore, select the Create A New Partition option and press ENTER to continue.

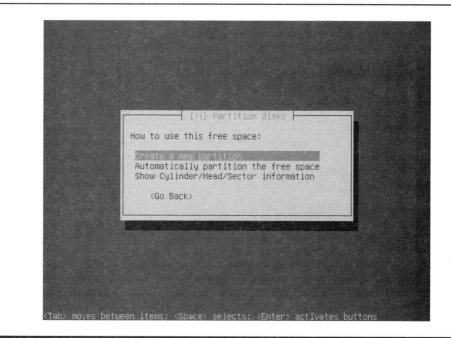

**Figure 2-12.** Options for using free space on a disk partition

7. You'll now have a chance to specify a partition size. The default would take all available free space. For this exercise, create a partition for the /boot directory, and set the partition size to 100MB. Then press TAB to highlight Continue, and press ENTER to continue.

8. The first partition can be Primary or Logical. Select a Primary partition, and press ENTER to continue.

9. The partition can be configured at the beginning or the end of the drive. The beginning of the drive is most appropriate for the /boot directory. Select Beginning, and press ENTER to continue.

10. In the menu shown in Figure 2-13, you'll get to customize various elements of the partition. Note the default mount point, the top-level root directory (/), which is not appropriate for a 100MB partition. Highlight the Mount Point line and press ENTER to continue.

11. Select the /boot directory from the menu that appears. For more information on other directories, see Chapter 5. Press ENTER to continue.

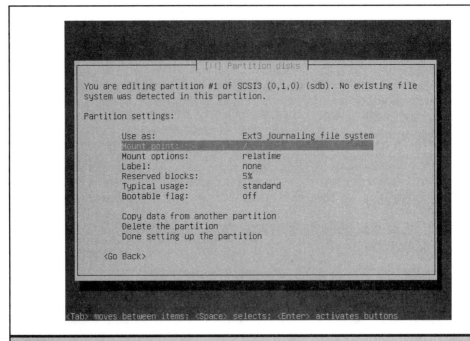

```
                    ┤ [!!] Partition disks ├
 You are editing partition #1 of SCSI3 (0,1,0) (sdb). No existing file
 system was detected in this partition.

 Partition settings:

         Use as:                    Ext3 journaling file system
         Mount point:               /
         Mount options:             relatime
         Label:                     none
         Reserved blocks:           5%
         Typical usage:             standard
         Bootable flag:             off

         Copy data from another partition
         Delete the partition
         Done setting up the partition

     <Go Back>
```

```
 <Tab> moves between items; <Space> selects; <Enter> activates buttons
```

**Figure 2-13.** Customizing a partition

12. As the /boot directory partition, the Bootable Flag should be set to On. Assuming it's off (which is the default), highlight that option and press ENTER. The partition's Bootable Flag should now be set to On.

   The third extended filesystem (ext3) is the default format for Ubuntu partitions. Some administrators prefer to format smaller partitions to the second extended filesystem (ext2), as there is little benefit to the journaling associated with ext3. If you want to make this change, this is the appropriate time to do so.

13. Scroll to the bottom of the screen to the Done Setting Up The Partition option, and press ENTER to continue.

14. You're returned to a screen similar to the one shown in Figure 2-11. Select the remaining Free Space and press ENTER.

15. Repeat step 6. Select Create A New Partition.

16. Allocate all but a few hundred megabytes of the remaining space to the New Partition, and press ENTER to continue.

17. As with step 8, set this second partition as a Primary Partition, and press ENTER to continue.

18. As with step 9, the partition can be configured at the beginning or the end of the drive. For the purpose of this chapter, select Beginning, and press ENTER to continue. You'll see a screen similar to Figure 2-13.

19. Confirm that the mount point is set to the top-level root directory (/), as suggested in steps 10 and 11. Change it to that directory, if required.

20. Select Done Setting Up The Partition.

21. Review the partitioning table; you should now have at least two partitions.

22. Now create a third partition—one for swap space. Highlight the existing free space and press ENTER.

23. Again, select Create A New Partition and press ENTER. Swap space is normally approximately twice the existing RAM.

24. As with step 8, set this partition as a Primary Partition. But if you prefer, it will work essentially just as well as a Logical Partition. Make a selection, and press ENTER to continue.

25. The partition can be configured at the beginning or the end of the drive. Assume the beginning of the drive; select Beginning, and press ENTER to continue.

26. Highlight the Use As option and press ENTER.

27. In the Partition Disks: How To Use This Partition menu that appears, as shown in Figure 2-14, select Swap Area and press ENTER.

28. Confirm the result in the Partition Settings screen that appears. If acceptable, highlight Done Setting Up The Partition and press ENTER.

29. Review the final partition table, as shown in Figure 2-15. If satisfactory, scroll down and highlight the Finish Partitioning And Write Changes To Disk option. Press ENTER to continue.

30. Finally, you'll have a chance to write the changes to disk. Select Yes if so desired and press ENTER.

31. The installation program formats the partition that you've configured.

If you haven't allocated a partition or volume to the top-level root directory (/), an error message will appear. Repeat the allocation process if needed to assign a partition or volume to that directory. The allocation can be temporary, if you want to set up a RAID array as the top-level root directory (/). When these steps are successful, you're returned to the expanded Ubuntu Installer Main Menu.

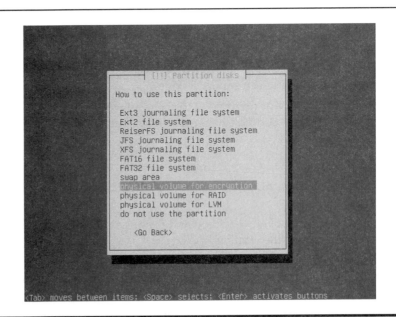

**Figure 2-14.** Configuring a swap partition

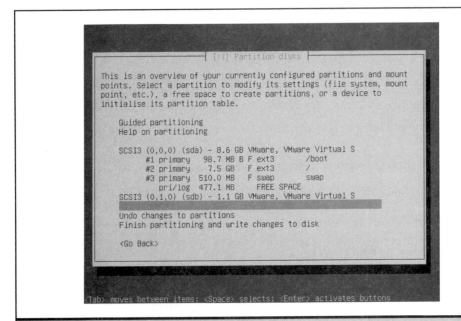

**Figure 2-15.** The partition table

# Configure MD Devices

Select the Configure MD Devices option from the expanded Main Menu. A multi-disk device is associated with RAID devices. While RAID stands for a Redundant Array of Independent Disks, that's not quite accurate, as RAID configuration through the installation program would be related to partitions, not disks.

The options are not usable unless you've configured RAID partitions in the section just completed. You'll learn how you can configure RAID partitions in Chapter 5, so select Finish and press ENTER to continue.

If successful, you're again returned to the expanded Main Menu.

# Install the Base System

Select the Install The Base System option from the expanded Main Menu. The basic Ubuntu Server installation process begins, using the options and partitions configured in preceding sections.

This is a good opportunity for a break, as this process takes a few minutes even from a CD mounted from an ISO file. Part of the installation can also come from the Ubuntu mirror selected earlier. When the base system installation is complete, you're returned to the expanded Main Menu.

# Set Up Users and Passwords

Select the Set Up Users And Passwords option from the expanded Main Menu. Then take the following steps:

1. Accept the option to Enable Shadow Passwords. (While it's not absolutely required, I strongly recommend it. For more information, see Chapter 10.) If required, press TAB until Yes is highlighted, and then press ENTER.

2. Decline the option to Allow Login As Root. The default for Ubuntu is to disable direct logins by the root user. If required, press TAB until No is highlighted, and then press ENTER.

3. Specify the name of the new user. While it's best to enter the full name of the user, it's not required. You're not required to enter anything at this step. Make any desired entry for the user's full name and press ENTER.

4. Specify the username for the first account. By default, this user has access to administrative privileges using the **sudo** command, as defined in Chapter 10. The username must begin with a lowercase letter. Enter a username (or accept the one that is suggested) and press ENTER.

5. Type in a password for the new user, and press ENTER.

6. Repeat step 5 to confirm; if the passwords don't match, you get to repeat steps 5 and 6.

When these steps are successful, you're returned to the expanded Main Menu.

## Configure the Package Manager

Select the Configure The Package Manager option from the expanded Main Menu. If you configured a mirror earlier in the Choose A Mirror Of The Ubuntu Archive section, be ready with that mirror here. Then take the following steps.

> **NOTE**  If any preceding steps have been skipped or there are problems such as a bad network connection to a mirror, this step prompts you to complete the missing steps.

1.  You're prompted to configure a network mirror to supplement the packages available from the CD. Unless you want to have the CD always in the drive, select Yes and press ENTER to continue.

2.  Select a protocol for file downloads; the Ubuntu installer supports access to mirrors via the HTTP or FTP protocols. Make a selection and press ENTER to continue.

3.  Unless you want to use the default country-specific mirror, scroll to the top of the list, select Enter Information Manually, and press ENTER to continue.

4.  Enter the URL to the hostname of the desired Ubuntu Archive Mirror. (Since the protocol was selected in step 1, I just enter the plain URL, without any directories. In my case, that's mirrors.kernel.org.) Type in the desired mirror and press TAB to highlight Continue. Press ENTER to continue.

5.  Enter the directory of the desired mirror with the Ubuntu repository files. In most cases, it's /ubuntu/, and that directory is normally entered by default. If in doubt, check the URL for yourself in an appropriate browser. Type in any desired entry, and press ENTER to continue.

6.  Enter any required proxy server information—if a proxy server regulates access between the local system and the Internet, enter the required information in this format *(http://[[user][:pass]@]host[:pass]/)*, where *pass* = password, *host* = hostname of proxy server, and *port* is the port number of the proxy server, if it's something other than the default, *3128:*.

    If no proxy server regulates access from the local network to the Internet, leave this entry blank. Make any required proxy server access information and press ENTER to continue.

7.  Now you'll see a question on whether you want to Use Restricted Software. As discussed in Chapter 1, restricted software does not comply with open source licenses but might be required in some cases to configure an Ubuntu system that "just works." I accept this option, but you can choose otherwise if you want to limit this installation to open source software. Make your selection using the TAB key, and press ENTER to continue.

8.  You'll see a similar question related to the universe repository. As discussed in Chapter 1, software in the universe repository is open source, but is not supported by Canonical or the Ubuntu project. I accept this option, but the choice is yours. Make your selection using the TAB key, and press ENTER to continue.

9. You'll see a similar question related to the multiverse repository. As discussed in Chapter 1, software in the multiverse repository is not open source and is not supported by Canonical or the Ubuntu project. I accept this option, but the choice is yours. Make your selection using the TAB key, and press ENTER to continue.

10. You'll see a similar question related to the backports repository. As discussed in Chapter 1, software in the backports repository takes new features, primarily from later releases, and incorporates them into the current distribution release. I accept this option, but the choice is yours. Make your selection using the TAB key, and press ENTER to continue.

For detailed information about the repositories discussed in this section, see Chapter 8. When these steps are successful (it takes a few minutes to download the database of packages from the selected repositories), you're returned to the expanded Main Menu.

## Select and Install Software

Select the Select And Install Software option from the expanded Main Menu. A few moments after selecting the option, you'll see the menu shown in Figure 2-16.

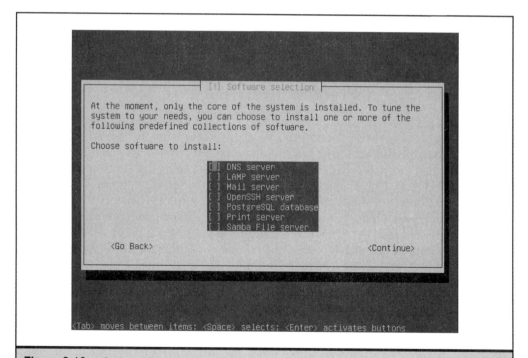

**Figure 2-16.**   Server software package groups

| Package Group | Description |
|---|---|
| DNS Server | Installs the Berkeley Internet Name Domain (BIND) name server; see Chapter 14 |
| LAMP Server | Adds the components for an integrated web server: Apache, MySQL, and PHP; see Chapter 15 |
| Mail Server | Includes the Postfix e-mail server; see Chapter 17 |
| OpenSSH Server | Adds the Secure Shell (SSH) service; see Chapter 7 |
| PostgreSQL database | Incorporates the PostgreSQL database server; alternative to MySQL |
| Print Server | Adds the Common Unix Printing System (CUPS) server; see Chapter 9 |
| Samba File Server | Includes the file server associated with Microsoft networks; see Chapter 16 |

**Table 2-4.**   Ubuntu Server Package Groups

The Ubuntu installer lets you select from several preconfigured groups of packages appropriate for servers, as described in Table 2-4. This step is unique to the Ubuntu Server installation process.

Make desired selections, press TAB to highlight Continue, and press ENTER to continue. If you selected the LAMP group, you're prompted for a password for the MySQL administrative root user. Enter the password and press ENTER to continue.

If you selected the Mail Server group, you're prompted for a basic Postfix configuration, as explained in Figure 2-17. The configuration of Postfix, with these options, is explained in more detail in Chapter 17. I select Internet Site to start the process of configuring the local server as an outgoing e-mail server. But that requires a real domain name on the Internet, such as mcgraw-hill.com. Make your choice and press ENTER to continue.

You're prompted to enter a system mail name, which should be a fully qualified domain name (FQDN), which is included in the header of outgoing e-mail. If this system will be directly connected to the Internet, the FQDN should include a real domain name. Type in an appropriate FQDN and press ENTER to continue. However, if you're using a domain name assigned by a home ISP, you may need the permission of that ISP.

When the installation of these packages is successful, you're returned to the expanded Main Menu.

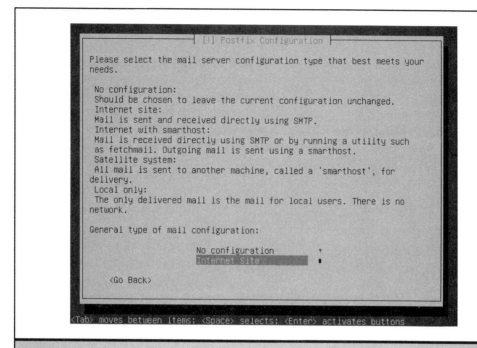

**Figure 2-17.**    Mail server group configuration options

## Build LTSP Chroot

Select the Build LTSP Chroot option from the expanded Main Menu. LTSP is short for the Linux Terminal Server Project, which Ubuntu and especially Edubuntu Linux uses for thin clients. Be aware that if you're setting up an LTSP server, you'll need the space for a client operating system, which could be several gigabytes in size. (It added approximately 2GB to the space required for my installation.)

If you select this option, you're asked whether to Set Up A LTSP Chroot Environment. You can always add the information for a thin client to the local system later, which is a good idea, especially if you're not sure about the free hard drive space on the local system. For more information on LTSP, see Chapter 20.

When these steps are successful (or if an error message appears about a failed LTSP installation), you're returned to the expanded Main Menu. The next three sections are based on options located below those shown in the expanded Main Menu in Figure 2-7.

These options are mutually exclusive; in other words, you can either install GRUB or LILO, or continue without a boot loader. While you should be aware of all three options, you'll run only one of the three. The standard on current Linux systems is GRUB. These options are part of the expanded Main Menu and shown in Figure 2-18.

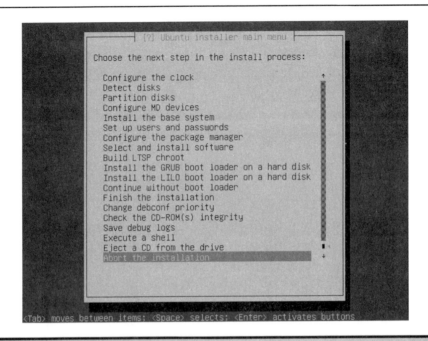

**Figure 2-18.**    More of the expanded Ubuntu Installer Main Menu

*NOTE*    GRUB and LILO are boot loaders that allow the user to select between operating systems or kernels when the system is being powered up. GRUB is an acronym for the Grand Unified Bootloader, the default for most Linux distributions, including Ubuntu. LILO is an acronym for the Linux Loader, and is still used for many specialty computers. These boot loaders are functionally similar to Microsoft's NTLDR and Windows Boot Manager.

## Install the GRUB Boot Loader on a Hard Disk

Select the Install The GRUB Boot Loader On A Hard Disk option from the expanded Main Menu shown in Figure 2-18. You're prompted to choose whether to install the GRUB on the master boot record (MBR) of the first hard drive. If you so select, the local system uses reads the MBR when booting, which refers to the /boot/grub/menu.lst file for more information.

If you want to install the GRUB boot loader on the MBR, select Yes. If you select No, you can install GRUB on a specific partition, which could be configured with a second boot loader, even Microsoft's NTLDR.

You can then set a password for the boot loader, and this is an excellent idea. When set up with a properly managed GRUB configuration file, a GRUB password can help secure your system from crackers who could otherwise use GRUB to gain administrative access. For more information on GRUB, see Chapter 4.

 **NOTE** In the Linux world, the term "hacker" is different from its meaning in popular culture. Among Linux users, a hacker is someone who just wants to create better software. In contrast, a cracker is someone who breaks into computer systems.

## Install the LILO Boot Loader on a Hard Disk

If you don't want to install GRUB and need a boot loader, select the Install The LILO Boot Loader On A Hard Disk option from the expanded Main Menu. You'll be prompted to choose whether to install LILO on the MBR or the first partition of the first hard drive. Those choices actually embed the /etc/lilo.conf configuration file in the MBR or the first bytes of the first partition.

## Continue Without Boot Loader

Select the Continue Without Boot Loader option from the expanded Main Menu, and you'll see a message associated with booting manually. This is a suitable option for some third-party boot loaders such as VCOM's System Commander. This is also an appropriate alternative if you've configured Microsoft's NTLDR or Boot Manager to boot Linux.

When you select Continue, you're returned to the expanded Main Menu.

## Finish the Installation

At this point, you could opt to select the Finish The Installation option from the expanded Main Menu. When you do, final options are configured, and network installation settings are disabled. You're asked whether the system clock, normally configured in the system BIOS menu, should be set UTC, which is essentially equivalent to Greenwich Mean Time or US Military Zulu time. It's required for systems configured for time changes such as Daylight Savings Time. However, it should be avoided on systems if set up in a dual-boot configuration with an operating system that can't handle UTC, such as Microsoft Windows. I say select Yes and press ENTER to continue.

Finally, you're prompted to remove any installation media, such as the Ubuntu Server Installation CD. In a moment, select Continue, and press ENTER to continue. But before you do this, select Go Back and review the final options from the expanded Main Menu.

## Change Debconf Priority

The **dpkg-reconfigure** command can help you reconfigure specific packages. One example is shown in Chapter 13, where it's used to reconfigure an X Window System server. If you want to change its behavior, select the Change Debconf Priority option from the expanded Main Menu. Then you can scroll between four priority levels, three of which are shown in Figure 2-19.

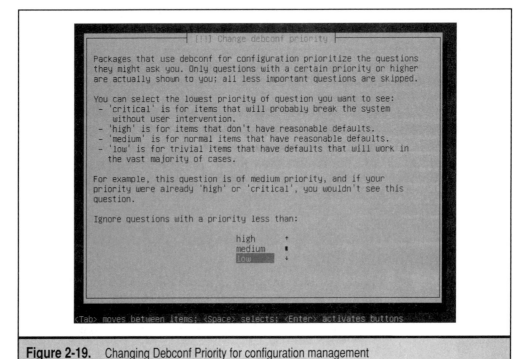

**Figure 2-19.** Changing Debconf Priority for configuration management

Make any desired changes and press ENTER to continue. (I set the priority to low on my systems, as I need to investigate configuration options in all of their gory details.) When successful, you're returned to the expanded Main Menu.

## Check the CD-ROM(s) Integrity

If you have doubts about the CD or DVD you're using, the better time to check it was earlier in the process—discussed back in the "Download the ISO File Online" section. But if you think you need to check the integrity of the media now, select the Check The CD-ROM(s) Integrity option from the expanded Main Menu. Be aware, if you're working with a mounted ISO file, say on a virtual machine, this option works equally well.

**NOTE**  Yes, the option and the title of this section does not follow the conventions of standard written English, but that's the nature of many options on Linux systems.

When you see the Check CD-ROM Integrity option, select Yes. The process begins automatically and takes some time, especially if you're working from a DVD. If successful, you'll see the same message that was shown if you chose the Check CD For Defects option when booting from the Ubuntu Server installation CD:

```
The CD-ROM integrity test was successful. The CD-ROM is valid.
```

**NOTE**   If you don't see the message shown, the CD/DVD drive may not have been completely detected. For example, on a VMware Server virtual machine, I've had to set up PC Card services via the Detect And Mount CD-ROM option.

You'll also see a Continue option highlighted. Press ENTER. You're prompted with a question to check the integrity of another CD/DVD. Select No, highlight Continue, press ENTER, and you're taken through the Detect And Mount CD-ROM process. Once it's complete, you're returned again to the expanded Main Menu.

## Save Debug Logs

If you want to analyze what happened with the installation, you can select the Save Debug Logs option from the expanded Main Menu. Debugging logs for the installation can be saved to a floppy disk, a local website, or a local partition. (As none of my systems include a floppy disk drive, I do not cover that option.)

When I selected Web, I got a message suggesting that a "simple web server" has been started. After reading the message, I pressed ENTER to continue. The logs are available from the IP address configured for the local server and can be read from remote systems with any ordinary browser, as shown in Figure 2-20. Just be aware that these files disappear once the installation process is complete.

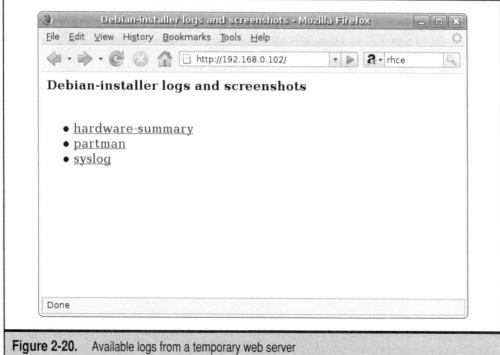

**Figure 2-20.**   Available logs from a temporary web server

Alternatively, you could select Mounted File System. You're prompted to enter a directory where the debug logs will be saved. To save these logs in the administrative user's home directory, I type in this:

```
/target/root
```

Debug logs are saved in the root administrative user's home directory, in the install/ subdirectory. These files remain available after installation is complete.

When successful, you're returned to the expanded Main Menu.

## Execute a Shell

Select the Execute A Shell option from the expanded Main Menu. If you select Complete from the option that appears, a command line ash shell is started, as shown in Figure 2-21.

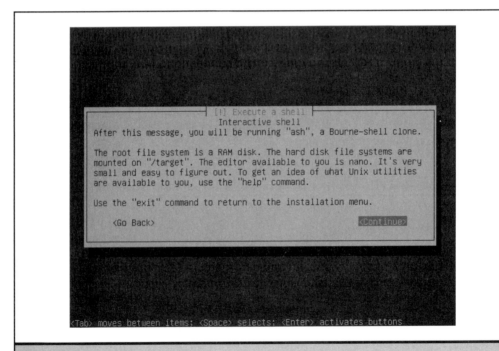

**Figure 2-21.** Ubuntu's installation shell

As described in Figure 2-21, hard disk filesystems as configured during the installation process are mounted on the /target directory. Standard directories after installation is complete are available as subdirectories of /target.

The ash shell is already available in the second and third virtual terminals, accessible by pressing ALT-F2 and ALT-F3. Incidentally, if you want to start configuring the system before installation is complete, you could run the following command from the ash shell prompt:

```
# chroot /target
```

This sets the top-level root directory to the filesystem that will be available to you after installation is complete. You have access to configuration files, man pages, and more using commands familiar to any Linux administrator.

The **exit** command leaves the chroot configuration. If you've accessed the ash shell, type **exit**, press ENTER, and you're returned to the expanded Main Menu.

## Eject a CD from the Drive

This option is generally not used, unless you actually need to change CD/DVDs and the eject button on the CD/DVD drive doesn't work.

## Abort the Installation

If for some reason you want to stop the installation process, you can select the Abort The Installation option, or, more simply, just press CTRL-ALT-DEL to reboot the system.

## Finish the Installation

The system reboots and starts for the first time. You'll have to press ENTER once after installation to see the login prompt shown in Figure 2-22.

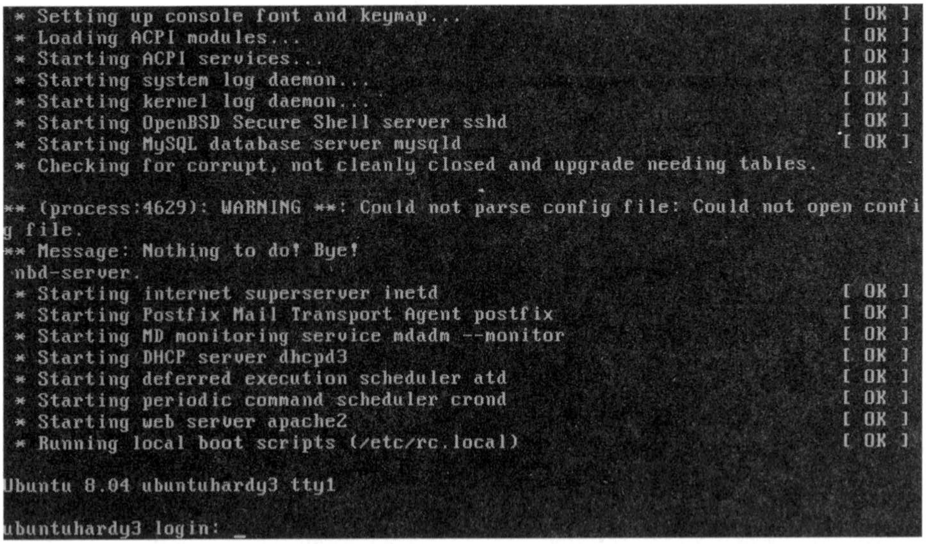

```
* Setting up console font and keymap...                        [ OK ]
* Loading ACPI modules...                                      [ OK ]
* Starting ACPI services...                                    [ OK ]
* Starting system log daemon...                                [ OK ]
* Starting kernel log daemon...                                [ OK ]
* Starting OpenBSD Secure Shell server sshd                    [ OK ]
* Starting MySQL database server mysqld                        [ OK ]
* Checking for corrupt, not cleanly closed and upgrade needing tables.

** (process:4629): WARNING **: Could not parse config file: Could not open confi
g file.
** Message: Nothing to do! Bye!
nbd-server.
* Starting internet superserver inetd                          [ OK ]
* Starting Postfix Mail Transport Agent postfix                [ OK ]
* Starting MD monitoring service mdadm --monitor               [ OK ]
* Starting DHCP server dhcpd3                                  [ OK ]
* Starting deferred execution scheduler atd                    [ OK ]
* Starting periodic command scheduler crond                    [ OK ]
* Starting web server apache2                                  [ OK ]
* Running local boot scripts (/etc/rc.local)                   [ OK ]

Ubuntu 8.04 ubuntuhardy3 tty1

ubuntuhardy3 login: _
```

**Figure 2-22.** Booting into Ubuntu Server

# NETWORK INSTALLATIONS

One way to configure a network installation takes advantage of the PXE boot option available on modern network cards and BIOSs. If you configure an appropriate DHCP and TFTP server, you can mount the installation CD on that server. It's then possible to boot the Ubuntu Server installation CD directly from the network boot system, which works even on systems without CD drives. If they're not already installed, you can add the servers described in this section with the following command:

```
$ sudo apt-get install dhcp3-server tftpd-hpa tftp
```

## Dynamic Host Configuration Protocol (DHCP) Services

A DHCP server automates the network configuration process for clients. In detail, DHCP allows a Linux computer to serve dynamic IP addresses. It supports the configuration of a range of IP addresses and allows you to reserve a specific IP address, based on the hardware address associated with a client's network card. It can assign more information such as the gateway and DNS IP address to every system that requests an IP address.

DHCP servers can simplify and centralize network administration if you're administering more than a few computers on a network. They are especially convenient for networks with a significant number of mobile users. The standard Ubuntu DHCP server is based on the dhcp3-server package. That server must be on the same system as the TFTP server for a network installation of this type to work.

Just be aware that many users already have a configured DHCP service. Even home users may already have a DHCP server on the router that connects their home networks to the Internet. Multiple DHCP servers on a single network can lead to problems. It's best to deactivate other DHCP servers before testing the DHCP servers described here.

Now review the configuration of the DHCP server. The default configuration file, which is /etc/dhcp3/dhcpd.conf, does not configure any IP addresses by default. So if you try to activate the DHCP3 server without modifying the configuration file, the attempt will fail. This section reviews only those directives required for a basic service on a standard private IPv4 network, customized for network booting. Detailed configuration options are described in Chapter 14.

In the /etc/dhcp3/dhcpd.conf configuration file, Dynamic DNS updates are not enabled based on the following directive:

```
ddns-update-style none;
```

In the following directives, you should substitute the domain name for the local private network with *example.org*. You should also substitute the FQDN or IP address of the DNS servers with *ns1.example.org* and *ns2.example.org*:

```
option domain-name "example.org";
option domain-name-servers ns1.example.org, ns2.example.org;
```

Of course, you need to configure a system for some local network. The following stanza takes advantage of the PXE Linux configuration file on the Ubuntu Server installation CD. It then configures the DHCP server on the 192.168.0.0/255.255.255.0 network. It assigns IP addresses between 192.168.0.200 and 192.168.0.220.

```
filename = "ubuntu/install/netboot/pxelinux.0";
subnet 192.168.0.0 netmask 255.255.255.0 {
 range 192.168.0.200 192.168.0.220;
}
```

There are a number of additional suggested options commented out in the default version of the /etc/dhcp3/dhcpd.conf configuration file. They provide hints for configuring the DHCP server for remote networks and reserved IP addresses, as well as allowing or denying DHCP access to a group of systems.

Once configured, turn off any other DHCP services, and start this one with the following command:

```
$ sudo /etc/init.d/dhcp3-server restart
```

Success or failure is logged in files such as /var/log/messages. First test this server from a remote client, with a command such as this:

```
$ sudo dhclient eth0
```

Now you're ready to make this work with a TFTP server. When you're finished with the remote installation process, deactivate this DHCP server with the following command:

```
$ sudo /etc/init.d/dhcp3-server stop
```

If you deactivated other DHCP servers in this section, it's now OK to reactivate those servers.

# Trivial File Transfer Protocol

There are several TFTP services available for Ubuntu. The focus of this section is on the tftpd-hpa package. If you have a firewall on the local system, pay attention to the associated port number(s) listed in this file. Just remember that to test the TFTP service, you also need the tftp client package.

The simplest way to configure the TFTP service is through the /etc/default/tftpd-hpa configuration file. I use the following directives in my version of this file:

```
RUN_DAEMON="yes"
OPTIONS="-l -s /var/lib/tftpboot"
```

The directives are simple: The first is almost self-explanatory as it runs the /usr/sbin/ in.tftpd daemon. The second feeds command line options to the daemon. As can be verified with the in.tftpd man page, these options run the server in standalone mode, using the /var/lib/tftpboot directory as the root directory for clients. The information from this file is fed to the associated service script, /etc/init.d/tftpd-hpa.

# Configure a Network Installation

Now with a TFTP and DHCP server configured, you're ready to set up a network installation of Ubuntu Server. If you've downloaded an ISO file associated with an Ubuntu installation CD or DVD, all you need to do is mount that file on the TFTP directory. For example, the following command mounts the Ubuntu Server Hardy Heron CD on the appropriate TFTP directory:

```
$ sudo mount -o loop ubuntu-8.04-server-i386.iso /var/lib/tftpboot/ubuntu
```

Create the noted mount directory if needed. Make sure the TFTP and DHCP3 servers described earlier are active. Boot the system where you want to install Linux over a network using the PXE environment described next, and it will boot the installation CD over the network.

# PXE Booting

Most modern systems include some sort of network boot card and a BIOS that can take advantage of that capability. As a wide variety of options are available from the boot menu, they are not all described here. If available, the option should be listed in your computer's hardware documentation. If the PXE environment is selected, it should show messages such as these:

```
Network boot from some network card

CLIENT MAC ADDR: 00 0C 39 40 4E EA
GUID: 564DFD09-31C9-77F0-ED6C-CE86DA304EEA
DHCP:
```

If the server is properly configured, especially with the pxeclient.0 file described in the discussion of the DHCP server, the client PXE environment should automatically detect the DHCP server, along with the client files as configured. If successful, the PXE boot process should bring up the screen shown in Figure 2-23. At that point, you should be able to start the same Expert mode installation by typing in **expert** and pressing ENTER at the **boot:** prompt.

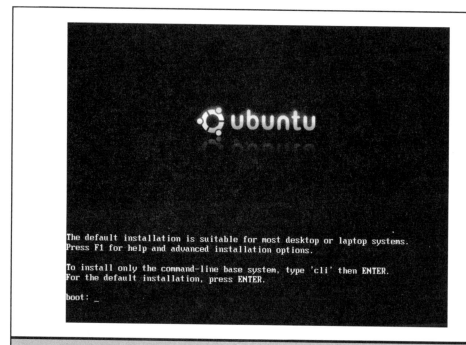

**Figure 2-23.** Starting a network installation

**NOTE** If PXE booting is not available on the target client's network card or BIOS, it's possible to create a boot CD or floppy disk that simulates the PXE boot process. For more information, see www .rom-o-matic.net.

# SUMMARY

In this chapter, you learned how to install Ubuntu Server Edition, based on Expert mode. It can be installed from an Ubuntu Server CD available from an ISO file downloaded online or perhaps from one purchased from a third-party source. In some cases, the ISO file itself can be used to emulate the CD to test Ubuntu Server. Ubuntu works well with most current hardware, but some components may require packages with closed source licenses.

The Ubuntu Server boot screen provides a wide variety of installation options. Four consoles are available: The first provides installation messages; the next two provide virtual consoles; and the fourth gives system messages that can help diagnose problems.

Ubuntu Server installation options include choices associated with the language, keyboard, hardware detection, additional installer components, network configuration, SSH access during the installation process, installation and package mirrors, clocks, partitions, users and passwords. There are even custom package groups appropriate to a server as well as options to support the configuration of a thin client using the work of the LTSP.

Finally, with a DHCP and TFTP server, network installations can be configured, with a bit of help from a PXE boot network card and BIOS.

# CHAPTER 3

# Automated Installations
# with Kickstart

As described in Chapter 2, the Ubuntu Server installation can take some time. Imagine repeating this process a dozen, even 100 times, when installing Ubuntu Server in an enterprise. Yes, you could install many services on a single server, as shown in Chapter 2, but that's appropriate only for a test system. Production systems today dedicate specific servers for individual services.

In fact, some organizations dedicate multiple servers to single service. (For example, I understand some enterprises dedicate a dozen servers just to the Domain Name Service [DNS].) With the advantages associated with virtualization, I suspect even some smaller organizations now configure 100 or more virtual servers (on fewer physical systems).

To keep the workload manageable, administrators need to be able to automate the Ubuntu installation process. Automation of any Linux installation requires an "answers file" that configures the installation with information that would otherwise require real-time manual input.

As befits the choices associated with open source software, Ubuntu includes two different ways to automate the installation process. As Ubuntu developers (as of this writing) focus on the Kickstart tool developed by Red Hat for its Linux distributions, I focus on that choice.

# HOW TO KICKSTART AN INSTALLATION

Kickstart was developed by Red Hat to provide automated installation of Red Hat–based Linux distributions. Courtesy of the GNU General Public License (GPL), Ubuntu developers have adapted it for installations of various Ubuntu releases. If you know Kickstart for Red Hat, Kickstart for Ubuntu should be easy.

The principles of Kickstart for Ubuntu and Red Hat are the same. The questions asked during the installation can be automatically answered with a single text file. Once the text file is configured, it's possible to install nearly identical systems quickly.

As of this writing, Kickstart support in Ubuntu is far from complete. For the latest information, review the associated wiki at https://help.ubuntu.com/community/KickstartCompatibility.

## Install the Kickstart Software

Before using Kickstart on an Ubuntu release, install the applicable Kickstart configuration tool. One method uses the following command:

```
$ sudo apt-get install system-config-kickstart
```

If you're starting with the Ubuntu Server installation created in Chapter 2, you have not yet configured a GUI. In that case, this command installs a whole group of extra packages, sufficient for remote access to the graphical Kickstart software configuration tool.

In the sections that follow, you'll use that graphical Kickstart Configurator to create an automated configuration file. You'll analyze and customize that file with a command line editor, and then set up that file to automate another installation of Ubuntu.

## Remote Access to GUI Tools

If you haven't installed a GUI on a system, you can't run GUI-based tools on that system. However, as discussed in Chapter 13, X servers and X clients can be run on different systems. In other words, the Kickstart configuration tool is an X client, which can be run on a remote system with an X server.

So, assuming you've installed the Secure Shell (SSH) server during the installation process, first make sure it's active on the Ubuntu server with the following command:

```
$ sudo /etc/init.d/ssh start
```

Now you should be able to log in from a remote system, through a user account on the Ubuntu Server system. From any connected remote system, log in with the following command (substitute your account name for *michael*):

```
$ ssh -X michael@ubuntuhardyserver
```

Be aware that the **-X** switch enables forwarding of X client information. If the hostname or fully qualified domain name of the remote Ubuntu server system is not available in a local DNS server or in a local /etc/hosts configuration file, you'll need to substitute the IP address for the name of the server. (For more information on secure shell clients and servers, see Chapter 7.)

# Use the Kickstart Configuration Tool

The Kickstart configuration tool is a graphical tool. If you've installed Kickstart without a GUI on an Ubuntu Server system, Kickstart can be run from a remote system with a GUI. Just take the following steps:

1. On the Ubuntu server, run the **ifconfig** command to look for the local IP address. An excerpt of the output should appear similar to the following. (In my case, the IP address is 192.168.0.102. Your IP address will probably be different.)

```
eth0 Link encap:Ethernet HWaddr 00:0c:29:15:2a:4e
     inet addr: 192.168.0.102 Bcast:192.168.0.255 Mask: 255.255.255.0
```

2. Install the Kickstart Configurator on the Ubuntu Server system with the following command:

```
$ sudo apt-get install system-config-kickstart
```

3. Start the GUI in a remote system. (In this case, I do so on an Ubuntu laptop system, in the GNOME desktop environment.)

4. Open a command line interface in the noted GUI. One method is to choose Applications | Accessories | Terminal.

5. In the command line interface that appears, note the hostname or IP address of the Ubuntu server. Based on the IP address found in step 1, I log in to the Ubuntu server with my account, as shown below. Your IP address and account name will probably be different. If the hostname is configured in /etc/hosts or a locally authoritative DNS server, substitute the hostname for the IP address.

   ```
   $ ssh -X michael@192.168.0.102
   ```

6. If you're using **ssh** to connect to this particular Ubuntu server for the first time, a warning message should appear, as discussed in Chapter 7. Assuming both systems are on a private network, and you're confident that the network is secure, type **yes** to the following question and press ENTER.

   ```
   Are you sure you want to continue connecting (yes/no)?
   ```

7. Enter the password for the specified user on the Ubuntu server. (In my case, it's user michael's password.)

8. You're now logged into the Ubuntu server from a remote client, and can now access X clients. Run the following command to open the Kickstart Configurator:

   ```
   $ sudo system-config-kickstart
   ```

9. The Kickstart Configurator screen shown in Figure 3-1 should open from the Ubuntu server on the remote system.

---

**NOTE** While the sequence in the Kickstart Configurator—more closely follows the Red Hat installation process, the same steps will work with various Ubuntu releases.

---

There are several categories of options shown in the left pane of the Configurator screen. To learn more about Kickstart, experiment with some of these settings. Choose File | Save to save these settings with the filename of your choice, which can then be reviewed in a text editor. Alternatively, choose File | Preview to see the effect of different settings on the Kickstart file.

The following sections provide a brief overview of each option shown in the left pane. One of the weaknesses of Kickstart on Ubuntu is the lack of a default configuration file for the current system; in other words, unlike on a Red Hat system, no anaconda-ks.cfg file or any other Kickstart file exists based on the local system as installed.

---

**NOTE** Ubuntu developers are working on a Kickstart tool to generate a file based on the current configuration. For more information, see bug 15156 at https://bugs.launchpad.net.

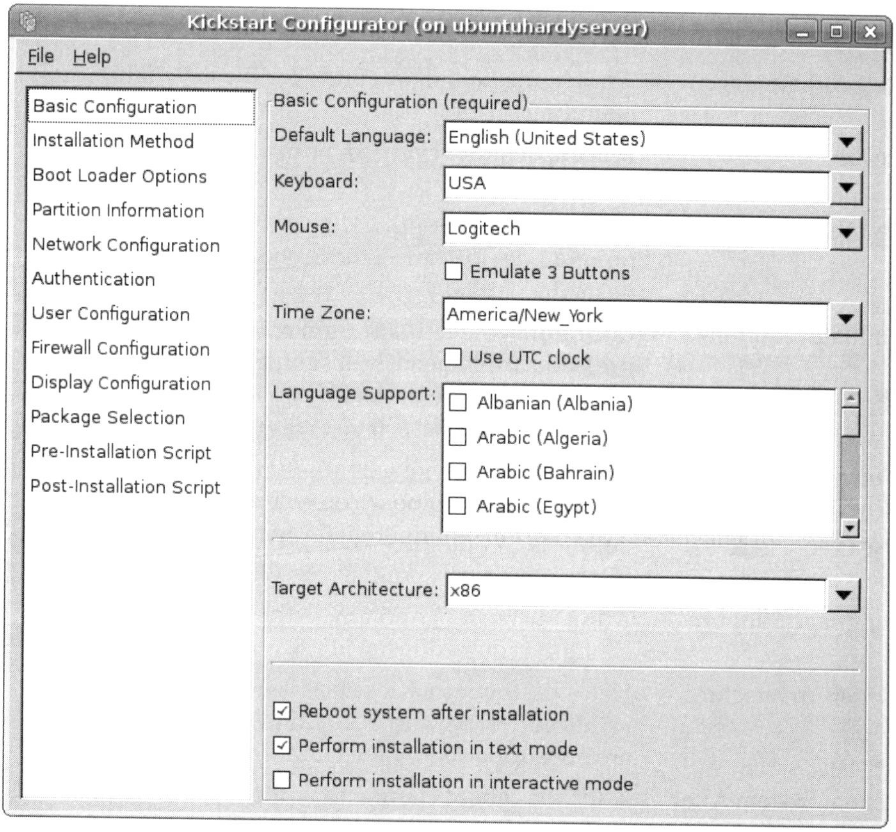

**Figure 3-1.**   The Kickstart Configurator

## Basic Configuration

In the Basic Configuration screen, you can assign settings for several components. Several of these settings include a variety of options available from drop-down text boxes or scroll windows. These components are described in Table 3-1.

## Installation Method

In the Kickstart Configurator screen's left pane, select Installation Method. The options are straightforward. The Ubuntu version of this tool supports only new installations; it does not support the Red Hat options associated with upgrades. The tool is somewhat interactive; for example, if you select an FTP installation method, the Kickstart Configurator

| Basic Installation Option | Description |
|---|---|
| Default Language | Assigns the default language for the installation and operating system. |
| Keyboard | Sets the default keyboard; normally associated with language. |
| Mouse | Configures the pointing device; if in doubt or if the pointing device varies, the Probe For Mouse option normally works. |
| Emulate 3 Buttons | Configures the left and right mouse buttons; when pressed simultaneously, it simulates the action of the middle mouse button. If you have a scroll wheel, press on it; if it clicks, it already works (and should be automatically recognized) as a middle mouse button. |
| Time Zone | Allows configuration of the time zone of the local system. |
| Use UTC Clock | Supports computers where the hardware clock is set to UTC, functionally equivalent to Greenwich Mean Time. |
| Language Support | Adds the current and any extra languages for configuration and installation. |
| Target Architecture | Helps customize a Kickstart file for different CPU architectures; be warned, architectures such as IA-64 are not supported by the Ubuntu project or Canonical. |
| Reboot System After Installation | Adds the **reboot** command to the end of the Kickstart configuration file. |
| Perform Installation In Text Mode | Supports automated installation in text mode; should always be selected for automated Ubuntu installations. |
| Perform Installation In Interactive Mode | Allows you to test the steps associated with a Kickstart-based installation; default answers as configured here are added during the installation process, which helps you review how it works with the installation program. |

**Table 3-1.**   Kickstart Basic Configuration Options

prompts for the name or IP address of the FTP server and the shared directory with the installation files. It also supports entries for an FTP username and password, if the FTP server does not support anonymous connections.

You can configure a Kickstart file to install various Ubuntu releases from a CD, a local hard drive partition, or an HTTP or FTP server. NFS (Network File System)–based installations are no longer supported. (I use virtual machines for most of my systems, so I configure the Ubuntu Server installation from a CD. Since the CD drive on a virtual machine is a virtual device, it isn't limited by the mechanical speeds of a physical CD/ DVD drive.)

## Boot Loader Options

In the Kickstart Configurator, select Boot Loader Options. The options in this section, shown in Figure 3-2, assume that you want to use the default Grand Unified Bootloader (GRUB) which supports encrypted passwords for an additional level of security during the boot process.

Linux boot loaders are normally installed on the master boot record (MBR). If you're dual-booting Linux and Microsoft Windows with GRUB, you can set up the Microsoft boot loader (or an alternative boot loader such as Partition Magic or System Commander or even the Microsoft boot loader) to point to GRUB on the first sector of the Linux partition with the /boot directory.

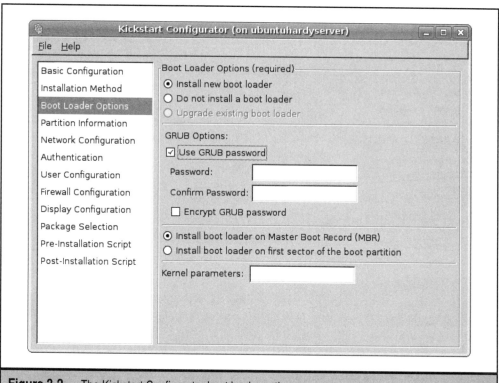

**Figure 3-2.** The Kickstart Configurator boot loader options

## Partition Information

Now select Partition Information. The options shown in Figure 3-3 determine how partitions are configured. While it appears to support the configuration of standard and RAID (Redundant Array of Independent Disks) partitions, it does not currently support the configuration of LVM (Logical Volume Management) groups. The Clear Master Boot Record option configures Kickstart to wipe the MBR from an older hard disk. (I've set up several partitions in Figure 3-3.)

If you're using a new hard drive—or want to erase all data on the current drive—make sure the Initialize The Disk Label radio button is active. Click the Add button to open the Partition Options dialog box shown in Figure 3-4. As you can see in Figure 3-4, the dialog box supports detailed configuration of each partition, per the following components:

▼ **Mount Point**   Assigns the directory where the configured partition is to be mounted.

■ **File System Type**   Sets the format for the configured partition; swap and software RAID file system type options are available.

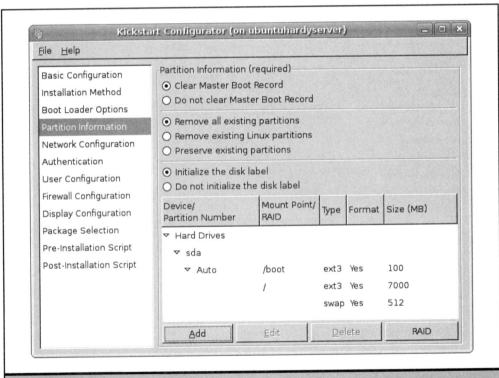

**Figure 3-3.**   The Kickstart Configurator partition information

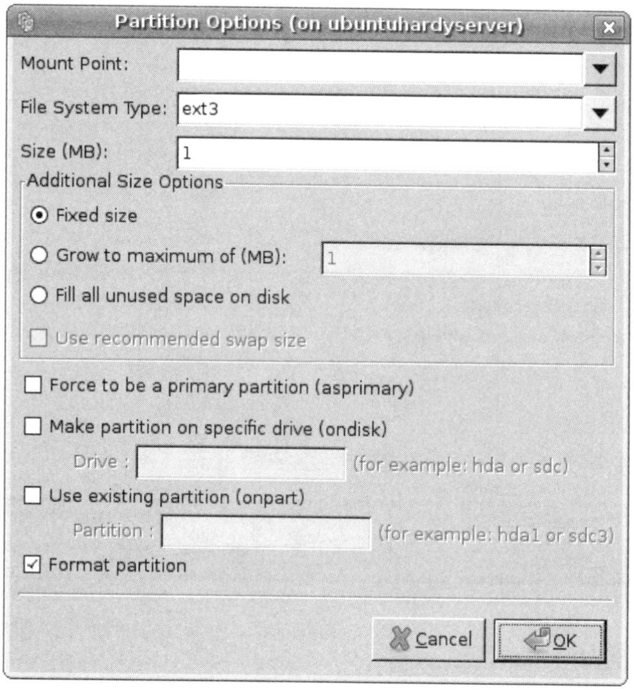

**Figure 3-4.** The Partition Options dialog box

- **Size** Configures a size for the partition.
- **Additional Size Options** Supports growable partitions to fill available free space on a hard drive.
- **Force To Be A Primary Partition** Configures the partition as a primary partition on the hard drive.
- **Make Partition On Specific Drive** Assigns a drive device for the partition; required if more than one hard drive is available.
- **Use Existing Partition** Assigns a specific existing partition, based on the device filename.
- ▲ **Format Partition** Sets the configured partition to be formatted during the installation process.

While it's possible to configure partitions on multiple drives using the Kickstart Configurator, such options are not (yet) recognized by the Ubuntu installation program. (When I tried to configure Kickstart partitions on two drives for this chapter, the Ubuntu installer consolidated the changes into the first hard drive.)

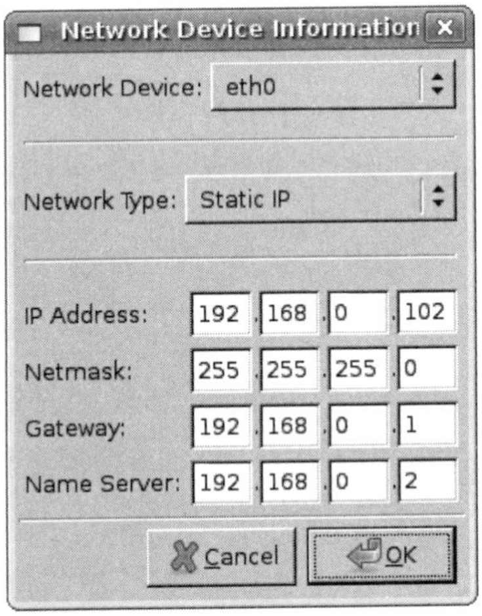

**Figure 3-5.** Network Device Information

## Network Configuration

Back in the Kickstart Configurator, select Network Configuration to configure IP addressing one or more network cards. Click the Add Network Device button to open the Network Device Information screen shown in Figure 3-5.

You can customize static IP addressing for a specific computer or configure the use of a DHCP (Dynamic Host Configuration Protocol) server. You can also make Kickstart look for a Bootstrap Protocol (BOOTP) server, which is a specially configured DHCP server on a remote network.

As the Ubuntu installation process takes packages from remote systems, errors in this section can stop the progress of an installation cold.

## Authentication

In the Kickstart Configurator, select Authentication. The options here support the configuration of two forms of security for local user passwords: Shadow Passwords, which encrypt user passwords in the /etc/shadow file, and MD5 encryption. This section also allows you to set up authentication information for various protocols. Be aware that, as of this writing, only local authentication is supported in the Ubuntu implementation of Kickstart. (I include descriptions of the other authentication methods, as I fully expect them to be functional for Kickstart installations, hopefully in the near future.)

▼ **NIS**  The Network Information Service configures one login database for a network with Unix and Linux computers.

■ **LDAP**  The Lightweight Directory Access Protocol is used for certain types of databases, such as directories.

- ■ **Kerberos 5**    The Kerberos system developed at the Massachusetts Institute of Technology (MIT) uses strong cryptography to authenticate users over a network.

- ■ **Hesiod**    Hesiod is associated with Kerberos 5.

- ■ **SMB**    Samba is based on the SMB, or Server Message Block protocol, updated for the Common Internet File System (CIFS), which allows configuration of your Linux computer on a Microsoft Windows–based network.

- ▲ **Name Switch Cache**    Associated with NIS for looking up passwords and groups.

## User Configuration

In the Kickstart Configurator, select User Configuration. As shown in Figure 3-6, this section supports options for the root account and an initial regular user. Ubuntu systems disable the root account by default, and in my opinion, this is an excellent security option. But if you don't enable a root account, you'll need to configure an initial user here. That user is allowed administrative root privileges by using his or her standard password.

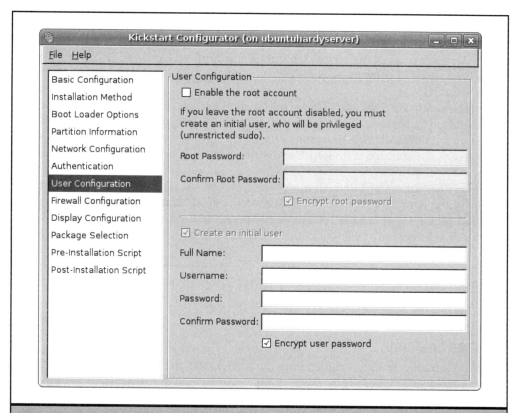

**Figure 3-6.**    User configuration of regular (initial) and root users

## Firewall Configuration

As of this writing, firewall configuration is disabled by default in the Ubuntu implementation of the Kickstart Configurator. Based on the default port options associated with Ubuntu Server, I'm not convinced that a firewall will ever be enabled in Kickstart.

Select the Firewall Configuration option. If this section were enabled, it would support the configuration of a default firewall for the subject computer. Generally, you would want a firewall only for those computers that are connected to outside networks such as the Internet. This section allows the easy configuration of a firewall to permit access to trusted services on the local system, including HTTP, FTP, SSH, Telnet, and SMTP (Simple Mail Transfer Protocol).

If other services are to be trusted, they can also be configured by TCP or UDP (User Datagram Protocol) packet, along with the port number, as defined in the /etc/services configuration file.

## Display Configuration

In the Kickstart Configurator, select Display Configuration. This section supports the configuration of the Linux GUI. While much debate centers on the superiority of GUI- or text-based administrative tools, text-based tools are more stable. For this reason (and more), many Linux administrators don't even install a GUI. By default, neither a GUI nor the X Window is installed in the Ubuntu Server Edition. However, if you're installing Linux on a series of computers, it's likely that most of the users are regular users who will want a GUI.

In this section are three tabs. Under the General tab, you can set a default color depth and resolution, indicate a default desktop (GNOME or KDE), configure X Window System to start by default, and disable or enable the Setup Agent (the First Boot process). As the Setup Agent is associated with Red Hat distributions, this option is disabled in Ubuntu releases.

Under the Video Card and Monitor tabs, you can set Linux to probe the hardware or specify the hardware from a list. Unless you have specialty hardware (or otherwise have had problems with these hardware components during the installation process in Chapter 2), it's generally best to leave these defaults as is.

**NOTE**   As this book is focused on Ubuntu Server Edition, I do not enable the configuration of the X Window System in the Kickstart Configurator.

## Package Selection

In the Ubuntu Server Edition implementation of Kickstart, the Package Selection section is currently not used. Hopefully, package group options, such as LAMP, DNS, PostgreSQL, and Samba, as described in Chapter 2, will appear.

## Installation Scripts

In the Kickstart Configurator, select Pre-Installation Script and Post-Installation Script. These sections support scripts that are run before and after installation, respectively, in the Kickstart configuration file. Post-installation scripts are more common, and they can help configure other parts of a Linux operating system in a common way. For example, if you want to install a directory with employee benefits information, you can add a post-installation script that adds commands such as **cp** to copy files from a network server.

## Final Comments on the Kickstart Configurator

After you've created desired installation settings, choose File | Save File to save the settings created with a filename of your choice. The standard from Red Hat distributions (which you do not have to follow) is ks.cfg.

Even though the Kickstart Configurator is open on a remote system, the ks.cfg file is saved on the Ubuntu server. The default save directory is the home directory of the associated user (in my case, that's the /home/michael directory). This file is discussed in the next section.

# Customize the Kickstart File

As the Kickstart Configurator is still a work in progress, you might want to customize or at least inspect the ks.cfg file that it creates. The options created by the Ubuntu implementation of the Kickstart Configurator are described here, line by line. Most directives in this file include helpful comments. Be aware that the lines in this file do not appear in the same order shown in the Kickstart Configurator; the order more closely resembles that of the Ubuntu installation process. Because Kickstart for Ubuntu is still a work in progress based on the work of Red Hat developers, some of the options described in the Red Hat installation guide, available from www.redhat.com/docs/manuals/enterprise, might work, subject to the limitations already described.

**NOTE** The following analysis is based on the Ubuntu Server installation created in Chapter 2. It refers to files on an Ubuntu Server system; if the contents of your versions of these files are different, that's probably OK. Just make sure to try out the configured Kickstart file on a test system before putting it into use on production systems.

The first line is commented out, primarily because the installation program automatically detects the CPU and installs from the appropriate repository. The system language and associated modules should correspond to the default language as defined in the /etc/default/locale configuration file.

```
#System language
lang en_US
#Language modules to install
langsupport en_US
```

In actuality, the setting is slightly different in /etc/default/locale, as shown here; but it should be sufficient to verify the code for US English:

```
LANGUAGE="en_US:en"
```

The keyboard is fairly standard as well, and the following directive from the Kickstart configuration file,

```
keyboard us
```

should correspond to the **XKBLAYOUT="us"** directive in the /etc/default/console-set-up configuration file.

The system mouse option is not important unless you're installing a GUI, as the default setting shown here is added only to the associated X server configuration file, /etc/X11/xorg.conf:

```
mouse
```

The following time zone would be local, except for the **--utc** switch, which corresponds to UTC or Zulu time, as described in Table 3-1. The time zones don't quite match what's shown during the installation process, but they do correspond to a configuration subdirectory and file in the /usr/share/zoneinfo directory:

```
timezone --utc America/Los_Angeles
```

As with other standard Ubuntu installations, passwords for the root user are strongly discouraged. The following setting respects that decision by disabling the root password. And that's different from a blank password, which still allows logins by the user of that password.

```
rootpw --disabled
```

Along with a disabled root user goes at least one regular user, with the encrypted password as shown:

```
user michael --fullname "Michael Jang" --iscrypted --password $1$CuWIEW
```

The following command reboots the system after a successful installation of an Ubuntu system:

```
reboot
```

As an automated graphical installation is not supported by Ubuntu's implementation of Kickstart, the following directive confirms that installation will proceed in text mode:

```
text
```

In contrast to the comment in the ks.cfg file, upgrade installations are not (yet) supported in Ubuntu's implementation of Kickstart. So the following directive proceeds with a regular installation:

```
install
```

The following directive directs Kickstart to use local CD media:

```
cdrom
```

Alternatively, if you've configured a web server with a copy of the CD, you might see the following directive in its place:

```
url --url http://192.168.0.102/ubuntu/
```

The GRUB boot loader is the default and is assumed. The following directive installs the boot loader on the MBR, with an MD5 encrypted password:

```
bootloader --location=mbr --md5pass=$1$ulmrQw$wPlSrPxzy2aAbyoixp51
```

Even though this directive comes after that which writes the GRUB boot loader to the MBR, it is executed first:

```
zerombr yes
```

Assuming you're ready to delete all data on the hard drive associated with this installation, the following directive clears all partitions from the hard drives and specifies the default label for the architecture, which happens to be *msdos*, as described in Chapter 2.

```
clearpart --all --initlabel
```

This is followed by directives associated with specific partition information. As shown next, I've tried to set up filesystems on partitions on different hard drives, as suggested by these directives. That didn't work; the top-level root directory (/), the /boot directory, and the /tmp directory were each configured on partitions on the first hard drive.

```
part /boot --fstype ext3 --size 100 --asprimary --ondisk sda
part / --fstype ext3 --size 7000
part swap --size 512
part /tmp --fstype ext3 --size 500 --ondisk sdb
```

Standard authentication on modern Linux systems include the Shadow Password Suite with MD5 encrypted passwords, as described in Chapter 10.

```
auth --useshadow --enablemd5
```

Network information can be static or dynamic. Dynamic configuration can be local with **--bootproto dhcp** or configured via a DHCP server on a remote network with **--bootproto bootp**. The following line specifies static addressing information. I've added **--hostname hardytest1** to the end of the command even though it's not available in the Kickstart Configurator. *Be aware that this command is and must be on a single line.* Line wrapping within the Kickstart configuration file is acceptable and helps with the formatting of this book.

```
network --bootproto=static --ip=192.168.0.103
--netmask=255.255.255.0 --gateway=192.168.0.1
--nameserver=68.87.85.98 --device=eth0 --hostname hardytest1
```

As noted earlier, firewall configuration through Kickstart is not enabled as of this writing. For more information, see Chapter 18. As befits a Linux server, the X server is not configured or installed on this system, based on the following directive:

```
skipx
```

## Boot an Installation with a Kickstart File

There are several ways to start an automated installation using a Kickstart configuration file. First, the Kickstart file could be included with the CD or attached to some other media such as a USB key. It's best to set it up on a server. As described in Chapter 15, the default directory for the Ubuntu implementation of Apache is /var/www. I've copied the Kickstart file created earlier in this chapter to the /var/www/kick directory.

A directory on a network server is a handy way to set up multiple Kickstart files. For example, you could set up ks1.cfg for the first server to be configured, ks2.cfg for the second server, and so on. Such files can easily be customized with different IP addresses, hostnames, and more. Once loaded, they're accessible by default, as shown in Figure 3-7.

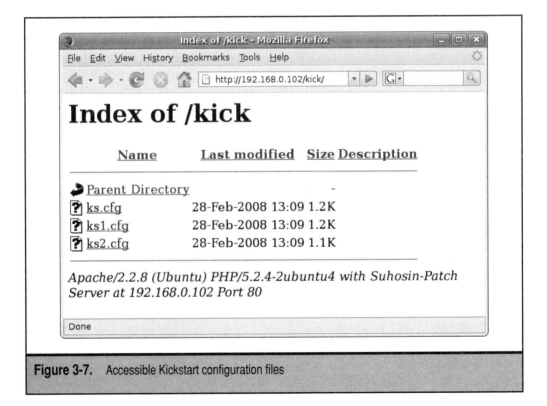

**Figure 3-7.**    Accessible Kickstart configuration files

You could boot the target server with a CD using the technique described in Chapter 2, from the **boot:** prompt. If you boot from an Ubuntu Server CD, you'll see the standard boot menu. Press the ESC key, and then when prompted that to leave the Graphical Boot Menu, accept by selecting OK, which leads to the **boot:** prompt.

Then start the installation process with the desired Kickstart file. The following directive, when run at the **boot:** prompt, starts the installation (install) program, using the Kickstart configuration file (ks.cfg) available from the web server at the IP address shown.

```
boot: install ks=http://192.168.0.102/kick/ks.cfg
```

If the Kickstart configuration file is properly configured, installation should proceed automatically, until the standard Ubuntu Server is installed and the login prompt is available. When you boot Ubuntu Server without a GUI, you might need to press ENTER before the following login prompt appears:

```
Ubuntu hardy hardytest1 tty1

hardytest1 login:
```

# SUMMARY

This chapter described the Kickstart automated installation tool as configured for Ubuntu systems. Ubuntu developers have focused on Kickstart as the primary tool for creating automated installations, even if it was originally developed for Red Hat Linux. Ubuntu developers have adapted the Red Hat GUI tool for Kickstart, which makes it easier to use and configure for less experienced users.

# CHAPTER 4

## The Boot Process and Rescue Mode

This chapter is focused on the boot process, and how it can be used to rescue and repair a damaged system. What happens if a junior administrator accidentally erases the GRUB configuration file? How can you manage Ubuntu from the root account? How can you check the integrity of a critical file system? These questions and more are answered in this chapter, along with the basics of the BIOS (Basic Input/Output System), the GRUB boot menu, the kernel ring buffer, and the relatively new Upstart system.

You'll also learn see how to access some rescue options available from the GRUB menu, the associated **grub>** prompt, and LiveCDs. This chapter is focused on the relatively short period between the powering up of a system to the time you're able to log into an Ubuntu server system.

# WHAT HAPPENS AFTER POWERING UP

After a system is powered up, the BIOS is the first program to run. Although the BIOS sequence is not directly related to Linux, it does set the stage for hardware detection. It loads the GRUB menu, courtesy of a pointer installed in the master boot record (MBR) of the primary hard drive. From the GRUB (Grand Unified Bootloader) menu, you can select Ubuntu boot and kernel options. Once the system boots from GRUB and loads the desired Linux kernel, the operating system is loaded as well. Boot messages are loaded through the kernel ring buffer, which can help diagnose a variety of boot issues. Then, before a login screen appears, there are services to start, daemons to run, and more.

**NOTE**    As this is not a hardware book, some of the descriptions of generic PC hardware presented here are oversimplifications. Addressing the full variety of BIOS programs and server/PC hardware is well beyond the scope of this book. One option for more information on server/PC hardware is *PC QuickSteps, Second Edition* (McGraw-Hill Professional, 2008).

## The BIOS Sequence

The BIOS is sometimes also known as a type of firmware. Some BIOSs serve as the overall firmware for computers, and other BIOSs are dedicated for individual components such as hard drive controllers, video cards, sound cards, and more. At one time, BIOS information was stored in read-only memory (ROM). Today, BIOS firmware on most components can be upgraded.

**NOTE**    BIOS firmware upgrades are another issue for Linux administrators. Many manufacturers make updates available only via Microsoft-based tools. The availability of such upgrades via Linux can be another consideration when the Linux administrator authorizes the purchase of hardware.

After a computer is powered up, the system BIOS starts the Power-On Self Test (POST) process. During the POST, the BIOS checks available RAM memory, looks for installed buses, such as those associated with PCI (Peripheral Component Interconnect) cards.

Many problems, such as loose connections on hardware cards, are associated with error codes, often depicted as audio "beeps." The meaning of a *beep code* is generally specific to the motherboard. Beeps are usually reserved for critical problems, such as RAM that isn't properly connected.

Once basic hardware is recognized, a BIOS menu is usually available. BIOS menus come in a wide variety of formats depending on manufacturer. Access to BIOS menus in current hardware is often hidden but available for a few seconds after the boot sequence starts. Access codes used in these menus are also manufacturer specific: you'll probably need to press a key, such as ESC, F1, F2, or DEL, to access a menu like the one shown in Figure 4-1.

BIOS menus often merely confirm detected components. For many hardware components, custom settings are not possible. For example, while the characteristics of detected hard drives are shown in some detail, most BIOS menus don't support custom hard drive power settings.

However, the options available in BIOS menus do share some common characteristics, including the following:

▼ **Boot Sequence**  Configures the search order for bootable media.

■ **Peripheral Controls**  Supports types of access to certain peripherals.

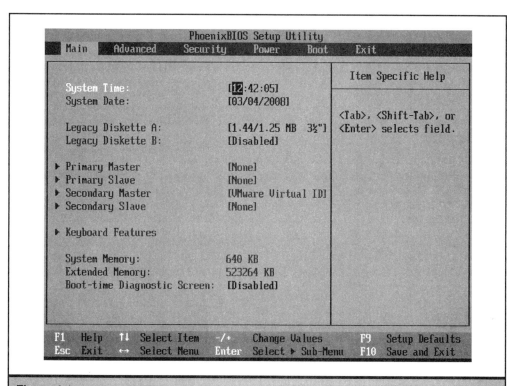

**Figure 4-1.**  A typical BIOS menu

- ■ **Password Protection** Secures the BIOS menu from changes; might also secure access to boot menu.
- ■ **Boot time diagnostic screen** Displays messages such as detected hard drives, if enabled.
- ▲ **Network boot access** Supports an option to move directly to the Preboot Execution Environment (PXE)–enabled boot system of the local network card.

Where video memory is shared with system RAM, the allocation of memory is often customizable through the BIOS menu. Many BIOS menus can be bypassed, based on a message similar to this:

```
Press F2 to Enter SETUP, Press F12 for Network Boot, Esc for Boot Menu
```

In this case, pressing the ESC key accesses a boot menu similar to that shown in Figure 4-2.

Available options might depict one or more removable devices, such as USB keys, floppy disk drives, or even secure digital media cards. They normally also depict one or more hard drives. Of course, the CD-ROM option is somewhat more generic than the menu choice suggests; it may boot a drive that can even write to DVDs. The Network Boot option demonstrates that the PXE boot characteristics of a local network card are integrated into the BIOS.

*TIP* Secure production systems should include password protection for the BIOS menu. Otherwise, crackers who gain physical access to your systems could be able to boot LiveCDs from other media such as CD/DVDs, USB keys, and so on. Of course, you could also install locks on such server physical access points.

## Making GRUB

GRUB is the default boot loader for most Linux distributions. In other words, when you boot a system with Linux installed, you may have access to a menu similar to that shown in Figure 4-3.

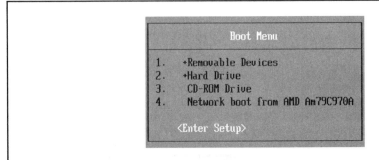

**Figure 4-2.** A boot media menu

## Virtualization

*Hardware virtualization* facilitates the configuration of multiple virtual machines on a single system. Linux supports several options for hardware virtualization. Red Hat enables Xen with a specialized kernel on its distributions. Newer releases of VMware products also take advantage of hardware virtualization. The default virtualization option for Ubuntu Server Edition is based on a Linux kernel module known as the Kernel-based Virtual Machine (KVM).

The current trend towards virtualization depends on supportive CPU hardware. Hardware virtualization does not require multiple CPUs, but it does take advantage of the multi-core CPU chips available from both Intel and AMD. The Intel multi-core CPUs allow virtualization to be disabled in the BIOS; most manufacturers disable it by default, and some manufacturers don't even allow users to enable virtualization, even if the multi-core CPU supports it. Not all Intel Dual Core/ Core 2 Duo or AMD X2 CPUs support hardware-assisted virtualization. Generally, hardware virtualization support is limited to AMD X2 CPUs of TL-50 and above, as well as Intel Dual Core CPUs of T2300 (or T5600) and above. If the target system includes an Intel multi-core CPU which supports virtualization, you probably will have to enable the feature in the BIOS.

One way to check for virtualization with an Ubuntu LiveCD. After booting from that media (and possibly making appropriate changes in the BIOS), review the /proc/cpuinfo file. If you see the **vmx** (Intel) or **svm** (AMD) flags in that file, the subject system supports hardware virtualization. (For more information on creating a virtual machine within an Ubuntu system, see Chapter 20, which is dedicated to the subject.)

Of course, when you see the following prompt, you'll have to press the ESC key before the timeout to see the menu:

```
GRUB Loading stage1.5

GRUB loading, please wait...
Press 'ESC' to enter the menu... 3
```

The menu options are straightforward. The first option boots from the customized Ubuntu Server Hardy Heron kernel. The second option boots from the same kernel in single-user mode. The third option is designed to run the memtest program, which may also be available from a BIOS menu, and stresses the local RAM looking for errors.

If you install a new kernel, that new kernel and at least the previously installed kernel are normally both made available from GRUB menu.

```
Ubuntu 8.04, kernel 2.6.24-16-server
Ubuntu 8.04, kernel 2.6.24-16-server (recovery mode)
Ubuntu 8.04, memtest86+




      Use the ↑ and ↓ keys to select which entry is highlighted.
      Press enter to boot the selected OS, 'e' to edit the
      commands before booting, or 'c' for a command-line.
```

**Figure 4-3.**  A typical GRUB menu

The code stanzas discussed in the following examples are from the GRUB configuration file on the laptop on which I boot Ubuntu Server, without the comments (which you can read for yourself). To review the version of this file on your own system, open the /boot/grub/menu.lst file. The first active directive points to the first stanza as the default. In other words, if you don't make a choice in 10 seconds (as depicted by the **timeout** directive), GRUB automatically chooses the first stanza.

**NOTE**  In this context, a *stanza* is a group of directives in a configuration file designed for a specific purpose. In the GRUB configuration file, a stanza specifies how an operating system is booted on a local machine.

```
default 0
timeout 3
```

Be aware that if you set **default 1**, the default choice is set to the *second* stanza.

Even though the following directive is commented out, the menu is hidden by default. If you don't want a hidden menu, add the **menu** directive.

```
#hiddenmenu
```

The default sets the GRUB menu in white with a black background. Colors can be changed, as suggested by the following directive:

```
color cyan/blue white/blue
```

The password options are important; if you don't protect the GRUB menu with a password, a cracker who gets this far can then set the local system to boot at any runlevel, including one that could provide administrative access without any other password. You could set the password in clear text with a directive such as this:

```
password somepassword
```

> *TIP* I strongly recommend password protection for the GRUB menu. I suggest that you should also disable or at least password-protect the "recovery mode" stanza configured in Ubuntu releases for GRUB. Otherwise, anyone who is able to reboot (or power cycle) your Ubuntu system and can start recovery mode can gain access to your system—with full administrative privileges.

It's possible to use the MD5 algorithm to encrypt the password, using the following steps:

1. Run the **grub-md5-crypt** command.
2. Enter the desired password and enter it again when prompted.
3. Copy the encrypted password as shown to the directive that follows. (The encrypted password is the jumble of letters, numbers, and punctuation at the end of the line.)

   ```
   password --md5 $1$2EPqO$5wO/9IAKFyED7SfVaJ9Qi0
   ```

   If this line is written *before* the individual stanzas, it password-protects the GRUB menu. If this line is written *within* a stanza, the user who selects that stanza is prompted to enter that password.

Now examine the individual stanzas. The Hardy Heron release introduces the Universal Unique Identifier (UUID), which is associated with the partition, RAID device, or logical volume configured for a certain directory. (For more information on UUIDs see Chapter 5.

The **title** directive specifies what's seen in the main GRUB menu:

```
title  Ubuntu, kernel 2.6.24-16-server
```

The **root (hd0,0)** directive specifies the partition with the /boot directory files:

```
root    (hd0,0)
```

In this case, it's the first partition of the first hard drive. (If it were **root (hd1,2)**, it would be the third partition of the second hard drive.) The **root** directive in the third line is different from **root (hd0,0)**.

The **kernel** directive points to the filename of the Linux kernel, located relative to **root (hd0,0)**. Then the **root** directive specifies the UUID, partition, label, or logical volume on which the top level root directory (/) is mounted. (These options are described in more detail in Chapter 5.) The **ro** means this top level root directory (/) is mounted read-only, until the system reads the /etc/fstab configuration file. The **quiet** and **splash** options hide associated messages, using a default Ubuntu splash screen. If you want to watch messages as an Ubuntu system boots, you could delete those two options.

```
kernel /vmlinuz-2.6.24-16-server root=UUID=766680a9-4090 ro quiet
splash
```

Finally, loading the initial RAM disk, **initrd** for short, loads the associated image file from the partition associated with the aforementioned **root (hd0,0)** directive. In other words, the initial RAM disk file, initrd.img-2.6.24-16-server, is located in the /boot directory.

```
initrd /initrd.img-2.6.24-16-server
```

The final **quiet** option suppresses messages after the initial RAM disk is loaded:

```
quiet
```

The Recovery Mode GRUB menu option configured for Ubuntu systems includes a similar stanza of directives. The one difference is in the **kernel** command line. As shown here, it specifies **single** in place of **quiet splash**. The **single** option starts Linux in single-user mode, often also known as *runlevel 1*. You can also password-protect access to recovery mode using the same technique described earlier in this section. Just make sure the **password** directive with the password is included as part of the recovery mode stanza.

```
root (hd0,0)
kernel /vmlinuz-2.6.24-16-server root=UUID=766680a9-4090 ro single
initrd /initrd.img-2.6.24-16-server
```

## The Meaning of Root in Linux

There are several meanings associated with the word *root* in Linux. In GRUB, a directive such as **root (hd0,1)**, which couples it with a partition, specifies the partition with the /boot directory. Also in GRUB, a directive such as **root=/dev/hda5** in the **kernel** command line specifies the partition or device where the top-level root directory (/) is mounted. The home directory for the root administrative user is /root, which exists even if the root user isn't given a password (which is the default in Ubuntu). The root prompt, normally a pound sign (#) in the default bash shell, indicates that you're logged in as the root user.

For contrast, the next stanza is, as suggested by its title, associated with Novell's SUSE Linux distribution. The boot directory is on the eighth partition of the first hard drive, as suggested by its title. The **kernel** command line cites the Linux kernel in /boot/vmlinuz, which confirms that the /boot directory is not located on a separate partition.

```
title  SUSE Linux Enterprise Server 10 (on /dev/sda8)
root   (hd0,7)
kernel /boot/vmlinuz root=/dev/sda8 vga=0x314 splash=silent showopts
initrd /boot/initrd
savedefault
boot
```

The differences between the SUSE and Ubuntu-style stanzas are subtle: In the case of the SUSE stanza, the top-level root directory (/) and the /boot directory are both on the same eighth partition of the first hard drive. Since the /boot directory is not directly mounted on a partition, the kernel and initial RAM disk files both have taken from the /boot/vmlinuz and /boot/initrd files. The **vga=0x314** option is a framebuffer mode, used during the boot process. (For more information on framebuffer modes, see http://tldp.org/HOWTO/Framebuffer-HOWTO.html.) As suggested by **splash=silent**, no SUSE splash screen appears during the boot process. The **showopts** option is indirect; options listed before this directive are hidden during the boot process. The **savedefault** option is generally ignored today; the **boot** option, which is the default, starts the boot process using the settings listed in the stanza.

To learn more, examine how Red Hat configures a GRUB stanza. The following boots my installation of Red Hat Enterprise Linux 5:

```
title Red Hat Enterprise Linux Server (2.6.18-8.1.8.el5)
        root (hd0,2)
        kernel /vmlinuz-2.6.18-8.1.8.el5 ro root=LABEL=/ rhgb quiet
        initrd /initrd-2.6.18-8.1.8.el5.img
```

The /boot directory is shown in the same format as in the Ubuntu-based stanza; in this case, it's located on the third partition of the first hard drive. As the partition is dedicated to the boot directory, the **kernel** directive finds the noted Linux kernel file in the local directory. As with the Ubuntu stanza, the **ro** means that the top level root directory (/) is mounted read-only, until enough of the system has booted. That top level root directory (/) is associated with the **LABEL=/** label, functionally similar to how Ubuntu uses the UUID. The **rhgb** option is associated with a Red Hat graphical boot; the **quiet** directive means that messages are hidden during the boot process.

Finally, examine how a Microsoft Windows system is booted from GRUB:

```
title       Windows XP Media Center Edition
root        (hd0,1)
chainloader +1
boot
```

The **root (hd0,1)** directive works like other similar root directives. In this case, it points to the second partition of the first hard drive. The **chainloader +1** directive points one sector from the start of the specified partition, which is where the Microsoft boot loader takes over.

**NOTE** Later, in the "Recovery and Single-User Mode" section, I'll show you how to take advantage of the GRUB menu to recover from some types of boot failures and more.

# Kernels and Hardware Detection

Once a system boots from GRUB into some specified Linux kernel, the kernel is loaded into the system—and is ready for more. The process is tracked in the *kernel ring buffer*, available via the **dmesg** command or in the /var/log/dmesg file. While it's a large file, you should know at least the basics of what's available through that file, as it can help diagnose a variety of boot issues.

The details associated with the kernel ring buffer varies with BIOS, with attached hardware, with power management schemes, and more. Some common characteristics are listed in Table 4-1; but they may appear in a different order—or not at all on a system, depending on the variations just described. The information for Table 4-1 was collected from my desktop and laptop systems, as well as a VMware Server running Ubuntu.

With this knowledge, you can search through the kernel ring buffer for problems, using filtering tools such as the **grep** command. For example, if a problem with detected hardware appears, search through the kernel ring buffer for the device file, the associated hardware specification, or even hardware addresses.

But before you can log in to Linux, services must be started, terminals configured, partitions mounted, and other tasks must be accomplished. And that's the province of a relatively new system known as Upstart.

# Upstart, RCs Scripts, and Services

If you haven't installed a new version of Linux lately, you might be in for a shock. There is no /etc/inittab configuration file in Ubuntu releases. Upstart, the replacement for the System V init program, is designed to meet the demands of the latest plug-and-play hotplug environments. During the boot process, Upstart is especially helpful with filesystems mounted on portable and network devices.

**NOTE** This section assumes that you have some basic knowledge of services and runlevels; thus, some of the explanations here are too brief for a relatively new Linux administrator. For more information on runlevels and script management, see Chapter 7.

As an affirmation of Upstart's success, Red Hat has adopted it as a replacement for System V init, starting with Fedora 9 released in the spring of 2008.

| Keyword | Description |
|---|---|
| Kernel | Specifies version and release date |
| RAM | BIOS RAM map; can include high and low memory |
| Zone | Messages such as "DMA zone" specifies the amount of reserved memory in the noted area |
| ACPI or APM | Detailed ACPI (Advanced Configuration and Power Interface) settings include but are not limited to interrupts, APIC (Advanced Programmable Interrupt Controller), and more APM (Advanced Power Management) is now obsolete. |
| Kernel command line | Directives and options from the kernel command line in the GRUB boot loader |
| CPU | Dual core and multiple CPU systems specify CPU#0, CPU#1, and so on |
| Memory | Detected RAM memory |
| SELinux or AppArmor | Messages associated with enabling such security feature |
| pnp | Linux plug and play support; can also list number of detected devices |
| TCP | Settings for network tables |
| Various devices | Can specify serial ports, mouse controllers, ISA (Industry Standard Architecture) cards, network devices, USB systems |
| Driver files | Can list device files such as eth0 for a network device, sda for a SCSI (Small Computer Systems Interface) or SATA (Serial Advanced Technology Attachment) drive |
| Mounted filesystems | Can include the format and partition device |

**Table 4-1.**   Typical Types of Kernel Ring Buffer Messages

## Upstart Service Scripts

Pay particular attention to the scripts in the /etc/event.d directory. Future Linux releases might see service scripts currently in the /etc/init.d directory move there to become a part of the Upstart system. One service script, the logging daemon, **logd**, was already moved there for the Hardy Heron release. The configuration file, /etc/event.d/logd, is straight-forward. First, logging is stopped in runlevels 0, 1, and 6 with commands like this:

```
stop on runlevel 0
```

Next, log output, unless otherwise configured, is sent to the console:

```
console output
```

The /sbin/logd daemon is run by default. If it is stopped for any reason, it is restarted, as depicted by the **respawn** directive:

```
exec /sbin/logd
respawn
```

## Upstart Scripts Replace /etc/inittab

If you remember the directives in the /etc/inittab configuration file, you'll recognize the contents of the other files in the /etc/event.d directory. As the hardware advantages of Upstart are essentially transparent to most users, this section focuses on how Upstart provides equivalent functionality to /etc/inittab.

The first line in a standard /etc/inittab file specifies the default runlevel. To review, for Debian-based distributions including Ubuntu, the default runlevel as signified by the following directive is 2:

```
id:2:initdefault
```

The default runlevel is now configured with Upstart's rc-default configuration file in the /etc/event.d directory. In essence, the script takes the default runlevel from /etc/inittab if the file exists and a directive like **id:2:initdefault** is included; otherwise, it's configured to set a runlevel of 2.

Next, some scripts are run independent of runlevel, as configured by the following:

```
si::sysinit:/etc/init.d/rcS
```

This effectively runs all scripts in the /etc/rcS.d directory. These are all "start" scripts, as they start with a capital *S*. In other words, they're started whenever Linux is booted. The same scripts are run through Upstart, courtesy of the /etc/event.d/rcS script.

The next directive from my old /etc/inittab specifies what needs to be done when Linux is booted into single-user mode, as specified by the recovery mode option described earlier in the GRUB configuration file. The *S* runlevel is synonymous with the **single** that appears in the GRUB configuration file, which starts single-user mode. The **wait** directive stays in the noted runlevel. The **sulogin** command, when invoked by the recovery mode option, boots and logs into the root account.

```
~~:S:wait:/sbin/sulogin
```

The equivalent Upstart functionality is available from the /etc/event.d/rcS-sulogin file, which invokes the **sulogin** command unless /etc/inittab exists on the system.

These directives from /etc/inittab provide options; only one is run, based on the specified runlevel. For example, if the default runlevel is 2, the associated command runs the scripts in the /etc/rc2.d directory:

```
l0:0:wait:/etc/init.d/rc 0
l1:1:wait:/etc/init.d/rc 1
```

```
l2:2:wait:/etc/init.d/rc 2
l3:3:wait:/etc/init.d/rc 3
l4:4:wait:/etc/init.d/rc 4
l5:5:wait:/etc/init.d/rc 5
l6:6:wait:/etc/init.d/rc 6
```

The equivalent Upstart script for runlevel 2 is /etc/event.d/rc2, which confirms the desired runlevel and then runs the following command:

```
exec /etc/init.d/rc 2
```

Linux systems are configured to accept the CTRL-ALT-DELETE key combination often associated with Microsoft systems. When the associated signal is received, the /etc/inittab file specifies the following directive, which starts the **shutdown** command in one second (**-t1**), limited by any existing rules specified in an /etc/shutdown.allow file (**-a**), if it exists, and reboots now (**-r now**).

```
ca:12345:ctrlaltdel:/sbin/shutdown -t1 -a -r now
```

In contrast, Upstart's /etc/event.d/control-alt-delete file executes the following command, with fewer limitations. Of course, the command can be modified to suit your needs.

```
exec /sbin/shutdown -r now "Control-Alt-Delete pressed"
```

Many server systems are protected by Uninterruptable Power Supplies (UPS). When connected to a Linux system, they can send one of three signals to the system, which was interpreted by /etc/inittab with the following commands:

```
pf::powerwait:/etc/init.d/powerfail start
pn::powerfailnow:/etc/init.d/powerfail now
po::powerokwait:/etc/init.d/powerfail stop
```

These options require the powstatd package, also known as the Configurable UPS Monitoring Daemon. It depends on the noted /etc/init.d/powerfail script as well as the /etc/powstatd.conf configuration file. But as **/sbin/powstatd** is now a regular daemon controlled by the complementary /etc/init.d/powstatd script, it's technically not part of Upstart.

Linux systems typically include six consoles, also known as *gettys*. In /etc/inittab, they're started with the following directives, where all six gettys are made available in runlevels 2 and 3.

**NOTE**   They're known as *gettys*, not *getties*, based on a somewhat odd acronym, as *a getty get a TTY*, short for *teletypewriter*. The *TTY* is the predecessor for the current command line console, which "gets" the TTY.

```
1:2345:respawn:/sbin/getty 38400 tty1
2:23:respawn:/sbin/getty 38400 tty2
3:23:respawn:/sbin/getty 38400 tty3
```

```
4:23:respawn:/sbin/getty 38400 tty4
5:23:respawn:/sbin/getty 38400 tty5
6:23:respawn:/sbin/getty 38400 tty6
```

In the Upstart system, each of these gettys are started with tty*x* files in the /etc/ event.d directory, where *x* represents the terminal number. While these files are more descriptive, they contain the same information. All six terminals are started in runlevels 2 and 3. When a user logs out of a terminal, the **respawn** directive regenerates that terminal with a new login screen. Communication in a text screen is plenty fast at 38400 bits per second.

# RESCUE OPTIONS

Problems happen, even in Linux: A key file might be erased, a newer administrator might introduce a syntax error in a boot file, drivers and even volumes can become corrupt, a download from a bad source can cause trouble for other systems. As real life happens, Linux administrators need to know their options for rescuing troubled systems. This includes such options as single-user mode, rescue options from installation CDs, and even the use of LiveCDs.

## Recovery and Single-User Mode

There are two ways to access a recovery mode from the GRUB menu. By default, Ubuntu releases include a recovery mode option in the GRUB configuration file, which provides root administrative access to the Ubuntu system, even when the root administrative account is not enabled.

### Recovery Mode

Earlier in this chapter, I suggested that you disable or at least password-protect the recovery mode option in the GRUB menu. The risk is that recovery mode does provide access to root administrative privileges on the local system. The title of the associated stanza in the GRUB configuration file will appear similar to this:

```
Ubuntu 8.04, kernel 2.6.24-16-server (recovery mode)
```

If you select this option, Linux boots without hiding any boot messages. It then starts a Recovery Menu, as shown in Figure 4-4, which offers three straightforward options: Resume Normal Boot, Drop To Root Shell Prompt, or Try To Fix X Server. The options are as depicted in the /usr/share/recovery-mode/recovery-menu configuration file, associated with the options configured in the /usr/share/recovery-mode/options directory.

▼  **Resume Normal Boot**   The boot process proceeds as if you booted a regular kernel in the standard runlevel 2.

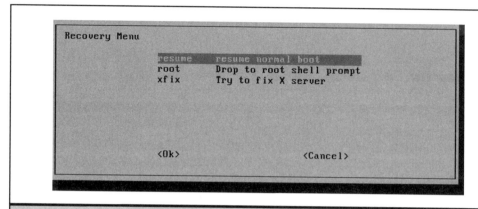

**Figure 4-4.**   The Recovery Menu

- **Drop To Root Shell Prompt**   The bash shell is started with a root user prompt; unless you've created a password for the root user, no password is required.
- **Try To Fix X Server**   Executes the **dpkg-reconfigure -phigh xserver-xorg** command, which prompts the administrator to reconfigure the default X server, if the xserver-xorg package is installed.

## Other GRUB Runlevels

Currently, it's not possible to access any nonstandard runlevel from GRUB menu on Ubuntu releases, except single-user mode. Access to other runlevels is a common feature via the GRUB menu in other distributions. However, bug 85014 suggests Ubuntu developers are working on this issue.

If the menu is password-protected using the method suggested in the first part of the chapter, you'll see the following message at the bottom of the menu, where *OS* is short for operating system:

```
Press enter to boot the selected OS or 'p' to enter a
password to unlock the next set of features.
```

**NOTE**   The *OS* in the GRUB menu is an oversimplification. The implication is that each choice in the GRUB menu starts a different operating system. In reality, it starts a different kernel, or even just a different stanza configured to start the same operating system and kernel in a different runlevel.

Once a password is entered (or if the GRUB menu is not password-protected), the message is a bit different:

```
Press enter to boot the selected OS or 'e' to edit the
commands before booting, or 'c' for a command-line.
```

Now to access single-user mode from the Ubuntu GRUB menu, take the following steps:

1. Highlight an operating system. For Ubuntu Hardy Heron server, choose Ubuntu 8.04 kernel-2.6.24-16-server.
2. Press E to access the associated stanza of commands.
3. Highlight the line that starts with the **kernel** directive.
4. Press E to edit the line with the **kernel** directive.
5. Press the SPACEBAR once and type in the desired runlevel. In this case, to set up single-user mode for root access, type **S** or **single** and press ENTER.
6. Press B to boot from the modified stanza.
7. When you see the menu shown in Figure 4-4, select root and press ENTER.

The computer should now boot in single-user mode, giving you access to the local system with root administrative privileges. Be aware that changes made to this stanza through the GRUB menu editor are temporary and will not appear the next time you boot or reboot this system.

## Using the GRUB Command Line

If the GRUB configuration file is accidentally erased, all is not lost. You could use a rescue mode as described in the next section. Alternatively, you could just enter the commands at the GRUB command line that appears when the GRUB configuration file is missing or misplaced. To follow along with this section, print out a copy of your GRUB configuration file, /boot/grub/menu.lst, or refer to the file as described in the first half of this chapter.

```
[ Minimal BASH-like editing is supported. For
  the first word, TAB lists possible command
  completions. Anywhere else TAB lists the possible
  completions of a device/filename. ESC at anytime
  exits. ]

grub>
```

You don't need to delete the GRUB configuration file to access this menu. If the GRUB menu is password-protected, press P and enter the password. Enter **c** for the command line shown here.

Several commands are available from the GRUB command line; enter **help** for a full list. Options include directives often found in GRUB configuration files such as **root,**

**kernel,** and **initrd**, as well as common shell commands such as **cat** and **find**. If at least the /boot directory is associated with a regular partition, the **find** command can help you identify the partition with those files. For example, the following command identifies a standard file in the /boot/grub/ directory, in the first hard drive, on the first partition:

```
grub> find /grub/device.map
(hd0,0)
```

If the /boot directory is not mounted on a separate partition, you'll need to enter the full path to find the partition with the /boot/grub/device.map file. And, yes, it will be on a partition, as the BIOS might not recognize an alternative such as a logical volume.

If the top-level root directory (/) is mounted on a regular partition, without benefit of a logical volume or RAID device, you could search for key files there, such as /etc/fstab:

```
grub> find /etc/fstab
(hd0,1)
```

If you're fortunate to find a file like /etc/fstab, the **cat/etc/fstab** command can read the contents of that file. But first you need to specify the partition with the following command:

```
grub> root (hd0,1)
```

If you don't remember the precise contents of the associated GRUB configuration file, some trial and error may be required. But the first command specifies the partition with the /boot directory, in this case:

```
grub> root (hd0,0)
```

Next, type in **kernel /**, and press the TAB key, once. You'll see available files on the speci fied partition, as shown in Figure 4-5. The TAB key also supports command completion. Experienced Linux users should already know that the Linux kernel file is vmlinuz-*.

```
grub> kernel /
```

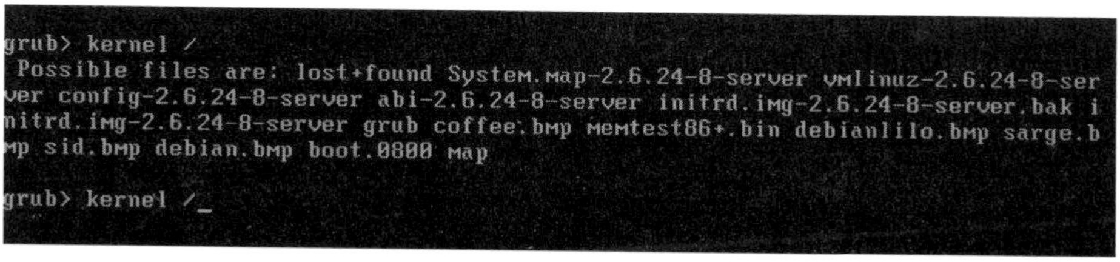

**Figure 4-5.** View available files using command completion

If you know the GRUB configuration file, you should already know this is where to specify the location of the top-level root directory (/). This may be tricky, especially if that directory is located on a RAID device or logical volume. For the purpose of this section, I'm assuming, and have an Ubuntu system, where that directory is mounted on a specific partition, in this case, /dev/sda2. It's mounted as read only (**ro**) until the operating system is loaded and the Upstart system can take over.

```
grub> kernel /vmlinuz-2.6.24-16 root=/dev/sda2 ro
```

But wait, the GRUB configuration file described earlier specified an UUID for the top-level root directory (/), if you know the partition where that directory is mounted, you don't need the UUID.

Finally, the initial RAM disk is normally loaded with the **initrd** command. In the same fashion, I can take advantage of command completion. First, I type in this:

```
grub> initrd /
```

Then I press the TAB key to see available files, which should include an initrd.img-2.6.24-16-server file:

```
grub> initrd /initrd.img-2.6.24-16-server
```

Finally, to start the boot process from the **grub>** prompt, I use the **boot** command:

```
grub> boot
```

If successful, the boot process should proceed as if it's been run directly from a regular GRUB configuration file. You can then re-create an appropriate /boot/grub/menu.lst configuration file using an example from another Ubuntu Server system.

## The Installation CD Rescue Mode

Sometimes, you just need a rescue disk. The example of a missing GRUB configuration file is a good way to test the rescue mode available from the Ubuntu installation CD. For the purpose of this section, I run the following command to disable the GRUB menu:

```
$ sudo mv /boot/grub/menu.lst /home/michael
```

Now that GRUB is disabled, use the Ubuntu Server installation CD—the ISO file described in Chapter 2 would work just as well. Boot from that CD, and when you get to the main Ubuntu Server installation menu, choose Rescue A Broken System and press ENTER.

The first few steps of rescue mode proceed like an installation. As shown in Figure 4-6, a Rescue Mode label appears in the upper-left corner.

The first few steps are essentially identical to the first few steps of the installation process described in Chapter 2. Remember that as these are text-mode installation screens, use the TAB and arrow keys to highlight a selection and press ENTER to confirm the choice.

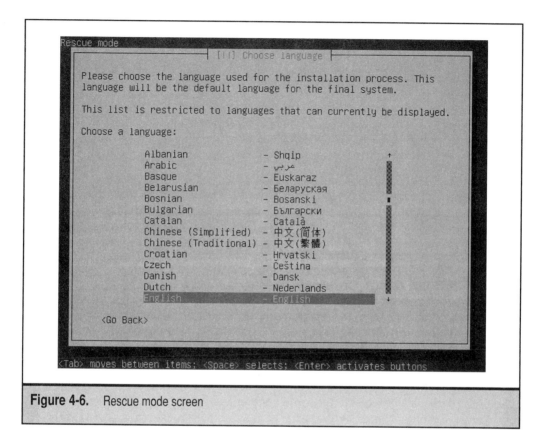

**Figure 4-6.**  Rescue mode screen

Rescue mode also provides full access to the other installation tools; just select Go Back, and you should recognize the installation menu.

1. Select a language and press ENTER.

2. Based on the selected language, a choice of countries or regions may be presented. Select the most appropriate option and press ENTER to continue.

3. When you see an option Detect Keyboard Layout, I prefer to select No. Otherwise, you're prompted to type in one of several different characters, several times. Make a choice and press ENTER to continue.

4. Select a Keyboard Origin and press ENTER.

5. Select a Keyboard Layout and press ENTER.

6. The Ubuntu installer now takes a few moments to detect critical hardware and install packages required for rescue mode.

7. Enter a hostname for the system, which does not have to match the hostname of the system being rescued.

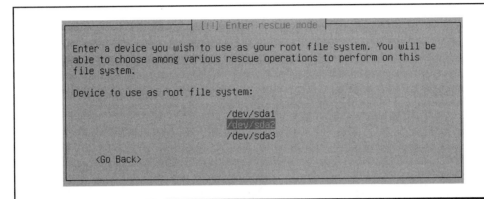

**Figure 4-7.** Selecting a root filesystem in rescue mode

8. Based on the national origin associated with the keyboard, review the options for time zones. Select a time zone most appropriate for your location and press ENTER.

9. In the Rescue Mode screen shown in Figure 4-7, you'll see a list of detected devices, which can be partitions, logical volumes, or RAID devices. Select the device associated with the top-level root directory (/) and press ENTER.

   If in doubt about the right device, shell access is available in the second and third virtual consoles, in the same manner as during the regular Ubuntu installation process. Press ALT-F2 or ALT-F3, and then press ENTER, to access the ash shell in one of these consoles. You can run basic commands such as **df, fdisk, cat,** and **mount** to review available files. You can then return to the Rescue Mode screen by pressing ALT-F1.

   Alternatively, just try all available options; if the top-level root directory (/) device is not found, an error message appears after the next step, at which point you can select Go Back and try a different device.

10. There are four options which appear, as shown in Figure 4-8. The first option depends on the device selected in step 9.

   ■ **Execute A Shell In /dev/*xyz***   The actual device file that appears (instead of *xyz*) depends on the device selected in step 9. This option mounts the device and looks for a shell in the associated volume. If a shell doesn't exist in that volume, you'll see an error message. If it exists, you're asked to confirm, before the device file is mounted on the top level root directory (/), and you're taken to a root user prompt. Generally this is the preferred option.

   ■ **Execute A Shell In The Installer Environment**   The device file selected earlier is mounted on the /target directory, a shell from the installation CD is used, and you're shown a root user prompt.

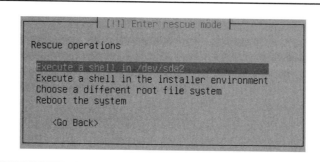

**Figure 4-8.** Selecting a rescue mode operation

- **Choose A Different Root Filesystem** This option opens the Ubuntu Installer Main Menu, defaulting to the Enter Rescue Mode option. Select this option, and repeat step 8.

- **Reboot The System** This option does not reboot the system, as of this writing.

11. Assuming you've selected one of the first two options from Figure 4-8, you should have access to a root prompt. If the /var directory is part of the top-level root directory (/) volume, you should have access to log files in the /var/log directory, to diagnose errors as needed.

12. Let's return to the original problem, a moved GRUB configuration file. Assume the **find** command was used to search and locate the menu.lst GRUB configuration file, say in your home directory. In that case, you can restore the menu.lst configuration file with the following command (substituting your user information):

```
# cp /home/michael/menu.lst /boot/grub
```

13. Once changes are complete, type **exit** to return to the screen shown in Figure 4-8. At that point, you can select Reboot The System. If this takes you to the Ubuntu Installer Main Menu, select Execute A Shell, select Confirm, and press ENTER. Then type in the **reboot** command.

## Using a LiveCD/DVD

Sometimes a LiveCD is better suited to repairing a troubled system. It's the best option if there are doubts about the integrity of a local filesystem. The boot process from an Ubuntu LiveCD leads to a menu slightly different from that of the Ubuntu Server CD. You'll see an option to Try Ubuntu Without Any Change To Your Computer, which boots a complete version of the current Ubuntu release direct from the CD, without using any files or partitions on local hard drive(s).

After the live Ubuntu system boots, administrators who prefer the command line, can choose Applications | Accessories | Terminal, or press CTRL-ALT-F*x*, where *x* is a number between 1 and 6, to access one of the standard six virtual terminals.

One advantage of the LiveCD is that no local partitions are mounted (unless you choose to mount them). That fact frees you to run commands such as **fsck** and **badblocks** to check the integrity of various partition, logical volume, and RAID device files.

From a command line in the LiveCD, the **sudo** command is not password-protected. So from a LiveCD command line, you could check the integrity of a partition such as /dev/sda1 with the following command:

```
$ sudo fsck /dev/sda1
```

**NOTE**   Similar advantages are available from other Linux LiveCD/DVD media. I often use the Knoppix DVD, which includes a wide variety of tools. But if you need to rescue a system, you're probably under some pressure and should therefore use a LiveCD/DVD with familiar tools.

# SUMMARY

This chapter focused on the boot process. While it included a general description of the BIOS menu, much of the focus was on the GRUB boot loader, and how the GRUB menu and individual entries can be password-protected and edited during the boot process. It also described the general messages associated with the kernel ring buffer, available in the /var/log/dmesg file.

It introduced the Upstart system, Ubuntu's replacement for /etc/inittab. Designed to run more smoothly, especially with hotpluggable storage devices, it's configured primarily in the /etc/event.d directory. The Red Hat community is adopting Upstart for its own releases. Eventually all service scripts in the /etc/init.d directory will be converted to Upstart scripts.

There are several different ways to rescue a Linux system. A recovery mode option exists in the default Ubuntu GRUB boot loader menu. If you choose to delete this option (and I recommend this), single-user mode is available with a bit of editing of the regular GRUB boot option. If the GRUB configuration file is corrupt or lost, you may be able to boot directly from the **grub>** prompt. Alternatively, a rescue mode is available from the installation CD. As the Ubuntu LiveCD provides a fully functional operating system, it can also be used to rescue another Ubuntu system.

# CHAPTER 5

## Filesystem Configuration

This chapter focuses on filesystems and how they can be configured on formatted partitions, software RAID (Redundant Array of Independent Disks) arrays, and logical volumes. Linux directories follow a protocol known as the Filesystem Hierarchy Standard (FHS). Several tools are available to create and format partitions and more.

While it's easier to configure logical volumes and RAID arrays during the standard installation process, that's not always possible. This chapter describes how you can configure partitions and then create RAID arrays and logical volumes after the Ubuntu Server operating system is installed.

# MAKE THE FILESYSTEM WORK FOR YOU

Everything in Linux is associated with a file. Partitions are represented by filesystem device files, such as /dev/sda1. Logical volumes and RAID arrays are also represented by filesystem device files. Other components such as CD/DVD drives are associated device files, such as /dev/dvd. The standard for organizing files and directories in Unix and Linux is through the Filesystem Hierarchy Standard (FHS). This section provides a basic overview of the FHS.

**NOTE**   You may be aware that many Linux distributions do not precisely follow every element of the FHS. Some elements in Ubuntu such as the Upstart system and the /etc/default configuration files were developed after the latest FHS release in 2004. Detailed information is available from the official FHS home page at www.pathname.com/fhs.

## The Filesystem Hierarchy Standard

While there are variations, modern Unix/Linux operating systems share several common directories. Some of these directories are dedicated for user files, drivers, kernels, logs, programs, utilities, and more. These directory categories, documented in the FHS, make it easier for users of other Unix-based operating systems to understand the basics of Linux.

On every Linux distribution, the filesystem starts with the top-level root directory, also known by its symbol, the single forward slash (/). Every other Linux directory is a subdirectory of that top-level root directory. Major directories are summarized in Table 5-1. Unless subdirectories are mounted separately, you can also find their files on the same partition, RAID array, or logical volume as the root directory. You might not see some of the directories shown in the table if you have not installed associated packages, as not all directories shown are officially part of the FHS.

Mounted directories are often known as *volumes* and can span multiple partitions in RAID arrays or logical volumes.

**NOTE**   In Linux, there are several different meanings associated with filesystem. A filesystem can refer to the FHS, an individual partition such as /dev/hda1, or a format such as ext3 or vfat.

| Directory | Description |
|---|---|
| / | Notes the top-level root directory. All other directories are subdirectories. |
| /bin | Adds essential command line utilities. Should not be mounted separately; otherwise, it could be difficult to get to these utilities when using a rescue mode. |
| /boot | Includes several Linux boot files, including the Linux kernel. If mounted separately, 100MB is usually sufficient for several kernels. Generally should not be mounted on a logical volume or RAID device. |
| /dev | Specifies hardware and software device drivers such as USB drives and console terminals. Do not mount this directory on a separate partition. |
| /etc | Sets most basic host-specific configuration files; several /etc subdirectories are specified in the FHS, including /etc/X11. |
| /home | Includes home directories for every user (except root). |
| /lib | Adds program libraries for /bin and /sbin command line utilities and the kernel. Do not mount this directory on a separate partition. |
| /media | Incorporates mount points for removable media and unassigned volumes. Examples include floppy disks (/media/floppy) and CD/DVDs (/media/cdrom). Unassigned volumes may be associated with partitions; for example, /dev/sda6 can be mounted as /media/sda6. |
| /misc | Includes a standard mount point for local directories mounted via the automounter; not a formal part of the FHS. |
| /mnt | Adds a legacy mount point; formerly used for removable media, commonly used for temporary filesystems. |
| /net | Includes a standard mount point for network directories mounted via the automounter; not a formal part of the FHS. |
| /opt | Incorporates a common location for third-party application files. |
| /proc | Specifies currently running kernel-related processes, including device assignments such as IRQ ports, I/O addresses, and DMA channels, as well as kernel configuration settings such as IP forwarding. |
| /root | Notes the home directory of the root user. |
| /sbin | Adds system administration binary commands. Don't mount this directory separately. |

**Table 5-1.**  Basic Filesystem Hierarchy Standard Directories

| Directory | Description |
|-----------|-------------|
| /smb | Includes the standard mount point for remote shared Microsoft network directories mounted via the automounter; not a formal part of the FHS. |
| /srv | Specifies a directory commonly used by network servers. |
| /tmp | Includes temporary files. |
| /usr | Adds small programs accessible to all users. Includes many system administration commands and utilities in subdirectories such as /usr/bin. |
| /var | Includes variable data, including log files and printer spools. |

**Table 5-1.** Basic Filesystem Hierarchy Standard Directories (*continued*)

## Partition Device Files

Before you review how to create partitions, take a step back and examine how partition device files work. Partitions can be created on several different types of media:

▼ **PATA drives** Since nearly the beginning of the PC era, the standard computer system has been configured to manage up to four IDE (Integrated Drive Electronics) hard drives, now known as PATA (Parallel Advanced Technology Attachment) drives.

■ **SATA drives** Current PCs can also handle SATA (Serial ATA) drives.

■ **SCSI drives** Servers commonly are configured with SCSI (Small Computer Systems Interface) drives. Depending on the SCSI hardware, up to 31 different SCSI hard drives may be attached.

■ **USB drives** It's not currently possible to boot Linux directly from a USB (Universal Serial Bus)–based hard drive or similar device such as a USB key, since you can't load Linux boot files directly from these drives. However, it is possible to set up a boot floppy or CD/DVD to start Linux from these drives. Directories other than /boot can be mounted on a USB drive.

▲ **IEEE 1394 drives** IEEE 1394 (Institute of Electrical and Electronics Engineers standard 1394, also known as FireWire or iLink) hard drives have similar abilities and limits to USB drives.

There are limits to how directories can be configured. While you can use as many PATA, SATA, SCSI, USB, and IEEE 1394 drives as your hardware can handle, the Linux boot files from the /boot directory must be installed on one of the first two *internal* hard drives; alternatively, you'd need to configure a boot floppy, CD, or USB key, depending on the capabilities of the BIOS.

| Partition Device | Device File |
|---|---|
| Floppy drive | First floppy = /dev/fd0 |
| PATA (IDE) hard drive or CD/DVD drive | First drive = /dev/hda, Second drive = /dev/hdb, Third drive = /dev/hdc, Fourth drive = /dev/hdd |
| SATA, SCSI, USB, IEEE 1394 drive | First drive = /dev/sda, Second drive = /dev/sdb … Twenty-seventh drive = /dev/sdaa, and so on |
| Primary partition | First PATA primary partition = /dev/hda1; Second SATA/SCSI primary partition = /dev/sda2 |
| Extended partition | /dev/sda$x$ or /dev/hda$x$; depending on configured primary partitions, $x$ could be 2, 3, or 4 |
| Logical partition | First SCSI/SATA logical partition = /dev/sda5; Second PATA logical partition = /dev/hda6 |

**Table 5-2.**    Partition Devices

On each drive, up to four primary partitions can be configured. One primary partition can be assigned as an extended partition, which can be subdivided into logical partitions. While more can be configured using tools such as **fdisk**, Linux recognizes no more than 16 partitions on a SATA/SCSI drive.

Ubuntu systems normally detect all partition devices listed in this section automatically. In the context of the Linux FHS, partition devices, are part of the /dev directory. Typical partition device files are described in Table 5-2.

## Create Partitions with fdisk

Older Linux veterans know the **fdisk** utility. It's the traditional partition management tool for Linux. This section describes a few of the basic **fdisk** commands. The expert mode available for **fdisk** illustrates the flexibility of this tool, which is much more capable than the Microsoft version, FDISK.EXE.

**NOTE**    This section assumes you're working on Ubuntu Server Edition with at least two SCSI hard drives. If you don't have such hardware available, SATA drives are also acceptable. Alternatively, a VMware Server–based virtual machine makes it easy to create virtual SCSI drives. That's what I used when writing this book.

## The Basics of fdisk

First, you need to know the device file of the drive to be configured. The easiest way to determine this is with the following command, which lists all connected drives—if they're detected:

```
$ sudo fdisk -l
```

You'll see drive sizes, listed in order, as well as partitions configured on each drive. A sample output is shown in Figure 5-1. Note the partitions configured on the first two drives. The actual drive order varies by hardware; portable drives such as those connected by USB and IEEE1394 devices appear after internal devices.

The following code shows how **fdisk** is used to open the second SCSI or SATA drive, /dev/sdb, to access an **fdisk**-based command line prompt. From this prompt, the **m** command lists basic **fdisk** commands.

```
$ sudo fdisk /dev/sdb

Command (m for help): m
Command action
   a   toggle a bootable flag
   b   edit bsd disklabel
   c   toggle the dos compatibility flag
```

```
michael@ubuntuhardyserver:~$ sudo fdisk -l
[sudo] password for michael:

Disk /dev/sda: 8589 MB, 8589934592 bytes
255 heads, 63 sectors/track, 1044 cylinders
Units = cylinders of 16065 * 512 = 8225280 bytes
Disk identifier: 0x00067c3f

   Device Boot      Start         End      Blocks   Id  System
/dev/sda1   *           1          12       96358+  83  Linux
/dev/sda2              13         924     7325640   83  Linux
/dev/sda3             925         986      498015   82  Linux swap / Solaris

Disk /dev/sdb: 1073 MB, 1073741824 bytes
255 heads, 63 sectors/track, 130 cylinders
Units = cylinders of 16065 * 512 = 8225280 bytes
Disk identifier: 0x5ac362c8

   Device Boot      Start         End      Blocks   Id  System
/dev/sdb1               1         130     1044193+  83  Linux

Disk /dev/sdc: 1073 MB, 1073741824 bytes
255 heads, 63 sectors/track, 130 cylinders
Units = cylinders of 16065 * 512 = 8225280 bytes
Disk identifier: 0x00000000

Disk /dev/sdc doesn't contain a valid partition table
michael@ubuntuhardyserver:~$ 
```

**Figure 5-1.**   fdisk lists available partitions

```
d    delete a partition
l    list known partition types
m    print this menu
n    add a new partition
o    create a new empty DOS partition table
p    print the partition table
q    quit without saving changes
s    create a new empty Sun disklabel
t    change a partition's system id
u    change display/entry units
v    verify the partition table
w    write table to disk and exit
x    extra functionality (experts only)

Command (m for help): q
```

There's a lot that you can do with the **fdisk** utility. If you're interested in **fdisk** in depth, run the **x** command to review associated extra functionality.

## Important fdisk Commands

To see what **fdisk** can do, type in the print command (**p**). Examine how it prints out the current partition table. The capacity of the drive and each configured partition is listed in cylinders. In the following case, the drive contains 130 cylinders, and 65 cylinders are used by the only configured partition on this drive.

```
Command (m for help): p

Disk /dev/sdb: 1073 MB, 1073741824 bytes
255 heads, 63 sectors/track, 130 cylinders
Units = cylinders of 16065 * 512 = 8225280 bytes
Disk identifier: 0x5ab062c8

   Device Boot      Start         End      Blocks   Id  System
/dev/sdb1                1          65      522081   83  Linux

Command (m for help):
```

From the available free space, you can create a new (**n**) partition which can be either a primary (**p**) or logical (**l**) partition. If an extended partition doesn't already exist, you can create it with the **e** command; that extended partition can then contain logical partitions.

When you assign space to a partition, you're assigning a block of cylinders on that hard disk. If you have free space, the **fdisk** default starts the new partition at the first available cylinder. The actual size of the partition depends on disk geometry, which can lead to a variance of several megabytes. In other words, if you specify a partition of 100MB, the actual size of the partition might be something like 96MB or 104MB.

## Use fdisk to Delete a Partition

To see how the **fdisk** utility works, take a look at how it deletes a partition. For the purpose of this section, I've configured the target partition without any data. To delete a partition from my second SCSI drive, I take the following steps:

1. I run the **sudo fdisk /dev/sdb** command. This opens the following **fdisk** prompt:

   ```
   Command (m for help):
   ```

2. I print the current partition table with the **p** command, which lists any configured partitions by device. For example, the first partition on the second SCSI drive is /dev/sdb1.

3. I delete the partition with the **d** command. If this is the only partition on the drive, it is automatically deleted. If there is more than one partition configured on this drive, I'm prompted for the partition number with a prompt like this:

   ```
   Partition number (1-4):
   ```

4. Before changes are made, they have to be written to disk with the **w** command. This deletes the partitions; at this point, data would be much more difficult to recover. It takes a few seconds to write the changes before returning to the command line.

   ```
   The partition table has been altered!
   Calling ioctl() to re-read partition table.
   Syncing disks.
   ```

It's no longer necessary to use the **sync** or **partprobe** command or reboot to implement the changes. I now have an empty hard disk or hard disk area in which to create needed partitions.

## Use fdisk to Create a Regular Partition

This section illustrates how to create a new partition for the /boot directory. Any existing partition associated with this directory can then be used as a backup. In this example, I create a partition on the second SCSI drive. In general, a partition created for the /boot directory should be on one of the first two physical drives. To add a suitable partition to my second SCSI drive, I take the following steps:

1. I run the **sudo fdisk /dev/sdb** command. This opens the following **fdisk** prompt:

   ```
   Command (m for help):
   ```

2. I print the current partition table with the **p** command, which lists any configured partitions by device. For example, the first partition on the second SCSI drive is /dev/sdb1.

3. I run the **n** command to create the new partition.

4. I specify the **p** command to set it as a primary partition. These steps assume the second SCSI disk has primary partitions available.

5. When I see the following prompt, I specify a partition number. If the number is already taken, **fdisk** provides a message to that effect and allows me to try again.

```
Partition number (1-4):
```

6. If partitions are already configured on the second SCSI disk, I recommend that this partition is configured to start at the first available cylinder. Normally, that's the default, as suggested by the prompt shown here:

```
First cylinder (1-256, default 1): 1
```

7. One of the strengths of **fdisk** is its ability to specify partition sizes in a normal format, such as bytes, kilobytes, or megabytes. To specify a size of 100MB, I follow the suggestions at the prompt shown here:

```
Last cylinder or +size or +sizeM or +sizeK (2-256,def 256): +100M
```

8. As a partition associated with the /boot directory should be bootable, I use the **a** command.

9. I run the print command (**p**) one more time to make sure that I made the right changes. Although I specify a 100MB partition, the geometry of the disk generally does not allow that precise size, as shown in the example. The effect is variable. On one disk, a 100MB partition actually covers 92MB. On another disk, a 100MB partition covers 99MB.

10. Assuming I'm pleased with the changes, I use the write command (**w**) to record the changes to the disk.

I can now format the partition. Then I can mount the partition and copy desired files to the new partition. Finally, I implement the changes in the /etc/fstab configuration file. This process is covered a bit later.

## Use fdisk to Create a Swap Partition

This section assumes a swap partition is available, appropriately sized for the RAM on the local system. This section illustrates how to create an additional swap partition using **fdisk**. You already know how to open a disk for editing with **fdisk**. Here, I create a swap partition on my second SCSI hard drive. For the purpose of this exercise, I assume there's at least 512MB of free space available. (For learning purposes, the swap partition can be smaller.)

1. I run the **sudo fdisk /dev/sdb** command to get to the following **fdisk** prompt:

```
Command (m for help):
```

2. I run the **l** command to list available file types. While the **fdisk** default creates a Linux Native type partition, many other types are available. Note the hex code for a regular Linux partition (**83**) and a Linux swap partition (**82**).

3. I run the **n** command to create a new primary or logical partition. I create it and specify with a size of 512MB.

4. I run the **p** command to review the new partition, and note the number assigned to the partition.

5. I run the **t** command, and type in **82** to change the file system type to a Linux swap partition.

6. I confirm the result by running the **p** command again.

7. I run the **w** command to write the changes to disk.

At this point, I can format the new partition, activate it as a swap device, and then configure it in /etc/fstab. This process is discussed a bit later.

## The parted Utility

One primary alternative to **fdisk** is *parted*, an excellent tool developed by the GNU Foundation. As with **fdisk**, **parted** can be used to create, check, and destroy partitions, but it can do more. It can also be used to resize and copy partitions, as well as the file systems contained therein. More information is available at www.gnu.org/software/parted.

*CAUTION*   Be extra careful with the **parted** utility. Changes made are immediately written to the target partition or drive, even before **parted** is closed.

This discussion assumes that you've run a command such as **sudo parted /dev/sda** to open a drive. When **parted** is open, the following prompt appears:

```
(parted)
```

If you use **parted** and then check configured partitions with **fdisk**, you might see errors such as this:

```
Partition 1 does not end on cylinder boundary.
```

Such an error is not a big deal. While **fdisk** partitions are associated with hard drive cylinders, **parted** is not so limited.

## The Basics of parted

Before you use **parted** to work with a partition, you need to know the device file of the drive to be configured. The easiest way to do this is with the following command, which in this case lists the partitions configured on the second SCSI or SATA drive:

```
$ sudo parted /dev/sdb print
```

You'll see the size of the noted drive, as well as partitions configured on that drive. The following code shows how I start the **parted** utility to open that second SCSI or SATA drive, /dev/sdb, to access the (**parted**) command line prompt:

```
$ sudo parted /dev/sdb
GNU Parted 1.7.1
Using /dev/sdb
Welcome to GNU Parted! Type 'help' to view a list of commands.
(parted)
```

As suggested by the comment, the **help** command lists available commands. If you're familiar with **fdisk**, you can see that **parted** can do more, as it can even format and resize partitions. Unfortunately, the format functionality is limited and does not allow you to create or resize ext3 partitions, at least as of this writing.

For more information on each of these commands, run **help** *command*. For example, the **help rm** command specifies how the **rm** command can be used to remove a partition. You don't have to follow the specified command format precisely; **parted** commands prompt you for any required information.

## Important parted Commands

At the (**parted**) command line prompt, start with the **print** command to review the current partition table, assuming one exists. If free space is available, you can use the **mkpart** command to make a new partition. You could even use the **mkpartfs** command to make and format a new partition. The **mkfs** command can format partitions, but not to the default ext3 filesystem. The **rm** command can delete partitions.

Remember that disks can have up to four primary partitions, corresponding to numbers 1 through 4. One of the primary partitions can be redesignated as an *extended* partition. The remaining partitions are logical partitions, numbered 5 and above. While the **parted** utility allows you to create more than 15 partitions, in this case, anything beyond /dev/sdb15 is not recognized by Linux.

## Deleting a Partition

It's easy to delete a partition: From the (**parted**) prompt, use the **rm** command to delete the partition that you no longer need. Of course, before deleting any partition, you should do the following:

▼ Save any data you need from that partition.

■ Unmount the partition.

■ Delete any entry in /etc/fstab, so Linux doesn't try to mount it the next time you boot.

▲ Start **parted** and run the **print** command to identify the number of the partition to be deleted.

For example, if you want to delete partition /dev/sdb2 from the (**parted**) prompt, run the following command:

```
(parted) rm 2
```

## Using parted to Create a Regular Partition

Here I create new partition for the /home/michael directory. Any existing partition associated with this directory can then be used as a backup. I do this on the third SCSI or SATA drive.

Whenever a new hard drive is installed, a new partition table is required. While the **sudo parted /dev/sdc** command opens a freshly installed third SCSI or SATA drive, a new label is required. I try to review the partition table with the **print** command and get the following message:

```
Error: Unable to open /dev/sdc - unrecognised disk label.
```

*CAUTION*   Don't run the **mklabel** command in the **parted** utility on any disk with data that you want to keep. All existing data on the disk will be deleted.

Before I can do anything else with this drive, I need to create a label. I consult the list of avaible commands, and note that I can do this with the **mklabel** command. As strange as it sounds, the default label to be used for a Linux hard drive is **msdos**, as shown with the following commands. You might recognize that label from the installation process as described in Chapter 2.

```
(parted) mklabel
New disk label type? msdos
```

Now I can add a partition to my third SCSI or SATA drive with the following steps:

1. If **parted** isn't already open, I run the **sudo parted /dev/sdc** command, which opens the (**parted**) prompt:

   ```
   (parted)
   ```

2. Now I create a new partition with the **mkpart** command. The **parted** utility prompts for required information. If an extended partition already exists, I can create a logical partition.

   ```
   (parted) mkpart
   Partition type? primary/extended? primary
   File system type? [ext2]? ext2
   Start? 0
   End? 100MB
   ```

3. Now I review the results, as follows:

```
(parted) print

Disk /dev/sdc: 1074MB
Sector size (logical/physical): 512B/512B
Partition Table: msdos

Number  Start    End     Size    Type     File system  Flags
   1     0.51kB  100MB   100MB   primary  ext2
```

> **NOTE**  If this is the first partition you've created on this drive, the File system column is empty, no matter what you have entered. You can address that issue with the **mkfs** command. If you then exit from **parted**, you can reboot or run the **partprobe** command to get Linux to read the new partition table.

## Using parted to Create a Swap Partition

Now repeat the process to create a swap partition. Make the start of the new partition 1 MB after the end of the preceding partition. Use the same commands, substituting the **linux-swap** file system type as appropriate:

```
(parted) mkpart
Partition type? primary/extended? primary
File system type? [ext2]? linux-swap
Start? 101MB
End? 1000MB
```

Here's the result:

```
(parted) print

Disk /dev/sdb: 10.7GB
Sector size (logical/physical): 512B/512B
Partition Table: msdos

Number  Start    End      Size    Type     File system  Flags
   1     0.51kB  100MB    100MB   primary  ext2
   2     101MB   1000MB   900MB   primary
```

Repeat the process to create a regular partition after the swap partition:

```
(parted) mkpart
Partition type? primary/extended? primary
File system type? [ext2]? ext2
Start? 1101MB
End? 2100MB
```

Now exit from **parted**. To get Linux to read the new partition table, reboot or run the **partprobe** command. Then exit from **parted** with the **quit** command.

> *CAUTION*   Sometimes you'll see errors when you run the **partprobe** command, even on a correctly configured system. For example, if you haven't put a disk into an existing floppy drive, errors related to the device file (usually fd0) can occur. If the disk in your CD/DVD drive is read-only you'll see a message to that effect.

# Format New Filesystems

It's not enough to create a new partition: it also has to be formatted. Linux supports a rich variety of filesystem formats, which can be somewhat inaccurately divided into "standard" filesystems without a journal and "other" filesystems that do contain a journal. Generally, journaling filesystems are better suited for larger partitions. This section reviews a list of basic standard and journaling filesystems and shows how they can be formatted. It does not include filesystems such as those associated with MINIX or The SCO Group. One more command is required to activate a swap filesystem.

## Standard Filesystem Formats

Linux is a clone of Unix that was developed from the Unix filesystems available at the time. The first Linux operating systems used the Extended Filesystem (ext). This has evolved into the standard Second Extended Filesystem (ext2), still in use for smaller partitions. For example, it's common to create a 100MB partition for the /boot directory; that partition is often formatted to ext2. A sample of standard filesystem formats is shown in Table 5-3. These formats appear in lowercase characters, as the associated commands (and the output to the **mount** command) generally also cite these formats in lowercase.

## Journaling Filesystem Formats

As hard disks and partitions grow in size, Linux users are moving toward filesystems with journaling features. Journaling filesystems have two main advantages: they're faster for Linux to check during the boot process, and if a crash occurs a journaling filesystem has a log (also known as a *journal*) that can be used to restore the metadata for the files on the relevant partition. The default filesystem for Ubuntu is ext3; several options are shown in Table 5-4.

## How to Format a Filesystem

There are several commands available which can format a Linux filesystem. All are based on the **mkfs** command, which includes extensions that describe the filesystem format, such as **mkfs.ext2, mkfs.ext3,** and **mkfs.reiserfs**. Closely related is the **mkswap** command, which formats a Linux swap partition. Of course, the commands discussed in this section should not be run on a mounted filesystem.

These commands are straightforward. The following command formats the /dev/sdb1 partition to the ext2 filesystem:

```
$ sudo mkfs.ext2 /dev/sdb1
```

| Filesystem Type | Description |
| --- | --- |
| ext | The first Linux filesystem, used only on early versions. |
| ext2 | A Linux filesystem in common use for smaller partitions such as the /boot directory; also known as the Second Extended Filesystem. |
| swap | The Linux swap filesystem is associated with dedicated swap partitions. |
| msdos, fat16, vfat | Microsoft formatted filesystems are generally recognized in Linux as the noted filesystem types. |
| iso9660 | The standard filesystem for CD/DVD media. |
| ntfs, fuseblk | The current Microsoft Windows filesystem. |
| proc, sysfs, tmpfs, devfs | Linux *virtual* filesystems. |
| /dev/pts | The Linux implementation for virtual terminals. |
| nfs | The Network File System, the system most commonly used to share files and printers between Linux and Unix computers. |
| cifs, smb | The Common Internet File System (CIFS) is the successor to the Samba/Server Message Block (SMB) system for shared directories. |

**Table 5-3.**  Some Linux Standard Filesystem Types

| Filesystem Type | Description |
| --- | --- |
| ext3 | The default filesystem |
| reiserfs | The Reiser File System is resizable and supports fast journaling; troubled due to the legal problems of its original developer |
| xfs | Developed by Silicon Graphics to support very large files, up to $9 \times 10^{18}$ bytes |

**Table 5-4.**  Journaling Filesystems

The following command formats /dev/sdc2 to the Linux swap filesystem:

```
$ sudo mkswap /dev/sdc2
```

You can convert partitions between the ext2 and ext3 formats. As the only difference is the journal, you could add a journal to the ext2 formatted /dev/sdb1 partition with the following command:

```
$ sudo tune2fs -j /dev/sdb1
```

The journal can be removed with the following command:

```
$ sudo tune2fs -O ^has_journal /dev/sdb1
```

## How to Set Up a Swap Partition

As suggested, swap partitions are a bit different from regular partitions. First, they're given swap filesystem types in utilities such as **fdisk** and **parted**. Next, they're formatted with the **mkswap** command. To activate a swap partition such as /dev/sdc2, you would need to run the following command:

```
$ sudo swapon /dev/sdc2
```

# Manage Filesystems in /etc/fstab

While you can run the **mount** command to activate and copy data to newly formatted partitions, that's not enough. Such partitions aren't recognized during the boot process unless they're configured in the /etc/fstab configuration file. To understand what's configured in this file, review it with a command like **less /etc/fstab**. As you can see in Figure 5-2, different filesystems are configured on each line.

As suggested by the opening comments in the file, there are six fields associated with each filesystem. Table 5-5 describes these fields, from left to right.

```
# /etc/fstab: static file system information.
#
# <file system> <mount point>   <type>  <options>        <dump>  <pass>
proc            /proc           proc    defaults         0       0
# /dev/sda2
UUID=766680a9-1892-4090-a37d-505380004319 /              ext3    errors=remount-ro 0        1
# /dev/sda1
UUID=079e50fd-f042-4aa6-8cf3-4fa33cd0fb18 /boot          ext3    defaults         0       2
# /dev/sda3
UUID=d890a210-a36e-4258-a7b2-db0ec2c8f5bb none           swap    sw               0       0
/dev/scd0       /media/cdrom0   udf,iso9660 user,noauto,exec,utf8 0    0
/dev/fd0        /media/floppy0  auto    rw,user,noauto,exec,utf8 0    0
/etc/fstab (END)
```

**Figure 5-2.** /etc/fstab

| Field Name | Description |
|---|---|
| **<file system>** | Identifies the device to be mounted; can be a device file such as /dev/sda1 or a Universally Unique Identifier (UUID); some distributions use a label. |
| **<mount point>** | Notes the directory where the filesystem will be mounted. |
| **<type>** | Labels the filesystem format type. |
| **<options>** | See Table 5-6. |
| **<dump>** | Shows a value of either 0 or 1. A value of 1 means that data is automatically saved to disk by the **dump(8)** command when you exit Linux. |
| **<pass>** | Drives the order that filesystems are checked during the boot process. The root directory (/) filesystem should be set to 1, and other local (nonremovable) filesystems should be set to 2. |

**Table 5-5.**   Description of /etc/fstab by Column

More information is required for the **<options>** column. Generally, **defaults** is the appropriate mount option for most /etc/fstab filesystems. Some major options are listed in Table 5-6. Opposites such as **sync** and **async**, **auto** and **noauto** are often available. Multiple options can be separated by commas. A more complete list is available with the **man mount** command.

| Option | Description |
|---|---|
| **async** | Data is read and written asynchronously. |
| **atime** | The file inode is updated each time the file is accessed; superseded by **relatime**. |
| **auto** | Tries to detect the filesystem format. |
| **defaults** | A combination of **rw, suid, dev, exec, auto, nouser,** and **async**. |
| **dev** | Used for character devices such as terminals and block devices such as partitions. |

**Table 5-6.**   /etc/fstab Mount Options

| Option | Description |
|--------|-------------|
| **exec** | Allows binaries (compiled programs) to be run on this filesystem. |
| **noauto** | Filesystem is not mounted during the boot process. |
| **nouser** | Only root users are allowed to mount the specified filesystem. |
| **relatime** | The file inode is updated only when needed; supersedes **atime**. |
| **ro** | Mounts the filesystem as read-only. |
| **rw** | Mounts the filesystem as read/write. |
| **suid** | Allows **setuid** or **setgid** permissions. |
| **sync** | Reads and writes occur at the same speed (synchronously). |
| **user** | Allows nonroot users to mount the filesystem. By default, this also sets the **noexec, nosuid**, and **nodev** options. |

**Table 5-6.** /etc/fstab Mount Options (*continued*)

Finally, consider those pesky UUIDs. If you've configured regular partitions on local drives, UUIDs aren't required. You can use the device file associated with the subject partition. But because Ubuntu is now configuring /etc/fstab with UUIDs to accommodate partitions on hot-swappable drives, you need to learn about them.

A UUID is configured for each standard partition in the /etc/fstab configuration file. The default Ubuntu /etc/fstab file includes comments for the associated partition device. For example, based on the /etc/fstab in Figure 5-2, you can replace the UUID expression associated with the /boot directory with /dev/sda1.

UUIDs are listed in the /dev/disk/by-uuid directory. Run the **ls -l /dev/disk/by-uuid** command and note the links from the UUIDs to device files. Compare these results to those of the **blkid** command. As shown in Figure 5-3, the **blkid** results correlate partition device files, UUIDs, and format types. But be aware, the **blkid** command is not updated when you generate a new UUID.

Similar output is available from the **sudo vol_id /dev/sda1** command. It identifies the filesystem, format, and UUID. Unlike the output to the **blkid** command, the UUID in this output is up to date.

If you've just created a new partition, such as the 100MB partition created earlier on the /dev/sdb2 device, your next steps are to format it and generate the UUID with the following command:

```
$ uuidgen /dev/sdb2 > uuidsdb2
```

```
michael@ubuntuhardyserver:~$ blkid
/dev/sda1: UUID="079e50fd-f042-4aa6-8cf3-4fa33cd0fb18" SEC_TYPE="ext2" TYPE="ext3"

/dev/sda2: UUID="766680a9-1892-4090-a37d-505380004319" SEC_TYPE="ext2" TYPE="ext3"

/dev/sda3: UUID="d890a210-a36e-4258-a7b2-db0ec2c8f5bb" TYPE="swap"
/dev/sdb1: UUID="95218342-4bbf-48b1-979b-ed40db204252" TYPE="ext2"
/dev/sdb2: UUID="c1ef75bf-a9bd-4cae-9c51-98032f9eebb0" SEC_TYPE="ext2" TYPE="ext3"

/dev/sdc1: UUID="0580963d-38df-42bb-94ec-863576d26475" TYPE="ext2"
/dev/sdc2: UUID="41c212e6-6600-414b-80eb-e98fd98406cd" TYPE="swap"
michael@ubuntuhardyserver:~$
```

**Figure 5-3.**  blkid output

Then apply the new UUID to the device with the following command. If you're familiar with the effect of back quotes (`` ` ``), you understand that the output of **cat uuidsdb2** is taken as input to the **tune2fs -U** command, which is applied to the /dev/sdb2 partition.

```
$ sudo tune2fs -U `cat uuidsdb2` /dev/sdb2
```

This might seem strange—a UUID is generated for a specific device, and then the UUID has to be applied to that device. The **uuidgen** command doesn't automatically apply the UUID to the device.

Review the format of the /etc/fstab configuration file. You can write the UUID directly to this file. To apply the new UUID to the mount directory, take the following steps. First, this is one case where you'll need direct root administrative access, available with the following command:

```
$ sudo su
```

Next, add an appropriate line to the end of the /etc/fstab configuration file. This command is a bit dangerous; back up the /etc/fstab configuration file first:

```
# cp /etc/fstab ~
```

You can then add the appropriate line to /etc/fstab with the following command:

```
# echo "UUID=`cat uuidsdb2` /mnt ext3 defaults 0 2" >> /etc/fstab
```

Run the **exit** command to leave the administrative interface. To confirm that the changes were added to the end of the /etc/fstab file, run the following:

```
$ less /etc/fstab
```

Now, try to mount the new partition (and all other new partitions) in /etc/fstab with the following command:

```
$ sudo mount -a
```

You'll get an error message suggesting that some special device in the /dev/disk/by-uuid directory does not exist. Aha! That's the UUID for the /dev/sdb2 partition device. You now need to create the link and can do so with the following command:

```
$ sudo ln -s /dev/sdb2 /dev/disk/by-uuid/`cat uuidsdb2`
```

Now try the aforementioned **sudo mount -a** command again; now that the UUID is properly linked, you'll get no messages. To confirm the change, run the **mount** command by itself, and you'll see that the /mnt directory is mounted on the /dev/sdb2 partition. If desired, you can further confirm success by rebooting your system.

To review, the following steps were used to set up a UUID:

1. Run the **uuidgen** command on a newly formatted partition.
2. Apply the new UUID to the partition with the **tune2fs -U** command.
3. Configure /etc/fstab with the new partition, mount point, and UUID.

# HOW TO MAKE RAID WORK

A RAID array is a series of disks or partitions that can save your data even if a catastrophic failure occurs on one of the disks. While some versions of RAID make complete data copies, others use the so-called *parity bit* to allow your computer to rebuild the data on lost disks. Software RAID is configured on a *meta device*, which is a composite of two or more devices. Here you'll learn about the different levels of software RAID available in Ubuntu, how to create a RAID partition, how to configure and activate a RAID array, and how to set up RAID in /etc/fstab.

**NOTE** Hardware RAID is beyond the scope of this book.

In this section, I create a RAID 1 array for my wife's home directory to make sure her data is protected. The applicable partitions are /dev/sdb1 and /dev/sdc1. I also install the mdadm package, which installs applicable commands and modules.

## RAID Definitions

Depending on how you look at it, each of the nine or ten different types of RAID arrays; all but one are associated with a different level of data redundancy. It's even possible to combine different types of RAID arrays. As the focus here is on the Ubuntu server, the following supported levels of software RAID are discussed: 0, 1, 5, and 6. In all cases, if RAID is to work as intended, each partition on a RAID array *should* be on a different physical hard drive. Although RAID 4 is also supported, it is an inferior option (in my opinion) and is therefore not included here. RAID 10 is also supported as a combination of RAID 1 and RAID 0.

This discussion assumes that software RAID arrays are set up on two or more physical partitions, but they can also be configured on entire hard disks.

## RAID 0

RAID 0 is designed to speed reads and writes; however, it provides no data redundancy. It requires at least two partitions, preferably on different physical hard drives. If possible, they should be connected to different hardware controllers.

In a RAID 0 array, reads and writes to the hard disks can occur simultaneously on two or more hard disks. All hard disks in a RAID 0 array are filled equally. But since RAID 0 does not provide data redundancy, a failure of any one of the partitions will result in total data loss. RAID 0 is also known as *striping without parity*.

## RAID 1

RAID 1 is designed to set up two copies of the same data on two separate partitions. To work as designed, these partitions must be located on separate physical hard drives. If one partition is damaged or deleted, all of the data is stored on the other partition.

RAID 1 is slower than RAID 0 because data has to be written twice. It is also relatively expensive. To support RAID 1, you need a second hard disk for every hard disk's worth of data. RAID 1 is also known as *disk mirroring*.

## RAID 5

A RAID 5 array requires three or more partitions. Each partition should be located on a separate physical hard drive. RAID 5 protects data by creating *stripes*, which is parity information distributed evenly across each partition. If one partition fails, the data can be reconstructed from the parity data on the remaining disks. RAID 5 is also known as *disk striping with parity*.

## RAID 6

RAID 6 literally goes one better than RAID 5. In other words, while it requires four or more disks, it has two levels of parity and can survive the failure of two member disks in the array. RAID 6 is also known as *disk striping with dual parity*.

# Create RAID Partitions

Earlier in this chapter, you learned how to create partitions with the **fdisk** and **parted** utilities. In this section, you'll learn how to set configured partitions as RAID partitions.

In **fdisk**, after you create a partition of the desired size, take the following steps:

1. Run the **t** command from the **fdisk** prompt.

2. If more than one partition is configured on the current drive, you're prompted for a partition number.

3. At the prompt that follows, type **l** to list available codes.

4. As you should see from the list that appears, the applicable code for a Linux RAID partition is **fd**; type it in.

5. Run the **p** command to confirm the changes.

6. Run the **w** command to write the changes to the disk and exit **fdisk**.

In **parted**, after you create a partition of the desired size, it's easy to set it up as a RAID partition. The steps are simple:

1. Run the following command from the (**parted**) prompt:

   ```
   (parted) set 1 raid on
   ```

2. Confirm the result with the **print** command.

3. Exit from parted with the **quit** command.

# Format and Configure a RAID Array

As data is stored in each component of a RAID array, each partition must be formatted. The method is the same as that for formatting a partition for direct use. For example, to format the target partitions to the ext3 filesystem, I run the following commands:

```
$ sudo mkfs.ext3 /dev/sdb1
$ sudo mkfs.ext3 /dev/sdc1
```

For this example, I've set up a spare partition on a fourth SCSI drive, /dev/sdd1, which I've also formatted. I can configure a RAID array in Ubuntu with the **mdadm** command. I configure the two partitions appropriate for a RAID 1 array, along with a spare, with the following command:

```
$ sudo mdadm --create --verbose /dev/md0 --level=1
 --raid-devices=2 --spare-devices=1 /dev/sdb1 /dev/sdc1 /dev/sdd1
```

First, unlike other commands, this command doesn't work with a backslash. I've artificially typed it in on two lines for formatting purposes. It's okay if the length of the command forces it to wrap to the next line.

The **--create /dev/md0** option sets up the array on device /dev/md0 and assumes this device file isn't already in use. The **--verbose** option displays more information about the process. The **--level=1** option sets up a RAID 1 array. The **--raid-devices=2** option configures two devices in the array. The **--spare-devices=1** option configures one device as a spare. That's three devices, for which I designate three partitions, /dev/sdb1, /dev/sdc1, and /dev/sdd1.

The command leads to a group of messages associated with each device; here is an excerpt of my output:

```
mdadm: /dev/sdd1 appears to contain an ext2fs file system
    size=506016K  mtime=Wed Dec 31 16:00:00 1969
mdadm: /dev/sdd1 appears to be part of a raid array:
    level=raid1 devices=2 ctime=Wed Mar 12 10:10:22 2008
mdadm: size set to 505920K
Continue creating array?
```

This output is to be expected; it means that /dev/sdd1 is formatted. Even though it refers to *ext2fs*, it's actually formatted to the ext3 filesystem. The message is the same because ext3 is the same format as ext2, except ext3 includes a journal. The message about being a *part of a raid array* is just a sign that the partition has been configured as a RAID partition using a tool such as **fdisk** or **parted**. The size of the array, per the *size set to* message, is based on the space available in each component of the array. The last line requests confirmation; the **y** command is a sufficient response to that prompt.

After creating the array, I need to wait from a few seconds to a few minutes before using the array, as it gets built. To monitor the build process, I run the **cat /proc/mdstat** command. If the array is still being built, I see a message similar to the following in the output:

```
[======>........]  resync=50.1%
```

Once the build process is complete, the /proc/mdstat file contains the following information, which identifies the array device as md0, an active RAID 1 array, using partitions sdd1, sdc1, and sdb1. The (**S**) identifies sdd1 as a spare.

```
md0 : active raid1 sdd1[2](S) sdc1[1] sdb1[0]
      505920 blocks [2/2] [UU]
```

I can then review this information (and more) in a human-readable format with the following command:

```
$ sudo mdadm --detail /dev/md0
```

If you use this command, don't pay attention to the UUID in the output to this file. A new UUID will be generated and used for the /etc/fstab configuration file in the next section. To make sure the array also has a journal, the associated device file also needs to be formatted:

```
$ sudo mkfs.ext3 /dev/md0
```

# Use an Active RAID Array

Now that the RAID array is active, it can be used. As noted earlier, I'm setting up this array for my wife's home directory, /home/donna. First, I back up the contents of her directory, temporarily, to the /mnt directory:

```
$ sudo cp -ar /home/donna /mnt/
```

Next, I mount the RAID array:

```
$ sudo mount /dev/md0 /home/donna
```

Then I can restore the files from Donna's home directory to its new location on the RAID array. Note the dot (.) at the end of the **/mnt/donna/**, which copies all files, including hidden files:

```
$ sudo cp -ar /mnt/donna/. /home/donna
```

# Maintaining RAID Arrays

RAID arrays sometimes need maintenance. Hard drives do fail on occasion. Even if you've configured a spare partition, the failed drive should be replaced. In other words, you need to know how to remove and delete a partition from an array and how to add a new partition to an array.

The following command simulates a failure in the /dev/sdc1 partition of the /dev/md0 RAID array:

```
$ sudo mdadm --verbose /dev/md0 -f /dev/sdc1
mdadm: set /dev/sdc1 faulty in /dev/md0
```

Because I had configured this earlier as a regular RAID device, the array has to be rebuilt; I can observe the progress if I run the **cat /proc/mdstat** command right after simulating a failure in the /dev/sdc1 partition.

But the /dev/sdc1 partition is still a part of the RAID array. To remove it, I run the following command:

```
$ sudo mdadm --verbose /dev/md0 -r /dev/sdc1
```

After I replace the drive associated with /dev/sdc, an appropriate replacement partition can be created. At that point, the /dev/sdc1 partition can be added to the array with the following command:

```
$ sudo mdadm --verbose /dev/md0 --add /dev/sdc1
```

# Make RAID Work in /etc/fstab

It's not enough to create, configure, and maintain a RAID array. I need to make sure the array gets properly mounted on Donna's home directory the next time this server is booted. I need to set up the array in the /etc/fstab configuration file.

UUIDs aren't required. I could use the device file associated with the RAID array—in this case, /dev/md0. However, if I choose to use the UUID, I could set up a new UUID number for this purpose. The following command saves the UUID generated by the **uuidgen** command to the uuidmd0 text file:

```
$ uuidgen /dev/md0 > uuidmd0
```

I then apply the new UUID to the RAID array device:

```
$ sudo tune2fs -U `cat uuidmd0` /dev/md0
```

Now I need to add the RAID array and Donna's home directory to the /etc/fstab configuration file. As it requires root administrative access, I first run this command:

```
$ sudo su
```

I can then add an appropriate line to the end of the /etc/fstab configuration file. This command is a bit dangerous, so I back up the /etc/fstab configuration file first:

```
# cp /etc/fstab ~
```

I can then add the appropriate line to /etc/fstab with the following command:

```
# echo "UUID=`cat uuidmd0` /home/donna ext3 defaults 0 2" >> /etc/fstab
```

While the **exit** command is not required, I use it to return to the regular prompt. I then create a link from the /dev/disk/by-uuid directory with the following command:

```
$ sudo ln -s /dev/md0 /dev/disk/by-uuid/`cat uuidmd0`
```

Now I can try the changes with the **sudo mount -a** command. If it works, I'll see Donna's home directory mounted on the RAID device in the output to the **mount** command. This should also work the next time this system is booted or rebooted.

# LOGICAL VOLUMES PROMOTE FLEXIBILITY

The concept of *logical volumes* makes it easier to increase or reduce the size of a filesystem after Linux is installed. For example, since extra space is available on the /var directory volume, and more space is needed for /home directories, you can use the logical volume tools to help you reassign the space. Alternatively, you can add a new physical disk and allocate its storage capacity using logical volume tools to an existing /home directory partition.

## Logical Volume Concepts

In a logical volume, physical hard disk partitions are set up in a bunch of equal-sized chunks known as *physical extents (PEs)*. These PEs from one or more partitions are mapped to *logical extents (LEs)*, which are then organized into *logical volumes (LVs)*. Volume groups can then be created from the space available in a LV. But that's a mouthful, especially if you're not familiar with logical volume concepts, so here are some definitions:

▼   **Physical volume (PV)**   A standard primary or logical partition configured to a logical volume format type.

■   **Physical extent (PE)**   A chunk of disk space; every PV is divided into a number of equal sized PEs.

■   **Volume group (VG)**   A group of PVs; configures the pool of space for logical volumes.

■   **Logical extent (LE)**   A chunk of disk space; every LE is mapped to a specific PE.

▲   **Logical volume (LV)**   A group of LEs; you can mount a filesystem such as /home and /var on a LV.

While it's easiest to create logical volumes during the Ubuntu installation process, it's not always possible. To set up a logical volume, you need to create a new PV using a command such as **pvcreate**, assign the space to a VG with a command such as **vgcreate**, and allocate the space from some part of available VGs to a LV with a command such as **lvcreate**.

To add space to an existing LV, you need to add free space from an existing VG with a command such as **lvextend**. If you have no existing VG space, you'll need to add to it with unassigned PV space with a command such as **vgextend**. If all your PVs are taken, you might need to create a new PV from an unassigned partition or hard drive with the **pvcreate** command.

But that might sound like a lot of gobbledygook to those unfamiliar with logical volumes, so the following sections break down the process. Just be sure to install the lvm2 package for access to required commands, like so:

```
$ sudo apt-get install lvm2
```

A substantial number of files reside in the lvm2 package. The dmsetup package is also installed as a dependency, which also configures the device mapper for creating logical volumes from volume groups.

As an overview, logical volume configuration files are stored in the /etc/lvm directory. For PV-related commands, run the **ls /sbin/pv\*** command. For VG-related commands, run the **ls /sbin/vg\*** command. For LV-related commands, run the **ls /sbin/lv\*** command. These files are described in more detail in the following sections.

Before you continue, run the following command to add the appropriate module:

```
$ sudo modprobe dm-mod
```

Otherwise, you'll have problems when creating a logical volume. A couple of other modules are required for certain actions related to copies and snapshots of logical volumes:

```
$ sudo modprobe dm-mirror
$ sudo modprobe dm-snapshot
```

## Create Physical Volumes

The first step to create a logical volume is to identify the available space on a physical disk. If you have just added an empty hard disk, you can create a PV on the entire disk. For example, if you've just added a fourth SATA hard disk (/dev/sdd), you could set up a PV on that disk with the following command:

```
$ sudo pvcreate /dev/sdd
```

You can also configure a new PV on a properly configured partition, using the **fdisk** and **parted** utilities discussed earlier in this chapter. If you've added a new partition called /dev/sdd1, for example, you'd follow this sequence of commands (in bold) to change the file type to *Linux LVM*:

```
$ sudo fdisk /dev/sdd
Command (m for help) : t
Partition number (1-4): 1
Hex code (type L to list codes): 8e
Command (m for help) : w
```

Next, confirm the results with the **sudo fdisk -l /dev/sdd** command; the output should be similar to the following:

```
Device Boot      Start       End      Blocks   Id  System
/dev/sdd1            1       100      803218+  8e  Linux LVM
```

Alternatively, if you've created a partition with the **parted** utility, the following sequence of commands changes the file type with the same result:

```
$ sudo parted /dev/sdd
GNU Parted 1.7.1
Using /dev/sdd
Welcome to GNU Parted! Type 'help' to view a list of commands.
(parted) set 1 lvm on
(parted) quit
```

After the partition is ready, you can run the following command to create a new PV on that partition (/dev/sdd1):

```
$ sudo pvcreate /dev/sdd1
```

To take full advantage of logical volumes, you should create such partitions and PVs on all available free space. There are a number of other PV-related commands available in the /sbin directory, summarized in Table 5-7. Because these commands require administrative privileges, they should generally be preceded with the **sudo** command.

## Creating a Volume Group

You can create a VG from two or more PVs using a straightforward command: just substitute the name of your choice for *volgroup1*:

```
$ sudo vgcreate volgroup1 /dev/sdc1 /dev/sdd1
```

Once a VG is available, it's easy to add more room. In this example, I've created a PV on /dev/sdb1 for this purpose and want to add more room to the VG named volgroup1. To that end, I created a /dev/sdb1 partition, configured with the Linux LVM partition type, and applied the **pvcreate** command to that partition. I then add that partition to the existing VG volgroup1 as follows:

```
$ sudo vgextend volgroup1 /dev/sdb1
```

| PV Command | Description |
|---|---|
| **pvchange** | Changes attributes of a PV: the **sudo pvchange -x n /dev/sdb1** command disables the use of PEs from the /dev/sdb1 partition. |
| **pvck** | Checks the metadata associated with a PV. |
| **pvcreate** | Initializes a disk or partition as a PV. If it's a partition, it should be configured with the logical volume filesystem. |
| **pvdisplay** | Displays currently configured PVs. |
| **pvmove** | Moves PVs in a VG from the specified partition to free locations on other partitions; prerequisite to disabling a PE. |
| **pvremove** | Removes a given PV from a list of recognized volume: for example, **pvremove /dev/sda10**. |
| **pvresize** | Changes the amount of a partition allocated to a PV. If you've expanded partition /dev/sda10, **pvresize /dev/sda10** takes advantage of the additional space. |
| **pvs** | Lists configured PVs and the associated VGs, if so assigned. |
| **pvscan** | Similar to **pvs**; provides a baseline of PVs, VGs, and sizes. |

**Table 5-7.**   Available Physical Volume Management Commands

To take full advantage of logical volumes, you need to understand the commands used to configure a VG and are available in the /sbin directory; these are summarized in Table 5-8. As these commands require administrative privileges, they should generally be preceded with the **sudo** command.

## Creating a Logical Volume

You can create a LV from the space configured for a VG using the **lvcreate** command. It's a straightforward command. The following command creates an LV on device /dev/volgroup1/logvol1: just substitute the name of your choice for *volgroup1*.

```
$ sudo lvcreate -L 200M volgroup1 -n logvol1
```

There are many variations on the **lvcreate** command; however, this usage is the most straightforward, as it specifies the size and name of the LV to be created. If you're in doubt about the space available in the VG, run the **vgs** command.

LVs are popular because they're easy to expand. If the **vgs** command confirms that space is available in the VG, more space can be allocated with the **lvextend** command. For example, the following command expands the size of the LV just created to 1GB:

```
$ sudo lvextend -L 1000M /dev/volgroup1/logvol1
```

| VG Command | Description |
|---|---|
| **vgcfgbackup** **vgcfgrestore** | Backs up and restores the configuration files associated with LVM; default backups are from the /etc/lvm directory to /etc/lvm/ backup. |
| **vgchange** | Allows you to activate or deactivate a VG. For example, the **vgchange -a y** command enables all local VGs. Similar to **pvchange**. |
| **Vgck** | Checks the metadata associated with a VG after an LV is created. |
| **vgconvert** | Supports conversions from LVM1 systems to LVM2: **vgconvert -M2 volgroup1** converts that VG. |
| **vgcreate** | Creates a VG from two or more configured PVs: for example, **vgcreate volgroup1 /dev/sdc1 /dev/sdd1** creates volgroup1. |
| **vgdisplay** | Displays characteristics of currently configured VGs. |
| **vgexport** **vgimport** | Exports and imports unused VGs from those available for LVs; the **vgexport -a** command exports and inactivates all inactive VGs. |
| **vgextend** | Extends the size of a VG; **vgextend volgroup1 /dev/sdb1** adds the space from a PV on /dev/sdb1 to volgroup1. |
| **vgmerge** | Merges unused VGs: if you have an unused VG volgroup2, for example, you can merge it into volgroup1: **vgmerge volgroup1 volgroup2**. |
| **vgmknodes** | Checks problems with VG device files, and recreates the devices as needed. |
| **vgreduce** | Removes a PV; for example, the **vgreduce volgroup1 /dev/sdb1** command removes the PV from volgroup1 if free space is available. |
| **vgremove** | Removes a LV; for example, the **vgremove volgroup1** command removes volgroup1, assuming it is not used by any LV. |
| **vgrename** | Allows renaming of LVs; for example, **vgrename volgroup1 volgroup2**. |
| **Vgs** | Displays basic information on configured VGs. |
| **vgscan** | Scans and displays basic information on configured VGs. |
| **vgsplit** | Splits an existing volume group, based on specified PVs. |

**Table 5-8.** Available Volume Group Commands

| LV Command | Description |
| --- | --- |
| lvchange | Changes the attributes of a LV; similar to **pvchange** and **vgchange; lvchange -a n /dev/volgroup1/logvol1** deactivates that LV. |
| lvconvert | Converts an LV, if there are sufficient PVs, for example, the **lvconvert -m 1 volgroup1/logvol1** command converts a regular LV to a mirror LV. |
| lvcreate | Creates a new LV in an existing VG; for example, **lvcreate -L 200M volgroup1 -n logvol1** creates a logvol01 of 200 M. |
| lvdisplay | Displays currently configured LVs. |
| lvextend | Adds space to a LV: for example, the **lvextend -L4G /dev/volgroup1/logvol01** command extends lvol01 to 4GB, assuming space is available. |
| lvreduce | Reduces the size of a LV; if data exists in the reduced area, it is lost. |
| lvremove | Removes an active LV. |
| lvrename | Renames a LV. |
| lvresize | Resizes a LV; can be done by **-L** for size, as with **lvcreate**. |
| Lvs | Lists all configured LVs. |

**Table 5-9.**   Available Logical Volume Commands

There are a number of other LV-related commands available in the /sbin directory, summarized in Table 5-9. As these commands require administrative privileges, these commands should generally be preceded with the **sudo** command.

In addition, there are also a series of **/sbin/lvm*** commands, most of which are not yet active for the current Linux logical volume packages.

## Activate Logical Volumes

After you've created an LV, a couple more steps are required—the volume must be formatted and mounted. These steps are similar to those associated with a new partition and a RAID array, as described earlier in this chapter. For the LV created in this section, /dev/volgroup1/logvol1, I've set up 1000MB of space for that volume. Now I'll set up the LV for the /home/book directory.

To format the new LV to the default ext3 filesystem, I run the following command:

```
$ sudo mkfs.ext3 /dev/volgroup1/logvol1
```

Now I create the /home/book directory if it doesn't already exist. To do so, I run the following command to mount the new LV on that directory:

```
$ sudo mount /dev/volgroup1/logvol1 /home/book
```

> **NOTE**   Remember that before expanding (or reducing the size of) an LV, you should make sure the data is backed up on the volume; then unmount it, and then expand (or reduce) the size of the LV. You can then remount the LV.

## Configure Logical Volumes in /etc/fstab

As with any new partition and RAID array, it's important to document the mount directory associated with the new LV in the /etc/fstab configuration file. I need to make sure the array gets properly mounted on the /home/book directory the next time this server is booted. To do so, I need to set up the array in the /etc/fstab configuration file.

I don't need to use UUIDs. I could just cite the device file associated with the LV—in this case, /dev/volgroup1/logvol1. If I choose to use UUIDs, I need to generate one using the **uuidgen** command. Despite the LV UUID shown in the output to the **lvdisplay** command, I need to set up a dedicated UUID for this purpose, which I save to a text file with the following command:

```
$ uuidgen /dev/volgroup1/logvol1 > uuidlv1
```

I then apply the new UUID to the LV device:

```
$ sudo tune2fs -U `cat uuidlv1` /dev/volgroup1/logvol1
```

Now I need to add the LV and the /home/book directory to the /etc/fstab configuration file. As command line–based appending requires root administrative access, I first run this:

```
$ sudo su
```

I can then add an appropriate line to the end of the /etc/fstab configuration file. This command is a bit dangerous, so I first back up the /etc/fstab configuration file:

```
# cp /etc/fstab ~
```

I can then add the appropriate line to /etc/fstab with the following command:

```
# echo "UUID=`cat uuidlv1` /home/book ext3 defaults 0 2" >> /etc/fstab
```

While the **exit** command is not required, I run that command to leave the administrative prompt. I still need to create a link from the /dev/disk/by-uuid directory, which is easy to do with the following command:

```
$ sudo ln -s /dev/volgroup1/logvol1 /dev/disk/by-uuid/`cat uuidlv1`
```

Now I can try the changes with the **sudo mount -a** command. If it works, I'll see the /home/book directory mounted on the LV device in the output to the **mount** command. It's actually mounted on a LV mapper; the device should be configured on a /dev/mapper/volgroup1-logvol1 device. The mounts in /etc/fstab should also now work the next time the system is booted.

# SUMMARY

This chapter described how you can manage filesystems after the operating system is installed. While it's easy to create partitions, RAID arrays, and logical volumes during the installation process, administrators need to know how to perform these tasks from the Ubuntu system command prompt. Each major part of the chapter included a description of how to make the UUID work for you.

To understand how filesystems can be configured, this chapter explained the FHS and how partitions can be created from a variety of drives. The **fdisk** and **parted** utilities are discussed in some detail. New partitions can be formatted to standard or journaling filesystems, and then set up for a directory in the /etc/fstab configuration file.

To understand how RAID arrays can be configured, this chapter explained the different levels of RAID, how RAID partitions can be created using **fdisk** and **parted**, how RAID arrays can be created and managed with the **mdadm** command, when RAID arrays should be formatted, and how they can be assigned to a directory in the /etc/fstab configuration file.

To understand how logical volumes can be configured, this chapter explained the workings of PVs, PEs, VGs, LEs, and LVs. It continued with a description on how logical volume partitions can be created using **fdisk** and **parted**. Such partitions can then be configured as PVs, which can then be collected together in VGs. On any system, a VG can be flexibly divided into LVs, which can then be formatted and assigned to a directory in the /etc/fstab configuration file.

# CHAPTER 6

## Command Line Tools and Shell Management

The default Ubuntu Server installation doesn't include a GUI (Graphical User Interface), and this book assumes that most server administrators already understand the fundamentals of the command line. Nevertheless, new Linux users may have learned to use the operating system primarily from the GUI and are more familiar with GUI tools. Because these users may not have a complete grounding in basic commands and shell configuration files, those topics are covered in this chapter. Such users should realize these fundamental skills serve as building blocks for more advanced topics.

As the default shell for Linux is the *bash* shell (at least for the first user), this shell is covered here. Be aware that Ubuntu developers are working toward converting from the long-time Linux standard bash shell to the lighter-weight Debian-based *dash* shell, a descendant of the Almquist Shell (or *ash* shell). Ubuntu administrators also need to know how to configure user startup scripts, and these are covered as well.

# COMMAND LINE FUNDAMENTALS

As Linux was developed as a clone of Unix, Linux shares many of the same commands developed for Unix. The *bash shell* is in essence a command line interpreter. Commands at the bash shell can run scripts, manage files, interact with hardware, and more. The interactivity and command completion characteristics of the bash shell can help you as an administrator.

There are also commands that are used to navigate the Filesystem Hierarchy Standard (FHS); read, manipulate, filter, and manage files; and configure combinations of commands. This section covers a few basic Linux commands and just a small subset of what you can do with each command. (A more complete discussion would require several hundred pages.)

## Interactivity and Command Completion

Server administration involves a lot of repetitive tasks. Commands are recorded in each user's history. While many tasks can and should be configured as scripts, sometimes it's fastest to repeat a recently executed command. That's where the characteristics of *interactivity* and *command completion* can help.

### The HISTORY Commands

Any command in a user history can be rerun at any time. By default, the last 500 commands run by a user are stored in that user's home directory, in the .bash_history configuration file. To review those commands from that file in reverse order use the UP and DOWN ARROW keys.

Alternatively, you can list the past 500 commands with the **history** command. As the output is effectively a database, you can *pipe* that command to the *pager* known as the **less** command, shown next. An excerpt from my current command history is shown in Figure 6-1.

```
$ history | less
```

```
459  mount
460  df
461  sudo lvscan
462  sudo vgs
463  sudo lvdisplay
464  uuidgen /dev/volgroup1/logvol1
465  uuidgen /dev/volgroup1/logvol1 > uuidlv1
466  sudo tune2fs `cat uuidlv1` /dev/volgroup1/logvol1
467  sudo tune2fs -U `cat uuidlv1` /dev/volgroup1/logvol1
468  sudo su
469  sudo ln -s /dev/volgroup1/logvol1 /dev/disk/by-uuid/`cat uuidlv1`
470  sudo mount -a
471  moun
472  mount
473  cat /etc/mtab
474  ls /dev/mapper/
475  ls -l /dev/mapper/
476  sudo reboot
477  cd /etc/modprobe.d/
478  ls
479  vi options
480  vi fuse
481  vi arch-aliases
:
```

**Figure 6-1.**    An excerpt of a command history

You can scroll up and down through all 500 commands using the PAGE UP and PAGE DOWN keys, as well as the UP and DOWN ARROW keys. You could read the history and even copy the text at some command line interfaces. But the power of the command line history comes from the options that allow you quickly to rerun previously executed commands of your choice. At the bash shell prompt, the exclamation point (!) is often used to refer to certain points in the command history.

There are four basic methods that can be used to take advantage of the command line history:

▼    Use the UP ARROW key at the command line interface. When the desired command is shown, press the ENTER key. Alternatively, once you see something *close* to the desired command, use the BACKSPACE and LEFT/RIGHT ARROW keys to customize the command before executing it.

■    Use the number associated with the desired command. Numbers appear in the left column in the output to the **history** command, next to each command. This is where the exclamation point comes into play: For example, if I want to reassign the UUID shown in Figure 6-1's command number 467, I'd preface it with the exclamation point:

```
$ !467
```

■ Use the first few alphanumeric characters associated with the command. For example, if I've run 481 commands from the local account, and based on the command history output shown in Figure 6-1, the following entry would execute the **sudo reboot** command (in preference to previous commands which also start with an *s*):

```
$ !s
```

▲ Use a search term within the commands. For example, based on my current command history, the following entry would execute the last run **tune2fs** command. Based on Figure 6-1, that would correspond to command 467:

```
$ !tune2fs
```

## Command Completion

*Command completion* allows you to use the TAB key like a wildcard to complete a command or a filename, or to display available options in terms of the *absolute path*. For example, if you installed the lvm2 package described in Chapter 5, you can review the associated commands by first typing the following:

```
$ lv
```

When you press the TAB key twice, you'll see the following output—a variety of commands related to the LV's discussed in Chapter 5.

```
lvchange   lvdisplay lvmchange   lvmsadc   lvremove lvs
lvconvert  lvextend  lvmdiskscan lvmsar    lvrename lvscan
lvcreate   lvm       lvmdump     lvreduce  lvresize
```

If only one command includes the initial entry, you can simply press the TAB key once. For example, I installed the system-config-kickstart package on my system, so when I type this,

```
$ syst
```

and then press the TAB key once, the command is automatically completed:

```
$ system-config-kickstart
```

# Navigate Around Directories

Directories are special types of files. They're used to organize other files. Drivers, devices, and the nodes associated with USB hardware are also special types of files. To navigate around these files, you need to understand some basic commands that are used to describe where you are, what is there with you, and how to move around associated directories.

## The Tilde (~)

Every regular Linux user has a home directory, and the tilde (~) is frequently used to represent the home directory of the currently active user. For example, if your username is *dickens*, your home directory is */home/dickens*. But if you allow logins as the root user, and log in as the root user, the home directory is */root*. In other words, the effect of the **cd ~** command, depends on the login username. Normally, if you logged in as user mj, the **cd ~** command brings you to the /home/mj directory. But if you've logged in as the root user, the command brings you to the /root directory.

The tilde can be used with other commands; for example, you can list the contents of the current user's home directory from anywhere in the directory tree with the **ls ~** command.

## Dots and Double Dots

The dot (.) and double dot (..) offer a couple of command options. A single dot represents files in the current directory. This notation is a handy way to copy regular and hidden files from the current directory. For example I created a new user (katie) manually and then copied default shell configuration files from the /etc/skel directory with the following command:

```
$ cp -ar /etc/skel/. /home/katie/
```

A single dot can also be useful for scripts that are not in the current value of PATH. The current directory is typically not in any user's PATH, so if you create a script named *testscript* in your home directory and want to test it there, you can do so with the following command:

```
$ ./testscript
```

**NOTE**  For more information on the PATH variable, see the "Variables and More" section later in this chapter.

The double dot represents a higher level directory. For example, if you're currently in any regular home directory, the following command lists all files and directories in the /home directory:

```
$ ls ..
```

Double dots can be combined; for example, the following command, run in any regular home directory, lists the contents of the top-level root directory (/):

```
$ ls ../..
```

## Paths

There are two path concepts associated with Linux directories: *absolute* paths and *relative* paths. An absolute path describes the complete directory structure based on the top level root directory (/). A relative path is based on the current directory and does not include the slash in front.

The difference between an absolute path and a relative path is important.

Especially when creating a script, absolute paths are essential. Otherwise, scripts executed from directories other than those designed for that script can lead to unintended consequences.

## pwd

The Ubuntu default at the bash shell includes the current directory within the prompt. But that's not the case in the dash shell. In many situations, you may not know where you are relative to the top level root (/) directory. The **pwd** command, short for *print working directory*, can provide this information.

## ls

The most basic version of the **ls** command lists the files in the current directory. But the Linux **ls** command, with the right switches, can be powerful. With the right switches, the **ls** command can tell you everything about a file, such as creation date, last access date, and size. It can help you organize the listing of files in just about any desired order. Important variations on this command include **ls -a**, which reveals hidden files; **ls -l** for long listings with permissions; **ls -t** for a time-based list; and **ls -i** for inode numbers. You can combine switches; for example, the **ls -ltr** command displays the most recently changed files last.

**NOTE**  The inode number of a file specifies the index or pointer to the file on a specific partition or volume. If two files have the same inode number, the files are identical.

## cd

It's easy to change directories in Linux. Just use the **cd** command with the absolute path of the directory. If you use the relative path, remember that your final destination depends on the present working directory.

# File Management

The file management commands cited in this section are used for the most basic tasks. For example, the **find** and **locate** commands can help with file searches. The **file** command can help identify file types. The **cat**, **more**, **less**, **head**, and **tail** commands can read the contents of individual files in different ways. The **cp**, **mv**, and **ln** commands can copy, move, and link files, respectively.

You should already know that most Linux configuration files are text files, Linux editors are text editors, and many of these Linux commands are designed to read text files.

# find

The **find** command searches through directories and subdirectories for a desired file. For example, to find the full path to the Samba configuration file, smb.conf, you could use the following command, which would start the search in the top-level root directory (/):

```
$ sudo find / -name smb.conf
```

When I ran this command, it found additional examples of Samba configuration files, useful for my research. But this kind of search can take time on older or heavily loaded systems. If you know that the file is located in the /etc subdirectory tree, you could start in that directory with the following command:

```
$ sudo find /etc -name smb.conf
```

But that may not be desirable, as that would deprive you of the locations of the other example Samba configuration files.

# locate

Ubuntu systems include a default database of all files and directories. Searches with the **locate** command are almost instantaneous, and don't require the full filename. The drawback is that the **locate** command database is normally updated only once each day, as documented in the /etc/cron.daily/mlocate script.

# file

As there are no standard file extensions in Linux, it can be difficult to determine if a file is a text file, a compressed archive, an executable binary, or something else. The **file** command can address this problem. For example, the **file \*** command, run in a home directory, tells me more about each of the files in that directory, as shown in Figure 6-2.

If you want to use the **file** command to identify hidden files as well, run the **file `ls -a`** command. It takes a list of the names of all files, including hidden files, and uses it as input to the **file** command.

# cat

The most basic command for reading files is **cat**. The **cat** *filename* command scrolls the text from the *filename* file. This command also works with multiple filenames; it concatenates the contents of the listed files as one continuous output to the screen. You can also redirect the output to the filename of your choice.

# more and less

Larger files demand a command that can help you scroll though the file text at your leisure. Linux has two such commands: **more** and **less**. With the **more** *filename* command, you can scroll through the text of a file, from start to finish, one screen at a time. The SPACEBAR can then be used to scroll down the file.

```
michael@ubuntuhardyserver:~$ file *
hardy-server-1386.iso:                        ISO 9660 CD-ROM filesystem data UDF
 filesystem data (unknown version, id 'NSR01') 'Ubuntu-Server 8.04 i386
 (bootable)
ks1.cfg:                                      ASCII English text
ks2.cfg:                                      ASCII English text
ks.cfg:                                       ASCII English text
landscapekey:                                 PGP armored data public key block
local.seed:                                   UTF-8 Unicode English text, with ve
ry long lines
lvmdump-ubuntuhardyserver-2008031360021.tgz: gzip compressed data, from Unix, la
st modified: Wed Mar 12 23:00:22 2008
menu.lst:                                     writable, regular file, no read per
mission
preseed.txt:                                  ASCII English text
test:                                         directory
uuidlv1:                                      ASCII text
uuidmd0:                                      ASCII text
uuidsdb2:                                     ASCII text
vgscan:                                       ELF 32-bit LSB executable, Intel 80
386, version 1 (SYSV), for GNU/Linux 2.6.8, dynamically linked (uses shared libs
), stripped
michael@ubuntuhardyserver:~$ []
```

**Figure 6-2.** Identify file types with the file * command

Ironically, the **less** command is more powerful than the **more** command. With the **less** *filename* command, you can scroll in both directions through the same text using the PAGE UP and PAGE DOWN keys. Both commands support vi-style searches.

## head and tail

While the **head** and **tail** commands are related, they are separate commands that work in opposite ways. By default, the **head** *filename* command looks at the first 10 lines of a file, and the **tail** *filename* command looks at the last 10 lines of a file. You can specify a different number of lines with the **-nxy** switch. For example, the **tail -n15 /etc/passwd** command lists the last 15 lines of the /etc/passwd file.

The **tail -f logfile** command is commonly used as a way to monitor log messages as they appear. It's often used with files in the /var/log directory.

## cp

The **cp** (copy) command allows you to take the contents of a file and write the copy to a file with the same or a different name, to a different directory if desired. For example, the **cp file1 file2** command takes the contents of *file1*, saving the contents in *file2*. One of the dangers of **cp** is that it can easily overwrite files in different directories, without confirming to make sure that's what you really want to do.

## mv

While you can't rename a file in Linux, you can move it. The **mv** command essentially puts a different label on a file. For example, the **mv file1 file2** command changes the name of *file1* to *file2*. Unless you're moving the file to a different partition, everything about the file, including the inode number, remains the same.

## ln

You can create linked files. One use for such links are hardware device files such as /dev/cdrom and the UUID files in the /dev/disk/by-uuid directory. Assuming the local system includes a CD/DVD drive, you can see a link with the following command:

```
$ ls -l /dev/cdrom
lrwxrwxrwx 1 root root 4 2008-03-09 22:11 /dev/cdrom -> scd0
```

Linked files can also be used to provide access to the same file to multiple users, even in their home directories.

*Hard links* include a copy of the file. As long as the hard link is made within the same partition, RAID array, or logical volume, the inode numbers are identical. Inode numbers can be verified with the **ls -i** *filename* command. You could delete a hard-linked file in one directory, and it would still exist in the other directory. For example, the following command creates a hard link from the actual Samba configuration file to smb.conf in the local directory:

```
$ ln /etc/samba/smb.conf smb.conf
```

On the other hand, a *soft link* serves as a redirect; when you open a file created with a soft link, you're directed to the original file. If you delete the original file, although the link is still visible, the file is lost. While the soft linked file is still there, it has nowhere to go. The following command is an example of how you can create a soft link:

```
$ ln -s /etc/samba/smb.conf smb.conf
```

# Quotes and Backslashes

Sometimes, a quote can be used to help define more complex commands. Sometimes, all you need is a backslash. Such characters can be used to help the shell process different combinations of spaces, variables, and commands.

## Different Kinds of Quotes

There are three types of quotes used at the Linux command line: the single quote ('), the double quote ("), and the back quote (`). Each creates different results when applied to standard input to the command. (The back quote key might be difficult to find on many keyboards: On the left side of my US keyboard, the back quote is the lowercase key between the ESC and TAB keys.)

Each type of quote leads to a different result, depending on whether the input is a command such as **ls** or a variable such as NAME. Everything between the quotes is sent as standard input to the command. The differences between the types of quotes are as described here:

Single quote (')        Variables and commands inside the quotes are *not* processed

Double quote (")        Variables such as NAME *are* processed, commands are *not*

Back quote (`)          Every expression is processed as if it were a command

The examples which follow use all three types of quotes. I've first set the value for NAME with the following command:

```
$ NAME=Dickens
```

The following illustrates the baseline command without quotes. As you can see, the shell processes the value of the NAME variable. Since a **$** appears in front of NAME:, the shell processes it as a variable.

```
$ echo Hooray $NAME, you wrote a book on date
Hooray Dickens, you wrote a book on date
```

Next, try the same command with single quotes. Note how the variable is not processed:

```
$ echo 'Hooray $NAME, you wrote a book on date'
Hooray $NAME, you wrote a book on date
```

Now try the same command with double quotes. The variable is processed:

```
$ echo "Hooray Dickens, you wrote a book on date"
Hooray $NAME, you wrote a book on date
```

You might wonder why anyone would use double quotes. It's a valuable option for situations such as files or directories of multiple words, such as a Microsoft-style "My Documents" directory.

So let's see what happens when back quotes are configured around the word *date*, making it work as a command:

```
$ echo "Hooray $NAME, you wrote a book on `date`"
Hooray Dickens, you wrote a book on Fri Jul 11 13:33:01 PDT 2008
```

But this doesn't work so well if the command in back quotes is surrounded by an expression in single quotes:

```
$ echo 'Hooray $NAME, you wrote a book on `date`'
Hooray $NAME, you wrote a book on `date`
```

## The Backslash (\)

In some cases, all you need is a backslash. For example, if you've configured a network connection to the C: drive on a Microsoft system, say on the /ms directory, you could use double quotes to find the contents of the Documents and Settings folder:

```
$ ls "/ms/Documents and Settings"
```

Or you could use backslashes to "escape the meaning" of the space:

```
$ ls /ms/Documents\ and\ Settings
```

The backslash can also be useful in other ways. For example, if you're looking for all instances of the asterisk (*) in the Samba configuration file, you might be tempted to run the following command:

```
$ grep * /etc/samba/smb.conf
```

But that doesn't work, because the asterisk (*) is a wildcard. As such, it would take the first available filename in the current directory and use it as a search term for text in the second file in that directory. Fortunately, the backslash can escape the meaning of wildcards, which makes the following search more fruitful:

```
$ grep \* /etc/samba/smb.conf
```

# Aliases

Commands can be long, and are prone to typos. You could create a script, save it, and make the script executable. Alternatively, you could create an *alias* for the long command. Here's an example: I run the **sudo apt-get update** command fairly often, so I can create an alias for that command, as follows:

```
$ alias agu='sudo apt-get update'
```

The process can be reversed using the **unalias** command. Assuming the alias is retained, you could then use the **agu** alias as if it were the **sudo apt-get update** command.

To review the current aliases available on an account, run the **alias** command. The .bashrc configuration file includes comments for other possible aliases:

```
# alias ll='ls -l'
# alias la='ls -A'
# alias l='ls -CF'
```

If you want to activate any of these aliases, remove the comment character, in this case, the pound sign (#) at the front of the line. The next time you open a command line console in this system, the alias will be active. You could also add more aliases to this file. (For more information on the .bashrc configuration file, see the "Optimize the Shell" section later in this chapter.)

## Wildcards in a Glob

Sometimes you may not know the exact name of a file or search term. This is when a wildcard is handy. The use of wildcards in Linux is known as *globbing*. Basic wildcards are shown in Table 6-1.

## File Filters

Linux is rich in commands that can help you filter the contents of a file. Simple commands can help you search, check, or sort the contents of a file. In addition, special types of files can contain other files, colloquially known as *tarballs*.

Tarballs are commonly used for distributing Linux packages. They are normally distributed in a compressed format with a .tar.gz or .tar.bz2 file extension, consolidated as a package in a single file. In this respect, they are similar to Microsoft-style compressed zip files.

### sort

You can sort the contents of a file in a number of ways. By default, the **sort** command sorts the contents in alphabetical order depending on the first letter in each line. For example, the **sort /etc/passwd** command would sort all users (including those associated with specific services and such) by username.

### grep and egrep

The **grep** command uses a search term to look through a file. It returns the full line that contains the search term. For example, **grep 'Michael Jang' /etc/passwd** looks for my name in the /etc/passwd file.

| Wildcard | Description |
|---|---|
| * | Any number of alphanumeric characters (or no characters at all). For example, the **ls ab\*** command would return the following filenames, assuming they exist in the current directory: ab, abc, abcd. |
| ? | One single alphanumeric character. For example, the **ls ab?** command would return the following filenames, assuming they exist in the current directory: abc, abd, abe. |
| [] | A range of options. For example, the **ls ab[123]** command would return the following filenames, assuming they exist in the current directory: ab1, ab2, ab3. Alternatively, the **ls ab[X-Z]** command would return the following filenames, assuming they exist in the current directory: abX, abY, abZ. |

**Table 6-1.**   Wildcards in the Shell

The **egrep** command is more forgiving; it allows you to use some unusual characters in a search, including **+**, **?**, **|**, **(**, and **)**. While it's possible to set up **grep** to search for these characters with the help of the backslash, the command can be awkward to use.

The **locate** command described earlier is basically essentially a specialized version of the **grep** command, that uses the **updatedb** command–based database of files on the local system.

## wc

The **wc** command, short for *word count*, can return the number of lines, words, and characters in a file. The **wc** options are straightforward: the **wc -w** *filename* command returns the number of words in the *filename* file. The **wc -l** *filename* command returns the number of lines in that file. The **wc -c** *filename* command returns the number of characters in that file.

## sed

The **sed** command, short for *stream editor*, allows you to search for and change specified words or even text streams in a file. For example, the following command changes the *first* instance of the word *Windows* to the word *Linux* in each line of the file opsys, and then writes the result to the file newopsys:

```
$ sed 's/Windows/Linux/' opsys > newopsys
```

However, this may not be enough. If a line contains more than one instance of *Windows*; the noted **sed** command would not change the second and later instances of that word. However, you can make it change *every* appearance of *Windows* by adding the global suffix, **g**:

```
$ sed 's/Windows/Linux/g' opsys > newopsys
```

## awk

The **awk** command, named for its developers (Aho, Weinberger, and Kernighan), is more of a database manipulation utility. It can identify lines with a key word and read out the text from a specified column in that line. Again, using the /etc/passwd file, for example, the following command will read out the username of every user with *Mike* in the comment column:

```
$ awk '/Mike/ {print $1}' /etc/passwd
```

# Command Combinations and Data Streams

It's possible to combine multiple commands in Linux, based on data flow. Linux uses three basic data streams. Data goes in, data comes out, and errors are sent in a different direction. These streams are known as *standard input* (*stdin*), *standard output* (*stdout*), and *standard error* (*stderr*). Normally, input comes from the keyboard and goes out to the screen, while errors are sent to a buffer. Error messages are also sent to the display (as text stream 2). In the following example, *filename* is stdin to the **cat** command:

```
$ cat filename
```

When you run **cat** *filename*, the contents of the *filename* file are sent to the screen as standard output.

You can redirect each of these streams to, or from, a file. For example, if you have a program named *database* and a datafile with a lot of data, the contents of that datafile can be sent to the database program with a left redirection arrow (<). As shown here, datafile is taken as standard input:

```
$ database < datafile
```

Standard input can come from the left side of a command as well. For example, if you need to scroll through the boot messages, you can combine the **dmesg** and **less** commands with a pipe (|):

```
$ dmesg | less
```

The output from **dmesg** is redirected as standard input to **less**, which then allows you to scroll through that output as if it were a separate file.

Standard output is just as easy to redirect. For example, the following command uses the right redirection arrow (>) to send the standard output of the **ls** command to the file named *filelist*:

```
$ ls > filelist
```

You can add standard output to the end of an existing file with a double redirection arrow (>>) with a command such as this:

```
$ ls >> filelist
```

If you believe that a particular program is generating errors, redirect the error stream from it with a command like this:

```
$ program 2> err-list
```

# Set the Default Linux Text Editor

Yes, the default text editor for Ubuntu is nano. It's an easy editor. No special commands are required to input and delete text from files being edited. The nano editor provides a straightforward interface, as shown in Figure 6-3.

However, the vi editor is still quite popular, and it is often the only editor available from some rescue systems. In addition, some users prefer the emacs editor. Some Unix users may even prefer the ed editor.

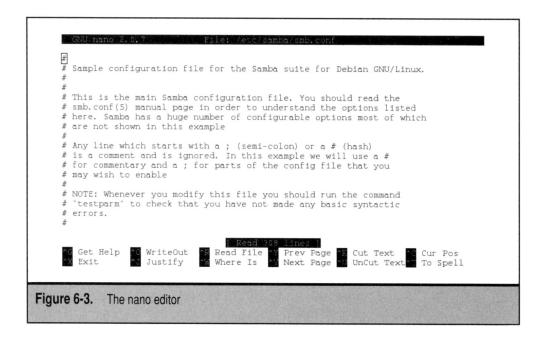

**Figure 6-3.** The nano editor

The following command provides options for revising the default editor for Ubuntu:

```
$ sudo update-alternatives --config editor
There are 4 alternatives which provide `editor'.

  Selection    Alternative
------------------------------------------------
           1    /usr/bin/vim.tiny
           2    /bin/ed
*+         3    /bin/nano
           4    /usr/bin/emacs22

Press enter to keep the default[*], or type selection number:
```

The results are reflected in the /etc/default/editor binary configuration file. As suggested by the menu, Ubuntu systems use a simplified version of the vi editor known as *vim.tiny*. I change my systems to use vi because it's the editor I know best.

**NOTE** There are several specialized variations of the vi command. Three variations are **vipw**, **vigw**, and **visudo**, which edit /etc/passwd, /etc/group, and /etc/sudoers, respectively.

# OPTIMIZE THE SHELL

As of this writing, Ubuntu developers still configure *administrative* users to the traditional bash shell. That includes the root user, if active, as well as the first regular user normally created during the installation process. Accounts created with the Users Settings tool are also normally assigned the bash shell.

However, Ubuntu developers are currently working on implementing the lighter weight dash shell. In fact, dash was implemented as the default shell for Edgy Eft (6.10), but the bash shell was restored for Feisty Fawn (7.04). Because dash has fewer features, the dash shell has broken some existing bash shell scripts.

In this section, you'll test configuration files and commands with the bash shell. All system-wide shell configuration files are kept in the /etc directory, including bash.bashrc, bash_completion, profile, and the scripts in the /etc/bash_completion.d directory.

These files and scripts are supplemented and can be overridden by hidden files in each user's home directory, in files such as .bashrc, .bash_history, .bash_logout, and .profile. I'll describe these files later in this section.

## Profiles in Bash

All system-wide shell configuration files are kept in the /etc directory. For the bash shell, these files are bash.bashrc and profile. These files and scripts are supplemented and can be overridden by hidden files in each user's home directory. The following sections examine these files.

### /etc/bash.bashrc

The /etc/bash.bashrc file is used for aliases and functions on a system-wide basis. Open this file in a text editor or read it using a pager with a command such as **less /etc/bash .bashrc**. Read the comments in the file. Even if you don't understand the programming commands, you should be able to see that this file sets the following bash shell parameters for each user. For example:

▼ It assigns a prompt, using the **PS1** variable, which appears just before the cursor at the command prompt.

■ It includes settings from /etc/bash_completion to enable command completion.

▲ It configures messages associated with **sudo** access (for more information, see Chapter 10).

The settings are called by the .bashrc file in each user's home directory. The default Ubuntu version of this file adds information on aliases. The settings are supplemented by the .bash_history and .bash_logout files in each user's home directory.

### /etc/profile

The /etc/profile file is used for system-wide environment and startup files. The following is the profile script from my copy of Ubuntu Server. It's a straightforward file. First, it looks for other configuration files in the /etc/profile.d directory. It then sets what's shown at the bash command prompt, for the regular and root user, as well as a default value for the **umask** variable, explained later in the "Manage Permissions, Octal and Super" section later in this chapter. Note how it calls the /etc/bash.bashrc file for other parameters.

```
# /etc/profile: system-wide .profile file for the Bourne shell (sh(1))
# and Bourne compatible shells (bash(1), ksh(1), ash(1), ...).
if [ -d /etc/profile.d ]; then
  for i in /etc/profile.d/*.sh; do
    if [ -r $i ]; then
      . $i
    fi
  done
  unset i
fi
if [ "$PS1" ]; then
  if [ "$BASH" ]; then
    PS1='\u@\h:\w\$ '
    if [ -f /etc/bash.bashrc ]; then
        . /etc/bash.bashrc
    fi
  else
    if [ "`id -u`" -eq 0 ]; then
      PS1='# '
    else
      PS1='$ '
    fi
  fi
fi

umask 022
```

# A Minor in Scripts

"Real" Linux administrators program their own scripts. They create scripts because they don't want to sit at their computers all the time. Scripts can allow Linux to back up directories automatically when nobody is in the office. Scripts can help Linux process databases when few people are using the system.

If you're not a programmer, don't worry, because this is not as difficult as it sounds. For example, utilities related to the **crontab** command automate the creation of a number of different scripts. (The cron system is discussed in more detail in Chapter 7.)

If you're at all familiar with shell commands and programming expressions, you can find some examples of Ubuntu shell programs in the /etc/cron.daily directory.

## Variables and More

Variables can change. Parameters are set. The bash shell includes a number of standard environment variables. Their default values are shown in the output to the **env** command. One critical variable is the value of PATH, which you can check at the command line with the **echo $PATH** command. The directories listed in PATH are automatically searched when you try to run a command. For example, if you want to run the **fdisk** command from the /sbin directory, you could do it with the following command:

```
$ /sbin/fdisk
```

However, as the /sbin directory is in the default PATH for the first regular user, you don't need the leading **/sbin** to call out the command; the following would work:

```
$ fdisk
```

But the PATH variable does not include /sbin for other regular users. So if you want to add the /sbin directory to your PATH, just run the following commands:

```
$ PATH=$PATH:/sbin
$ export PATH
```

If you want to set a user's PATH to include the /sbin directory, the appropriate location is in the .profile configuration file in that user's home directory. All you need to do is add the following line to the end of that file:

```
PATH=$PATH:/sbin
```

The next time that user opens a command line console, the /sbin directory is activated as part of that user's PATH.

# MANAGE PERMISSIONS, OCTAL AND SUPER

The basic security of a Linux computer is based on file permissions, associated with read, write, and execute access. Default file permissions are set through the **umask** shell variable. Ownership is based on the default user and group IDs of the person who created a file. Managing permissions and ownership involves commands such as **chmod**, **chown**, and **chgrp**. Special SUID (set user ID) and SGID (set group ID) permissions can give all users access to specific files.

There was a time when users had read access to the files of all other users. By default, users had permissions only in their own directories. With access control lists (ACLs), that has changed. Users can be given selective access to individual files, even in the directories of other users. Important commands for ACLs include **getfacl** and **setfacl**.

# Basic File Permissions

Linux file permissions are straightforward. Consider the following output from **ls -l** **/sbin/fdisk**:

```
-rwxr-xr-x 1 root root  85064 2008-03-06  20:24 /sbin/fdisk
```

The permissions are shown on the left side of the listing. Ten characters are shown. The first character determines whether this is a regular or a special file. The remaining nine characters are grouped in threes, applicable to the file owner (user), the group owner, and everyone else on that Linux system. In this case, the user owner and group owner are both root, as noted in the third and fourth columns. The characters are straightforward: **r** = read, **w** = write, **x** = execute. The character positions are described in Table 6-2.

# Commands to Modify Permissions and Ownership

Default permissions depend on the value of **umask**. At this time, the **umask** can only change standard read, write, and execute permissions. Key commands that can help you manage the permissions and ownership of a file are **chmod**, **chown**, and **chgrp**. The **chmod** command is especially powerful, as it can customize the special permissions on a file. The **chattr** command provides a twist in the way it manages file attributes.

## Modify Permissions with chmod

The **chmod** command uses the numeric value of permissions associated with the owner, group, and others. In Linux, permissions are assigned the following numeric values: **r** = 4, **w** = 2, and **x** = 1. For example, if you were crazy enough to give read, write, and execute permissions on **fdisk** to all users, you would run the **sudo chmod 777 /sbin/fdisk** command. If you wanted to give read and write permissions to the Samba configuration file to the administrative user and read-only permissions to all other users, you'd run the **sudo chmod 644 /etc/samba/smb.conf** command. Be aware, these numbers are different from the positions described in Table 6-2.

| Character Position | Description |
|---|---|
| 1 | Type of file: **-** = regular file, **b** = block device, **c** = hardware device, **d** = directory, **l** = linked file |
| 234 | Permissions granted to the owner of the file |
| 567 | Permissions granted to the group owner of the file |
| 890 | Permissions granted to all other users on the Linux system |

**Table 6-2.** Description of File Permissions

Alternatively, the **chmod** command can be used to make minor changes. First, look at the output of the following command:

```
$ ls -l /usr/games/newgame
-rw-r----- 1 dickens coolcats 15972 2007-12-12 05:59 /usr/games/newgame
```

The output reveals permissions and ownership for the script newgame in the /usr/ games directory. It has a user owner of dickens and a group owner of coolcats. In other words, dickens has read and write permissions, members of the coolcats group have read permissions, and all other users have no permissions on the script.

Next, enable execute permissions for the user owner, dickens, for the script with the following command:

```
$ sudo chmod u+x /usr/games/newgame
```

Analyze the switches in this command. The **u** represents the user owner, and the **+** adds the permission in question—in this case, **x**, the execute permission. Other examples include the following, which activates write permissions for members of the coolcats group on the noted script:

```
$ sudo chmod g+w /usr/games/newgame
```

Of course, the process can be reversed. The following command removes write permissions from members of the coolcats group:

```
$ sudo chmod g-w /usr/games/newgame
```

You can then allow coolcats members to execute the script with the following command:

```
$ sudo chmod g+x /usr/games/newgame
```

Finally, when you're ready to allow everyone access to the newgame script, you could run the following command, where **o** represents other users, not represented by the user owner or group owners:

```
$ sudo chmod o+r /usr/games/newgame
```

If you understand how scripts work, you realize that execute access is also required, and that can be activated for all (**a**) categories of users with the following command:

```
$ sudo chmod a+x /usr/games/newgame
```

## Change Ownership with chown and chgrp

The **chown** and **chgrp** commands adjust the user and group owners, respectively, as associated with the cited file. Before testing what it can do, take a look at this excerpt from the output to the **ls -l /etc/cups** command. Note that a couple of subdirectories have different owners:

```
drwxr-xr-x 2 root lp   4096 2008-01-29 12:50 ppd
```

The user owner of the ppd/ subdirectory is *root*, and the group owner is *lp*. If you want to change the owner of this directory, the **chown** command can help. For example, the following command makes *michael* the user who owns this directory:

```
$ sudo chown michael /etc/cups/ppd
```

The **chgrp** command works in a similar fashion. The following command changes the group owner of the noted directory to lpadmin:

```
$ sudo chgrp lpadmin /etc/cups/ppd
```

However, these commands don't change *ownership* in any files or directories in the /etc/cups/ppd directory. To make those changes in such directories, the **-R** switch can be used. In fact, that switch applies the changes *recursively*, so ownership is changed in all files and subdirectories:

```
$ sudo chown -R michael /etc/cups/ppd
```

The **chown** and **chgrp** commands can be combined in a way. The following command changes user and group ownership recursively with all features associated with the other noted **chmod** and **chgrp** commands:

```
$ sudo chown -R michael.lpadmin /etc/cups/ppd
```

## Set Default Permissions with umask

The way **umask** works in Linux might surprise you, especially if you're coming from a different Unix-style environment. You cannot configure **umask** to allow the creation of new files automatically with executable permissions. This promotes security: If fewer files have executable permissions, fewer files are available for a cracker to use to run programs to break through your system.

**NOTE** In the world of Linux, a *hacker* is a good person who simply wants to create better software. A *cracker* is someone who wants to break into your system for malicious purposes.

Every time you create a new file, the default permissions are based on the value of **umask**. In the past, the value of **umask** canceled out the value of numeric permissions on a file. For example, if the value of **umask** was 000, the default permissions for any file created by that user would be 777 − 000 = 777, which corresponds to read, write, and execute permissions for all users.

When you type the **umask** command in Linux, you'll see a four-number output such as **0245**. As of this writing, the first number in the **umask** output is always **0** and is not used.

In addition, no matter what the value of **umask**, new files in Linux can no longer be automatically created with executable permissions. In other words, a **umask** value of **0454** is functionally equivalent to a **umask** value of **0545**. You need to use commands such as **chmod** subsequently to set executable permissions on a specific file.

## Control Attributes with chattr

Filesystem attributes can help you control what anyone can do with different files. One attribute that protects a file from deletion, even by the root user, is *immutability*. For example, you could protect /etc/samba/smb.conf from tinkering by other administrators with the following command:

```
$ sudo chattr +i /etc/samba/smb.conf
```

Then, when a user with administrative privileges tries to delete the file, she gets the following message:

```
$ sudo rm /etc/samba/smb.conf
rm: cannot remove '/etc/samba/smb.conf': Operation not permitted
```

Of course, as an administrator, that user could remove the immutable attribute with the following command:

```
$ sudo chattr -i /etc/samba/smb.conf
```

Immutability requires that an administrator think twice before tinkering with a file, thus helping to minimize careless mistakes.

# Special File Permissions

Permissions can be a risky business, but you need to give all users access to some programs. Setting full read, write, and execute permissions for all users on a Linux system can be dangerous. One alternative is setting the SUID and the SGID permission bits for a file.

Specialized permissions are available, known as *set user ID (SUID)*, *set group ID (SGID)*, and the *sticky bit*. To review a file with SUID permissions, run the **ls -l /usr/bin/passwd** command. The **s** that appears in the user execute permissions column is the SUID bit.

```
-rwsr-xr-x 1 root root 29104 2008-02-14 12:56 /usr/bin/passwd
```

Because the **passwd** command is accessible to all users, one can infer that the SUID bit provides root level execute access to the **passwd** command. Without this particular SUID bit, regular users would not be able to change their own passwords. Similar rules exist for the SGID bit.

```
-rwsr-xr-x 1 root root 29104 2008-02-14 12:56 /usr/bin/passwd
```

To review a directory with the sticky bit, run the **ls -l /** command. Pay attention to the /tmp directory. The **t** is where execute permissions for other users would otherwise exist; **t** is the symbol for the sticky bit.

In contrast, the **t** that appears in the permissions associated with the /tmp directory is the sticky bit:

```
drwxrwxrwt  11 root root  4096 2007-07-10 21:00 tmp
```

Now I'll show you how to activate (and deactivate) these bits on sample files.

## The SUID Bit

The SUID bit allows normal users to run a script or program as the user owner of that script or program. As just suggested, the SUID bit on the **/usr/bin/passwd** command allows it to be run by anyone as the root user. With Pluggable Authentication Modules (PAM), as discussed in Chapter 10, regular users can change only their own passwords.

To set the SUID bit on a file, run the following command:

```
$ sudo chmod u+s filename
```

Alternatively, if you're also setting read and execute permissions for only the user (and read-only permissions for everyone else), the following command would work:

```
$ sudo chmod 4544 filename
```

The first **4** in **4544** represents the SUID bit; the **544** represents the other user permissions just described.

## The SGID Bit

The SGID bit is commonly used for directories shared by a specific group of users. For example, the SGID bit set on a /home/supervisors directory, with a group owner of supervisors, allows each member of the supervisors group to add files to and read files from that directory. To set the SGID bit on a directory, run the following command:

```
$ sudo chmod g+s directory
```

Alternatively, if you want read and write permissions for just the group owner (and read permissions for everyone else), the following command would work:

```
$ sudo chmod 2474 directory
```

The **2** in **2474** represents the SGID bit; the **474** represents the other permissions just described.

## The Sticky Bit

The sticky bit is usually applied to a directory. It allows files in the directory to be added and deleted by their owners. To set the sticky bit on a file, run the following command:

```
$ sudo chmod o+t directory
```

Alternatively, if you want read, write, and execute permissions for all users on this directory, set the sticky bit on a directory with the following octal command:

```
$ sudo chmod 1777 directory
```

The **1** in **1777** represents the sticky bit; the **777** represents the other permissions just described.

Of course, variations are possible. For example, the following command sets read and write permissions for all users, with the SUID and sticky bits:

```
$ sudo chmod 5666 directory
```

The **5** in **5666** represents the SUID and sticky bits (4+1); the **666** represents the other permissions just described.

# Access Control Lists

Even if you configure user home directories manually, users do not normally have write access to files in other user's home directories. But this can be changed on a per-file basis using the Linux implementation of ACLs.

Before ACLs can be configured, at least execute permissions must exist on the associated directories. For example, to make sure appropriate access is available to the home directory for the book, I can make sure execute permissions are available with the following command:

```
$ sudo chmod a+x /home/book
```

The control associated with regular permissions is limited; appropriate ACLs can allow administrators to grant read, write, and execute access to a variety of users and groups.

## Configuring a Filesystem for ACLs

Before you can configure a file or directory with ACLs, you need to mount the associated filesystem with the same attribute. If you're testing a system for ACL, you can remount an existing partition appropriately. For example, if /home is mounted on /dev/sda3, remount it with ACL settings using the following command:

```
$ sudo mount -o remount -o acl /dev/sda3 /home
```

Naturally, to make sure this is the way /home is mounted on the next reboot requires editing /etc/fstab; for the noted parameters, the applicable line might be similar to this:

```
UUID=05a3f3c2-cd11-4c64   /home   ext3    defaults,acl    0,2
```

Depending on the configuration, you might see a partition device name such as **/dev/sda3** in place of the UUID.

## Working with ACLs

Now, with a properly mounted filesystem and appropriate permissions, you can manage ACLs on your system. To review default ACLs, run the **getfacl** *filename* command. For this example, I've created a text file named smb.conf in the home directory for the book, and I get the following ACLs for that file:

```
$ getfacl /home/book/smb.conf
# file: home/book/smb.conf
```

```
# owner: book
# group: book
user::rw-
group::r--
other::r--
```

> **NOTE**   If you don't see the **getfacl** or **setfacl** commands, install the acl package.

Now when I assign ACLs for the file named smb.conf for myself (user michael), I first need to assign appropriate ACLs for the /home/book directory. The following command sets the ACLs, which support read and execute permissions for myself on the book home directory, as well as an effective rights mask that should equal or exceed the user ACLs:

```
$ sudo setfacl -m user:michael:r-x /home/book
$ sudo setfacl -m mask:r-x /home/book
```

Now I can configure individual files with ACLs. First, I deny access to all users but the owner:

```
$ chmod 700 /home/book/abc
```

To check the result, I log into my own account and try opening smb.conf from the home directory for the book. I get the *[permission denied]* message.

Now I set the ACLs for file smb.conf with the following commands:

```
$ sudo setfacl -m user:michael:r-- /home/book/smb.conf
$ sudo setfacl -m mask:r-x /home/book/smb.conf
```

Now I can open /home/book/smb.conf from my own account. Others can be given similar permissions; just repeat the next to last **setfacl** command, substituting the desired username for *michael*. For example, the following command provides similar privileges to user elizabeth:

```
$ sudo setfacl -m user:elizabeth:r-- /home/book/smb.conf
```

# SUMMARY

This chapter provided a basic overview of fundamental Linux commands, using history, command completion, navigation, and basic file management. Quotes, backslashes, aliases, wildcards, and symbols that take advantage of data streams can help you combine commands and more.

The characteristics of Linux commands depend on the default shell, currently the bash shell. Related configuration files are stored in the /etc/ directory and can be modified by hidden files in user home directories. The behavior of the shell can be affected by variables and more. Shell parameters and variables can be used in scripts.

Basic file permissions include read, write, and execute; special file permissions include the SUID, SGID, and sticky bits. Permissions and ownership can be modified with commands such as **chmod**, **chown**, and **chgrp** and otherwise fixed with commands such as **chattr**. ACLs can customize permissions on a per file and per user basis.

# CHAPTER 7

## Basic Administrative Tools

This chapter addresses several basic administrative services and commands not covered elsewhere. The Secure Shell (SSH) is one excellent way to configure remote access, one convenient to administer servers without monitors. The cron and at daemons can help administrators schedule jobs when needed. Administrators should know how to configure those services necessary to their systems. When problems arise, administrators need to understand the data collected by the wide variety of Linux log files.

# CREATE A SECURE SHELL SERVER

People take personal security seriously. They lock their doors. They avoid dangerous neighborhoods. They secure personal information. In the Internet world, far too many people effectively leave their doors unlocked—as they allow their computers to be accessible without firewalls. They browse websites known to be dangerous or risky.

And they transmit personal information such as passwords without encryption. All that a determined cracker needs to get into such an unsecured system is access from any coffeehouse wireless network.

Linux is a clone of Unix. Furthermore, the open source licenses associated with Linux encourage developers to share source code. Unfortunately, this free exchange of information can present security challenges. Many of the original Unix networking tools work in clear text. In other words, others who connect to your networks may be able to read your data, when transmitted without encryption.

The Secure Shell utilities are one answer, with associated standards of encryption. SSH commands provide strong encryption, which I believe in most cases will encourage a cracker to look for an easier target.

## Installation

One way to install the most standard SSH server package is with the **sudo apt-get install openssh-server** command. The associated client should already be installed by default. It's useful to install the SSH server on all systems that you want to administer remotely. An appropriately configured SSH connection can log on remote users without even transmitting a password over a network, once appropriate authentication keys are exchanged.

Once installed, the SSH server package is set to start by default in runlevel 2, but not in runlevel 1, also known as *single user mode*. As discussed in Chapter 4, recovery mode boots Linux in single user mode. In other words, if you configure a remote Ubuntu server to boot in recovery mode, you won't normally be able to use SSH to administer the remote server.

## Configuring the SSH Server

You don't have to do much to configure an SSH server for basic operation. Install the package described previously. Once installed, the server is active by default. If a firewall or other security block exists, you may need to open the appropriate TCP/IP port (22).

The SSH server is driven by a couple of configuration files, /etc/default/ssh and /etc/ssh/sshd_config.

## Default SSH Server Settings

The SSH script in /etc/init.d/ssh starts the associated daemon (/usr/sbin/sshd), with any custom switches configured in the /etc/default/ssh configuration file. As suggested by the **sshd** man page, switches can limit access to IPv4 or IPv6 addresses, use a non-standard configuration file, specify a different TCP/IP port, and so on.

## The SSH Server Configuration File

The SSH server configuration file is /etc/ssh/sshd_config. This section analyzes the default version of this file, which includes a number of default settings. The first directive is a default, and should be commented out if you configure access on a different port in /etc/default/ssh:

```
Port 22
```

If the local server is a gateway, or for some other reason has multiple active network cards, you may choose to activate one or both of the following directives, and then specify the IP address of the interface connected to the network for the SSH server. Be sure to substitute an IP address (or hostname); otherwise, these default directives would listen to all addresses.

```
#ListenAddress ::
#ListenAddress 0.0.0.0
```

The following directive specifies SSH version 2, which is more secure:

```
Protocol 2
```

The next directives uses default host keys, created during the installation process. Read/write access to these keys is limited to the root administrative account. The names refer to the RSA and DSA encryption algorithms. RSA is an acronym associated with its developers (Rivest, Shamir, and Adleman). DSA is short for the Digital Signature Algorithm, which is a US government standard.

```
HostKey /etc/ssh/ssh_host_rsa_key
HostKey /etc/ssh/ssh_host_dsa_key
```

The next directive minimizes the risk associated with unprivileged processes:

```
UsePrivilegeSeparation yes
```

The next two directives don't matter unless you've set Protocol 1 to configure SSH version 1, as described earlier:

```
KeyRegenerationInterval 3600
ServerKeyBits 768
```

The following directive sends all log messages related to authentication to /var/log /secure. In other words, whenever someone logs into your system (or tries and fails), it's recorded. For more information on log levels, see the "Manage Those Log Files" section later in this chapter.

```
SyslogFacility AUTH
LogLevel INFO
```

The following directives relate to authentication. The **LoginGraceTime** is in seconds. Logins to the root administrative account are permitted by default. On many Linux distributions, I'd recommend changing the **PermitRootLogin** directive to no, but as long as you don't activate the root account with a password, as discussed in Chapter 10, this is less important. The **StrictModes** directive checks ownership within the user's login directory; without it, others might have access to a user who does not properly set permissions on his or her own files.

```
LoginGraceTime 120
PermitRootLogin yes
StrictModes yes
```

The **RSAAuthentication** directive applies only to SSH protocol 1. **PubkeyAuthentication** supports private/public authentication keys, as described next in "Passphrases." The **AuthorizedKeysFile** directive specifies the default location for authorized encrypted login keys, the .ssh/authorized_keys subdirectory of each user's home directory. All are defaults.

```
RSAAuthentication yes
PubkeyAuthentication yes
#AuthorizedKeysFile     %h/.ssh/authorized_keys
```

The next two directives apply only if SSH protocol 1 is used:

```
IgnoreRhosts yes
RhostsRSAAuthentication no
```

If you prefer authentication based on hosts, as opposed to user accounts, you could enable the following directives. But I would not recommend this, as it can leave your system more vulnerable to crackers who could find a vulnerable account.

```
HostbasedAuthentication no
#IgnoreUserKnownHosts yes
```

Of course, you could allow users to log in remotely without a password, but I would not recommend that either:

```
PermitEmptyPasswords no
```

The challenge/response authentication associated with telephone modem connections is generally disabled because of interaction problems with Pluggable Authentication Modules (PAM), as described in Chapter 10.

```
ChallengeResponseAuthentication no
```

The **PasswordAuthentication** directive is important. Even though it is commented out, it reflects the default. Disable it only if you want to keep the SSH server from using passwords transmitted over the network. (You'll see how that can work in the next section.)

```
# PasswordAuthentication yes
```

The following directive authorizes password authentication, based on local user passwords:

```
PasswordAuthentication = yes
```

Other directives are available for Kerberos-based authentication, if you configure a Key Distribution Center (KDC) or the Generic Security Services Application Program Interface (GSSAPI). Those directives are not further explained or repeated here, as that would require another chapter and is beyond the scope of this book.

The following directives are important and enable remote access to a GUI tool:

```
X11Forwarding yes
X11DisplayOffset 10
```

You can enable a daily message to clients who log in via SSH, in /etc/motd, if you enable the following directive:

```
PrintMotd no
```

The following directive adds a message associated with the time and date of the last login of the subject user:

```
PrintLastLog yes
```

The following directive restores a connection if a wireless network is temporarily interrupted:

```
TCPKeepAlive yes
```

I normally keep this directive disabled, as it would otherwise affect my ability to run GUI tools remotely. I know it's not what a "real Linux administrator" would do, but as many administrators do use GUI tools, I cover some of them in this book and therefore retain the following directive:

```
# UseLogin no
```

The **MaxStartups** and **Banner** directives, if activated, can regulate the number of logins via SSH, and the message given to users who connect, respectively:

```
#MaxStartups 10:30:60
#Banner /etc/issue.net
```

The following directive takes language-related environment variables from the client and uses them on the server, if the language options are available:

```
AcceptEnv LANG LC_*
```

The final directives support the use of SSH encryption for secure FTP file transfers and the use of the PAM system for access to utilities specified in the /etc/pam.d directory. It enables the use of SSH for FTP clients with the **sftp** command.

```
Subsystem  sftp   /usr/lib/openssh/sftp-server
```

Now that you've examined the default version of the SSH server configuration file, I'll discuss some of the changes that I normally make. Whether you make the same changes depends on the circumstances.

If you choose to configure a password for the root administrative user, as described in Chapter 10, disable logins by the root user with the following directive:

```
PermitRootLogin no
```

Users with administrative privileges can still access the root account after connecting via SSH. While that means the password would be transmitted over the network, it's done only after the encrypted SSH connection is established.

I also like to limit the users allowed to access a system via SSH. The key is the **AllowUsers** directive. You can limit by user with a directive such as this:

```
AllowUsers michael donna
```

Alternatively, you can limit access by each user to certain hosts with a directive such as this:

```
AllowUsers michael@enterprise5vm donna@poohbear.example.net
```

I configure my desktop system with passphrases to avoid transmitting passwords over a network. For that system, once I've configured passphrases, I disabled password authentication by adding the following directive:

```
PasswordAuthentication no
```

Crackers who then try to break into this system with passwords will be out of luck.

# Passphrases

If you don't want to allow passwords to be transmitted over a network, it's time to learn about passphrases. They're configured from client systems. For example, I've configured my laptop system with passphrases for my desktop and virtual machine server.

The process is straightforward. On the client (in my case, it's a laptop), create the private/public key pair with the **ssh-keygen** command. The default version of this command uses RSA encryption, with the following prompts. Normally, you should stick with the prompted location, which creates an RSA private and public key in the current user's .ssh/ subdirectory.

```
Generating public/private rsa key pair.
Enter file in which to save the key (/home/michael/.ssh/id_rsa):
```

Use a passphrase. Don't leave the passphrase entry blank. Otherwise, someone who gets hold of the client will be able to access your servers. Another advantage is that the passphrase is checked only against the encrypted local key, and is not transmitted over the network. When the private/public key pairs are successfully created, you'll see a location for these keys in the .ssh/ subdirectory, with a key fingerprint.

```
Enter passphrase (empty for no passphrase):
Enter same passphrase again:
Your identification has been saved in /home/michael/.ssh/id_rsa.
Your public key has been saved in /home/michael/.ssh/id_rsa.pub.
The key fingerprint is:
```

If 1024-bit encryption is not good enough, you could set up a more complex encryption scheme with a command like this:

```
$ ssh-keygen -t rsa -b 4096
```

Just don't set the bits too high, or it may take too long for the system to create the key pair. A 2048-bit key is considered good. On my system, a 4096-bit encryption key pair took about 15 seconds to create. (The US federal specification for DSA keys uses 1024 bits.)

Next, copy the public key to the remote SSH server. As noted in the output to the **ssh-keygen** command, the public key file created is id_rsa.pub, in the user's home directory, in the .ssh/ subdirectory. You could take the client public key file (id_rsa.pub), copy it to the remote SSH server system, and append the contents to the authorized_keys file in the remote user's home directory, in the .ssh/ subdirectory. This is possible with commands such as **scp** and **rsync**—or even with a portable device such as a USB key.

Alternatively, the **ssh-copy-id** command can help. The following command copies the public key just created (the **-i** specifies it as the "identity file") to the noted location on the SSH server:

```
$ ssh-copy-id -i .ssh/id_rsa.pub 192.168.0.102
```

Now client access should work with just the passphrase. Both password- and passphrase-based access to an SSH server is covered in the upcoming section "Client Access." But first, a warning about passphrases.

# A Warning

Canonical has an important warning for anyone who has created a passphrase on Ubuntu systems built from distributions released between April 2007 and April 2008. If you've run or administer systems based on Ubuntu's Feisty Fawn (7.04), Gutsy Gibbon (7.10), or the initial Hardy Heron (8.04) release, be warned. A problem was found with the random number generator associated with the creation of passphrases for SSH authentication. In short, the random number generator isn't as random as intended. This problem also affects Debian Linux and related systems released in the same timeframe.

To address this problem, make sure that you've installed or updated your systems with the latest versions of the openssh-server and openssh-client packages. One way to do so is with the following command:

```
$ sudo aptitide install openssh-server openssh-client
```

If your system might be at risk, this command should install the openssh-blacklist package as well as updated versions of the openssh-server, openssh-client, and the associated Secure Sockets Layer (SSL) library package.

The installation process for the updated packages should also warn you that "Vulnerable host keys will be regenerated." If you see this message, press TAB and then press ENTER.

Once the cited packages are upgraded and installed, try the **ssh-vulnkey** command. It checks standard locations described in the previous section for vulnerable passphrase-related SSH keys. If there's a problem, the **ssh-vulnkey** command will tell you so with output similar to this:

```
COMPROMISED: 2048 8d:f2:b3:03:5b:18:fd:3a:97:9e:64:f5:14:4e:29:74
michael@UbuntuGG
```

If you have an SSH key in a non-standard location, run the **ssh-vulnkey** command with the full path to the applicable file. If one or more of your keys is compromised, you'll have to create and copy new keys using the techniques described in the preceding section.

# Client Access

Based on the defaults, SSH client configuration is generally not required. All you need in order to access the SSH server is the username and hostname or IP address of that server. I generally use a command similar to this:

```
$ ssh michael@ubuntuserver.example.net
```

If needed, substitute the IP address for the ubuntuserver.example.net hostname. The response depends on the value of **PasswordAuthentication** on the SSH server and whether a public encryption key has been transmitted from client to server, as described earlier.

If **PasswordAuthentication** is still enabled, the first time the client connects, you'll see a warning message:

```
The authenticity of host '192.168.0.102 (192.168.0.102)' can't be
established.
 RSA key fingerprint is 13:b4:5d:97:99:6c:ea:2e:7b:9d:7b:23:3a:a3:15:a4.

Are you sure you want to continue connecting (yes/no)?
```

Assuming you verify by entering **yes** at the prompt, information on the SSH server is added to the .ssh/known_hosts file in that user's home directory. Then the SSH server asks for the user's password:

```
michael@ubuntuserver.example.net's password:
```

If the correct password is given, you're logged into the SSH server, with all the privileges associated with the login account. If the public encryption key has been properly transmitted, and you're working from the text console, the following message appears (with the appropriate user information), requesting the passphrase used to create that key:

```
Enter passphrase for key '/home/michael/.ssh /id_rsa':
```

Alternatively, if you're working from the GNOME desktop environment, a graphical window requesting the passphrase should appear. In either case, type in the original passphrase (including spaces and punctuation) to connect.

If you've transmitted the encryption key, allow access on the SSH server with the **PasswordAuthentication** directive, and see the *user password* request just described, there's a problem with the encryption keys. In that case, repeat the **ssh-keygen** process described earlier.

Once the passphrases have been verified from the desired clients, disable the **PasswordAuthentication** directive in the SSH server configuration file (/etc/ssh /sshd_config). Then limit access—in the SSH server configuration file—to users (like myself, in this case) with a directive such as **AllowUsers michael**. This way, you don't have to worry about passwords being transmitted over the network, reducing the risk that crackers who use a protocol analyzer (also known as a "sniffer") on the network find the passwords they'd need to access the server.

Custom configuration of the SSH client is possible through the /etc/ssh/ssh_config file. Changes are rarely required to the file. Just be aware that if you want to take advantage of the **X11 Forwarding** directive on the SSH server, the defaults in the client configuration file means you'll need to use the **ssh -X** *username@host* command to log in from the SSH client.

**NOTE**    For users who still have to administer and even run Microsoft Windows systems, there are SSH client services available to administer remote Linux systems from Microsoft clients.

## Telnet if You Must

Many experienced users still prefer the older Telnet service for remote connections. Therefore, it's possible that, as an administrator, you'll have to install and support this service. It's available from the telnetd package for the server and the telnet package for the client.

There are a couple of options that can be used to provide additional security. Such security requires installation of the telnetd-ssl and telnetd packages on the server and the telnet-ssl package on the client. With the SSL, passwords can be encrypted between the server and client. A successful connection includes messages that confirm an SSL connection, as shown here:

```
$ telnet-ssl ubuntuhardyserver
Trying 192.168.0.102...
Connected to ubuntuhardyserver.mommabears.com.
Escape character is '^]'.
[SSL - attempting to switch on SSL]
[SSL - handshake starting]
SSL: Server has a self-signed certificate
SSL: unknown issuer: /O=Internet Widgits Pty Ltd/OU=ubuntuhardyserver
telnetd/CN=ubuntuhardyserver./emailAddress=root@ubuntuhardyserver.
[SSL - OK]
Ubuntu hardy
ubuntuhardyserver login: michael
Password:
```

Be aware, even encrypted passwords can be intercepted and (eventually) decrypted, which is why I recommend the use of passphrases, as described earlier in this chapter.

# SCHEDULE IMPORTANT JOBS

Without the cron system, administrators would have to wake up in the middle of the night to run jobs such as system backups that would otherwise overload important systems. The cron and at systems are essentially alarm clocks that can start jobs on a schedule.

Major Linux distributions, including Ubuntu, install the cron and at daemons by default. Most distributions are configured to check the /var/spool/cron directory for cron jobs by user, and *at* jobs. (In this context, *at* is the service, not the conjunction.) It also checks for scheduled jobs for the computer under /etc/crontab and in the /etc/cron.d directory.

The behavior of the Linux cron is different from its behavior in Unix, where the cron daemon wakes up only when it needs to launch a program. Because cron always checks for changes, you do not have to restart cron every time you make a change.

# Standard cron Jobs

The /etc/crontab configuration file is set up in a specific format. Comments start with a #. Variables such as SHELL and PATH can be set. Time is configured in a certain sequence and serves as an alarm to run the command(s) that follow. In Linux, standard cron jobs are run through /etc/crontab on an hourly, daily, weekly, and monthly basis. Scripts for this purpose are run from the /etc/cron.hourly, /etc/cron.daily, /etc/cron.weekly, and /etc/cron.monthly directories. Standard cron jobs that don't follow such schedules can be stored in the /etc/cron.d directory.

When a regular command is run in the cron service, the actions of the shell are based on environmental variables. To see the environmental variables, run the **env** command. Some of the standard variables include HOME as the home directory, SHELL as the default shell, and LOGNAME as the username.

You can set different variables within the /etc/crontab file, or environmental variables with the following syntax:

```
Variable=Value
```

You can set these variables to different values in your crontab file. For example, the default /etc/crontab file includes the following variables:

```
SHELL=/bin/sh
PATH=/usr/local/sbin:/usr/local/bin:/sbin:/bin:/usr/sbin:/usr/bin
```

Note that the values of PATH and SHELL are different from those for the standard environment variables.

> **NOTE** The MAILTO variable can notify you via e-mail when a job is run. Just add MAILTO=me@somewhere.com to route cron messages associated with that script to that e-mail address.

Pay attention to the following comment line in the /etc/crontab file; it provides clues to what goes in each column:

```
# m h dom mon dow user command
```

From left to right, this represents the minute, hour, day of the month, month, day of the week, user, and command. These columns are detailed in Table 7-1.

An asterisk (*) in any column means that cron runs that command for all standard values of that column. For example, an * in the hour field means that the command is run every hour as limited by the other settings. Here's another example:

```
5  4  3  2  *  root apt-get update
```

This line runs the **apt-get update** command every February 3rd at 4:05 A.M. The asterisk in the day of week column simply means that the day of the week does not matter.

| Field | Value |
|---|---|
| Minute | 0–59 |
| Hour | Based on a 24-hour clock; for example, 20 = 8 P.M. |
| Day of month | 1–31 |
| Month | 1–12, or jan, feb, mar, etc. |
| Day of week | 0–7; 0 and 7 both represent Sunday; or sun, mon, tue, etc. |
| User | The user to run the command as |
| Command | The command or job to run |

**Table 7-1.**    Entries in a **crontab** Command Line

There are other ways to configure time settings in the crontab file. For example, a **7–10** entry in the month field would run the specified command in July, August, September, and October. A list such as **1,2,3,4** in the hour field would run the specified command at 1:00 A.M., 2:00 A.M., 3:00 A.M., and 4:00 A.M. The user column is configured only in the /etc/crontab file; it runs the commands actual command in the sixth field.

For more examples, review some of the scripts in the /etc/cron.daily directory. Three key scripts include logrotate, for rotating log files; mlocate, which updates the locate file database; and standard, which backs up the shadow password suite database files (/etc/passwd, /etc/shadow, /etc/group, /etc/gshadow) and others in the /var/backups directory.

## User cron Jobs

Regular users can run the **crontab** command to create and manage cron jobs for their own accounts. There are four switches associated with the **crontab** command:

▼   **-u** *user*   Allows the root user to edit the crontab of another specific user.

■   **-l**   Lists the current entries in the crontab file.

■   **-r**   Removes cron entries.

▲   **-e**   Edits an existing crontab entry. By default, crontab in Ubuntu uses the **nano** editor, unless you've changed the default editor with the **update-alternatives** command, described in Chapter 6.

To configure cron jobs for your own account, start with the **crontab -e** command, which opens the default editor. You can then add variables and schedule the commands or scripts that you need to be run on a schedule. The format is the same as just described for the /etc/crontab configuration file, except that no username is required. Of course, that means that your account needs permissions to run the commands or scripts in question.

## Configure at Jobs

While the cron daemon supports jobs run on a regular schedule, the at daemon (atd) supports jobs run on a one-time basis. Think of the at daemon as functionally similar to the print process. Jobs associated with this daemon are spooled in the /var/spool/cron/at directory and run at the specified time.

You can configure the at daemon to run the script or command of your choice. For example, as user michael, I've created a script named dreamliner in my home directory to process some airplane sales database to another file in the same directory called sales.

When run, the **at time** command can be configured to run a job—once—at a specified *time*. That *time* can be now; in a specified number of minutes, hours, or days; or at the time of your choice. Several examples are illustrated in Table 7-2.

Any of the commands shown in Table 7-2 can be used to open an at job. When you run an **at time** command, it starts an **at>** prompt. You can specify the command or script that you want run at the specified time at that prompt. Let's say I'm about to leave work at around 10 P.M. and I want the dreamliner script to be run at 11:00 tonight. I'd run the following commands:

```
$ at now + 1 hour
at> /home/michael/dreamliner > /home/michael/sales
at> Ctrl-D
```

The CTRL-D key combination exits the **at>** prompt and returns to the originating shell interface. Current jobs are stored in a spool and can be reviewed with the **atq** command. If you have a problem with a job, pay attention to the number assigned to it.

| Period | Example | Description |
|---|---|---|
| Minutes | at now + 20 minutes | Configured jobs start in 20 minutes |
| Hours | at now + 6 hours | Configured jobs start in 6 hours |
| Days | at now + 2 days | Configured jobs start in 48 hours |
| Weeks | at now + 1 week | Configured jobs start in 7 days |
| n/a | at teatime | Configured jobs start at 4:00 P.M. |
| n/a | at 3:00 10/30/08 | Configured jobs start on October 30, 2008, at 3:00 A.M. |

**Table 7-2.**   Examples of the **at** Command

```
#!/bin/sh
# atrun uid=1000 gid=1000
# mail michael 0
umask 22
XDG_SESSION_COOKIE=f933a8df06f871bf44b1fc9647d9353d-1205943698.952263-98703164;
export XDG_SESSION_COOKIE
SSH_CLIENT=192.168.0.6\ 34979\ 22; export SSH_CLIENT
SSH_TTY=/dev/pts/0; export SSH_TTY
USER=michael; export USER
LS_COLORS=no=00:fi=00:di=01\;34:ln=01\;36:pi=40\;33:so=01\;35:do=01\;35:bd=40\;3
3\;01:cd=40\;33\;01:or=40\;31\;01:su=37\;41:sg=30\;43:tw=30\;42:ow=34\;42:st=37\
;44:ex=01\;32:\*.tar=01\;31:\*.tgz=01\;31:\*.svgz=01\;31:\*.arj=01\;31:\*.taz=01
\;31:\*.lzh=01\;31:\*.lzma=01\;31:\*.zip=01\;31:\*.z=01\;31:\*.Z=01\;31:\*.dz=01
\;31:\*.gz=01\;31:\*.bz2=01\;31:\*.bz=01\;31:\*.tbz2=01\;31:\*.tz=01\;31:\*.deb=
01\;31:\*.rpm=01\;31:\*.jar=01\;31:\*.rar=01\;31:\*.ace=01\;31:\*.zoo=01\;31:\*.
cpio=01\;31:\*.7z=01\;31:\*.rz=01\;31:\*.jpg=01\;35:\*.jpeg=01\;35:\*.gif=01\;35
:\*.bmp=01\;35:\*.pbm=01\;35:\*.pgm=01\;35:\*.ppm=01\;35:\*.tga=01\;35:\*.xbm=01
\;35:\*.xpm=01\;35:\*.tif=01\;35:\*.tiff=01\;35:\*.png=01\;35:\*.svg=01\;35:\*.m
ng=01\;35:\*.pcx=01\;35:\*.mov=01\;35:\*.mpg=01\;35:\*.mpeg=01\;35:\*.m2v=01\;35
:\*.mkv=01\;35:\*.ogm=01\;35:\*.mp4=01\;35:\*.m4v=01\;35:\*.mp4v=01\;35:\*.vob=0
1\;35:\*.qt=01\;35:\*.nuv=01\;35:\*.wmv=01\;35:\*.asf=01\;35:\*.rm=01\;35:\*.rmv
b=01\;35:\*.flc=01\;35:\*.avi=01\;35:\*.fli=01\;35:\*.gl=01\;35:\*.dl=01\;35:\*.
xcf=01\;35:\*.xwd=01\;35:\*.yuv=01\;35:\*.aac=00\;36:\*.au=00\;36:\*.flac=00\;36
:\*.mid=00\;36:\*.midi=00\;36:\*.mka=00\;36:\*.mp3=00\;36:\*.mpc=00\;36:\*.ogg=0
0\;36:\*.ra=00\;36:\*.wav=00\;36:; export LS_COLORS
MAIL=/var/mail/michael; export MAIL
PATH=/usr/local/sbin:/usr/local/bin:/usr/sbin:/usr/bin:/sbin:/bin:/usr/games; ex
port PATH
PWD=/home/michael; export PWD
LANG=en_US.UTF-8; export LANG
HISTCONTROL=ignoreboth; export HISTCONTROL
SHLVL=1; export SHLVL
HOME=/home/michael; export HOME
LOGNAME=michael; export LOGNAME
SSH_CONNECTION=192.168.0.6\ 34979\ 192.168.0.102\ 22; export SSH_CONNECTION
LESSOPEN=\|\ /usr/bin/lesspipe\ %s; export LESSOPEN
LESSCLOSE=/usr/bin/lesspipe\ %s\ %s; export LESSCLOSE
cd /home/michael || {
        echo 'Execution directory inaccessible' >&2
        exit 1
}
/home/michael/dreamliner > /home/michael/sales
```

**Figure 7-1.** An at job includes extensive environment variable information

Details of spooled jobs are stored in the /var/spool/cron/atjobs directory. For example, the contents of the noted job are shown in Figure 7-1. Note the detail before the actual command at the bottom of the file.

If you want to cancel an at job, it can be removed with the **atrm** command. For example, if the output to the **atq** command reveals it as job 5, it can be removed with the following command:

```
$ atrm 5
```

## Job Scheduling Security

Access to both the at and cron daemons can be limited. The process is similar to that available for TCP Wrappers-based services. User access to the cron daemon can be regulated in the /etc/cron.allow and /etc/cron.deny files. If these files don't exist (which is the default), cron usage is not restricted. If users are named in /etc/cron.allow file, all other users won't be able to use cron. If there is no /etc/cron.allow file, the users named in /etc/cron.deny can't use cron.

The right way to configure these files is with one line per user. For example, the following entries in /etc/cron.deny would keep users dickens and katie from configuring their own cron jobs:

```
dickens
katie
```

This assumes no /etc/cron.allow exists to override the options in /etc/cron.deny.

The at daemon can be secured, based on the same rules. The corresponding configuration files are /etc/at.allow and /etc/at.deny. The default version of /etc/at.deny includes standard service users such as bin, ftp, and games. If a cracker breaks into one of those accounts, he or she wouldn't be able to run an at job.

# CUSTOMIZE SERVICES AND RUNLEVELS

With the introduction of the Upstart system, described in Chapter 4, services and runlevels are organized differently. With Ubuntu's heritage as a Debian-based distribution, Ubuntu's runlevels are already organized differently from Red Hat-style distributions. So if you're more familiar with other Linux distributions, you may only partially recognize how runlevels are organized on an Ubuntu system.

To recap the lessons of Chapter 4, when you boot Linux, scripts that begin with an *S* in the /etc/rcS.d and /etc/rc2.d directories are started. Minimizing the number of scripts that are started during the boot process can help secure your system. Fewer active services mean fewer ways for crackers to break into your system.

## Script Actions in Different Runlevels

When reviewing an Ubuntu Server, it's useful to review the scripts that are started when the system boots. To do so, run the following commands:

```
$ ls /etc/rcS.d
$ ls /etc/rc2.d
```

By default, all the scripts in these directories start with an *S*. In other words, they are *start scripts*. Be aware that the scripts are run in numeric, and then alphabetic order. In other words, on my system's runlevel 2, documented in the /etc/rc2.d directory, the S01policykit script is run first, and the S99rmnologin script is run last.

In contrast, examine the scripts in the halt (0), single user (1), and reboot runlevels (6) with the following commands:

```
$ ls /etc/rc0.d
$ ls /etc/rc1.d
$ ls /etc/rc6.d
```

Most of the scripts listed in these runlevels start with a *K*, which means they're stopped when the system moves to runlevel 0, 1, or 6. If both *K* and *S* scripts are stored in a runlevel directory, the *K* scripts are run first, in numeric order.

*TIP* When you run a command such as **ls -l /etc/rcS.d**, the output appears in different colors, which can be difficult to read against the white background common for a command line terminal in the GUI. Placing a backslash (\) before the command can address this issue by disabling special colors.

## Manage when a Service Starts and Stops

Be aware that most services are run by default when installed in Ubuntu. So the safest way to disable a service is to remove it from the server. Just apply the **apt-get remove** command to the package in question, as discussed in Chapter 8.

There are times that you might want a service, but aren't ready to activate it. For example, if you're studying the conversion of a Microsoft network to Samba, you'll want to install the associated packages. In addition, you'll want to make sure the service doesn't start when the system is running. In this case, the first step is to ensure the service is stopped with a command like the following:

```
$ sudo /etc/init.d/samba stop
```

This stops the service from running until the next time the system reboots.

Of course, you may need to reboot for other reasons such as kernel updates. In that case, you'll need to manage when a service starts and stops during the boot process. There are three methods to that end. One method is based on the **update-rc.d** command. The simplest way to use that command is to deactivate the scripts in the /etc/rc*x*.d directories (where *x* corresponds to the runlevel) as follows. Don't substitute the desired *service* yet.

```
$ sudo update-rc.d -f service remove
```

If you want to restore the defaults, you could run the following command:

```
$ sudo update-rc.d service defaults
```

The problem is that the defaults used by the **update-rc.d** command might not correspond to the original scripts in associated /etc/rc*x*.d directories. On my system, Samba scripts are K19samba and S20samba. The order is important; in runlevels 0, 1, or 6, it's helpful to stop the Samba service before stopping the Linux implementation of the Windows Internet Name Domain, through the K20winbind script, assuming the winbind package is installed.

Similarly, the S20samba script is started just before the S20winbind script in appropriate runlevels. So to make sure the script start and stop order is respected, you should record the start and kill script numbers and remove the service from all runlevels with the following command:

```
$ sudo update-rc.d -f samba remove
```

Naturally, if you've installed the winbind package, you'll want to remove the associated scripts for that service as well.

When you're ready to activate Samba and Winbind for the local network, you can do so appropriately with the following commands:

```
$ sudo update-rc.d samba start 20 2 3 4 5 . stop 19 0 1 6 .
$ sudo update-rc.d samba start 20 2 3 4 5 . stop 19 0 1 6 .
$ sudo update-rc.d winbind start 20 2 3 4 5 . stop 20 0 1 6 .
```

If that seems like too much trouble, and you don't have a GUI, a low-level graphical tool can help. It's available from the sysv-rc-conf package and can be started with a command of the same name. As shown in Figure 7-2, the tool has an intuitive interface. Be aware that space corresponds to the SPACEBAR, and the carat (^) symbol is associated with the CTRL key.

The GUI method is based on the Service Settings tool shown in Figure 7-3, which can

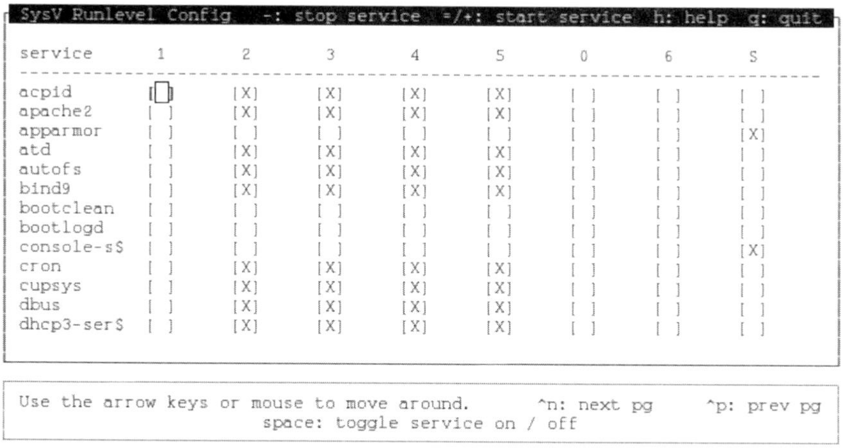

**Figure 7-2.** Controlling services from a command line console

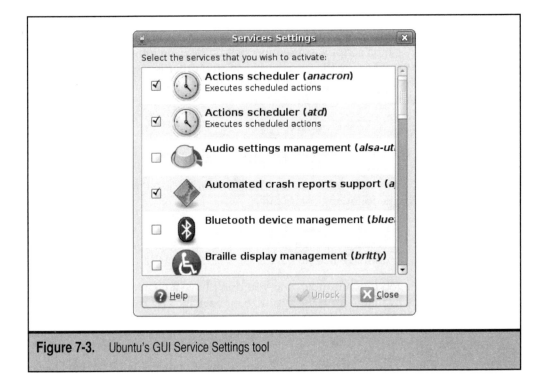

**Figure 7-3.** Ubuntu's GUI Service Settings tool

be used to deactivate the start script in the /etc/rcS.d or /etc/rc2.d directory. Starting with the Hardy Heron release, this tool is available only to authorized users. If your account is authorized in the PolicyKit, as described in Chapter 10, an active Unlock button will be shown in the Service Settings window (and other similar administrative tools), which allows selected users to control GUI administrative tools.

The Service Settings tool is a front end to the command line interface just described. But as you can see, the utility associated with the **sysv-rc-conf** command is more versatile.

# MANAGE THOSE LOG FILES

To maintain a system and keep it secure, it's important to track what happens on the system. If you're aware of key events, such as when most users connect, log files can help you to spot unusual activity. Ubuntu systems use a number of packages to monitor activity on a system. These packages include utilities that can help you identify problems and their causes.

There are several log-related scripts installed by default on Ubuntu systems. Three are related to the boot process but are currently not active. These scripts have been replaced by the Upstart service, specifically the upstart-logd package. The kernel log daemon, klogd, logs kernel messages and events. The system log daemon, syslogd, logs all other process activity. You can use the log files that syslogd generates to track activities on your system. If you are managing multiple systems, you can configure the syslogd daemon to log messages to a central host system.

Both daemons are typically active by default and can be activated with the sysklogd and klogd scripts in the /etc/init.d directory. Once these daemons start, the syslogd daemon uses /etc/syslog.conf to determine the log information to collect. The klogd daemon normally runs only with the syslogd daemon.

There are several excellent log management tools available. To review the variety of log management tools available for the current Ubuntu release, run the following commands:

```
$ apt-cache search "log analyzer"
$ apt-cache search "log analysis"
```

# General Log Configuration

You can configure what syslogd records through the /etc/syslog.conf configuration file. As shown in this section, the default version of the file includes a set of rules for different facilities (if the corresponding packages are installed). If you make changes to this file, just remember to restart the syslogd daemon with the **/etc/init.d/sysklogd restart** command.

In the analysis of any log file, it's important to understand the levels of log messages available. Each level is known as a *priority*. Log priorities, in increasing order of importance, are listed here:

▼ **debug** Used for troubleshooting; provides the highest detail

■ **info** Notes for information

■ **notice** Significant events that might require attention

■ **warn** Equivalent to *warning*

■ **err** Equivalent to *error*

■ **crit** Important errors such as those that can affect data integrity

■ **alert** A problem that requires immediate attention

▲ **emerg** Normally shown to all users; equivalent to *panic*

There's an inverse relationship between the order of importance and the number of messages. In other words, there are fewer messages at higher priorities. In addition, a generic *none* priority logs all messages at all levels.

The first line takes messages from the auth and authpriv facilities; both relate to the authentication process. Log messages related to login attempts, access to other accounts, and access to the administrative account are sent to the /var/log/auth.log file. The asterisk (*) means that all log messages in the noted categories are affected.

```
auth,authpriv.*              /var/log/auth.log
```

The next line means that all log messages—except those related to authentication—are sent to the /var/log/syslog configuration file:

```
*.*;auth,authpriv.none       -/var/log/syslog
```

The directive that follows, if activated (the **#** is a comment character), would log all cron jobs in the noted file:

```
#cron.*                      /var/log/cron.log
```

The **daemon.*** directive sends messages related to the starting and stopping of daemons to the noted file. I find a surprising number of hardware detection messages in this file as well.

```
daemon.*                     -/var/log/daemon.log
```

While kernel messages are controlled by the klogd daemon, log messages are still configured through this file. You'll find many messages in common with the kernel ring buffer, available in the /var/log/dmesg file. Additional messages relate to dynamic settings associated with the /proc and /sys directories.

```
kern.*                       -/var/log/kern.log
```

The following directive is normally obsolete, unless you use the Line Printer Daemon (LPD) or Line Printer, Next Generation (LPRng) print services. As you'll see throughout Chapter 9, the default Ubuntu print service is CUPS, the Common Unix Printing System.

```
lpr.*                        -/var/log/lpr.log
```

Any e-mail services such as Sendmail or Postfix, discussed in Chapter 17, are logged as **mail** messages in the file noted:

```
mail.*                       -/var/log/mail.log
```

A few user-initiated processes are also logged. On Ubuntu, one example is based on the RSA and DSA keys created for the SSH network connections and described in the first part of this chapter.

```
user.*                       -/var/log/user.log
```

The following three directives relate to e-mail and are sequentially cumulative. In other words, **mail.warn** includes all messages in **mail.err**; **mail.info** includes all messages in **mail.warn**. If you configure an e-mail server with extensive traffic, you could substitute

terms such as **mail.=warn** for **mail.warn**, which would limit messages in /var/log/mail
.warn to warning log messages.

```
mail.info                    -/var/log/mail.info
mail.warn                    -/var/log/mail.warn
mail.err                     /var/log/mail.err
```

If the InterNetNews (INN) Usenet-style server is installed, the following directives
would actually matter:

```
news.crit                    /var/log/news/news.crit
news.err                     /var/log/news/news.err
news.notice                  -/var/log/news/news.notice
```

The following directive is effectively one line, courtesy of the backslashes. It takes
debug and only debug level messages from all but authentication, news, and e-mail
related services:

```
*.=debug;\
        auth,authpriv.none;\
        news.none;mail.none     -/var/log/debug
```

The next directive is similar but it sends all *info-*, *notice-*, and *warn*-level logging messages, except those related to authentication, cron jobs, daemon management, mail, and
news services, to the /var/log/messages file:

```
*.=info;*.=notice;*.=warn;\
        auth,authpriv.none;\
        cron,daemon.none;\
        mail,news.none          -/var/log/messages
```

The following line supports messages to a GUI text console, based on the aforementioned syslogd daemon, mail, and news messages—as well as all messages at the *debug*,
*info*, *notice*, and *warn* levels. This directive works only if you're running a GUI and have
access to the **xconsole** command.

```
daemon.*;mail.*;\
        news.err;\
        *.=debug;*.=info;\
        *.=notice;*.=warn       |/dev/xconsole
```

If you've connected to the server remotely and administer it from a GUI, run the **xconsole**
command. The GUI does not have to be installed on the server, but the x11-apps
package does need to be installed. Log messages are shown in an X Window console,
similar to those shown in Figure 7-4.

Alternatively, if you aren't using a GUI, you could send messages to a local terminal.
One option suggested by comments in the file is /dev/tty8, the eighth virtual console. If you're not currently in the GUI, press ALT-F8 to access this console. Otherwise,
if you're working in the GUI, press CTRL-ALT-F8 to access the console. (You could then

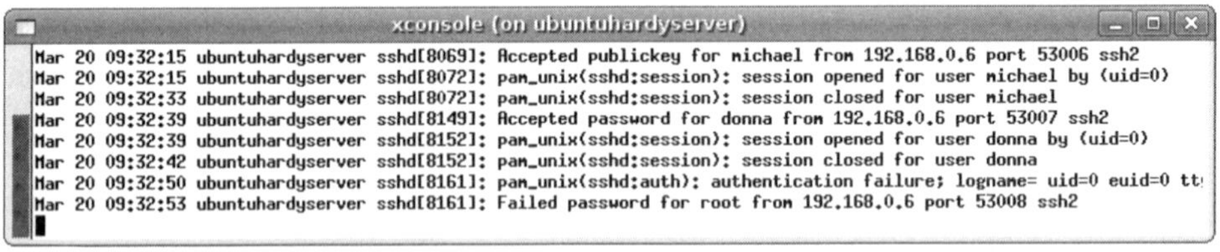

```
                      xconsole (on ubuntuhardyserver)
Mar 20 09:32:15 ubuntuhardyserver sshd[8069]: Accepted publickey for michael from 192.168.0.6 port 53006 ssh2
Mar 20 09:32:15 ubuntuhardyserver sshd[8072]: pam_unix(sshd:session): session opened for user michael by (uid=0)
Mar 20 09:32:33 ubuntuhardyserver sshd[8072]: pam_unix(sshd:session): session closed for user michael
Mar 20 09:32:39 ubuntuhardyserver sshd[8149]: Accepted password for donna from 192.168.0.6 port 53007 ssh2
Mar 20 09:32:39 ubuntuhardyserver sshd[8152]: pam_unix(sshd:session): session opened for user donna by (uid=0)
Mar 20 09:32:42 ubuntuhardyserver sshd[8152]: pam_unix(sshd:session): session closed for user donna
Mar 20 09:32:50 ubuntuhardyserver sshd[8161]: pam_unix(sshd:auth): authentication failure; logname= uid=0 euid=0 tt
Mar 20 09:32:53 ubuntuhardyserver sshd[8161]: Failed password for root from 192.168.0.6 port 53008 ssh2
```

**Figure 7-4.**   Monitor log messages in an X Window console

return to the GUI with the CTRL-ALT-F7 key combination.) If that's best for you, substitute **/dev/tty8 for /dev/xconsole** (or for any of the other log files listed earlier in the file).

One more alternative is available for those who prefer to administer via an SSH connection. The console associated with the first SSH connection is /dev/pts/0. In fact, if the following line is added to /etc/syslog.conf,

```
auth,authpriv.*     /dev/pts/0
```

and then the **/etc/init.d/sysklogd restart** command is run, attempts by others to log into the remote server, successful and otherwise, immediately appear on the local console.

Logs can even be sent to remote servers. In fact, one common option is to set up a dedicated log server. For example, if the following line is added,

```
auth,authpriv.*     @log.example.net
```

log messages are sent to the noted log.example.net server. If a firewall exists between the two systems, make sure TCP/IP port 514 is open on the firewall.

## General Log Files

General log files and their functionality are described in Table 7-3. This section does not include logs related to services such as Samba. It does include settings shown in the default /etc/syslog.conf file. All files shown are in the /var/log directory. If you haven't installed or activated the associated package, you may not see the log file on your system. Some general services are not part of the standard /var/log directory, and others are discussed in the next section.

## Service-Specific Log Files

To complete the discussion of collected log files, Table 7-4 lists typical logs and log directories in the /var/log directory; these are related primarily to services such as Apache and Samba. Table 7-4 is not a complete list; additional service-specific log files may be available.

| Log Files | Description |
|---|---|
| acpid | Specifies events related to the Advanced Configuration and Power Interface |
| auth.log | Notes authentication-related messages |
| boot | Now obsolete; associated services replaced by Upstart |
| btmp | Lists failed local or Telnet login attempts; readable with the **lastb** command |
| daemon.log | Adds messages associated with certain daemons |
| debug | Includes debug-level messages, unless related to authentication, news, or mail |
| dist-upgrade/ | Includes log files related to the **apt-get dist-upgrade** command |
| dmesg | Records basic boot and related messages |
| dpkg.log | Adds data on any use of **dpkg** (or front ends such as **apt-get install**) |
| faillog | Lists failed login attempts; readable with the **faillog** command. |
| fsck/ | Includes log files associated with **fsck** and related commands |
| installer/ | Includes log files associated with the installation process; might be available only from a text-mode installation |
| kern.log | Adds kernel-related messages, after the boot process is complete |
| lastlog | Lists login records for all users; readable with the **lastlog** command |
| mail.* | Specifies several log files related to mail services |
| messages | Includes messages from other services as defined in /etc/syslog.conf |
| news/ | Includes log files associated with news services, if installed |
| syslog | Adds all general log messages, except those related to authentication |
| udev/ | Includes log files associated with Linux plug-and-play detection |
| user.log | Adds messages associated with user-run services |
| wtmp | Read with the **lastb -f /var/log/wtmp** command |
| Xorg.0.log | Adds setup messages for the X Window System |

**Table 7-3.**   General Log Files and Directories

| Log Files | Description |
|---|---|
| apache2/ | Includes log files associated with the Apache web server |
| apparmor/ | Adds log files associated with the AppArmor security framework |
| apt/ | Specifies log files associated with the **apt-get** and related commands |
| cups/ | Includes CUPS print logs related to access, pages, and errors |
| fontconfig.log | Specifies installed fonts |
| gdm/ | Adds messages associated with the GNOME Display Manager, if installed |
| landscape/ | Includes connection and command messages associated with Landscape, as discussed in Chapter 8 |
| mysql.* | Specifies logs related to the MySQL database server |
| postgresql/ | Adds log files associated with the PostgreSQL database server |
| pycentral.log | Includes messages associated with building Python packages |
| samba/ | Adds several access and service logs for the Samba server |
| scrollkeeper.log | Includes information related to GNOME utilities |

**Table 7-4.**   Service-Specific Log Files and Directories

## Log Rotation

Logs can easily become very large and difficult to analyze. The logrotate package configures a daily cron job, which in most cases creates new log files every week. The governing /etc/logrotate.conf configuration file can also be used to compress, e-mail, and remove desired log files. Generally, five weeks of logs are kept for a number of services. As logging is configured with many individual services, you may see even a longer history of logs in the /var/log directory.

## SUMMARY

This chapter covered several basic administrative tools. The SSH server can help you administer remote systems. The cron and at daemons can help you schedule administrative jobs as needed. Service scripts configured in appropriate runlevels can promote security. As problems can be diagnosed in log files, the general configuration file, /etc/syslog .conf, can help optimize how you manage your Ubuntu servers.

# CHAPTER 8

## Manage Updates and Local Repositories

U buntu system administrators need to know how to manage updates. Administrators of large networks should also know how to mirror remote repositories locally. Since Ubuntu is built on Debian Linux, many of the skills and key commands are the same.

Modern Linux distributions configure packages in a variety of repositories. For each Ubuntu release, client updates are configured in the local /etc/apt/sources.list configuration file. Updates and other maintenance commands are also possible with Landscape, Canonical's system management service. (Be aware that while trial subscriptions are available, the continued use of Landscape requires an appropriate subscription through Canonical.)

**NOTE**  For more information on updates, repositories, and general Linux package management, see this author's *Linux Patch Management*, published by Prentice Hall.

# THE BASICS OF DPKG AND APT

Because Ubuntu releases are based on and still use packages developed for Debian Linux, Ubuntu distributions use the Debian packaging system. So it should be no surprise that Ubuntu systems use many of the same commands available in Debian Linux, including package management commands such as **dpkg** and **apt-\***.

The **dpkg** command is a package manager. The **apt-\*** commands do much more, as they can install packages with dependencies from remote repositories. Repositories such as Ubuntu main and universe are configured in every system's /etc/apt/sources.list configuration file.

**NOTE**  A *dependency* refers to a package that is a prerequisite to another. For example, if you installed the sysv-rc-conf package in Chapter 7, you may have noticed that other packages such as libcurses-ui-perl were also installed. These additional packages are called dependencies.

Once you understand the **dpkg** and **apt-\*** commands and how they work with repositories, you're ready to learn about the **aptitude** utility and the Synaptic Package Manager. Finally, you'll take a brief look at the Task Selector, which can help install packages by group.

## A Background in dpkg

The **dpkg** command is fundamental to the Debian packaging system used on Ubuntu releases. If you're familiar with Red Hat–style distributions, it's functionally equivalent to the **rpm** command. The options are rich and varied. As has been done for **rpm**, the options associated with **dpkg** could be collected into a book-length work.

This section explains the switches that I use most often. To test these switches, you'll want a ready archive of packages. Even if this is a completely new installation, an archive should be available in the /var/cache/apt/archives directory. The package you select for this purpose should have as few dependencies as possible. If the package is already installed, back up any associated configuration file and apply the **dpkg -P** command to purge that package.

One example discussed in Chapter 7 is the sysv-rc-conf utility, available from the sysv-rc-conf_*_all.deb package. To prepare for this section, I've run the **sudo apt-get install sysv-rc-conf** command. Then I purged the package with the **sudo dpkg -P sysv-rc-conf** command.

The **dpkg** command requires administrative privileges; in most cases, preface the **dpkg** with the **sudo** command. Now install the package. The following command should work on any available package developed for Ubuntu releases, assuming no dependencies. You may need to include the directory path to the package.

```
$ sudo dpkg -i  sysv-rc-conf_*_all.deb
```

If a message appears which cites "dependency problems," one solution is to include those other packages in the **dpkg** command. While that's not required with the **apt-get** commands described shortly, the focus of this section is on the **dpkg** command.

To verify that a desired package is installed, the **dpkg -l** command can help. Be aware that it works only with the name of the package—in this case:

```
$ dpkg -l sysv-rc-conf
Desired=Unknown/Install/Remove/Purge/Hold
| Status=Not/Installed/Config-f/Unpacked/Failed-cfg/Half-inst/t-aWait/
T-pend
|/ Err?=(none)/Hold/Reinst-required/X=both-problems (Status,Err:
uppercase=bad)
=||/ Name            Version         Description
+++-==============-===============-================================
ii  sysv-rc-conf    0.99-6          SysV init runlevel configuration
```

If you've spelled the package correctly, the status of the package is shown in the output. The first two or three letters on the left of the package name, in this case, the **ii** to the left of **sysv-rc-conf**, indicate the status of the package. Hints are shown in the output. The first letter is the "Desired" status, where **i** is short for install and **p** is short for purge. The second letter is the actual status; in this case, **n** is short for not installed and **i** is short for installed.

Run the **dpkg -l** command by itself, and marvel as it displays the full list of currently installed packages. For those of you more familiar with RPM-based distributions, note the similarity with the **rpm -qa** command.

For any installed package, it's easy to identify the list of files installed with that package. Just apply the **dpkg -L** command to it, and you should see the full list of files and directories installed through that package:

```
$ dpkg -L sysv-rc-conf
```

If you're not sure about the source of a particular file, apply the **dpkg -S** command to the full path to that file. For example, when I run the following command, I see that it's based on the passwd package:

```
$ dpkg -S /etc/default/useradd
passwd: /etc/default/useradd
```

Be aware that the **dpkg -S** command doesn't work on every file, as some files are composite configuration files created from two or more packages.

Finally, a couple of options are available for uninstalling the package. The **dpkg -r** command removes a package, without removing associated configuration files. The **dpkg -P** command purges the configuration files along with the package.

# Ubuntu Repository Organization

Ubuntu repositories for the United States are available from http://us.archive.ubuntu .com. From this URL, examine the top level repository directories. Click the ubuntu/ subdirectory, and then click the dists/ subdirectory to see the listing shown in Figure 8-1.

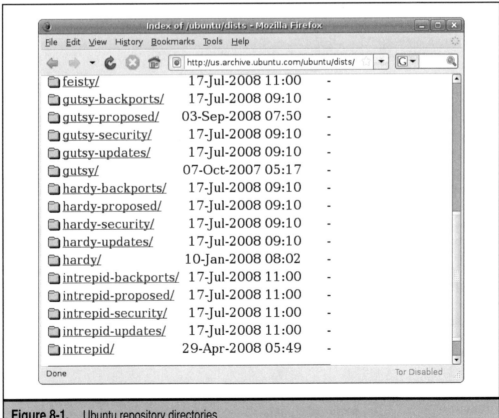

**Figure 8-1.**   Ubuntu repository directories

| Directory | Description |
|---|---|
| hardy/ | Includes standard files associated with Hardy Heron installation; many of the packages contained can also be found on the installation CD |
| hardy-backports/ | Adds packages that incorporate features from later releases |
| hardy-proposed/ | Specifies packages not yet ready for production |
| hardy-security/ | Notes package updates made available for security reasons |
| hardy-updates/ | Includes packages that update features |

**Table 8-1.** Repository Categories

Note the five categories associated with the Hardy Heron release. These are all effectively subdirectories. There are four repositories included in each of these subdirectories: main, restricted, universe, and multiverse.

Let's expand on this concept. The subdirectories shown in Figure 8-1 can be explained in Table 8-1. If you're working with a different release, substitute the code name for *hardy* accordingly.

In each of the categories listed in the table are four repositories, described as follows:

▼ **main**   Includes packages that are released under open source licenses and supported by Canonical.

■ **restricted**   Limited to packages that are *not* released under open source licenses and are supported by Canonical.

■ **universe**   Encompasses packages that are released under open source licenses and are supported by Canonical.

▲ **multiverse**   Restricted to packages that are *not* released under open source licenses and are supported by Canonical.

If you explore further, each of these repositories is subdivided by architecture, in subdirectories such as binary-i386/ and binary-amd64/. Starting with the Hardy Heron release, packages built for other architectures are not supported by Canonical.

If a package is supported by Canonical, you may be able to get help for the package with a support subscription as discussed at www.canonical.com/services/support.

## Repository Source Management

Local repositories are configured in the /etc/apt/sources.list file. In this section, I analyze this file on my Ubuntu Hardy Heron system. The default version of this file includes several comments that suggest alternative commands. What you see in this file depends in part on what repository options were configured during the installation process described in Chapter 2's "Install Ubuntu Server."

The first commands in comments would apply if you keep the installation CD constantly connected. As I prefer to keep the CD/DVD drive, even on a virtual machine, free for other things, I don't activate this repository. Of course, if you're running a virtual machine, you could just configure another CD/DVD drive.

The commands that follow are based on the default Ubuntu Server installation, based on US defaults. If you've configured a connection to a more local mirror, the URL will be different from http://us.archive.ubuntu.com/ubuntu/.

The first two active directives point to the main and restricted repositories for the Hardy Heron release. The first directive starts with the **deb** command, which is associated with standard binary packages. The second directive starts with the **deb-src** command, which connects to accompanying source code packages in the same repositories.

```
deb http://us.archive.ubuntu.com/ubuntu/ hardy main restricted
deb-src http://us.archive.ubuntu.com/ubuntu/ hardy main restricted
```

The directives that follow are associated with Hardy Heron updates, upgrades to what may have been included during the original installation process:

```
deb http://us.archive.ubuntu.com/ubuntu/ hardy-updates main restricted
deb-src http://us.archive.ubuntu.com/ubuntu/ hardy-updates main
restricted
```

The next set of directives point to the Hardy Heron universe repository. The associated comment notes that the Ubuntu team will not support any packages contained therein, and said packages won't get any security updates. There are four directives in this group that point to the binary and source code in both the *hardy* and *hardy-updates* subdirectories:

```
deb http://us.archive.ubuntu.com/ubuntu/ hardy universe
deb-src http://us.archive.ubuntu.com/ubuntu/ hardy universe
deb http://us.archive.ubuntu.com/ubuntu/ hardy-updates universe
deb-src http://us.archive.ubuntu.com/ubuntu/ hardy-updates universe
```

Four additional directives follow, which are almost identical to those shown above, except they substitute *multiverse* for *universe*. As described in the previous section, the multiverse repository does not conform to open source licenses.

In my opinion, it's important to activate backports, especially on LTS (long term support) releases. As LTS releases such as Hardy Heron are supported for three years on the desktop and five years on the server, backports allow you to update Hardy Heron with features from later releases. Be aware that despite the format limitations on this printed page, **main restricted universe multiverse** all appear on the same line.

```
deb http://us.archive.ubuntu.com/ubuntu/ hardy-backports main
restricted universe multiverse
```

```
deb-src http://us.archive.ubuntu.com/ubuntu/ hardy-backports main
restricted universe multiverse
```

If you're interested in third-party packages, one repository of interest is the *partner* repository. Unlike the other repositories, the *partner* repository may not be available on the mirror of your choice. If you're interested in partner packages such as the Opera web browser, activate these directives:

```
# deb http://archive.canonical.com/ubuntu hardy partner
# deb-src http://archive.canonical.com/ubuntu hardy partner
```

**NOTE**   Not all software from Ubuntu partners is available from this repository. For a list of current Ubuntu partners, navigate to http://webapps.ubuntu.com/partners/software/.

Finally, the following six directives are associated with the Hardy Heron security repositories. Note the references to main, restricted, universe, and multiverse packages. You may have noted the Ubuntu warnings on how they don't provide support for packages in the universe or multiverse repositories. But when security updates are made available to Ubuntu, the responsible developers include it in the appropriate repositories.

```
deb http://security.ubuntu.com/ubuntu hardy-security main restricted
deb-src http://security.ubuntu.com/ubuntu hardy-security main restricted
deb http://security.ubuntu.com/ubuntu hardy-security universe
deb-src http://security.ubuntu.com/ubuntu hardy-security universe
deb http://security.ubuntu.com/ubuntu hardy-security multiverse
deb-src http://security.ubuntu.com/ubuntu hardy-security multiverse
```

**NOTE**   While other repositories are often directed toward mirror sites, many experts recommend that you do *not* connect to mirrors for security-related repositories. Some security updates can be time-sensitive.

Finally, there are a variety of groups who try to use Ubuntu's success, with additional features beyond what's available even in the partner, universe, and multiverse repositories. One well-known example is Ultamatix (http://ultamatix.com), which builds on the work of the former Automatix, which automatically installs a number of multimedia and desktop applications. These are known as *third-party repositories*. Not all third-parties who create specialized repositories work closely with Ubuntu developers, so take extra care before using the software from these projects.

One risk of third-party repositories is related to dependencies. If the dependency is not available or conflicts with a key Ubuntu package, it can impact other packages. Such impacts on other packages can lead to problems with even more packages. This is known as *dependency hell*. Therefore, if you're unsure about a third-party repository, check online feedback. Read about any problems that other users have encountered with that repository.

## Find the Right Mirror

During the installation process, you may have configured a connection to an appropriate national mirror. However, a national mirror may not be the best mirror for you. For example, when I trace the route to the http://us.archive.ubuntu.com mirror from the US West Coast, it actually connects to a server in the United Kingdom. Any mirror located in the continental United States is more likely to better serve my systems.

**NOTE**   One way to trace the route to a remote server is with the **traceroute** command. Alternatively, IP address locators available online can help identify the geographic position of a remote server.

So to find the best connection to a mirror, it's best to find a mirror close to me. A current list of Ubuntu mirrors is available online from https://launchpad.net/ubuntu/+archivemirrors. When selecting a mirror, consider the following factors:

▼   **Geographic distance**   A mirror physically close to you is less likely to be subject to Internet traffic problems.

■   **Desired protocol**   Not all mirrors support access through HTTP, FTP, and rsync servers.

▲   **Speed**   Depending on the number of users who connect to a mirror, faster mirrors usually lead to faster downloads.

If you have access to a GUI, the process can be somewhat automated. Open the Software Sources application: From the GNOME desktop, choose System | Administration | Software Sources. If you want to open this application over a remote SSH connection, run the **sudo software-properties-gtk** command. In the Ubuntu Software tab shown in Figure 8-2, click the Download From drop-down text box. Click Other to open the Choose A Download Server window shown in Figure 8-3.

You can use the tool to evaluate the configured list of download servers. Try it out for yourself; click Select Best Server. When I clicked this button, it selected a server several states away. However, there are a number of excellent alternative mirror sites with the same connection speed located closer to me. So remember to make your own judgment on the results, and evaluate it against the aforementioned list of Ubuntu mirrors.

## Fundamental apt Commands

The early part of this chapter described one of the problems with the **dpkg** command: installation trouble when dependencies exist. While it is possible to force a package installation, overriding existing dependencies can be risky. Installed packages without access to dependencies can lead to problems with associated commands and applications.

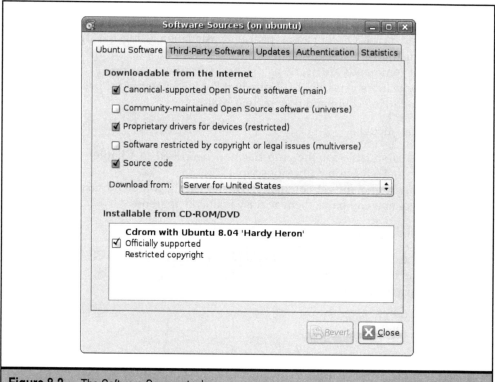

**Figure 8-2.**   The Software Sources tool

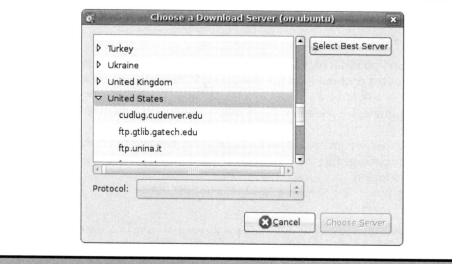

**Figure 8-3.**   Choose a Download Server

That's where the **apt-\*** commands can help. Specifically, the **apt-get install** *package* and **apt-get remove** *package* commands installs and removes the package of your choice, with all dependencies. Of course, as package installation using the **dpkg** command requires administrative privileges, so does the **apt-get** command.

The **apt-get** commands are nearly as rich and versatile as the **dpkg** command; some would say they're more versatile. To ensure that the local database of packages is up-to-date, run the following command on a regular basis:

```
$ sudo apt-get update
```

This command is suitable for the cron daemon described in Chapter 7 and may be appropriate for the /etc/cron.daily/apt script.

There's more to the **apt-get** command. The following command takes a look at all current packages and compares them against available upgrades:

```
$ sudo apt-get upgrade
```

Based on the current state of packages, a few packages may be listed, with messages that they should have been installed or removed. Such packages can be caught with one of the following commands:

```
$ sudo apt-get -f install
$ sudo apt-get -f remove
```

Another approach uses the **dselect-upgrade** option. The **-u** displays upgraded packages:

```
$ sudo apt-get -u dselect-upgrade
```

If you really want to update all packages on the local system, the following package checks all packages against what's available:

```
$ sudo apt-get -u dist-upgrade
```

If you want to update all packages to the next release, change the release name in the /etc/apt/sources.list configuration file. For example, changing all instances of *hardy* to *intrepid* in that file would be a prelude to a release upgrade. Just be aware that such an action would upgrade to a release without long-term support, and may affect a support contract.

The /var/cache/apt/archives directory can easily become filled with gigabytes of possibly obsolete package files. You could clean out all packages from this directory with the following command:

```
$ sudo apt-get clean
```

Alternatively, you could just clear out those packages that have become obsolete (and in most cases are superseded by more recent packages) with the following command:

```
$ sudo apt-get autoclean
```

# More apt Commands

The **apt-get** command is just one of the many available **apt-** based commands. Others discussed in this section include **apt-cache**, **apt-file**, and **apt-ftparchive**. The **apt-ftparchive** command will be used to help to create a repository mirror later in this chapter.

For a more complete list of **apt-** commands and options, see the Debian Linux apt HOWTO, available online from www.debian.org/doc/manuals/apt-howto/.

## apt-cache

The simplest way to review available repositories for package information is with the **apt-cache** command. Assuming the local repository databases are up-to-date, the following command searches for all packages related to the Linux Terminal Server Project (LTSP), the default Ubuntu implementation of the diskless client:

```
$ apt-cache search ltsp
```

If you want a preview of the dependencies associated with a package, the **depends** and **rdepends** switches can help. For example, the following command provides a list of dependencies, or packages that should be installed before the Samba file server can be installed. If you read the list carefully, you'll see suggested packages associated with some optional features of Samba, as well as recommended packages, conflicts, and updates of currently installed packages associated with dependencies.

```
$ apt-cache depends samba
```

If you're interested in reverse dependencies, the **rdepends** switch can help. For example, to find packages that require Samba to be installed first, run the following command:

```
$ apt-cache rdepends samba
```

But the information provided by **apt-cache** might not be up-to-date. Before running any **apt-\*** command, make sure the local system has the latest repository updates with the following command:

```
$ sudo apt-get update
```

## apt-file

The **apt-file** command uses the repository databases to help search within uninstalled packages. For example, if you're running a later version of an Ubuntu distribution, the /etc/inittab file won't normally be installed. If you prefer a boot process using the file, you could search for it from connected repositories with the following command:

```
$ apt-file search /etc/inittab
```

Of course, this assumes the local repository and file databases are up-to-date. If unsure, run the **apt-get update** command. If you need to install the **apt-file** command, run the **sudo apt-get install apt-file** command.

The first time you run the **apt-file** command after installation, you'll need to update the associated cache with the following command:

```
$ sudo apt-file update
```

### apt-ftparchive

The **apt-ftparchive** command can be used to configure a repository for client access. Specifically, the following version of this command, when run in a directory with a bunch of Ubuntu packages, creates an appropriate Packages.gz file database:

```
$ sudo apt-ftparchive packages . | gzip -9c > Packages.gz
```

The dot (.) in the command refers to all files in the current directory. Of course, you could substitute the name of the directory with the packages to be configured into a repository, and send the output to the appropriate directory searched by clients.

On the main Ubuntu Hardy Heron archive in the United States assuming a standard i386 repository, the directory with the Packages.gz file is

```
/ubuntu/dists/hardy/main/binary-i386
```

The organization of Ubuntu repositories were discussed earlier in this chapter in the "Ubuntu Repository Organization" section.

## Update Management Tools

Two of the popular alternatives to the **apt-*** commands are **aptitude** and the Synaptic Package Manager. The **aptitude** command works in two basic modes. As a command, **aptitude** can in most situations be used as a "drop-in" replacement for the **apt-get** command. As such, a separate section for **aptitude** as a command would be redundant. When run by itself, **aptitude** opens an intuitive tool that does not require a GUI. One more popular option is the Update Manager, available through the **update-manager** command.

### Package Management with aptitude

The **aptitude** tool is powerful. It's only a front end, but it provides menu-driven support to all **apt-*** based commands. It does not require a GUI. You don't even need to preface the **aptitude** command with **sudo**; it prompts you for the appropriate password when required. The interface, shown in Figure 8-4, is accessible even over a remote connection.

Packages are subdivided into the categories shown in Figure 8-4. The basic categories are generally self-explanatory; for example, Upgradable Packages specify a list of installed packages for which upgrades are available. Virtual Packages help developers organize packages. For example, apache2-mpm is a virtual package that helps organize other Apache multi-processing module packages. Finally, the Tasks category specifies packages not included in other categories.

Use the UP ARROW, DOWN ARROW, and ENTER keys to navigate around aptitude. For example, Figure 8-5 provides more information about the aptitude package. At this point, if you press ENTER, you'd see more information about the package, including dependencies.

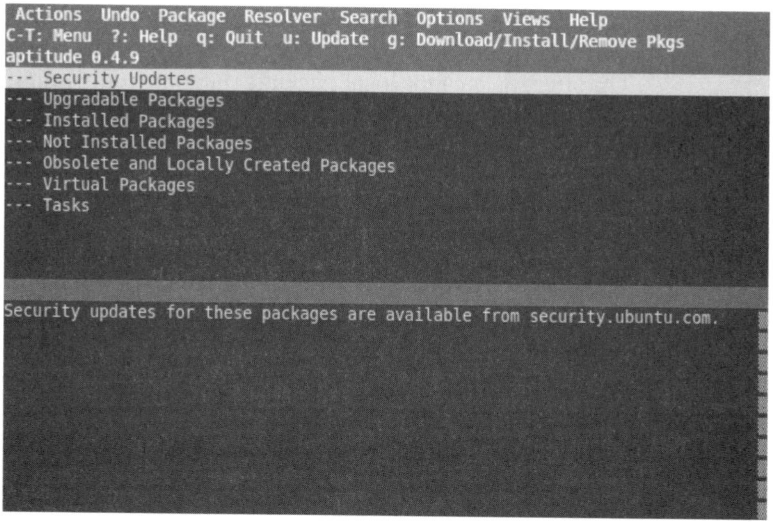

**Figure 8-4.**    The **aptitude** tool

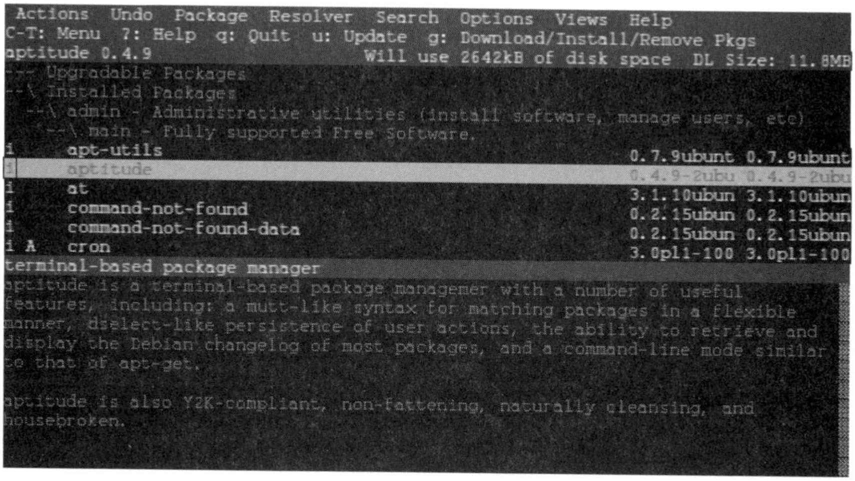

**Figure 8-5.**    The **aptitude** tool describes the aptitude package.

| Command | Description |
| --- | --- |
| u | Updates the current local package database; equivalent to **sudo apt-get update** |
| + | Adds the package to the list to be installed |
| - (dash) | Adds the package to the list to be removed |
| _ (underscore) | Adds the package to the list to be purged |
| g | Installs and removes the aforementioned packages |
| CTRL-T | Provides access to the drop-down menus; to exit, press ESC and any arrow key |
| ? | Opens a detailed list of key-driven commands |

**Table 8-2.**   Basic Commands from the **aptitude** Tool

To go back up the **aptitude** command tree, press Q as many times as needed.

In the screen shown in Figure 8-5, up to three letters can be associated with each package. The first letter for all packages in the Installed category is *i*, which means the current state of the package is installed. The second letter specifies a pending action. A third letter, such as *A*, specifies that the package was automatically installed.

The basic commands are straightforward, as described in Table 8-2, which includes several commonly used commands beyond what's shown in Figure 8-5.

## Synaptic Package Manager

The **synaptic** command opens the Synaptic Package Manager, shown in Figure 8-6. While this is a GUI tool, it is and has been a popular administrative option for years on Debian-based distributions, including Ubuntu.

In some ways, the Synaptic Package Manager is similar to **aptitude**, as it serves as a front end to several of the **apt-\*** commands. It provides a visual overview of available packages, including descriptions, dependencies, and more. It also provides a front end to the Software Sources tool described earlier in this chapter. As with the **aptitude** command, administrative actions are not enabled unless **synaptic** is run with administrative privileges.

This section covers only the basic capabilities of the Synaptic Package Manager. First, note the buttons in the top toolbar. The Reload option is a front end to the **apt-get update** command, which updates databases to the latest information available from the repositories cited in the /etc/apt/sources.list file. The Mark All Upgrades button checks the local repository database against currently installed packages and marks all packages

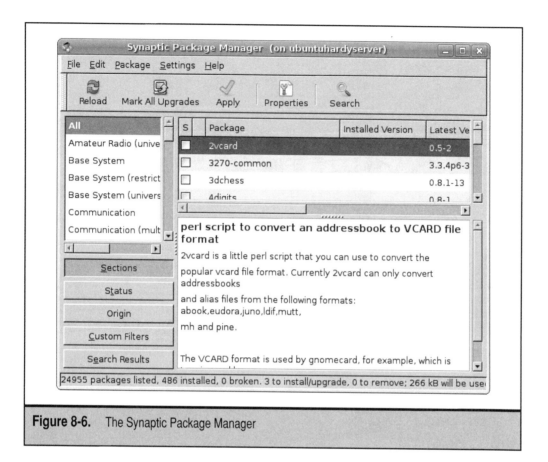

**Figure 8-6.**    The Synaptic Package Manager

with available upgrades. If you click this button (or configure a package for installation or removal), the Apply button becomes active, which prompts you to start the download and installation of all marked upgrades.

**NOTE**    If you're running Synaptic from a remote server where the GUI is not installed, some icons could be missing. In that case, make sure the hicolor-icon-theme package is installed.

If you haven't marked any other packages for installation or removal, click the Status button in the lower-left section, and then click the Installed (upgradable) option that appears in the upper-left section. You'll see a group of packages to be upgraded in the upper-right pane, as shown in Figure 8-7.

It's a fairly common practice to avoid kernel upgrades in certain circumstances. Software such as database managers may be certified only to a specific kernel version. Special drivers may be built to a specific kernel version. In either case, a kernel upgrade would mean trouble. If you don't want to upgrade a kernel, disable any active updates

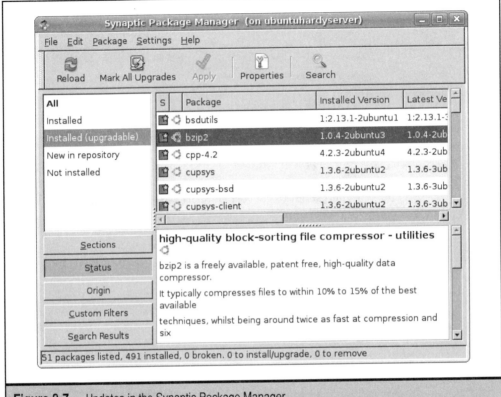

**Figure 8-7.** Updates in the Synaptic Package Manager

for the linux-headers and linux-image packages. To do so, right-click the package name and select Unmark from the pop-up menu that appears.

A click of the Properties button opens an unnamed window that provides detailed information about the highlighted package, including dependencies and installed files. The Search button supports a search through the database; it's a front end to the **apt-cache** command.

Note the organization of the Synaptic window. Categories are listed in the upper-left pane. Packages in the highlighted category are shown at the upper-right pane. A description of the highlighted package is shown in the lower-right pane.

The lower-left pane includes five buttons with options for sorting packages. Associated categories are then listed in the upper-left pane. Briefly, the Sections button provides a functional grouping of packages. The Status button divides packages by installation status. The Origin button classifies packages by their original repository. The Custom Filters button divides packages by those that are marked for changes, those that are upgradable, custom searches, and more. Finally, the Search Results button lists the output of custom searches.

Choose Settings | Repositories. The window that appears should be familiar—it's the Software Sources application.

There are a substantial number of other options available. Choose Settings | Preferences. Explore the tabs that appear in the Preferences window. These options can help you see how updates can be customized on any Ubuntu system.

## Update Manager

The Update Manager is another important GUI tool for package management. It can be started with the **update-manager** command in a GUI. It compares the current list of packages against the local database of available updates.

The Update Manager is a straightforward tool. As shown in Figure 8-8, packages for which updates are available are listed and selected by default. Administrative password confirmation is not required until you click the Install Updates button. As the comparison is made against a local database, you can run the **sudo apt-get update** command first to make sure that local databases are up-to-date—or just click the Check button, which performs the same function.

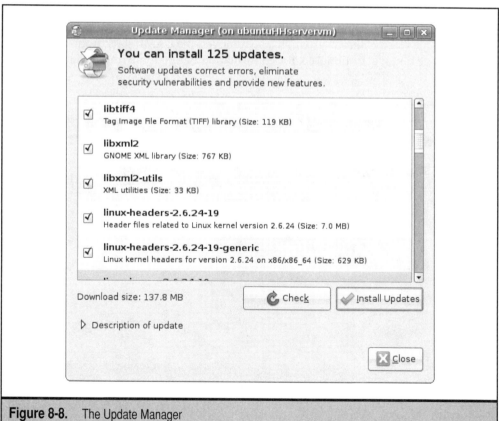

**Figure 8-8.**   The Update Manager

If for some reason you don't want to update a kernel, disable the updates for the linux-headers and linux-image packages by deselecting them in the Update Manager. When you click Install Updates, kernel updates are not updated in the list, unless so required as dependencies.

## The Task Selector

The Task Selector is a simple tool to install groups of packages after an Ubuntu system is installed. Like the Update Manager and Synaptic Package Manager, it's a front end to the **aptitude** command—which itself is a front end to the **apt-get** command. To open it, run the **sudo tasksel** command. The advantage, as shown in Figure 8-9, is the listing of major package groups. You can navigate with arrow and TAB keys. To select a desired package group, highlight it and press the SPACE BAR to add an asterisk to the group. Then press ENTER to activate the download and installation of associated packages.

The Task Selector does not, however, list the individual packages to be installed. For example, when I install the LAMP stack, the "Please Wait" message appeared without progress for nearly four minutes. And if the network is slow, you might not see progress for quite some time. So be patient. If desired, recheck the network connection.

I don't recommend using the Task Selector to remove a package group, because the results can be unpredictable. For example, when I removed the Mail Server package group from one Hardy Heron system, it also removed the LAMP stack from that system. Other package removal options ask for confirmation before removing packages seen as dependent.

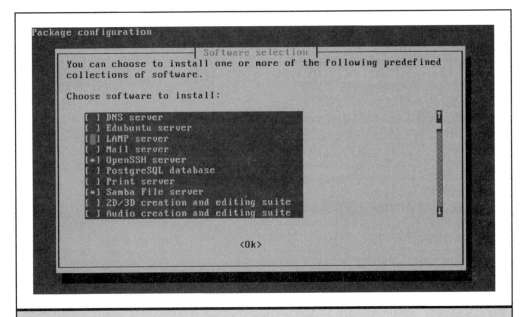

**Figure 8-9.**   The Task Selector opens a command line Software Selection tool

# KEEP THE SERVER UP-TO-DATE

Perhaps a fundamental skill for a Linux administrator is not only the ability to update a system—but the judgment required as to when to keep a server up-to-date. You could run the **sudo apt-get upgrade** command on a regular basis. You could even automate updates by setting up this command as a script in the /etc/cron.daily directory. But not all updates are desirable. In fact, some updates can affect the functionality of some applications—and even invalidate support for others.

I've grouped updates in three categories, which by necessity overlap. For example, a kernel update could be made available for security reasons, and the update could also affect the functionality or certification of an application.

## Security Updates

As strange as it may sound, some administrators don't install all security updates. For example, if the Samba file server is not in use, and you don't plan to install Samba in the near future, there's no reason to update a system for a Samba security update. Even if you're using Samba, the update can relate to a feature you're not using. The security updates to be installed depend on the services that are needed.

Ubuntu Security Notices (USN) are designed to help the administrator understand whether a security update is needed. The latest USN are available from www.ubuntu .com/usn. If you have a browser that supports RSS (Really Simple Syndication) feeds, it's possible to subscribe to these notices. Alternatively, you could subscribe to the Ubuntu Security Announcements mailing list, available from https://lists.ubuntu.com/.

**NOTE** The unattended-upgrades package provides a front end to the security update process. It runs with the **unattended-upgrades** command, based on the configuration in the /etc/apt/apt.conf.d/ 50unattended-upgrades configuration file.

## Kernel Updates

New kernels can be especially difficult for some systems. Kernel updates can plug security holes. But that can cause problems, because some applications such as database management tools may be certified to a certain version of a kernel. In that case, upgrades would then invalidate support for that database.

Specialized drivers may be available only for certain kernels; if source code is not available for that driver, it's not possible to recompile that driver to the new kernel. In that case, an updated kernel could even break that driver.

Kernel updates are enabled by default by the major command tools, including **apt-get**, **aptitude**, the Synaptic Package Manager, and the Update Manager. Updates can be deselected in the Package Manager and the Update Manager as described earlier in the "Update Management Tools" section. If you'd rather use the **aptitude** command, updates to the Ubuntu server kernel can be disabled with the following command:

```
$ sudo aptitude hold linux-image-`uname -r`
```

The next time you upgrade packages with a command such as **sudo aptitude upgrade**, the package related to the current Linux kernel is not upgraded. Just be careful; if a new Linux kernel package is included as a dependency, further work is required to identify those other packages that also should not be upgraded.

## Application Updates

Knowing when to update an application can be problematic. Most packages associated with Ubuntu systems are developed by third parties. While appropriate packages are supported by Canonical, you still need to decide when to update an application. Some application updates could introduce features that disable the work done by your users.

In addition to the aforementioned USN security notices, other information can be found at Ubuntu's news site. Known as The Fridge, it provides "news, grassroots marketing, advocacy, team collaboration, and great original content." Available at http://fridge.ubuntu.com, this community news site details release announcements, conference events, hot new features, project reports, and more.

Of course, another alternative is the Internet home page for the application in question. For example, you may want to read the latest information from the OpenOffice.org website before downloading the hundreds of megabytes of data such an update entails, especially on a group of computers.

# CREATE A REPOSITORY MIRROR

When there are a significant number of Ubuntu systems on a network, large updates, if run simultaneously, can easily overload even business-level Internet connections. It seems like every time I turn around, there's an update to the OpenOffice.org suite, which leads to a several hundred megabyte update—for each system.

If you administer a substantial number of Linux systems, it may be more cost-effective to create a local mirror of at least certain repositories, such as those associated with updates. For that purpose, Ubuntu distributions include tools that can copy and synchronize from a remote mirror. If you also want to keep systems up-to-date with custom packages, there are several tools that can help configure the repository database.

Of course, once a local mirror is created, it won't help unless local clients are configured to use that local mirror. And local mirrors need to be kept up-to-date, so you should set up a regular job such as an automated cron job to keep the mirror up-to-date.

## Mirror Configuration

There are two basic methods to synchronize a local client to a remote repository. The **rsync** command is the traditional method associated with synchronizing local and remote groups of files. The **apt-mirror** command is more focused, and in my opinion, a better choice at least for the initial mirroring of the remote repository. The focus of this section is on **apt-mirror**; you could subsequently use the **rsync** command to keep the repository created up-to-date.

As the apt-mirror package is rarely installed with an Ubuntu installation, you'll need to install it with a command such as:

```
$ sudo apt-get install apt-mirror
```

You could use the **sudo apt-mirror** command immediately, with associated configuration files, as is. However, when I tried it on my Hardy Heron server, it warned me that it would download more than 40GB of files. And that would have overloaded the free space currently available on that system.

So I modified the configuration files associated with the apt-mirror package. The files I changed included /etc/apt/mirror.list and /usr/bin/apt-mirror.

## /etc/apt/mirror.list

The default version of the /etc/apt/mirror.list configuration file lists default paths in comments, as well as configured repositories. You may also note a new apt-mirror user and group in the /etc/passwd and /etc/group files, respectively. I'll come back to those files shortly.

Now return to the /etc/apt/mirror.list configuration file. The first directive in the file sets the directory where files are copied. The default is /var/spool/apt-mirror; you could create a partition with sufficient space for the /var/ directory.

```
# set base_path    /var/spool/apt-mirror
```

Because of the demands of an Ubuntu system mirror, I set up a separate partition on a new hard drive, configured it on the /apt-mirror directory, and modified the /etc/apt /mirror.list file accordingly:

```
set base_path /apt-mirror
```

The following directives (and associated comment—and *privlages* is misspelled in the configuration file) list the directories that need to be created, with privileges:

```
# if you change the base path you must create the directories
# below with write privlages
# set mirror_path  $base_path/mirror
# set skel_path    $base_path/skel
# set var_path     $base_path/var
# set cleanscript $var_path/clean.sh
```

I suspect that most readers will have already installed the Apache Web server. It's also useful for repositories. You could create repositories in the standard Apache directory tree, /var/www/. But soft links from this directory are also fairly easy to configure. I therefore ran the following commands to create the appropriate directories, as subdirectories of the value of the **base_path** directive:

```
$ sudo mkdir /apt-mirror
$ sudo mkdir /apt-mirror/mirror
```

```
$ sudo mkdir /apt-mirror/skel
$ sudo mkdir /apt-mirror/var
$
```

These commands create the noted directories with write privileges for the owner. But to make this work, I also need to set the owner for all these directories (and sub-directories) as the apt-mirror user and group. One way to do this is with the following command. The **chown -R** command changes ownership on the /apt-mirror directory, and subdirectories, recursively:

```
$ sudo chown -R apt-mirror.apt-mirror /apt-mirror
```

Now I return to the /etc/apt/mirror.list configuration file. The default uses the running host architecture. If I were creating a mirror on a 64-bit system, the following suggests that the default would be to copy from 64-bit repositories:

```
# set defaultarch   <running host architecture>
```

If the mirror is for clients of a different architecture from the local server, I would have to specify that as well. For example, if I were creating a mirror for 32-bit systems on a 64-bit server, I would add the following directive:

```
set defaultarch i386
```

The directives which follow include a series of URLs which specify the repositories to be mirrored. These URLs should be changed to list only those repositories that need to be mirrored. For example, I limit what is mirrored by including only the following URLs and commenting out all others. The **clean** directive frees space from obsolete packages from associated repositories.

```
deb http://us.archive.ubuntu.com/ubuntu hardy-updates main restricted
clean http://us.archive.ubuntu.com/ubuntu
```

I specify the national repository that applies to me, substituting *us.archive.ubuntu .com* for the instances of *archive.ubuntu.com* shown in the configuration file. I also limit the copying to the main and restricted repositories. I could also add the universe and multiverse repositories to this directive. The repositories you choose to copy depends on available disk space and your willingness to download tens of gigabytes of data.

I don't even consider mirroring the security-related repositories, as it's more impor-tant that security updates are based on the latest available releases.

While the http://us.archive.ubuntu.com/ubuntu repository is the most up-to-date, I could substitute a mirror such as http://mirrors.kernel.org/ubuntu. The decision is whether to copy the mirror or the more up-to-date but distant repository. There are good arguments for both, and the decision depends in part on how frequently the selected mirror site is kept up-to-date. I choose to copy from the mirror, so I substitute accordingly in /etc/apt/mirror.list:

```
deb http://mirrors.kernel.org/ubuntu hardy-updates main restricted
clean http://mirrors.kernel.org/ubuntu
```

Any other URL shown in this file is deactivated by adding a comment character (#) in front. As discussed earlier, if you changed the default **base_path** defined earlier for the /etc/apt/mirror.list configuration file, a change is also required to the /usr/bin /apt-mirror script. Since I changed it to /apt-mirror, I change it in the /usr/bin/apt-mirror script as well:

```
"base_path"    => '/apt-mirror',
```

## To Mirror an Ubuntu Repository

Now I've set up a volume with sufficient free space, at least for those repositories to be mirrored locally. I've modified the /etc/apt/mirror.list configuration file and /usr/bin/ apt-mirror script to mirror the main and restricted repositories for the i386 CPU architecture on the /apt-mirror directory.

I can then run the **sudo apt-mirror** command, which executes the /usr/bin/apt-mirror script. Instead of the 40GB of files that would have been downloaded earlier, the **apt-mirror** command in my configuration downloaded just over 1GB of files. This works if there's sufficient free space available in the /apt-mirror directory.

The required free space will vary. The amount of information downloaded to your system depends on the repositories selected in /etc/apt/mirror.list and the packages in those repositories. As package and security updates increase over time, make sure that any volume you reserve for this purpose has room for significant growth.

Once the process is complete, examine the structure of the /apt-mirror directory (or whatever directory you use). Because I've copied the updates from the http://mirrors .kernel.org/ubuntu site, the **apt-mirror** command as configured copies the selected repository sections to the /apt-mirror/mirror/mirrors.kernel.org/ubuntu directory.

## Use the Local Mirror

Of course, none of this works unless you point local systems to the noted mirror. While it's possible to set up other share protocols, the most convenient protocol for a local repository is HTTP. It's the same default Web protocol, and it takes advantage of the preconfigured Apache Web server included with a LAMP-based Ubuntu Server installation. For more information on Apache and LAMP (Linux, Apache, MySQL, PHP), see Chapter 15.

Be aware, the standard directories associated with the Apache Web server are located in /var/www, which differs from the previously created /apt-mirror directory. I set up access via Apache using a soft link, with the following command:

```
$ sudo ln -s  /apt-mirror/mirror/mirrors.kernel.org/ /var/www/mirror
```

I can then modify appropriate /etc/apt/sources.list configuration files on desired clients. Based on the update repositories that have been mirrored, I'd replace the connections to remote repositories with the following directive:

```
deb http://192.168.0.104/mirror/ubuntu hardy-updates main restricted
```

# MANAGE WITH LANDSCAPE

Landscape is Canonical's web-based system management service. It allows administrators to manage the Ubuntu systems on their networks from a single web-based interface. While Landscape is not freely available, it is a convenient administrative front end that makes it possible to monitor and administer individual systems without always having to connect to each system. For readers familiar with other system management tools, Landscape is functionally similar to the Red Hat Network, Microsoft's Systems Management Server (or System Center Configuration Manager), and Novell's ZENworks Suite.

More information, including the conditions for a free trial, is available from www.canonical.com/projects/landscape. When I asked for a free trial, I was sent an e-mail invitation to open an account, as depicted in this chapter. The account is limited to five systems. Full access is available with a dedicated Landscape subscription, or any Canonical support subscription.

## Landscape Features

Landscape supports the system management of Ubuntu computers. It allows you to administer users, security updates, and even custom repositories. Several systems with common requirements can be managed as a group. Packages can be managed individually by system or group.

The Landscape system monitoring tools allow you to review resource usage, manage processes, and audit actions performed by other administrators. It also supports a hardware inventory of each system. It includes direct feedback to the Canonical support team. As they have read-only access to your information available in Landscape, it helps them diagnose any problems you may have. To keep the focus on Ubuntu Server, I do not go into extensive detail on Landscape features.

## Work with Landscape

There are several basic tools associated with Landscape. But you need to know how to set up and register a client. You'll then learn how easy it is to monitor registered client systems.

When you register with Landscape (even with a trial subscription), you should receive an e-mail confirmation, with an embedded link. Navigate to the associated URL and follow the instructions. Remember any  included passphrase, as you'll need it when logging into Landscape, as shown in Figure 8-10. The passphrase used here can and probably should be different from the registration password. You'll also need the registration password when registering Landscape systems.

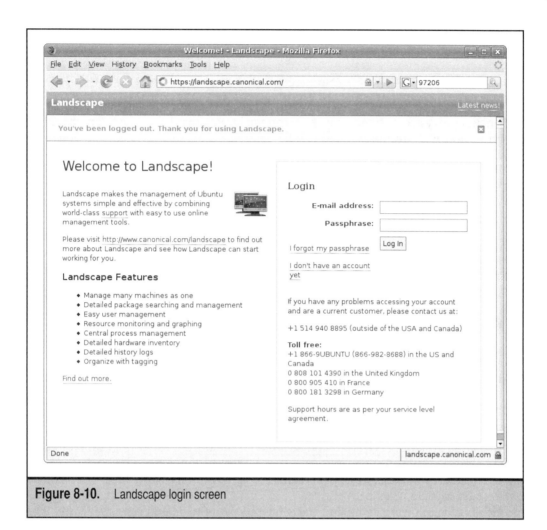

**Figure 8-10.**    Landscape login screen

**NOTE**    Access to Landscape is available with a Canonical support subscription. A 60-day trial may be available from www.canonical.com/landscape/register. For more information, see www.canonical .com/projects/landscape.

## Register a Client

To register an Ubuntu client with Landscape, you need to update the associated /etc/ apt/sources.list configuration file with the appropriate repository. For example, you would add the following line for the Hardy Heron release:

```
deb http://landscape.canonical.com/packages/hardy  ./
```

If you're working with a different release, substitute for *hardy* accordingly.

While it's not absolutely required, you should download the appropriate GPG (GNU Privacy Guard) key with the following command:

```
$ gpg --keyserver-options no-http-proxy --keyserver keyserver.ubuntu.com \
--recv-key C605E80D
```

If there is a proxy server somewhere between the local network and the Internet, replace **no-http-proxy** with **http-proxy**, and you'll be prompted for such as needed. If you don't acquire the GPG key, some sort of "GPG error" and "Warning" messages will appear.

If the download is successful, you'll see a message about a public key associated with the "Landscape Development Team," along with several keys in the current user's home directory, in the .gnupg/ subdirectory. You can then make the key available to the **apt-\*** commands as follows:

```
$ gpg --armor --export C605E80D | sudo apt-key add -
```

The message I see when this command is successful is

```
OK
```

Now you can update the local repository cache:

```
$ sudo apt-get update
```

And install the Landscape client package:

```
$ sudo apt-get install landscape-client
```

The command installs a number of dependent packages. I tried it on three different Hardy Heron systems; between 8 and 36 were installed from my configuration to help enable remote administration. In the first case, most of the dependent packages were already installed. In either case, expect this command to take some time to download and install associated packages.

Finally, the following command starts the process of registering the client. You'll be prompted for required information. The computer title can be a descriptive human-readable name; my entries are in boldface:

```
$ sudo landscape-config
The Landscape client must be started on boot to operate correctly.
Start Landscape client on boot? (Y/n): y
Starting Landscape client: landscape-client
 .
This script will interactively set up the Landscape client. It will
ask you a few questions about this computer and your Landscape
account, and will submit that information to the Landscape server.
```

```
After this computer is registered it will need to be approved by an
account administrator on the pending computers page.

Please see https://landscape.canonical.com for more information.

The computer title you provide will be used to represent this
computer in the Landscape user interface. It's important to use
a title that will allow the system to be easily recognized when
it appears on the pending computers page.

This computer's title: Office Desktop Computer
```

You'll also need the account name, the registration password (which is the passphrase described earlier), any applicable proxy server information. While Landscape allows script management of clients from the web-based interface, it doesn't normally allow it from the client. This should be enabled on systems controlled by administrators:

```
Enable script execution? [y/N] y
```

Be aware that this information is saved in clear text in the /etc/landscape/client.conf configuration file.

If you enable script execution, the landscape-config utility prompts for users with appropriate permissions:

```
Script users: michael,donna
```

Finally, the **landscape-config** utility prompts you to request a new registration for this computer:

```
Request a new registration for this computer now? (Y/n): y
Please wait... System successfully registered.
```

Next, you can confirm the connection from your administrative Landscape account by navigating to https://landscape.canonical.com/dashboard. Log into the account and click Pending Computers. The options are intuitive and are available to subscribers.

## Monitor a System

The administrative power of Landscape comes from the way computers can be configured. The standard Landscape screen is shown in Figure 8-11, and the different monitoring options are shown at the bottom of the screen.

**Info**  Basic information for each configured system is included in the Info screen.

**History**  User and group configuration actions associated with the local system are listed in the History screen.

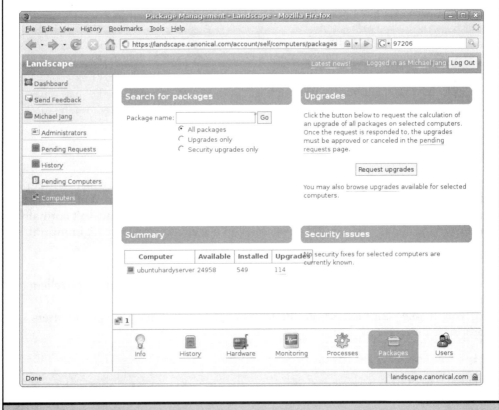

**Figure 8-11.** Landscape control screen

**Hardware** A list of detected hardware devices are shown in the Hardware screen. More information based on how the hardware was detected is available by hyperlink. Similar information is available from the client command line with the **hal-device** command.

**Monitoring** The Monitoring screen includes graphical information on RAM, swap space, load, disk usage, and temperature. Similar information is available from the client command line with the **top** and **df** commands.

**Scripts** The Scripts screen allows you to configure and run a script, based on the shell interpreter of your choice, run as the user of your choice. As Landscape provides an administrative interface, scripts can even be run as the root user.

**Processes** The Processes screen displays all currently running processes. Similar information is available from the client command line with variations on the **ps x** command.

**Packages** The Packages screen supports lists of currently installed and upgradable packages. A list of currently installed packages can be shown with the **dpkg -l** command; a list of upgradeable packages is available from the **apt-get upgrade** command.

**Users** The Users screen supports management of users and groups. The options available from this screen are effective front ends to user management commands such as **useradd**, **usermod**, **groupadd**, and **groupmod**.

# SUMMARY

This chapter addressed the tools needed to manage updates and local repositories. To understand how to install and update Ubuntu packages, you need to have at least a basic understanding of the **dpkg** and **apt-\*** commands. To make updates work effectively, you need to know how to configure the update configuration file, /etc/apt/sources .list. Several available tools can help the administrator in this regard, including **aptitude**, the Synaptic Package Manager, and the Update Manager.

Administrators need certain skills to know how to keep a server up-to-date. Furthermore, administrators need the ability to judge when to keep a server up-to-date. Security updates may or may not affect what you do. Kernel updates could break drivers and invalidate support for important applications. Application updates could introduce undesirable features.

Administrators responsible for a substantial number of systems might want to create a local mirror of certain repositories. The apt-mirror package facilitates the creation of a local mirror. As security issues can be time-sensitive, local mirrors should not include security repositories.

Finally, Canonical offers Landscape as a web-based management tool for multiple Ubuntu systems.

# CHAPTER 9

## Printer Configuration

This chapter focuses on CUPS (Common Unix Printing System), the way it works, the available configuration tools, the options for printer management, as well as the assignment of print administrators. CUPS is functionally compatible with the latest print services from several other operating systems, all of which work through the Internet Print Protocol (IPP).

Of course, CUPS can be configured by directly editing associated configuration files. But the language in a CUPS configuration file is specialized and might be beyond what you have time to learn. This chapter covers two excellent graphical tools that can help configure CUPS, but these GUI tools can't do everything. To that end, this chapter also covers how to take advantage of the special print administrators group configured in the Ubuntu implementation of CUPS, and how to control printers from the command line.

**NOTE**   Extensive CUPS documentation is readily available, even with the CUPS packages. Once CUPS is installed and running, navigate to http://localhost:631/help/ on the local system.

# CUPS AND THE INTERNET PRINTING PROTOCOL

CUPS is a complete system for print management that includes a server, supports client commands, detects a wide variety of printers, and more. The CUPS packages include print drivers and even a web-based management tool.

While you could still install the Line Printer Daemon (LPD) and Line Printer, Next Generation (LPRng) services, CUPS is the default print service for most Linux distributions, including Ubuntu. IPP, the default protocol for CUPS, can serve as a front end to the wide variety of print protocols in current use. The key is the Universal Resource Identifier (URI), which is a superset of the well-known URL.

**NOTE**   For the pedantic, the latest documentation includes changes to the words behind the URI and URL acronyms. Uniform Resource Identifier is replacing Universal Resource Identifier; Uniform Resource Locater is replacing Universal Resource Locater. Even for most geeks, the differences are trivial.

In this section, you'll learn how to install applicable CUPS packages. You'll also take a brief look at the CUPS configuration files and examine how a variety of printers can be configured through CUPS.

## The Installation of CUPS

Although the standard CUPS server packages are installed by default for the Ubuntu desktop, they're not included in the standard Ubuntu Server installation, unless the Print Server software group is selected during the installation process. Even if you've already installed CUPS, it's a good idea to see what CUPS packages are available and then choose

| Package | Description |
|---|---|
| cupsys | Adds the CUPS server |
| cupsys-bsd | Includes commands familiar to LPD/LPRng administrators, such as **lpq**, **lpr**, and so on |
| cupsys-client | Incorporates print client commands |
| cupsys-common | Supports both CUPS client and server packages |
| foomatic-* | Adds open source drivers and other printer support |
| hal-cups-utils | Includes plug-and-play support for CUPS based on the hardware abstraction layer (HAL) |

**Table 9-1.**  Important CUPS Packages

what should be installed (or what additional packages should be installed). To that end, the following command lists all available packages associated with the CUPS service:

```
$ aptitude search cups
```

If you compare this list against the packages already installed during the installation process, the differences are trivial. Additional packages related to specialized printers and the GIMP (GNU Image Manipulation Program) are also available, known as *Gutenprint plugins*. Several packages important for a print server are listed in Table 9-1. The list is not complete; for example, the bluez-cups package facilitates connections to Bluetooth-enabled printers.

If you need to add CUPS-related packages to the local system, use a command such as **apt-get install** or a tool such as **aptitude** or Synaptic to install those packages.

# A Variety of Local and Network Printers

CUPS can be used to manage printers on local and network printer ports. CUPS normally detects locally connected printers on the standard variety of physical printer connections, including standard parallel (LPT), serial, USB, IEEE1394, and SCSI ports.

CUPS also supports a wide variety of network print protocols, most importantly IPP. Several major network print protocols supported by CUPS are listed in Table 9-2. Note the bolded labels in the table, which indicates the output associated with the **lpinfo** command, which is described next.

For a full list of local and network print protocols on a CUPS server, use the **lpinfo** command. For example, the following output from the **lpinfo -v -h 192.168.0.50** command verifies available local (**direct**), print to **file**, and **network** printer options from the print server at the noted IP address. The list is not complete and depends on available hardware.

| Network Print Protocol | Description |
|---|---|
| IPP | (**ipp**) The Internet Print Protocol uses TCP/IP Port 631 for communication. |
| LPD/LPRng | (**lpd**) The Line Print Daemon (and Line Printer, Next Generation) protocols are based on older System V or Berkeley Standard print servers. |
| SMB/CIFS | (**smb**) Configured CUPS printers can be shared on SMB/CIFS networks. Listed in the print tools as "Windows Printer via SAMBA." |
| Bluetooth | CUPS can connect to Bluetooth-enabled printers. |
| AppSocket/HP JetDirect | (**socket**) The AppSocket/HP JetDirect interface uses TCP/IP port 9100; can also connect to some dedicated print servers. |
| PAP | The Printer Access Protocol is associated with printers connected to the AppleTalk network. |
| HP Fax | (**hpfax**) Associated with fax options available through the HP Linux Imaging and Printing (HPLIP) package |
| HP Printer | (**hp**) Associated with printer options available through the HPLIP package. |

**Table 9-2.** CUPS Supported Network Print Protocols

For example, if this system did not have a parallel port, **direct parallel:/dev/lp0** would not appear in the output.

```
network socket
network beh
direct hal
direct hpfax
direct hp
network http
network ipp
network lpd
file cups-pdf:/
direct parallel:/dev/lp0
direct scsi
network smb
```

Some additional explanation is required: The **network beh** option uses the so-called "Backend Error Handler" to manage errors such as paper jams. The **direct hal** output uses HAL to detect local printers. The **direct hpfax** output can be associated with a fax machine. The **direct hp** output is associated with output direct to specialized printers from HP.

# The Universal Resource Identifier (URI)

Perhaps the most important bit of CUPS configuration data is the URI, which is a superset (inverse of subset) of the more well-known URL. In other words, a URI includes regular HTTP and FTP URLs, as well as IPP interfaces such as this:

```
DeviceURI ipp://192.168.0.30/printers/LaserJonHP
```

*Local URIs* are based on printers directly connected to the local system, and *networked URIs* are based on printers accessed over a network. First, I present several examples of local URIs, which are almost self-explanatory. The first URI is based on an HP printer LaserJet 4L connected via a parallel port:

```
DeviceURI hp:/par/LaserJet_4L?device=/dev/parport0
```

The next two URIs suggests parallel and USB ports, respectively, with no specified printer. You might see this based on a generic print driver, or even a connected and known printer that just wasn't detected. As long as you've specified an appropriate print driver, the generic nature of the URI is not important.

```
DeviceURI parallel:/dev/lp0
DeviceURI usb:/dev/usb/lp0
```

The device that follows is based on a connection to a specific HP OfficeJet printer for fax-based print jobs:

```
DeviceURI hpfax:/officejet_7100_series?
```

The following devices are based on local printers connected to LPD/LPRng, SCSI, and serial ports:

```
DeviceURI lpd
DeviceURI scsi
DeviceURI serial
```

Examples of networked **DeviceURI**s include the following. The first option is one way to connect to a CUPS configured printer. While the first address uses HTTP, the IPP is actually the protocol used as port 631 is specified. For that reason, the port number is not required in the second option as the URI starts with an *ipp://*.

```
DeviceURI http://ubuntuserver:631/printer/LaserJonHP
DeviceURI ipp://ubuntuhardyserver/printer/LaserJonHP
```

The **socket://** is somewhat generic; port 9100 is commonly used for some HP and Apple printers:

```
DeviceURI socket://192.168.0.5:9100/
```

The following URI connects to a printer configured to an LPD or LPRng server:

```
DeviceURI lpd://192.168.0.10/LaserJonHP
```

# Major CUPS Configuration Files

CUPS does its good work based on the configuration files in the /etc/cups directory. Available configuration options go beyond what most administrators need. When the CUPS service starts, it loads the parallel printer module by default, as specified in the /etc/default/cupsys configuration file. (Yes, some computers—including two of mine—still have parallel ports.)

The basic functionality of other CUPS configuration files is described in Table 9-3. These files reflect the features available in CUPS version 1.3.6, included with the Ubuntu Hardy Heron release. In addition, the /etc/cups/printers.conf or /etc/cups/classes.conf

| /etc/cups File | Description |
|---|---|
| acroread.conf | Adapts CUPS for the Adobe Acrobat Reader |
| classes.conf | Lists print classes, which consist of one or more printers |
| cupsd.conf | Includes the main CUPS configuration file |
| cups-pdf.conf | Configures a virtual printer that creates PDF files |
| mime.convs | Adds file format filters |
| mime.types | Specifies allowable file types |
| /etc/printcap | Sets a share list; can be included via /etc/cups/cupsd.conf when the CUPS service is run and is used by Samba |
| pdftops.conf | Adapts CUPS for the xpdf Acrobat file reader |
| ppd/ | Inserts configured PPD (PostScript Printer Description) print drivers |
| printers.conf | Documents configured printers |
| raw.convs | Adds file format filter for raw input |
| raw.types | Specifies allowable file type for raw input |
| snmp.conf | Configures automated network printer discovery |
| ssl/ | Sets a directory with SSL certificates |

**Table 9-3.** CUPS Configuration Files

files might not exist until appropriate printers or print classes have been configured. Specialty packages can add more configuration files not described here. All but the /etc/printcap configuration file are in the /etc/cups directory.

For most services, it's best to edit configuration files directly from the command line. This is also true for CUPS—if you know the commands and directives well.

In my opinion, CUPS directives are more cryptic than those for the average Linux service. I've found that the comments in /etc/cups files aren't as descriptive as those for other services. The available GUI editing tools are excellent. If you don't want to install a GUI on a print server, the GUI tools can still be used from a remote client.

Administrators can configure services remotely. I'll describe the few minor changes required based on the default version of the main CUPS configuration file, /etc/cups/cupsd.conf. Other critical CUPS configuration files include /etc/cups/printers.conf, /etc/cups/classes.conf, and /etc/printcap.

## /etc/cups/cupsd.conf

Even if you don't learn the CUPS configuration files in detail, it is important to understand a few key directives. The default Ubuntu version of the cupsd.conf file is excellent and the comments make it easier to make those few critical changes. But before moving on to the file, examine some implicit default directives.

For example, the default **ServerRoot** directive sets the default top-level directory for CUPS configuration files:

```
ServerRoot /etc/cups
```

In addition, log files are normally stored in the /var/log/cups directory, and the default options for these directives specify their types and locations:

```
ErrorLog /var/log/cups/error_log
AccessLog /var/log/cups/access_log
PageLog /var/log/cups/page_log
```

There used to be a default reference to the /etc/printcap configuration file, designed to help share printers with the Linux Samba file server, as described in Chapter 16. It was created by using the standard CUPS configuration file. That is no longer the case; if you intend to share CUPS-configured printers in this way on a Microsoft-based network, you'll need to add the following directive:

```
Printcap /etc/printcap
```

The file is created when the CUPS service is restarted.

**NOTE** Sharing on a Microsoft-based network is no longer required for printers, as Microsoft clients can connect directly to printers using the IPP protocol.

Now examine the settings in the default version of the cupsd.conf configuration file. The Ubuntu configuration is much simpler than what you might see on other

Linux distributions. Specifically, it makes it easy to configure dedicated print administrators. The following directive limits administrative access to members of the lpadmin group, as defined in /etc/group. Of course, you can change this definition or add selected printer administrators to the lpadmin group in /etc/group.

```
SystemGroup lpadmin
```

The configuration of the lpadmin group is described later in this chapter in the "Configure Print Administrators" section.

The following directives specify where connections can be made. The default settings limit access to the localhost system, and only when CUPS is running:

```
Listen localhost:631
Listen /var/run/cups/cups.sock
```

Of course, you may want to allow access to all systems at least on the local network. Port 631, as shown in /etc/services, is the default TCP/IP port for IPP. But the **Listen** directive sometimes confuses people. It should also be set to the IP address of the applicable local network card. For example, as my print server connects to my LAN via a network card configured to IP address 192.168.0.50, I want to change the first **Listen** directive to this:

```
Listen 192.168.0.50:631
```

Generally, most print administrators will want to search configured printers on the LAN. By default, this is enabled in the Ubuntu implementation of /etc/cups/cupsd.conf with the following directive:

```
Browsing On
```

The default **Browse\*** directives that follow are optimized for sharing. The **BrowseOrder** directive shown looks first to the **BrowseAllow** directive, and then to a **BrowseDeny** directive if it exists. If you want to make sure to limit these directives to the local network, change the value associated with the **BrowseAllow** directive from all to a network address such as 192.168.0.0/24.

```
BrowseOrder allow,deny
BrowseAllow all
```

The network address is not required. The **BrowseAddress** directive shown here allows broadcast access to allowed clients on the local network.

```
BrowseAddress @LOCAL
```

The **DefaultAuthType Basic** directive uses the /etc/passwd and /etc/group configuration files to search for allowed users. It works with the **SystemGroup** directive described earlier. Other authentication options may be preferable, as this setting allows passwords of print administrators to be transmitted over the network in clear text. However, if print administration occurs behind a secure firewall, clear text authentication might be acceptable.

```
DefaultAuthType Basic
```

One option to clear text passwords is *Digest* encrypted authentication, based on the following directive:

```
DefaultAuthType Digest
```

Digest authentication depends on usernames and passwords in /etc/cups/passwd .md5, which can be created with the **lppasswd** command. For more information see the "Configure Print Administrators" section later in this chapter. For alternative authentication levels, review the **AuthType** directive in the CUPS documentation.

The following stanza is encapsulated by the **<Location />** container. As it relates to the top-level CUPS directory, it determines whether CUPS-configured printers are shared. By default, they are not.

```
<Location />
  Order allow,deny
</Location>
```

This stanza limits access to the local system with an implicit **Allow localhost** directive. If you want to allow access to systems on the local network, you could add the **Allow @LOCAL** directive.

```
<Location />
  Order allow,deny
  Allow localhost
  Allow @LOCAL
</Location>
```

Alternatively, if you want to allow access to all systems even on remote networks, change **Allow @LOCAL** to **Allow all**.

The next stanza relates to remote administrative access. The default shown here allows only administrative access from the local system:

```
<Location /admin>
  Order allow,deny
</Location>
```

To allow administrative access from other systems on the network, you could add the **Allow @LOCAL** directive. I prefer to specify the IP addresses of the local network; one example is the bolded directive:

```
<Location /admin>
  Order allow,deny
  Allow localhost
  Allow 192.168.0.0/24
</Location>
```

Similar action is required with the next stanza, which regulates network access to the CUPS configuration files using a CUPS configuration tool. The **AuthType Default** directive refers back to the value of **DefaultAuthType**. The **Require user @SYSTEM** directive refers back to the **SystemGroup** directive. I add the same **Allow** directive shown in the preceding stanza to limit access to systems on the noted network:

```
<Location /admin/conf>
  AuthType Default
  Require user @SYSTEM
  Order allow,deny
  Allow localhost
  Allow 192.168.0.0/24
</Location>
```

> **NOTE**   Most of the remaining directives in the default Ubuntu version of the CUPS configuration file relate to print job policies, and allow configuration by members of the lpadmin group. More information is available in the CUPS documentation.

Once you're satisfied with the changes, the following command makes the CUPS daemon read the new version of the /etc/cups/cupsd.conf configuration file:

```
$ sudo /etc/init.d/cupsys reload
```

Of course, you could restart the service, but that might cut off any pending print jobs in the local printer spool.

## /etc/cups/printers.conf

Once a CUPS printer is configured, key settings are written to the /etc/cups/printers .conf configuration file. After you've configured some printers, examine this file on the print server. Examine how key directives can be used. For example, the following directive specifies a stanza associated with the default printer:

```
<DefaultPrinter LaserJet_4L>
```

Of course, without the **Default**, this directive just becomes a stanza container for a regular configured printer.

The **DeviceURI** specifies the URI of the printer. The URI can specify local printers; the following example of an URI from one of my printers.conf files specifies a parallel port device:

```
DeviceURI hp:/par/LaserJet_4L?device=/dev/parport0
```

The **DeviceURI** can also specify a network port. The following examples specify a connection via a Samba server, a connection to a dedicated print server, and a direct IPP connection. Of course, you should see only one **DeviceURI** for any configured printer.

```
DeviceURI smb://user:passwd@MSHOME/UBUNTUSERVER/LaserJet-4L
DeviceURI http://192.168.0.5/lp1
DeviceURI ipp://192.168.0.50:631/printers/UbuntuPrinter
```

The file is often updated dynamically. For example, the **State** directive can be set to **Idle** or **Stopped**; this indicates whether the printer queue is active. The **State** can also be changed with the **cupsaccept** or **cupsreject** command. Similarly, the **Accepting** directive can be set to **Yes** or **No**, which indicates whether the printer is active and accepting jobs, or disabled. The value of the directive can be changed with the **cupsenable** and **cupsdisable** commands.

## /etc/cups/classes.conf

CUPS can accommodate printers in groups, also known as a *CUPS class*. Once configured, they're listed in a container in the classes.conf file. The directives in this file are similar to those in printers.conf. And that's consistent, since a print group functions like an individual printer.

The differences between individual printers and print classes are straightforward: While individual printers are configured in *Printer* containers, print classes are configured in *Class* containers. The printers that are configured in the group are defined by the **Printer** directive. For example, the following directives

```
Printer HPLaserJet4
Printer LaserJonHP
```

specify that the *HPLaserJet4* and *LaserJonHP* printers are both members of the specified class in the printers.conf file. Any job sent to this print class are sent to the first available member printer of that class.

## /etc/printcap

As CUPS is designed to replace the LPD/LPRng print services, it uses many of the same configuration files. LPD/LPRng printers are configured in the /etc/printcap configuration file. If the **Printcap** directive is active, CUPS printers are also included in the /etc/printcap configuration file. In either case, /etc/printcap provides a list of detected and configured printers.

# THE GUI CONFIGURATION TOOLS

There are two major GUI configuration tools available for CUPS on Ubuntu: a web-based tool, as well as a more conventional GUI tool named Printer Configuration. The web-based tool is available on all major Linux distributions in which CUPS is installed. In addition, the Printer Configuration tool was originally developed for Red Hat distributions. Neither tool requires the installation of additional packages on the CUPS print server. These sections also describe how to use the web-based tools to administer a remote CUPS server. Remote access assumes appropriate changes to the /etc/cups/cupsd.conf configuration file, as described earlier.

# The CUPS Configuration Tools

For the purpose of this chapter, I've configured a CUPS server on a system named ubuntuhardyserver.example.net. I've reconfigured the /etc/cups/cupsd.conf configuration files to allow remote access and administration. Now to administer the CUPS server on a remote system, using the web-based interface, I open a browser and navigate to https://ubuntuhardyserver.example.net:631. If needed, I accept the default website certificate. It opens the tool shown in Figure 9-1.

The Printer Configuration tool can be installed on a Hardy Heron client with the following command:

```
$ sudo apt-get install system-config-printer-common \
system-config-printer-gnome
```

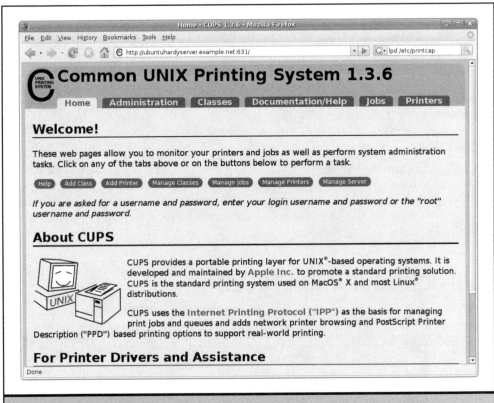

**Figure 9-1.** CUPS web-based administrative interface

Next, to administer the CUPS server on the ubuntuhardyserver.example.net system, take the following steps from a GUI client:

1.  Open a command line and enter the **system-config-printer** command.
2.  When the Printer Configuration window appears, click the Goto Server button.
3.  When the Connect To CUPS Server window appears, enter the hostname or IP address of the desired CUPS server—in my case, I enter **ubuntuhardyserver .example.net**.
4.  Specify a username with print administrative privileges. That user should be a member of the lpadmin group, as defined in the /etc/group file on the CUPS server.
5.  Click Connect.
6.  When prompted, enter the password for the specified username. You should now have access to the Printer Configuration tool on the remote CUPS server, as shown in Figure 9-2.

**NOTE**   Older Ubuntu releases used the gnome-cups-manager package to administer printers from the GUI. Ubuntu developers no longer maintain that package.

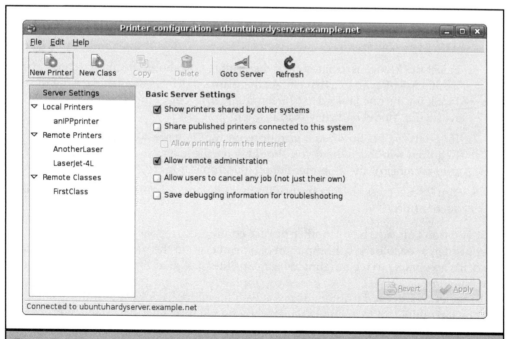

**Figure 9-2.**   CUPS Printer Configuration tool

# Add a New Printer

In this section, I'll show you how to add a new printer using a web-based configuration tool. From a web browser, navigate to the hostname or IP address of the CUPS server described in the preceding section. Then take the following steps:

1. Click Add Printer.

2. In the Add New Printer page that appears, enter a Name, Location, and Description for the printer. The Name is especially important as it is what's used to share the printer via CUPS or Samba. It must be a single alphanumeric word. The Location and Description can be human-readable multi-word descriptions. Click Continue.

3. In the Device page that appears, click the drop down box, and select the device associated with the location of the printer. Table 9-2 lists available network print protocols. If a local port is available on the system, it's listed with options such as LPT #1, SCSI, and USB. If you select a local port, skip to step 5.

4. Specify the URI for the printer. If the guidance in this chapter is not sufficient, more examples are shown from the Network Printers link. Click Continue.

5. Select the Manufacturer associated with the printer. Over 50 manufacturers are available. If you don't see a long list of manufacturers, make sure the foomatic-db package is installed. Click Continue.

   Alternatively, if you have a Postscript Printer Description (PPD) file, click Browse and that file can be uploaded into CUPS. Many PPD files associated with Microsoft drivers can work for CUPS. Click Add Printer and skip to step 7.

6. Select the Model associated with the printer. You should be able to choose from a database of available drivers. As there are six drivers available for my printer, I look for the one labeled as "(recommended)". Select the driver associated with your Model and click Add Printer.

7. If you haven't configured a printer recently, you'll see an Authentication Required window, where you should enter the username and password of a user member of the aforementioned lpadmin group.

8. You'll see a message that the printer that you've configured has been configured successfully.

If you don't already have another printer configured, repeat the above steps for another printer, to enable the configuration of a print class in the next section. For test purposes, it's acceptable to reconfigure the same printer a second time, as long as you use a different name.

To review configured printers from the web-based tool, click the Administration tab near the top of the tool to open the screen shown in Figure 9-3. Click Manage Printers.

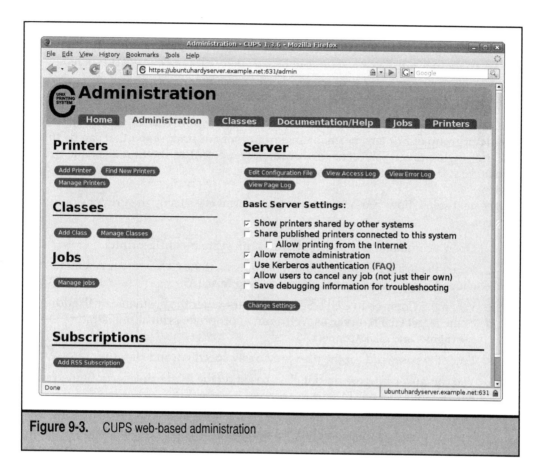

**Figure 9-3.**   CUPS web-based administration

The Manage Printers window displays installed and detected printers. Here you'll see options that allow you to do the following for each printer:

▼   Print a test page.

■   Stop the printer.

■   Reject additional print jobs.

■   Move jobs to another printer.

■   Cancel all jobs on the printer.

■   Unpublish the printer.

■   Modify the printer, which allows you to reconfigure options such as the URI and driver.

■   Set printer options based on the capabilities of the printer.

■   Delete the printer.

■   Set the printer as the default.

▲   Set allowed users to limit access to the printer.

If you activate some of these options, the opposite option appears in this tab. For example, if you choose Unpublish The Printer, an option appears to Publish The Printer. Just be aware that a printer must be "published" before it can be properly shared.

## Add a Print Class

One key advantage of CUPS is is the ability to configure print classes. A print class often includes a group of printers, normally in a print room or print center that can be shared like any single printer. Jobs sent to a print class are sent to the first available printer in that class. If none of the printers in a class are being used, the selection is made at random.

The next steps show you how to configure a print class using the Printer Configuration tool.

1.  Open a command line in the GUI, and run **system-config-printer**.
2.  When the Printer Configuration tool appears, if the CUPS server is remote, choose File | Goto Server. Otherwise, skip to step 5.
3.  When the Connect To CUPS Server appears, enter the hostname or IP address of the target CUPS server, as well as an appropriate print administrator username, and click Connect.
4.  Enter the password for the user previously specified, and click OK.
5.  You can now configure a print class based on the local printers configured in the previous section. To start the process, choose Edit | New Class.
6.  In the New Class window that appears, select the desired printers from the Others column shown in Figure 9-4, and click the left-facing arrow.
7.  Once the desired printers are moved to the Members Of This Class column, click Apply.

You should now be able to review the newly created print class, along with other printers, in the main Printer Configuration window. The printers and print classes that I've configured are shown in Figure 9-5.

As you can see, several general options can be configured for the server. When a printer is selected, detailed options are tabbed and fall into the categories described in Table 9-4.

## Samba Shared Printers

This section makes a few assumptions. It assumes that the Samba server package is installed. Even if you selected the Samba File Server during the installation process, it is worth the trouble to run the following command:

```
$ sudo apt-get install samba
```

It also installs Samba client packages, which can help test Samba from the server.

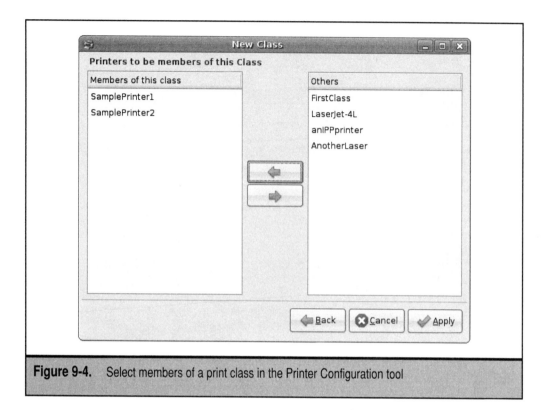

**Figure 9-4.**    Select members of a print class in the Printer Configuration tool

It also assumes that you've configured the **Browsing On** and the **Printcap /etc/printcap** directives in the /etc/cups/cupsd.conf configuration file, as described earlier in the chapter. If the CUPS service has been at least reloaded, an /etc/printcap configuration file should exist, with lines for each configured printer or print class.

The final assumption is that the Samba server is active, which can be confirmed with the following command:

```
$ sudo /etc/init.d/samba status
```

If these assumptions are true, you should be able to verify that printers configured for this CUPS server are shared over a locally configured Microsoft-style network with the following command:

```
$ smbclient -L localhost
Password:
```

Unless you've already configured Samba passwords for your account, leave the Password entry blank. Shared printers are browsable by default. Samba passwords, as you'll see in Chapter 16, are by default different from standard Linux passwords.

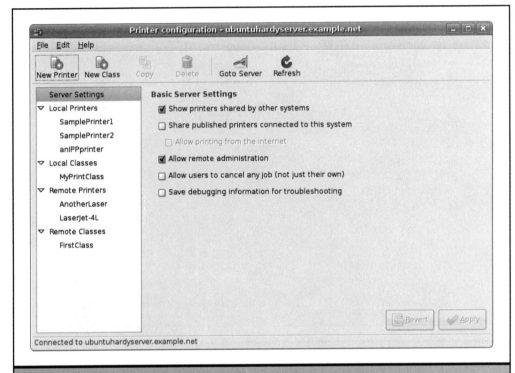

**Figure 9-5.**    Printer Configuration window showing printers

| Tab | Description |
| --- | --- |
| Settings | Includes the description, location, and URI. Can be configured as the default; test pages, and other printer specific functionality may also be available. |
| Policies | Supports changes to the state of the printer, error policies, and banners. |
| Access Control | Allows access limits by user. |
| Printer Options | Supports options depending on printer capabilities; not available for a print class. |
| Job Options | Configures actions associated with each print job. |
| Members | Allows changes in print class members. |

**Table 9-4.**    CUPS Printer Configuration Tabs

# MORE PRINT MANAGEMENT OPTIONS

Many organizations assign print administration tasks to specific users. With the options available in CUPS, it's fairly easy to set up a dedicated group of print administrators. In this section, you'll learn how print administrators can be configured and how to set up a separate authentication database for this purpose.

Even with the capabilities of the GUI tools listed so far in this chapter, many Linux administrators prefer to manage printers from the command line. The major available commands for managing CUPS-configured printers are included here.

## Configure Print Administrators

Print administrators are configured through the /etc/cups/cupsd.conf configuration file. As suggested in the earlier discussion of that file, the following directive specifies that members of the lpadmin group, in /etc/group, are configured as print administrators:

```
SystemGroup lpadmin
```

The following line in /etc/group gives users katie and dickens administrative privileges to CUPS on the local system:

```
lpadmin:x:108:katie,dickens
```

This limitation on print administrators does not work unless there is an appropriate directive in key stanzas. For example, the following directive limits access to members of the lpadmin group:

```
Require user @lpadmin
```

But there's a drawback. The standard **DefaultAuthType Basic** directive means that print administrator passwords are sent over the network in clear text. Even if you've limited access to the local network behind a secure firewall, that would not keep an internal cracker from detecting passwords. And as these same usernames and passwords are also used for regular logins, the security risks are serious.

One alternative I like is **DefaultAuthType Digest**, which encrypts the password and uses a different password database. That adds two barriers for the cracker. But to take advantage of its benefits, you need to set up the passwords. For example, as my username is a part of the lpadmin group, I can add it to the CUPS password database with the following command:

```
$ sudo lppasswd -a -g lpadmin michael
```

The command adds (**-a**) my account, as part of the lpadmin group (**-g lpadmin**), to the database. Once I enter the passwords, the information is encrypted and added to the /etc/cups/passwd.md5 configuration file.

# Print Management Commands

CUPS administrators often work from the command line. Many of the key CUPS commands were developed from LPD-based cousins. Only a few of the more commonly used commands are reviewed in detail here.

Three major commands are used to manage print queues: **lpr**, **lpq**, and **lprm**, to add print requests, list queued print requests, and remove print requests, respectively. One more command can help administer print queues: **lpc**. While these commands were developed for the LPD/LPRng services, they also work well with CUPS. Several other commands originally developed for LPD/LPRng services have also been modified for CUPS.

Native CUPS commands include **cupsaccept** and **cupsreject** for print queues; **cupsenable** and **cupsdisable** to manage printers; and **cupsctl** command to review key settings from the /etc/cups/cupsd.conf configuration file. Other CUPS-related commands are specialty commands. For the most part, they are related to graphics and PPD drivers.

Several commands require print administrative authentication. If you've configured **DefaultAuthType Basic** in the /etc/cups/cupsd.conf configuration file, that requires you to specify a print administrative user, a member of the lpadmin group, along with that user's regular password. If you've configured **DefaultAuthType Digest**, the password required is the one that was created earlier with the **lppasswd** command and stored in the /etc/cups/passwd.md5 authentication database file.

Some of the commands in this section can be used to administer a remote CUPS server, typically with an **-h** *printserver* switch. That requires a CUPS configuration file that allows remote access and administration.

## lpc: Line Print Control

To view all known queues, run the **lpc status** command; it displays the results shown in Figure 9-6. As you can see, the output helps you easily scan all configured print devices and queues.

Administrators migrating from LPD/LPRng services may realize that commands such as **lpc up** *queue* don't work with CUPS. Alternative commands described shortly include **cupsaccept** and **cupsreject**.

## lpr: Line Print Request

Any user can use the **lpr** *filename* command to send print requests to any print queue. By default, it sends the text from the *filename* to the default printer specified in the /etc/cups/printers.conf configuration file. If you want to send the print job elsewhere, say to the printer named PSC_1210, run the **lpr -P PSC_1210** *filename* command. A space is now allowed between the **-P** and the name of the printer.

## lpq: Line Print Query

Any user can inspect the contents of a print queue with the **lpq** command. When run by itself, the **lpq** command displays the current queue on the default printer. When run with

```
michael@ubuntuhardyserver:~$ lpc status
anIPPprinter:
        printer is on device 'ipp' speed -1
        queuing is enabled
        printing is enabled
        no entries
        daemon present
AnotherLaser:
        printer is on device 'ipp' speed -1
        queuing is enabled
        printing is enabled
        no entries
        daemon present
FirstClass:
        printer is on device 'ipp' speed -1
        queuing is enabled
        printing is enabled
        no entries
        daemon present
SamplePrinter1:
        printer is on device 'http' speed -1
        queuing is enabled
        printing is enabled
        no entries
        daemon present
SamplePrinter2:
        printer is on device 'http' speed -1
        queuing is enabled
        printing is enabled
        no entries
        daemon present
michael@ubuntuhardyserver:~$ []
```

**Figure 9-6.**   Printer configuration options

the **-a** switch, it displays the queue for all configured printers. As with the **lpr** command, the **-P** *printer* option inspects the queue of the named *printer*. If you want to manage print jobs, pay attention to the job number, as shown in the output to the **lpq -P SamplePrinter1** command:

```
SamplePrinter1 is not ready
Rank Owner    Job  File(s)                   Total Size
1st  michael 6     passwd                       2048 bytes
2nd  michael 7     vmlinuz-2.6.24-12-server 1988608 bytes
```

## lprm: Line Print Job Removal

With the **lprm** command, you can delete the jobs of your choice. In the print queue previously shown, you might note with horror that there's a pending print job for the Linux kernel. To cancel that print job, use the **lprm** command with the job number:

```
$ lprm 7
```

## lpmove: Move a Print Job

If a printer goes down—because of a printer jam, lack of toner, or whatever, and it hasn't yet entered the printer buffer—you could use the **lpmove** command to move the print job. Refer back to the output to the **lpq -P SamplePrinter1** command. If print job 6 still isn't running, you could move it to SamplePrinter2 with the following command:

```
$ lpmove 6/SamplePrinter1 SamplePrinter2
```

## lpstat: Printer Status

Another handy command is the **lpstat -t** command, which provides an overall view of configured printers and current status. If CUPS is running properly, the first message is

```
scheduler is running
```

Other excerpts are shown here. First, the default printer is listed:

```
system default destination: anIPPprinter
```

Next, configured print classes are shown, with the individual printer members of each class:

```
members of class FirstClass:
        LaserJet-4L
        UbuntuPrinter
members of class MyPrintClass:
        SamplePrinter1
        SamplePrinter2
```

The devices for each printer are shown with associated URIs:

```
device for anIPPprinter: ipp://ubuntuserver.mommabears.com:631/printers/
LaserJet-4L
device for AnotherLaser: ipp://ubuntuserver.mommabears.com:631/printers/
AnotherLaser
device for FirstClass: ipp://ubuntuserver.mommabears.com:631/classes/
FirstClass
device for LaserJet-4L: ipp://ubuntuserver.mommabears.com:631/printers/
LaserJet-4L
device for MyPrintClass: ///dev/null
device for SamplePrinter1: http://192.168.0.50:631/printers/LaserJet-4L
device for SamplePrinter2: http://192.168.0.50/printers/LaserJet-4L
```

The next group of messages specify whether each printer is accepting print jobs:

```
anIPPprinter accepting requests since Wed 26 Mar 2008 01:43:33 PM PDT
AnotherLaser accepting requests since Thu 27 Mar 2008 07:42:46 AM PDT
```

```
FirstClass accepting requests since Thu 27 Mar 2008 07:42:47 AM PDT
LaserJet-4L accepting requests since Thu 27 Mar 2008 07:42:48 AM PDT
MyPrintClass not accepting requests since Wed 26 Mar 2008 07:14:35 PM
PDT -
SamplePrinter1 accepting requests since Thu 27 Mar 2008 09:25:49 AM PDT
SamplePrinter2 not accepting requests since Wed 26 Mar 2008 06:40:36 PM
PDT -
        Rejecting Jobs
```

If there is no currently active print job, the printer is listed as idle or possibly disabled:

```
printer anIPPprinter is idle.  enabled since Wed 26 Mar 2008 01:43:33
PM PDT
printer AnotherLaser is idle.  enabled since Thu 27 Mar 2008 07:42:46
AM PDT
printer FirstClass is idle.  enabled since Thu 27 Mar 2008 07:42:47 AM
PDT
printer LaserJet-4L is idle.  enabled since Thu 27 Mar 2008 07:42:48 AM
PDT
printer MyPrintClass disabled since Wed 26 Mar 2008 07:14:35 PM PDT -
        reason unknown
printer SamplePrinter1 disabled since Thu 27 Mar 2008 09:25:49 AM PDT -
        Paused
printer SamplePrinter2 is idle.  enabled since Wed 26 Mar 2008 06:40:36
PM PDT
        Rejecting Jobs
```

Any pending print jobs are listed after all this excellent information.

## lpadmin: Administer the Printer

The **lpadmin** command can adjust and modify printers, as configured in the /etc/cups/printers.conf configuration file. The following command sets the default printer to SamplePrinter1:

```
$ lpadmin -d SamplePrinter1
```

Printers can be limited by user; if you'd like to keep a couple of users from accessing a printer, just substitute **deny** for **allow**:

```
$ lpadmin -p SamplePrinter1 -u allow:michael,donna
```

If you want to correct an error in a printer's URI, the following command enters a different URI:

```
$ lpadmin -p SamplePrinter2 -v \
http://192.168.0.50:631/printers/LaserJet-4L
```

Try this command for yourself. Copy the current version of the /etc/cups/printers .conf configuration file to a location such as your home directory, and run one of the **lpadmin** commands.

## cupsaccept and cupsreject: Queue Management

The queues on every configured printer can be managed with the **cupsaccept** and **cupsreject** commands. The commands are straightforward; the **cupsreject** *printer* command disables the queue on the noted printer. After the **cupsreject** command is run, any job that is sent to that printer leads to the following message:

```
lpr: Destination "printer" is not accepting jobs.
```

You can review the result in the output to the **lpc status** command; as you can see here, queuing is disabled for the *printer*. Similar information is also available in the /etc/ cups/printers.conf configuration file described earlier.

```
PSC_1210:
    printer is on device 'http' speed -1
    queuing is disabled
    printing is enabled
    no entries
    daemon present
```

The status can be reversed with the **cupsaccept** *printer* command.

## cupsenable and cupsdisable: Printer Management

Printers can be activated and deactivated with the **cupsenable** and **cupsdisable** commands. The commands are straightforward. The **cupsdisable** *printer* command disables the noted printer. After the **cupsdisable** command is run, print jobs are still accepted by a printer, but you'll see the following message associated with *printer* in the output to the **lpc status** command:

```
printing is disabled
```

But the **cupsdisable** command isn't the only thing that can disable a printer. Ordinary problems such as a printer running out of paper and toner can disable a printer. Once the problem is fixed, the following command works as a reset to re-enable the *printer*:

```
$ cupsenable printer
```

## cupsctl: Review and Modify cupsd.conf

The **cupsctl** command provides another way to modify the settings in the /etc/cups/ cupsd.conf configuration file. If you're unsure about the syntax of CUPS, the **cupsctl** command may work better for you. By itself, **cupsctl** highlights important directives. Several major options are highlighted in Table 9-5.

| cupsctl switch | Description |
|---|---|
| --remote-admin | Enables remote administration via other CUPS tools |
| --remote-printers | Allows configured printers to be browsed |
| --share-printers | Supports connections from systems other than localhost |
| --user-cancel-any | Allows a user to cancel any print job |

**Table 9-5.**   CUPS Configuration Files

*NOTE*   Be aware that the options in Table 9-5 can be reversed: For example, remote administrative access can be disabled with the **--no-remote-admin** switch.

# SUMMARY

This chapter focused on print services using CUPS. It's the default print service for current Linux distributions and it can also be used to manage printers from other major print services. As it runs through IPP, it's also compatible with the latest print services from other major operating systems. CUPS relies on configuration files in the /etc/cups directory.

With a little tweaking, CUPS can be configured remotely using GUI tools. The web-based and Printer Configuration tool makes it easy to set up a new printer as well as a print class. These tools also facilitate a number of administrative settings for each printer as well as the overall print service.

CUPS enables special print administrators, who can be segregated into a separate authentication database. Of course, a number of commands can be used to customize and administer CUPS. Many have been adapted from the LPD/LPRng service; others are native to CUPS.

# CHAPTER 10

## User, Group, and Administrator Management

This chapter describes the tools you need to administer local users, groups, and other administrators. Current local Linux user authentication databases are based on the Shadow Password Suite, which can be managed from the command line and with various GUI tools. If your focus is network authentication, read Chapter 12.

When you administer users and groups, you may regulate the resources they use. To this end, quotas can regulate the amount of space and number of files available to individual users and groups.

Few administrators can work alone. Even on small business networks, authority for certain tasks such as printer management can be delegated, as discussed in Chapter 9. With Pluggable Authentication Modules (PAM), Ubuntu regulates authenticated access to important tools. With the **sudo** tools, special users and groups can be given different levels of administrative privileges. With the newly implemented PolicyKit, a finer-grained control of administrative tools is possible.

# THE SHADOW PASSWORD SUITE

Older versions of Linux included encrypted passwords in the /etc/passwd configuration file. Because that file is accessible to all users, a cracker could copy this file and decrypt everyone's password. If privileges to /etc/passwd were made more restrictive, it would lead to other problems. This security flaw led to the development of the Shadow Password Suite.

This section examines the details of each file associated with the Shadow Password Suite. You'll create a new user with the User Settings tool, with commands at the console, and by directly editing these text files: /etc/passwd, /etc/shadow, /etc/group, and /etc/gshadow.

## Shadow Password Files

Historically, all you needed to manage Linux users and groups was the information included in the /etc/passwd and /etc/group files. These files include passwords and are, by default, readable by all users.

The Shadow Password Suite was created to provide an additional layer of protection. It is used to encrypt user and group passwords in shadow files (/etc/shadow and /etc/gshadow) that are readable only by users with administrative privileges. These files include additional useful information, such as password/account life and group administrators.

The Shadow Password Suite is enabled by default in Ubuntu. Standard commands for creating new users and groups automatically set up encrypted passwords in the Shadow Password Suite files, as described in the sections that follow.

## /etc/passwd

Read the /etc/passwd file. One way to browse this file is with the **less /etc/passwd** command. Regular users on most systems are normally listed near the bottom of the file. Scroll around this file and look for lines like the following:

```
michael:x:1000:1000:Michael Jang,,,:/home/michael:/bin/bash
```

Each column in /etc/passwd, delineated by a colon, is described in Table 10-1.

## /etc/group

Every Linux user is assigned to one or more groups. By default in Ubuntu, every user gets his own private group. By default, the user is the only member of that group, as defined in the /etc/group configuration file. Read the /etc/group file; you should see lines similar to this:

```
michael:x:1000:
donna:x:1001:
scanner:x:104:hplip,michael,donna
```

| Column | Example | Purpose |
|---|---|---|
| Username | michael | The login name; cannot start with a numeral or an uppercase letter. |
| Password | x | Associated with a password. Can be an *x* or an asterisk (*). An *x* refers to /etc/shadow for the password. An asterisk means the account is disabled, even if there's a password in /etc/shadow. |
| User ID | 1000 | The unique numeric user ID (UID) for that user. By default, Ubuntu starts user IDs at 1000. |
| Group ID | 1000 | The numeric group ID (GID) associated with that user. By default, the GID matches the UID. |
| User Info | Michael Jang | Intended for comments about the user, such as a full name, phone number, e-mail address, or physical location. Can be blank. |
| Home Directory | /home/michael | The standard location for a home directory is /home/*username*. |
| Login Shell | /bin/bash | By default, Ubuntu assigns users to the bash shell. |

**Table 10-1.** Columns in /etc/passwd

The contents of the file are straightforward. The users michael and donna are members of their own groups as well as the scanner group. The four columns in /etc/group are described in Table 10-2.

## /etc/shadow

Read the /etc/shadow file. By default, it's accessible only to the administrative user. One command that allows you to browse this file with arrow and PAGE UP/PAGE DOWN keys is **sudo less /etc/shadow**. If you've added regular users to your system, those users should be listed near the bottom of this file. Scroll around this file, and you should see a series of lines like the following:

```
michael:$1$Oe1/BrGD$:1000:1000:Mike,,,:/home/michael:/bin/bash
```

While similar to /etc/passwd, the /etc/shadow file can include additional information such as password life and account expiration. Each column in /etc/shadow, delineated by a colon, has a purpose, as described in Table 10-3. The command switches listed in the table are associated with and can be modified using the **chage** command, described later in the "Configure Users at the Command Line" section.

**NOTE**    In Linux, the exclamation point character, the !, is also known as a bang.

One key difference between this file and others involves the root account, normally the first one listed in the /etc/shadow file. By default, direct logins to that account are disabled. Unless you've changed this default, a bang or exclamation point will appear in the second column of this line, which disables direct logins as root.

| Column | Example | Purpose |
|---|---|---|
| Groupname | michael | Each user gets his own group, with the same name as his username. You can also create unique group names. |
| Password | x | The password; an *x* points to /etc/gshadow for the actual password, if it exists. Groups do not require a password. |
| Group ID | 1000 | The numeric GID. |
| Group Members | michael, donna | A list of the usernames that are members of the group. |

**Table 10-2.**    Columns in /etc/group

| Column | Field | Description |
|--------|-------|-------------|
| 1 | Username | Username |
| 2 | Password | Encrypted password; requires an *x* in the second column of /etc/passwd. An **!** in this column means the account is disabled. |
| 3 | Password history | Date of the last password change, in number of days after January 1, 1970. |
| 4 | mindays | Minimum number of days that a password must be kept (**-m**). |
| 5 | maxdays | Maximum password lifetime, in days (**-M**). |
| 6 | warndays | Number of days before password expiration for a warning (**-W**). |
| 7 | inactive | Number of days after password expiration when an account is made inactive (**-I**). |
| 8 | disabled | Number of days after password expiration when an account is disabled (**-E**). |

**Table 10-3.**   Columns in /etc/shadow

## /etc/gshadow

Every Linux user is assigned to a group. By default in Ubuntu, every user gets his own private group. As with /etc/shadow, each regular user is normally the only member of that user's private group, as defined in the /etc/group configuration file. As the /etc/gshadow file is readable only by administrative users, you can only read that file with a command like the **sudo less /etc/gshadow** command, which should reveal lines similar to the following:

```
michael:!::
donna:!::
scanner:!::hplip,michael,donna
```

The contents are straightforward. These lines tell you that users michael and donna are members of their own groups as well as the scanner group. The four columns in each /etc/gshadow line are described in Table 10-4.

| Column | Example | Purpose |
|---|---|---|
| Group name | donna | Each user is a member of his own group, with the same name as his username. Many other group names exist. |
| Password | ! | Encrypted password; requires an $x$ in the second column of /etc/group, and ! if there's no group password. |
| Group Administrators | michael | The numeric GID associated with that user. By default, Ubuntu creates a new group for every new user. |
| Group Members | michael, donna | Lists the usernames that are members of the group. Can be blank if the user is the only member of the group. |

**Table 10-4.** Columns in /etc/gshadow

# If You Need to Deactivate the Shadow Password Suite

If you prefer a system in which the Shadow Password Suite is disabled, the **shadowconfig** command can help. It's a simple command: While **sudo shadowconfig off** disables the Shadow Password Suite, **sudo shadowconfig on** enables it. Older releases used commands such as **pwconv** and **grpconv** to activate (coupled with **pwunconv** and **grpunconv** to deactivate) the suite. In contrast, take a look at the script in the /sbin/shadowconfig file. You'll see those commands appropriately configured within the script.

# A User and Group Configuration Tool

Ubuntu supports configuration of users and groups with the Users Settings GUI tool. It supports fairly fine-grained customization of user and group settings. Starting with the Hardy Heron release, permission to use this tool is limited by the PolicyKit package, as described in the last section of this chapter. If your account has permissions to manage system configuration tools, you can open Users Settings from a command line interface in the GUI with the following command:

```
$ users-admin
```

**NOTE**   Prior to the implementation of the PolicyKit with Ubuntu's Hardy Heron release, administrative tools could be started by prefacing them with the **sudo** command. That's no longer necessarily true.

This opens the Users Settings tool, shown in Figure 10-1. It displays currently configured users with standard accounts. In this case, it shows two regular users on the local system along with the root administrative user.

If you're not already familiar with the Users Settings tool, review and back up the files of the Shadow Password Suite (/etc/passwd, /etc/group, /etc/shadow, and /etc/gshadow) before and after making changes with the tool. Then any changes made with the Users Settings tool can be reversed if needed.

## Creating a User

To create a user in the Users Settings tool, click Add User. This opens the New User Account window shown in Figure 10-2. This window includes three tabs: Account, User Privileges, and Advanced. Standard user information can be configured under the

**Figure 10-1.**   The Users Settings tool

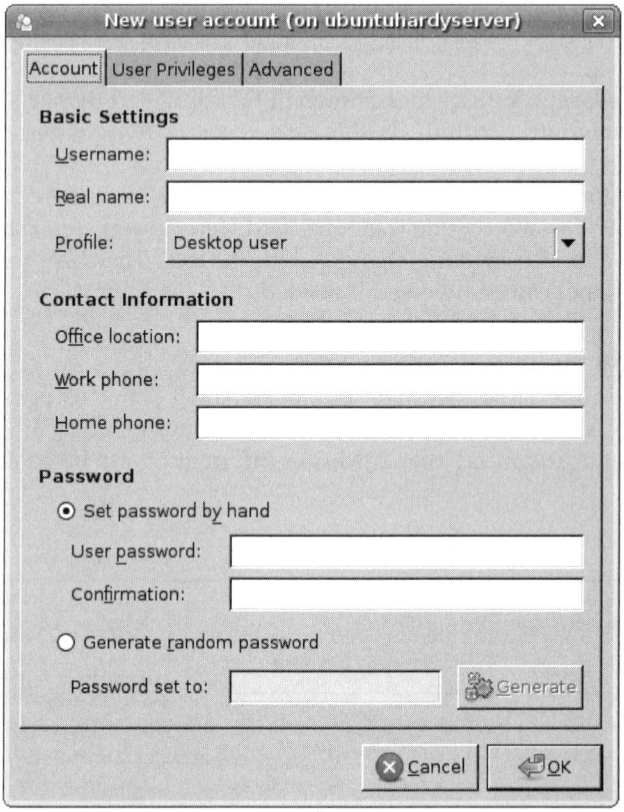

**Figure 10-2.**   Basic account information

Account tab, as described in Table 10-5. When you add a user, the changes can affect all four files of the standard authentication database: /etc/passwd, /etc/group, /etc/shadow, and /etc/gshadow.

For the purpose of this section, I've selected Desktop User on the Account tab. When I click the User Privileges tab, I see a series of options shown in Figure 10-3. (What you see is probably different, depending in part on installed hardware.)

Each of the check box options is associated with a specific group, as defined in /etc/group and described in Table 10-6. In other words, if you activate a specific group under the User Privileges tab, that user is made a member of that group.

| Option | Description |
|---|---|
| Username | Login name; must be one word, starting with a lowercase letter |
| Real Name | More information about the user; you don't have to include the real name |
| Profile | With three options, associated with default group memberships under the User Privileges tab: Administrator, Desktop User, and Unprivileged |
| Office Location | More information about the user, in human-readable format |
| Work Phone | More information about the user, in human-readable format |
| Home Phone | More information about the user, in human-readable format |
| Set Password By Hand | Radio button that activates the User Password and Confirmation text boxes |
| User Password | Enter the desired password; administrators should then instruct the user how to change his or her password |
| Confirmation | Enter the desired password a second time to confirm the selection |

**Table 10-5.**   Basic Options for New Users

When I select the Advanced tab, I see four options, as shown in Figure 10-4:

▼   The Home Directory is set to /home/*username*, per the *username* set in the Account tab.

■   The Shell is set to /bin/bash, the bash shell. Ubuntu developers are working toward changing this to the dash shell (the Debian Almquist shell). Users created with the **useradd** command are already assigned the dash shell by default.

■   The Main Group is blank by default; it's a drop-down box. If you select a Main Group, the new user is added as a member of that group in the /etc/group and /etc/gshadow configuration files.

▲   The User ID is a number. Traditionally, regular users in Linux must have a UID of 100 or higher. Ubuntu systems assign UIDs of 1000 or higher, leaving lower UIDs for special and system users.

As changes are not required, I click OK or Cancel to return to the main Users Settings window.

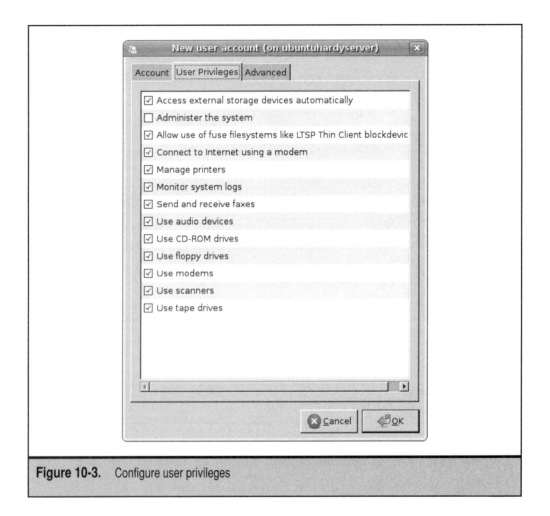

**Figure 10-3.** Configure user privileges

## Create a Group

Now I'll show you how to create a new group using the Users Settings tool. From the Users Settings window, click Manage Groups. This opens the Groups Settings window. Click Add Group to open the New Group window shown in Figure 10-5.

The options are straightforward. Like the username, group names must start with a lowercase letter. The Group Members window lists eligible users that you can select to make a part of the new group. The only slightly tricky bit for a special group is the Group ID; it can't be the same as any existing GID in /etc/group and should be different from any standard range of UID numbers. When I create special groups, I use GIDs in a different range, such as 50000 and up, to avoid any conflict with configured and new UIDs.

| Option | /etc/group Name |
|---|---|
| Access External Storage Devices Automatically | plugdev |
| Administer The System | admin |
| Allow Use Of Fuse Filesystems Like LTSP Thin Client Blockdevice | fuse |
| Connect To Internet Using A Modem | dip |
| Monitor System Logs | adm |
| Send And Receive Faxes | fax |
| Use Audio Devices | audio |
| Use CD-ROM Drives | cdrom |
| Use Floppy Drives | floppy |
| Use Modems | dialout |
| Use Scanners | scanner |
| Use Tape Drives | tape |

**Table 10-6.**   User Privileges Group Options

# Configure Users at the Command Line

Alternatively, you can create and configure users with the **useradd** command. For example, to add a new user named humu, just type **useradd humu** to add this user to the /etc/passwd file. This also creates a private group in the /etc/group file. Assuming the Shadow Password Suite is active, the command also creates parallel entries in the /etc/shadow and /etc/gshadow files.

The **useradd** command also assumes that the default shell is /bin/sh, which is actually linked to the dash shell. As suggested earlier in the chapter, the default shell can vary depending on the Ubuntu release. If you want to specify the bash shell while creating an account for user humu, run the following command:

```
$ sudo useradd -s /bin/bash humu
```

By default, this command configures a home directory in /home/humu, but it doesn't automatically create that directory. You'll need to create the directory and add the standard files from the /etc/skel directory. This process is described shortly.

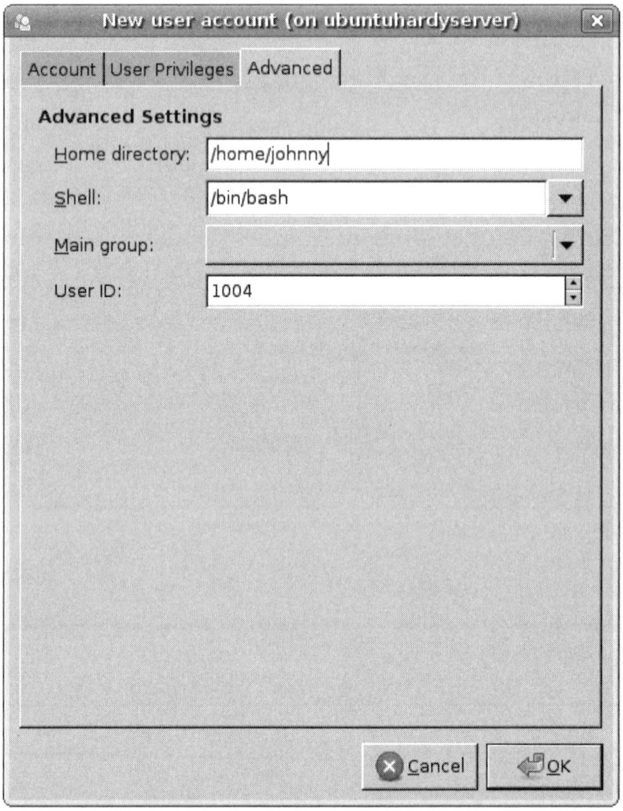

**Figure 10-4.** Advanced user privileges

The **useradd** command is versatile and includes a number of command options shown in Table 10-7.

## Modify or Delete a User Account

The removal of a user account is a pretty straightforward process. The easiest way to delete a user account is with the **userdel** command. By itself, this command does not delete the user's home directory. However, it does delete the user's account information from /etc/passwd and /etc/shadow—as well as the user's private group from /etc/group and /etc/gshadow. Alternatively, the **userdel -r** *username* command deletes the user's home directory along with all the files stored in that directory.

If you just want to make a few changes, use the **chage** command, described shortly.

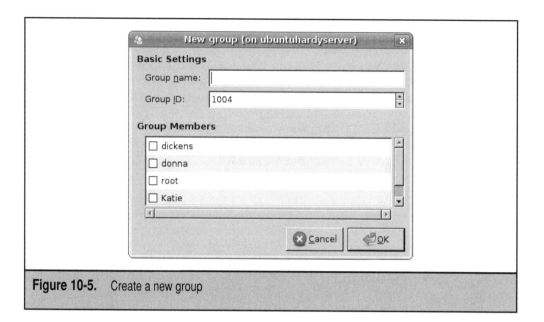

**Figure 10-5.**   Create a new group

## Create Groups at the Command Line

Sometimes administrators need to configure special groups of users, such as supervisors, engineers, drafters, and mechanics. While the **useradd** and **userdel** commands can create and remove groups, the **groupadd** and **groupdel** commands work only with group information in the /etc/group and /etc/gshadow configuration files.

Once these groups are created, the administrator can add appropriate users to the groups with the tools described throughout this chapter.

| Option | Purpose |
|---|---|
| **-u** *UID* | Overrides the default *UID*, which normally starts at 1000 and continues sequentially |
| **-g** *GID* | Overrides the default *GID*, which normally matches the *UID* |
| **-c** *info* | Includes a comment about the user, such as his or her name |
| **-d** *dir* | Overrides the default home directory for the user, /home/*username* |
| **-s** *shell* | Overrides the default shell for the user, /bin/sh (the dash shell) |

**Table 10-7.**   User Privileges Group Options

## Assign a Password

If you've created a username from the command line, use the **sudo passwd** *username* command to assign a new password to that user. For example, the **sudo passwd pm** command lets you assign a new password to user pm. You're prompted to enter a password twice. Relatively insecure passwords such as dictionary words and sequential numbers are allowed, but is strongly discouraged.

Users automatically have permissions to create and change the password for their own accounts. When you create a new user, you should set up a password, tell that user the password, and then have the user run the **passwd** command to create his or her own password. If that password is lost, you can re-create a password for that user with the **passwd** *username* command.

> **NOTE**   Good passwords are important. Any cracker who has connected into a network might be able to read or decrypt user passwords. It's best if all users set up complex passwords, with uppercase and lowercase characters, numerals, and punctuation. One example is OT,Ie9eoc. (short for "On Tuesday, I'll eat 9 ears of corn.").

## Create and Populate a Home Directory

As the title in part suggests, once a new user is created with the **useradd** command, the administrator (presumably you) must still create and populate a home directory. Earlier, I created a user named humu with the **useradd humu** command. I can create humu's home directory with the following command:

```
$ sudo mkdir /home/humu
```

But that home directory (for now) is owned by the root user. I'll change ownership in a moment. First, I'll populate that home directory with files from the /etc/skel directory, which is used for default environment files.

The Users Settings tool automatically copies these files to the home directory when a new account is created. They contain essential user files associated with the bash shell. Administrators can include additional files in that directory, such as corporate policies. To review all files in this directory, including those hidden from standard view, I run the following command:

```
$ ls -a /etc/skel
```

To set up standard files for user home directories, I can add them to the **/etc/skel** directory. New users added thereafter can be configured with the files in that directory.

I copy these files to user humu's home directory with the command shown here.

```
$ sudo cp -a /etc/skel/. /home/humu/
```

Any subdirectories and files embedded therein are copied courtesy of the **-a** switch. Note the dot (**.**) at the end of the /etc/skel/. directory, which copies all hidden files.

Now I can change the ownership of all files in user humu's home directory. The following **chown** command, with the recursive (**-R**) switch, changes both the user and group owner of the /home/humu directory as well as all files and subdirectories. The **humu.humu** specifies that the user humu and the group humu will be the new owner of the /home/humu directory and all files contained therein:

```
$ sudo chown -R humu.humu /home/humu
```

## Manage Accounts with chage

You can use the **chage** command to manage the expiration date of a password—and an account. Password aging information is stored in the /etc/shadow file. For example, if you wanted to require that user test1 keep a password for at least two days, use the **chage test1 -m 2** command. Current password and account aging information is available for user michael with the following command:

```
$ chage -l michael
```

Options for the **chage** command are described in Table 10-8. Dates can be expressed either in a total number of days after January 1, 1970, or in a *YYYY-MM-DD* format, where *YYYY* is the four-digit year, *MM* the two-digit month, and *DD* the two-digit day of the month.

| Option | Purpose |
|---|---|
| -d | Specify the number of days, after January 1, 1970, when the password was changed. |
| -E | Specify the number of days, after January 1, 1970, when the account expires. |
| -I | Set the number of days after password expiration when an account is disabled. |
| -l | Specify current password and account aging information. |
| -m | Note the minimum number of days to keep a password. |
| -M | Note the maximum number of days after which a password must be changed. |
| -W | Note the number of days when a warning is given before a password expires. |

**Table 10-8.** Options for the chage Command

# DELEGATE ADMINISTRATIVE AUTHORITY

Ubuntu disables the root account by default. While it's possible to set up a password for the root user, this is discouraged to limit the risks to the system. Ubuntu includes a specific configuration in the authentication database that allows access to administrative commands by at least the first regular user. By editing the /etc/sudoers configuration file, you can customize these privileges by administrative command and user.

## Super User Concepts

Based on the standard password authentication database, passwords for standard users are stored in the /etc/shadow configuration file. This file includes an encrypted password in the second column for regular users and a "bang" (!) that disables the password for the root (and other system) users.

Review the /etc/group configuration file. As implied back in Table 10-6, the admin group is available for administrative purposes. The first regular user created on an Ubuntu system should be a member of this group. But that works only with the following directive in the /etc/sudoers configuration file, which allows password-protected access—to members of the admin group—for all administrative commands:

```
%admin ALL=(ALL) ALL
```

When I first examined the /etc/sudoers configuration file, I thought the required password for users and groups configured in this file was the administrative password. I was wrong. The line shown above actually allows administrative access based on the password of the regular user. Yes, that means if someone were to crack my account password, that user would have administrative access to my system.

But at least it makes me think a bit before running an administrative command. For example, if I accidentally tried to run the **sudo mkfs** command on an unmounted partition, I would get the following message, which serves as an "Are You Sure?" warning:

```
[sudo] password for michael:
```

One variation is the **sudoedit** command, which automatically opens the text file that follows in the default text editor. For example, the following command automatically opens the /etc/shadow file:

```
$ sudoedit /etc/shadow
```

The **sudoedit** command is equivalent to **sudo -e**. As a root password is normally not configured on Ubuntu systems, the **su** command does not normally work by itself because it requires the password of the root user. So here's a small trick for those of you accustomed to administering Linux from the root account. The following command logs in to the root account from a regular account, using that regular user's password:

```
$ sudo su
```

| Option | Description |
|--------|-------------|
| -e | Runs the **sudoedit** command; should be applied to an administrative file |
| -K, -k | Eliminates the **sudo** 15-minute timestamp; the next time **sudo** is used, the password is required |
| -l | Specifies the commands that can be run with administrative privileges for the subject user |
| -V | Prints out the version number |

**Table 10-9.** Important **sudo** Command Switches

If you do want to create a password for the root user, run the **passwd** command after running **sudo su**. Furthermore, if you really want the full environment of the root account, run the following command from the root user prompt:

```
# su -
```

Alternatively, the **su -** *username* command can be used to log in to the account of another user. You'll be prompted for the password of that user.

One of the weaknesses of the **sudo** command is that once a correct password is given and accepted, further **sudo** commands are accepted without a password for the next 15 minutes. In the Linux world, this is known as a *ticket*. In the sections that follow, I'll analyze the default /etc/sudoers configuration file and show you how to configure it to allow a special group to access a specific administrative command. A few of the important **sudo** switches are described in Table 10-9.

# Partial Authorization in sudoers

The super user configuration file is /etc/sudoers. This file regulates access to the **sudo** command. Don't open it in a text editor just yet. One way to review this file from the command line console is via the following command:

```
$ sudo less /etc/sudoers
```

The first active line in this file sets **Defaults**. The following directive uses basic environment variables associated with the administrative account. The PATH for the administrative account is more extensive than is standard for most users. As such, authorized users who run the **sudo** command have access to key root account environment variables.

```
Defaults       env_reset
```

For contrast, examine the first directive from an older version of /etc/sudoers, shown next. The bang (!) negates the effect of a directive. Here's a breakdown of this first line: The **!lecture** negates the first time "lecture" is given to users who run the **sudo** command. The **tty_tickets** requires users to confirm with their passwords when running **sudo** in different consoles, also known as *ttys*. The **!fqdn** directive disables the use of fully qualified domain names (FQDNs) in this file. I like this last setting, as it avoids problems with access to DNS servers.

```
Defaults        !lecture,tty_tickets,!fqdn
```

The next active line provides sudo privileges to the root user:

```
root    ALL=(ALL) ALL
```

The format of /etc/sudoers commands is as follows:

```
user  system=run_as_username   command
```

This helps explain the last standard active directive. When the percent sign (%) precedes a name associated with users, it specifies a group. So the next line specifies permissions for users in the admin group. The first **ALL** specifies all systems; one alternative is to substitute **localhost** limit access to the local system. The **(ALL)** allows access to all usernames. That's not a problem, as the line still limits access to users in the admin group. Finally, the last **ALL** supports administrative access to all commands.

```
%admin    ALL=(ALL) ALL
```

If you're sufficiently confident to disable the password requirement, the following would enable password-free access from users in the admin group to all administrative commands:

```
%admin    ALL=(ALL) NOPASSWD: ALL
```

I discourage this kind of change, however, as it removes a safeguard against administrative mistakes.

Now you're ready to customize this file.

## Partial Authorization for a Wheel

The /etc/sudoers file can be edited with the **visudo** command; access to this command requires administrative privileges. Therefore in Ubuntu, you'd run the following command to open /etc/sudoers in a text editor:

```
$ sudo visudo
```

Now you're ready to make changes. As an example, if you've created a group named power in /etc/group and want to allow members of that group to reboot the system, add the following line. The **localhost** means that members of the power group can reboot only when on the local system—in other words, they can't log in remotely and reboot that system.

```
%power    localhost=(ALL)   /sbin/reboot
```

This is just the briefest of introductions to the /etc/sudoers configuration file. The **man sudoers** command provides an extensive manual to this configuration file.

# QUOTA CONFIGURATION

*Quotas* are used to limit the ability of a user or group to consume disk space. This helps prevent a small group of users from monopolizing disk capacity and potentially interfering with other users or the entire system. Disk quotas are commonly used by Internet service providers (ISPs), by web-hosting companies, on FTP sites, and on corporate file servers to ensure continued availability of their systems.

Without quotas, one or more users can upload files on an FTP server and occupy all free space on a partition. Once the affected partition is full, other users are effectively denied upload access to the disk. This is also a reason to mount different filesystem directories on different partitions. For example, if partitions were configured only for the root (/) directory and swap space, someone uploading files could fill up all of the space in your root directory (/). Without at least a little free space in the root directory (/), the system could become unstable or even crash.

There are two ways to set quotas for users and groups: Limits can be set by inodes or by kilobyte-sized disk blocks. Every Linux file requires an inode. In other words, limits can be set by the number of files or by absolute space. Different quotas can be set for different filesystems. For example, each user can have different quotas on the /home and /tmp directories if the directories are mounted on separate volumes or partitions.

If the quota package isn't already installed, you can install it with the **sudo aptitude install quota** command.

## Quotas in /etc/fstab

As described in Chapter 5, the file /etc/fstab is used to specify how Linux mounts filesystems during the boot process. The Options column of this file configures how Linux mounts a directory, which can also be configured for user and group quotas.

**CAUTION**   Before editing a key configuration file such as /etc/fstab, back it up! If any changes lead to a catastrophic failure, you can boot the system in rescue mode and then restore the original configuration file.

The relevant parts from my Hardy Heron /etc/fstab configuration file, with user and group quota settings on the /home directory volume, are shown in Figure 10-6.

```
    # /etc/fstab: static file system information.
    #
    # <file system> <mount point>   <type>  <options>      <dump>  <pass>
    proc            /proc           proc    defaults       0       0
    # /dev/mapper/ubuntuhardyserver-root
    UUID=41c78ad2-23f1-409b-bc78-1d00255c4df9 /             ext3     relatime,error
    s=remount-ro 0      1
    # /dev/sda1
    UUID=63ce6ed9-6ee4-455f-9bb5-8d31bd71dc3c /boot         ext3     relatime
            0       2
    # /dev/mapper/ubuntuhardyserver-home
    UUID=cc388f0e-4f23-401f-b61d-f7e9fbf47d20 /home         ext3     relatime,usrqu
    ota,grpquota      0       2
    # /dev/mapper/ubuntuhardyserver-swap_1
    UUID=959fda25-a7ce-410c-bc59-720612f479c1 none          swap     sw
        0       0
    /dev/scd0       /media/cdrom0   udf,iso9660 user,noauto,exec,utf8 0        0
    ~
```

**Figure 10-6.**   /etc/fstab with quota settings

Unlike past Linux distributions, it's acceptable for lines in /etc/fstab to wrap to the next line. Note how the **usrquota** and **grpquota** settings are applied to the /home directory volume. If you don't have a separate /home directory partition, apply the quota settings to the volume with the top-level root directory (/).

You can test changes to /etc/fstab by rebooting the computer or remounting a filesystem. For example, if you've just added **usrquota** and **grpquota** entries to the /home directory filesystem, test it with the **mount -o remount /home** command. The following excerpt from the /etc/mtab file illustrates the result (the following code represents one line):

```
/dev/mapper/ubuntuhardyserver-home /home ext3
rw,relatime,usrquota,grpquota 0 0
```

## Quota Management Commands

Before quotas can be activated, appropriate quota files must be created. For user and group quotas, you'll need the aquota.user and aquota.group files in the selected filesystem before quotas can be activated. You no longer need to create those files manually; once you've remounted the desired directory, the appropriate **quotacheck** command creates them automatically. For the /home directory described previously, you'd use the following commands:

```
$ sudo mount -o remount /home
$ sudo quotacheck -cugm /home
```

The **quotacheck** as shown includes the following command options:

▼ **-c**  Performs a new scan

■ **-u**  Scans for user quotas

■ **-g**  Scans for group quotas

▲ **-m**  Remounts the scanned filesystem

The **quotacheck** command checks the current quota information for all users, groups, and partitions. It stores this information in the appropriate quota partitions. Once the command is run, the aquota.user and aquota.group files should appear in the configured directory—in this case, /home.

## Quotas by Size and Inode

The **edquota** command can be used to create and customize disk quotas for users. This file edits the aquota.user or aquota.group file with the default editor. In this section, I'll edit quotas for user donna to restrict the amount of disk space she is allowed to use. I use the following command to edit user donna's quota configuration:

```
$ sudo edquota donna
```

The **-u** switch is the default **edquota** command option; if you want to edit the quotas of a group, the **-g** switch is appropriate. If the default editor is nano, you can expand the command line window. To fit on a page in this book, I reduced the spacing between quota columns in Figure 10-7.

Pay attention to the formatting and take note of the seven columns. The volume name associated with the /home directory is /dev/mapper/ubuntuhardyserver-home. The name is so long that it displaces the quota numbers from the associated columns. The Blocks column specifies the user's current disk usage, in 1 kilobyte blocks. The Inodes column specifies the current number of files and directories owned by that user.

A *0* in any column disables the limit. Figure 10-7 specifies a 10MB soft and a 20MB hard limit; along with a soft limit of 10,000 inodes and a hard limit of 20,000 inodes. If I specify a hard limit in either case, it should be larger. Soft and hard limits can be set for both blocks and inodes. By default, any limit in the quota configuration set to 0 disables

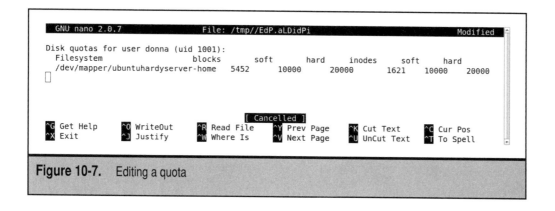

**Figure 10-7.**   Editing a quota

the limit for the user. The meanings of soft and hard limits are often confused; here's an explanation of both:

▼ **Soft limit**   The maximum amount of space a user or group can have on a volume. If a grace period has been set, the soft limit acts as an alarm. The user or group is then notified of a quota violation. Soft limits with a grace period require a hard limit.

▲ **Hard limit**   Necessary only when grace periods are in use. If grace periods are enabled, this will be the absolute limit a user can use. Any attempt to consume resources beyond this limit will be denied.

You can see that user donna is currently using 5452 blocks and has 1621 files (inodes) on this volume. Each block takes up 1KB of space; thus, user donna's files total approximately 5.4MB.

You can implement quotas in Ubuntu; restart the associated service with the following command:

```
$ sudo /etc/init.d/quota restart
```

## Quota Grace Periods

The *grace period* is the number of days a user is allowed to exceed the soft limits of the implemented quota. After the grace period is over, the user must get under exceeded soft limits to continue. The default grace period for all users is seven days, and cannot be customized by the user. To change the grace period, run the **edquota -t** command. When I run this command on a user, I see the following output:

```
Grace period before enforcing soft limits for users:
Time units may be: days, hours, minutes, or seconds
    Filesystem                 Block grace period      Inode grace period
/dev/mapper/ubuntuhardyserver-home      7days                       7days
```

No space appears between the *7* and *days*. This is a quirk associated with quota grace periods. The **edquota** utility does not recognize a space between the number and the unit (for example, *7days*, not *7 days*). You could add a space when editing the configuration, but when the grace period is saved, **edquota** deletes those spaces.

The **edquota** command allows you to use an already configured user's quota as a template for new users. To use this feature, you need to run the **edquota** command with the **-p** switch; for example, the following command applies the quotas configured for user donna to users (**-u**) michael, randy, and nancy:

```
$ sudo edquota -up donna nancy michael randy
```

Quotas can be configured for a group, and it's useful to create a dedicated directory for a group. To do so, run **edquota** with the **-g** *group_name* argument, where *group_name* is specified in the /etc/group file.

## Quota Reports

As an administrator, you might like to see reports about who is using the most disk space. You can generate reports on users, groups, and everybody with files in a volume. To view a report showing quota information for all users, run the **sudo repquota -a** command. You'll see a list of quotas for all users.

If you have multiple filesystems with quotas, you can use the **repquota** command to isolate a specific filesystem. For example, if you want to view the quota report for the filesystem with the /home directory, run the following command:

```
$ sudo repquota -u /home
```

Alternatively, if you want to view quota information on user donna, run the following **quota** command:

```
$ sudo quota -uv donna
Disk quotas for user donna (uid 1001):
 Filesystem  blocks   quota   limit   grace   files   quota   limit   grace
/dev/mapper/ubuntuhardyserver-home
             5452   10000       0            1621   10000       0
```

An individual user can check his or her own usage with the **quota** command.

# PLUGGABLE AUTHENTICATION MODULES (PAM)

PAM files can be used to regulate access to specified administrative tools via configured authentication databases. "PAM-aware" packages associated with LDAP, Samba, and even web services can be installed with the following command:

```
$ sudo apt-get install libpam-ldap libpam-smbpass libpam-http
```

There are a number of PAM-aware packages; in other words, they incorporate configuration files in the /etc/pam.d directory. Associated packages range from those that install the CUPS (Common Unix Printing System) and SSH (Secure Shell) servers, the **sudo** and **passwd** commands, and common files associated with the Dovecot and Samba services.

Many of the configuration files in the /etc/pam.d directory are named after applications. These applications are PAM-aware. In other words, you can change the way users are verified for applications such as the console login program. Just modify the appropriate configuration file in the /etc/pam.d directory.

## PAM Configuration File Format

PAM is configured in service-specific files in the /etc/pam.d/ directory. While the /etc/pam.conf configuration file exists, it is not used in current implementations of PAM. Each file in the /etc/pam.d directory includes a group of dynamically loadable library modules that govern how applications verify their users. Each line in the /etc/pam.d directory conforms to the following format:

```
module_type   control_flag   module [arguments]
```

## PAM Module Type

There are four module type settings available for PAM configuration files: **auth**, **account**, **password**, and **session**:

▼ **Authentication management (auth)**   Establishes the identity of a user. For example, a PAM **auth** module type can prompt for a username and/or a password.

■ **Account management (account)**   Allows or denies access according to the account policies. For example, a PAM **account** module type can deny access according to time, password expiration, or a specific list of restricted users.

■ **Password management (password)**   Manages other password policies. For example, a PAM **password** module type can limit the number of times a user can try to log in before a console is reset.

▲ **Session management (session)**   Applies settings for an application. For example, the PAM **session** module type can set default settings for a login console.

## PAM Control Flag

The *control flag* determines what PAM does if the module succeeds or fails. Five different control flags are available, as described in Table 10-10.

| Control Flag | Description |
|---|---|
| required | If the module works, PAM proceeds to the next line in the file. If it fails, the command associated with the configuration file fails. |
| requisite | Similar to **required**; if the module fails, the associated command also fails. |
| sufficient | If the module works, the login or other authentication proceeds. No other lines in the configuration file are processed. |
| optional | PAM ignores module success or failure. |
| include | A directive which includes directives from a cited file; for example, the **@include common-auth** line includes all directives from the common-auth file. |

**Table 10-10.**   PAM Control Flags

## PAM Modules and Arguments

Modules cited in PAM configuration files are stored in the /lib/security directory. In older Linux distributions, the full path to the PAM module was required. For more information, each module in the noted directory normally has a man page, which includes available arguments. Now consider the following lines from the /etc/pam.d/common-password configuration file:

```
# password required        pam_cracklib.so retry=3 minlen=6 difok=3
# password required        pam_unix.so use_authok nullok md5
```

In the first line, **pam_cracklib.so** is the module. As specified in the associated man page (accessible with the **man pam_cracklib** command), several arguments are possible. In this case, users who type in the wrong password are prompted to retry three times (**retry=3**), passwords must be at least six alphanumeric characters in length (**minlen=6**), and at least three of the characters in the new password must be different from the current password (**difok=3**).

In the second line, as noted in the pam_unix man page, the new rule supersedes previous rules (**use_authok**), zero length passwords are allowed (**nullok**), and passwords are encrypted using the MD5 algorithm associated with the Shadow Password Suite.

If I activate these lines, per the instructions in the /etc/pam.d/common-password file (commenting out a different line), the next time I change a password, I'm subject to the rules associated with the pam_cracklib module.

# PAM Configuration Files

This section continues with an analysis of the /etc/pam.d/login configuration file, as it's an excellent example of how PAM standardizes the user authentication process. The first officially active line from /etc/pam.d/login allows root logins at the login console—if the terminal is listed in the /etc/securetty configuration file:

```
auth requisite pam_securetty.so
```

For more information, run the **man pam_securetty** command and review the /etc/securetty file.

The next line prevents logins from users other than root, if the /etc/nologin file exists. As the root user isn't configured for logins on default Ubuntu installations, don't create this file! (If it exists, you'd have to boot into recovery mode to rescue the system.)

```
auth requisite pam_nologin.so
```

This, and the last line in /etc/pam.d/login, relates to Security Enhanced Linux, which is not normally used in Ubuntu. For more information, see Chapter 18.

```
session     required    pam_selinux.so close
```

With two lines, the environment, default language, and keyboard are set:

```
session required pam_env.so readenv=1
session required pam_env.so readenv=1 envfile=/etc/default/locale
```

The following line includes all **auth** modules from the /etc/pam.d/common-auth file.

```
@include common-auth
```

The next directive supports group membership based on users, terminals, and times as defined in the /etc/security/group.conf configuration file. As noted in that file, such an option is inherently not secure.

```
auth        optional    pam_group.so
```

If you activate this directive, it's possible to limit access by day and time of day, as configured in the /etc/security/time.conf configuration file:

```
# account    requisite  pam_time.so
```

If activated, the following directive can regulate logins by terminal and user, based on limits in the /etc/security/access.conf configuration file:

```
# account    required   pam_access.so
```

If activated, the following directive configures session-based limits by user or group, based on rules specified in the /etc/security/limits.conf configuration file:

```
session    required   pam_limits.so
```

One bit especially useful for administrative users is the last login date and time. For example, it could help identify if someone logged into your account while you were on vacation. As shown here, the file has optional flags, where the success or failure of this module shouldn't affect the session.

```
session    optional   pam_lastlog.so
```

The next option specifies the display of the "message of the day" upon a successful console login. By default, the standard message of the day is available in the /etc/motd file.

```
session    optional   pam_motd.so
```

Users who have just logged in can see if they have any new mail, courtesy of this option:

```
session    optional   pam_mail.so standard
```

The remaining active commands in this file refer to other files also in the /etc/pam.d directory. As suggested by their filenames, the **account**, **session**, and **password** directives from each of the noted files are included in this PAM file:

```
@include common-account
@include common-session
@include common-password
```

# THE POLICYKIT

The PolicyKit is relatively new for Linux. Originally developed to enable finer grained policies with respect to hardware, the PolicyKit has been extended to allow access from regular, normally unprivileged users. For the Hardy Heron release of Ubuntu, it's focused primarily on GUI-based administrative tools and utilities. It's intended to provide a finer-grained control than is realistic or possible using the **sudo** and PAM tools discussed earlier in this chapter.

In fact, starting with the Hardy Heron release, many system configuration GUI tools now cannot be used by administrators unless appropriate configuration changes are made through the PolicyKit. Such administrative users should also be a member of the admin group, as defined in the /etc/group and /etc/gshadow configuration files.

> **NOTE** Ubuntu's implementation of the PolicyKit for the Hardy Heron release is based in part on the way it was implemented for Fedora Linux. If you're interested in future directions for the PolicyKit on Ubuntu, install the latest Fedora Linux distribution. Alternatively, the latest PolicyKit manual is available from http://hal.freedesktop.org/docs/PolicyKit/.

The PolicyKit is implemented in commands and a GNOME-based GUI tool. The XML (eXtensible Markup Language) code used by the PolicyKit is, in my opinion, arcane. The Ubuntu implementation for the PolicyKit is still under development. Therefore, this chapter focuses on the GUI tool, followed by brief references to associated commands. This is appropriate because the PolicyKit controls access to GUI-based configuration and administration tools.

Some users are skeptical about the PolicyKit, at least with respect to its current implementation on the Ubuntu Hardy Heron release. It's certainly been a challenge for Ubuntu developers to implement the PolicyKit without having tested it on a previous release.

You can install the PolicyKit and associated tools with a command such as this:

```
$ apt-get install policykit-gnome
```

## Keeping It Simple

Normally, the PolicyKit enables "unlock" access to administrative tools to members of the admin group, as configured in the /etc/group and /etc/gshadow configuration files. Members of this group who start an administrative tool can have access via the Unlock key, which is now included in most GNOME-based administrative tools.

For example, when user bub opens the Users Settings tool with the **users-admin** command, full access is disabled by default. However, when user bub clicks the Unlock key, the Authenticate window appears, as shown in Figure 10-8. The same Authenticate window appears when a user clicks Unlock in any other PolicyKit-enabled GUI administrative tool.

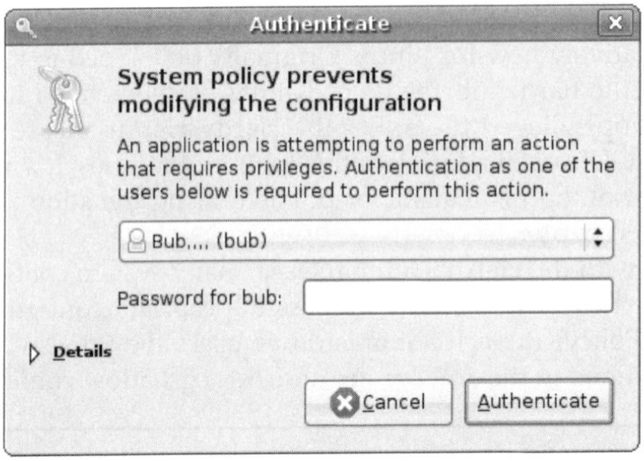

**Figure 10-8.** Authenticating an administrative user

When user bub enters his password in the text box, access to the administrative tool is unlocked. Alternatively, user bub can click the username drop-down text box to browse the current list of administrative users. Access can be enabled with the password of any user that appears in the list.

# PolicyKit Concepts

The PolicyKit model assumes that applications are run by two distinct types of processes: mechanisms and policies. *Mechanisms* run in privileged mode and are associated with administrative utilities and commands. *Policies* have their own unprivileged processes and define the conditions for executing those administrative utilities.

The mechanism is split into three groups: the subject, the object, and the action. The *subject* is the application. The *object* is the file or device being changed or modified. The *action* specifies how the object is being modified.

The subject is the administrative command or tool. The object can be device files that are formatted, configuration files that are modified for new users, and physical devices such as a CD/DVD drive. The action is based on the functionality of the tool, which might for example format a device, add a user, or open a CD/DVD drive.

The basic PolicyKit is configured in the /etc/PolicyKit/PolicyKit.conf configuration file. PolicyKit settings for specific users are stored in the /var/lib/PolicyKit directory. As of the Hardy Heron release, Ubuntu policies regulate access to GNOME-based tools but not regular command line utilities.

## Configure with the PolicyKit GUI Tool

True Linux geeks work from the command line. But more Microsoft administrators are converting to Linux. For this audience, many, and perhaps most, readers learn more about tools based on newer concepts from the GUI.

To start the GUI PolicyKit configuration tool, run the following command:

```
$ sudo polkit-gnome-authorization
```

It opens the Authorizations tool, shown in Figure 10-9.

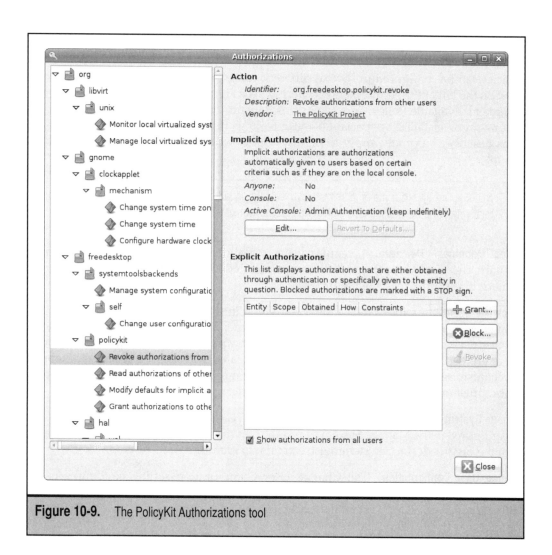

**Figure 10-9.** The PolicyKit Authorizations tool

Those of you familiar with the latest Fedora Linux releases may already know the capabilities of this tool. If you just want to look around the tool, open it without the administrative **sudo**. Unless your account is administratively enabled to modify PolicyKit settings, changes cannot be written. A number of these options are rather fine-grained and can be used to manage hardware in extensive detail. In many cases, the control goes beyond the capabilities of the hardware available to me; such settings are not tested.

**NOTE** The descriptions in this section include PolicyKit identifiers, whose names might be wrapped in the text due to their lengths. In this chapter, hyphens that appear in identifiers are required and part of the identifier names.

## PolicyKit Identifiers

Policies can be configured in several different categories. Some are accessible from the pane on the left of the Authorizations window (see Figure 10-9). The list you see may not include all available PolicyKit options. This depends in part on any additional services that might be installed or special PolicyKit settings that might be configured. Most options described normally apply to regular users—who are *not* members of the admin group.

**NOTE** I've split out major administrative settings in additional detail. To keep the descriptions relatively even, the subsections in this area are not consistent.

**Virtual Machines**   By default, regular users are allowed to monitor but not manage virtual machines. These capabilities are associated with the org.libvirt.unix.monitor and org.libvirt.unix.manage identifiers.

**Clock Management**   Clock management is divided into three functions for the PolicyKit: Change System Time Zone, Change System Time, and Configure Hardware Clock. Regular users do not have permissions to adjust any of these parameters, at least through the operating system. These capabilities are associated with the org.gnome.clockapplet .mechanism.settimezone, org.gnome.clockapplet.mechanism.settime, and org.gnome .clockapplet.mechanism.configurehwclock identifiers.

**Manage System Configuration**   PolicyKit-enabled access to system configuration tools can be configured in the Manage System Configuration category. This capability is associated with the org.freedesktop.systemtoolsbackends.set identifier.

**Change User Configuration**   The Change User Configuration setting configures users' access to their own accounts with system configuration tools. This capability is associated with the org.freedesktop.systemtoolsbackends.self.set identifier.

**Revoke PolicyKit Authorizations**   Users configured in the Revoke Authorizations From Other Users category can revoke the PolicyKit-based permissions of others. This capability is associated with the org.freedesktop.policykit.revoke identifier.

**Read Authorizations Of Other Users**    Users configured in the Read Authorizations Of Other Users category can read the PolicyKit-based permissions of other users. This capability is associated with the org.freedesktop.policykit.read identifier.

**Modify Defaults For Implicit Authorizations**    Users configured in the Modify Defaults For Implicit Authorizations category can modify default PolicyKit-based permissions. This setting is associated with the org.freedesktop.policykit.modify-defaults identifier.

**Grant Authorizations To Other Users**    Users configured in the Grant Authorizations To Other Users category have significant power; they can grant PolicyKit-based permissions to other users. This setting is associated with the org.freedesktop.policykit.grant identifier.

**Wake On LAN**    When enabled, settings in the Wake On LAN category restores activity to a system in hibernation. As suggested by the name, the trigger is network activity. This section is subdivided into three functions for the PolicyKit: If Wake On LAN Is Supported, If Wake On LAN Is Enabled, and Enable or Disable Wake On LAN. Regular users do not have permissions to adjust any of these parameters. These capabilities are associated with the org.freedesktop.hal.wol.supported, org.freedesktop.hal.wol.enabled, and org.freedesktop.hal.wol.enable identifiers.

**Filesystem Storage Management**    The PolicyKit Storage category controls permissions for the management of filesystems in six different areas, as described in Table 10-11. As PolicyKit settings regulate access via GUI tools, this primarily affects tools such as Nautilus as a file browser.

**Power Management**    The PolicyKit Power Management category controls permissions for various power settings in a number of different areas, as described in Table 10-12. Some of these settings are beyond the capabilities of the hardware available to me, so I haven't tested them. As PolicyKit settings regulate access via GUI tools, this won't affect hardware-enabled options such as power buttons.

**Killswitch Management**    The PolicyKit Killswitch category controls permissions for three types of wireless devices: wireless wide area network (WAN) cards, wireless local area network (LAN) cards, and Bluetooth devices. These capabilities are associated with the org.freedesktop.hal.killswitch.wwan, org.freedesktop.hal.killswitch.wlan, and org.freedesktop.hal.killswitch.bluetooth identifiers.

**Docking Station Management**    PolicyKit-enabled removal from docking stations, common with laptop systems, can be configured in the Dockstation category. This capability is associated with the org.freedesktop.hal.dockstation.undock identifier.

**Device Access**    The PolicyKit Device Access category controls access permissions to a number of systems, as described in Table 10-13. As PolicyKit settings regulate access via GUI tools, this won't affect hardware-enabled options such as volume buttons.

| PolicyKit Storage Setting | Description |
|---|---|
| Unmount File Systems Mounted By Other Users | Allows specified users administrative control over filesystems mounted by other users; per the org.freedesktop.hal.storage.unmount-others identifier |
| Mount File Systems From Removable Drives | Gives specified users permission to mount filesystems from removable drives such as USB and CD/DVD drives; per the org.freedesktop.hal .storage.mount-removable identifier |
| Mount File Systems From Internal Drives | Gives specified users permission to mount filesystems from local partitions and volumes; per the org.freedesktop.hal.storage.mount-fixed identifier |
| Eject Removable Media | Allows specified users permission to eject (and unmount) suitable media such as CD/DVD drives; per the org.freedesktop.hal.storage.eject identifier |
| Set Up Decryption For Encrypted Removable Storage Devices | Supports decryption of removable storage devices, per the Linux Unified Key Setup (LUKS) standard; uses the org.freedesktop.hal.storage.crypto-setup-removable identifier |
| Set Up Decryption For Encrypted Fixed Storage Devices | Supports decryption of internal storage devices, per the LUKS standard; uses the org.freedesktop.hal .storage.crypto-setup-removable identifier |

**Table 10-11.**    PolicyKit Filesystem Storage Settings

## Implicit and Explicit Authorizations

Two levels of authorization are possible in each of the PolicyKit categories just described. *Implicit* and *explicit* authorizations are discussed in the following sections.

**Implicit Authorizations**    As noted in the PolicyKit tool, implicit authorizations can be configured to authorize access by user or by console. Control can be based on user status on the console.

Implicit authorizations are available in all of the policy areas described in the preceding section. Select the category of your choice. In the Implicit Authorizations category of the PolicyKit Authorizations tool, click Edit to open the Edit Implicit Authorizations window shown in Figure 10-10.

| PolicyKit Power Setting | Description |
|---|---|
| Suspend The System | Gives specified users power to set suspend mode on the local system; per the org.freedesktop.hal.power-management.suspend identifier |
| Shut Down The System When Multiple Users Are Logged In | Allows a user to shut down a system even if other users are currently connected; per the org.freedesktop.hal.power-management.shutdown-multiple-sessions identifier |
| Shut Down The System | Allows a user to shut down a system; per the org.freedesktop.hal.power-management.shutdown identifier |
| Configure The System To Prefer Power Savings | Supports changes to the power management scheme; per the org.freedesktop.hal.power-management.set-powersave identifier |
| Reboot The System When Multiple Users Are Logged In | Allows a user to reboot a system even if other users are currently connected; per the org.freedesktop.hal.power-management.reboot-multiple-sessions identifier |
| Reboot The System | Allows a user to reboot a system; per the org.freedesktop.hal.power-management.reboot identifier |
| Detect Ambient Light Using Sensor | Supports configuration of systems that can detect current (ambient) light levels; per the org.freedesktop.hal.power-management.light-sensor identifier |
| Set Laptop Panel Brightness | Allows a user to set the brightness level on a system, primarily associated with portable devices; per the org.freedesktop.hal.power-management.lcd-panel identifier |
| Set Keyboard Backlight | Allows a user to set the keyboard backlight level on a system; per the org.freedesktop.hal.power-management.keyboard-backlight identifier |
| Hibernate The System | Allows a user to set a system to hibernate; per the org.freedesktop.hal.power-management.hibernate identifier |
| Configure CPU Frequency Scaling | Supports control of CPUs speeds; per the org.freedesktop.hal.power-management.cpufreq identifier |

**Table 10-12.** PolicyKit Power Management Settings

| PolicyKit Device Access Setting | Description |
|---|---|
| Directly Access Video Capture Devices | Allows access to cameras and similar devices; per the org.freedesktop.hal.device-access.video4linux identifier |
| Directly Access The Uinput Control Device | Supports control of specialty human interface devices (HIDs) such as a keyboard and mouse; not required for all HIDs. Per the org.freedesktop.hal.device-access.input identifier |
| Directly Access Sound Devices | Allows access to sound hardware; per the org.freedesktop.hal.device-access.sound identifier |
| Directly Access Scanners | Allows access to scanners; per the org.freedesktop.hal.device-access.scanner identifier |
| Directly Access PDA Devices | Allows access to Personal Digital Assistants (PDAs); per the org.freedesktop.hal.device-access.pda identifier |
| Directly Access Firewire IIDC Devices | Supports access to FireWire (IEEE 1394) devices associated with live video; per the org.freedesktop.hal.device-access.ieee1394-iidc identifier |
| Directly Access Firewire AVC Devices | Supports access to FireWire (IEEE 1394) devices associated with live video based on the Advanced Video Coding (AVC) standard; per the org.freedesktop.hal.device-access.ieee1394-avc identifier |
| Directly Access DVB Devices | Allows access to Digital Video Broadcasting (DVB) devices associated with HDTV; per the org.freedesktop.hal.device-access.dvb identifier |
| Directly Access Optical Drives | Enables access to CD/DVD drives; per the org.freedesktop.hal.device-access.cdrom identifier |
| Directly Access Digital Cameras | Enables access to digital cameras; per the org.freedesktop.hal.device-access.camera identifier |
| Directly Access Audio Players | Enables access to music players; per the org.freedesktop.hal.device-access.audio-player identifier |

**Table 10-13.** PolicyKit Device Access Settings

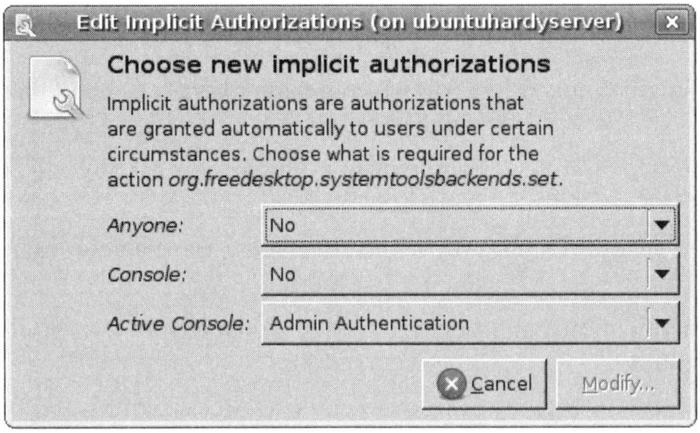

**Figure 10-10.** Implicit Authorizations for the PolicyKit

Implicit authorizations support modulated levels of access by regular users. The levels of implicit authorization shown in Figure 10-10 fall into three sub-categories. Several of the implicit authorizations for Anyone are described in Table 10-14. The descriptions are general, as they apply to all PolicyKit settings.

In general, the Admin Authentication options are limited to users configured as members of the admin group, as defined in /etc/group and /etc/sudoers. In contrast, regular Authentication options support access by all regular users.

Experiment with these options, especially those in the Manage System Configuration area. Once selections are made in the Edit Implicit Authorizations window shown in Figure 10-10, click Modify. You can then open a second console and access tools such as the Network Settings tool with the **network-admin** command. Find the several combinations that activate the Unlock key. Different combinations support access either via an admin group account in /etc/group or via a regular user account.

There are two groups of scenarios that activate the Unlock key, based on some combination of Authentication and Admin Authentication options described in Table 10-14. Admin Authentication takes advantage of users configured in /etc/sudoers. User dickens is a member of this group. So when I select her account and enter her password, I get full access to the now unlocked administrative tool, as shown in Figure 10-11.

In general, any option that supports *indefinite* authentication is a security risk. As the changes survive a reboot, the next user who logs into that account gets at least the same level of administrative access. To remove an indefinite authentication, say for user michael, open the associated PolicyKit configuration file. For user michael, that would be the user-michael .auths file in the /var/lib/PolicyKit/ directory. The problem directive looks like this:

```
scope=always:action-id=org.freedesktop.systemtoolsbackends.set:
when=1207257157:auth-as=1000:constraint=active
```

| Authorization | Description |
|---|---|
| Admin Authentication (one shot) | Supports one-time *console* access, if enabled in /etc/sudoers |
| Admin Authentication | Supports one-time access for anyone or the console, if enabled in /etc/sudoers |
| Admin Authentication (keep session) | Allows access during the console session, if enabled in /etc/sudoers |
| Admin Authentication (keep indefinitely) | Enables access, if enabled in /etc/sudoers; changes survive a reboot |
| Authentication (one shot) | Supports one-time access, confirmed by the user password |
| Authentication | Supports one-time access, confirmed by the user password |
| Authentication (keep session) | Supports access throughout a session, confirmed by the user password |
| Authentication (keep indefinitely) | Supports access that survives a reboot |

**Table 10-14.** Implicit Authorizations for Anyone

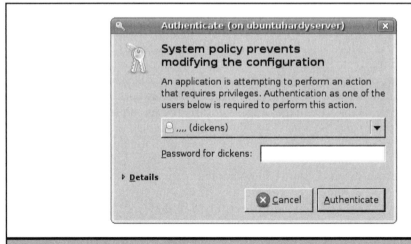

**Figure 10-11.** Unlocking with an administrative account

One problem is **scope=always**, which is a permanent authorization for tools associated with the noted **id**, in this case, org.freedesktop.systemtoolsbackends.set. In other words, system tools such as the Network Settings tool are permanently unlocked for user michael. If you run into this issue, I suggest that you delete the line and avoid the "keep indefinitely" implicit authorizations. The best option in my opinion is to click Revert To Defaults under all Implicit Authorizations policy categories.

**Explicit Authorizations**   In the PolicyKit Authorizations tool, Explicit Authorizations can help you regulate access in the defined policy areas. Before making any changes, open a typical GUI system configuration tool such as the Network Settings tool. It can be started with the **network-admin** command. Unless you've already made changes to default PolicyKit authorizations, everything is grayed out. If you try starting this tool from the administrative account, the result is the same.

As suggested by the buttons associated with Explicit Authorizations, you can Grant, Block, or Revoke authorization. In the PolicyKit Authorizations tool, select Manage System Configuration and click Grant to open a Grant Authorization window similar to the one shown in Figure 10-12.

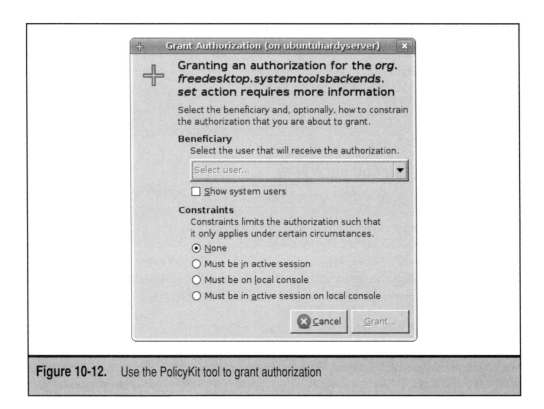

**Figure 10-12.**   Use the PolicyKit tool to grant authorization

To grant authorization to a specific user from the Grant Authorization window, under Beneficiary, click the Select User drop-down box and select an active user. For the purpose of this exercise, I select user michael.

If you activate the Show System Users check box, you could conceivably select from system users such as root and bin. I do not recommend this, as it could lead to security problems.

Select appropriate constraints. Do not leave the constraints set to None, unless the tool in question is run automatically without a console, such as by an administrative *cron* or *at* job (described in Chapter 7). If you connect from a remote system, such as with an SSH login, do not use either of the local console options. For those who connect via SSH, select Must Be In Active Session, and then click Grant.

Now user michael should have authenticated access to administrative utilities such as the Network Settings tool with the **network-admin** command from user michael's prompt. As user michael is explicitly authorized, the **sudo network-admin** command is not required, and in fact it would not work with such administrative utilities.

Return to the main GUI Authorizations tool window. The Block button in the lower right area works in a similar fashion to Grant; it supports blocking of specific users based on similar options just described for the Grant Authorization window.

The Revoke button deletes the custom settings granted or blocked for a specific user, as highlighted in the Explicit Authorizations area.

# PolicyKit Commands

This section provides an all too brief overview of the commands associated with the PolicyKit. The commands either customize or check the syntax of PolicyKit configuration files. The directives and XML format associated with these files are described at http://hal.freedesktop.org/docs/PolicyKit/.

## Verify PolicyKit Configuration Files

The main PolicyKit configuration file is /etc/PolicyKit/PolicyKit.conf. If you make changes to this file, the syntax can be checked with the following command:

```
$ polkit-config-file-validate /etc/PolicyKit/PolicyKit.conf
```

Standard PolicyKit policy files are available in the /usr/share/PolicyKit/policy/ directory. If you make changes to files in this directory, the syntax can be checked with the **polkit-policy-file-validate** command.

## Actions on the PolicyKit

Two commands are associated with PolicyKit actions: **polkit-auth** and **polkit-action**. To review current authorizations on your account, the following command lists the basic authorizations:

```
$ polkit-auth
```

It assumes you're looking for authorizations for the current user. For more information, the **--explicit-detail** option can help. When I run that command on my own account (michael), I get the following output, which can be compared directly to the GUI PolicyKit Authorization tool. The first stanza specifies authorization for the current user to access system configuration tools:

```
org.freedesktop.systemtoolsbackends.set
  Authorized:   Yes
  Scope:        Indefinitely
  Obtained:     Thu Oct  3 14:51:10 2008 from root (uid 0)
  Constraint:   Session must be active
```

Do not be concerned about the "indefinite" scope, as it does not carry over to the actual tools. The setting was created by a user with administrative access. In other words, it was probably created by a user with sudo-based administrative privileges. In all cases, the constraint assumes an active session, which means the user must be logged in to use the authorized privilege.

The next stanza allows the current user to revoke the PolicyKit privileges of others:

```
org.freedesktop.policykit.revoke
  Authorized:   Yes
  Scope:        Indefinitely
  Obtained:     Thu Oct  3 17:49:59 2008 from root (uid 0)
  Constraint:   Session must be active
```

This stanza allows the current user to grant PolicyKit privileges to others:

```
org.freedesktop.policykit.grant
  Authorized:   Yes
  Scope:        Indefinitely
  Obtained:     Thu Oct  3 17:50:25 2008 from root (uid 0)
```

The following stanza allows the current user to run tools such as the Users Settings tool to modify user information:

```
org.freedesktop.systemtoolsbackends.self.set
  Authorized:   Yes
  Scope:        Indefinitely
  Obtained:     Thu Oct  3 17:51:03 2008 from root (uid 0)
  Constraint:   Session must be active
```

The following stanza means the current user can read the authorizations granted to others:

```
org.freedesktop.policykit.read
  Authorized:   Yes
  Scope:        Indefinitely
```

```
Obtained:    Thu Oct  3 17:52:00 2008 from root (uid 0)
Constraint:  Session must be active
```

In this case, the current user has permissions to review the PolicyKit authorizations for other users—for example, I can review user donna's authorizations with the following command:

```
$ polkit-auth --user donna --explicit-detail
```

The final stanza means the current user has permissions to modify the default authorizations for other users:

```
org.freedesktop.policykit.modify-defaults
  Authorized:  Yes
  Scope:       Indefinitely
  Obtained:    Thu Oct  3 17:52:12 2008 from root (uid 0)
  Constraint:  Session must be active
```

The **polkit-auth** command can also be used to **--grant**, **--block**, or **--revoke** an authorization. Since I now know that my michael account is authorized, the following command grants access to system configuration tools to user donna:

```
$ polkit-auth --user donna --grant org.freedesktop.policykit.
systemtoolsbackends.net --constraint active
```

The other PolicyKit command is **polkit-action**, primarily related to default settings. But it can also show available options and defaults. For example, the following command lists defaults associated with system configuration tools:

```
$ polkit-action --action org.freedesktop.systemtoolsbackends.set
```

## Restore Default PolicyKit Settings

If there are problems with the PolicyKit and you don't remember the default settings based on the PolicyKit Authorizations tool or any other commands that have been run, they can be reset with the following commands. The first two commands reset the defaults for system administration tools and user customization tools:

```
$ polkit-action --reset-defaults   org.freedesktop.systemtoolsbackends.set
$ polkit-action --reset-defaults   org.freedesktop.systemtoolsbackends.self.set
```

The following two commands reset the defaults for users who can revoke the PolicyKit-based authority given to others and resets the defaults for users who can read the PolicyKit-based authority given to others:

```
$ polkit-action --reset-defaults org.freedesktop.policykit.revoke
$ polkit-action --reset-defaults org.freedesktop.policykit.read
```

The final two commands reset the defaults for users who can modify and grant the PolicyKit-based defaults given to others:

```
$ polkit-action --reset-defaults org.freedesktop.policykit.modify-defaults
$ polkit-action --reset-defaults org.freedesktop.policykit.grant
```

# SUMMARY

The first part of the chapter described user and group authentication as configured through the files of the Shadow Password Suite. You should now be able to create users and groups from GUI tools, from the command line, and by directly editing appropriate files. Users and groups also can be regulated by quotas—based on disk usage and numbers of files.

The traditional Linux method for delegating administrative authority is based on the /etc/sudoers configuration file as well as PAM configuration files in the /etc/pam.d directory. Ubuntu has implemented the PolicyKit for finer-grained control of administrative authority, starting with the Hardy Heron release.

# CHAPTER 11

# Network Configuration and Troubleshooting

U buntu builds on the Linux/Unix heritage as a network-centric operating system.

Network problems can be difficult to diagnose. But with an understanding of how networking is started during the boot process, how networks transmit messages, and how networks route data, you'll be able to diagnose network problems systematically. In this chapter, you'll learn how to configure basic network interfaces and routing tables. You'll examine how Ubuntu works with latest wireless network cards. Finally, you'll also learn how to manage network configuration files directly from the command line and with Ubuntu utilities.

Basic IP addressing is not covered in this book. The latest Ubuntu releases can work well with both IP version 4 (IPv4) and IP version 6 (IPv6) addressing. For simplicity, IPv4 addresses are used throughout the book.

*TIP*   For a primer on IP addressing and related protocols, read *TCP/IP Protocol Suite*, by Behrouz Forouzan, published by McGraw-Hill (2005).

# BASIC NETWORKING

This section shows you how to configure the network card with a numeric IPv4 as well as a hardware MAC (Media Access Control) address. Network communication depends on routing tables. Communication through network gateways depend on properly configured forwarding.

*TIP*   Some administrators choose to disable IPv6 addressing. One way to do so is to disable the directive with the ipv6 module in the /etc/modprobe.d/aliases file and add a **blacklist ipv6** line to the /etc/modprobe.d/blacklist file.

As with other systems, networking is documented and read from configuration files. As wireless networking is becoming a feasible alternative for servers, key wireless configuration commands are described in this part of the chapter. To ease the process, Ubuntu includes a GUI Network Settings tool.

*NOTE*   Because high-speed network connections are almost mandatory for servers, dial-up modems are not discussed in this book. However, since nearly half of US home Internet users still connect online via telephone modem, those of you who support home users need to know how to configure a telephone modem in Linux. One guide is available from https://help.ubuntu.com/community/DialupModemHowto.

## Configure a Network Interface Card

A network interface card (NIC) enables computers to communicate over a wired or wireless network. The primary command used to configure a NIC is the **ifconfig** command. The following sections break down the output from the **ifconfig** command and explain how to use the command to change network settings.

## Current ifconfig Settings

When run by itself, the **ifconfig** command displays current settings associated with configured NICs on the local system. The following output displays two NIC adapters. The *eth0* adapter is the first Ethernet adapter on this system, and the *lo* adapter is known as the *loopback device*, which verifies proper installation of basic network software.

```
$ ifconfig
```

Consider the first line from the output, shown next. Note the hardware address (HWaddr), associated with the first Ethernet card (eth0).

```
eth0  Link encap:Ethernet  HWaddr 00:0c:29:15:2a:4e
```

The second line displays the current IPv4 addresses, associated with the inet addr label. It also displays the broadcast address (Bcast) and network mask (Mask).

```
inet addr:192.168.0.104  Bcast:192.168.0.255  Mask:255.255.255.0
```

The next line specifies the current IPv6 address:

```
 inet6 addr: fe80::20c:29ff:fe15:2a4e/64 Scope:Link
```

The next line indicates that the eth0 adapter is up and running in broadcast mode, can send multicast messages, and is allowed to send up to 1500 bytes per packet:

```
UP BROADCAST RUNNING MULTICAST  MTU:1500  Metric:1
```

The next lines are associated with received (RX) and transmitted (TX) packets, along with errors associated with a busy network or perhaps interference on a wireless network. The last line notes the IRQ (interrupt request) port and base address, also known as the I/O (input/output) address.

```
    RX packets:36632 errors:0 dropped:0 overruns:0 frame:0
    TX packets:35606 errors:0 dropped:0 overruns:0 carrier:0
    collisions:0 txqueuelen:1000
    RX bytes:5935531 (5.6 MB) TX bytes:19185284 (18.2 MB)
    Interrupt:16 Base address:0x1400
```

Similar information is available for the loopback adapter (lo). As no physical network card exists for the loopback adapter, no IRQ or I/O address is assigned to that adapter.

## Change the Network Configuration with ifconfig

The **ifconfig** command can also be used to configure network interfaces. For example, the following command assigns a new IP address to the eth0 NIC:

```
$ sudo ifconfig eth0 192.168.100.1
```

To see the effect of this change, run the **ifconfig eth0** command. The following excerpt shows the relevant output:

```
$ ifconfig eth0
eth0  Link encap:Ethernet  HWaddr 00:0c:29:15:2a:4e
      inet addr: 192.168.100.1 Bcast:192.168.100.255  Mask:255.255.255.0
      inet6 addr: fe80::2e0:4cff:fee3:d106/64 Scope:Link
```

Note that the broadcast address and network mask have also changed, based on default IPv4 settings for this particular address. However, there is no change in the IPv6 address.

With other switches, the **ifconfig** command can be used to modify other settings associated with a NIC. For example, if a non-standard network mask can be specified with a command like the following:

```
$ sudo ifconfig eth0 192.168.100.1 netmask 255.255.0.0
```

Run the **ifconfig** command again, and you'll see that the broadcast address has also been changed to conform to the new IP address and network mask. Two other commonly used switches deactivate and activate the adapter. The following commands deactivate and activate the eth0 adapter:

```
$ sudo ifconfig eth0 down
$ sudo ifconfig eth0 up
```

## Configure a Hardware Address

There are cases when an administrator needs to clone the hardware address of a NIC. For example, some Internet service providers (ISPs) expect to connect to a NIC with a specific unique hardware address. If a NIC has to be replaced for any reason, you can specify the hardware address of your choice. For example, the following command specifies the noted hardware address for the new eth0 NIC:

```
$ sudo ifconfig eth0 hw ether 000c29152a4f
```

This command is simple enough, but it's not the only place where hardware addresses are used. You'll run into hardware addresses again later in this chapter in ARP (Address Resolution Protocol) tables as well as wireless access points.

## Configure Routing Tables

Routing tables help network cards send messages to the right place. Routing tables at the IP address level can and should specify the path messages take to every applicable IP address. Routing tables that use hardware addresses should specify the hostname or IP address available on a local network. Hardware addresses cannot be routed to remote networks.

## An IP Address Routing Table

Believe it or not, routing tables can be configured with the **route** command. The command can be run without an option and is equivalent to **netstat -r**. The following is a sample output:

```
$ route
Kernel routing table
Destination   Gateway        Genmask          Flags Metric  Ref   Iface
localnet      *              255.255.255.0    U     0       0     eth0
default       192.168.0.1    0.0.0.0          UG    100     0     eth0
```

The Destination column lists networks by their IP addresses, hostname, or label. In this output, the *localnet* label is associated with the local network; the *default* label specifies all other IP addresses, as defined in the /etc/networks configuration file. The Gateway column specifies the gateway addresses.

Contrast the preceding output to the output from the **route -n** (or **netstat -nr**) command, from another system:

```
$ route -n
Kernel routing table
Destination   Gateway        Genmask          Flags Metric  Ref   Iface
192.168.0.0   0.0.0.0        255.255.255.0    U     0       0     eth0
192.168.1.0   0.0.0.0        255.255.255.0    U     0       0     eth1
0.0.0.0       192.168.0.1    0.0.0.0          UG    0       0     eth0
```

I prefer to use the **-n** switch, as it does not rely on reverse lookups of DNS servers or /etc/hosts configuration files.

If the destination is on the LAN, no gateway is required, as indicated by the "default" IP address (0.0.0.0). The Genmask column lists the network mask. Networks look for a route appropriate to the destination IP address. The IP address is compared against the destination networks, in order. When the IP address is found to be part of one of these networks, it's sent in that direction. Note the connection between the 192.168.0.0 network to the eth0 NIC, and the 192.168.1.0 network to the eth1 NIC.

If there is a gateway IP address, it's sent to the computer with that address. The Flags column describes how this is done. Flag descriptions are listed in Table 11-1. The last key column is Iface, which stands for the interface device in question.

## Add a Network Route

In Linux network configuration, the **route** command can be used to set up a default gateway for the network. Strictly speaking, a default gateway is the route used if the desired destination address does not exist elsewhere in the routing table. It's the gateway to the default IP address, 0.0.0.0. This output from the **route -n** command suggests no current default gateway address:

```
192.168.0.0   *    255.255.255.0   U    0     0    eth0
```

| Flag | Description |
|------|-------------|
| G | The route uses a gateway. |
| U | The network adapter (Iface) is up. |
| H | Only a single host can be reached via this route. |
| D | This entry was created by an Internet Control Message Protocol (ICMP) redirect message. |
| M | This entry was modified by an ICMP redirect message. |

**Table 11-1.**   The **route** or **netstat** Flag Indicates the Route

A default gateway, in this case, can be added to the routing table with the following command:

```
$ sudo route add default gw 192.168.0.1 dev eth0
```

If there's only one physical network device, the **dev eth0** is not required. Here's a second scenario. Assume you've added another Ethernet card, say with a USB device. Assume it's device eth1, connected to a second network. If any DHCP (Dynamic Host Configuration Protocol) server on the local network is properly configured, the **sudo dhclient eth1** command should add the appropriate information to the routing table.

Alternatively, if you prefer to configure the eth1 NIC statically, use the **ifconfig** command described earlier in this chapter to assign an appropriate IP address. If that doesn't add appropriate information to the routing table, say through the eth1 NIC to the 192.168.100.0 network, you can add it with the following command:

```
$ sudo route add 192.168.100.0 dev eth1
```

## Hardware Routing

The ARP associates the hardware address of a network adapter with an IP address. That hardware address is also known as the MAC address.

The **arp** command displays a table of hardware and IP addresses on the local computer—an *ARP table*. With the **arp** command, you can detect problems such as duplicate addresses on the network, or you can manually add ARP table entries as required. Here's a sample **arp** command, showing all ARP table entries in the local database. I add the **-n** switch to avoid issues with searches through /etc/hosts or DNS servers.

```
$ arp -n
Address          HWtype  HWaddress          Flags Mask   Iface
192.168.0.6      ether   00:18:DE:38:44:71  C             eth0
```

```
192.168.11.254   ether   00:50:56:EC:7D:50   C           eth1
192.168.11.1     ether   00:50:56:C0:00:01   C           eth1
192.168.0.1      ether   00:09:5B:FA:BB:76   C           eth0
```

An empty ARP table suggests that you haven't made any recent connections to other computers. Courtesy of the **-n** switch, the Address column lists IP addresses. The HWtype column shows the hardware type of the remote adapter; *ether* is short for Ethernet. The HWaddress column shows the hardware address of the remote adapter.

The **arp** command can help diagnose problems with duplicate IP addresses, which can stop a network completely. To remove the offending machine's **arp** entry from the local ARP table, use the **arp -d** command:

```
$ sudo arp -d 192.168.11.254
```

This removes all ARP information for the noted IP address. To add an entry to the current ARP table, use the **arp -s** command:

```
$ sudo arp -s 192.168.11.254 00:50:56:EC:7D:50
```

This entry will add the noted IP address with the given hardware address to the ARP table.

# Configure Forwarding

A router is a key device in network communication. Linux systems are commonly configured as routers. Router configuration is an important skill for Ubuntu administrators.

To configure Ubuntu as a router, all you need to do is configure a kernel variable. The following command confirms the default for IPv4 addressing, where Linux is *not* configured as a router:

```
$ cat /proc/sys/net/ipv4/conf/default/forwarding
0
```

If the local computer has two or more network cards, you can configure the system as a router. To do so, enable IP forwarding in /etc/sysctl.conf with the following directive:

```
net.ipv4.ip_forward=1
```

Of course, if IPv6 networking is active, you'll also want to add the following directive:

```
net.ipv6.conf.all.forwarding=1
```

This is different from the command in comments in the default version of the /etc/sysctl .conf configuration file. (For more information, see Debian bug 469557 at http://bugs .debian.org.) But the associated variable file, /proc/sys/net/ipv6/ip_forward, does not exist. Interestingly enough, when the **net.ipv4.ip_forward** variable is set to 1, the **net.ipv4.conf.all.forwarding** variable is also set to 1.

You don't need to reboot to activate these changes; the following command rereads the /etc/sysctl.conf configuration file:

```
$ sudo sysctl -p
```

Finally, to confirm the changes, run the following commands:

```
$ cat /proc/sys/net/ipv4/ip_forward
$ cat /proc/sys/net/ipv6/conf/all/forwarding
```

Be aware that the directive in /etc/sysctl.conf and the associated file in the /proc directory has varied in the past with Ubuntu releases, so don't be surprised if the directive changes again. Refer to the current /etc/sysctl.conf file for the latest information.

# Network Configuration Files

There are a number of other important network configuration files included on an Ubuntu system. The information requested by a client can be customized by an appropriate DHCP client configuration file. Databases that translate domain names, such as www .mhprofessional.com, to IP addresses, such as 12.163.148.249, can be configured either locally in /etc/hosts or can be referenced by /etc/resolv.conf. To prevent conflicts, a name search order can be configured in either /etc/host.conf or /etc/nsswitch.conf. Most other network configuration files are listed in the /etc/network directory.

## A DHCP Client

Ubuntu supports a variety of DHCP clients. While most clients are focused on IPv4 addressing, some administrators prefer to administer their IPv6 networks with appropriate DHCP clients. The default DHCP client uses the /etc/dhcp3/dhclient.conf configuration file from the dhcp3-client package. Many of the options are listed in the dhcp-options man page. A few of the more important suggested directives are examined here.

To activate a directive, remove the comment character (#) from the front of the applicable line. To use the first directive, substitute the actual local hostname for *<hostname>*:

```
send host-name "<hostname>";
```

The **request** directive pulls specified information from the DHCP server. If the hostname was specified for the **send host-name** directive, delete the **host-name** option from the list specified from the following **request** directive. More information on noted commands and directives is shown in Table 11-2.

```
request subnet-mask, broadcast-address, time-offset, routers,
        domain-name, domain-name-servers, host-name,
        netbios-name-servers, netbios-scope;
```

| Directive | Description |
|---|---|
| send | Provides information for the directives that follow |
| host-name | Specifies the hostname |
| request | Asks for information related to the directives that follow |
| subnet-mask | Specifies the subnet mask, also known as the network mask |
| broadcast-address | Specifies the broadcast address |
| time-offset | Specifies the time offset, in seconds, relative to UTC |
| routers | Notes the IP address for connected routers |
| domain-name | Notes the domain name for the local network |
| domain-name-servers | Associated with the DNS (Domain Name System) server |
| netbios-name-servers | Acquires Windows Internet Name Service (WINS) servers |
| netbios-scope | Identifies configured logical NetBIOS (Network Basic Input/Output System) networks on the LAN |

**Table 11-2.**   Key Directives from **dhclient.conf**

The default version of /etc/dhcp3/dhclient.conf includes commented stanzas that can help configure a fixed IP address, and conditions for a specific IP address lease.

## /etc/hosts

Before DNS services became popular, databases of hostnames and IP addresses were set up in a static text file, /etc/hosts. When just a few nodes were on the network that eventually turned into the Internet, it was practical to maintain identical /etc/hosts files on each computer.

As the number of computers on a smaller network is not as overwhelming, some smaller networks still use /etc/hosts, synchronized by the Network Information Service (NIS) server described in Chapter 12. The following is an excerpt from my /etc/hosts, which lists the IP address, fully qualified domain name, and alias for one system:

```
192.168.0.60    linux1.mommabears.com  laptop
```

## /etc/resolv.conf

There are many millions of hosts on the Internet. Even if it were possible to collect all domain names and IP addresses into a /etc/hosts file, the file would overwhelm every computer. And it would overwhelm every network administrator who would have to make sure that all the /etc/hosts files on the Internet match—and are updated every time a new website appears. That's why DNS was developed. The most common DNS server on Linux systems is based on the Berkeley Internet Name Domain (BIND). In /etc/resolv.conf, the IP address of each DNS server is listed with a simple line similar to this:

```
nameserver 192.168.0.1
```

## Which Comes First, DNS or /etc/hosts?

Many networks configure an /etc/hosts file for the local network and a DNS server for other networks and/or the Internet. When your computer looks for an IP address, some older applications refer to the fairly simple /etc/host.conf configuration file to determine the database to search first.

```
order hosts,bind
multi on
```

The first line means the local system first looks through /etc/hosts before looking to the DNS servers configured in /etc/resolv.conf. The **bind** refers to DNS, as it is short for the Berkeley Internet Name Domain. The **multi on** line means that a search returns all valid IP addresses for a hostname configured in /etc/hosts. If more than one IP address is associated with a hostname, that's usually an error.

Most applications look to one line in the /etc/nsswitch.conf configuration file for the name search order. The order means that the local database (/etc/hosts) is searched before DNS servers.

```
hosts: files dns
```

Other databases can be included in the search order, which is one reason the /etc/nsswitch.conf file supersedes /etc/host.conf in most cases. For example, if there's an active NIS server, a Samba database of hostnames, and an LDAP server, you might see the following line in /etc/nsswitch.conf (the order can vary):

```
hosts: files dns nis ldap winbind
```

## /etc/network/interfaces

The default network settings for an Ubuntu system are stored in the /etc/network/interfaces configuration file. This file could seem cryptic to newer Linux users, so I'll analyze one version from my system, line by line. First, the **auto** directive identifies the network interface to be configured—in this case, the loopback adapter, as noted by the **lo** label:

```
auto lo
```

Without the **auto** directive, the specified interface is not activated the next time you administratively run the **/etc/init.d/networking restart** script or the **ifup -a** command.

But that directive does not actually configure a loopback adapter. The interface also needs to be configured, and that's the purpose of the **iface** directive. It applies IPv4 networking, as defined by the **inet** directive (IPv6 networking would be configured with **inet6**), along with the **loopback** address, to the loopback adapter, **lo**:

```
iface lo inet loopback
```

The next set of directives illustrates that their order is not critical. The directive that follows, as suggested by the **static** directive, specifies a static configuration, using IPv4 addressing, for interface eth0:

```
iface eth0 inet static
```

To configure a DHCP client, replace **static** with **dhcp**. In that case, no further information is required for the interface, as it would normally be configured by the remote DHCP server.

Assuming a static configuration, the specified IP **address** is shown here:

```
address 192.168.0.104
```

The **netmask** (short for network mask) and **gateway** addresses are configured next. The **gateway** directive specifies the IP address associated with the default route.

```
netmask 255.255.255.0
gateway 192.168.0.1
```

If you didn't configure DNS servers on the DHCP server, you could do so with the following directive:

```
dns-nameservers 68.87.69.146 68.87.85.98
```

Finally, the following configures a specific wireless network ID, based on the Extended Service Set ID (ESSID). The **wireless-essid** directive shown here names my home wireless network ID, katiedickens (named after our dog and cat):

```
wireless-essid katiedickens
```

Additional directives are available for the /etc/network/interfaces file. Commonly used directives, including those already described, are listed in Table 11-3.

## Other /etc/network/ Configuration Files

Other /etc/network configuration files include scripts that are also run when networking is started or stopped. These scripts are all located in subdirectories of /etc/network and are described in Table 11-4. Scripts in the if-up.d/ or if-pre-up.d/ subdirectories are activated by the **ifup** command. Scripts in the if-down.d/ or if-post-down.d/ subdirectories are deactivated by the **ifdown** command.

| Directive | Purpose |
|---|---|
| **auto** | Identifies the network device file, such as **lo** and **eth0** |
| **allow-hotplug** | Supports hotplug and play access to network interfaces |
| **iface** | Identifies the network address system and type associated with a device |
| **lo** | Notes the loopback adapter |
| **eth0** | Specifies the first Ethernet card; uses the same name as network device files, such as eth1, ath0, wlan0, and so on |
| **static** | Specifies a static IP address |
| **dhcp** | Points the associated device to a DHCP server |
| **bootp** | Points the network device to a DHCP server on a remote network |
| **inet** | Configures IPv4 networking |
| **inet6** | Configures IPv6 networking |
| **address** | Precedes a static IP address |
| **netmask** | Precedes a static IP address network mask |
| **gateway** | Precedes a default gateway IP address for the network |
| **hwaddress** | Precedes a hardware address |
| **hostname** | Specifies the hostname |
| **network** | Specifies the network address |
| **dns-nameservers** | Assigns a DNS server |

**Table 11-3.** Common /etc/network/interfaces Directives

Several other services can be configured in the directories listed in Table 11-4. For example, when I configure the SSH and Postfix servers on another Ubuntu system, associated scripts are added to the /etc/network/if-up.d/ directory.

# Wireless Networking

Experienced users may shudder at the thought of connecting servers via wireless networks for at least two reasons: such networks are less reliable than wired networks, and are more prone to interference. But as 802.11n networks come online, more users will configure servers connected via wireless networks. To that end, Ubuntu server administrators need to

| Script | Subdirectory of /etc/network | Purpose |
|---|---|---|
| wireless-tools | if-pre-up.d/, if-post-down.d | Activates and deactivates wireless interfaces |
| wpasupplicant | all | Reads and uses WPA keys for a wireless network, as available; identical in all four directories |
| mountnfs | if-up.d/ | Mounts NFS filesystems configured in /etc/fstab |
| ntpdate | if-up.d/ | Starts the NTP service, if configured to start on boot |

**Table 11-4.** Typical /etc/network Scripts

know the basic configuration commands associated with wireless networking. The **iwlist**, **iwconfig**, and **iwgetid** commands are covered in this section.

But first, it's important to realize that Linux and Ubuntu don't support all wireless cards. Determining which cards are supported can be difficult. Ubuntu provides a current list of supported cards at https://help.ubuntu.com/community/WifiDocs/ WirelessCardsSupported. As suggested in Chapter 1, some wireless support is based on proprietary drivers in the Ubuntu restricted repository.

If your wireless card is not listed in the noted wiki or one of the many other Linux-related wireless projects, the next step is to find more information on the installed card, with the **lspci** command. More information is available with the **-v** and **-vv** switches.

If you have one of the few wireless devices not yet recognized by Ubuntu, the ndiswrapper packages might help, on x86 systems. Once these packages are installed, they include a "wrapper" that translates an installed Microsoft driver for Linux. For more information, see http://ndiswrapper.sourceforge.net. I avoid ndiswrapper where real Linux drivers are available.

Now on to the wireless configuration commands.

## iwlist

The **iwlist** command can be used to find information on available access points, which can then be used to change wireless networks. The **iwlist** command by itself provides information on its functionality, in the following format:

```
Usage: iwlist [interface] scanning [essid NNN] [last]
```

The [interface] is the device file associated with the network adapter, such as eth1 or wlan0. As noted in the associated man page, scanning can be shortened to scan. You can specify the name of the wireless network to be listed by its ESSID. If you've previously scanned for available wireless networks, the last option reads the results of that previous scan.

To view available wireless network access points, I often run the following command:

```
$ iwlist eth1 scan
```

If you're already connected to a wireless network, you might first need to disconnect from that network; a simple method for test purposes is with the following command, which tries to connect to some nonexistent network ESSID of **adsj**:

```
$ sudo iwconfig eth1 essid adsj
```

When I then run the **iwlist eth1 scan** command from my living room in a semi-urban neighborhood, I see 21 wireless access points (of which 10 are not encrypted).

## iwconfig

The **iwconfig** command is designed to configure a wireless network interface. By itself, it lists the wireless extensions associated with existing network adapters. If the network adapter is a wired connection, the corresponding message looks like this:

```
eth0      no wireless extensions
```

If the network adapter is wireless, it provides a lot of information about the interface, in some ways, the information is similar to that shown earlier in this chapter in the output to the **ifconfig** command. When I run **iwconfig eth1** on my system, I get the following output:

```
eth1 IEEE 802.11g  ESSID:"katiedickens"
     Mode:Managed Frequency:2.412 GHz Access Point: 00:14:D1:C0:36:44
     Bit Rate:54 Mb/s    Tx-Power:15 dBm
     Retry limit:15    RTS thr:off    Fragment thr:off
     Power Management:off
     Link Quality=84/100 Signal level=-42 dBm Noise level=-61 dBm
     Rx invalid nwid:0  Rx invalid crypt:0   Rx invalid frag:0
     Tx excessive retries:0  Invalid misc:3537   Missed beacon:0
```

This information is broken down in Table 11-5. Several of these parameters can be customized with the right **iwconfig** options.

While the connection protocol may be fixed, the **iwconfig** command can be used to change other parameters. For example, the following command points the wlan0 wireless adapter to a wireless network access point named *default*:

```
$ sudo iwconfig wlan0 essid default
```

| iwconfig Output | Description |
|---|---|
| IEEE 802.11g | Notes the connection protocol; others include 802.11a, 802.11b, and so on; *unassociated* means no valid connection |
| ESSID | Points to the wireless network name |
| Mode | Specifies the functionality of the device |
| Frequency | Notes the transmission frequency |
| Access Point | Lists the hardware address of the remote access point |
| Bit Rate | Notes the current maximum transmission rate |
| Tx-Power | Specifies current transmission power, in decibels |
| Link Quality | Measures the quality of the connection |
| Rx | Reads the number of problems in received packets |
| Tx | Reads the number of problems in transmitted packets |

**Table 11-5.**   Output from the **iwconfig** Command

If the network in question is not open, this command isn't enough. You'll need the encryption key. The following command connects to the network named *Friend* with the noted encryption (**enc**) key. The **enc** and **key** options are synonymous.

```
$ sudo iwconfig eth1 essid Friend enc 2C0BB80617
```

On occasion, you might encounter two adjacent wireless networks with the same ESSID. In that case, you can specify the desired connection with the hardware address of the access point:

```
$ sudo iwconfig eth1 ap 00:14:D1:C0:36:45
```

## iwgetid

The **iwgetid** command identifies specific information also found in the output to the **iwconfig** command. By itself, it identifies the current ESSID. Other important switches are intuitive; for example, the **iwgetid -a** command identifies the current access point hardware address, and the **iwgetid -c** command identifies the current channel. For a full list, see the man page or run the **iwgetid -h** command.

# The Network Settings Tool

The Network Settings tool is a GUI option for configuring network devices on an Ubuntu system. It requires administrative privileges associated with the PolicyKit discussed in Chapter 10. Assuming your account has appropriate privileges, start the Network Settings tool with the **network-admin** command. Ubuntu detects and configures most network adapters automatically; those adapters are displayed in the window shown in Figure 11-1.

In most cases, network adapters are automatically detected during the installation process. If you find that one or more network adapters aren't displayed in the Network Settings window, review the output from the **lspci**, **lsusb**, or **lspcmcia** command. You might just need to find, install, and load the associated network driver.

The Network Settings tool includes four series of configuration options, organized by tabs: Connections, General, DNS, and Hosts.

## Connections Tab

The Connections tab of the Network Settings window displays detected network adapters. There are three adapters shown in Figure 11-1; the two of interest are two wired connections. To configure a detected connection, highlight it and click Properties. It supports

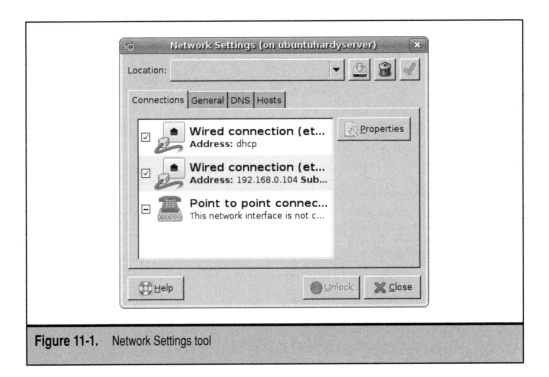

**Figure 11-1.** Network Settings tool

static and DHCP client-based connections, as well as the so-called "Zero Configuration Networking," implemented by Apple as Bonjour, by Microsoft as Automatic Private IP Addressing (APIPA), and by Linux as Avahi. Related packages can be reviewed with the **apt-cache search avahi** command.

## General Tab

There are two settings available under the General tab: Host Name and Domain Name. The Host Name corresponds to the name of the system, also known as the hostname. Changes made to this setting are reflected in the /etc/hostname and /etc/hosts configuration files.

If you set a Domain Name, it should be set to the domain name for the local network. For private networks, one option is to use the example.com, example.net, and example .org domain names, which are normally reserved for documentation. The Domain Name assigned here is recorded in the /etc/resolv.conf configuration file.

## DNS Tab

There are two options provided on this tab: DNS Servers and Search Domains. DNS Servers can be added and deleted, if you know their IP addresses. Some ISPs allow businesses or even home networkers to use their DNS servers; otherwise, you can create your own DNS server, as described in Chapter 14.

The Search Domains option adds a domain name suffix to a hostname. For example, when I added google.com to the list, I could type *news* into the address text box in a *graphical* browser. It adds google.com to the end of *news*, and then my browser navigated to news.google.com.

## Hosts Tab

The Hosts tab provides a view of the local /etc/hosts configuration file. Of course, it supports deleting the entries of your choice from this file. If you want to add an entry to this file, you'll need the IP address and alias(es) such as the hostname or fully qualified domain name (FQDN) of the system.

# NETWORK TROUBLESHOOTING

Anyone can look through log files and search online for similar problems. But that's not enough to understand what's really happening. To troubleshoot a network, you need to know how networks start during the boot process. Then you can intelligently troubleshoot a wired network connection and a wireless connection. You should also know how to troubleshoot routing issues as well as network services.

Messages associated with network problems are often sent to log files. For more information on available log files, see Chapter 7.

# Networking in the Boot Process

Ubuntu has a well-deserved reputation as an operating system that "just works." But problems do arise. To understand what might go wrong, it's important to understand how networking starts and is configured during the boot process.

As Linux is loaded, network hardware is eventually detected and appropriate network modules are loaded. If a problem occurs when hardware should be detected, it may be revealed through the kernel ring buffer discussed in Chapter 4 and available in the /var/log/dmesg log file. If a new problem occurs with an existing hardware component, the problem can require a comparison between the latest and an earlier version of that log file.

Once Linux is loaded, it starts a series of scripts in two different directories: /etc/rcS.d and /etc/rc2.d. The only network-related script from these directories is /etc/rcS.d/S40networking, which is linked to the /etc/init.d/networking script. As the script starts with an *S*, it is a *start* script. Read through the script. It uses the **ifup** and **ifdown** commands, which reads settings in the /etc/network/interfaces configuration file and appropriate /etc/network/ subdirectories, as described earlier in the section "Network Configuration Files."

Changes to these configuration files can affect how the network works on the system.

# Troubleshoot a Network Connection

Troubleshooting a network connection can be a straightforward, step-by-step process. With the **ping** command, you can make sure current interfaces work on the local system, test connections to remote systems on the local network, and test connections to remote networks. When you run the **ping** command to a URL such as www.mhprofessional.com, be prepared to press CTRL-C to stop the **ping**, or run the command with the **-c** *n* switch. For example, the **ping -c 4 www.mhprofessional.com** command sends four pings. When I have doubts about my network, I usually test network connections in the following order:

1. Run the **ping 127.0.0.1** command to verify that the network connection can see the local system. If problems arise, the loopback adapter might not be active. If you suspect this, try the **ifconfig** command. If you don't see the lo adapter in the output, the loopback adapter is more likely to be the problem.

2. Run the **ping localhost** command. If you see an "unknown host" message, there could be a problem with the /etc/hosts configuration file, which should contain the following line:

   ```
   127.0.0.1 localhost
   ```

3. Run the **ping** command on the local IP address associated with the network card. If unsure, the IP address is shown in the output to the **ifconfig** command. For example, as the IP address on my eth0 adapter is 192.168.0.104, I run the following command:

   ```
   $ ping -c 4 192.168.0.104
   ```

   If you have more than one network card, run the **ping** command on the IP address associated with each network card.

4. Run the **ping** command on the local hostname, as shown in /etc/hostname. Problems with this command might indicate that the hostname is not properly shown in /etc/hosts or is not properly configured in the database of a locally authoritative DNS server.

5. Run the **ping** command on the IP address of another system on the LAN. If you don't know any other IP address on the LAN, try the gateway address, as revealed in the output to the **route -n** command. Problems with this command may indicate a physical or some other type of break in the LAN.

6. Run the **ping** command on the hostname or FQDN of another system on the LAN. Problems with this command might indicate that the hostname of the remote system is not properly shown in /etc/hosts or is not properly configured in a locally authoritative DNS server.

7. Finally, **ping** an external address such as www.mcgraw-hill.com. If there's a problem with this command, try a different external address. If there's still a problem, you might need to do a bit more troubleshooting, as described in the next section.

   If you suspect a problem with one of the applicable DNS servers, you might try applying the **ping** command to the IP address of that server.

The IPv6 version of the **ping** command is **ping6**, which can be used in the same way; of course, **ping6** works with IPv6 addresses.

## Troubleshoot a Network Route

Assuming the network you're on has a connection to the Internet (or some other external network), two problems are possible if a **ping** can't reach a remote destination: The DNS server listed in the /etc/resolv.conf configuration file described earlier might be wrong, or there's a break in the network between the local system and the destination.

The IP address in /etc/resolv.conf should be that of the DNS server you configure or that of the ISP associated which serves your network.

If the DNS server checks out, the **traceroute** command can help. One interesting experiment is to run the **traceroute** command on a URL in a different country. For example, if you're not located in Europe, try the **traceroute www.ubuntu.com** command. You'll see the addresses of routers in many interesting places.

The **traceroute** command can help diagnose problems with enterprise-level networks. If you have a problem connecting to a remote office, run the **traceroute** command on a URL or IP address of the remote system. It might identify the router or gateway that is not forwarding packets.

The IPv6 version of the **traceroute** command is **traceroute6**, which can be used in the same way, of course, with IPv6 addresses.

## Troubleshoot Network Channels

The **ping** and **traceroute** commands do not provide enough information to troubleshoot network problems. You could **ping** a remote system and still be unable to connect to it. There are 65,000 TCP/IP ports available. While successful **ping** and **traceroute** commands can receive responses through port 7, that does not mean other ports are open for other services. For that purpose, the **netstat** and **nmap** commands can help.

If you need more information than **netstat** or **nmap** can provide, the **tcpdump** command captures packets on the network. Many administrators use the Wireshark utility to read each packet in a GUI. In fact, Wireshark is one way to determine whether users or administrators are transmitting passwords in clear text over a network.

## Review Network Connections with netstat

You've already seen how the **netstat -nr** command can specify the current routing table. But it can do so much more—on the local system. Try the **netstat -altun** command. Analyze the switches. The **-a** inspects all sockets where a service is listening and where a connection is established. The **-l** specifies all ports to which the local system is listening for connections. The **-t** specifies connections associated with TCP (Transmission Control Protocol) data; the **-u** specifies connections associated with UDP (User Datagram Protocol) data. The **-n** works as it did before with the **netstat** command, as it specifies IP addresses in numeric format. One sample output from one of my Ubuntu Hardy Heron servers is shown in Figure 11-2.

Connections are defined by protocol (TCP or UDP), local and remote (Foreign) address, the TCP/IP port number, and its current status (State). TCP connections can be regulated with the TCP Wrappers security system. TCP/IP port numbers can be used to regulate remote access. Each of these security options is discussed in Chapter 18.

For example, take the line associated with port 631:

```
tcp   0   0 0.0.0.0:631    0.0.0.0:*     LISTEN
```

```
Active Internet connections (servers and established)
Proto Recv-Q Send-Q Local Address          Foreign Address       State
tcp      0      0 0.0.0.0:9571            0.0.0.0:*             LISTEN
tcp      0      0 0.0.0.0:9572            0.0.0.0:*             LISTEN
tcp      0      0 127.0.0.1:3306          0.0.0.0:*             LISTEN
tcp      0      0 0.0.0.0:139             0.0.0.0:*             LISTEN
tcp      0      0 192.168.11.128:53       0.0.0.0:*             LISTEN
tcp      0      0 192.168.0.104:53        0.0.0.0:*             LISTEN
tcp      0      0 127.0.0.1:53            0.0.0.0:*             LISTEN
tcp      0      0 0.0.0.0:631             0.0.0.0:*             LISTEN
tcp      0      0 0.0.0.0:25              0.0.0.0:*             LISTEN
tcp      0      0 127.0.0.1:953           0.0.0.0:*             LISTEN
tcp      0      0 127.0.0.1:6010          0.0.0.0:*             LISTEN
tcp      0      0 0.0.0.0:445             0.0.0.0:*             LISTEN
tcp      0      0 127.0.0.1:44791         127.0.0.1:6010        ESTABLISHED
tcp      0      0 127.0.0.1:6010          127.0.0.1:44790       ESTABLISHED
tcp      0      0 127.0.0.1:44790         127.0.0.1:6010        ESTABLISHED
tcp      0      0 127.0.0.1:6010          127.0.0.1:44791       ESTABLISHED
tcp6     0      0 :::80                   :::*                  LISTEN
tcp6     0      0 :::53                   :::*                  LISTEN
tcp6     0      0 :::22                   :::*                  LISTEN
tcp6     0      0 :::631                  :::*                  LISTEN
tcp6     0      0 ::1:953                 :::*                  LISTEN
:
```

**Figure 11-2.** Sample output with local network connections

The 0.0.0.0 is the default IP address. The local system is listening to connection requests on Port 631. As discussed in Chapter 9, that port is associated with CUPS (Common Unix Printing System). In other words, the local system is listening to CUPS print requests from all addresses—unless you've configured CUPS on a non-standard TCP/IP port number.

## Identify Open Ports with nmap

The **netstat** command works only on a local system. To see the face a server presents to a network, the **nmap** command can help. I run it from my laptop, reviewing open ports from my Ubuntu Server system. From the output, I can review available services based on the IP address (or hostname) of the target server:

```
$ nmap 192.168.0.104

Starting Nmap 4.53 ( http://insecure.org ) at 2008-04-08 13:13 PDT
Interesting ports on ubuntuhardyserver.example.net (192.168.0.104):
Not shown: 1707 closed ports
PORT      STATE SERVICE
22/tcp   open   ssh
25/tcp   open   smtp
53/tcp   open   domain
80/tcp   open   http
139/tcp  open   netbios-ssn
445/tcp  open   microsoft-ds
631/tcp  open   ipp

Nmap done: 1 IP address (1 host up) scanned in 2.939 seconds
```

On an Ubuntu system, open ports as defined by the output to the **nmap** command are associated with running services. To verify this, stop a service revealed by **nmap** output. For example, based on the preceding output, I can stop the Apache web server on the remote system with the following command:

```
$ sudo /etc/init.d/apache2 stop
```

The next time I run the **nmap** command to review open ports on my Ubuntu server, port 80, associated with the HTTP protocol, is no longer open.

*CAUTION*   Be aware that the **nmap** command is a common tool for crackers trying to crack remote systems. As such, **nmap** messages may be regulated or rejected by some ISPs or server administrators.

## Possible Firewall Issues

Just because a port is open doesn't mean that it's accessible. Firewalls don't have to block traffic to secure a system. A firewall can regulate how traffic is sent over a network. One common **iptables** directive can regulate the number or rate associated with responses to a **ping** command. Similarly, a firewall can log connection attempts through open ports.

# Troubleshoot Network Services

This section provides a general overview of the troubleshooting of network services. If a service is not working, it might not be running. For example, when there's a network problem, the first thing I usually do is to start or restart networking based on the configuration files described in the first part of the chapter, with commands such as:

```
$ sudo /etc/init.d/networking start
$ sudo /etc/init.d/networking restart
```

Strictly speaking, networking is not a network service. However, if a problem occurs with a network service, it's a good idea to make sure networking is running properly. Alternatively, the service script, when run on its own, reveals available options. For example, the following output suggests options associated with the DHCP server script:

```
$ sudo /etc/init.d/dhcp3-server
Usage: /etc/init.d/dhcp3-server {start|stop|restart|force-reload|status}
```

The command options are almost self-explanatory: the options can start, stop, restart, and display the current status of the DHCP server service. The **force-reload** option can be used without restarting the DHCP server, to re-read a newly revised configuration file.

Another example relates to the Postfix e-mail server:

```
$ sudo /etc/init.d/postfix
 * Usage: /etc/init.d/postfix {start|stop|restart|reload|flush|check|
abort|force-reload}
```

A couple of additional command options are available. The **flush** option removes e-mail from any configured queue. The **check** option reviews the syntax of the associated configuration files.

Some common troubleshooting tools are syntax checkers, which are service-specific. For example, the **testparm** command inspects the syntax of the main Samba server configuration file. The **apache2ctl -t** command inspects the syntax of included Apache configuration files.

# SUMMARY

This chapter described the configuration and troubleshooting of network interfaces. As this book is focused on Ubuntu Server, it assumes the server system is connected through a high-speed network. Servers need Internet connections with appropriately configured IP address and hardware routing tables. I've also shown you how to configure IP forwarding, as many servers are also configured as routers or gateways between private networks and the Internet. Since high-speed networking is coming to wireless networks, the chapter included a discussion of configuration tools for wireless adapters.

Network troubleshooting can be done systematically, using the tools described in this chapter. Networks are started systematically during the boot process, using a few key configuration files. Network connections can be troubleshot systematically with the **ping** and **traceroute** commands. With the **netstat** and **nmap** commands, you can review open channels. With some general knowledge of basic network service scripts, you can address many related issues.

# CHAPTER 12

## Manage Network Authentication

While all Linux systems support local authentication by default, network administrators usually configure a single authentication database over a network. A single authentication database means users need to remember only one password, and the administrator need not maintain separate databases on each system.

Two common options to this end are the Network Information Service (NIS) and the Lightweight Directory Access Protocol (LDAP). These services can also manage databases of configuration files and more. As the focus of this chapter is network authentication, the descriptions in this chapter are limited to that topic.

There are other network authentication options available. Some administrators prefer the older Samba authentication system based on Microsoft NT 4 domains. While no longer supported by Microsoft, these systems are still supported on Linux and is therefore a viable option. Samba on Linux can be easily configured as a Primary Domain Controller (PDC) or a member of a Windows 2000/2003 Active Directory (AD). When Samba 4 is finally released, it will be configurable as an AD domain controller. For more information, see http://samba.org/samba/docs/man/Samba-HOWTO-Collection/samba-pdc.html.

As NIS clients and servers can be configured from the same Ubuntu packages, the associated sections are described by configuration file. However, as LDAP clients and servers are configured from separate packages, those sections are organized differently.

# NETWORK INFORMATION SERVICE

The NIS provides a centralized database for multiple systems on a local network. It's the traditional option for Unix and Linux systems. It's easier to maintain one database on a central server as opposed to distributed databases on every client. Users can be sure that the same username and password works on every client.

You'll see how to install NIS on an Ubuntu system, how to configure domains, how to manage related configuration files, and how to set up appropriate database maps. Both client and server implementations of NIS are contained in the same package.

> **NOTE** NIS is inherently insecure. Access should be limited to select clients on the local network. Related TCP/IP ports should be fixed and blocked by an appropriate firewall. Fixed IP addresses for at least the NIS servers can also enhance security.

## Prepare a Network for NIS

When I prepare a network for NIS, I designate one system as a master server. For test purposes, I also assign a second system as an NIS client.

On the NIS master server, I set up several different users that do not already exist on the slave or client. Once the setup of NIS servers and clients is complete, I can then log into the NIS client systems as one of those users from the NIS server.

Note that an NIS server cannot work alone. Unless appropriate home directories already exist on all NIS clients, users who log into an NIS client may not have a home directory. To that end, many networks that use NIS also share the /home directory from the NIS server using the Network File System (NFS) described in Chapter 16.

## Installation and NIS Domains

As both client and server are all rolled into a single package, the following command can be run to install NIS on all target client and server systems:

```
$ sudo apt-get install nis
```

The make and portmap packages are dependencies; in other words, this command makes sure they're installed. The make package allows you to recompile a group of configuration files and more. It's useful for processing changes to the NIS service—as well as other systems such as the Linux kernel, as discussed in Chapter 19. The portmap package is required for NIS as well as similar services such as NFS, discussed in Chapter 16.

When installing NIS, the first part of the configuration process begins automatically. You're presented with a screen that requests the name of the NIS domain. It can be, but doesn't have to be, the same name used for the domain name for the local network. If you're configuring an NIS client, enter the current NIS domain name.

If you don't already have an NIS server, the service tries to bind to one as a client. If this is the first NIS system on the local network, it won't succeed. If you want to change the NIS domain name in the future, you can run the **sudo dpkg-reconfigure nis** command or just modify it directly in the /etc/defaultdomain configuration file and reload or restart the NIS service.

## Make portmap Responsive

Before the portmap service can be networked with NIS (or other services such as NFS), it needs to be available to more than just the local system. To do so, make sure the following directive in the /etc/default/portmap configuration file is commented out:

```
#OPTIONS="-i 127.0.0.1"
```

The /etc/default/portmap file is designed to include switches and options that are applied when starting the portmap service. More information on such switches are available from the portmap man page.

If you'd rather configure the NIS server before allowing NIS clients to connect, don't make the noted change until the NIS server is configured to your satisfaction.

# Configuration Files

After portmap has been configured, you're ready to customize appropriate configuration files. The /etc/defaultdomain configuration file sets the default NIS domain for all systems. The /etc/default/nis file sets basic configuration conditions for the local system and can help configure an NIS server and client. The /etc/init.d/nis script uses these configuration conditions. The /etc/yp.conf file configures NIS clients. The /etc/ypserv.conf and /etc/ypserv.securenets files are used for NIS servers. The associated /var/yp/Makefile is extensive and is therefore covered after this section, in "The NIS Makefile."

## /etc/defaultdomain

The /etc/defaultdomain configuration file is simple; it specifies the domain name for the NIS system on the local network. Of course, you can edit this configuration file directly and then restart or reload the service with the /etc/init.d/nis script. Alternatively, the **sudo dpkg-reconfigure nis** command described earlier performs both functions.

## /etc/default/nis

The /etc/default/nis configuration file makes it easier for administrators to set up a system as a client or server. It's cited by the /etc/init.d/nis script to start and stop NIS services. Most of the directives are straightforward, especially with the comments. The first directive can be changed from false to support configuration as a *master* or *slave* NIS server.

```
NISSERVER=false
```

Even if you're configuring a system as an NIS server, that system should also be configured as a client. So unless you're experimenting with special situations, there's no reason to change the following directive:

```
NISCLIENT=true
```

The files of the Shadow Password Suite are located in the /etc directory. Unless you configure substitute authentication files in another directory, there's no reason to change the following directive:

```
YPPWDDIR=/etc
```

Many administrators allow users to change personal information associated with their usernames, associated with the comment field listed in the /etc/passwd configuration file. If that applies to you, add the **chfn** command to the following directive. The default version of this directive allows users to change their login shell, which is desirable for gurus who prefer to work at different command line interfaces.

```
YPCHANGEOK=chsh
```

If you're configuring an NIS slave server as a backup to an NIS master, add the hostname or fully qualified domain name (FQDN) of the NIS master to the following directive. IP addresses are encouraged to avoid problems with name resolution.

```
NISMASTER=
```

The following directives support command options for the **ypserv**, **ypbind**, **yppasswdd**, and **ypxfrd** daemons, respectively:

```
YPSERVARGS=
YPBINDARGS=
YPPASSWDDARGS=
YPXFRDARGS=
```

In order, these daemons are associated with the NIS server, configure the binding process between NIS servers and clients, support user configured password changes, and allow authentication database transfers between NIS master and slave servers. One practice that supports port-specific firewall tools is restrictions on associated ports. Look for empty port numbers in the /etc/services configuration file. Depending on the firewall used, access can be limited to ports below 1024. For example, I assign the following port numbers with the noted directives:

```
YPSERVARGS="-p 801"
YPBINDARGS="-p 802"
YPPASSWDDARGS="-p 803"
YPXFRDARGS="-p 804"
```

Additional directives and variables in the /etc/init.d/nis script can be configured in /etc/default/nis. However, the default version of the subject configuration file includes all directives needed to configure a system as an NIS client or server.

## /etc/ypserv.conf

While /etc/ypserv.conf is the nominal configuration file for NIS servers, it's often left unchanged. Most NIS server settings are already configured in /etc/default/nis, and other changes can be made to the /var/yp/Makefile. In most cases, directives in this file are intended to promote system security; I believe a better approach is through the /etc/ypserv.securenets configuration file.

However, three default commands are listed in the default version of this file. No additional configuration is required in the /etc/ypserv.conf configuration file, but some use it to limit access to systems on the local network. Directives in this file are formatted in four columns, separated by colons:

▼ **Host**   Corresponds to the allowed IP address(es), such as 192.168.0.1, 10.0.0.0/255.0.0.0, and 172.16.0.0/16.

■ **Domain**   Specifies the NIS domain name for which the directive applies.

■ **Map**   Notes the database in the /var/yp configuration file with the compiled authentication information.

▲ **Security**   Corresponds to access limits. May be set to none, which always allows access; port, which allows access on ports below 1024; and deny, which always denies access.

## /etc/ypserv.securenets

The default settings in the /etc/ypserv.securenets configuration file support access by the localhost system (on the 127.0.0.0 network), and all clients (based on the default IPv4 address of 0.0.0.0), with the following directives:

```
255.0.0.0  127.0.0.0

0.0.0.0  0.0.0.0
```

I strongly recommend that you delete or at least comment out the second directive and replace it. You could limit access to a specific local network with a directive such as this:

```
255.255.255.0   192.168.0.0
```

Some administrators prefer to specify NIS clients by IP address. Of course, such clients must be given static IP addresses for this level of security to work. And don't forget to add the IP address of the NIS server to the list.

```
host 192.168.0.153
host 192.168.0.104
host 192.168.0.50
```

## Client Configuration in /etc/yp.conf

The /etc/yp.conf configuration file is the primary NIS client configuration file. With reliable network connections, all that's required in this file is to add the hostname or IP address of NIS master and slave servers. The following directives assume NIS servers on the noted IP addresses:

```
ypserver 192.168.0.104
ypserver 192.168.0.50
```

If you're uncertain about the hostnames or IP addresses of NIS servers, you could add a **broadcast** directive. But because it's important to limit access to NIS, a broadcast would be less than secure. If there are problems connecting from an NIS client, check the communications channels first. Check the network. Check any open ports on any firewall between the client and server. Check broadcast ports. Such troubleshooting techniques are discussed in Chapter 11.

Some other distributions also include the name of the NIS domain, but the NIS domain should already be configured in the /etc/defaultdomain configuration file.

## The NIS Makefile

The primary configuration file for NIS is the /var/yp/Makefile file, which has to be compiled. Once properly configured, it incorporates the authentication files of the Shadow Password Suite. The Makefile includes a lot of detail. The following directive, if active, allows the NIS server to use DNS to identify NIS clients. If you've configured clients in the aforementioned /etc/ypserv.securenets file, there's no need to activate this directive.

```
B=-b
```

If slave (backup) NIS servers have been configured, change the following from *true* to *false*. The NIS server looks for the names or IP addresses of slave servers in the /var/yp/ypservers configuration file.

```
NOPUSH=true
```

As discussed in Chapter 10, regular users and groups are configured with a minimum UID and GID of 1000. Other Linux distributions can have different minimums. Some administrators prefer to configure several "local-only" users. Either situation would justify a change to the following directives:

```
MINUID=1000
MINGID=1000
```

Starting with Linux kernel 2.6, assignable UIDs and GIDs were expanded to 32 bits ($2^{32}$), which explains the following maximum UID and GID directives. Of course, if you want to reserve some high number UIDs and GIDs for other purposes such as Samba-based authentication, these numbers should be changed to a lower value.

```
MAXUID=4294967295
MAXGID=4294967295
```

By default, shared NFS directories are configured to map the root user to the nobody user on the remote system, with limited privileges. Alternatively, this could be set to 0. For more information on NFS, see Chapter 16.

```
NFSNOBODYUID=65534
NFSNOBODYGID=65534
```

Some distributions that cannot handle maps of the /etc/shadow and /etc/gshadow configuration files have the following directives set to *true*, but it's not necessary, as Ubuntu can handle these files, which are part of the Shadow Password Suite:

```
MERGE_PASSWD=false
MERGE_GROUP=false
```

The following are database variables and should not be changed, unless you've installed nonstandard versions of the **awk** or **make** commands:

```
AWK = /usr/bin/awk
MAKE = /usr/bin/make
UMASK = umask 066
```

The following specify base directories to be used. Some administrators change the values of YPSRCDIR and YPPWDDIR to /etc/NIS, to differentiate files shared over NIS from local configuration files. Of course, if you do so, you'll have to copy or create appropriate versions of these files (such as /etc/hosts) in the /etc/NIS directory. Generally, there's no reason to change the values of any of the other directives, unless this Makefile is copied from a 32-bit to a 64-bit system (or vice versa).

```
YPSRCDIR = /etc
YPPWDDIR = /etc
YPBINDIR = /usr/lib/yp
YPSBINDIR = /usr/sbin
YPDIR = /var/yp
YPMAPDIR = $(YPDIR)/$(DOMAIN)
```

The directives that follow later in the /var/yp/Makefile file specify the location of a number of configuration files. As this section is focused on authentication, note how the following directives (given that YPPWDDIR=/etc) relate to the files of the Shadow Password Suite.

```
GROUP       = $(YPPWDDIR)/group
PASSWD      = $(YPPWDDIR)/passwd
SHADOW      = $(YPPWDDIR)/shadow
GSHADOW     = $(YPPWDDIR)/gshadow
```

The directives which come after in the Makefile go beyond authentication, and are therefore beyond the scope of this chapter.

## Database Maps

Now the configured Makefile can be used to process the files you want to share into a database map. You can perform this activity with the following command:

```
$ sudo /usr/lib/yp/ypinit -m
```

This command processes files cited in /var/yp/Makefile into the /var/yp/`domainname` directory, where the `**domainname**` command in the directory returns the NIS domain name configured when the *nis* package was installed. It prompts for the hostnames of NIS clients, as follows:

```
At this point, we have to construct a list of the hosts which will run NIS
servers. ubuntuhardyserver.example.org is in the list of NIS server hosts.
Please continue to add the names for other hosts, one per line. When you
are done with the list, type a <control D>.
    next host to add: ubuntuhardyserver.example.org
    next host to add:
```

You should then add the hostnames (or IP addresses) of each NIS host at the next host to add prompt. As directed, when the list is complete, press CTRL-D. At that point you'll see the following message that lists configured NIS servers by their hostname and IP address:

```
The current list of NIS servers looks like this:

ubuntuhardyserver.example.org
192.168.0.153


Is this correct? [y/n: y]
```

Future changes to any of the files of the Shadow Password Suite can be added to the NIS database with the following command:

```
$ make -C /var/yp
```

## NIS Security

You've already learned about one NIS security measure: how access can be limited to hosts on specific IP addresses in the /etc/ypserv.securenets configuration file. You've also learned how ports can be fixed in the /etc/default/nis configuration file. Fixed NIS ports enable security and access using the **iptables** command discussed in Chapter 18.

As NIS uses TCP packets, security can also be configured through the TCP wrappers files, also discussed in Chapter 18. The three services that apply are portmap, ypserv, and ypbind. I allow access to the local network in the /etc/hosts.allow configuration file with the following directives:

```
portmap : 192.168.0.0/24
ypserv : 192.168.0.0/24
ypbind: 192.168.0.0/24
```

Of course, TCP wrappers do not limit access unless an appropriate directive is included in the /etc/hosts.deny configuration file.

In general, if there are concerns about security conflicts, options such as TCP wrappers can be temporarily disabled. Alternatively, you could substitute other measures such as those described in Chapter 18.

## An NIS Client

NIS server systems already include the /etc/yp.conf configuration file and ypbind service for NIS clients. For systems in which you want to configure just an NIS client, the following command installs the needed packages:

```
$ sudo apt-get install portmap nis
```

You're prompted for the NIS domain name; for the example discussed earlier, that name is example.org. As is done for the NIS server, the name you enter is included in the /etc/defaultdomain configuration file. The name can be reconfigured by directly editing that file or by running the **sudo dpkg-reconfigure nis** command.

Yes, this command also installs the server configuration files. But the default version of the /etc/default/nis configuration file sets up a client, courtesy of the following two directives:

```
NISSERVER=false
NISCLIENT=true
```

To configure a system as an NIS server, just change the **NISSERVER** directive as discussed earlier to *master* or *slave.*

But problems do arise when an NIS client searches for an NIS server, especially when there are problems with name resolution. So it is best to have a fixed IP address for the NIS server, which can then be included in the /etc/yp.conf configuration file:

```
ypserver 192.168.0.104
```

## Testing NIS

With the server and clients configured, you're now ready to test the NIS system. First, on the server, restart the NIS service with the following command:

```
$ sudo /etc/init.d/nis restart
```

Error messages may appear in the /var/log/daemon.log or /var/log/syslog files. If problems come from remote NIS clients, the following commands stops the NIS client and then places the ypbind daemon into debugging mode:

```
$ sudo /etc/init.d/nis stop
$ sudo ypbind -d
```

If the NIS client connects to the server, you should be able to log in to the client with an account that exists only on the NIS server. You can set up a user on the NIS server for that purpose and try logging on in the NIS client, using that account. If successful, that user should be logged into the appropriate home directory, assuming it exists. If that directory doesn't exist, NIS assumes that such user home directories are the top-level root directory (/). And that is insecure.

> **NOTE** If you prefer home directories on local clients, read the "Lightweight Directory Access Protocol" section later in this chapter. Pay attention to how the LDAP migration tools modify the /etc/pam.d /common-session configuration file. It includes a directive that automatically creates a home directory on a local client.

To complete the configuration, it's helpful to set up a shared NFS /home directory from a server with the home directories for the networked users. For more information on NFS, see Chapter 16.

## NIS Slave Services

An NIS slave server is a backup to the NIS master server. The only differences are the values for the first two directives in the /etc/init.d/nis configuration file, which should read like so:

```
NISSERVER=slave
NISCLIENT=true
```

Don't forget to make appropriate changes to other NIS configuration files, as described in this chapter, before restarting the NIS service on the slave server.

## NIS in the Search Order

On an NIS client system, take a look at the /etc/nsswitch.conf configuration file. By default, the following directives read the local password database first:

```
passwd: compat
group: compat
shadow: compat
```

If you make the following change, the NIS client looks first to the authentication information available on an NIS server. Of course, if you reverse `files` and `nis`, locally available users can log in more quickly.

```
passwd: nis files
group: nis files
shadow: nis files
```

# LIGHTWEIGHT DIRECTORY ACCESS PROTOCOL

A more secure alternative for network authentication is based on the Lightweight Directory Access Protocol (LDAP). Because it is commonly used for other operating systems, it does provide interoperability. In this section, I configure a single LDAP server and appropriate LDAP clients. Once configured in appropriate Pluggable Authentication Module (PAM) files in the /etc/pam.d directory, an LDAP server can be used as the central authentication server for a network.

This section assumes an installation on an Ubuntu Server system where either NIS or a Microsoft authentication database has not been installed. Variations, especially as they relate to the incorporation of NIS databases, may change what you see during the installation process.

Some LDAP configuration files are fussy. An extra blank space at the end of a line in a configuration file can lead to errors. When possible, use the automated tools described in this section to configure LDAP.

**NOTE**   Web-based LDAP configuration tools are available. Ubuntu developers are working on incorporating the Fedora Directory Server. The ldap-account-manager package configures a web-based LDAP management tool. Once installed on the LDAP server, navigate to http://serverIPaddress/lam. Another option is the Webmin tool.

## Installation

Because separate packages are used for LDAP clients and servers, the installation commands and packages are separated into different sections here. The functionality of some more important LDAP packages is summarized in Table 12-1. The last time I checked, there are nearly 200 LDAP-related packages available for Ubuntu.

### Install an LDAP Server

To install the packages required for an LDAP server, run the following command:

```
$ sudo apt-get install ldap-account-manager ldap-auth-config ldapscripts\
slapd ldap-utils migrationtools
```

With dependencies, this command installs all the packages required to configure and manage an LDAP server for network authentication. If various Apache server and LDAP client packages are not already installed, it includes those packages as dependencies.

The installation process requires answers to several questions presented in low-level graphical screens. Use the TAB and ENTER keys to change and make selections. If you've installed any of these packages before, some questions may not appear. For example, in one iteration, I was asked whether to allow the debconf system to manage LDAP

| Package | Description |
|---|---|
| auth-client-config | Modifies PAM and /etc/nsswitch.conf files for LDAP |
| authtool | Supports workstation configuration for LDAP or NIS |
| ldap-account-manager | Installs web-based front end for LDAP accounts |
| ldap-auth-config | Required for a Linux client to authenticate to an LDAP server |
| ldap-auth-client | Required for a Linux client to authenticate to an LDAP server |
| ldapscripts | Supports management of users and groups |
| ldap-utils | Includes client programs to access an LDAP server |
| libnss-ldap | Supports LDAP access via /etc/nsswitch.conf |
| libpam-ldap | Supports LDAP access using PAM |
| migrationtools | Allows conversions of files for an LDAP server |
| nss-updatedb | Maintains authentication information; associated with libnss-ldap and libpam-ldap |

**Table 12-1.**    Important LDAP Packages

configuration. I do so as it enables the use of the **dpkg-reconfigure** command for that purpose.

1. Enter the desired LDAP administrative password. That password should (but does not have to be) different from the regular administrative password.

2. Confirm the desired LDAP administrative password.

3. Specify the Universal Resource Identifier (URI) address of the LDAP server. As this section assumes the local system is the LDAP server, the address you should enter is the IP address of the network card that serves the intended LAN. Substitute the IP address from your system.

```
ldap:///192.168.0.104
```

The URI is a subset of the well-known URL. Another example of its use is available in the discussion of CUPS, the Common Unix Printing System, in Chapter 9. The protocol options shown in the screen include ldaps:///, which corresponds to the secure version of the LDAP protocol, and ldapi:///, which enables communication over a Unix domain socket.

4.  Now specify the distinguished name for the LDAP search database. While not required, it's common to base it on the domain name for the local network. For example, if your LAN uses the example.org network, the entry would be

    ```
    dc=example,dc=org
    ```

5.  Next, specify the version of LDAP to use; the current standard and the one I select is LDAP 3.

6.  You're asked whether to Make Local Root Database Admin. If you select Yes, the local server root administrative user also gets administrative access over the LDAP server. I select Yes.

7.  The next question asks if the LDAP database requires a login. As long as the local administrative account has access to the local database, this is not required. I select No.

8.  LDAP databases can have an administrative account with a name other than root. That account name is the *Common Name*, or *cn* in an LDAP configuration file. The remainder of the account should match the previous choices for the Distinguished Name for the Search Base. Based on step 4, I enter this:

    ```
    cn=admin,dc=example,dc=org
    ```

9.  The last question asks for the LDAP root account password. It does not have to match the administrative password created in steps 1 and 2. Be careful, you get to enter the password only once in this step before installation proceeds.

Additional configuration options are available for some of the installed packages. For example, to go through the basic configuration options for the ldap-account-manager package, run the following command:

```
$ sudo dpkg-reconfigure ldap-account-manager
```

Just to see if the database is properly created, run the following **ldapsearch** command to search the example.org database, using simple authentication:

```
$ ldapsearch -xb dc=example,dc=org
```

The output should be similar to that shown in Figure 12-1.

## Install an LDAP Client

To install the packages required for an LDAP server, run the following command:

```
$ sudo apt-get install ldap-auth-client ldap-auth-config libnss-ldap \
  libpam-ldap auth-client-config
```

With dependencies, this command installs all packages required to configure and manage an LDAP client for network authentication. (If you try this command on an LDAP server, you'll confirm that these packages are installed on that system.) With dependencies, this command installs all packages required to configure and manage an LDAP client for network authentication.

```
michael@ubuntuhardyserver:~$ ldapsearch -xb dc=example,dc=org
# extended LDIF
#
# LDAPv3
# base <dc=example,dc=org> with scope subtree
# filter: (objectclass=*)
# requesting: ALL
#

# example.org
dn: dc=example,dc=org
objectClass: top
objectClass: dcObject
objectClass: organization
o: example.org
dc: example

# admin, example.org
dn: cn=admin,dc=example,dc=org
objectClass: simpleSecurityObject
objectClass: organizationalRole
cn: admin
description: LDAP administrator

# search result
search: 2
result: 0 Success

# numResponses: 3
# numEntries: 2
michael@ubuntuhardyserver:~$ █
```

**Figure 12-1.** Verifying an LDAP server

The installation process requires answers to several questions. Use the TAB and ENTER keys to change and make selections. If you've installed any of these packages before, some questions may not appear.

1. Specify the URI address of the LDAP server. It's best if you use the IP address of the LDAP server, so substitute this for the address shown here. The protocol should match that used when configuring the LDAP server in the previous section.

   ```
   ldap:///192.168.0.104
   ```

2. Now specify the distinguished name for the LDAP search database. While not required, it's common to base it on the domain name for the local network. For example, if your LAN uses the example.org network, the entry would be

   ```
   dc=example,dc=org
   ```

3. The remaining steps to configure an LDAP client match steps 4 through 9 of those required to create an LDAP server. The answers should also be the same.

Be aware that the local LDAP administrative password can be stored in the /etc/ldap.secret file, in clear text. Read permissions to this file are available only to the regular administrative account, but a clear text password is risky enough—I believe it's wise to make that LDAP administrative password different from any user or root administrative password.

# Configure LDAP on the Server

Now it's time to configure the LDAP servers and clients. On the server, I'll show you how to convert the authentication files of the Shadow Password Suite. But first are the files that identify the LDAP server. Some may have been properly configured during the installation process.

## The Common LDAP Configuration File (/etc/ldap.conf)

The /etc/ldap.conf configuration file is the client—which should also be configured on the server. On this file, you need to identify the distinguished name of the LDAP search database. The original version of this file set it to **base dc=padl,dc=com**; it should be set to your LDAP domain. For the configuration described so far in this chapter, it's

```
base dc=example,dc=org
```

You also need to specify the URI to the LDAP server. While nominally it could be set to the localhost system, it should be set to the same IP address as seen over the network for the LDAP server. Then the /etc/ldap.conf configuration file can be copied to clients. In my case, it's

```
uri ldapi://192.168.0.104
```

The following directive binds the administrative user to the noted admin account, authenticated by the password stored in clear text in the /etc/ldap.secret configuration file:

```
rootbinddn cn=admin,dc=example,dc=org
```

If there are network problems, the default configuration would appear to "hang" on clients, which is why I add the following directive:

```
bind_policy soft
```

One other configuration file must be configured for LDAP clients: /etc/nsswitch.conf. However, it's commonly configured just on the client and is described with the migration tools described shortly.

## LDAP Server Configuration File

The main LDAP server configuration file is /etc/ldap/slapd.conf. Generally, no changes are required to this file; everything that an LDAP server needs should be configured during the installation process as described. Most changes can be made with the following command:

```
$ sudo dpkg-reconfigure slapd
```

However, if problems occur, LDAP does not normally send any messages to standard log files. If you wanted to configure logging, add appropriate options to the **loglevel** directive. Fourteen levels are available and are listed in the man page for the slapd.conf file. To diagnose problems I had while writing this chapter, I changed the **loglevel none** directive to:

```
loglevel 1 64 128
```

This processes trace function calls, configuration files, and LDAP access control lists.

## Scripts from the migrationtools Package

Before the migrationtools package was created, populating an LDAP authentication database was a time-consuming process. Administrators had to write their own scripts to convert user and group account information into LDAP Data Interchange Format (LDIF). Some administrators might have even added users to LDIF databases one by one.

Several scripts are included with the migrationtools package to ease conversions from an authentication database configured to the Shadow Password Suite. Most of these scripts are located in the /usr/share/migrationtools directory.

**NOTE**   The migrationtools package also includes scripts that can convert NIS databases, normally stored in the /var/yp/`domainname` directory.

Before converting any databases, you should adjust a couple of defaults in the migrate_common.ph script, in the /usr/share/perl5 directory. About 70 lines into this file, you'll see the following directives:

```
$DEFAULT_MAIL_DOMAIN = "padl.com";
$DEFAULT_BASE = "dc=padl,dc=com";
```

Despite what you see in the comments of the default version of the script, these variables actually correspond to the LDAP domain as configured for the server. Based on what has been configured in this chapter, these variables should be changed to

```
#$DEFAULT_MAIL_DOMAIN = "padl.com";
$DEFAULT_BASE = "dc=example,dc=org";
```

I've commented out the DEFAULT_MAIN_DOMAIN variable, as that would require Kerberos authentication. That would add another level of complexity to the LDAP configuration process.

Navigate to the aforementioned /usr/share/migrationtools directory. Then basic information can and should be collected into an LDAP database with the following command:

```
$ ./migrate_base.pl > /tmp/base.ldif
```

Now with the following commands, you can migrate the /etc/passwd and /etc/shadow configuration files to the passwd.ldif database file. Access commands to /etc/shadow are embedded in the **migrate_passwd.pl** script, activated by administrative (**sudo**) access. The converted database, in LDAP format, can be sent to the arbitrarily named /tmp/passwd.ldif file:

```
$ cd /usr/share/migrationtools/
$ ./migrate_passwd.pl /etc/passwd /tmp/passwd.ldif
```

If successful, the /tmp/passwd.ldif should contain entries similar to those shown in Figure 12-2. The figure illustrates the entry for user katie, with information from her entries in both the /etc/passwd and /etc/shadow configuration files. I've included the start of user dickens' entry to illustrate that this database applies for multiple users.

Of course, information from the /etc/group configuration file should also be collected into an LDAP database with the following command:

```
$ ./migrate_group.pl /etc/group /tmp/group.ldif
```

```
dn: uid=katie, ou=People, dc=example, dc=org
uid: katie
cn: Katie
objectClass: account
objectClass: posixAccount
objectClass: top
objectClass: shadowAccount
userPassword: {crypt}!
shadowLastChange: 13970
shadowMax: 99999
shadowWarning: 7
loginShell: /bin/sh
uidNumber: 1002
gidNumber: 1002
homeDirectory: /home/katie
gecos: Katie,,,,

dn: uid=dickens, ou=People, dc=example, dc=org
uid: dickens
cn: dickens
objectClass: account
objectClass: posixAccount
objectClass: top
```

**Figure 12-2.** An LDAP user entry

One problem with the migration tools is how they fail to define users and groups in LDAP format. As I expect developers to address this problem in the future, you won't always need to create the following database file, which I'll call /tmp/usergroup.ldif. Be careful with this file; extra spaces, even at the end of a line, can cause errors.

```
dn: ou=People,dc=example,dc=org
ou: People
objectclass: organizationalUnit

dn: ou=Group,dc=example,dc=org
ou: Group
objectclass: organizationalUnit
```

Now you can set up the LDAP authentication database. The **ldapadd** command adds information from appropriate database files. The **-x** uses simple authentication. The **-W** prompts for the LDAP password, so you don't have to include it in clear text at the command line. The **-D** precedes the **binddn** in quotes. The **-f** reads from the file that follows.

Be careful when running these commands; unless you've run the **sudo** command in the past few minutes, you're prompted for the current user's password before being prompted for the LDAP administrative password. In addition, these commands won't work unless the noted files in the /tmp directory exist, per the instructions earlier in this section.

```
$ sudo ldapadd -xWD "cn=admin,dc=example,dc=org" \
-f /tmp/usergroup.ldif
$ sudo ldapadd -xWD "cn=admin,dc=example,dc=org" \
-f /tmp/group.ldif
$ sudo ldapadd -xWD "cn=admin,dc=example,dc=org" \
-f /tmp/passwd.ldif
```

Now that you have a database on the server, you should configure the LDAP clients.

## Configure LDAP on the Client

The LDAP client must point to the correct LDAP server, as specified in the /etc/ldap .conf configuration file. Once this file is received on the LDAP client, the **auth-client-config** script can be used to integrate LDAP access to key files associated with the login system. For example, when I run the following command,

```
$ sudo auth-client-config -a -p lac_ldap
```

it looks through files in the /etc/auth-client-config/profile.d/ directory. It finds the stanza labeled *[lac_ldap]* in the ldap-auth-config file in that directory. That stanza reconfigures five files. First it replaces the **passwd**, **group**, and **shadow** directives in the /etc/nsswitch.conf configuration file with

```
passwd: files ldap
group: files ldap
shadow: files ldap
```

which searches first through the local authentication database files before referring to a configured LDAP server.

It also changes the common-account, common-auth, common-password, and common-session files in the /etc/pam.d directory. Once changed, the script enables access from the LDAP client to the LDAP database on the server. The most interesting change is to the /etc/pam.d/common-session configuration file, which creates a new local home directory for the user if it doesn't already exist, courtesy of the following directive:

```
session   required   pam_mkhomedir.so skel=/etc/skel/
```

It creates that new user's home directory locally, in /home/username, whether or not the user's name and password are on the LDAP server or in local configuration files. It also populates that directory with the contents of the /etc/skel directory.

# SUMMARY

Many Linux administrators administer dozens of clients. To avoid the difficulties of maintaining the same usernames and passwords on every client, Linux administrators rely on network authentication systems, including NIS and LDAP.

NIS is the traditional method for centralizing authentication databases on Linux and Unix systems. The client and server on Ubuntu systems comes from the same package. Most NIS server settings can be configured in the /etc/default/nis and /var/yp/Makefile files. The NIS network can be configured with the **ypinit -m** command. NIS clients can be configured to use NIS databases through the /etc/nsswitch.conf file. While there are ways to minimize the risks, NIS is inherently insecure.

Perhaps the common alternative to NIS is LDAP. With the migrationtools package, it's much easier to convert the users and groups configured in the Shadow Password Suite. With a few modifications, these scripts can convert authentication databases to LDIF formatted files, which can then be imported into LDAP servers. The **auth-client-config** command can then be used to convert login configuration files, including /etc/nsswitch.conf and the /etc/pam.d/common-* PAM files.

# CHAPTER 13

## A Minimal Graphical Environment

D espite the prevailing bias by many Linux gurus against the GUI, at least a few Ubuntu administrators rely on the graphical environment to control and configure their systems. They find it convenient to be able to open several command line connections to different systems, side-by-side, in a single screen. Some (mostly third-party) packages aren't even installable without a GUI. To that end, this chapter describes how to install various GUI environments on an Ubuntu Server system.

Not all administrative tools are available at the command line interface; for example, most printer configuration is now done from either the graphical or the web-based interfaces described in Chapter 9.

In many cases, I find that X over SSH is sufficient to administer remote Ubuntu Server systems with GUI tools. If you choose this method, fewer packages are required to run an X client over SSH—even when compared to a minimal GUI on the server.

However, if you choose to run a full GUI, there are three major GUI desktop environments officially supported by Ubuntu: GNOME, KDE , and Xfce. All can be installed on an Ubuntu Server system. As Xfce is the lightest weight of the three environments, I arbitrarily focus this chapter on that GUI.

If you prefer GNOME, KDE, or another desktop environment, you can certainly install those. The basic principles for installation are the same. And many excellent books already cover both GNOME and KDE. All Ubuntu desktop environments include the X.org X Window Server, which serves as the foundation for these graphical interfaces. Of course, if you do not need or want GUI tools to administer Ubuntu Server systems, you do not need to install a GUI and can proceed to the next chapter.

**NOTE**   I personally prefer KDE. However, the default GUI for Ubuntu is GNOME, and the lightest weight GUI of the three supported GUI environments is Xfce. As this is an Ubuntu Server book, it's not appropriate to cover all three GUI desktops in detail.

# BASIC GRAPHICAL DEFINITIONS

There are three basic groups of packages associated with a GUI. The definitions of each group are fuzzy, as developers from each area have incorporated the functionality of others. These groups include the X Window Server, the desktop environment, and the window manager. Linux makes it possible to substitute alternatives for each of these groups of packages.

**NOTE**   For the editors among you, the X.org server is the "X Window System." However, I specify "Server" to emphasize the client-server model associated with the Linux GUI.

## The X Server

The X server is the "engine" of the GUI. Most current Linux systems include this technology developed by the X.org group. Older versions of Linux included an X server from the XFree86 project at www.xfree86.org. The change was made when the XFree86 group changed its licensing. Even for most administrators, the changes are trivial, such as a few different names for files and commands.

Generally, the X server is automatically installed as a dependency when you select a desktop environment and possibly a window manager. However, a lot can be done to customize the X server, which is discussed later in this chapter in the "Configure the X Server" section.

## The Desktop Environment

The desktop environment is commonly associated with the icons, windows, toolbars, folders, wallpapers, and desktop widgets. The GNOME, KDE, and Xfce desktop environments are briefly discussed in this chapter. Desktop environments normally include their own default window managers.

GNOME is part of the GNU project. While GNOME includes a number of applications such as the GNOME Office suite, the desktop environment is at the heart of its interface. While the latest releases of Ubuntu include the Compiz window manager, GNOME has its own alternative window manager. GNOME is built on GTK+ (GIMP Toolkit), which is a cross-platform set of widgets for creating graphical interface systems. The window managers commonly paired with GNOME give it a "look" somewhat like older Apple Macintosh operating systems.

KDE is also a free software project. GNOME was developed in part because KDE relied on the Qt application development framework. GNOME developers were not comfortable with KDE, as Qt software was not released under the GNU General Public License until 2005. (As for the *Qt* acronym, the *t* stands for toolkit and the *Q* was included for trivial reasons.) By 2005, GNOME was well established, including as the default desktop environment for Ubuntu. KDE also includes its own window manager. With appropriate settings, KDE has some visual similarities to current Microsoft operating systems.

Xfce is also a free software project—which also currently uses the GTK+ toolkit. It was originally developed as a Linux clone of the still proprietary Common Desktop Environment (CDE). However, its use of the XForms toolkit limited the popularity of this desktop environment, as XForms was not released under an open-source license until 2004. Well before then, Xfce was rewritten under the same GTK+ toolkit used for GNOME.

## The Window Manager

A window manager is a system that controls the placement and appearance of windows in a GUI. While the major desktop environments include their own window managers, several other window managers can be installed. For example, current versions of Ubuntu include the Compiz window manager.

Many Linux window managers were developed from the F Virtual Window Manager (FVWM) and Tom's Window Manager (TWM). Both FVWM and TWM also provide minimalist desktop environments. The code from these window managers provides the basis for many other alternatives.

One of these window manager derivatives is known as Enlightenment. It happens to be the default window manager for the GNOME desktop environment on the gOS operating system, a derivative of Ubuntu that is installed on some PCs sold by Walmart. With Enlightenment, gOS works on top of GNOME to provide a look and feel closer to current Macintosh operating systems.

# GRAPHICAL ENVIRONMENT OPTIONS

Ubuntu focuses on three main options for the graphical environment: GNOME, KDE, and Xfce. While there are many other excellent graphical environments available, these are associated with the three main Linux desktop releases from Canonical: Ubuntu (GNOME), Kubuntu (KDE), and Xubuntu (Xfce).

However, all of these releases, as well as Ubuntu Server, share the same repositories. In other words, you can install KDE on Ubuntu, GNOME on Xubutnu, and Xfce on Ubuntu Server. You'll see how to install all three desktop environments on an Ubuntu Server system in the following sections. The numbers of packages and required disk space that appear here are based on an Ubuntu Server system in which no other GUI-related packages have been installed.

As this book is based on the Ubuntu Server, which does not include a GUI in the default installation, these sections are based on such an Ubuntu Server configuration and assume you log into the Ubuntu server at the command line using an account with **sudo** privileges. They also assume that the local repository database is up to date, courtesy of the **sudo apt-get update** command.

As the GUI focus of this chapter is on the Xfce desktop environment, the small installation sections on the GNOME and KDE desktop environments are included solely for reference.

## Install Xfce

To install Xfce from the command line interface, you could install any or all of the Xfce packages available from the Hardy Heron repositories. But the implicit objective is not to install a standard GUI desktop, but to install a GUI with a fairly minimal number of packages.

The **apt-cache search xfce** command reveals 108 packages. As Xfce is built from the same toolkit as GNOME, GNOME-based GUI administrative tools can also be installed on that desktop environment. Be aware, several described throughout the book are based on GNOME. You could install all 108 packages, and you can even install additional desktop applications such as the OpenOffice.org suite. For the purposes of this chapter, examine what happens when you install just those packages needed for administrative purposes. Specifically, install the basic Xfce desktop meta-package (which automatically installs others required for the GUI) and the associated command line terminal:

```
$ sudo apt-get install xfce4 xfce4-terminal xauth xorg
```

I've included the xorg meta-package for the X server and the xauth package for authentication. Based on the aforementioned conditions, this command calls a number of dependencies, installing close to 200 packages, including those associated with the default X server. As this requires a download of more than 50MB, it can take some time. Of course, you might also want to install any desired GUI administrative packages, some of which are described throughout the book.

A graphical login manager is not required, unless you're actually running the GUI locally. If you are, the default used from the Xubuntu system is the GNOME display manager, available from the gdm package. However, the Xubuntu login screen has a different appearance.

One advantage of gdm is its support for remote graphical logins, described later in this chapter. If you're administering this system remotely using graphical tools, you may also want to install the update-manager and synaptic packages described in Chapter 8, along with the packages associated with other GUI administrative tools as described throughout the book. If successful, you should be able to start the GUI with the **startx** command, which leads to the desktop shown in Figure 13-1.

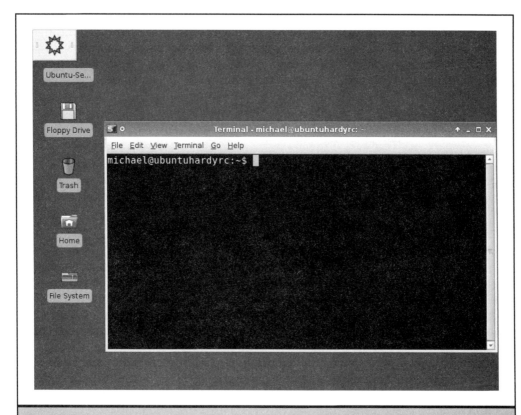

**Figure 13-1.**    A minimal Ubuntu Hardy Heron Xfce desktop environment

Alternatively, if you wanted to install a complete Xfce desktop environment, run the following command:

```
$ sudo apt-get install xubuntu-desktop
```

The xubuntu-desktop package is a meta-package that configures much more than a minimal environment. It installs around 600 packages and requires about a gigabyte of additional space—along with the features most GUI users expect, such as a word processor, a graphics editor, multimedia applications, and so on.

While most GUIs start with a login screen; in many cases, administrators will connect remotely. I've already described this process using the **ssh** command in Chapter 7.

## Install GNOME

To install the GNOME desktop environment from the command line interface, you could install any or all of the GNOME packages available from the Hardy Heron repositories. But the implicit objective is not to install a standard GUI desktop, but to install a GUI with a fairly minimal number of packages.

The **apt-cache search gnome** command reveals nearly 1400 packages. This incorporates GNOME-based GUI administrative tools, including several described in different chapters. You could install all 1400 packages, and you can even install additional desktop applications such as the GIMP. For the purpose of this chapter, I show you how to install just those packages needed for administrative purposes. Specifically, this includes the simplified GNOME desktop meta-package, gnome-core (which automatically installs others required for the GUI), and the associated command line terminal:

```
$ sudo apt-get install gnome-core gnome-terminal xauth xorg
```

I've included the xorg package for the X server and the xauth package for authentication. This command calls a number of dependencies, installing close to 200 packages, including those associated with the default X server. As this requires a download of more than 50MB, it can take some time. You can abort the download by entering **n** at the following prompt:

```
Do you want to continue [Y/n]?
```

If you proceed, and the download/installation is successful, you should be able to start the GUI with the **startx** command, which leads to the desktop shown in Figure 13-2.

A graphical login manager is not required, unless you're actually running the GUI locally. If you are, the default Ubuntu login manager is the GNOME display manager. If you're administering this system remotely using graphical tools, you may also want to install the update-manager and synaptic packages described in Chapter 8.

Alternatively, if you wanted to install a complete GNOME desktop environment, run the following command:

```
$ sudo apt-get install ubuntu-desktop
```

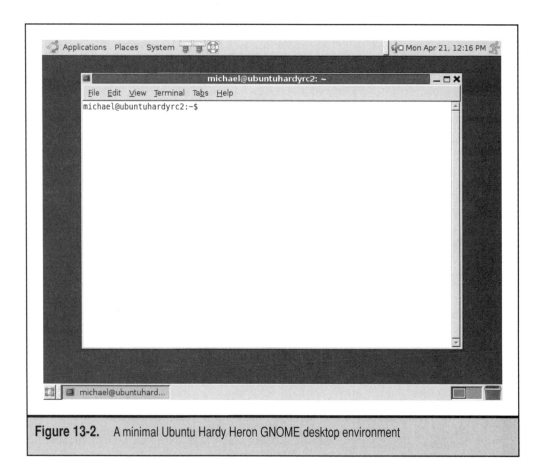

**Figure 13-2.**   A minimal Ubuntu Hardy Heron GNOME desktop environment

The ubuntu-desktop package is a meta-package that configures much more than a minimal environment. It installs around 600 packages and requires about 1.5 gigabytes of additional space—along with the applications most GUI users expect, such as the OpenOffice.org suite.

If you prefer GNOME, you can proceed with this installation. Just be aware of the extra demands on system resources relative to Xfce.

## Install KDE

To install the KDE desktop environment from the command line interface, you could install any or all of the KDE-related packages available from the Hardy Heron repositories. But the implicit objective is not to install a standard GUI desktop, but to install a GUI with a fairly minimal number of packages.

The **apt-cache search kde** command reveals around 1600 packages. This incorporates KDE-based GUI administrative tools. I've described GNOME-based tools throughout the book, as GNOME is the default for Ubuntu, and these tools are more compatible with the Xfce desktop. However, excellent equivalent KDE tools are available.

You could install all 1600 KDE-related packages, and you can install additional desktop applications such as Kopete Instant Messenger or even KDE's office suite, KOffice. For the purpose of this chapter, examine what happens when you try to install just those packages needed for administrative purposes. Specifically, run the following installation command for the basic KDE desktop meta-package (which automatically installs others required for the GUI) and the associated command line terminal:

```
$ sudo apt-get install kde-core konsole xauth xorg
```

I've included the xorg package for the X server and the xauth package for authentication. Based on the aforementioned conditions, this command calls a number of dependencies, installing around 150 packages, including those associated with the default X server. As this requires a download of more than 50MB, it can take some time. You can abort the download by entering **n** at the following prompt:

```
Do you want to continue [Y/n]?
```

A graphical login manager is not required, unless you're actually running the GUI locally. If you are, KDE has its own login manager, which is part of the kdm package. If you're administering this system remotely using graphical tools, you may also want to install the update-manager and synaptic packages described in Chapter 8, along with the packages associated with other GUI administrative tools as described throughout the book.

Alternatively, if you wanted to install a complete KDE desktop environment, run the following command:

```
$ sudo apt-get install kubuntu-desktop
```

The kubuntu-desktop package is a meta-package that configures much more than a minimal environment. It installs around 600 packages and requires about 1.5 gigabytes of additional space. If successful, the first time you log into a KDE desktop environment, you'll be asked to create a group of settings, starting with the screen shown in Figure 13-3.

These steps ask you to select the following:

▼ The local country and language

■ System behavior for mouse clicks and the keyboard

■ CPU allocation for graphical effects

▲ The thematic look and feel of the desktop

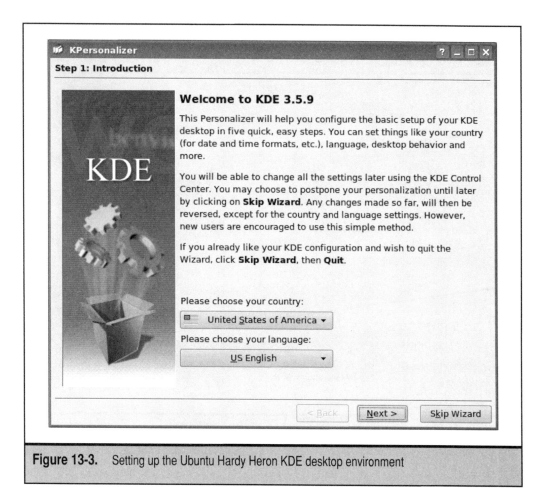

**Figure 13-3.**   Setting up the Ubuntu Hardy Heron KDE desktop environment

Once complete, you should see a KDE desktop environment screen. If you selected the defaults, it should appear similar to that shown in Figure 13-4. What you see might be quite different, depending on selected settings.

The next time you want to start the GUI, run the **startx** command. Of course, if you prefer a graphical login screen, make sure to install the kdm package. If you prefer KDE, you could proceed with this installation. Just be aware of the extra demands on system resources relative to Xfce.

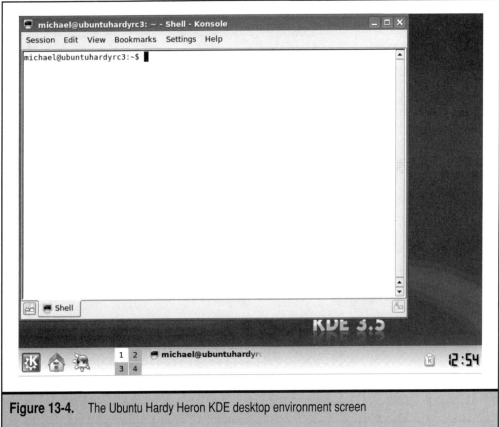

**Figure 13-4.** The Ubuntu Hardy Heron KDE desktop environment screen

# CONFIGURE THE XFCE DESKTOP ENVIRONMENT

This section provides a brief guide to configuring the Xfce desktop environment. Xfce provides a desktop, control options, and some useful applications. It also provides a foundation for installing several different GUI-based administrative tools described throughout the book. The following sections highlight some of the more useful Xfce and administrative packages. You'll learn how to configure the X server, and manage basic Xfce tools and menus. Finally, you'll learn how to configure remote access to an Xfce desktop environment.

To help illustrate available packages, I install the Synaptic Package Manager described in Chapter 8 with the following command:

```
$ sudo apt-get install synaptic
```

# Selected Xfce Packages

If you've already installed the Xfce desktop environment in the first part of this chapter, many related packages should already be installed. To find appropriate additional packages, you can use the search feature available from the Synaptic Package Manager. Just click the Search button, type **xfce** in the Search text box, and press ENTER to review Xfce-related packages. Several important Xfce packages are listed in Table 13-1.

The selected packages are arbitrary; others might be more well suited to your needs. Other packages suited to GUI-based administration are described in Table 13-2.

I've installed all the packages listed in Tables 13-1 and 13-2 on the Xfce desktop configured in this chapter. Once installed, I can run them locally. Alternatively, with the SSH (Secure Shell) server described in Chapter 7, they can also be run from a remote system.

# Configure the X Server

There are two ways to manage screen resolution from the command line interface. First, there's the **dpkg-reconfigure** tool, which can be applied with the X server package, **xserver-xorg**, as follows:

```
$ sudo dpkg-reconfigure xserver-xorg
```

| Package | Description |
| --- | --- |
| desktop-profiles | Helps configure desktop profiles for different users |
| kdocker | Supports application docking in a system tray |
| mail-notification | Allows an e-mail manager to notify on receipt of new e-mail |
| network-manager-gnome | Includes the network management tool |
| xfce4 | Adds a meta-package that includes others |
| xfce4-appfinder | Finds installed applications |
| xfce4-cpugraph-plugin | Provides a graphical view of CPU system load |
| xfce4-netload-plugin | Provides a graphical view of load on network interfaces |
| xfce4-session | Supports saving the state of running applications on logout |
| xfce4-taskmanager | Allows monitoring of running processes |
| xfce4-terminal | Adds a GUI-based command line terminal |
| xfprint4 | Includes a GUI printer manager |

**Table 13-1.** Useful Xfce Packages

| Package | Description |
|---|---|
| gconf2 | Customizes GNOME settings |
| gnome-system-tools | Includes administrative tools for networks, users, and shares |
| policykit-gnome | Supports administrative permission management |
| synaptic | Allows updates of existing and installable packages |
| system-config-kickstart | Configures Kickstart configuration files |
| system-config-printer | Configures printers |
| system-config-samba | Configures shares on a Samba server |
| update-manager | Supports custom updates |
| virt-manager | Allows configuration of virtual machines |

**Table 13-2.** Administrative Packages Suitable for the Xfce Desktop Environment

Alternatively, there are also options associated with the **Xorg** command, which can automatically detect most hardware and create a proposed X server configuration file, xorg.conf, in the local directory. A GUI tool is also available for reconfiguring the X server, based on the displayconfig-gtk package, which can be installed with the following command:

```
$ sudo apt-get install displayconfig-gtk
```

## Configure the X Server with a Graphical Tool

The Screen And Graphics Preferences tool can help configure the X server. It can be started with the **sudo displayconfig-gtk** command. In the Screen And Graphics Preferences window shown in Figure 13-5, you can configure multiple monitors if the hardware supports it. For example, a laptop with an external video port would show Screen 1 and Screen 2.

As suggested by the Location drop-down box, this tool supports multiple X server configurations. It's appropriate for a system such as a laptop that may be connected to a docking port. Once you're satisfied with one configuration, click the disk icon with the DOWN ARROW, and save the configuration under a specific location. Repeat the process with the second configuration.

There are two tabs associated with this tool. The Screen tab configures monitors, and the Graphics Card tab configures the driver and video memory associated with the graphics card.

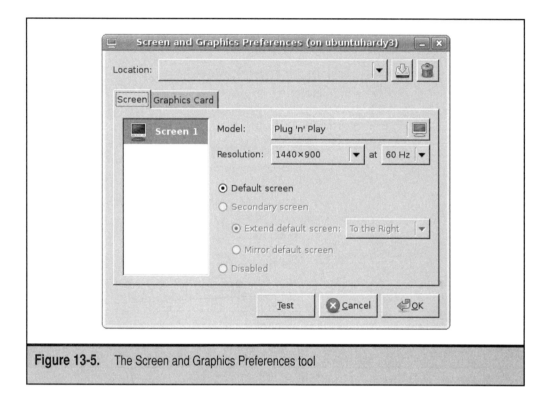

**Figure 13-5.** The Screen and Graphics Preferences tool

The Driver option under the Graphics Card tab opens a menu of available drivers, as shown in Figure 13-6. If you click the Choose Driver By Name drop-down box, it allows you to select from a list of available drivers. If you're not sure what driver is best suited to the local system, the generic VESA and VGA drivers should work in most cases. However, as generic drivers, they probably won't enable the features that make current video cards so desirable.

**NOTE** VGA is short for Video Graphics Array, a standard for older cathode ray tube monitors. VESA is short for the Video Electronics Standards Association, which provides a number of standards; when cited in Linux, the standard is associated with Super VGA hardware.

Alternatively, if you select Choose Driver By Model, you can choose from one or more graphics cards from nearly 40 different manufacturers. Once selected, you may be able to choose a video memory if the graphics card and associated Linux driver so supports it.

Once a graphics card is configured, it's appropriate to configure a monitor as described under the Screen tab. To select a monitor, click the text button adjacent to Model. It opens a Choose Screen window, as shown in Figure 13-7, which supports monitor selection by make and manufacturer. Widescreen monitors can be configured as needed. If desired,

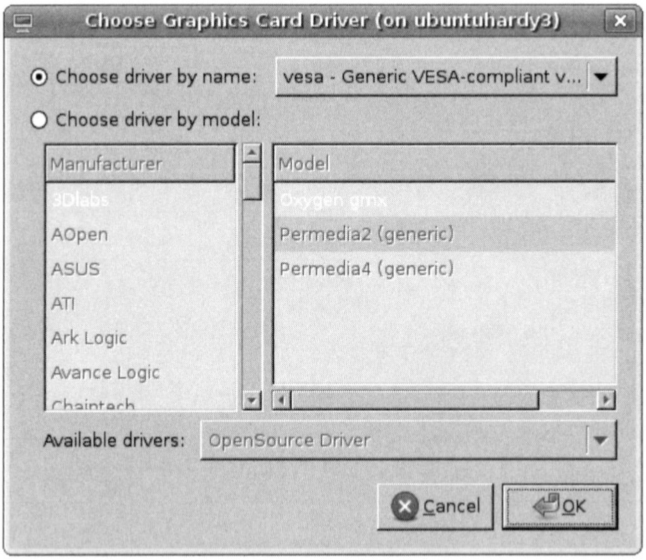

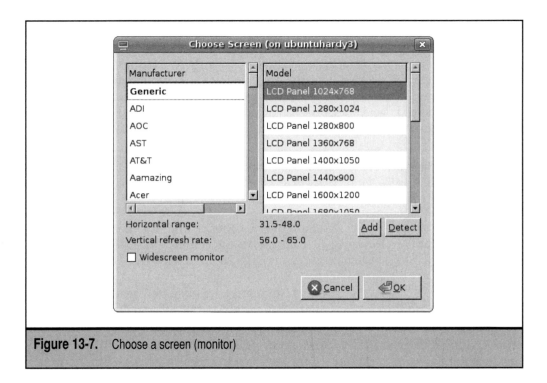

**Figure 13-6.** Select a graphics card driver

**Figure 13-7.** Choose a screen (monitor)

click the Detect button to detect the most current monitor hardware and suggest an appropriate driver.

Once changes are complete and the tool is closed, changes are saved to the X server configuration file, /etc/X11/xorg.conf. The message that suggests that all users must log off is a prerequisite to restarting the X server, which is when the changes to the xorg.conf file are applied.

## Configure the X Server from the Command Line

Those of you familiar with other Linux distributions may be familiar with the command line configuration tool for the X server. On older distributions, it was known as **xf86config**; on the latest distributions, it's known as **xorgconfig**. The **dpkg-reconfigure xserver-xorg** command brings the administrator through a similar series of steps.

It's a straightforward process to use the noted command to configure the X server. But before starting this process, back up the current X server configuration file, /etc/X11/xorg.conf. In fact, you may want to print the file, as reference for this exercise. With that in mind, the following command saves the current X server configuration file to the current user's home directory:

```
$ cp /etc/X11/xorg.conf ~
```

If you need to stop the tool any time during the process, open a new command line window, and find the process identifier with the **ps aux | grep dpkg-reconfigure** command. The process identifier is shown in the second column; here's an example when I run the noted command:

```
root      4986  2.4  3.1  13444 7988 pts/0     S+   18:23
    0:00 /usr/bin/perl -w /usr/sbin/dpkg-reconfigure xserver-xorg
```

In this case, the process identifier is 4986, at which point I can stop the process with the following command:

```
$ sudo kill 4986
```

If you prefer to configure the X server in less detail, include the **-phigh** switch, which creates a new xorg.conf configuration file automatically, without questions. But for this chapter, start the process with the following command:

```
$ sudo dpkg-reconfigure xserver-xorg
```

Now take the following steps:

1. The command opens a low-level graphical screen similar to that shown in Figure 13-8 and depicted in the steps that follow. It's not possible to "click" an option with the mouse in these screens; options can be selected with the TAB, ENTER, and arrow keys.

2. Select whether or not you want to use a framebuffer. Some trial and error may be appropriate for optimal performance. Select Yes or No and press ENTER to continue.

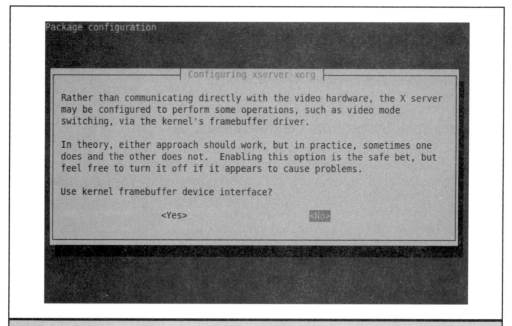

**Figure 13-8.**  Choose whether to enable a kernel framebuffer in this screen

3. You can choose to autodetect the keyboard layout; for the purpose of this exercise, select No and press ENTER to continue.

4. Review the description associated with keyboard layouts; normally users of US English keyboards will enter *us*. The ISO codes described in the instructions for alternative language keyboards are available in the iso_3166.tab file, in the /usr/share/iso-codes directory. Type in the desired keyboard or ISO code and select OK to continue.

5. Now you can select an X Keyboard Extension ruleset, listed in the menu as XKB. Normally, you should just accept the xorg default. Other options are listed in the /usr/share/X11/xkb/rules/ directory. Type a different selection if desired, and select OK to continue.

6. Read the options associated with the XKB rulesets. After reading, select OK to continue.

7. Type in the associated keyboard model, if appropriate. Users of US keyboards should generally accept the default, pc105, unless the precise model is known. Options are listed in the /usr/share/X11/xkb/symbols/ directory. Type a different selection if desired, and select OK to continue.

8. Read the options associated with keyboard variants. If you need a keyboard variant, enter it in the text box here. If uncertain, variant options are listed in the /usr/share/X11/xkb/symbols/ directory. Normally, a US keyboard does not require a variant, and this entry can be left blank. Type any desired selection and choose OK to continue.

9. Read the description of additional keyboard options available for options such as "Meta" keys, write down any desired options, and select OK to continue.

10. Enter any desired keyboard options based on the information in step 9, and select OK to continue.

11. If you see a comment about a dummy template and a "something is probably wrong" message, don't be overly concerned. In this case, everything is probably okay.

12. The configuration will be written to the /etc/X11 directory, in an xorg.conf file, with an extension associated with the date. For example, my system includes an xorg.conf.20080430083845 file, written on April 30, 2008, at 8:38 A.M.

    I can then review the proposed xorg.conf file; if it makes sense, I can copy it to the default location, /etc/X11/xorg.conf.

## Create a Proposed X Server Configuration

There is another way to create an X server configuration: try the **Xorg -configure** command. As long as a GUI is not currently open, that command should automatically detect appropriate hardware and create an xorg.conf file in the local directory.

If you've configured a graphical login manager, it's easiest to get the **Xorg -configure** command working from a different runlevel. In that case, move to runlevel 1 as follows:

```
$ sudo init 1
```

When you see the Recovery menu, select the Drop To Root Shell Prompt option. You can then run the **Xorg -configure** command. As the proposed X server configuration file is in the local directory, you can immediately return to runlevel 2 with the **exit** command.

**NOTE** With earlier versions of the X.org server, the **X -configure** command was equivalent to **Xorg -configure**. Some configurations might not react well to this command; if the screen goes blank, you may have to reboot the system to make the screen reappear.

Whatever you do to create a new X server configuration file, evaluate the new xorg .conf file. Guidelines are available in the following section.

## The X Server Configuration File, xorg.conf

This section examines the /etc/X11/xorg.conf file in detail. If you haven't configured the X server in some time, the directives in xorg.conf are similar to previous /etc/X11/ XF86Config files on older Linux distributions. In either case, xorg.conf is organized into stanzas. The directives in this file reflect just one configuration; you may see more or fewer directives in your version of xorg.conf. In some cases, settings that are automatically detected and/or are defaults may not appear in the configuration file.

In the comments is a note for how you can reconfigure the xorg.conf file from the command line, using the **dpkg-reconfigure xserver-xorg** command described earlier in this chapter. Older versions of the xorg.conf configuration file had a **ServerLayout** stanza at the start of the file. That stanza is now listed at the end of the file.

Two standard input devices are a keyboard and a mouse. That's reflected in the first two stanzas, entitled **InputDevice**. The first configures a keyboard as a regular US keyboard with 105 keys. The second configures a mouse. The **Emulate3Buttons** option, when active, configures the X server to activate middle mouse button functionality when you click the left and right mouse buttons simultaneously.

```
Section "InputDevice"
    Identifier   "GenericKeyboard"
    Driver       "kbd"
    Option       "XkbRules" "xorg"
    Option       "XkbModel" "pc105"
    Option       "XkbLayout" "us"
EndSection

Section "InputDevice"
    Identifier   "ConfiguredMouse"
    Driver       "vmmouse"
    Option       "CorePointer"
    Option       "Device" "/dev/input/mice"
EndSection
```

The following section specifies the video card **Device**. Note how it also identifies the hardware location through the **Busid**, the vmware **Driver**, as well as the standard **Screen 0**, which configures the GUI on the first available virtual terminal after the command line terminals, normally virtual terminal 7.

```
Section "Device"
        Identifier   "Configured Video Device"
        Boardname    "VMware virtual video card"
        Busid        "PCI:0:15:0"
        Driver       "vmware"
        Screen       0
EndSection
```

The next stanza specifies the display **Monitor**. Note how it also identifies the display parameters, as well as the limits on the horizontal scan (**Horizsync**) and vertical refresh

(**Vertrefresh**) rates. This section reflects a conservative configuration, when uncertain about the true capabilities of a flat panel or laptop monitor.

```
Section "Monitor"
        Identifier    "Configured Monitor"
        Vendorname    "Generic LCD Display"
        Modelname     "LCD Panel 1024x768"
        Horizsync     31.5 - 48.0
        Vertrefresh   56.0 - 65.0
EndSection
```

The **Screen** stanza collects information from the **Monitor** and graphics card (**Device**) stanzas. It is often coupled with a color depth (**Defaultdepth**) and available display **Modes**.

```
Section "Screen"
        Identifier      "Default Screen"
        Monitor         "Configured Monitor"
        Device          "Configured Video Device"
        Defaultdepth    24
        SubSection "Display"
                Depth   24
                Virtual 1024    768
                Modes           "1024x768@60"   "800x600@60"
        EndSubSection
EndSection
```

The **ServerLayout** section identifies the **"Default Screen"** just described in the **Screen** stanza. It can also be used for other screen configurations, such as second monitors.

```
Section "ServerLayout"
        Identifier      "Default Layout"
        Screen          "Default Screen"
EndSection
```

Stanzas that may or may not be included include **Module** and **ServerFlags**. A **Module** stanza would include driver modules loaded when the X server is started. **ServerFlags** would be associated with global options.

# Basic Xfce Tools

The Xfce desktop environment is similar to other GUI desktops, including GNOME, KDE, and even Apple Macintosh and Microsoft Windows. It includes a panel, a menu button, and icons. If you've installed the xubuntu-desktop meta-package described in the first part of the chapter, you've also installed a number of GNOME applications and utilities.

Those of you who've used Xfce in the past may notice how it's evolving more toward GNOME. Figure 13-9 displays the Xfce desktop environment shown when the xubuntu-desktop meta-package is installed. You'll note that it's much more complex than the minimal environment shown in Figure 13-1.

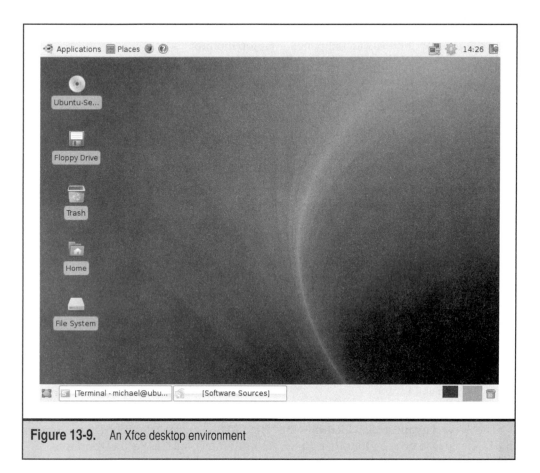

**Figure 13-9.** An Xfce desktop environment

The panel at the bottom includes minimized applications. The panel at the top includes menus, as well as icons associated with the time, network configuration, and available updates. Icons are shown on the left side of the screen as well.

Older versions of the Xfce desktop (as well as the minimal Xfce desktop shown in Figure 13-1) supported access to the main menu with a right-click. Now you need to click the Applications button to access the menu. The Applications submenu options are summarized in Table 13-3.

Three other options are shown on the Applications menu. The Help option opens Xubuntu documentation in the default web browser. The About Xfce option provides more information on the current version and licensing of the desktop environment. The Quit option opens a window that allows you to switch users, log out, restart, shut down, suspend, or hibernate the system, if the hardware allows it.

Finally, the Places menu supports access to custom versions of the Thunar file browser, with access to the current user's home directory and more. Thunar is functionally similar to GNOME's Nautilus and KDE's Konqueror.

| Submenu Option | Description |
|---|---|
| Settings | Accesses settings, printer, login window, Smart Common Input Method (SCIM) options when installed |
| Accessories | Opens lower level applets such as the terminal and text editors |
| Games | Allows access to the games from the gnome-games package |
| Graphics | Supports access to graphical tools such as the GIMP |
| Multimedia | Takes the user to multimedia applications |
| Network | Accesses basic networking/Internet applications |
| Office | Opens applications associated with office suites |
| System | Accesses administrative tools |

**Table 13-3.** Xfce Desktop Applications Options

# Remote GUI Access

Before proceeding to configure remote GUI access on Ubuntu, you need to know a couple of things about the workings of the Linux GUI. Normally on a network, the local computer is the client and the remote computer acts as the server. X Window clients and servers work on a different paradigm. The X server controls the graphics on the local computer. The X server draws images on the client screen and takes input from the local keyboard and mouse. In contrast, X clients are local or remote applications such as xclock that you can run on the local X server. X client data is transmitted over a network.

I'll describe three ways to configure remote access to a GUI system. I've suggested one method in Chapter 7—with SSH. Once configured as described in that chapter, you can access GUI applications from a remote client. All you need to do is add the **-X** switch to the **ssh** login command; for example, I administer an Ubuntu server on my desktop from my laptop by first logging into that remote system with the following command:

```
$ ssh -X michael@ubuntuhardy
```

I can then open GUI tools, including administrative tools, from the remote system on my laptop. The other major ways to access a GUI desktop remotely involve X Display Manager Control Protocol (XDMCP) and the Virtual Network Computing (VNC) service.

## Remote Access via XDMCP

To configure access via XDMCP, you need a graphical login manager on both the client and the remote X server. To modify the GNOME graphical login manager, which is also used for the Xfce desktop environment, use the Login Window Preferences tool,

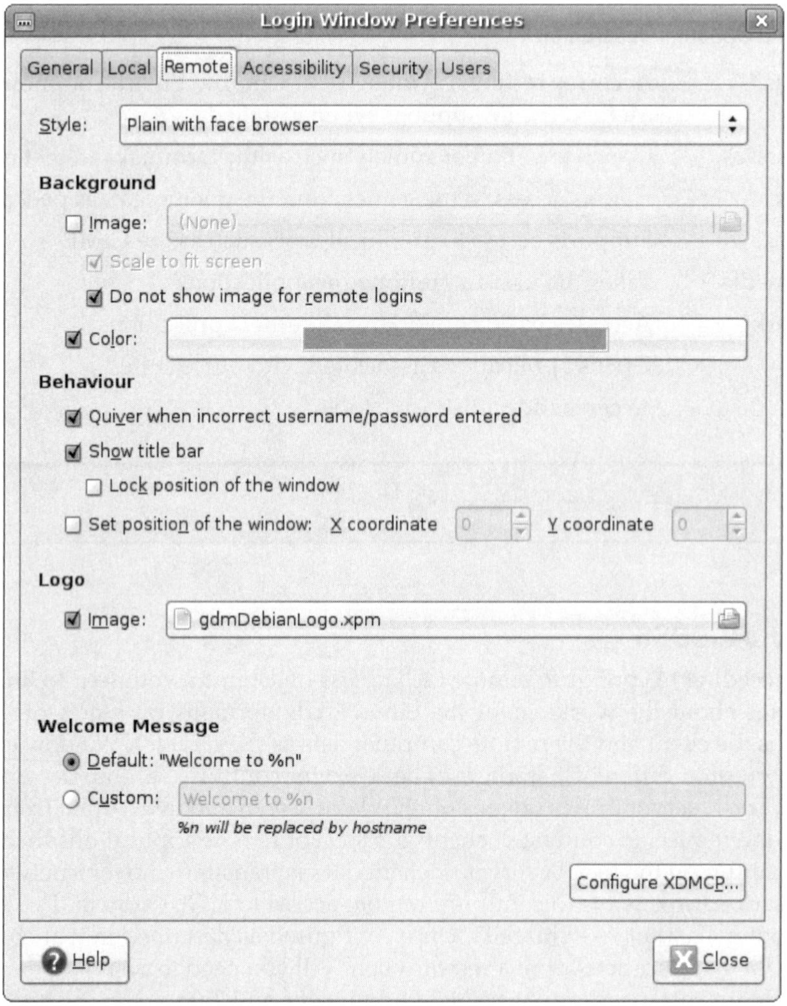

**Figure 13-10.** Configure remote access

available from the **sudo gdmsetup** command. As suggested by Figure 13-10, it's fairly easy to configure remote access using the login manager. Under the Remote tab, the Style drop-down text box can disable remote access, enable the same remote and local access screens, or enable a Plain With Face Browser screen.

I configured remote access from the screen shown in the figure, which added the following directive to the /etc/gdm/gdm.conf-custom file, which is incorporated into the main display manager configuration:

```
RemoteGreeter=/usr/lib/gdmgreeter
```

Once remote access is configured in this way, you should be able to connect from a remote desktop manager using the following steps:

1. From the GNOME login screen, click Options; from the KDE login screen, click Menu. If you're in the Xfce login screen, press F10.

2. From the pop-up menu that appears, select Remote Login Via XDMCP or Remote Login.

3. After a few moments, a screen should appear with a list of hosts configured for remote access. An example from a GNOME login screen is shown here.

4. Highlight the desired host, and click Connect or Accept. The display manager from the remote system should appear.

5. Log into the remote system using an appropriate username and password.

6. After logging out of the remote system, you should see the display manager for the local client.

## Remote Access via VNC

VNC can help you administer remote systems. There are several options available for VNC servers and clients in the Ubuntu repositories. This section describes just one server, *vino*, and one client, *vinagre*. Both are built with GTK libraries, suitable for Xfce and GNOME.

Install the vino package on a target server with the **sudo apt-get install vino** command. You can then configure the VNC server with the **vino-preferences** command, which opens the Remote Desktop Preferences tool shown in Figure 13-11.

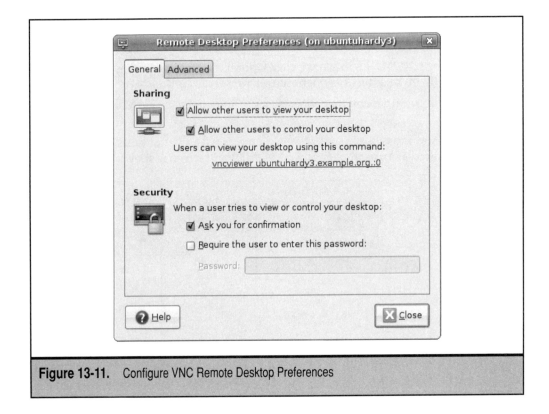

**Figure 13-11.** Configure VNC Remote Desktop Preferences

Options under the Advanced tab can block access, configure security, and notify the local user when someone has connected via VNC. To configure the local system as a VNC server whenever that user logs in, you'll need access to the Autostarted Applications tool, available through the **xfce4-autostart-editor** command. If the command is not available, install the xfce4-session package. The Autostarted Applications tool is elementary and determines the applications that start automatically when a user logs into the GUI. Such applications are configured in each user's home directory, using files in the .config/autostart/ subdirectory.

Install the VNC client package with a command such as **sudo apt-get install xvnc4viewer**. On the client, run the **xvnc4viewer** command to open the VNC Viewer: Connection Details window. Enter the IP address or hostname of the target system and click OK.

If you've configured the VNC server to confirm when a remote client is trying to connect, a user on that server has to click Refuse or Allow. If Allow is clicked on the server, the client gets a view similar to what's shown in Figure 13-12.

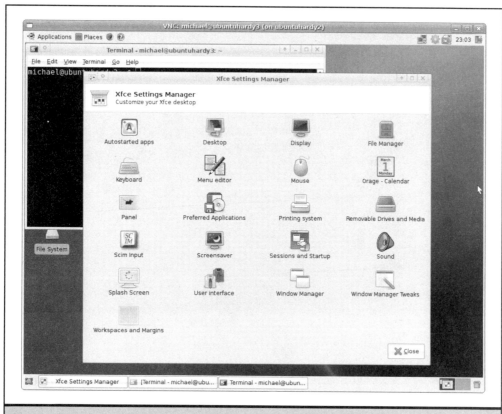

**Figure 13-12.**   A Remote VNC connection

# SUMMARY

This chapter described the basic process for installing a GUI on an Ubuntu Server system. You can install a basic set of packages for the GNOME, KDE, or Xfce desktop environments, or you can install the associated desktop meta-packages: xubuntu-desktop, ubuntu-desktop, or kubuntu-desktop.

The X server can be reconfigured in several ways. The basic method to reconfigure the X server is with the **sudo dpkg-reconfigure xserver-xorg** command. A graphical tool is available from the displayconfig-gtk package, which installs a tool that can be started with a command of the same name. The **Xorg -configure** command can also set up a proposed X server configuration file in the local directory.

The Xfce desktop environment shares characteristics with GNOME, as befits their common GTK development tools. Remote logins can be configured through graphical display managers. Remote access can be configured with appropriate VNC servers and clients.

# CHAPTER 14

## DHCP and DNS

This chapter focuses on the DHCP (Dynamic Host Configuration Protocol) and DNS (Domain Name System) services that connect Linux and other clients to networks such as the Internet. A DHCP server uses the Dynamic Host Configuration Protocol to automate the network configuration process, either from a preconfigured range of IP addresses or one or more specific reserved IP addresses. It can be used to configure additional network settings. In this chapter, you'll see how to configure a DHCP server for local and remote networks.

A DNS server translates human-readable domain names such as www.mommabears .com to IP addresses such as 10.245.43.5, and vice versa. DNS servers are configured in a distributed database; each server has its own delegated "zone of authority" for one or more domains. In this chapter, you'll see how to configure four different types of DNS servers.

While Ubuntu can handle both IPv4 and IPv6 addresses, the chapter and this book focus on IPv4 addresses. More people are familiar with IPv4, and in most cases IPv6 users can simply substitute their 128-bit addresses. In a few cases, IPv6 directives are slightly different from those of IPv4 and are also referenced in this chapter.

# CREATE A DYNAMIC HOST CONFIGURATION PROTOCOL (DHCP) SERVER

DHCP servers are designed to ration IP addresses on a network. They can also simplify the configuration of more than just IP addresses; DHCP servers can be configured to specify gateways, default routes, and more.

There are several DHCP server packages available for Ubuntu. The older dhcpd package was used just for IPv4 addresses. Ubuntu has therefore moved to the dhcp3-server package, which can handle IPv4 and IPv6 addresses. Once configured, the Ubuntu DHCP server can assign more information such as the gateway and DNS IP address(es) to every system that requests an IP address.

If you're testing Ubuntu Server, take care to avoid conflicts with any other DHCP routers. As I write this book from my home, I disable the DHCP server on the router that connects my home network to the Internet. I then activate the Ubuntu DHCP server. Multiple DHCP servers on a single network can make it difficult to diagnose problems.

## Install the DHCP Server Packages

There are two primary packages associated with a DHCP server: the main server, and a relay if you need that server to assign network information for remote networks. While this chapter focuses on the standard dhcp3-* server packages, you may prefer to install one of the alternatives, such as the lightweight udhcpd server or IPv6-only wide-dhcpv6-server. Most of the directives in the associated configuration files do not change.

**NOTE** Even though plenty of IPv6 addresses are (currently) available, DHCP servers are still needed for IPv6 networks, at least to distribute information such as DNS server and gateway IP addresses.

## Install a DHCP Server

To install the default Ubuntu DHCP server with the accompanying GUI configuration tool, run the following command:

```
$ sudo apt-get install dhcp3-server gdhcpd
```

Note that you'll learn how to configure the appropriate configuration file before opening the GUI DHCP server configuration tool.

## A DHCP Relay

If you need to configure a connection to another network, it would be simplest to configure the DHCP server on a gateway system with direct connections to all target networks. But that's not always possible. In that case, you'll want to install the dhcp3-relay package on a gateway computer with a connection to the network with the DHCP server—as well as the remote target network. One installation method uses the following command:

```
$ sudo apt-get install dhcp3-relay
```

When installing the dhcp3-relay package, you're asked to specify the hostname or IP address of the actual DHCP server in a screen similar to that shown in Figure 14-1.

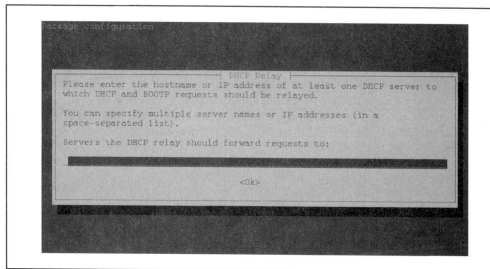

**Figure 14-1.** Configure the DHCP Relay server

Subsequent steps require the interface to remote networks, such as eth0. The DHCP relay service listens for DHCP client requests on that network. You're also asked for command options to the **dhcrelay3** command.

If you make a mistake or need to change these settings, the following command repeats the same steps:

```
$ sudo dpkg-reconfigure dhcp3-relay
```

However, messages between networks don't get delivered unless messages are forwarded as discussed in Chapter 11. In addition, you need to make sure no firewall is blocking traffic on the applicable TCP/IP port. Per the /etc/services configuration file, the BOOTP (Bootstrap Protocol) uses port 67.

## The Configuration File

Now review the configuration of the DHCP3 server. The default version of the configuration file, /etc/dhcp3/dhcpd.conf, does not configure any IP addresses. So if you try to activate this server without modifying the configuration file, it won't assign any IP addresses. This section reviews default configuration directives, along with the directives you need to add to set up a DHCP3 server on a standard private IPv4 network.

**NOTE** Be aware of the semicolon ( ; ) at the end of each line; a common cause for errors in DHCP configuration files is administrators who forget to add that bit of punctuation.

In the /etc/dhcp3/dhcpd.conf configuration file, Dynamic DNS updates are not enabled based on the following directive:

```
ddns-update-style none;
```

The standard alternative value is **interim**, which allows the DHCP server to update a configured Dynamic DNS server with assigned information.

In the following directives, you should substitute the domain name of the local private network for *example.org*. You should also substitute the fully qualified domain name (FQDN) or preferably the IP address of the DNS servers for *ns1.example.org* and *ns2 .example.org*:

```
option domain-name "example.org";
option domain-name-servers ns1.example.org, ns2.example.org;
```

If you don't substitute IP addresses for the DNS servers listed, there's a risk. If the IP address information for the DNS servers is not available locally, the client may not be able to find the DNS servers.

IP addresses are leased for a certain number of seconds, before they have to be renewed. The lease time is as defined by the following directives: the **default-lease-time** is the standard, and the **max-lease-time** is the maximum before a renewal is required:

```
default-lease-time 600;
max-lease-time 7200;
```

If this DHCP server is primary for the local network, you should activate the following directive. If it's primary for just a specific subnet, add the **authoritative** directive to the subnet stanza, which is explained shortly:

```
#authoritative;
```

By default, logging from this service is sent to the local system. Depending on the severity of the log, this directive means that DHCP server log messages are available in /var/log/debug and /var/log/messages, as defined in the /etc/syslog.conf configuration file.

```
log-facility local7;
```

If you want to isolate DHCP server messages, add an appropriate message to the /etc/syslog.conf file. For detailed information, see Chapter 7. For example, to log all messages of info level and higher in the /var/log/dhcpserver.log configuration file, add the following directive to /etc/syslog.conf:

```
local7.info     /var/log/dhcpserver.log
```

Before this works, you have to create an empty version of the log file; one method is with the **sudo touch /var/log/dhcpserver.log** command.

Of course, you need to configure a system for some local network. The following sample stanza, if active, would configure the DHCP server on the 10.254.239.0/255.255 .255.224 network. Available IP addresses range between 10.254.239.1 and 10.254.239.31. The **range** directive limits the DHCP server to assigning addresses between 10.254.239.10 and 10.254.239.20.

The **option routers** directive specifies a gateway host, which is added to subject client routing tables. You can, and in my opinion should, substitute IP addresses for the hostname, unless you have a reliable DNS server.

```
#subnet 10.254.239.0 netmask 255.255.255.224 {
#   range 10.254.239.10 10.254.239.20;
#   option routers rtr-239-0-1.example.org, rtr-239-0-2.example.org;
#}
```

The next sample stanza would work for a remote network connected via BOOTP, using the aforementioned dhcp3-relay server on a properly configured gateway system.

The **broadcast-address** directive assumes the gateway between the local network and the remote network can be found on IP address 10.254.239.31:

```
#subnet 10.254.239.32 netmask 255.255.255.224 {
#   range dynamic-bootp 10.254.239.40 10.254.239.60;
#   option broadcast-address 10.254.239.31;
#   option routers rtr-239-32-1.example.org;
#}
```

There are a number of other suggested options which can be found in the comments of the default version of the configuration file. For example, the following directive assigns a DNS server. DHCP clients write the information shown to their versions of the /etc/resolv.conf configuration file. You should replace *ns1.internal.example.org* with a pointer to your DNS server. I strongly recommend replacing *ns1.internal.example.org* with the IP address of your DNS server. Otherwise, you'll need an entry for the FQDN and the corresponding IP address in every client's /etc/hosts configuration file.

```
#   option domain-name-servers ns1.internal.example.org;
```

Many systems require or should have a static IP address. For example, I'm a believer that DNS servers should have fixed IP addresses. Even if reliable /etc/hosts files exist on each client, gateways for traffic outside the network need fixed IP addresses. The following stanza is not included in the default version of dhcpd.conf. It's included here as an example of how you could configure a fixed IP address. This stanza specifies the hardware address of the network card, 98:76:54:FE:DC:BA, on a system named gateway1, with the noted IP address:

```
host gateway1 {
    hardware ethernet 98:76:54:FE:DC:BA
    fixed-address 10.254.239.31
}
```

The remainder of the /etc/dhcp3/dhcpd.conf configuration file includes hints for configuring the DHCP server for remote networks and reserved IP addresses, as well as allowing or denying DHCP access to a group of systems. Feel free to activate and customize the hints appropriate to your network.

Once the configuration is complete, turn off any other DHCP services and start this one with the following command:

```
$ sudo /etc/init.d/dhcp3-server start
```

Even if you've changed the /etc/syslog.conf file, as described earlier, success or failure of the DHCP server is also logged in the /var/log/messages log file. Test this server from a remote client, with a command such as this:

```
$ sudo dhclient eth0
```

Then review the logs to see what happened. If an IP address lease has been granted, details will be available in the /var/lib/dhcp3/ directory, in the dhcpd.leases file.

If you're just experimenting and want to reactivate an existing DHCP server, first deactivate this DHCP server with the following command:

```
$ sudo /etc/init.d/dhcp3-server stop
```

## The GUI DHCP Server Configuration Tool

Ubuntu now has a GUI configuration tool available, courtesy of the gdhcpd package. As it's built with GTK+ libraries, it does not require many additional packages on the Xfce (or even the GNOME) desktop environments. I prefer to customize most services directly through their text configuration files. However, one value I find for GUI tools is how it helps newer administrators learn more about subject services.

Before running the tool, back up the current version of the configuration file. For example, the following command backs up that file in the current user's home directory:

```
$ cp /etc/dhcp3/dhcpd.conf ~
```

Now open the GDHCPD configuration tool with the following command that opens the interface shown in Figure 14-2.

```
$ sudo gdhcpd
```

The scope shown in Figure 14-2 is slightly different from what was configured in the preceding section. Note the additional information that can be configured in the Client Settings area. When I click the Reread button, the following stanza is added to the /etc/dhcp3/dhcpd.conf configuration file:

```
subnet 192.168.0.0 netmask 255.255.255.0 {
    interface eth0;
    range 192.168.0.100 192.168.0.110;
    default-lease-time 1200;
    max-lease-time 6400;
    option domain-name "example.org";
    option subnet-mask 255.255.255.0;
    option broadcast-address 192.168.0.255;
    option routers 192.168.0.1;
    option domain-name-servers 192.168.0.1;
}
```

As you can see from the graphical DHCP configuration tool, other options are available. The Single Hosts tab allows you to configure characteristics such as a fixed IP address. The Leases tab reviews the status of leased IP addresses in the aforementioned leases file, /var/lib/dhcp3/dhcpd.leases. The Verify tab allows you to run the shell commands.

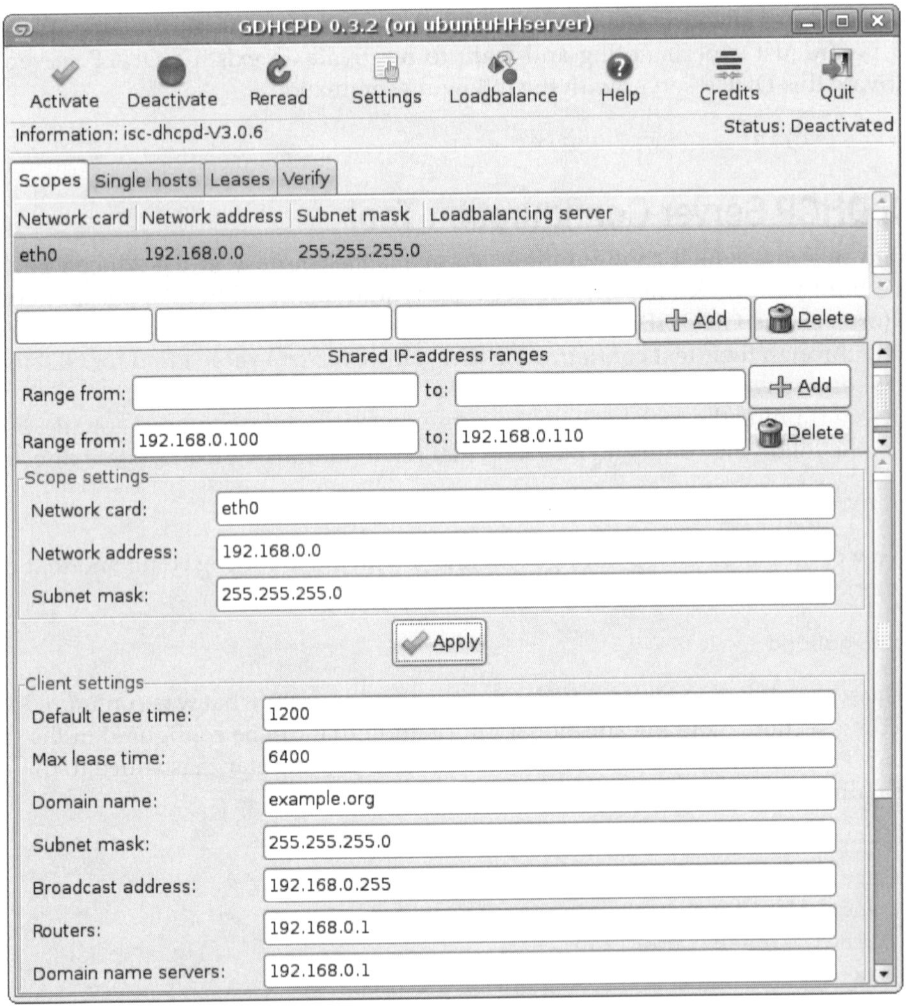

**Figure 14-2.** The Graphical DHCP configuration tool

# THE DOMAIN NAME SYSTEM

DNS maintains a database that can help your computer translate domain names such as www.ubuntu.com to IP addresses such as 91.189.94.249. As no individual DNS server has enough room to store the entire Internet in its database, each server is configured by default to refer requests to other DNS servers. A DNS server is also known as a name server or nameserver, as befits its description in the main DNS client configuration file, /etc/resolv.conf.

This section describes how to create four different types of DNS servers: forwarding, caching, slave, and master. The names are descriptive; for example, a forwarding DNS server forwards requests. A caching name server stores the results of forwarded requests; repeated requests that can use the cache are not forwarded. As the data directly available to a master server is generally limited to a local network, it needs to be able to forward requests as well. Finally, slave DNS servers (also known as *secondary master* servers) need access to the authoritative database on the master DNS server.

The basic DNS client was discussed in Chapter 11, along with how access to DNS servers is configured in the /etc/resolv.conf configuration file. In the first part of this chapter, you also learned how it can be configured by a DHCP server with the **domain-name-servers** directive.

## Install DNS Packages

The default DNS packages are based on the Berkeley Internet Name Domain (BIND). Development of the basic BIND server continues under the auspices of the Internet Systems Consortium (ISC). There are several excellent alternative DNS services available. A search of the Hardy Heron repositories reveals nearly 200 DNS related packages, including several servers. One alternative that I like is the djbdns package from http://cr.yp.to/djbdns.html, even though the license does not support open source–style modification. However, BIND is the "traditional" open source DNS service, and therefore BIND is what's covered in this chapter.

To install BIND and appropriate documentation, run the following command:

```
$ sudo apt-get install bind9 bind9-host bind9-doc resolvconf
```

The package name indicates that Ubuntu now uses BIND version 9, specifically 9.4.2-10, which is an Ubuntu build of the latest stable release available as of this writing. While the resolvconf package is not required, it can help with forwarding requests to other DNS services.

Pay attention to the **dig**, **nslookup**, and **host** commands; they can help you test any local or remote DNS server. If they don't exist on your system, make sure the dnsutils and bind-host9 packages are installed. These commands will be described after the first local DNS server is configured.

**NOTE**   Ubuntu now has a GUI DNS tool available from the gbindtool package. I chose not to cover the GUI tool in this book, as I found it obtuse. However, if you're learning to manage DNS for the first time, try it on a test computer. Review the effects on the configuration files discussed in this chapter. It could help you learn more about this service.

## Focus on BIND

The structure of BIND services can be complex. Larger enterprises may want to hide their master DNS servers, as DNS can be a focus of cracker attacks. Slave or caching DNS services may be presented for use by clients. Such hidden DNS servers are sometimes also known as *stealth servers*.

To that end, four different types of DNS servers can and will be configured in this chapter. Any of these not presented to clients are stealth servers.

▼ **A master DNS server**    Stores authoritative records for the domain. Requests for the IP address of other hosts may be cached or forwarded.

■ **A secondary master DNS server**    Relies on a master DNS server for data. It's also known as a slave DNS server. Requests for the IP address of other hosts may be cached or forwarded.

■ **A caching-only DNS server**    Stores recent requests like a Proxy server. If the answer is not in the local cache, it refers to other DNS servers.

▲ **A forwarding-only DNS server**    Refers all requests to other DNS servers.

## Ubuntu File Structure for BIND

Before making any configuration changes for the BIND service, you need to understand the files available for the service. Most BIND data and configuration files are stored in the /etc/bind/ directory. But when the BIND service starts, it first refers to the /etc/default/ bind9 configuration file. It includes basic options for the service; for more information, see the man page for the **/usr/sbin/named** command. Default BIND configuration files are listed in Table 14-1 and are in the /etc/bind/ directory unless otherwise noted. These files do not include the forward or reverse zone data files for the local network.

| DNS Configuration File | Description |
| --- | --- |
| db.0 | Reverse zone file for the default zone |
| db.127 | Reverse zone file for the loopback interface |
| db.255 | Reverse zone file for the broadcast zone |
| db.empty | Reverse zone designated for private IP address networks |
| db.local | Zone file for the loopback interface |
| db.root | List of root servers for the Internet |
| named.conf | Primary BIND9 configuration file |
| named.conf.local | BIND9 configuration file for administrator input |
| named.conf.options | BIND9 configuration file for caching and forwarding |
| rndc.key | Authentication key for DNS requests; can be changed with the **rndc-confgen** command |
| zones.rfc1918 | File for reverse lookups of private IP address networks |
| /etc/default/bind9 | File with start parameters for the BIND9 service |

**Table 14-1.**    DNS Server Configuration Files

BIND data for slave/secondary servers can be stored in the /var/cache/bind/ directory.

The basic configuration files in the /etc/bind9 directory are the named.* files. The named.conf.local file; is intended for use as a zone configuration file for the local network. The db.* files in the /etc/bind directory are intended as forward and reverse zone data files. Administrator input will primarily go into the named.conf.local and customized db.* files for the local network.

While you do not have to use the filenames listed in Table 14-1, you do need to make sure the files are properly cited in the /etc/bind/named.conf.* configuration files.

# Configure a Caching-Only Server

When the BIND service is installed from the bind9 package, the configuration files are already set up as a caching name server. All you need to do is make sure the DNS client uses the caching name server on the local system.

But let's back up a bit. Assume no DNS server is configured on the local system. In that case, DNS servers are added to the /etc/resolv.conf configuration file during the boot process, as the DHCP client acquires this information from the DHCP server.

How you edit the /etc/resolv.conf file depends on whether the resolvconf package has been installed. If you did not install the resolvconf package, the /etc/resolv.conf file can be edited directly. Otherwise, edit the /etc/resolvconf/resolv.conf.d/head file. To refer the client to the local caching DNS server, include the following directive:

```
nameserver 127.0.0.1
```

While there's a warning in comments about not modifying the /etc/resolvconf/ resolv.conf.d/head file "by hand," that's not relevant for the purpose of this chapter. We're just performing a test of whether the DNS client can read and reflect the information in appropriate files. Once the directive is added, activate the BIND9 DNS service with the following command:

```
$ sudo /etc/init.d/bind9 start
```

Check the /etc/resolv.conf file. If the resolvconf package is properly installed, it should automatically update that file. Otherwise, you may need to update the/etc/ resolv.conf file by hand.

Now take a quick look at the first active line in the main BIND9 configuration file. The following directive in /etc/bind/named.conf

```
include "/etc/bind/named.conf.options";
```

includes and imports all directives from the /etc/bind/named.conf.options file.

Now when requesting a web page such as www.mhprofessional.com, the client system asks the local DNS server for the associated IP address. This process is known as a *name query*. If the final DNS server is outside your network, this request can take time. The new caching-only name server stores these queries locally, which can save significant time while you or others on your network browse the same sites on the Internet.

As the default version of the /etc/bind/named.conf.options file is configured as a caching name server, it deserves a detailed review. All of the directives in this file are enclosed as *options*, as follows:

▼ The **directory** directive specifies the location of the DNS cache, in this case, the /var/cache/bind/ directory.

■ The **auth-nxdomain no** directive means the local DNS server is not authoritative and therefore must refer to other DNS servers for real information. You would not find this directive on a master or slave DNS server.

■ The **listen-on-v6 (any;)** directive specifies the use of any TCP/IP port number for IPv6 addresses.

■ Another possible additional directive would limit access to the standard TCP/IP port associated with DNS (53), as well as the IP address of the local system and the local network card (substitute as needed for 192.168.0.15):

```
listen-on port 53 { 127.0.0.1; 192.168.0.15; }
```

The IPv6 version of this directive is **listen-on-v6 port 53**.

▲ Another interesting directive would limit access to the local system and a specific local network (substitute your network address for 192.168.0.0/24):

```
allow-query { 127.0.0.1; 192.168.0.0/24; }
```

**NOTE**   If you have a firewall, it might expect DNS communication on TCP/IP port 53. If it does, you'll want to activate the **query-source address * port 53** directive (or add the **query-source-v6 address * port 53** directive for IPv6 addresses). For example, many **iptables** firewalls assume DNS communication via UDP (User Datagram Protocol) through port 53.

Once the /etc/bind/named.conf.options file is configured as desired, you can start the local caching DNS name server with the following command:

```
$ sudo /etc/init.d/bind9 restart
```

If problems arise, messages may appear in the console. For detailed messages relating to success or failure of DNS, including syntax errors, examine the daemon.log and syslog files in the /var/log directory.

# BIND Command Utilities

This section describes BIND tools that can manage and test the DNS server. These tools use the **nslookup**, **host**, and **dig** commands. In addition, one more command is important for controlling the BIND service: **rndc**. It's known as the *name server control utility*.

## The Name Server Control Utility, rndc

The **rndc** commands are straightforward; however, they don't tell you much until the DNS server is properly configured. When you run **rndc** by itself, the output guides you through the available options. Many options are straightforward: **rndc stop** and **rndc start** don't require much explanation, as they stop and start the local DNS service. The **rndc reload** command rereads any changes you've made to the configuration or DNS database files. The **rndc status** command confirms that DNS is running, along with information on the DNS database.

## nslookup

The **nslookup** command provides information on the DNS server, its address, as well as the address of the target hostname or IP address. When applied to the McGraw-Hill Professional website, the returned information is simple, as shown next. The DNS server used by the client is on the local system, as depicted by the loopback IP address of 127.0.0.1, using TCP/IP port number 53. And there's a live IP address associated with mhprofessional.com.

```
$ nslookup mhprofessional.com
Server:        127.0.0.1
Address:       127.0.0.1#53

Non-authoritative answer:
Name:   mhprofessional.com
Address: 12.163.148.249
```

However, when I apply the **nslookup** command to the noted IP address, I get more interesting information, including the fully qualified domain name. In other words, mhprofessional.com is just another name associated with IP address 12.163.148.247. In DNS-speak, it's a *canonical name*. The other "authoritative answers" specify the DNS servers with authority over the zone associated with mhprofessional.com. If you don't see any "authoritative answers," it's likely that a DNS server is not active on the local system.

```
$ nslookup 12.163.148.249
Server:        127.0.0.1
Address:       127.0.0.1#53

Non-authoritative answer:
249.148.163.12.in-addr.arpa     name = newbooks.eppg.com.

Authoritative answers can be found from:
148.163.12.in-addr.arpa nameserver = corp-hts-ns1.mcgraw-hill.com.
148.163.12.in-addr.arpa nameserver = corp-ukc-ns1.mcgraw-hill.com.
148.163.12.in-addr.arpa nameserver = corp-55w-ns1.mcgraw-hill.com.
corp-55w-ns1.mcgraw-hill.com    internet address = 198.45.19.135
corp-ukc-ns1.mcgraw-hill.com    internet address = 198.45.26.133
corp-hts-ns1.mcgraw-hill.com    internet address = 204.17.166.247
```

## host

The **host** command, when applied to a FQDN such as mhprofessional.com, lists just the basic information associated with that domain name:

```
$ host mhprofessional.com
mhprofessional.com has address 12.163.148.249
mhprofessional.com mail is handled by 0 mail.eppg.com.
```

The **host** command, when applied to an IP address, can also identify the authoritative DNS server for the domain:

```
$ host 12.163.148.249
249.148.163.12.in-addr.arpa domain name pointer newbooks.eppg.com.
```

The **host** command can do more. For authoritative domains, it can also list all members of the domain. Once you've configured a DNS server (later in this chapter), use the **host -la example.org** command (or the domain name for the local network) to list the members of the domain. For example, the following output illustrates the result on my network:

```
Trying "example.org"
;; ->>HEADER<<- opcode: QUERY, status: NOERROR, id: 50927
;; flags: qr aa ra; QUERY: 1, ANSWER: 13, AUTHORITY: 0, ADDITIONAL: 0

;; QUESTION SECTION:
;example.org.                        IN      AXFR

;; ANSWER SECTION:
example.org.            172800  IN      SOA     ns1.example.org.
    michael.example.org. 2008111301 7200 3600 86400 604800
example.org.            172800  IN      NS      ns1.example.org.
example.org.            172800  IN      MX      10 mail.example.org.
ftp.example.org.        172800  IN      CNAME   ubuntuhardy.example.org.
mail.example.org.       172800  IN      A       192.168.0.104
ns1.example.org.        172800  IN      A       192.168.0.104
ubuntuGG.example.org.   172800  IN      A       192.168.0.6
ubuntuhardy.example.org. 172800 IN      A       192.168.0.104
ubuntuhardy2.example.org. 172800 IN     A       192.168.0.153
ubuntuhardy3.example.org. 172800 IN     A       192.168.0.154
ubuntuserver.example.org. 172800 IN     A       192.168.0.50
www.example.org.        172800  IN      CNAME   ubuntuhardy.example.org.
example.org.            172800  IN      SOA     ns1.example.org.
    michael.example.org. 2008111301 7200 3600 86400 604800

Received 356 bytes from 192.168.0.153#53 in 2 ms
```

```
michael@ubuntuhardy:~$ dig mhprofessional.com

; <<>> DiG 9.4.2 <<>> mhprofessional.com
;; global options:  printcmd
;; Got answer:
;; ->>HEADER<<- opcode: QUERY, status: NOERROR, id: 30646
;; flags: qr rd ra; QUERY: 1, ANSWER: 1, AUTHORITY: 3, ADDITIONAL: 0

;; QUESTION SECTION:
;mhprofessional.com.            IN      A

;; ANSWER SECTION:
mhprofessional.com.    879      IN      A       12.163.148.249

;; AUTHORITY SECTION:
mhprofessional.com.    755      IN      NS      NS3.MHEDU.com.
mhprofessional.com.    755      IN      NS      NS2.MHEDU.com.
mhprofessional.com.    755      IN      NS      NS1.MHEDU.com.

;; Query time: 1 msec
;; SERVER: 127.0.0.1#53(127.0.0.1)
;; WHEN: Mon Apr 28 10:11:48 2008
;; MSG SIZE  rcvd: 112

michael@ubuntuhardy:~$ []
```

**Figure 14-3.**    The **dig** command provides important information

## dig

The domain information groper, also known as the **dig** command, is the DNS lookup utility. By itself, the **dig** command lists authoritative DNS servers for the specified URL. For example, Figure 14-3 lists the IP address associated with mhprofessional.com, followed by the three authoritative DNS servers, NS1.MHEDU.com through NS3.MHEDU.com.

# Configure a Forwarding Server

A forwarding DNS server is simple. It requires the addition of a single directive to the DNS configuration file. A template is already available in the /etc/bind/named.conf .options file. As noted, the directives in this file are automatically incorporated in the /etc/bind/named.conf file. To include the DNS addresses of other servers, you can take advantage of the following directive:

```
// forwarders {
//      0.0.0.0;
// };
```

The double forward slash (//) is a comment character associated with the C++ and Java programming languages. To configure specific forwarders, say from your ISP, substitute those IP addresses for 0.0.0.0. Be aware that some ISPs require permission to use their

DNS servers as forwarders. For the purpose of this exercise, I substitute a couple of the root servers from the /etc/bind/db.root configuration file:

```
forwarders {
      128.8.10.90;
      192.203.230.10;
};
```

If the data can't be found in those DNS servers, it's up to those servers to ask others for the information. As the IP addresses I cite here are from the "root" servers, they are authoritative name servers for the Internet. But as such, their response times may be slower.

# Configure a Standard DNS Server

To configure a standard DNS server, you need a domain name as well as hostnames and IP addresses for systems on the local network. You'll also need to know which systems are designated as name servers and mail servers. From this information, you can create appropriate data for forward and reverse searches in individual zone files.

For the purpose of this chapter, I've configured several systems on my network on the example.org domain. The example.com, example.net, and example.org domains are explicitly reserved for documentation, as you can see by entering any of these domain names in an Internet connected browser.

Forward searches return IP addresses such as 192.168.0.50 for domain names such as ubuntuserver.example.org. Similar searches can be stored in a database such as /etc/hosts or a DNS zone file. I use the db.example.org file for this purpose. Reverse searches require an inverse version of the same database. I use the db.192 file for the inverse database.

I've designated the ubuntuhardy.example.org system on IP address 192.168.0.104 as the name server and e-mail server. I've also configured several clients on the same IP address network, in both the forward (db.example.org) and reverse (db.192) zone files.

## Configuring named.conf.local for a Local Network

The /etc/bind/named.conf.local file is reserved for administrators to create a regular DNS server. What you add to this file is automatically incorporated in the main /etc/bind/named.conf configuration file. For this purpose, I add the following stanza that points to a forward zone file:

```
zone "example.com" {
      type master;
      file "/etc/bind/db.example.org";
      allow-transfer { 192.168.0.104; 192.168.0.153; };
};
```

The stanza specifies that a *master* DNS server is being configured for the example.org zone—also known as the DNS "zone of authority." In other words, this DNS server is the primary authoritative database for the example.org zone. The **allow-transfer** directives shown limit access to specific slave or secondary DNS servers at defined IP addresses. I include the IP address of the local master server system (in my case, 192.168.0.104); otherwise, that master DNS server won't work after transferring its database to the slave DNS server.

Data associated with that zone can be found in the noted file, /etc/bind/ db.example.org, which I'll populate shortly. But first, I add the following stanza for a reverse zone file:

```
zone "0.168.192.in-addr.arpa" {
        type master;
        file "/etc/bind/db.192";
        allow-transfer { 192.168.0.104; 192.168.0.153; };
};
```

The **zone** directive information in quotes is based on the reverse of the IP network address. I've configured the systems on my home network in the 192.168.0.0/24 subnet. The network address is 192.168.0.0. The part of that network address that is constant is 192.168.0. The reverse of that constant is 0.168.192. The **in-addr.arpa** is the standard directive suffix for reverse databases. The stanza looks for a reverse database in the /etc/ bind/db.192 configuration file.

Strictly speaking, a reverse zone file (and therefore a reverse zone stanza) is not required for a functional DNS server. Of course, without a reverse zone file, reverse searches based on IP address won't be possible, at least for the associated zone of authority.

## The Forward Zone File

To create a master DNS server, you'll need to create at least a forward zone file. Based on the configuration so far, the forward zone will be configured in a db.example.org file in the /etc/bind directory. To create this file, I start from the forward zone file for the localhost system, /etc/bind/db.local, with the following command:

```
$ sudo cp /etc/bind/db.local /etc/bind/db.example.org
```

Now to decipher some of the language in this file: **$TTL 604800** means that the default Time To Live (TTL) for data on this DNS server is seven days (which corresponds to 604800 seconds). It's also common to have a shorter TTL, which can be expressed in other units. For example, **2D** or **3D** corresponds to two or three days. If you prefer, individual TTLs can be specified for each entry in this file.

The SOA (Start Of Authority) record is the preamble to all zone files. It describes the zone where it comes from and the administrator e-mail for this DNS server. The @ specifies the current zone of authority, which, per the way I modified the /etc/bind/named .conf.local file, is example.org. So far, this file refers to the localhost system and specifies the root user's e-mail address. In other words, **root.localhost** translates to root@localhost.

I'll change this to the FQDN for this server and an appropriate e-mail address; the following line specifies michael@example.org:

```
@    IN    SOA    ns1.example.org. michael.example.org. (
```

Pay attention to the periods at the end of each host and domain name; without them, the DNS server will stop with a syntax error. The parentheses and the lines that follow specify a number of other parameters:

▼ The serial number is based on the date and version number. Based on the one shown below, this is the first database file created on November 13, 2008:

```
2008111301      ; Serial
```

■ The refresh frequency determines how long the local DNS *slave* server waits before checking for updates from any master DNS servers. I've changed it to every 2 hours:

```
7200            ; Refresh
```

■ The retry interval specifies how often the local DNS slave server retries contacting the master server—in this case, every hour:

```
3600            ; Retry
```

■ If there is no response from a DNS master server before the end of the expiration period—in this case, 24 hours— the local server stops accepting requests for the given domain:

```
24H             ; Expire
```

■ The TTL is the minimum amount of time other DNS servers should keep the local zone information in the cache—in this case, one week:

```
604800 )        ; Negative Cache TTL
```

▲ If you're creating a forward database from scratch, semicolons are a good idea for empty lines:

```
;
```

The **IN** specifies Internet-style data. The **NS** is the name server resource record, which refers to the name of the DNS server computer—in my case, ns1.example.org:

```
        IN    NS    ns1.example.org.
```

I delete the lines associated with IPv4 and IPv6 localhost addresses:

```
@       IN    A     127.0.0.1
@       IN    AAAA  ::1
```

I add a specification for the current mail server; the **MX** is the Mail Exchange record, which directs e-mail information to a particular computer:

```
        IN      MX      10 mail.example.org.
```

If there's more than one e-mail server, you can add more than one MX record to the forward database file. For example, the following two lines would direct e-mail traffic first to the mail.example.org system:

```
        IN      MX      10 mail.example.org.
        IN      MX      20 mail1.example.org.
```

Of course, standard entries for computers use the example.org zone. The **A** specifies the authoritative record for the zone. For example, as this is the zone of authority for example.org, the ubuntuserver.example.org internet datum (IN) authoritative record corresponds to an IP address of 192.168.0.50.

```
ubuntuserver    IN   A     192.168.0.50
ubuntuhardy     IN   A     192.168.0.104
ubuntuhardy2    IN   A     192.168.0.153
ubuntuhardy3    IN   A     192.168.0.154
```

More than one record can be associated with an IP address, courtesy of the Canonical name (**CNAME**) directive. For example, the following directives point the ftp.example.org and www.example.org FQDNs to the ubuntuhardy system:

```
mail            IN   CNAME   ubuntuhardy
www             IN   CNAME   ubuntuhardy
```

You can use additional **CNAME** directives to specify the same address for other servers such as those associated with FTP or even rsync servers. However, the **CNAME** directive no longer works for e-mail servers. Save this file. If you've only configured the forward zone in /etc/bind/named.conf.local, it's time to reread the configuration files with the **rndc reload** command. However, as I haven't done this yet, I'll need to create the reverse zone file first.

## The Reverse Zone File

A *reverse zone* file allows a DNS server to convert backward, from an IP address to a hostname. Reverse zone lookups are used by many servers of different kinds (FTP, IRC, WWW, and others) to decide whether they even want to talk to a computer asking for information. It's a common way for a mail server to check whether an e-mail has come from a valid domain. The necessary stanza has been previously added to the /etc/named.conf.local configuration file.

To create the reverse zone file, start with the reverse zone file for the localhost system, /etc/bind/db.127, with the following command:

```
$ sudo cp /etc/bind/db.127 /etc/bind/db.192
```

Be sure to make similar basic changes, as were made to the forward zone file:

```
$TTL    2D
@       IN      SOA     ns1.example.org. michael.example.org. (
                        2008111301      ; Serial
                        7200            ; Refresh
                        3600            ; Retry
                        24H             ; Expire
                        604800 )        ; Negative Cache TTL

;
@       IN      NS      ns1.example.org.
104     IN      PTR     ubuntuhardy.example.org.
153     IN      PTR     ubuntuhardy2.example.org.
154     IN      PTR     ubuntuhardy2.example.org.
50      IN      PTR     ubuntuserver.example.org.
```

Restart the BIND service with the **sudo /etc/init.d/bind9 restart** command. Now run the previously discussed **nslookup**, **host**, and **dig** commands on selected FQDNs and IP addresses. If the results do not look similar to the actual zone file, look for error messages in /var/log/daemon.log.

**NOTE**    The reverse zone database allows a server such as sendmail or Apache to verify whether the name of a requesting computer matches its IP address. This check can help prevent spoofing.

## Configure a Secondary Master (Slave) Server

A secondary master (slave) DNS server depends on a master DNS server for the database of hostnames and IP addresses. To create a secondary master DNS server, go to a system other than the master DNS server. Install the bind9 package on that server, and open the /etc/bind/named.conf.local file on that server. The information you enter here is similar to that for the master server:

```
zone "example.org" {
    type slave;
    file "db.example.org";
    masters { 192.168.0.104; };
};
```

The task for a slave server is easier; it periodically checks with the master DNS server—in this case the computer with an IP address of 192.168.0.104. If the serial number in the master database files (db.example.org, db.192) is higher than the local (slave) versions of this file, the latest DNS database information is transferred.

When the transfer is authorized, the slave automatically reads the master DNS server data and creates or updates the local db.example.org zone file in the /var/cache/bind/ directory.

# Common DNS Pitfalls

The Domain Name Service is an Internet-wide database of domain names and IP addresses. The syntax of DNS configuration files can be tricky. There are differences between BIND 8 and BIND 9, some of which have been mentioned, and most of which are beyond what can be covered in this book. A few common DNS errors are described in the following sections.

## Syntax Errors

Perhaps the most common DNS problem is a syntax error. Related log messages are available in the /var/log/syslog and /var/log/daemon.log files. Example errors include the following:

```
dns_rdata_fromtext: /etc/bind/db.example.org:13: near
'mail.example.org.': not a valid number
```

This message points to line 13 in the /etc/bind/db.example.org database file. And the not a valid number message points me to a difference between BIND versions 8 and 9—specifically the priority number, in this case 10, was not required in BIND 8:

```
        IN      MX      10      mail.example.org.
```

The following message suggests that one or more configuration files cited something other than example.org as the authoritative zone. I had to read each DNS configuration file until I identified the problem—I had accidentally typed *example.com* in one directive.

```
bad zone transfer request: 'example.org/IN':
non-authoritative zone (NOTAUTH)
```

The following message can have two causes. One might be extra spaces where they don't belong; another might be a syntax error such as a bracket } in place of a right parenthesis ).

```
loading from master file /etc/bind/db.example.org failed:
extra input text
```

Here's an example of another syntax error—in this case, on line 9 of the db.example .org database file. A space is required between the 604800 and the right parenthesis:

```
/etc/bind/db.example.org:9: near '604800)': syntax error
```

## Timing Issues

Sometimes, you won't see changes online for a few hours. When changes are made to a DNS server responsible for an Internet zone of authority, it takes some time to propagate the change to other DNS servers on the Internet. When I've changed web hosts, I'm told to wait up to 48 hours until propagation is complete. Therefore, whenever you change something such as the IP address associated with a web server, it's advisable to keep the old IP address available for that web server until the new IP address has time to propagate.

## The Serial Number

Perhaps the single most common DNS error occurs when an administrator makes updates to a zone file and restarts DNS. Unless he or she updates the serial number on the zone files, the updates aren't propagated to other DNS servers.

# SUMMARY

DHCP servers do more than just ration IP addresses on a network. They can be set up to configure much of the network configuration for network clients. DHCP servers can be configured to assign static IP addresses as needed. DHCP relay services can help the DHCP server configure clients on remote networks.

DNS servers are essential for larger networks. The standard DNS server is based on the BIND service, which can be configured as a master, slave (secondary), caching, and forwarding name server. DNS servers depend on custom configuration files that support forward and reverse searches.

# CHAPTER 15

## Web Servers and Apache's LAMP

L AMP is an acronym used to refer to a bundle of common software used to run dynamic web servers. When installed during the Ubuntu Server installation process, it's short for Linux, Apache, MySQL, and PHP. Other LAMP bundles may substitute or include the Perl and Python programming languages instead of or in addition to PHP.

This chapter covers the installation and configuration of a website on an Ubuntu server system, based on the LAMP installation. The chapter focuses on Apache configuration. Virtual hosts on Apache allow the configuration of multiple websites, even if the server is limited to a single IP address. Secure virtual hosts provide the website security now expected online by the general public.

# THE SPECIALIZED LAMP INSTALLATION

If you didn't select LAMP during the installation process, as shown in Figure 15-1, you can install the associated packages using the commands described in this section. More than 300 packages are associated with Apache, many of which include modules for everything from various forms of authentication, to adapters for programming languages, to connectors to databases. I'll describe just a few packages installed with the LAMP stack. Details are included at the beginning of the major sections in this chapter.

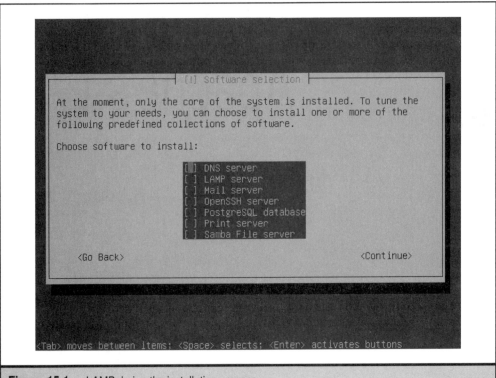

**Figure 15-1.**   LAMP during the installation process

Many administrators configure LAMP on a server without a GUI. But you might find it helpful to have a browser available on that server for hosts with access limited to the local system. For that purpose, text-based browsers such as ELinks are available from the main repository.

## Install the LAMP Stack

This section is based on an Ubuntu server installation, with only the Secure Shell (SSH) server selected to support remote access. The following command is one way to install the LAMP stack of packages:

```
$ sudo apt-get install apache2 mysql-server libapache2-mod-php5 php5-mysql
```

With dependencies, based on the Hardy Heron release, this command installs Apache version 2.2.8-1 and PHP5. If you want to install a legacy version of Apache or PHP, it's possible that Ubuntu will make it available in the current backports repository sometime in the future. But there are no guarantees. Other versions can be downloaded and compiled from the source code available from http://httpd.apache.org.

Until the Hardy Heron release, PHP4 was available from the universe repository. If you prefer this version of PHP, another option for the PHP4 source code is the home page at www.php.net.

A second way to install the packages of the LAMP stack is with the **sudo tasksel** command first described in Chapter 8. It opens a low-level graphical screen shown in Figure 15-2, and it may be the easiest way to install all needed packages of the LAMP stack.

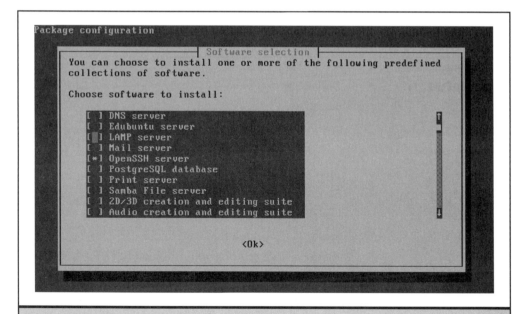

**Figure 15-2.** Installing LAMP with the **tasksel** utility

Just make sure LAMP Server is selected with an asterisk from the Choose Software To Install list. Press TAB to highlight OK, and then press ENTER. The installation process begins automatically. The actual command that is run is revealed in the output to the **ps aux | grep apt** command as shown here:

```
/usr/bin/perl -w /usr/bin/debconf-apt-progress -- apt-get -q
--no-install-recommends -y install lamp-server^
```

The process may appear to freeze for some time, as the packages are downloaded. No messages appear if the Internet connection (between your system and the Internet—or between the remote repository and the Internet) happens to be slower than usual.

During the installation process for the LAMP stack, you're prompted to create a password for the MySQL root user. If you want to change that MySQL server password at a later time, run the following command:

```
$ sudo dpkg-reconfigure mysql-server-5.0
```

Once the process is complete, a number of packages are installed for the LAMP stack.

## Installed Packages in the LAMP Stack

Examine each component of the LAMP stack, one by one. The first component, the Linux operating system, is already installed. The next component, the Apache web server, can include a large number of modules. Not all of them are installed with the LAMP stack. However, there are a surprising number of Perl packages installed with the Ubuntu LAMP stack. When I run the **apt-cache search apache** command, more than 300 related packages are available. When the LAMP stack is installed, some related Apache packages are shown in Table 15-1.

| Apache Package | Description |
|---|---|
| apache2 | The basic Apache server package |
| apache2-mpm-worker | An Apache daemon suited to high-traffic servers |
| apache2-utils | Apache commands for authentication, logs, and more |
| apache2.2-common | Standard modules and configuration files |
| libapr1 | The Apache portable runtime library |
| libaprutil1 | The Apache utilities library |
| libpcre3 | Expressions compatible with Perl 5 |
| libpq5 | Runtime library for communication with a PostgreSQL database |

**Table 15-1.** Basic Apache Packages

| MySQL Package | Description |
|---|---|
| libdbd-mysql-perl | Interface between Perl 5 and MySQL |
| libdbi-perl | Interface between Perl 5 and an SQL database |
| libmysqlclient15off | The MySQL client library |
| libnet-daemon-perl | Module for portable Perl daemons |
| libplrpc-perl | Perl extensions for remote procedure calls |
| mysql-client-5.0 | MySQL client commands |
| mysql-common | Files required for MySQL client libraries |
| mysql-server | Meta package for the MySQL server |
| mysql-server-5.0 | mysql-server version 5.0 commands |

**Table 15-2.**   Basic MySQL Packages

Some dependent packages go beyond the LAMP stack as defined. Included packages allow Apache connections to Perl and PostgreSQL. For detailed information about any package, run the **apt-cache show** *packagename* command. You can also install the packages from Table 15-1 with the following command:

```
$ sudo apt-get install apache2
```

With dependencies, the installation of the LAMP stack installs MySQL server version 5.0.51a. The installation also includes the basic packages listed in Table 15-2.

Alternatively, the following command installs the basic MySQL server, with the other packages included as dependencies:

```
$ sudo apt-get install mysql-server
```

With dependencies, the installation of the LAMP stack installs PHP server version 5.0.51a. The installation also includes the basic packages listed in Table 15-3.

| PHP Package | Description |
|---|---|
| libapache2-mod-php5 | Module for HTML embedded PHP5-based scripting |
| php5-common | Common files for PHP5 packages |
| php5-mysql | Package for embedding scripts in web pages |

**Table 15-3.**   Basic PHP Packages

Alternatively, the following command installs the basic PHP5 language, with the other packages included as dependencies:

```
$ sudo apt-get install php5-mysql
```

## If You Prefer Perl

While PHP is the default for the Ubuntu implementation of the LAMP stack, one common alternative is Perl. There are a large number of Perl packages installed by default, even without the LAMP stack. However, if you prefer Perl for websites, 34 related packages are available, as revealed by the following command:

```
$ apt-cache search perl | grep apache
```

One essential package for this purpose is libapache2-mod-perl. You may want to install other packages as shown in the output to the previous **apt-cache** command, depending on the functionality you need.

## If You Prefer Python

Another alternative to PHP in the LAMP stack is the Python programming language. There are a large number of Python packages installed by default, even without the LAMP stack. However, if you prefer Python for websites, three related packages are available, as revealed by the following command:

```
$ apt-cache search python | grep apache
```

Related packages include libapache2-mod-python, the Python Apache2 module, and libapache2-mod-wsgi, the associated web server gateway interface.

# CONFIGURE MYSQL AND PHP5

Before configuring Apache in the LAMP stack, you'll want to make sure the other components are ready. If a firewall is installed on the local system, or between the local network and target clients, you'll want to enable access through that firewall. (For more information on firewalls, see Chapter 18.) But several things for MySQL and PHP5 must be configured before configuring the Apache web server.

**NOTE** This book covers what a Linux server administrator needs to do. It does not go into the functions of a database administrator for MySQL or a programmer of PHP5, Perl, or Python. For more information, see *PHP: A Beginner's Guide* by Vikram Vaswani (McGraw-Hill Professional, 2008).

## Configure MySQL for Websites

First, there are several additional MySQL packages available, customized as Apache modules. One way to review the list is with the following command:

```
$ apt-cache search mysql | grep apache
```

The output reveals five packages, briefly described in Table 15-4.

Websites with higher traffic often include systems that require database access on different computers. For example, it's probably a good idea to keep shipping, tracking, inventory, and other e-commerce components on remote systems. To that end, it's important to allow MySQL access to more than just the localhost system. As shown in the output to the **netstat -atun** command discussed in Chapter 11, networking through the associated TCP/IP port is limited to the 127.0.0.1 IP address:

```
tcp   0   0 127.0.0.1:3306   0.0.0.0:*   LISTEN
```

To change this default, edit the /etc/mysql/my.conf configuration file. First, note the configured TCP/IP port number, which can be verified in the /etc/services file:

```
port = 3306
```

Note the **bind-address** directive, which is what limits access to the local system. To make it listen to other systems on the local network, change it to the IP address of a specific local network card; the line should look like this:

```
bind-address  =  192.168.0.154
```

| MySQL Module Package | Description |
|---|---|
| libapache2-mod-auth-mysql | For HTTP authentication through a MySQL database |
| libapache2-mod-log-sql | Module to log requests to a database |
| libapache2-mod-log-sql-dbi | For database independent logging |
| libapache2-mod-log-sql-mysql | A MySQL interface for database independent logging |
| libapache2-mod-log-sql-ssl | Encrypted connection for logging requests |

**Table 15-4.** Basic Apache-Related MySQL Packages

If you prefer to allow access to multiple networks, and the local system has multiple network cards, one option is the default IP address:

```
bind-address  =  0.0.0.0
```

Obviously, this may be a security risk; access from external networks should be at least limited to the relevant TCP/IP port 3306. To implement the change, restart the mysql service with the following command:

```
$ sudo /etc/init.d/mysql restart
```

MySQL is a complex database system. It includes 37 commands that start with **mysql\*** just in the standard Ubuntu server PATH. To get a taste of the capabilities, run the **mysqladmin | less** command. Scroll to the bottom of the output. Open a second command line terminal and try some of the options. For example, the **mysqladmin create newdata** command creates a new database named newdata. The **mysqladmin ping** command checks to see if the MySQL service is in operation. The **mysqladmin variables** command lists current database variables.

## Configure PHP for Websites

PHP is a popular option for configuring websites as it integrates well with MySQL and Apache. Ubuntu docs at https://help.ubuntu.com/community/ApacheMySQLPHP suggest that you may need to increase the default memory limit on configured scripts. The main PHP configuration file related to Apache is php.ini, in the /etc/php5/apache2/ directory, and the default memory limit is 16MB. Higher limits are possible, but memory limits are designed to keep poorly written scripts from consuming too much memory.

# INSTALL AND CONFIGURE APACHE

Now to the meat of the chapter, at least with respect to the functions of a Linux administrator. Over half of the websites on the Internet still run on the Apache web server, per www.netcraft.com. As many excellent books have been written about Apache, this chapter will cover only the basic functionality of this web server. As noted in the introduction, this chapter focuses on the version of Apache included with the Ubuntu Server Hardy Heron release 2.2.8-1.

This section explains the basic Apache configuration files, how to configure a standard web host, as well as how to set up multiple virtual hosts using a single IP address. If you need a secure virtual host, you probably also need, and therefore must first create, a standard virtual host. For more information, read the documentation online at http://httpd.apache.org/docs-2.2/; one alternative is *Apache Cookbook: Solutions and Examples for Apache Administrators*, published by O'Reilly.

**NOTE** Apache evolved from code written at the National Center for Supercomputing Applications (NCSA). It included so many patches that it became known as "a patchy" server.

Toward the end of this chapter, in the "Prepare Apache Documentation for Web Access" section, you'll learn how to access Apache documentation locally, based on the files installed from the apache2-doc package.

## Learn the Apache Configuration Files

The best way to learn the Apache configuration files is to trace its messages from when a system starts. During the boot process, Apache is started, courtesy of the /etc/init.d/apache2 script. The init.d script allows further access from the **/usr/bin/apache2ctl** control command.

The init.d script starts the Apache daemon, /usr/sbin/apache2, as modified by the settings configured in the /etc/default/apache2 file. It then reads and uses the Apache configuration files, stored in the /etc/apache2/ directory. The main /etc/apache2/apache2.conf file includes directives from other files in the same directory. Relevant files and subdirectories in the /etc/apache2/ directory are described in Table 15-5.

Some key directives in these configuration files point to other directories. The /etc/apache2/sites-enabled/000-default file configures the default Apache website, in the /var/www directory. The /etc/apache2/apache2.conf file sends log messages to the access.log and error.log files in the /var/log/apache2/ directory.

| Apache Configuration File | Description |
|---|---|
| apache2.conf | Main Apache configuration file |
| conf.d/ | Subdirectory that contains files with specific directives |
| envvars | Apache environment variables |
| httpd.conf | Empty Apache configuration file for administrative input |
| mods-available/ | List of available Apache modules |
| mods-enabled/ | List of enabled Apache modules |
| ports.conf | The TCP/IP ports associated with Apache |
| sites-available/ | List of available Apache websites |
| sites-enabled/ | List of configured Apache websites |

**Table 15-5.** Apache Configuration Files

The organization of Apache configuration files differs from other major Linux distributions. For example, Red Hat Enterprise Linux 5 configures virtual hosts directly in the main Apache configuration file and secure virtual hosts in the ssl.conf file in the conf.d/ subdirectory.

Most global changes to Apache defaults should be made to the httpd.conf file. New hosts should be configured in dedicated files in the sites-enabled/ subdirectory.

## Apache Default Settings

The default Apache settings in the /etc/default/apache2 configuration file relate to local caching, using the mod_disk_cache module. The cache is regulated using the **htcacheclean** command. The first directive, shown here,

```
HTCACHECLEAN_RUN=auto
```

means that the command is run only if the module is activated. You can activate the module with the following command:

```
$ sudo a2enmod disk_cache
```

The other options in the /etc/default/apache2 configuration file are fairly well explained in the comments; each option is associated with the **htcacheclean** command:

- ▼ **HTCACHECLEAN_RUN**   If set to yes, cleans the Apache cache when the service is started.
- ■ **HTCACHECLEAN_MODE**   If set to cron mode, where cleaning is configured as a regular job, the cache may not be cleared for 24 hours.
- ■ **HTCACHECLEAN_SIZE**   Limits the disk space allocated to the cache.
- ■ **HTCACHECLEAN_DAEMON_INTERVAL**   If HTCACHECLEAN_MODE is set to daemon mode, the cache is cleared based on this interval, in minutes.
- ■ **HTCACHECLEAN_PATH**   Specifies the directory with the cache.
- ▲ **HTCACHECLEAN_OPTIONS**   By default, set to "nice" (**-n**), which means that the cache is cleaned only when system resources are available.

## Apache Global Settings

Global settings for the Apache web server are configured by default in the /etc/apache2 /apache2.conf configuration file. Most numbers specified in this file are in seconds. This section describes the configured directives in that file. First, there's the **ServerRoot** directive, which specifies the top-level directory associated with Apache:

```
ServerRoot /etc/apache2
```

As Apache can spawn many additional processes for additional clients, some processes use the **AcceptMutex** directive (when set to **flock** or **fcntl**) to add the noted lock file:

```
LockFile /var/lock/apache2/accept.lock
```

The following directive specifies the location of the file that stores the Process Identifier, the **PidFile**, which includes the process number associated with the first invocation of the Apache service:

```
PidFile = $(APACHE_PID_FILE)
```

The **Timeout** directive limits the amount of time that goes by, in seconds, before the server provides a "Server not found message":

```
Timeout 300
```

Especially suited for web pages with multiple images, the following **KeepAlive** directive allows multiple requests over the same connection:

```
KeepAlive On
```

However, too many **KeepAlive** requests can overload a server; thus **MaxKeepAlive Requests** and **KeepAliveTimeout** directives are available:

```
MaxKeepAliveRequests 100
KeepAliveTimeout 15
```

These directives are followed by stanzas associated with the prefork and worker Multi-Processing Modules (MPMs). The *prefork MPM* stanza specifies available servers and limits the number of clients before enough requests "fork" a process; it includes directives, as explained in the default comments:

```
# prefork MPM
# StartServers: number of server processes to start
# MinSpareServers: minimum number of server processes which are kept spare
# MaxSpareServers: maximum number of server processes which are kept spare
# MaxClients: maximum number of server processes allowed to start
# MaxRequestsPerChild: maximum number of requests a server process serves
<IfModule mpm_prefork_module>
    StartServers          5
    MinSpareServers       5
    MaxSpareServers      10
    MaxClients          150
    MaxRequestsPerChild   0
</IfModule>
```

In contrast, the *worker MPM* stanza takes advantage of the multiple threads available for each Apache process. Multiple threads per process means that Apache can do more for web clients with the same resources.

```
# worker MPM
# MinSpareThreads: minimum number of worker threads which are kept spare
# MaxSpareThreads: maximum number of worker threads which are kept spare
```

```
# ThreadsPerChild: constant number of worker threads in each server process
# MaxRequestsPerChild: maximum number of requests a server process serves
<IfModule mpm_worker_module>
    StartServers          2
    MaxClients          150
    MinSpareThreads      25
    MaxSpareThreads      75
    ThreadsPerChild      25
    MaxRequestsPerChild   0
</IfModule>
```

The default user and group that run Apache are defined by the **User** and **Group** directives. A common option for the standard **User** and **Group** is *www-data*, which is the associated user and group in the /etc/passwd and /etc/group configuration files.

```
User ${APACHE_RUN_USER}
Group ${APACHE_RUN_GROUP}
```

Courtesy of the **AccessFileName** directive, additional directives are often included in a custom .htaccess file, which is commonly used to limit access by certain users and IP addresses. Files that start with a dot (.) are hidden by default.

```
AccessFileName .htaccess
```

While .htaccess files are hidden in the Linux directory tree, they would be visible to crackers on clients with the right skills—without the following stanza:

```
<Files ~ "^\.ht">
    Order allow,deny
    Deny from all
</Files>
```

The standard **DefaultType** directive is suited to a plain text web page. Alternatives include application/octet-stream and image/gif for different types of data.

```
DefaultType text/plain
```

If you change **HostnameLookups** to **On**, the server searches for and logs the URL associated with client IP addresses—a reverse DNS search.

```
HostnameLookups Off
```

The following two directives specify that all log messages of **warn** level or higher are sent to the noted **ErrorLog** file. Other log levels are discussed in the "Log Management" section of Chapter 7.

```
ErrorLog /var/log/apache2/error.log
LogLevel warn
```

I jump ahead a bit in the default configuration file to other log-related directives. These directives specify the format associated with messages sent to the /var/log/apache2 directory. The first **LogFormat** line is wrapped to fit the formatting limits of this book. Detailed logging format parameters, such as **%h** for host, **%u** for user, and **%t** for time, are described at http://httpd.apache.org/docs/2.2/mod/mod_log_config.html.

```
LogFormat "%h %l %u %t \"%r\" %>s %b \"%{Referer}i\"
    \"%{User-Agent}i\"" combined
LogFormat "%h %l %u %t \"%r\" %>s %b" common
LogFormat "%{Referer}i -> %U" referer
LogFormat "%{User-agent}i" agent
```

The following four lines include all directives from the noted configuration files. The first two load enabled modules of the file types from the directories specified. The third includes user-defined directives in the /etc/apache2/httpd.conf file. The fourth directive includes the TCP/IP ports from the specified /etc/apache2/ports.conf file.

```
Include /etc/apache2/mods-enabled/*.load
Include /etc/apache2/mods-enabled/*.conf
Include /etc/apache2/httpd.conf
Include /etc/apache2/ports.conf
```

The **ServerTokens** and **ServerSignature** directives provide information on the server configuration, often sent with error messages. The default values are shown here:

```
ServerTokens Full
ServerSignature On
```

These values specify a lot of information about the web server system. For example, when I navigate to a nonexistent page, I get the information shown in Figure 15-3, which includes the Apache version number, the available secure connection protocol, port number, and more.

The final two lines include all directives from the files configured in two directories. In Ubuntu, the /etc/apache2/conf.d/ directory is intended to include files with single directives, but such files can include more. As you'll see shortly, it can include a file that enables local access to the Apache documentation.

```
Include /etc/apache2/conf.d/
Include /etc/apache2/sites-enabled/
```

The directives shown in the default version of the /etc/apache2/apache2.conf file don't include defaults for other directives, but they do provide a basic idea on the workings of the Apache web server.

One example of a default directive is in comments—the following commented stanza is associated with error pages in different languages. Review the files in the /usr/share/

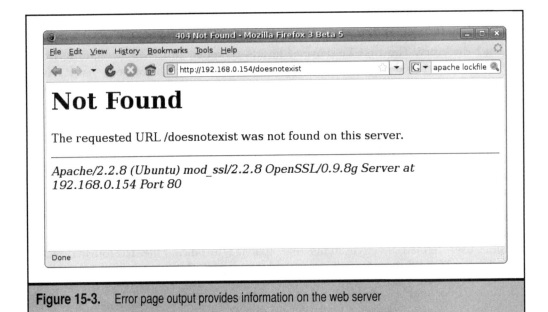

**Figure 15-3.**     Error page output provides information on the web server

apache2/error/ directory. You'll see different languages in these files, at least as listed in the **LanguagePriority** directive.

```
#    Alias /error/ "/usr/share/apache2/error/"
#
#    <Directory "/usr/share/apache2/error">
#        AllowOverride None
#        Options IncludesNoExec
#        AddOutputFilter Includes html
#        AddHandler type-map var
#        Order allow,deny
#        Allow from all
#        LanguagePriority en cs de es fr it nl sv pt-br ro
#        ForceLanguagePriority Prefer Fallback
#    </Directory>
```

# The Apache Control Command

As suggested earlier, the **apache2ctl** command is in part a front end to the Apache daemon. But it can do more. Run the command by itself, and you'll see the following output, which suggests the functionality:

```
Usage: /usr/sbin/apache2ctl start|stop|restart|graceful|graceful-stop|
configtest|status|fullstatus
        /usr/sbin/apache2ctl <apache2 args>
```

The options are generally straightforward; for example, the **sudo apachectl start** command starts the Apache service. The **graceful** and **graceful-stop** options restart and stop the Apache service, respectively, without interrupting any currently active connections.

> **TIP**   Whenever you want to check the syntax of Apache configuration files, run the **sudo apache2ctl configtest** command. When you're ready to test the result, restart the service with the **sudo apache2ctl graceful** command, and then check the result in a browser. It reloads the Apache configuration file without disconnecting current users.

The **configtest** option is most useful; it serves as a syntax checker for the main /etc/apache2/apache2.conf configuration file. As you'll see shortly, that file includes directives from the files that will actually be edited to serve actual websites. It incorporates the functionality formerly available from the **apache2 -t** command.

The **apache2ctl** command also works with the options listed in the **apache2** man page. One **apache2** command option related to **configtest** is the **-S** switch, which displays the TCP/IP port numbers, URLs, and configuration files for each regular and secure virtual host. After you configure virtual hosts, later in this section, try the **apache2ctl configtest** and **sudo apache2ctl -S** commands and observe the output.

> **NOTE**   Older versions of the **apache2ctl** command included the **startssl** option, for secure websites. Such support is and was also part of the various **start** and **stop** options.

Finally, the **apache2ctl status** command provides information about the server and associated activity. Sample output is shown in Figure 15-4.

The **apache2ctl fullstatus** command includes information on process identifiers (PIDs), secure server (SSL/TLS) connections, major modules, and more.

# Examine the First Host

The first host is configured in the /etc/apache2/sites-enabled/ directory, in the 000-default configuration file. It's a virtual host, linked to the file named *default*, in the /etc/apache2/sites-available/ directory. Examine this file in detail. The first directive is configured for virtual hosts based on domain names—on a single IP address.

```
NameVirtualHost *
```

You could limit access to a specific TCP/IP port. Commonly used ports include the HTTP standard of 80, the secure HTTPS standard of 443, and one commonly used for networks behind a proxy server, 8080. For example, you might set up specific HTTPS virtual hosts with a directive like this:

```
NameVirtualHost *:443
```

```
michael@ubuntuhardy3:~$ apache2ctl status
                    Apache Server Status for localhost

   Server Version: Apache/2.2.8 (Ubuntu) mod_ssl/2.2.8 OpenSSL/0.9.8g
   mod_perl/2.0.3 Perl/v5.8.8

   Server Built: Feb 2 2008 04:03:01

   --------------------------------------------------------------------

   Current Time: Friday, 02-May-2008 19:42:37 PDT

   Restart Time: Friday, 02-May-2008 17:02:39 PDT

   Parent Server Generation: 4

   Server uptime: 2 hours 39 minutes 58 seconds

   1 requests currently being processed, 5 idle workers

___W__......................................................
............................................................
............................................................
............................................................

   Scoreboard Key:
   "_" Waiting for Connection, "S" Starting up, "R" Reading Request,
   "W" Sending Reply, "K" Keepalive (read), "D" DNS Lookup,
   "C" Closing connection, "L" Logging, "G" Gracefully finishing,
   "I" Idle cleanup of worker, "." Open slot with no current process
michael@ubuntuhardy3:~$ []
```

**Figure 15-4.**   Apache Server Status

If you specify a port number, with **NameVirtualHost**, you'll need to specify the same port number with the **VirtualHost** directive in the same file. In any case, the **NameVirtualHost** directive can be used once for regular and once for secure hosts. In other words, the second regular and secure virtual host won't have the **NameVirtualHost** directive.

If you prefer virtual hosts based on IP addresses, substitute the desired IP address for the asterisk. In that case, every virtual host would require a different IP address.

```
<VirtualHost *>
```

Naturally, you'll want to change this directive to point to a working e-mail address:

```
ServerAdmin webmaster@localhost
```

Normally, each website should have a different **DocumentRoot**; a default index.html file is available in the /var/www directory:

```
DocumentRoot /var/www/
```

The following **Directory** stanza specifies limits on the top-level directory for the virtual host. The **Options FollowSymLinks** directive supports symbolic links. For example, for the "Prepare Apache Documentation for Web Access" section, later in this chapter, I create a link from the directory with HTML configured Apache documentation to the /var/www/manual directory with the **ln -s** command. The **AllowOverride None** directive disallows the use of .htaccess files for additional configuration.

```
<Directory />
        Options FollowSymLinks
        AllowOverride None
</Directory>
```

The following **Directory** stanza specifies limits on the /var/www directory, which contains the web page files for the virtual host. The **Indexes** in the **Options** directive supports file lists, if an index.html file does not exist in the /var/www directory. The **MultiViews** setting supports content negotiation based on file type. The **Order allow,deny** directive supports limited access, based on domain names or IP addresses.

```
<Directory /var/www/>
        Options Indexes FollowSymLinks MultiViews
        AllowOverride None
        Order allow,deny
        allow from all
</Directory>
```

The following directive and stanza configures Common Gateway Interface (CGI) scripts and Sever Side Includes (SSIs). If CGI scripts are installed, they are normally included in the /usr/lib/cgi-bin directory. The **ScriptAlias** directive supports access by appropriate owners in the /var/www/cgi-bin directory, based on the **+SymLinksIfOwnerMatch** option.

```
ScriptAlias /cgi-bin/ /usr/lib/cgi-bin/
<Directory "/usr/lib/cgi-bin">
        AllowOverride None
        Options +ExecCGI -MultiViews +SymLinksIfOwnerMatch
        Order allow,deny
        Allow from all
</Directory>
```

For the noted stanza to work, you'll need to create a link from the **DocumentRoot** directory to /var/www/cgi-bin with the following command:

```
$ sudo ln -s /usr/lib/cgi-bin /var/www/cgi-bin
```

The next two directives are straightforward, sending error messages of warn level or higher to the noted error.log file, and access messages to the noted access.log file:

```
ErrorLog /var/log/apache2/error.log
LogLevel warn
CustomLog /var/log/apache2/access.log combined
```

As noted, the following **ServerSignature** directive allows a footer in error messages.

```
ServerSignature On
```

The following directive limits access to documentation to the localhost system, as specified by the **Allow from** directive. The address 127.0.0.0/255.0.0.0 could be changed to allow access to the desired network with a setting such as 192.168.0.0/24.

```
Alias /doc/ "/usr/share/doc/"
<Directory "/usr/share/doc/">
    Options Indexes MultiViews FollowSymLinks
    AllowOverride None
    Order deny,allow
    Deny from all
    Allow from 127.0.0.0/255.0.0.0 ::1/128
</Directory>
```

The last directive in the file closes the virtual host stanza:

```
</VirtualHost>
```

## Configure Virtual Hosts

Before you configure a virtual host, make a copy of the 000-default file in the /etc/apache2/sites-enabled directory. For the purpose of this chapter, you could do so with the following commands:

```
$ cd /etc/apache2/sites-enabled
$ sudo cp 000-default website1
```

Then create a dedicated web page and logging directories. I've specified some arbitrary directories here. The directory names you use must also be specified in the virtual host file.

```
$ sudo mkdir /var/www/website1
$ sudo mkdir /var/log/apache2/website1
```

Now open the website1 file. First, add at least one general directive, which reflects the name of the website:

```
ServerName site1.example.org
```

It's common to add **ServerAlias** directives for other host or domain names that might be used, such as this:

```
ServerAlias www.example.org
```

Then to reflect the new directories just created, change the following directives:

▼   **ServerAdmin**   Set to the e-mail address of the administrator for the website

■   **DocumentRoot**   Configure to the directory with the website files—in this case, /var/www/website1

■   **<Directory** */dir***>**   Replace */dir* with the **DocumentRoot** directory

■   **ErrorLog**   Set to the dedicated directory for the log file

▲   **CustomLog**   Set to the dedicated directory for the log file

These are just minimal basic changes based on the default configuration included with the Ubuntu implementation of the Apache web server. Depending on any custom configuration, other similar changes may be required.

Once the first virtual host is configured, you can add web pages to the **DocumentRoot** directory. To test the virtual host, all you need is a text file. For example, for this virtual host, I create an index.html file in the /var/www/website1 directory. I add simple text to this file, as illustrated in Figure 15-5.

To test or configure this virtual website for remote clients, I'll either need to change the /etc/hosts configuration file on each client or add the specified website name to the DNS (Domain Name System) database.

I can now repeat this process for as many virtual hosts as I need. Given the following directive in the main Apache configuration file (/etc/apache2/apache2.conf),

```
Include /etc/apache2/sites-enabled/
```

all files in this directory are included in the Apache configuration.

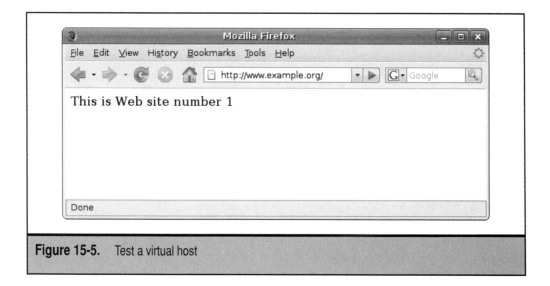

**Figure 15-5.**   Test a virtual host

# Configure Secure Virtual Hosts

In the public eye, a secure website is known to use encrypted communication. Slightly more aware users know secure websites by the protocol, HTTPS. Security is provided by the Secure Sockets Layer (SSL) protocol and its successor, Transport Layer Security (TLS). Documentation references for HTTPS still use SSL, so that is used here.

To configure a secure virtual host, you'll need to take four basic steps. First, enable the SSL module, already available from the default Apache packages installed on Ubuntu. Next, create the SSL certificate—either with the help of an official certificate authority (CA) or by creating a "self-signed" certificate. Next, change the configuration files associated with a regular virtual host to limit its purview to the standard TCP/IP port (80) for regular websites. Finally, you can create a secure virtual host, based on the virtual host template just used for regular websites.

## Enable the SSL Module

The SSL module is included in one of the default Apache Server packages, apache2.2-common. To include the SSL module in the Apache configuration, run the following command:

```
$ sudo a2enmod ssl
```

The next time Apache is restarted, the ssl.conf and ssl.load files are included in the list of enabled modules in the /etc/apache2/mods-enabled directory. If for some reason you want to reverse the process, the **a2dismod** command can help.

## Create the SSL Certificate

Without a private-public SSL key pair, connections to secure websites using the *https://* in a web browser won't be secure. Properly secured websites on the Internet use an official key pair generated by a CA. But such official key pairs can be expensive and are not required to learn how to configure a secure virtual website. Encryption is based on a public-private key infrastructure, based on the X.509 standard of the Internet Engineering Task Force. The filenames with encryption keys listed in this section (server.key, server.csr, and server.crt) are arbitrary. The commands listed in this section create the noted files in the local directory.

One way to create a self-signed certificate is with the **openssl** command. To do so, take the following steps.

Create the server.key file. The following command generates RSA (**genrsa**) parameters for an encryption key, using the triple DES (**-des3**) encryption standard, in the server .key file, of 1024 bytes:

```
$ sudo openssl genrsa -des3 -out server.key 1024
```

The command requires a passphrase, which can be a word or even a sentence. At least four characters are required. Like the best passwords, the best passphrases include a combination of uppercase and lowercase letters, numbers, and even punctuation.

**401**

After the server.key is available, create a Certificate Signing Request (CSR). The CSR can be sent to a CA for processing for a digital identity certificate. The **openssl req** command uses the X.509 standard to create a new key (**-new -key**), which sends output (**-out**) to the server.csr file. It starts a sequence of commands that require your input. Input is shown in boldface:

```
$ openssl req -new -key server.key -out server.csr
```

The command requires the passphrase you just used to create the server.key file. The passphrase is not shown.

```
Enter pass phrase for server.key:
You are about to be asked to enter information that will be incorporated
into your certificate request.
What you are about to enter is what is called a Distinguished Name or a DN.
There are quite a few fields but you can leave some blank
For some fields there will be a default value,
If you enter '.', the field will be left blank.
-----
```

The options that follow are straightforward. If you're setting up a server.csr to send to a CA, the entries should reflect your true identity:

```
Country Name (2 letter code) [AU]: US
State or Province Name (full name) [Some-State]: OpenSource
Locality Name (eg, city) []: My City
Organization Name (eg, company) [Internet Widgits Pty Ltd]: GroupofTwo
Organizational Unit Name (eg, section) []: One Section
Common Name (eg, YOUR name) []: Michael Jang
Email Address []: michael@example.org
```

The remaining questions provide additional verification to the CA:

```
Please enter the following 'extra' attributes
to be sent with your certificate request
A challenge password []:IeIC3teS
An optional company name []:company subtitle
$
```

Now you can submit the server.csr file to a CA for processing. Incidentally, one official CA is Thawte, founded by the same Mark Shuttleworth of the Canonical Foundation.

If you choose to create your own self-signed certificate (and I do for the purpose of this chapter), run the following command:

```
$ openssl x509 -req -days 30 -in server.csr -signkey server.key
 -out server.crt
```

With most commands, it's possible to include a backslash (\) to escape the meaning of a carriage return, thereby supporting the format requirements of this book. However, that feature is not available with the **openssl** command. Read both lines as a single command.

Now that a server certificate (server.crt) and server key (server.key) are available in the local directory, the following command moves them to the appropriate directories, which will be used when configuring a secure virtual host:

```
$ sudo cp server.crt /etc/ssl/certs/
$ sudo cp server.key /etc/ssl/private/
```

Now you're just about ready to create a secure virtual host. But first you need to prepare any existing regular hosts.

## Prepare Existing Hosts

Based on the files created earlier in the chapter for regular virtual hosts, you'll need to make a few changes. The first virtual host was configured in the /etc/apache2/sites-enabled/000-default file, with a single **NameVirtualHost** directive. It was configured for regular websites. Before you can set up a secure virtual host, this file with directives for a regular website must be limited to TCP/IP port 80. To do so, replace the existing version of the **NameVirtualHost** directive with the following:

```
NameVirtualHost  *:80
```

While the **NameVirtualHost** directive is used only in the 000-default virtual host configuration file, other standard virtual host files include a **<VirtualHost \*>** container that must be changed as follows:

```
<VirtualHost *:80>
```

## Create a Secure Virtual Host

Now to set up a secure virtual host, start with the 000-default file in the /etc/apache2/sites-enabled directory as a template. For the purpose of this section, use it as a template. Copy the file as follows:

```
$ cd /etc/apache2/sites-enabled
$ sudo cp 000-default secure1
```

The basic changes made here are similar to those made for regular virtual hosts, with a few differences. The first secure virtual host requires a **NameVirtualHost** directive that points to the TCP/IP port associated with secure web services:

```
NameVirtualHost *:443
```

While this particular **NameVirtualHost \*:443** directive is required only once, every secure virtual host requires a pointer to the same TCP/IP port, with the following virtual host container header:

```
<VirtualHost *:443>
```

Four special directives are required inside the virtual host container for a secure system. The first is straightforward, as it activates the SSL protocol engine:

```
SSLEngine on
```

SSL runtime options are controlled by the **SSLOptions** directive. The options shown here support access to secure websites without a password (**+FakeBasicAuth**), use the SSL keys just created (**+ExportCertData**), and deny access to inappropriate systems (**+StrictRequire**).

```
SSLOptions +FakeBasicAuth +ExportCertData +StrictRequire
```

Some documentation suggests the inclusion of the **+CompatEnvVars** option for additional CGI/SSI environment variables, but that option is no longer available for the Ubuntu implementation of Apache. (For more information, see bug 179959 at https://bugs.launchpad.net.)

The next two directives access certificate and key files just created:

```
SSLCertificateFile /etc/ssl/certs/server.crt
SSLCertificateKeyFile /etc/ssl/private/server.key
```

Other changes to the default virtual host container follow the same rules required for a regular virtual host. Don't forget to create appropriate directories and HTML files for the secure website, as well as dedicated log directories for any website that you want to track. Once the process is complete, restart the Apache service. You should then be able to access the secure website in the same way you access any other secure website.

## Prepare Apache Documentation for Web Access

If you'd rather have the Apache documentation available on the local network, it's a fairly easy process to install it. Just take the following steps:

1. Run the **sudo apt-get install apache2-doc** to install the noted package. This action installs the current Apache documentation primarily in the /usr/share/doc/apache2-doc/manual directory—in several languages.

2. Review the apache2-doc configuration file in the /etc/apache2/conf.d directory. With the **Alias** directive shown here,

   ```
   Alias /manual /usr/share/doc/apache2-doc/manual/
   ```

   the HTML files associated with Apache documentation can be made available in a properly configured /var/www/manual directory.

3. Create a link from /var/www/manual to /usr/share/doc/apache2-doc/manual/ with the following command:

   ```
   $ sudo ln -s /usr/share/doc/apache2-doc/manual /var/www/manual
   ```

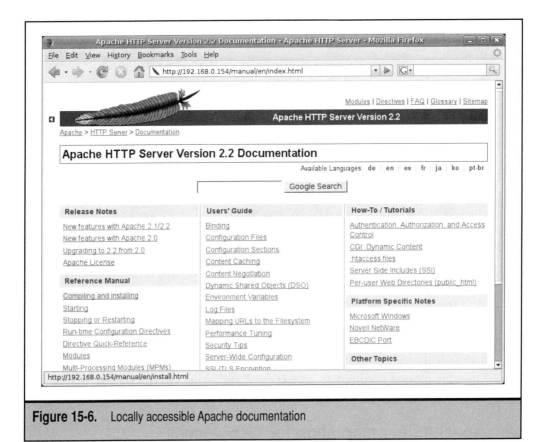

**Figure 15-6.** Locally accessible Apache documentation

4. Look at this directive, which follows symbolically linked directories. It allows access to the main Apache documentation page in the manual/ subdirectory, as shown in Figure 15-6.

```
Options Indexes FollowSymlinks
```

I navigated to http://*ServerIPaddress*/manual; courtesy of the default value of the **LanguagePriority** directive, I get the English language web page.

For your information, note the available languages near the top of the web page. Included are German (de), English (en), Spanish (es), French (fr), Japanese (ja), Korean (ko), and Brazilian Portuguese (pt-br).

# SUMMARY

Website administrators may be interested in the Ubuntu implementation of the LAMP stack. The components are Linux, Apache, MySQL, and PHP. Other LAMP stacks can substitute Perl or Python for PHP, and packages for those alternatives are also available. As MySQL and PHP configuration is generally the province of database administrators and programmers, the focus of this chapter is the Apache web server.

Most Apache configuration files are located in the /etc/apache2/ directory. Enabled modules are stored in the /etc/apache2/mods-enabled/ directory. Enabled virtual hosts are configured in files in the /etc/apache2/sites-enabled/ directory. Virtual hosts can share the same IP address. Information from these files are incorporated in the /etc/apache2/apache2.conf configuration file. Overall syntax can be checked with the **apache2ctl configtest** command.

Apache makes it easy to create and configure the security keys, CSRs, and certificates required for a secure website using TCP/IP port 443. With a few additional configuration changes, you can set up secure virtual hosts on the same IP address that is used for regular virtual hosts.

# CHAPTER 16

## Create a File Server

There are two major file servers associated with Linux: the Network File System (NFS) and Samba. While some excellent GUI tools are available for creating file servers, this chapter shows you how to configure these services from the command line. If you know how to use these services, you can do more in less time by directly editing key configuration files. The Ubuntu implementation of the Shared Folders GUI tool can manage NFS and Samba systems, and you'll see how to use that tool. But you'll be miles ahead of the competition if you learn to edit the server configuration files directly.

NFS is a protocol designed to allow easy access to directories on remote systems. Access to NFS-mounted directories is transparent; some networks configure a /home directory from a central server. Assuming the network is fast enough, users won't be able to tell the difference between an NFS mounted /home directory from a remote system and a local /home directory. As NFS was originally designed for Unix, Linux inherits its advantages as an easy and powerful way to share filesystems with other Linux and Unix workstations.

Samba is the open source implementation of the Server Message Block (SMB) protocol originally developed by IBM and adapted by Microsoft. As a file and printer sharing service, it supports sharing with other Linux and even Microsoft workstations. It incorporates the changes made by Microsoft with the Common Internet File System (CIFS). Samba can also be configured in many Microsoft server roles; when Samba 4.0 is released, you'll be able to configure it as an Active Directory (AD) domain controller.

# TWO NETWORK FILE SERVERS

NFS is the standard for sharing files and printers on a directory with Linux and Unix computers. Originally developed by Sun Microsystems in the mid-1980s, NFS has been cloned for Linux and has been used reliably for years, and it continues to be popular in organizations with Unix- or Linux-based networks.

One weakness of NFS sharing is the lack of encryption. By default, NFS shares are not encrypted, and there is no way under current NFS sharing daemons to encrypt such data over a network. Two versions of the service are available for Ubuntu. As the NFS kernel server is part of the main repository, it's the preferred standard. It's based on NFS version 4. The NFS user server does not support file locks, but it is supposedly easier to troubleshoot. However, I focus on the NFS kernel server in this chapter.

 *CAUTION* Don't install both the NFS user server and NFS kernel server on the same system. The interactions can lead to trouble.

Whatever kernel server is selected, it can work with user quotas, as discussed in Chapter 10's section "Quota Configuration." If you choose to configure quotas, pay attention to the /usr/sbin/rpc.rquotad service. NFS shares can be mounted with quotas enabled, a terrific convenience for a /home directory shared from a central server.

To some extent, it does not matter which version of NFS is installed. NFS servers are relatively easy to configure. Just be aware that NFS security depends on consistency in user ID numbers between servers and clients. The NIS (Network Information Service) and LDAP (Lightweight Directory Access Protocol) services discussed in Chapter 12 makes this easier with a single user database.

In this chapter, you'll learn how to configure the /etc/exports configuration file, export those shares, and then connect from an appropriate NFS client. Alternatively, you could use Ubuntu's Shared Folders tool, which can be started with the **shares-admin** command, discussed toward the end of this chapter.

# The Kernel Server

For the NFS kernel server, three packages are closely associated with NFS: portmap, nfs-common, and nfs-kernel-server. As they're not installed by default, you may need to use a command such as the following to integrate them into your system:

```
$ sudo apt-get install portmap nfs-common nfs-kernel-server
```

This installation includes NFS kernel server configuration files in /etc/exports as well as three others in the /etc/default directory.

# The User Server

The installation of the NFS user server is simpler. The installation of the nfs-user-server package requires only the support of the portmap daemon. As they're not installed by default, you could use a command like the following to integrate them into your system:

```
$ sudo apt-get install nfs-user-server portmap
```

# Related Services

There are three services installed with the NFS kernel server: nfs-kernel-server, nfs-common, and portmap. The first NFS kernel server configuration file is in the /etc/default directory. Control scripts for each service are located in the /etc/init.d directory. The portmap service is especially important, as it enables communication on specific TCP/IP ports.

These configuration files start the service, before the actual NFS shares are configured in the /etc/exports configuration file. You'll see how you can configure that file shortly.

## NFS Kernel Server

The base configuration file for the NFS kernel server is /etc/default/nfs-kernel-server. It includes command options that are fed to the /etc/init.d/nfs-kernel-server script. These options are described in Table 16-1.

This script starts the main rpc.nfsd and rpc.mountd services, based on configured shares in the /etc/exports configuration file. While you may note many of the same

| nfs-kernel-server Option | Description |
|---|---|
| **RPCNFSDCOUNT** | Number of NFS server daemons to start; higher numbers are suitable for busy networks but require more server resources |
| **RPCNFSDPRIORITY** | May range between –20 and +19; if NFS is interfering with other services, a positive **RPCNFSDPRIORITY** priority may be appropriate |
| **RPCMOUNTDOPTS** | Port-based firewalls block NFS, unless the port for NFS related services are fixed |
| **NEED_SVCGSSD** | Boolean (yes or no) option that can activate the Generic Security Services Application Program Interface (GSSAPI) |
| **RPCSVCGSSDOPTS** | Option primarily for debugging and logging the GSSAPI |

**Table 16-1.**    /etc/default/nfs-kernel-server Options

options from Table 16-1 in the /etc/init.d/nfs-kernel-server script, the options that govern are in the /etc/default/nfs-kernel-server configuration file.

## NFS Common

The base configuration file for the NFS common server is /etc/default/nfs-common. It includes command options that are fed to the /etc/init.d/nfs-common script. These options are described in Table 16-2.

These options are fed to the /etc/init.d/nfs-common service script. This script starts the main rpc.statd, rpc.gssd and rpc.imapd services, which work with configured NFS shares in the /etc/exports configuration file. While you may note many of the same options from Table 16-2 in the /etc/init.d/nfs-common script, the options that govern are in the /etc/default/nfs-common configuration file.

## The portmap Service

The base configuration file for the port mapper daemon is /etc/default/portmap. It suggests one command option that is fed to the /etc/init.d/portmap script:

```
#OPTIONS="-i 127.0.0.1"
```

Options are fed to the service script, /etc/init.d/portmap. This script starts the port mapper service, which enables NFS (and NIS) communication via regular TCP/IP ports.

| nfs-common Option | Description |
|---|---|
| **NEED_STATD** | Boolean (yes or no) option that can activate the network status monitor for remote procedure calls (RPCs) |
| **STANDOPTS** | Port-based firewalls block NFS, unless the port for NFS related services are fixed |
| **NEED_IDMAPD** | Boolean (yes or no) option that can activate the ID Name Mapper Daemon (IDMAPD) |
| **NEED_GSSD** | Boolean (yes or no) option that can activate the Generic Security Services Daemon (GSSD) |

**Table 16-2.**    /etc/default/nfs-common Options

The portmap service must be running for NFS shares to work—on clients and servers. If you're having trouble connecting to an NFS server, make sure the portmap daemon is running with the following command:

```
$ sudo /etc/init.d/portmap restart
```

Once the portmap service is started, you should be able to run the **rpcinfo -p** command to review those services that use portmap. The following excerpts from the output from my Ubuntu Server system tell me that portmap (portmapper), rpc.statd (status), rpc.nfsd (nfs), and the rpc.mountd (mountd) daemons are running. If you prefer a port-based firewall such as iptables, pay attention to the port numbers. For example, this output tells me that communication is possible using NFS versions 2, 3, and 4, using both TCP (Transmission Control Protocol) and UDP (User Datagram Protocol) packets.

To enable communication through a firewall, you'll need to fix the port numbers, primarily in the aforementioned /etc/default/ configuration files.

```
program vers proto   port
 100000    2   tcp    111   portmapper
 100000    2   udp    111   portmapper
 100024    1   udp  37952   status
 100024    1   tcp  53773   status
 100003    2   udp   2049   nfs
 100003    3   udp   2049   nfs
 100003    4   udp   2049   nfs
 100021    1   udp  32987   nlockmgr
 100021    3   udp  32987   nlockmgr
 100021    4   udp  32987   nlockmgr
```

```
100003    2    tcp   2049   nfs
100003    3    tcp   2049   nfs
100003    4    tcp   2049   nfs
100021    1    tcp  54171   nlockmgr
100021    3    tcp  54171   nlockmgr
100021    4    tcp  54171   nlockmgr
100005    1    udp  45402   mountd
100005    1    tcp  40733   mountd
100005    2    udp  45402   mountd
100005    2    tcp  40733   mountd
100005    3    udp  45402   mountd
100005    3    tcp  40733   mountd
```

# Configure Exports

The actual configuration of NFS shares may seem fairly simple. However, the diversity of available configuration options reflects the richness of the NFS service.

Shares are configured in the /etc/exports file. Each line in this file lists the directory to be exported, the hosts to which it will be exported, and the options that apply to this export. You can export a particular directory only once. Take the following examples from an /etc/exports file:

```
/pub         (ro,sync) one.example.org(rw,no_subtree_check,sync)
/home        *.example.org(rw,no_subtree_check,sync)
/tftpboot    nodisk.example.org(rw,no_root_squash,no_subtree_check,sync)
```

There are three basic components in each of these lines. The first component is the directory to be shared. The second component is the hostname or IP address of those systems that are allowed access to the share. If that second component is missing, the directory is shared with all systems. The final component, in parentheses, lists the conditions associated with the share.

**NOTE**  Be very careful with /etc/exports; one common cause of problems is an extra space between (or at the end of) expressions. For example, if a space is added after the comma in **(ro,sync)**, the directory won't get exported.

The directory to be shared requires no further explanation. Examine the following sections for more information on the hostnames or IP addresses, and the conditions associated with the share.

## Limiting Shares to Specific Systems

Limits on NFS shares can be specified by hostname or IP address. You can specify single hostnames, IP addresses, or no limits at all. To specify a group of hostnames and IP addresses, you need to understand the use of wildcards in /etc/exports.

In Linux, the use of wildcards is also known as *globbing*. The /etc/exports file uses "conventional" wildcards: for example, *.example.org specifies all computers within the example.org domain.

For IPv4 networks, wildcards often require some form of the subnet mask. For example, 192.168.0.0/255.255.255.0 specifies the 192.168.0.0 network of computers with IP addresses that range from 192.168.0.1 to 192.168.0.254. The /etc/exports file also supports the use of CIDR (Classless Inter-Domain Routing) notation. In CIDR, since 255.255.255.0 masks 24 bits, CIDR represents this with the number *24*. If you're configuring a network in CIDR notation, you can represent this 192.168.0.0/255.255.255.0 network as 192.168.0.0/24.

## Limit NFS Shares with Options

There are a number of options that regulate access to NFS shares. In the example /etc/exports file shown earlier, the /pub directory is exported to all users as read-only (**ro**). It is also exported to one specific computer with read/write (**rw**) privileges. The /home directory is exported, with read/write privileges, to any computer on the .example.net network. Finally, the /tftpboot directory is exported with full read/write privileges (even for root users, with the **no_root_squash** option); but the export is limited to the nodisk .example.net computer.

These shared directories do not check higher level directories for permissions (**no_subtree_check**). The shared directories, as configured, also include the **sync** flag. This requires all changes to be written to disk before a command such as a **file copy** is complete. While this option reduces the risk of lost data when a network connection is dropped, it can increase the load on the NFS server, as discussed earlier with the **RPCNFSDPRIORITY** directive in the /etc/default/nfs-kernel-server configuration file. A number of other options are listed in Table 16-3.

# Share Exports

It's not enough to configure /etc/exports. The first time the file is created, you'll need to activate those exports with the **exportfs -a** command. The next time you boot Ubuntu, the NFS kernel server start script (/etc/init.d/nfs-kernel-server) automatically runs the **exportfs -r** command, which synchronizes exported directories.

When you add a share to /etc/exports, the **exportfs -r** command adds the new directories. However, if you're modifying, moving, or deleting a share, it is safest to temporarily unexport all filesystems first with the **exportfs -ua** command before re-exporting the shares with the **exportfs -a** command.

Once exports are active, they're easy to check. Just run the **showmount -e localhost** command on the server. And then there's the client.

# From an NFS Client

If you're looking for the export list for a remote NFS server, just add the name (or IP address) of the NFS server. For example, the **showmount -e nfsUbuntuServer** command

| /etc/exports Option | Description |
|---|---|
| ro | Allows read-only access |
| rw | Supports read/write access |
| sync | Requires synchronous reads and writes |
| async | Allows reads, with data to be written held in memory |
| secure | Specifies communication through TCP/IP ports below 1024 |
| insecure | Allows communication through TCP/IP ports above 1024 |
| wdelay | Groups writes from multiple systems together |
| no_wdelay | Allows immediate writes to a shared NFS directory |
| hide | Prevents sharing of subdirectories |
| no_hide | Includes subdirectories of shared directories |
| subtree_check | Checks higher level directories for permissions |
| no_subtree_check | Does not check higher level directories for permissions |
| insecure_locks | Disables file locking; needed for older NFS clients |
| secure_locks | Allows file locking |
| all_squash | Maps all connected users to anonymous |
| root_squash | Maps requests from the root user to anonymous |
| no_root_squash | Allows the root user full administrative access to the shared directory |
| anonuid=xyz | Specifies the UID of the anonymous user |
| anongid=xyz | Specifies the GID of the anonymous group |

**Table 16-3.** /etc/exports Options

looks for the list of exported NFS directories from the nfsUbuntuServer computer. That command might not work for a couple of reasons: firewalls and the local /etc/hosts or authoritative DNS server. Name-resolution problems based on troubled /etc/hosts or DNS servers can be addressed by substituting the IP address of the NFS server. You'll see output similar to the following:

```
Export list for nfsUbuntuServer
/home/michael *
```

Now to mount this directory locally, you'll need an empty local directory. Create a directory such as /mnt/remote if required. You can then mount the shared directory from the nfsUbuntuServer1 computer with the following command:

```
$ sudo mount -t nfs nfsUbuntuServer1:/home/michael /mnt/remote
```

This command mounts the /home/michael directory from the computer named nfsUbuntuServer1. It also specifies the use of the NFS protocol (**-t nfs**) and mounts the share on the local /mnt/remote directory. Depending on traffic on your network, this command may take more than a few seconds, so be patient. Once the connection is made, you'll be able to access files on the remote directory as if it were a local directory.

# SHARING ON MICROSOFT NETWORKS

As Microsoft's work helped SMB evolve into the Common Internet File System (CIFS), Samba has evolved as well. Samba is fully configurable as a Primary Domain Controller (PDC), so many organizations are using it as a "drop-in" replacement for related Microsoft domains, as the Windows NT 4 Server operating system is no longer supported by Microsoft. Samba is also fully configurable as an AD domain server. When Samba 4.0 is released, it will be fully configurable as an AD domain controller.

SMB network communication over a Microsoft-based network is also known as *NetBIOS over TCP/IP (NBT)*. Through the collective works of Andrew Tridgell and the Samba team, Linux systems provide transparent and reliable SMB support over TCP/IP via a package known as Samba. You can do four basic things with Samba:

▼ Share a Linux directory tree with Windows and Linux/Unix computers

■ Connect to a shared Windows directory from Linux/Unix clients

■ Share a Linux printer with Windows and Linux/Unix computers

▲ Connect to a Windows printer from Linux/Unix clients

Some of the printer-sharing features associated with Samba were discussed in Chapter 9. Overall, Samba emulates many of the advanced network features and functions associated with the Win9$x$/ME and NT/2000/XP/2003/Vista/2008 operating systems through the SMB protocol. Complete information can be found at the official Samba website at www.samba.org. It is easy to configure Samba to do a number of things on a Microsoft-based network.

## A Bit of Background on Samba

Samba services provide interoperability between Microsoft Windows and Linux/Unix computers. But before you begin configuring Samba, you need a basic understanding of how Microsoft Windows networking works with TCP/IP.

The original Microsoft Windows networks were configured with computer hostnames, known as NetBIOS names, limited to 15 characters. These unique hostnames provided a simple, flat hostname system for the computers on a LAN. All computer identification requests were made through broadcasts. This overall network transport system is known as NetBEUI, which is not "routable." In other words, it does not allow communication between two different LANs. As a result, the original Microsoft-based PC networks were limited in size to 255 nodes.

While Microsoft networks could use the Novell IPX/SPX protocol stack to route messages between networks, that was not enough. As the Internet grew, so did the dominance of TCP/IP. Microsoft adapted its NetBIOS system with SMB to work with TCP/IP. Since Microsoft published SMB as an industry-wide standard, anyone could set up their own service to work with SMB. As Microsoft has moved toward CIFS, Samba developers have adapted well.

# Install Samba

Perhaps the simplest way to install the Samba file server is with the tasksel utility described in Chapter 15. All you need to do is enter **sudo tasksel** at the command line, and then select the Samba File Server package group. That action installs the samba, samba-common, samba-doc, libpam-smbpass, winbind, smbfs, and smbclient packages.

The samba package includes the Samba and NetBIOS services, as well as commands that can help monitor and manage the local system in a Microsoft-style network. The samba-common package creates important directories, includes more management commands, and refers to a variety of sample configuration files. The samba-doc package includes HTML-formatted book-length works that can be made accessible to Apache in the same way as Apache documents were made accessible in Chapter 15. The libpam-smbpass package supports a single Linux/Windows database of passwords. The winbind package installs a clone of the Microsoft Windows Internet Name Service (WINS). The smbfs and smbclient packages install Samba clients on the local system and must also be installed on other Samba clients.

# Common Samba Commands

Some key commands associated with Samba are listed in Table 16-4. This table does not include commands that require extensive knowledge of Microsoft systems such as NT quotas or access control lists.

Here are some examples of the use of some of these commands. The **smbtree** command, as shown in Figure 16-1, illustrates shared directories and printers from other Samba servers on a network. Note how it lists systems on workgroups (or domains) named WORKGROUP and MSHOME. The **-U michael** option adds shares available to the user michael, such as his home directory.

If you'd rather browse Samba shares on a specific system, the **smbclient** command can help. For example, the **smbclient -L //hostname** command reviews shared directories and printers from the Samba server on the computer named *hostname*. As with the **smbtree** command, Samba shares accessible to a specific user can be viewed with the **-U** *username* option. For example, if the **[homes]** share is activated in the Samba server

| Samba Command | Description |
|---|---|
| **findsmb** | Lists systems that respond to SMB name queries (and are thus Samba servers that might have shared directories or printers). |
| **mount.cifs** | Mounts shared Samba directories; as the SUID bit is enabled, can be run by regular users. Successor to the **smbmount** command. |
| **net** | Supports access similar to the Microsoft **NET** command. |
| **nmblookup** | Broadcasts a lookup request to a Samba/CIFS server. |
| **pdbedit** | Manages user accounts in a Security Accounts Manager (SAM) database. |
| **smbclient** | Lists shares in a specified Samba server; can be used as an FTP-style client on a Samba server. |
| **smbcontrol** | Sends messages to Samba servers. |
| **smbpasswd** | Creates a Microsoft network password for a given user. |
| **smbstatus** | Displays the status of current connections from a Samba server. |
| **smbtree** | Lists the shared directories from all connected Samba servers. |
| **tdbbackup** | Backs up Samba databases in the /var/lib/samba directory. |
| **umount.cifs** | Unmounts shared Samba directories; as the SUID bit is enabled, can be run by regular users. Successor to the **smbumount** command. |

**Table 16-4.**   Selected Samba Commands

configuration file, the following command would reveal the home directory of the given user as a shared directory:

```
$ smbclient -L //hostname -U username
```

Once a Microsoft network shared directory is configured on a remote system (even from a Samba server), you can mount it from a Linux client with the **mount.cifs** command. For example, if the share name from the computer named sambahost is **[backups]** as defined in the Samba configuration file, the directory can be mounted on the local /mnt directory with the following command:

```
$ mount.cifs //sambahost/backups /mnt
```

```
michael@UbuntuGG:~$ smbtree -U michael
Password:
WORKGROUP
        \\UBUNTUHARDYSERV              ubuntuhardyserver server (Samba, Ubuntu)
                \\UBUNTUHARDYSERV\IPC$                IPC Service (ubuntuhardyserver server (Samba
, Ubuntu))
                \\UBUNTUHARDYSERV\print$              Printer Drivers
        \\UBUNTUHARDY3                 ubuntuhardy3 server (Samba, Ubuntu)
                \\UBUNTUHARDY3\PDF             PDF
                \\UBUNTUHARDY3\print$         Printer Drivers
                \\UBUNTUHARDY3\IPC$           IPC Service (ubuntuhardy3 server (Samba, Ubuntu))
MSHOME
        \\UBUNTUSERVER                 ubuntuserver server (Samba, Ubuntu)
                \\UBUNTUSERVER\michael        Home Directories
                \\UBUNTUSERVER\AnotherLaser   Second copy
                \\UBUNTUSERVER\LaserJet-4L    No Information Available
                \\UBUNTUSERVER\UbuntuPrinter  No Information Available
                \\UBUNTUSERVER\FirstClass     sfadj;lk
                \\UBUNTUSERVER\print$         Printer Drivers
                \\UBUNTUSERVER\mnt            Donna's Backup
                \\UBUNTUSERVER\IPC$           IPC Service (ubuntuserver server (Samba, Ubuntu))
        \\UBUNTUGG                     UbuntuGG server (Samba, Ubuntu)
                \\UBUNTUGG\SambaDesktop       Connected to the Desktop
                \\UBUNTUGG\AnotherLaser       Second copy
                \\UBUNTUGG\FirstClass         sfadj;lk
                \\UBUNTUGG\LaserJet-4L        No Information Available
                \\UBUNTUGG\PSC_1210           PSC_1210
                \\UBUNTUGG\IPC$               IPC Service (UbuntuGG server (Samba, Ubuntu))
                \\UBUNTUGG\tmp                Temporary Files
                \\UBUNTUGG\print$             Printer Drivers
michael@UbuntuGG:~$ ▌
```

**Figure 16-1.**    The **smbtree** command displays shares

This command does not require administrative privileges, courtesy of the SUID bit associated with the **mount.cifs** command. This can be confirmed with the **ls -l /sbin/mount.cifs** command.

# Analyze the Configuration File

If you want to configure a Samba server, you'll need to edit the main Samba configuration file, /etc/samba/smb.conf. This file is long and includes a number of commands that require a good understanding of Microsoft Windows networking. Fortunately, the default version of this file also includes helpful documentation with suggestions and typical configurations that you can use.

To help you with this process, I analyze the default Ubuntu version of this file. The code shown next is essentially a complete view of this file. In some cases, I've replaced or supplemented the comments in the file with my own explanations. You might want to browse your own /etc/samba/smb.conf file as well. If you're familiar with versions of this file from older Ubuntu releases, they have been archived in the /usr/share/samba/ directory, with names such as samba.conf.dapper.

With several exceptions, I limit the analysis to the active directives in the default version of the file. In some cases, that means I leave out any description of several categories of directives.

The smb.conf file includes two types of comments. The hash symbol (#) at the start of a line is used for a general text comment. This is typically verbiage that describes a feature. The second comment symbol is the semicolon (;), used to comment out Samba directives (which you might later wish to uncomment to enable the disabled feature).

**Global Settings: Browsing** Examine the settings under the **[global]** heading, in the Browsing section. First, with respect to the **workgroup** variable, this Samba server will become a member of that Microsoft workgroup or domain. If a variable is not listed, the value reverts to the default, WORKGROUP. Some of you may recognize WORKGROUP as the old name of the default Microsoft peer-to-peer workgroup, and MSHOME as the more current default. The same variable is used if you're joining this computer to a Microsoft-style domain. (Yes, the comment shown here is grammatically questionable.)

```
# Change this to the workgroup/NT-domain name your Samba server will part of
   workgroup = WORKGROUP
```

The **server string** directive that follows is used in place of the current Microsoft Windows description field for a server. The **%h** is a variable that reads the local hostname; so for a Samba server named ubuntuhardyserver,

```
# server string is the equivalent of the NT Description field
    server string = %h Server (Samba, Ubuntu)
```

the description field would read "ubuntuhardyserver Server (Samba, Ubuntu)," which can be verified in the output to the **smbtree** command.

If you change this setting to **yes**, name searches can go through available DNS databases:

```
dns proxy = no
```

Several directives in the default version of the Samba configuration file are related to a WINS server, which can also resolve hostnames. A WINS server can be used as a substitute or supplement for a DNS server but is generally unused except on older Microsoft-style networks.

**Networking** Some Samba servers may be configured on systems with multiple network cards. In some cases, each of these cards will serve different networks. If this situation applies to you, and you want to configure Samba to serve only one network, the following two directives should be of interest. First, you'll want to identify the network that you want served. This could be accomplished with either of the following directives:

```
interfaces = 192.168.0.0/24
interfaces = eth1
```

Of course, you should substitute the network address or device as the value for the appropriate directive. As suggested by the comments, only one **interfaces** directive should be used.

If the local system serves as a firewall system or alternatively in a less-secure DMZ (demilitarized zone) between a secure network and the Internet, you may want to activate the following directive:

```
; bind interfaces only = true
```

**Debugging/Accounting**   The next active command sets up separate log files for every computer that connects to this Samba server. For example, if a computer named allaccess connects to this Samba server, the value for **%m** is set to **allaccess**, and the log file is written to /var/log/samba/log.allaccess. The **max log size** parameter limits log sizes to 1000Kb, with a minimum amount of information, as determined by the **syslog** directive. For more detailed log information, you could set **syslog** as high as 4.

```
log file = /var/log/samba/log.%m
max log size = 1000
syslog = 0
```

If a crash occurs, the following directive uses the **mail** command to e-mail a notice to the current root user; this can be configured to send messages to a given e-mail address in the /etc/aliases file.

```
panic action = /usr/share/samba/panic-action %d
```

**Authentication**   The **security** directive may be a bit confusing. This command means that connections check the local password database. It is appropriate if you're configuring this computer as a Domain Controller (DC), specifically a PDC.

```
security = user
```

Several options can be used for this directive: **domain** is for a member server on a Microsoft domain—but not a DC; **ads** is for a member server on an Active Directory domain.

Now-obsolete versions of Microsoft operating systems did not encrypt passwords; this line is now the default, which means passwords are encrypted on all Samba systems unless this line is changed:

```
encrypt passwords = true
```

The following directive is critical, as it points to the password database. Standard options for this directive are **smbpasswd**, **tdbsam**, and **ldapsam**, which correspond to Windows NT 4, Windows 2000/2003, and LDAP authentication databases, respectively.

```
passdb backend = tdbsam
```

The next active directive configures authentication support through the Pluggable Authentication Modules (PAM) described in Chapter 10, as applicable.

```
obey pam restrictions = yes
```

The directive that follows prohibits access by the root administrative user, promoting security:

```
invalid users = root
```

The following directives synchronize changes made on a Microsoft Windows client to a local Linux-based authentication database. First, the **unix password sync** directive attempts to synchronize the local /etc/passwd database with any changes made to the smbpasswd database. Due to the limitations of formatting in this book, the **passwd chat** command, with options, is split into three lines. If you choose to copy this code, do not include a carriage return character between the lines.

```
unix password sync = yes
passwd program = /usr/bin/passwd %u
passwd chat = *Enter\snew\s*\spassword:* %n\n \
*Retype\snew\s*\spassword:* %n\n \
*passwd:*password\supdated\ssuccessfully* .
```

The **pam password change** directive uses PAM, as discussed in Chapter 10, to regulate access to Linux password changes. Finally, the **map to guest** directive shown here rejects login attempts with bad passwords, unless the user does not exist. In that case, the user is mapped to a guest account, if it exists.

```
pam password change = yes
map to guest = bad user
```

**Domains**  If you're configuring a Microsoft NT 4–style domain, you'll want to activate the following directive:

```
; domain logons = yes
```

In addition, PDCs should have the following directive set to **yes**; Backup Domain Controllers (BDCs) should have the following directive set to **no**:

```
domain master = yes
```

In an NT 4–style network, logon profiles for remote users are stored on the local Samba server. When a user logs in, those profiles become a part of that user's registry. Two options for storing the profile are shown here:

```
;    logon path = \\%N\profiles\%U
;    logon path = \\%N\%U\profile
```

For our purposes, the %N corresponds to the name of the server, and the %U corresponds to the username. Other options are available, but as NT 4 domains are a less common option today, I leave you to the aforementioned Samba documents from the samba-doc package for more information.

If **domain logons** are configured, these directives set the logon drive as the H: drive on the client. The home directory on the server is associated with the name of the server (%N) and the logon username (%U). A script can be configured in the logon.cmd file for each user in the **logon home** directory.

```
;    logon drive = H:
;    logon home = \\%N\%U
;    logon script = logon.cmd
```

**Printing**   If you're sharing printers using Samba, sharing is enabled by default, as suggested by the following directive:

```
; load printers = yes
```

However, to configure printers, you'll need to select a print system. If you're using the CUPS service described in Chapter 9, activate the following directives:

```
;    printing = cups
;    printcap name = cups
```

If you've set up the /etc/printcap configuration file with the **Printcap** directive in /etc/cups/cupsd.conf as discussed in Chapter 9, the **printcap name** directive should be changed to this:

```
printcap name = /etc/printcap
```

**Miscellaneous**   If you have a group of Samba servers, the following directive allows you to create a common configuration file:

```
;    include = /home/samba/etc/smb.conf.%m
```

Then directives in a specific server named smb1 can be added to an smb.conf.smb1 file.

If you have a group of user IDs on a Samba network, it's often best to segregate them from local user IDs—or even user IDs from another authentication service such as NIS. To that end, the following directives suggest a range of user and group ID numbers. Different ranges are possible; since kernel 2.6, user and group IDs through $2^{32}$ (more than 4 billion) are available.

```
;    idmap uid = 10000-20000
;    idmap gid = 10000-20000
;    template shell = /bin/bash
```

Regular users are allowed to configure their own shares with the following directives. The first directive limits the number of shares on the local server to limit problems with server performance. The second directive allows regular users to configure shares for guest users.

```
;    usershare max shares = 100
     usershare allow guests = yes
```

**Share Definitions**   Authenticated clients who connect to a local Samba server will want access to their home directories. This is available if you activate the following stanza of directives. In other words, home directories are limited and available to users who log in with an appropriate password.

```
; [homes]
;    comment = Home Directories
;    browseable = no
```

To minimize the effect of spelling errors, **browseable** is a synonym for **browsable** in the Samba configuration file.

The following directives suggest appropriate, almost self-explanatory options. Yes, shares from a home directory can be made read-only. Read, write, and execute permissions for new directories and files can be limited to the owner of the home directory:

```
;   read only = yes
;   create mask = 700
;   directory mask = 700
```

As most users will want writable access to their home directories, you may want to set the following directive; to minimize the effect of spelling errors, **writeable** is a synonym for **writable** in the Samba configuration file.

```
writable = yes
```

The following directive limits access to the username associated with the home directory:

```
;   valid users = %S
```

I often add stanzas similar to that shown here to share files. Be aware; it's the name in the square brackets that appears as the "shared directory." The name you include between those brackets does not have to match any existing folder or directory.

```
[tmp]
   comment = Temporary file space
   path = /tmp
   read only = no
   public = yes
```

Directories for printers—and print drivers are shared by default. The **[printers]** share does not need to be browsable or writable, as you wouldn't want any users to view or write regular files in the print spool directory:

```
[printers]
   comment = All Printers
   browseable = no
   path = /var/spool/samba
   printable = yes
   guest ok = no
   read only = yes
   create mask = 0700
```

Finally, there's the share for print drivers. If Microsoft print drivers are made available in the /var/lib/samba/printers directory, Microsoft clients will be able to install those print drivers without requiring access to Microsoft installation files. Write access is limited to Linux and Microsoft administrative users.

```
[print$]
        comment = Printer Drivers
        path = /var/lib/samba/printers
        browseable = yes
        read only = yes
        guest ok = no
;       write list = root, @ntadmin
```

### Test Changes to /etc/samba/smb.conf

After making any changes to /etc/samba/smb.conf, you should always test your system before putting it into production. You can do a simple syntax check on the Samba configuration file with the **testparm** command. This does not actually check to determine whether the service is running or functioning correctly; it checks only basic text syntax and command stanzas.

## A Basic Domain Member

A member server of a domain passes authentication requests to others. The key directives for a basic domain member include the following directives in the /etc/samba/smb.conf configuration file:

```
security        = server
password server = <NT Server Name>
```

The **password server** directive should be set to the hostname or IP address of the system with the authentication database, normally a PDC. In that case, substitute accordingly for *<NT Server Name>*. Alternatively, if **password server = \***, the system automatically searches the network for a PDC, but that can delay logins.

## A Domain Controller

If the system is a PDC or BDC, security in the /etc/samba/smb.conf configuration file should be set as follows:

```
security = user
```

Generally, either a PDC or a BDC should be configured as the master browser for the domain to facilitate NetBIOS searches over the network:

```
local master = yes
```

If both a PDC and BDC is set as a master browser, higher numbers for the **os level** are appropriate (65 is commonly used for a PDC):

```
os level = 33
```

## Part of an Active Directory Network

Until Samba 4 is released, Samba is limited to being a member server on an AD network. To that end, a Samba server on an AD network can be configured as a basic domain member, with the help of the following **security** directive:

```
security = ads
```

## Implement Changes

Of course, changes must be implemented by the Samba script. In most cases, I restart the script with the following command:

```
$ sudo /etc/init.d/samba restart
```

I could reload the configuration file without restarting Samba, which means existing connections don't have to be broken:

```
$ sudo /etc/init.d/samba reload
```

Of course, this assumes you've addressed issues related to the password database described throughout this section—and unless you've implemented LDAP authentication, you won't be able to use the same database as that used for a Linux network.

# A GRAPHICAL NETWORK SHARING TOOL

If the NFS or Samba servers aren't yet installed, and you start the Shared Folders tool, the window shown in Figure 16-2 will appear, offering to install both NFS and Samba services. If you've read this chapter sequentially, chances are these services are already installed; otherwise, Samba connects to the Synaptic Package Manager to install both services. The installed NFS service is the NFS kernel server.

## Prepare to Share

Before you begin, back up the current versions of the /etc/exports and /etc/samba/ smb.conf configuration files. The simplest option is to back up these files to your home directory with the following commands:

```
$ cp /etc/exports ~
$ cp /etc/samba/smb.conf ~
```

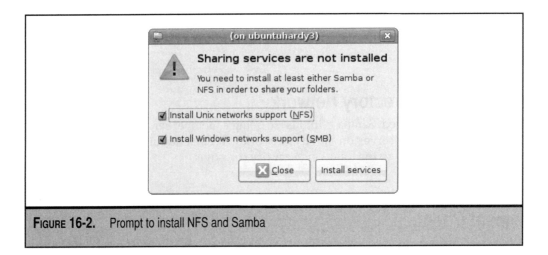

Now open the Shared Folders tool. The first time it's open, the window shown in Figure 16-3 will be blank. If the options are all grayed out, it means you haven't configured appropriate permissions in the PolicyKit or user members of the admin group, as discussed in Chapter 10. Otherwise, click unlock. In the Authenticate window that appears, select a user member of the lpadmin group and enter that user's password. Click Authenticate. The Add option should now be clickable.

The Shared Folders tab lists the shared directories configured on both Samba and NFS services. Directories are listed whether you've configured them through the Shared Folders tool or shared them by directly editing the associated configuration files.

**Figure 16-3.**   The Shared Folders configuration tool

The General Properties tab configures some basic settings for the Samba server. The Users tab configures allowed users for the Samba server.

The following sections describe how to share a directory via Samba and then another directory via NFS. Once configured, the settings can be reviewed and changed via the Properties button.

## Create a Samba Share

In this section, you'll examine how to configure a directory for sharing via the Samba server. This does not address any firewalls that may exist or network problems that may arise between server and client computers. This also assumes the gnome-system-tools, samba, and samba-common packages are installed, and your account has appropriate PolicyKit-based administrative privileges. Finally, the Shared Folders tool should be open in a GUI; one method is by using the **shares-admin** command. As suggested earlier, click Unlock, and specify the username and password of a user member of the admin group. Then take the following steps:

1.  Click Add in the Shared Folders tab.

2.  In the Share Folder window that appears, as shown in Figure 16-4, the Share Through drop-down text box typically includes two options: Windows Networks (SMB) and Unix Networks (NFS). Since this exercise shares a directory via Samba, select the Windows Networks (SMB) option.

3.  The Path drop-down text box allows you to select the path to the directory you want to share. The default should be the directory from which you ran the **shares-admin** command—in this case, /home/michael. For a different directory, choose Other from the Path drop-down text box and navigate to the desired directory. For this exercise, select the /tmp directory.

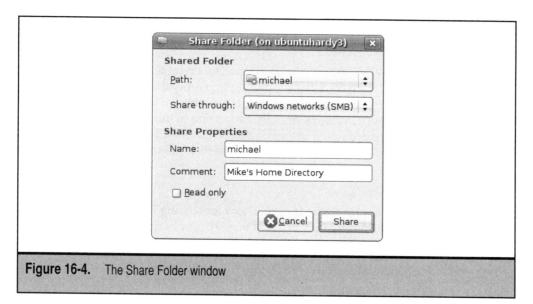

**Figure 16-4.**   The Share Folder window

4. Retain the default for the Name text box under Share Properties. This should match the last bit of the shared directory and will be the name seen and used by clients for sharing.

5. Add a comment as desired; this comment will be visible on clients in the output to the **smbtree** command.

6. Deselect the Read Only option and click Share.

7. The directory that you just configured for sharing should appear in the main Shared Folders window, under the Shared Folders tab. Highlight that directory.

8. Click Properties. The settings just created should appear. Make any changes if desired and click Share.

9. Click the General Properties tab. Enter the name of the domain or workgroup in the corresponding text box. If you want to configure this system as a WINS server, select the corresponding check box. If you want to configure this system to look to a different system as the WINS server, enter its hostname or IP address in the corresponding text box.

10. Click Close to exit from the Shared Folders window.

11. Now open the Samba configuration file, /etc/samba/smb.conf. The share for the /tmp folder should appear at the bottom of the file.

The options added in these steps added the following directives to the Samba configuration file:

```
[tmp]
path = /tmp
comment = Temporary Files
available = yes
browsable = yes
public = yes
writable = yes
```

If you configured a WINS server, or a connection to a remote WINS server, there will also be entries associated with the **wins support** and possibly the **wins server** directives.

The Shared Folders tool also includes a Users tab, with a list of current users from the /etc/passwd configuration file. It's essentially a front end to the **smbpasswd** command. If you select a user, you're prompted to enter a Samba password for that user. Be careful; unlike other password programs, you get to enter the new password only once.

# Create an NFS Share

In this section, you'll see how to configure a directory for sharing via the NFS kernel-based server. This does not address any firewalls that may exist or network problems that may arise between server and client computers. This also assumes the gnome-system-tools, samba, and samba-common packages are installed, and your account has appropriate PolicyKit-based administrative privileges. Finally, the Shared Folders tool should be open in a GUI; one method is with the **shares-admin** command. As suggested earlier, click Unlock, and specify the username and password of a user member of the admin group. Then take the following steps:

1. Click Add in the Shared Folders tab.

2. In the Share Folder window that appears, as shown in Figure 16-5, click the Share Through drop-down box, and select the Unix Networks (NFS) option.

3. Use the Path drop-down text box to select the path to the directory you want to share. Choose Other in the Path drop-down text box, and navigate to the desired directory. For this exercise, select the /home directory.

4. Click Add. If you selected the correct option in step 3, the Add Allowed Hosts window shown in Figure 16-6 should appear.

5. Select the Allowed Hosts drop-down text box, and review the three available options:

   ■ **Specify Hostname**   Allows you to enter the hostname or FQDN in the Host Name text box. That FQDN can include wildcards, such as *.example .net to represent all systems on the example.net network.

   ■ **Specify IP Address**   Lets you enter a single allowed IP address in the IP Address text box.

   ■ **Specify Network**   Permits you to specify a network, as two text boxes appear for the Network IP address and associated network mask.

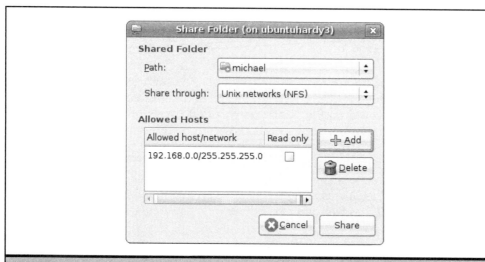

**Figure 16-5.**   The Share Folder window

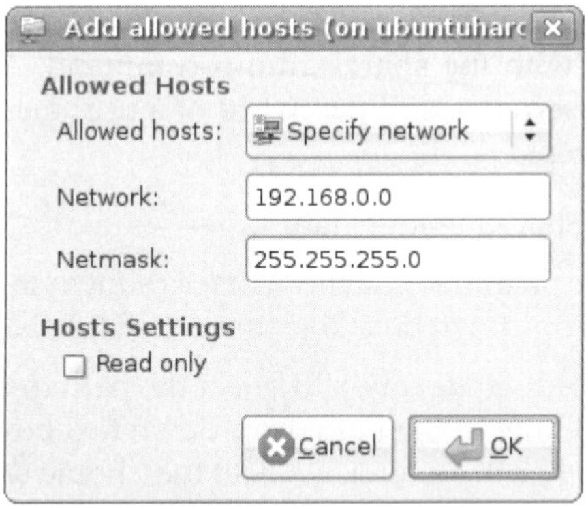

**Figure 16-6.** Add Allowed Hosts window

6. If you want the share to be writable, deselect the Read Only option near the bottom of the window. Click OK to continue.

7. Click Share to return to the Shared Folders window.

8. Close the Shared Folders window.

9. Review the result in the /etc/exports configuration file.

10. Run the **sudo exportfs -r** and **showmount -e localhost** commands. You should see the /home directory share just configured.

# SUMMARY

This chapter includes a basic overview of two file sharing services: NFS and Samba. As it was originally designed for Unix, NFS is well suited for efficient file sharing. And the NFS kernel server is based on the latest version of NFS: version 4. While NFS shares are configured in /etc/exports, settings are also configured in several files in the /etc/ default directory.

Samba is the open source implementation of current Microsoft networking protocols. Samba can be configured to share printers and directories with other Linux systems with Samba clients, as well as Microsoft clients. Samba can also be configured as a Microsoft NT 4–style PDC or BDC, as well as a member server on an Active Directory network.

# CHAPTER 17

# Other Services: Mail, FTP, and NTP

his chapter includes a collection of useful services. First, Linux administrators need to know how to configure e-mail servers; the default e-mail service for Ubuntu Server is Postfix. The standard Ubuntu FTP server is the very secure FTP service, vsFTP. And Network Time Protocol (NTP) services can help administrators synchronize multiple systems serving the same clients. While alternatives are available, these services are configured in Ubuntu's main repository, and they therefore get a higher level of support by Canonical and the Ubuntu community.

While Postfix is the default e-mail service, a common alternative is sendmail. Once installed and configured, either service can be configured as a local network mail server. Ubuntu includes the open source version of sendmail; the alternative commercial version is known as Sendmail (with a capital *S*). Both Postfix and sendmail are configured in this chapter.

The vsFTP daemon is the default for Ubuntu, which supports both basic and secure FTP server services. The vsFTP daemon can be configured with specific allowed users, secure directories, and more.

The NTP service is important for networks with multiple servers. Unless the times of different servers are synchronized, logs can be confusing, inventory might be mislocated, financial transactions might be complete before they're made, and so on.

# MAIL SERVICES

There are a number of components associated with e-mail services—clients, servers, and delivery agents. The configuration of clients such as Evolution and Thunderbird are fairly trivial for Ubuntu administrators and are not covered in this book on Ubuntu Servers. Linux offers a number of alternative methods for handling incoming and outgoing e-mail.

This section defines the components associated with mail services and then describes the configuration of Postfix and sendmail.

## Components of E-mail Systems

E-mail systems include up to four major components. Most users have mail user agents (MUAs) as their e-mail clients. Many administrators already configure mail servers, also known as mail transfer agents (MTAs). But an MTA doesn't do everything; a mail delivery agent (MDA) is required to carry the e-mail from a mail server to mailboxes. Finally, a mail retrieval agent (MRA) connects to files on a remote directory being used as a mailbox. Alternatives for each component are listed in Table 17-1.

The only components that are absolutely required are MTAs and MUAs. The basic functionality of an MDA is included in services such as sendmail and Postfix. MRAs are built into standard MUAs such as Evolution, Thunderbird, and even Microsoft's Outlook Express.

| E-mail Component | Examples |
|---|---|
| Mail transfer agent (MTA) | sendmail, Postfix |
| Mail user agent (MUA) | mail, Evolution, Thunderbird |
| Mail delivery agent (MDA) | procmail, maildrop |
| Mail retrieval agent (MRA) | fetchmail |

**Table 17-1.** E-mail Components

E-mail systems depend on reliable name resolution. That means you should install a DNS server on the local network, as described in Chapter 14. And that DNS server should be authoritative for the local network; otherwise, e-mail between users on the local network may not be delivered.

The sendmail and Postfix services rely on the Simple Mail Transfer Protocol (SMTP) to send e-mail. MUAs rely on other protocols to receive e-mail. When a separate MDA is configured, it may be used to transmit e-mail to specific account directories.

While it's good to test and learn both Postfix and sendmail, don't install both servers simultaneously on the same system. The interactions could lead to lost e-mail. For this chapter, you'll first install, configure, and test Postfix. You then uninstall Postfix before proceeding to install, configure, and test sendmail. Whether you prefer Postfix or sendmail is in some ways a matter of personal taste. In general, sendmail includes more features, but Postfix is easier to configure. The features associated with Postfix are, in the opinion of many, more than sufficient for the enterprise. But many excellent Linux administrators disagree.

There are several excellent books dedicated to the configuration of both services. Two that I like are *The Book of Postfix: State-of-the-Art Message Transport*, published by No Starch Press (2005), and *sendmail, 4th Edition*, published by O'Reilly (2007). The following sections just scratch the surface.

# Simple Postfix Configuration

The first time the Postfix SMTP service is installed, you're prompted with questions during the installation process. For example, if you install Postfix with the following command,

```
$ sudo apt-get install postfix
```

you're prompted to configure Postfix in a number of text-based screens. Figure 17-1 illustrates several choices, as described in Table 17-2.

For the purpose of this chapter, press TAB to highlight OK and then press ENTER to continue. Then select Internet Site to set up Postfix to send and receive e-mail with a minimum of additional agents.

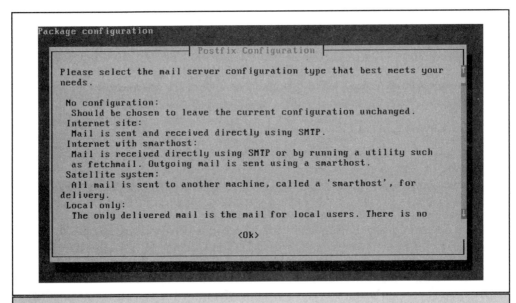

**Figure 17-1.** Postfix configuration types

Next, you're prompted to set up a mail name, which is the domain name added to usernames as a full e-mail address. If Internet delivery is configured for outgoing e-mail, the entry shown in Figure 17-2 has to be a valid domain name. Assuming you have one, enter a domain name for a domain that you own or control, and then press ENTER to continue.

| Desired Configuration | Description |
|---|---|
| No Configuration | No changes are made to default Postfix configuration files |
| Internet Site | Configures send and receive access via SMTP |
| Internet With Smarthost | Incorporates an MRA such as fetchmail |
| Satellite System | Sets up outgoing e-mail for a second SMTP server |
| Local Only | Configures e-mail for local users only |

**Table 17-2.** Postfix Configuration Options During Installation

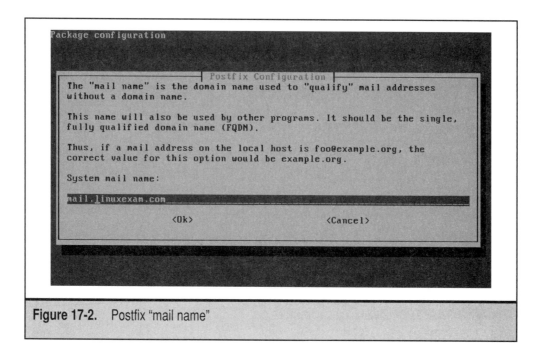

**Figure 17-2.** Postfix "mail name"

The configuration process continues. With the custom features just set, Postfix configuration files are stored in the /etc/postfix directory. To reconfigure these features and more, run the following command:

```
$ sudo dpkg-reconfigure postfix
```

The steps associated with this command prompt you to redirect e-mail that is sent to the postmaster, root, and other system accounts, preferably to a real e-mail account. It proposes a comma-delimited list of e-mail domains, which probably should be changed. You're allowed to force synchronous updates; this is not necessary unless the Internet connection is unreliable. In that case, synchronous updates are recommended to prevent loss of e-mails in the queue.

Next, as shown in Figure 17-3, you're prompted to enter the local networks for which this Postfix server should relay e-mail. IP network addresses may be entered in CIDR (Classless Inter-Domain Routing) notation.

If you configure procmail for local delivery, e-mails to local users are copied to appropriate locations in user home directories. You may be allowed to configure synchronous updates, which isn't necessary if the associated filesystem includes journaling features. Examples of common journaling filesystems are ext3, xfs, and reiserfs. You can also configure Procmail to deliver e-mail to local users.

Next, you may be given a chance to limit the size of the mailbox. The default of 0 corresponds to no limit. A limit might be advisable so spam or other big e-mail attachments don't overload the storage available on the local system.

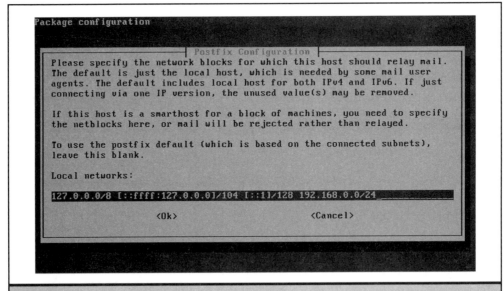

**Figure 17-3.** Postfix governs these networks

While you're allowed to change the character that helps define a local address, the default, a plus sign (+), is rarely changed. Finally, you can select whether the Postfix server uses IPv4, IPv6, or both for addressing. Unless you're certain that network hardware can handle IPv6 addresses, I recommend sticking with IPv4. And I do so in this chapter for ease of illustration.

Before doing anything else, back up the files in the /etc/postfix directory. The key file to customize is main.cf, explained in detail here. (It's a fairly simple file as configured for Ubuntu, with only 40 lines in my personal configuration.)

Back up this file and open it in a text editor. While the first line is commented, it cites the default file with the mail server URL, which you should have added with the **dpkg-reconfigure postfix** command earlier in this section:

```
#myorigin = /etc/mailname
```

E-mail servers often display a banner when administrators connect. That banner is based on the following directive, where $myhostname is the FQDN (fully qualified domain name) of the local system, and $mail_name is the name of the local server.

```
smtpd_banner = $myhostname ESMTP $mail_name (Ubuntu)
```

The banner is displayed when connecting with the **telnet** command. For example, when I connect to the local Postfix server, using the standard SMTP port number of 25, I see the following:

```
$ telnet localhost 25
Trying 127.0.0.1...
Connected to localhost.
Escape character is '^]'.
220 ubuntuhardy3.example.org ESMTP Postfix (Ubuntu)
```

The FQDN of the e-mail server is ubuntuhardy3.example.org, and the $mail_name is Postfix. If allowed by your ISP, you could try this command on the FQDN of the ISP's e-mail server.

The **biff** setting is normally disabled, as it can cause performance problems. If enabled, it supports notification whenever Postfix processes the incoming e-mail queue:

```
biff = no
```

The **append_dot_mydomain** directive, if enabled, appends the domain name to e-mail addresses. This functionality is handled by modern e-mail clients (MUAs) such as Evolution and Thunderbird, so the directive is disabled:

```
append_dot_mydomain = no
```

Sometimes, target e-mail servers are down. But like other SMTP e-mail services, Postfix keeps trying to deliver messages. While the following directive is commented, it does reflect the default, which notifies the sender if an e-mail isn't delivered in four hours:

```
# delay_warning_time = 4h
```

The **readme_directory** is pointed at Postfix documentation files, if the postfix-doc package is installed. If installed, the directive is

```
readme_directory = /usr/share/doc/postfix
```

If the postfix-doc is not installed, the directive is

```
readme_directory = no
```

The following directives enable Transport Layer Security (TLS), the current implementation of the Secure Sockets Layer (SSL) protocol. It enables encrypted communication to and from the Postfix server. In order, they enable the TLS certificate, the encryption key, and the use of TLS. The final two directives configure a cache good for a session, so any password doesn't have to be transmitted continuously.

```
smtpd_tls_cert_file=/etc/ssl/certs/ssl-cert-snakeoil.pem
smtpd_tls_key_file=/etc/ssl/private/ssl-cert-snakeoil.key
smtpd_use_tls=yes
```

```
smtpd_tls_session_cache_database = btree:${data_directory}/smtpd_scache
smtp_tls_session_cache_database = btree:${data_directory}/smtp_scache
```

The remaining directives specify options configured earlier with the **dpkg-recon figure postfix** command, plus a few more options. Some of the options have already been described. The **alias_maps** and **alias_database** directives specify the file that associates target users and destination e-mail addresses.

```
myhostname = ubuntuhardy3.example.org
alias_maps = hash:/etc/aliases
alias_database = hash:/etc/aliases
myorigin = /etc/mailname
```

The **mydestination** directive corresponds to the domains to which the local Postfix server considers itself to be authoritative:

```
mydestination = linuxexam.com, ubuntuhardy3.example.org,
localhost.example.org, localhost
```

If you configured access through a different e-mail SMTP server, it will be designated as the **relayhost**. Otherwise, the following directive leaves full responsibility for sending and receiving e-mail to the local system:

```
relayhost=
```

The **mynetworks** directive specifies the IP addresses served by the Postfix server. The first three entries are essentially different names for the localhost system. The final setting is the local network address, in CIDR notation:

```
mynetworks = 127.0.0.0/8 [::ffff:127.0.0.0]/104 [::1]/128 192.168.0.0/24
```

The **mailbox_size_limit** directive sets a size limit for each user's mailbox, in bytes:

```
mailbox_size_limit = 10000000
```

The **recipient_delimiter** specifies the character associated with local users:

```
recipient_delimiter = +
```

If there are multiple network interfaces, the **inet_interfaces** directive should be set to the network device that serves the target network. For now, it's set to serve all interfaces:

```
inet_interfaces = all
```

The **inet_protocols** directive can specify the IP versions readable by Postfix; it may be set to **ipv4**, **ipv6**, or **all**:

```
inet_protocols = ipv4
```

If you've installed the postfix-doc package, pay attention to one more directive which points to the directory with Postfix documentation in HTML format:

```
html_directory = /usr/share/doc/postfix/html
```

I use this directory to access Postfix documentation locally, using the techniques documented in Chapter 15.

Remember, if you also want to consider sendmail (or another SMTP e-mail server), it's best to uninstall the Postfix service first. I choose not to purge the associated configuration files with the **apt-get purge** command, as I may yet decide that Postfix is the best option for a local SMTP e-mail server. To that end, I uninstall Postfix with the following command:

```
$ sudo apt-get remove postfix
```

After removal is complete, you should still see the same configuration files in the /etc/postfix directory.

## Simple sendmail Configuration

If you choose to install the sendmail SMTP service, be prepared to do most configuration by directly editing an appropriate configuration file. When installing sendmail with the following command,

```
$ sudo apt-get install sendmail
```

several additional packages are installed (if they're not already included), as described in Table 17-3.

| sendmail Package | Description |
| --- | --- |
| m4 | A macro processor intended to compile the sendmail.mc file |
| procmail | An MDA sometimes used by sendmail for local e-mail addresses |
| sendmail-base | Architecture-independent files for sendmail |
| sendmail-bin | For user authentication databases including NIS (Network Information Service) and LDAP (Lightweight Directory Access Protocol) |
| sendmail-cf | Example sendmail configuration files |
| sensible-mda | Connector between sendmail and an MDA |

**Table 17-3.** Packages Installed with the sendmail SMTP Service

The sendmail configuration files are stored primarily in the /etc/mail directory. Alternative configuration files are available in the /usr/share/sendmail/cf directory. The key files that will be configured indirectly are sendmail.cf for incoming mail and submit .cf for outgoing mail. Other sendmail configuration files in the /etc/mail directory are described in Table 17-4. The sendmail service requires compiled versions of several configuration files, with the .db (database) extension. In a bit, I'll explain how the database and configuration files are created.

| /etc/mail File | Description |
| --- | --- |
| access, access.db | Supports outgoing access rules |
| address.resolve | Specifies different e-mail addresses for local, firewall, and remote delivery |
| aliases, aliases.db | Notes the target user for e-mail sent to other users; linked to /etc/aliases |
| databases | Includes automatically configured databases |
| helpfile | Notes help messages available to administrators who connect remotely via port 25 |
| local-host-names | Supports aliases for local hostnames |
| m4/ | Notes the directory with m4 macro processor files |
| Makefile | Contains rules for compiling files in /etc/mail |
| peers/provider | Includes support to a remote SMTP server |
| sasl/ | Notes the directory with Simple Authentication Security Layer (SASL) files for authentication |
| sendmail.cf | Specifies the main sendmail configuration file |
| sendmail.cf.errors | Notes errors in the current sendmail configuration |
| sendmail.conf | Adds alternative configuration file for sendmail |
| sendmail.mc | Includes macros that can be used to generate a new version of sendmail.cf |
| service.switch | Specifies the search order for hostnames; the format is similar to /etc/nsswitch.conf |
| service.switch-nodns | Specifies the search order for hostnames; the format is similar to /etc/nsswitch.conf |

**Table 17-4.** sendmail Configuration Files

| /etc/mail File | Description |
|---|---|
| smrsh/ | Adds files for the sendmail control shell |
| submit.cf | Specifies the main outgoing sendmail configuration file |
| submit.mc | Includes macros that can be used to generate a new version of submit.cf |
| tls/ | Notes the directory with sendmail Transport Layer Security (TLS) certificates |
| trusted-users | Lists special users that can send e-mail without warnings |

**Table 17-4.**  sendmail Configuration Files (*continued*)

Most of the work required is in customizing the sendmail.mc configuration file. But first, you should know a bit about the language found in the sendmail.mc and submit.mc macro files.

## How sendmail Configuration Files Are Read

When the sendmail service is started, it reads the .cf (configuration) and .db (database) files in the /etc/mail directory. The configuration files are sendmail.cf and submit.cf. The sendmail.cf file is a long (around 2000 lines) file that may seem difficult to decipher but includes a wealth of helpful comments. The submit.cf file is nearly as long. This file provides detailed rules (organized into rulesets) on how sendmail should process e-mail addresses, filter spam, talk to other mail servers, and more. The database files limit access primarily by IP address and provide aliases for specified users.

The sendmail.cf file is complex and may appear cryptic. Fortunately, most directives in this file need not be changed. And Linux simplifies this process—all you really need to do is customize a smaller file full of macros, sendmail.mc. There's a similar relationship between the submit.cf and submit.mc files.

Once you've configured these files (and any other files in the /etc/mail directory), you can use the **sendmailconfig** command to compile new custom sendmail.cf and submit.mc files. As these files are still fairly complex, I'll highlight those directives associated with configuring sendmail for basic operation.

The macros in the sendmail.mc and submit.mc files perform the following tasks:

▼ Activate or deactivate features.

■ Define variables and values.

▲ Include descriptive comments.

The most basic macro is **dnl**, which is effectively a comment character. Information from this macro to the end of the line is not compiled or included in the actual sendmail configuration.

The **include** directive instructs sendmail to read the contents of the named file and insert it at the current location in the output. Some of these files are in the /etc/mail directory; some administrators include macro files (with .mc extensions) in various /usr/share/sendmail/cf directories.

The **define** directive sets files or enables features that you want to use. The following example in sendmail.mc disables certain commands:

```
define(`confPRIVACY_FLAGS',dnl
`needmailhelo,needexpnhelo,needvrfyhelo,restrictqrun,restrictexpand,
nobodyreturn,authwarnings')dnl
```

The **FEATURE** directive, not surprisingly, enables specific features. For example, one **FEATURE** directive refers to the /etc/mail/access.db file for allowed systems.

**DAEMON_OPTIONS** directly controls the sendmail daemon. The default active **DAEMON_OPTIONS** directive does not accept any mail from outside the local system, as defined by the localhost address:

```
DAEMON_OPTIONS(`Family=inet, Name=MTA-v4, Port=smtp, Addr=127.0.0.1')dnl
```

There are a seemingly inconsistent pair of quote characters in most of these lines. Specifically, in this command, the directives inside the parentheses start with a back quote (`) and end with a single quote (').

## Configuring and Securing sendmail.mc

Before making any changes to the sendmail.mc configuration file, back it up. You need to make only a couple of adjustments to get your system ready for use on the Internet. By default, the following line limits sendmail access to the local system, despite the IP addresses in the /etc/mail/access file:

```
DAEMON_OPTIONS(`Family=inet, Name=MTA-v4, Port=smtp, Addr=127.0.0.1')dnl
```

To allow access to other computers, remove the address information. That can be limited to the local network in the /etc/mail/access file:

```
DAEMON_OPTIONS(`Family=inet, Name=MTA-v4, Port=smtp')dnl
```

There are four **DAEMON_OPTIONS** directives in the default /etc/mail/sendmail .mc configuration file, as shown. IPv6 addressing is disabled by default.

```
dnl DAEMON_OPTIONS(`Family=inet6, Name=MTA-v6, Port=smtp, Addr=::1')dnl
DAEMON_OPTIONS(`Family=inet,  Name=MTA-v4, Port=smtp, Addr=127.0.0.1')dnl
dnl DAEMON_OPTIONS(`Family=inet6, Name=MSP-v6, Port=submission, Addr=::1')dnl
DAEMON_OPTIONS(`Family=inet,  Name=MSP-v4, Port=submission, Addr=127.0.0.1')dnl
```

If you activate IPv6 addressing, and disable the IPv4 and IPv6 address limits, these directives would read like so:

```
DAEMON_OPTIONS(`Family=inet6, Name=MTA-v6, Port=smtp')dnl
DAEMON_OPTIONS(`Family=inet,  Name=MTA-v4, Port=smtp')dnl
DAEMON_OPTIONS(`Family=inet6, Name=MSP-v6, Port=submission')dnl
DAEMON_OPTIONS(`Family=inet,  Name=MSP-v4, Port=submission')dnl
```

Note the **Port** directives; the smtp and submission port numbers, as defined in /etc/services, are TCP/IP port numbers 25 and 587.

Next, in the /etc/mail/submit.mc file, the following directive configures a source IP address of 127.0.0.1. It should be changed to a real IP address. Many servers block e-mails from private IP addresses, as that would be a simple way to send spam from an unidentifiable location. But a private IP address should work for e-mails within a local network. If you intend to configure this system to connect online, you should give it a real IP address—and if there's a router between the local network and the Internet, that router should transmit messages on the aforementioned TCP/IP ports to the sendmail system.

```
FEATURE(`msp', `[192.168.0.154]', `MSA')dnl
```

But that's not enough. If you want to allow remote computers or networks access to your sendmail server, you'll need to add their names or addresses to the /etc/mail/access file. And there are four directives of interest in this file, as described in Table 17-5.

| access Directive | Description |
|---|---|
| Connect | Specifies systems that may be allowed to use this service |
| GreetPause | Sets a delay, in milliseconds, against floods of spam e-mail |
| ClientRate | Limits the number of connections, per minute |
| ClientConn | Limits the number of simultaneous connections |

**Table 17-5.** Key Directives in the /etc/mail/access File

The **Connect** directive can be used to allow or deny access to the sendmail service. For example, the following directive would allow access to my private network, 192.168.0.0/24:

```
Connect:192.168.0          RELAY
```

Pay attention to the notation. For this file, no dot (.) appears at the end of the IP address.

Next is the **GreetPause** directive, which can slow the rate of e-mail connections from spamming servers. The first **GreetPause** directive disables from the local network; the second **GreetPause** directive enables a 5 second (5000 millisecond) delay from all other systems. The second directive should already be included in /etc/mail/access by default.

```
GreetPause:192.168.0   0
GreetPause:            5000
```

The **ClientRate** directive limits the number of connections from a single system, on a per-minute basis. Assuming the users on the local network can be trusted, the following directives disable the **ClientRate** limit from the local network, and then sets a limit of 10 e-mails per minute from all other systems. The second directive should already be included in /etc/mail/access by default.

```
ClientRate:192.168.0   0
ClientRate:            10
```

Finally, the **ClientConn** directive limits the number of simultaneous connections from a single system. Assuming the users on the local network can be trusted, the following directives disable the **ClientConn** limit from the local network, and then sets a limit of 10 simultaneous connections from all other systems. The second directive should already be included in /etc/mail/access by default.

```
ClientConn:192.168.0   0

ClientConn:            10
```

Back up the current files in the /etc/mail directory. Then you can generate a new set of sendmail configuration files with the following command:

```
$ sudo sendmailconfig
```

The **sendmailconfig** script processes the files in the /etc/mail directory, with a series of questions. The first question is a bit misleading, as there's no sendmail.conf configuration file, but the question should be accepted to enable **sendmailconfig** to process the other files.

```
Configure sendmail with the existing /etc/mail/sendmail.conf? [Y] Y
```

Next, you're asked whether to use the current sendmail.mc macro file:

```
Configure sendmail with the existing /etc/mail/sendmail.mc? [Y] Y
```

And finally, you're prompted to reload the currently running sendmail service:

```
Reload the running sendmail now with the new configuration? [Y] Y
```

If there are errors you can find them in the /etc/mail/sendmail.cf.errors file. Read this file and follow the suggestions. The default configuration leads to errors such as this:

```
*** ERROR: FEATURE() should be before MAILER()
```

If you configure the **MAILER** directives at the end of the /etc/mail/sendmail.mc macro file, the errors will disappear the next time you run the sudo **sendmailconfig** command.

# FTP SERVICES

The File Transfer Protocol is one of the original network applications associated with the TCP/IP protocol suite. It follows the standard model for network services, as FTP requires a client and a server. The FTP client is installed by default on most operating systems, including Ubuntu.

vsFTP is the server available from the main repository, and therefore it could be considered the default FTP service. vsFTP is the default FTP service installed on other distributions, including Red Hat. According to the associated website (http://vsftpd.beasts .org), vsftpd is used to power the main FTP services for Red Hat, SUSE, and even the released Linux kernels. I therefore focus on vsFTP in this book.

## Other FTP Servers

While vsFTP is the default for Ubuntu and several other Linux distributions, many other fine FTP services are available, some of which are described in Table 17-6. The associated package name is in parentheses.

## The Very Secure FTP Service

Before configuring the vsFTP server, you need to install it. One method is with the following command:

```
$ sudo apt-get install vsftpd
```

| FTP Server | Description |
|---|---|
| Advanced TFTP (atftpd) | A multi-threaded TFTP server for multiple connections |
| Netkit FTP (ftpd) | An FTP server with an SSL option; other FTP servers are preferred in the Ubuntu documentation |
| Secure FTP (krb5-ftpd) | An FTP server that uses Kerberos for authentication |
| Pure-FTPd (pure-ftpd) | A complex FTP server with support for chroot directories, quotas, and more |
| Trivial FTP (tftpd) | The standard TFTP server, sometimes used for terminal servers |
| TwoFTPd (twoftpd) | A two-part FTP server, including an authenticating front-end without code |
| WU-FTPD (wu-ftpd) | A popular FTP server that hasn't been maintained since 2001 |

**Table 17-6.** Description of Selected FTP Servers

Two key vsFTP configuration files are /etc/vsftpd.conf and /etc/ftpusers. The vsftpd.conf configuration file is the standard. The /etc/ftpusers file is commonly used by other FTP servers to configure users who are not allowed access through the server.

The directives in this file are straightforward. I urge you to read the file for yourself; the comments provide good explanations of many of the directives. A few of these directives are listed in Table 17-7. (Because some directives are long, line wrapping is unavoidable.) Commented directives from the default version of the vsftpd.conf file include the pound character (#) in front. Many commented directives are default settings.

This section focuses on those directives that you might change to enhance the security or customize access to regular users. The directives in the default vsftpd.conf file are just a small fraction of the directives that are available; other directives are listed in the vsftpd.conf man page.

Once the configuration is complete, restart the server with the following command. You can connect from the local system or from a remote system on the same network.

```
$ sudo /etc/init.d/vsftpd restart
```

As I've enabled anonymous access, I'd expect to be able to access this FTP server with the username *anonymous*. And when the vsftpd package is installed, FTP server uploads and downloads are configured by default in the /home/ftp directory.

| Command | Description |
|---|---|
| listen=YES | Supports a control script in /etc/init.d; note the **listen_ipv6** directive available for IPv6 communication |
| anonymous_enable=YES | Allows anonymous access; can be set to **NO** |
| # local_enable=YES | Can support regular user logins |
| # write_enable=YES | Can support writes by authenticated regular users |
| # local_umask=022 | Can override the default umask of 077; requires **local_ enable=yes** |
| # anon_upload_ enable=YES | Enables uploads by anonymous users |
| # anon_mkdir_write_ enable=YES | Enables new directories by anonymous users |
| dirmessage_enable=YES | Allows directory messages; by default, located in .message file |
| xferlog_enable=YES | Activates logging of uploads and downloads |
| connect_from_port_ 20=YES | Supports data transfers through TCP/IP port 20 |
| #chown_uploads=YES | Allows changing the ownership of uploaded files |
| #chown_ username=whoever | Sets the ownership for uploaded files |
| #xferlog_file=/var/log/ vsftpd.log | Specifies the default log for file transfers |
| #xferlog_std_ format=YES | Specifies the standard log format |
| #idle_session_ timeout=600 | Notes that sessions are timed out in 10 minutes |
| #data_connection_ timeout=120 | Notes that attempted data connections are timed out in two minutes |
| #nopriv_user=ftpsecure | Defines an unprivileged user, not included in /etc/passwd |
| #async_abor_enable=yes | Required for some FTP clients; enabling this option is discouraged |
| #ascii_upload_ enable=yes | Enables uploads in ASCII mode; documentation suggests this is a "terrible feature" |

**Table 17-7.**   Some vsFTP Server Configuration Commands

| Command | Description |
|---|---|
| #ascii_download_enable=yes | Enables downloads in ASCII mode; documentation suggests this is a "terrible feature" |
| #ftp_banner=Welcome to blah FTP service | Configures a banner |
| #deny_email_enable=YES | Can set up a list of denied anonymous e-mail addresses |
| #banned_email_file=/etc/vsftpd.banned_emails | Specifies file with unallowed e-mail addresses; requires **deny_email_enable=YES** |
| #chroot_local_user=YES | Can limit local users to their home directories |
| #chroot_list_enable=YES | Can set up a list of users associated with **chroot** |
| #chroot_list_file=/etc/vsftpd.chroot_list | If **chroot_local_user=YES**, users in the noted file are not allowed to **chroot** |
| #ls_recurse_enable=YES | Can set up the **ls -R** command for subdirectories |
| secure_chroot_dir=/var/run/vsftpd | Points to a directory that should be empty, and not writable by the FTP user |
| pam_service_name=vsftpd | Configures Pluggable Authentication Module (PAM) security |
| rsa_cert_file=/etc/ssl/certs/ssl-cert-snakeoil.pem | Points to a certificate for secure connections |
| rsa_private_key_file=/etc/ssl/private/ssl-cert-snakeoil.key | Notes a certificate key for secure connections |

**Table 17-7.** Some vsFTP Server Configuration Commands (*continued*)

# FTP Client

The standard FTP client software is a basic command line, text-oriented client application that offers a simple but efficient interface. Most web browsers offer a graphical tool that can be used as an FTP client; to that end, the gFTP and KFTPgrabber tools are available from Ubuntu repositories. However, the FTP client I prefer is **lftp**.

Any FTP client supports views of files in a directory tree. Most FTP clients are simple. For example, you can use the **ftp** command to connect to a server such as ftp.kernel.org as follows:

```
$ ftp ftp.kernel.org
```

I prefer the **lftp** client, as it supports interchanges similar to those available at the command line. By default, the **lftp** client automatically attempts an anonymous login. It also supports command completion, which can help you access files and directories with longer names.

Most commands at the FTP prompt are run at the remote host, similar to a Telnet session. Most command line FTP clients still allow access to the local shell. From the FTP client prompt, just preface the desired local command with a bang (!) to run regular shell commands.

# THE NETWORK TIME PROTOCOL SERVICE

When multiple servers are being used for the same purpose, it's important that their clocks are kept in sync. It's annoying enough when e-mails appear to arrive before they've been sent. Furthermore, if inventory numbers don't match sales, customers will be disappointed. In addition, if a system crashes, the wrong time on the backup system can mean less data is recovered. In this section, you'll learn how to create and configure your own Network Time Protocol (NTP) server. But first, you'll configure a client.

## Configure an NTP Client

In most cases, Ubuntu has already been configured as an NTP client during the installation process. It's available through the ntpdate package, whose settings are configured in the /etc/default/ntpdate configuration file. This file is simple, with three options. The first refers to the /etc/ntp.conf configuration file, which is the standard for a local NTP server, if installed:

```
NTPDATE_USE_NTP_CONF=yes
```

The second option specifies a remote NTP server. The noted ntp.ubuntu.com server is the default available during the boot process:

```
NTPSERVERS="ntp.ubuntu.com"
```

Alternative NTP servers are described shortly—including how you can configure a local NTP server. If you choose or configure an alternative, substitute appropriately.

Finally, options to the NTP client service, **/usr/sbin/ntpdate**, can be included in the following directive:

```
NTPOPTIONS=""
```

However, unless you have the NTP server installed locally, this configuration doesn't work. To make it work, you'll have to do two things. First, change the directive that points to an NTP server configuration file:

```
NTPDATE_USE_NTP_CONF=no
```

Then you could configure a regular job to update the time on a regular basis. For more information, see Chapter 7. Alternatively, you could just run the following command:

```
$ sudo ntpdate-debian
14 May 07:28:03 ntpdate[29374]: adjust time server 91.189.94.4 offset
-0.392028 sec
```

## Select a Remote NTP Server

The standard Ubuntu NTP server, ntp.ubuntu.com, is located in the United Kingdom. Distant NTP servers are less accurate, as distance leads to delays. If you want to find a public NTP server closer to you, one place to start is http://support.ntp.org/bin/view/ Servers/WebHome. When searching for a geographically closer NTP server, be aware that you should connect to a "Stratum Two" time server. Even then, permission may be required from the NTP server administrator. Too many connections to an NTP server can degrade performance, leading to delays. And delays are never good for a time server.

One option to Stratum Two servers is available from the Public NTP Time Server project. For more information, navigate to http://pool.ntp.org. It provides public access to a cluster of time servers worldwide.

## Basic Configuration

While an Ubuntu system includes an NTP client by default, an NTP server requires a bit more. To install the NTP server, run the following command:

```
$ sudo apt-get install ntp
```

It includes several configuration files. The first is /etc/default/ntp, which includes options associated with the NTP daemon, /usr/sbin/ntpd. The default setting in this file is this:

```
NTPD_OPTS='-g'
```

The -g switch allows the NTP service to adjust the time once by over the "panic" threshold of 1000 seconds. That can help if you've accidentally picked the wrong time zone during the installation process.

The NTP service then refers to the /etc/ntp.conf configuration file. The first directive describes how NTP collects statistics. Variations from remote NTP servers are listed in the noted file:

```
driftfile /var/lib/ntp/ntp.drift
```

If problems arise with the NTP service, logs are filed in the noted directory. Despite being commented out, /var/lib/ntpstats is the default directory for this purpose:

```
# statsdir /var/lib/ntpstats/
```

The following directive specifies the statistics to be collected. The **loopstats** directive is associated with updates to the local clock. The **peerstats** directive logs updates from peer NTP servers listed in this configuration file. The **clockstats** directive is associated with the clock driver.

```
statistics loopstats peerstats clockstats
```

The directives that follow specify how statistics are collected for each criteria in the **statsdir** directory. For example, statistics associated with **loopstats** are collected in the /var/lib/ntpstats/loopstats file, every day.

```
filegen loopstats file loopstats type day enable
filegen peerstats file peerstats type day enable
filegen clockstats file clockstats type day enable
```

During the installation process, Ubuntu checks with its default NTP server. The information described earlier from the /etc/default/ntpdate file should match the following directive:

```
server ntp.ubuntu.com
```

If you have a local NTP server, you'd also want the following directive:

```
server 127.127.1.0
```

This is an arbitrary address—it's in the "loopback" IP address network, but don't confuse it with the standard loopback address of 127.0.0.1. The noted server address is dedicated to NTP services.

These lines configure default restrictions for IPv4 and IPv6:

```
restrict -4 default kod notrap nomodify nopeer noquery
restrict -6 default kod notrap nomodify nopeer noquery
```

The **kod** prevents so-called "Kiss of Death" packets from bringing down the server. The **notrap** option denies the message trap service; the **nomodify** option prevents other NTP servers from modifying this one. These options should not be changed.

To configure a local NTP server, you don't need the **nopeer** and **noquery** options to enable others to synchronize and request information. If the users on the local network are trustworthy, leave out the **kod** option. To enable access to the 192.168.0.0 network with the noted subnet **mask**, you could add the following IPv4 directive:

```
restrict -4 192.168.0.0 mask 255.255.255.0 notrap nomodify
```

You can add more **restrict** directives, as needed, for other networks. The IPv6 version of this directive would be similar on the noted subnet:

```
restrict -6 0011:838:0:1:: mask ffff:ffff:ffff:ffff:: kod notrap nomodify
```

The following default **restrict** directives limit administrative access to the local system for the IPv4 and IPv6 loopback addresses:

```
restrict 127.0.0.1
restrict -6 ::1
```

If you want to add a remote administrative interface, specify its IP address with another directive:

```
restrict 10.11.12.13
```

That's all that you absolutely have to change to configure a local NTP server. Of course, after saving these changes, activate the NTP server with a command like this:

```
$ sudo /etc/init.d/ntp restart
```

# SUMMARY

This chapter covered the configuration of three somewhat disparate services: e-mail, FTP, and NTP. Two major options for e-mail servers are Postfix and sendmail. While Postfix is the standard for Ubuntu, sendmail remains popular. Postfix is easier to configure, and the process is facilitated by the prompts with the **sudo dpkg-reconfigure postfix** command.

While many excellent FTP services are available, the standard for Ubuntu is vsFTP. It's fairly easy to configure for anonymous or user-based access through the /etc/vsftpd .conf configuration file.

Administrators of multiple servers should be interested in NTP. Consistent clocks can help ensure reliable inventories, proper backups, and more. This chapter described how you can update local systems with the NTP client and configure a local NTP server.

# CHAPTER 18

## Backups and Security

S ecurity is a sensitive topic. Many administrative gurus have their own takes on the
best ways to ensure a secure system.

In this chapter, you'll examine several ways to configure AppArmor (short for Application Armor), an alternative to SELinux (Security Enhanced Linux). At this point, there
is no consensus on whether AppArmor or SELinux is better. Red Hat distributions use
SELinux. SUSE distributions use AppArmor. Ubuntu wants to offer both; however, as of
the Hardy Heron release, the Ubuntu implementation of SELinux is incomplete.

This chapter also describes the use of TCP Wrappers to help secure TCP-based services. It also describes how to use the **iptables** command to keep systems and networks
more secure.

Before we get into security, remember, the intent is to protect data. And part of the
data protection process requires regular backups.

# BACKUPS

Different backup methods are associated with different levels of risk. You may be willing
to do more for more sensitive information. On the other hand, if the data in question is
simply a bunch of log files from reliable servers on the local network, regular backups
may be less important. In contrast, administrators who have spent hours configuring
custom servers want to protect their creations. Enterprises depend on customer databases for their business. Finally, most users "know" that their data is more important
than yours!

While there are many backup systems and commands available for Linux, two basic
options are the focus of this chapter. The tape archive command, **tar**, is the traditional
method for creating an archive suitable for copying to remote media, including high-
speed tape drives. The **rsync** command allows you to create custom backups of specific
directories, supporting partial backups that do not include those temporary system-
dependent files and directories.

## The Tape Archive (tar) Command

The **tar** command is simple and filled with features. It can package groups of files into
a single compressible archive. Packages created with the **tar** command are sometimes
known as *tarballs*, which is still a common method for distributing packages. Tarballs are
still an option for distributing packages for all major Linux distributions.

It's time for an example. If you want to back up the files in user michael's home directory, the following command collects all files from the noted home directory, recursively
(with all subdirectories), into a compressed archive:

```
$ tar cvzf michaelbackup.tar.gz /home/michael
```

This command creates (**c**) the backup. As the backup is created in verbose (**v**) mode,
you can monitor the creation of the archive. But if you have confidence in the process,

verbose mode is not required. The archive is compressed in gzip format (**z**). An alternative is bzip2 format (**j**), which supports a bit more compression. The archive is sent to a file (**f**), as specified by the name that follows, in this case, *michaelbackup.tar.gz*.

The process can be reversed: just substitute **x** (extract) for **c** in the noted command. So if I were restoring files from michael's home directory from the backup, I'd run the following command:

```
$ tar xzvf michaelbackup.tar.gz
```

## Compression Algorithms

There are two basic compression algorithms available for the **tar** command. The **gzip** command, short for GNU zip, uses the DEFLATE algorithm, which is incidentally the same algorithm used for .zip files common on Microsoft systems. Alternatively, Linux also includes the **zip** command, which can archive a group of files with the same algorithm. The **z** switch to the **tar** command incorporates the compression functionality of the **gzip** command.

**NOTE** When I transmit compressed archives to Microsoft users, I use the **zip** command. For example, just before I started writing this chapter, I ran the **zip -R ch17 89217w.doc f17\*** command to create the ch17.zip file, based on the document and associated figures. I then transmitted the ch17 .zip archive to McGraw-Hill for further processing.

The second compression regime is known as bzip2, which uses the Burrows-Wheeler transform data compression algorithm. It provides more compression but is slower than the **gzip** and **zip** commands. The **j** switch to the **tar** command incorporates the compression functionality of the **bzip2** command.

When groups of files are compressed with the **tar** command, an extension is normally added to the archive filename. In the aforementioned command, the .tar.gz extension is added as a descriptive label: the .tar is associated with an archive created with the **tar** command, and the .gz indicates the compression algorithm. An alternative popular extension with the same meaning is .tgz.

When groups of files are compressed using the bzip2 regime, a different extension is normally added to the archive file. If the **j** switch is used in the aforementioned command, the .tar.bz2 extension is added as a descriptive label: the .tar is associated with an archive created with the **tar** command, and the .bz2 indicates the compression algorithm. An alternative popular extension with the same meaning is .tbz2.

As suggested, the **gzip** and **bzip2** commands can be used separately. They compress individual files in the noted format, with the .gz and bz2 extensions, respectively. The **gunzip** and **bunzip2** commands reverse the process.

## Command Switches for tar

The **tar** command is one of the few Linux commands that do not require a dash (–) with command switches. Several important command switches are shown in Table 18-1.

| tar Switch | Description |
|---|---|
| c | Create an archive |
| d | Compare an archive and a current directory |
| f | Specify an archive filename |
| j | Use bzip2 (Burrows-Wheeler) compression |
| k | Restore only files which don't already exist |
| r | Add files to the end of an archive |
| t | List current files from an archive |
| v | Verbose mode; useful for troubleshooting |
| z | Use gzip (DEFLATE) compression |

**Table 18-1.** Command Switches for **tar**

## Sync Remotely

The **rsync** command transfers files between directories. It takes just as much time to copy files with the **rsync** command—the first time. The power of the **rsync** command is revealed after the first time. The only data that's transmitted is data that has changed—specifically, only the parts of each file that have changed. That makes **rsync** suitable for backups even over slow networks.

If you're not experienced with the **rsync** command, try a basic version of this command. First, create a /backup directory, owned by your username (in my case, michael), with the following commands:

```
$ sudo mkdir /backup
$ sudo chown michael.michael /backup
```

Then copy all files from your home directory to the /backup directory with the following command:

```
$ rsync -a /home/michael/. /backup/
```

This command copies all files from the home directory to the /backup directory. The dot (.) specifies all files and directories, regular and hidden. By convention, Linux hidden files and directories start with a dot. The **-a** specifies the archive switch, which is explained shortly.

Make some changes in your home directory. Run the same **rsync** command again. That command compares every file in the source and destination directories. Except for the file information that is compared, the only data that is transmitted is the information that's changed in new or newly revised files. However, if you've deleted a file from that home directory, that file still exists in the /backup directory.

Now go a bit further. The following command copies the information from my home directory to a remote system named backup.example.org, in the /backup subdirectory. There are differences; some subtle, some more direct.

```
$ rsync -ave ssh --log-file=log /home/michael backup.example.org:/backup/
```

The **-v** switch specifies verbose mode. As such, it's not required but provides messages that can be helpful if there is trouble. The **-e** switch allows you to specify the use of a different shell. By default, the **rsync** command would use the **rsh** command for remote connections. The **ssh** command is more secure, as it enables encrypted connections. The **--log-file=***log* sends the verbose messages to the local file named *log*; substitute the name of your choice.

The /home/michael directory used in the command, without the trailing forward slash, synchronizes my home directory and subdirectories, with the target location. The files are sent to the target, the backup.example.org system, to the directory named /backup/. If desired, substitute the IP address for the URL. When the backup is complete, you'll be able to find the files from your home directory on the backup .example.org system—in my case, in the /backup/michael directory.

There are many more switches available in the **rsync** man page; a few are listed in Table 18-2.

| rsync Switch | Description |
|---|---|
| **-a** | Sets archive mode; substitutes for **-rlptgoD** |
| **-D** | Includes device files, in the /dev directory |
| **-e** | Changes the transfer command from **rsh** to an alternative such as **ssh** |
| **-g** | Preserves group ownership |
| **-H** | Includes hard linked files |
| **-l** | Includes symbolically linked files |
| **--log-file=file** | Specifies a file to send messages; suited to verbose mode (**-v**) |
| **-o** | Preserves user ownership |
| **-p** | Preserves permissions |
| **-r** | Acts recursively |
| **-v** | Sets verbose mode |
| **-z** | Compresses data |

**Table 18-2.** Command Switches for **rsync**

As suggested by the table, the advantage of archive mode (**-a**) is how it preserves additional characteristics of each file, including ownership, permissions, last revision times, and symbolic links.

## Other Backup Tools

Linux offers many capable backup tools. The **cpio** command literally copies input files from a command such as **find** and creates a backup from those files. The **dump** and **restore** commands are well suited to running full, differential, and incremental backups. These tools are suited to tape drives; higher speed tape drives can save data at hundreds of MB/s. Several specialized Linux backup tools are available, such as Afbackup, Amanda, the Backup Manager, Bacula, and Box Backup—and these backup tools are only a drop in the bucket—those whose names begin with the first two letters of the alphabet.

There are also hardware tools available. If you prefer to back up to DVD media, options for so-called "jukeboxes" that can save data on hundreds of DVDs are available. But with the rapidly dropping prices of hard drive media, options related to RAID devices (as discussed in Chapter 5) are more popular. Hot-swappable hardware, even those connected via USB 2.0 or IEEE 1394 devices, make it easier to back up critical data remotely. Network Attached Storage (NAS) options make it possible to store and backup data in remote locations, facilitating disaster recovery.

## SECURITY WITH APPARMOR

AppArmor is an alternative to SELinux. Both systems are available under the GNU General Public License (GPL) and provide mandatory access control (MAC). In brief, MAC-based security can help ensure that files, directories, and users associated with one system can't be used to break into a second system. Normally, if a cracker breaks into a server with the games user, that could be a problem, as the games user in /etc/passwd has an administrative user ID (below 1000). But with MAC-based security, that cracker won't be able to use that account to break through other systems.

In other words, AppArmor makes it more difficult for crackers to use or access any file or service if they break in. AppArmor includes profiles that can be set in enforce, complain, or unconfined modes.

One problem with AppArmor is that it doesn't work if it's installed on the same system with SELinux. So if you prefer the SELinux techniques of MAC-based security, uninstall the AppArmor packages first. The related packages installed by default are apparmor and apparmor-utils. As of this writing, the Hardy Heron release of Ubuntu includes SELinux support only for the CUPS print service described in Chapter 9.

Some administrators prefer AppArmor, because it is easier to configure and can support access control for networked filesystems mounted via NFS.

Through the Gutsy Gibbon release, the use of AppArmor required loading of the associated apparmor module. If properly installed, it should be listed in the output to the **lsmod** command. Starting with the Hardy Heron release, AppArmor was integrated in the default kernel. If you install SELinux, you must explicitly disable AppArmor during the boot process, adding the following directive at the end of the kernel command line:

```
apparmor=0
```

**NOTE** AppArmor development is centered around Novell's SUSE Linux. In contrast, SELinux development is centered around the Red Hat distributions. The implementation of both systems on Ubuntu is still a work in progress.

# AppArmor Packages

The default AppArmor packages are apparmor and apparmor-utils. These and other related packages are described in Table 18-3. If AppArmor is your security package of choice, read the table and decide which of these packages to install.

Detailed information associated with AppArmor is available from the apparmor-docs package. It stores the latest available technical documentation in PDF format, compressed using the **gzip** system. The file is techdoc.pdf.gz, in the /usr/share/doc/apparmor-docs directory. One way to access the file is to copy it to your home directory, and then apply the **gunzip** command:

```
$ sudo cp /usr/share/doc/apparmor-docs/techdoc.pdf.gz ~
$ gunzip techdoc.pdf.gz
```

| Package | Description |
| --- | --- |
| apparmor | Includes the AppArmor service, parser, and profiles; standard profiles can be found in the /etc/apparmor and /etc/apparmor.d directories |
| apparmor-docs | Adds AppArmor documentation from SUSE developers |
| apparmor-profiles | Includes profiles that may not be fully tested |
| apparmor-utils | Installs AppArmor configuration commands |
| libapparmor1 | Adds the AppArmor "change hat" function for different roles |
| libapache2-mod-apparmor | Includes an Apache module for AppArmor configuration |
| libpam-apparmor | Includes a PAM module for AppArmor configuration |

**Table 18-3.** AppArmor Packages for Ubuntu

The techdoc.pdf file should now be available in your home directory, accessible from any standard PDF reader.

# AppArmor Modes

There are four modes associated with AppArmor. Each mode can protect a command or process, configure when systems are logged, disable profile enforcement, or disable AppArmor completely.

- ▼ **enforce** Protects the noted process; access is limited as specified in the associated profile.
- ■ **complain** Sets up learning mode, which logs appropriate information; similar to SELinux's permissive mode.
- ■ **audit** Sets up a logging mode; similar to SELinux's permissive mode.
- ▲ **not confined** Does not apply AppArmor protections. Profiles may still exist for the process.

# Unsuitable AppArmor Commands

Most commands can be configured with AppArmor. The few that have been tested are located in the /etc/apparmor.d directory, and you can add more. There are several commands that shouldn't be controlled with AppArmor, such as **awk**, **ls**, and **kill**. These commands are listed in the logprof.conf file, in the /etc/apparmor directory.

**NOTE** Expert options for AppArmor can be configured in the /etc/apparmor/logprof.conf configuration file.

# AppArmor Status

Assuming AppArmor is properly installed, you can review the current status on the local system with the **sudo apparmor_status** command. From the output, you can confirm that the apparmor module is properly loaded, as well as the number of configured profiles and processes. Both profiles and processes can be set to enforce, complain, and unconfined modes. It's functionally equivalent to the following command:

```
$ sudo /etc/init.d/apparmor status
```

If you're running an older version of Ubuntu (Gutsy Gibbon or earlier), make sure the apparmor module is loaded in the output to the **lsmod** command. If it isn't loaded, install the apparmor-modules-source package.

# AppArmor Boot Process

Starting with the Hardy Heron release, AppArmor is automatically installed by default. It's started like any other normal service, in this case from the **apparmor** script in the

/etc/init.d/ directory. The script incorporates the functions from the /etc/apparmor /rc.apparmor.functions configuration file. It also incorporates the profiles configured in the /etc/apparmor.d/directory.

# AppArmor Profiles

Standard AppArmor profiles are available in the /etc/apparmor.d directory. The profiles included in this directory have been tested. Take a look at the first available profile, bin.ping, which regulates access to the **ping** command, in the /bin directory. If you don't see a desired profile, make sure the associated package is installed first. The bin.ping profile is included in the apparmor-profiles package. The AppArmor profile for the default DNS service is not included until the bind9 package is installed.

AppArmor profiles often have **#include** directives, which incorporate the directives from other files. This particular line incorporates directives from the global file, from the tunables subdirectory:

```
#include <tunables/global>
```

The next line indicates that the command is set in "complain" mode. The first forward bracket encompasses the options that follow:

```
/bin/ping flags=(complain) {
```

The next three options incorporate directives from the abstractions/ subdirectory:

```
#include <abstractions/base>
#include <abstractions/consoles>
#include <abstractions/nameservice>
```

The following options are also straightforward, if you're familiar with the settings. They provide capabilities to the **ping** command, allowing access to raw network packets (**net_raw**), and to other users, courtesy of **setuid** mode. Network communication is enabled for raw IPv4 (**inet**) packets.

```
capability net_raw,
capability setuid,
network inet raw,
```

The final two lines set permissions of a sort for the **ping** command as well as related access to the /etc/modules.conf configuration file. That file does not exist in the Hardy Heron release. The permissions are known as access modes.

```
/bin/ping mixr,
/etc/modules.conf r,
}
```

## AppArmor Access Modes

Access modes are the building blocks of AppArmor. The full list is available from the man page for the apparmor.d directory. Some are straightforward; others require more explanation. The modes are summarized in Table 18-4.

Several of these modes are mutually exclusive. For example, AppArmor can't be set to write and append to a file. Only one option from the **ux**, **Ux**, **px**, **Px**, and **ix** modes can be configured on a single file.

## AppArmor Commands

There are two **apparmor_\*** commands. The **apparmor_status** command was described earlier. The **apparmor_parser** command is called during the AppArmor initialization process. The remaining AppArmor commands are **aa-\*** commands. The following command reveals them as links to other scripts, also in the /usr/sbin directory:

```
$ ls -l /usr/sbin/aa-*
```

| Access Mode | Description |
| --- | --- |
| r | Read |
| w | Write (cannot be combined with **a**) |
| a | Append (cannot be combined with **w**) |
| ux | Sets unconfined execute (disables AppArmor protection) |
| Ux | Sets unconfined execute (child processes also run without AppArmor protection) |
| px | Works only with programs with AppArmor profiles |
| Px | Works only with programs with AppArmor profiles (should be rarely used) |
| ix | Allows calls of other AppArmor protected programs, in execute mode |
| m | Makes programs executable |
| l | Supports file links |
| k | Allows file locking |

**Table 18-4.**    AppArmor Access Modes

*TIP* Linked files on the command line may be shown in colors that are difficult to read, especially on the white background associated with terminals in a GUI. To disable the effect of color in a terminal, start a command with a backslash (\).

The **aa-status** command is functionally equivalent to **apparmor_status**. The **aa-unconfined** command provides information on network services not currently regulated by AppArmor.

## AppArmor Audits

The **aa-audit** command takes a specified profile already in the /etc/apparmor.d/ directory, which enables logging whenever the applicable program is accessed. For example, after I run the following command, I'm prompted to enter the name of a program:

```
$ sudo aa-audit
[sudo] password for michael:
Please enter the program to switch to audit mode: ping
Setting /etc/apparmor.d/bin.ping to audit mode.
$
```

If the program or command doesn't have a profile in the /etc/apparmor.d/ directory, nothing is done. But as described earlier, there is a profile for the **ping** command in the bin.ping file. The **flags** directive is changed, as shown:

```
/bin/ping flags=(audit)
```

Now every time anyone on the local system runs the **ping** command, that attempt is logged in the /var/log/messages and /var/log/syslog files. Be aware that some profiles may send logging information to files in the /var/log/apparmor/ directory.

## AppArmor Complaints

The **aa-complain** command takes a specified profile already in the /etc/apparmor.d/ directory, which enables complain mode whenever the applicable program is accessed. It works in a similar way to the **aa-audit** command; in effect, it reverses the effect of the **aa-audit** command when applied to the **ping** command.

## AppArmor Enforcement

The **aa-enforce** command takes a specified profile already in the /etc/apparmor.d/ directory, which enables enforce mode whenever the applicable program is accessed. It works in a similar way to the **aa-audit** command. Messages are not normally logged unless a violation of some sort occurs.

# Extra AppArmor Profiles

If you're looking for more control with AppArmor, additional profiles are available from the apparmor-profiles package, in the /usr/share/doc/apparmor-profiles/extras/ directory.

Be aware that the profiles in this directory are not fully tested. When they are, expect to see more profiles in the /etc/apparmor.d/ directory.

As of the Hardy Heron release, these profiles include commands such as **man** and **passwd**, applications such as Adobe Acrobat Reader and Evolution, clients such as **dhclient** and **portmap**, as well as services such as sendmail and vsFTP. One example on how you can use these profiles is shown in the README file in this directory. If you want to use one of these extra profiles, the appropriate file can be copied to the /etc/apparmor.d/ directory.

An alternative to these profiles is the **aa-genprof** command, which can call or generate profiles. If a profile exists, the command modifies it as need. If you select a command listed in the /etc/apparmor/logprof.conf file, the **aa-genprof** command will refuse to create the profile. In that case, try the **aa-autodep** command, which can suggest appropriate profile rules.

# SECURITY WITH TCP WRAPPERS

As suggested by the name, *TCP Wrappers* provides protection for services that communicate using TCP packets. An overview of these services is available in the /etc/services configuration file. For example, the following excerpt confirms that Secure Shell services use TCP packets for communication over port 22:

```
ssh    22/tcp
```

The following sections describe how you can protect such services using TCP Wrappers. It's based on appropriate directives in the /etc/hosts.allow and /etc/hosts.deny configuration files.

## The TCP Wrappers Process

Systems that communicate with TCP packets channel those packets through TCP Wrappers. The request is checked against a series of rules. If the specified rules allow, control is then returned to the service.

TCP Wrappers rules are specified in the /etc/hosts.allow and /etc/hosts.deny files. The process is sequential: clients and users listed in hosts.allow are allowed access; clients and users listed in hosts.deny are denied access. Because rules in these files may appear to conflict, the TCP Wrappers system takes rules in the following order:

1.   The rules from /etc/hosts.allow are read. If the rules in this file allow access, it is granted. Control is immediately passed back to the service.

2.   The rules from /etc/hosts.deny are read. If the rules in this file deny access, it is denied. Information may be sent back to the client, as suggested by the rule.

3.   If there is no rule associated with the host, client, or service in either file, access is granted, and control is passed back to the service.

# TCP Wrappers with /etc/hosts.allow and /etc/hosts.deny

There is a specific format associated with directives in both /etc/hosts.allow and /etc/hosts.deny. The basic format for commands in each file is as follows:

```
daemon_list : client_list
```

One simple directive for these files is

```
ALL : ALL
```

This directive specifies all services (daemons) and makes the rule applicable to all hosts (clients) on all IP addresses. If this line is configured in /etc/hosts.deny (without other information in /etc/hosts.allow), access is blocked to all services that transmit TCP packets.

Most administrators will want to create finer-grained filters. For example, the following directive in /etc/hosts.allow allows access through the SSH service to one IP address:

```
sshd : 192.168.0.100
```

If that's coupled with an **ALL : ALL** directive in the /etc/hosts.deny file, that would serve as an effective barrier to all who try to connect via SSH except from the noted IP address. But you're not limited to IP addresses; there are alternatives for specifying clients, as shown in Table 18-5.

To configure multiple services for a client, you can use commas, or specify each service on a different line. Exceptions to a specific rule can be made with the **EXCEPT** directive. Examples of each of these configurations from my /etc/hosts.deny are shown here:

```
ALL : .cracker.com
sshd: 10.0.0.0/255.0.0.0 EXCEPT 10.192.168.25
apache2, vsftpd : 192.168.0.1
```

| Client | Description |
|---|---|
| **ALL** | All clients |
| **192.168.** | All IP addresses starting with 192.168 |
| **10.0.0.0/255.0.0.0** | All IP addresses with the noted subnet mask |
| **.example.org** | All clients in the example.org domain |
| **user@ pc1.example.org** | Specifies a user, on the system with the noted URL; can substitute an IP address |

**Table 18-5.**    Sample Commands in /etc/hosts.allow and /etc/hosts.deny

| Variable | Description |
|----------|-------------|
| %a | Client address |
| %A | Host address |
| %c | Client information |
| %d | Process name |
| %h | Client hostname |
| %H | Server hostname |

**Table 18-6.**   Some tcp_wrappers Variables

The first line stops communication with **ALL** services from computers in the cracker.com domain. The second line closes the SSH service to any computer on the 10.0.0.0 network, except the one with an IP address of 10.192.168.25. The last line specifies that the Apache and vsFTP services are closed to the computer with an IP address of 192.168.0.1.

If you want to send messages to the client, such as a warning to restricted users, the **twist** or **spawn** command can help. They support access to shell commands. For example, take the following line in a /etc/hosts.deny file:

```
sshd : .cracker.com : twist /bin/echo Sorry %c, access denied
```

This sends a customized error message for users from the cracker.com domain who try to connect via SSH. If the name and host is included in the connection request, it is sent back as the value of the **%c** variable. Several common variables are described in Table 18-6.

# PORT SECURITY WITH IPTABLES

Firewalls are almost ubiquitous today, perhaps the most common way to protect a private LAN from outside networks. Firewalls based on the **iptables** command are popular for several reasons. First, it can be configured to examine every network packet that passes through its protective rules. It can also be configured to filter out data associated with security risks. The **iptables** command is known as a *packet filter*.

## Port Security Concepts

Linux networking is associated primarily with the TCP/IP protocol stack, also known as the Internet Protocol suite. The TCP/IP stack is organized in several layers. Two of the more important protocols in the stack are TCP (Transmission Control Protocol) and UDP (User Datagram Protocol). Equivalent is the Internet Control Message Protocol (ICMP) associated with the **ping** command. Data transmitted with these protocols use 1 or more of approximately 65,000 ports. Many of these ports are defined in the /etc/services configuration file.

The data that travels through these ports may be broken down in units generally known as *packets*. On some types of networks, they're known as *cells*. Whatever the term, data is transmitted in groups with headers—which includes administrative information, help reconnecting packets, the type of data, the source address, and destination address. Packets are reassembled when they reach the destination computer.

**NOTE**   TCP/IP networking is a rich and complex topic. For more information, see Behrouz Forouzan's *TCP/IP Protocol Suite, Third Edition*, published by McGraw-Hill (2005).

The **iptables** command can take advantage of header information to determine whether to allow the packet to pass. It's customized for IPv4 networks. The iptables package also includes an **ip6tables** command suited for IPv6 networks. The way the **iptables** and **ip6tables** commands can regulate such traffic over the ports of the TCP/IP protocol suite is similar to how cable TV providers can allow and block the transmission of certain channels through their wires.

While I focus on the **iptables** command for IPv4 networks in this chapter, everything described here can apply to IPv6 networks as well. In most cases, all you need to do is substitute the **ip6tables** command.

# Configuring iptables

Firewalls based on the **iptables** command is organized in "chains" of rules. Each rule in a chain is compared against each network packet. Every **iptables** command specifies information that can be found in a packet header. If a match is found, it also specifies the actions to take. Firewalls are a complex subject; for more information, see *Linux Firewalls* (Third Edition; Novell Press, 2005), by Suehring and Ziegler.

The **iptables** command is organized in the following format:

```
iptables -t tabletype <action direction> <packet pattern> -j <what to do>
```

Let's analyze this command, bit by bit. The first bit after the command is the **-t** *tabletype* switch. There are two basic *tabletype* options for **iptables**:

▼   **filter**   Sets a rule for filtering packets.

▲   **nat**   Configures Network Address Translation (NAT), also known as masquerading. It allows systems with private IP addresses to use the public IP address presumably available on the system with the firewall.

If there is no **-t** switch, the **iptables** command assumes by default that a filter rule is being created.

The next bit is the *<action direction>*. The following list shows six basic actions associated with **iptables** filtering rules. Be aware, other options are available. The double-dashed switch in parentheses is a synonym; for example, **-A** has the same effect as **--append**.

▼ **-A (--append)** Appends a rule to the end of a chain.

■ **-I (--insert)** *num* Inserts a rule in a chain, at *num* in the sequence of existing rules.

■ **-R (--replace)** *num* Replaces a rule in a chain, at *num* in the sequence of existing rules.

■ **-D (--delete)** *num* Deletes a rule from a chain, normally at *num* in the sequence of existing rules; can also apply to a full **iptables** chain.

■ **-L (--list)** Lists the currently configured rules in the chain.

▲ **-F (--flush)** Flushes all of the rules in the current **iptables** chain.

The next bit is the direction. If you're appending (**-A**), inserting (**-I**), replacing (**-R**), or deleting from (**-D**) a chain, you'll want to apply it to network data traveling in one of three directions:

▼ **INPUT** All incoming packets are checked against the rules in this chain.

■ **OUTPUT** All outgoing packets are checked against the rules in this chain.

▲ **FORWARD** All packets being sent to another computer are checked against the rules in this chain.

The following bit is a *<packet pattern>*. Your firewall checks every packet against this pattern. One pattern is the source or destination IP address:

▼ **-s** *ip_address* Packets are checked for a specific source IP address.

▲ **-d** *ip_address* Packets are checked for a specific destination IP address.

Another pattern can be based on whether the packet is being transmitted using the TCP, UDP, or ICMP protocol, specified with the **-p** and **-m** switches. This pattern is often combined with the destination port number, specified with the **--dport** switch. For example, if you add the **-p tcp --dport 80** extension, the rule regulates systems that are trying to connect to a web server using the standard HTTP port number (80). Some matching information specifies the type of connection; one that I use is based on matching the state of a new or recent connection:

```
-m state --state NEW -m recent
```

Finally, once an **iptables** command rule finds a match, it needs instructions on what to do with that packet. That's the last part of the command, **-j** *<what to do>*. There are three basic options for the action that can be taken with the packet:

▼ **DROP**   The rule drops the packet without sending a message to the requesting computer.

■ **REJECT**   The rule drops the packet and sends an error message to the requesting computer.

▲ **ACCEPT**   The rule allows the packet to proceed.

The following commands include examples of how the **iptables** command can be used to configure a firewall. Before proceeding, I always check for currently configured rules with the following command:

```
$ sudo iptables -L
```

If there are existing **iptables** rules, they will be classified in three different categories: **INPUT**, **FORWARD**, and **OUTPUT**. From my desktop system, I see the following output, which regulates connection attempts to my SSH server:

```
# Generated by iptables-save v1.3.6 on Fri Dec 28 08:00:41 2007
*filter
:INPUT ACCEPT [4571:32432]
:FORWARD ACCEPT [0:0]
:OUTPUT ACCEPT [393:34208]

-A INPUT -i eth1 -p tcp -m tcp --dport 22 -m state --state NEW -m recent
--set
-A INPUT -i eth1 -p tcp -m tcp --dport 22 -m state --state NEW -m recent
--update --seconds 60 --hitcount 3 -j DROP COMMIT
```

These rules do go into more detail than anything so far in this section. But with the information cited to this point, you should be able to verify the following description from the *Linux Firewalls* book or even, with a little work, the man page for the **iptables** command.

While the **iptables** command is not explicitly cited, the output is associated with the **iptables -L** command. It is based on a rule, appended (**-A**) to the chain named **INPUT**. It uses the network interface (**-i**) on the second Ethernet card (**eth1**), to regulate data coming in through that card. The protocol for this communication is TCP (**-p tcp**); incoming packets are also matched to the TCP protocol (**-m tcp**). The destination port shown (**--dport**) corresponds to TCP/IP port 22, which is the standard for Secure Shell (SSH) connections. It looks at the header state of each packet to see if the header is new (**-m state --state NEW**) or recently added to the current cache (**-m recent**). The source address of such connections are added to the cache (**--set**).

Now the cache of packets is ready for matching tests. The second command uses the cache, limiting its use to the last 60 seconds (**--update --seconds 60**). In other words, if a failure occurs in SSH connection attempts, the remote user can try again after a minute. The number of logins from a cached IP address is limited to 3 (**--hitcount 3**). Additional attempts to log in through port 22 are dropped (**-j DROP**).

These limits allow me and my friends to connect to this system, giving us a couple of chances to recover in case of silly errors such as an accidental use of the CAPS LOCK key. However, it prevents crackers from trying more than three passwords from their dictionary lists before the connection is unceremoniously dropped. Several variations on this command are discussed online by administrators who need remote secure SSH–based access.

Before I added this level of **iptables**-based firewall protection, my log files, specifically /var/log/auth.log, often grew to several megabytes of text, based on cracker attempts using port scanners to break into my system. Alternative security settings are available, such as changing the default port associated with the secure shell, and I use some of these options. But the objective in this section is to describe the use of the **iptables** command.

Another commonly used **iptables** command regulates the use of the **ping** command. This particular **iptables** command stops users from the computer with an IP address of 192.168.200.25 from pinging your system, as it drops packets that use the associated ICMP protocol:

```
$ sudo iptables -A INPUT -s 192.168.200.25 -p icmp -j DROP
```

The following is a similar command that limits the number of **ping** packets that are accepted over a network connection, in this case to 2 per second:

```
$ sudo iptables -A INPUT -p icmp -m limit --limit 2/s -j ACCEPT
```

The following command guards against TCP SYN attacks from outside the network. Assume that your network IP address is 192.168.1.0. The bang (!), which looks like an exclamation point, inverts the meaning; in this case, the command applies to all IP addresses except those with a 192.168.1.0 network address (and a 255.255.255.0 subnet mask):

```
$ iptables -A INPUT -s !192.168.1.0/24 -p tcp -j DROP
```

The default rule for **INPUT**, **OUTPUT**, and **FORWARD** is to **ACCEPT** all packets. One way to stop packet forwarding is to add the following rule:

```
$ iptables -A FORWARD -j DROP
```

A second way to stop packet forwarding is to disable the setting in the kernel. As discussed in Chapter 11, packet forwarding for IPv4 and IPv6 networks can be disabled by setting the following parameters in the /etc/sysctl.conf configuration file:

```
net.ipv4.ip_forward = 0
net.ipv6.conf.all.forwarding = 0
```

Then activate these settings with the **sudo sysctl -p** command.

## Configuring iptables in Ubuntu

Ubuntu does not have the infrastructure associated with **iptables** on other distributions such as Red Hat Enterprise Linux. In other words, you'll have to create files to store any **iptables** rules, as well as scripts to restore these rules, whenever the system is rebooted or restored into the default runlevel.

One simple method to save firewall rules is to create an /etc/firewall configuration file. The **iptables-save** command can save current rules to a specified filename. One option is to save the rules to the firewall file in the local directory to avoid having to log in as the root administrative user:

```
$ sudo iptables-save > firewall
$ sudo cp firewall /etc/firewall
```

Now the firewall configuration is saved in an appropriate administrative directory. To test the result, flush the firewall with the **sudo iptables -F** command. Now restore the firewall from the newly created configuration file with the following command:

```
$ sudo iptables-restore < /etc/firewall
```

But you don't want to have to remember to run this command every time Linux boots. To add this command to the boot process, you need to find an appropriate configuration script. One option for a network configuration script is /etc/init.d/networking. You could include the **iptables-restore < /etc/firewall** command in that script, and the configured **iptables** rules are automatically restored whenever networking is activated.

If you would rather use a graphical tool to configure the firewall, several options are available, including Shorewall, ebox-firewall, FireHOL, and Lokkit. I have not tested any of these packages. However, the **iptables** command and TCP/IP ports are the same on other Linux distributions, at least those with the Linux version 2.6 kernel, so if there's a firewall configuration available from another Linux system, you might be able to transfer that configuration.

# SUMMARY

Backups and security go hand in hand. For the most part, they share the same objective—protecting critical data. This chapter covers some of the basic command line tools that can facilitate backups. The **tar** command can create archives suitable for backups, even to tape archives. The **rsync** command is well suited to synchronizing data over remote networks; once a backup is complete, only revised data is sent over the network.

AppArmor is the system selected by Ubuntu for mandatory access control (MAC), which provides another layer of security for files, directories, and users. AppArmor's protection is based on profiles in the /etc/apparmor.d/ directory. It can be configured with various **apparmor_\*** and **aa-\*** commands. Additional profiles that have not been fully tested are available from the apparmor-profiles package.

TCP Wrappers support the configuration of a firewall for services that communicate with TCP packets. Such services can be controlled with configuration options in the /etc/hosts.allow and /etc/hosts.deny configuration files.

Firewalls can be configured with the **iptables** command. Groups of **iptables** commands can be chained together in a set of rules. Once a set of **iptables** rules are created, they can be saved in a configuration file with the **iptables-save** command. To make sure the rules are restored during the boot process, the rules can be read through the configuration file with the **iptables-restore** command.

# CHAPTER 19

# Kernel Management

The kernel is the core of the operating system. The kernel enables communication between the operating system and the hardware. The kernel manages and provides the environment for each process. While kernel management can be tricky, it has an undeserved reputation for being difficult.

The simplest way to manage a kernel is to upgrade it in almost the same way that you might upgrade a regular package. If you need to customize modules, related kernel packages are available and are relatively simple to configure. But the nitty-gritty of kernel management is custom configuration.

The Linux kernel is highly configurable. It can be customized to every last hardware detail on local servers or clients. But most administrators are not so picky. In many cases, it's sufficient to install the latest updated kernel package from the appropriate Ubuntu repository. Alternatively, you could just compile drivers using regular or restricted modules and avoid the complications associated with recompiling the kernel.

**NOTE**    While the ability to compile a kernel is a common and necessary skill for Linux system administrators, the use of a custom compiled kernel on a system supported by Canonical may affect that support. It could also affect the support provided by third parties; for example, some database systems are certified only to specific "builds" of a kernel and have not been tested with a custom kernel you may have created.

# WHY RECOMPILE A KERNEL?

Most regular users and many administrators will rarely, if ever, have to recompile a kernel. But there are several potential advantages, including the following:

▼    Faster kernel services

■    Better support for certain drivers

■    Availability of needed drivers as modules

■    Lower kernel memory footprint

▲    Additional support for server-specific hardware, such as RAM above 4GB and virtualization

Ideally, you would take the time to customize each kernel to match every hardware component, to work only with those filesystems that you need, and more. But that would be rather time consuming, and the troubleshooting of kernel errors can lead to additional difficulties.

But in many cases, the solution is simple. Ubuntu provides an updated kernel package as appropriate for security and feature updates. It can be installed just as easily as any other package upgrade. In some cases, you can compile third-party drivers using source code packages associated with regular or restricted modules, based on the updated packages available from Ubuntu.

**NOTE** Whenever I recompile a kernel, the process is long. But I get a sense of accomplishment similar to the first time I solved Schrodinger's Equation (a partial differential equation that predicts the path of an electron around a nucleus) for an advanced college mathematics class.

# The Right Reasons

Ideally, kernels should be compiled with only the elements needed on a local system. The more that is left out of the kernel, the more efficiently the kernel and the operating system can run. For example, if you have no need for a sound card, such support can be removed from the kernel. The action of removing unneeded devices and drivers has several advantages:

▼ A smaller kernel, which loads faster during the boot process

■ Faster response time from the kernel

▲ More CPU and RAM resources available for other hardware

But you shouldn't remove all unneeded drivers. It can be helpful to have drivers available in the kernel for upgrades. For example, if you're just about ready to upgrade the server with 10 Gigabit Ethernet cards, it's best to keep those drivers supported by the kernel. Once those cards are installed, they should be automatically detected without having to recompile or otherwise modify the kernel once again.

# Basic Kernel Concepts

It's helpful to review some kernel concepts before proceeding. Kernels can be configured as one big monolithic file or organized with a core and a group of modules. There are many different kernel-related packages available. Updated kernels built by Ubuntu and uploaded to appropriate repositories are fairly easy to use. The kernel numbering system, if you aren't familiar with it, can be confusing. (Linux geeks should recognize that some readers may be converting from either Microsoft or Unix-based operating systems.)

## Monolithic vs. Modular

There are monolithic kernels, microkernels, and modular kernels. A *monolithic* kernel includes device and driver modules built directly into the kernel. Such a configuration enables faster communication. But the required size of a monolithic kernel for a typical Linux server would be inefficiently large. In addition, some systems just can't boot a kernel that's too large.

A *microkernel* enables only the basic communication between an operating system and hardware. Its smaller size is suited to embedded devices, especially with their limited hardware resources.

A *modular* kernel is sort of a hybrid, a microkernel with modular devices and drivers. These modules are loaded during the boot process. Modules aren't directly integrated into the kernel but are extensions that can be loaded and unloaded as needed. The advantage of a module means that an associated hardware failure won't lead to the failure of the entire kernel. Modular kernels are standard on most Linux distributions.

A modular kernel provides flexibility. It's usually relatively easy to compile drivers as modules. Each module can then be added as needed. Modules keep the initial kernel size low, which decreases the boot time and improves overall performance. If Linux has trouble loading a kernel module, the **modprobe** or **insmod** command can load modules as needed.

## Kernel Packages

There are a substantial number of kernel-related packages available. The packages, names, and versions will vary by release. The names cited here are listed as extensions to files in the /boot directory. For example, the *generic* kernel image is the standard for Ubuntu desktop or laptop systems; the associated kernel image file for the first Hardy Heron release is /boot/vmlinuz-2.6.24-16-generic. The corresponding *server* kernel image file, vmlinuz-2.6.24-16-server. And remember, as this is a book on Ubuntu Server, I use that kernel in this book. (I also use the kernel released with the first Hardy Heron update, 8.04.1, version 2.6.24-19-server.)

There is also a *virtual* kernel image, associated with simulated hardware. It is a kernel optimized for use as a guest within a virtual machine. This is different from kernels designed for the Xen virtual machine monitor. It's also different from the modules that enable the use of the VirtualBox open source edition on Ubuntu, as discussed in Chapter 20. In addition, there are *debug* kernel images available for developers.

## The Kernel Numbering System

The version numbers shown with Linux kernels are confusing enough for many less experienced users. The iterations associated with how Ubuntu builds the Linux kernel for Ubuntu releases add one more layer of complexity. The standard Ubuntu kernel includes a version number—for example, my current Ubuntu Server kernel file is vmlinuz-2.6.24-19-server. The version system conforms to a *majorversion.majorrevision.patch-build* format. The vmlinuz name is the standard for Linux kernel images.

The first number (2) specifies the *major* version number, associated with huge changes to the kernel. Major version number changes are reserved for completely new kernel designs. (I do not know if we'll see a new major version number in this decade.)

The second number (6) means two different things. It is the sixth major *revision* of version 2 of the kernel. Because it is an even number, it is associated with a stable production kernel. Up to version 2.6, odd second numbers were associated with developmental kernels, but that even/odd system has changed. When version 2.7 is released, it will also be a production kernel. Changes in the second number are rather infrequent; version 2.6.0 was released at the end of 2003.

The third number (24) is known as the *patch version* number, which typically includes small changes, bug fixes, security fixes, and enhancements.

The fourth number (-16-server) is added by Ubuntu. In this case, it's the sixteenth build of Linux kernel 2.6.24, customized for Ubuntu Server. Other Ubuntu builds include a different fourth number, such as -16-generic for desktop/laptop systems.

Ubuntu customizes kernels released by the developers of the Linux kernel. They're available from ftp.kernel.org. These kernels are released under a slightly different four-number system. The first two numbers are identical to the Ubuntu system. The third number specifies a major patch; the fourth number specifies a bug fix or security update.

To verify the version number currently running on the local system, run the **uname -r** command. In several places in the book, a command such as `uname -r` is included in the name of a directory or a file. When embedded with the back quotes (`` ` ``), the command substitutes the currently running kernel version number in the name of directory or file.

# EASY KERNEL UPGRADES

With the long-term (5-year) support associated with the Hardy Heron release of Ubuntu Server, it's almost certain that there will be security advisories that suggests an update to a new Linux kernel. At that point, Ubuntu should have an appropriate kernel available from standard repositories.

## Get a New Kernel with apt

Updating the kernel is easier in Debian-based systems. With connections to appropriate repositories, an update is a straightforward process. With the **apt-get install** command, it's easy to upgrade a kernel:

```
$ sudo apt-get install linux-server linux-headers-`uname -r` \
linux-image-server linux-restricted-modules-`uname -r`
```

Of course, if some of these packages, such as linux-restricted-modules-`uname -r`, are not currently installed, they need not be upgraded. In fact, if you prefer to limit Ubuntu to GPL and other open source software, do not install the linux-restricted-modules package.

## Make Sure the Boot Loader Is Right

Once the installation process is complete, the new kernel is included in the /boot/ directory and the GRUB configuration file is automatically updated, with parallel options for the old and new kernels. To make this possible, the installation of the new kernel leaves in the old kernel and initial RAM disk (initrd) files in the /boot directory. In essence, GRUB treats the new kernel as if it were an entirely new operating system.

If the new kernel doesn't work for some reason, you can still boot the system with the old kernel. As the installation of a new kernel from an Ubuntu repository doesn't automatically overwrite the last old kernel, you can boot into that kernel from the GRUB menu.

Examine your /boot/grub/menu.lst file. There should be a stanza that points to the appropriate files with the original Linux kernel and initial RAM disk. For example, here is an excerpt from my Ubuntu Server version of this file (which includes a dual-boot configuration with Microsoft Windows):

```
title           Ubuntu 8.04, kernel 2.6.24-16-server
root            (hd0,0)
kernel          /boot/vmlinuz-2.6.24-16-server root=UUID=1f0ef060-
                7f75-4915-ba08-19fdaadaff22 ro quiet splash
initrd          /boot/initrd.img-2.6.24-16-server

title           Windows XP Media Center Edition
root            (hd0,1)
savedefault
makeactive
chainloader     +1
boot
```

For Ubuntu, the Linux kernel is in the vmlinuz-`uname -r` file; the initial RAM disk is in the initrd.img-`uname -r` file, both in the /boot directory.

# UPGRADE A KERNEL FROM SOURCE

One of the strengths of Linux is the ease with which the kernel can be customized to meet your precise needs. But before this process is started, you need the Linux kernel source code.

If you choose to recompile the Linux kernel, make sure several GBs of free space are available in the partition or volume that contains the /usr directory. In this section, the source code and packages are downloaded, which can help you build and modify the current kernel configuration.

## Start with the Latest Kernel Source Code

The title of this section is purposely vague. You could start with the latest kernel, as in the one loaded on the local Ubuntu Server system, as built by Ubuntu developers. You could also start with the latest kernel, as released by the kernel developers as led by Linus Torvalds. One way to install the Linux kernel source code, as patched by Ubuntu, is with the following command:

```
$ sudo apt-get install linux-source
```

For the Hardy Heron release of Ubuntu Server, this command installs the linux-source-2.6.24.tar.bz2 tarball archive, in the /usr/src directory. Many administrators would navigate to that directory before unpacking the archive with the following commands:

```
$ cd /usr/src
$ sudo tar xjvf linux-source-2.6.24.tar.bz2
```

The command takes some time as it unpacks the many thousands of files associated with the development of the Linux kernel. Once unpacked, the files are stored in the linux-source-2.6.24 subdirectory.

As substantial kernel documentation is based on having the kernel source code available in the /usr/src/linux directory, I like to create a link to that directory and can do so with the following command:

```
$ sudo ln -s /usr/src/linux-source-2.6 /usr/src/linux
```

If you're not impressed with the changes made by Ubuntu developers, use the latest generic Linux kernel. To download that kernel, navigate to www.kernel.org. The associated home page includes information for the latest stable version of the Linux kernel as well as developmental kernels. Linux kernels from www.kernel.org are available in compressed tarballs in both tar.gz and tar.bz2 formats. The tarball can be processed in the same way as the source code just downloaded from the Ubuntu repository.

**NOTE** Be aware that if you use the source code from www.kernel.org, it may affect any support contract that you may have with Canonical.

## Get the Right Tools

The Linux source code is not enough. You need additional packages to get the tools to compile and customize the kernel. The basic packages required to compile the kernel can be installed with the following command:

```
$ sudo apt-get install fakeroot linux-kernel-devel ccache
```

The fakeroot package is especially important for Ubuntu systems, where the root administrative user is rarely enabled. It includes wrappers around key commands such as **chown** and **chmod** to enable a regular user to assume root privileges temporarily for the purpose of building a package, especially necessary for building a Linux kernel.

The linux-kernel-devel package is a front end to a series of packages required to compile the Linux kernel, including GCC (GNU C language Compiler) compilers, the GIT revision control system, and the **make** command to compile groups of programs.

Technically, that's enough to build and compile a Linux kernel. The ccache package just speeds the process. You could directly edit a .config file in the aforementioned /usr/src/linux directory, and then compile it using the tools described later in this chapter.

```
michael@ubuntuhardy3:/usr/src/linux$ sudo make config
scripts/kconfig/conf arch/x86/Kconfig
#
# using defaults found in /boot/config-2.6.24-16-server
#
*
* Linux Kernel Configuration
*
*
* General setup
*
Prompt for development and/or incomplete code/drivers (EXPERIMENTAL) [Y/n/?]
Local version - append to kernel release (LOCALVERSION) []
Automatically append version information to the version string (LOCALVERSION_AUT
O) [N/y/?]
Arbitrary version signature (VERSION_SIGNATURE) [Ubuntu 2.6.24-16.30-server]
Support for paging of anonymous memory (swap) (SWAP) [Y/n/?]
System V IPC (SYSVIPC) [Y/n/?]
POSIX Message Queues (POSIX_MQUEUE) [Y/n/?]
BSD Process Accounting (BSD_PROCESS_ACCT) [Y/n/?]
  BSD Process Accounting version 3 file format (BSD_PROCESS_ACCT_V3) [Y/n/?]
Export task/process statistics through netlink (EXPERIMENTAL) (TASKSTATS) [Y/n/?
]
  Enable per-task delay accounting (EXPERIMENTAL) (TASK_DELAY_ACCT) [N/y/?]
  Enable extended accounting over taskstats (EXPERIMENTAL) (TASK_XACCT) [Y/n/?]
    Enable per-task storage I/O accounting (EXPERIMENTAL) (TASK_IO_ACCOUNTING) [
Y/n/?]
User Namespaces (EXPERIMENTAL) (USER_NS) [N/y/?]
PID Namespaces (EXPERIMENTAL) (PID_NS) [N/y/?]
Auditing support (AUDIT) [Y/?] y
  Enable system-call auditing support (AUDITSYSCALL) [Y/n/?]
Kernel .config support (IKCONFIG) [N/m/y/?]
Kernel log buffer size (16 => 64KB, 17 => 128KB) (LOG_BUF_SHIFT) [17]
Control Group support (CGROUPS) [Y/n/?]
  Example debug cgroup subsystem (CGROUP_DEBUG) [N/y/?]
  Namespace cgroup subsystem (CGROUP_NS) [Y/n/?]
  Cpuset support (CPUSETS) [Y/n/?]
```

**Figure 19-1.** Customize the kernel the hard way

Alternatively, you could even use the **sudo make config** command in that directory and answer a series of several hundred questions, as shown in Figure 19-1. But the **make config** process is a bit much even for the most hard-core Linux geeks, as a single error during the process means that you'll have to answer all of the questions again.

There are graphical tools available which can help customize the kernel. If you don't have a GUI, there's a low-level ncurses-based screen with the same functionality. To install the packages required for the ncurses tool, a command such as the following installs the right ncurses libraries:

```
$ sudo apt-get install libncurses5 libncurses5-dev
```

Assuming you've installed the other packages described so far in this chapter, you'll be able to start the noted kernel configuration tool from the /usr/src/linux directory with the **sudo make menuconfig** command.

If you prefer a GUI tool, a command such as the following installs the required Qt library tools and packages:

```
$ sudo apt-get install qt3-dev-tools libqt3-mt-dev
```

Assuming you've installed the other packages described so far in this chapter, you'll be able to start the noted kernel configuration tool from the /usr/src/linux directory with the **sudo make xconfig** command.

*NOTE*   The xconfig GUI kernel configuration tool may not work remotely unless a graphical environment is installed on the target system.

It's even possible to configure a kernel remotely; I've opened both tools over a remote Secure Shell connection.

# DESIRED CHANGES

There are thousands of options associated with the Linux kernel. Current settings can be found in the /boot/config-`uname -r` file. The kernel on my Ubuntu Server includes over 3000 settings. The next major section covers the configuration tools as well as the variety of available options.

Sometimes the changes you might consider are all contained in a patch. If you've configured a stock kernel for an Ubuntu system, patches available from the Linux kernel library at www.kernel.org can be used to upgrade a kernel.

## Include a Patch

If you've downloaded the source code for a kernel, it can be patched. If you keep abreast of the latest Linux news, or at least the change log associated with patched kernels, you'll know the features or fixes available with the latest patch.

Patches usually work fairly well if you're upgrading from one patch version to the next higher version. For example, the patch-2.6.24.2.gz or patch-2.6.24.2.bz2 file can be used to upgrade the kernel from version 2.6.24.1 to 2.6.24.2. There are also more substantial patches available—for example, either the patch-2.6.25.gz or patch-2.6.25.bz2 file can be used to upgrade the kernel from version 2.6.24 to 2.6.25. Third parties may also have kernel patches available.

Kernel patches are readily available from sites such as ftp.kernel.org. For example, if you want to upgrade from kernel version 2.6.24.3 to kernel version 2.6.24.4, download the patch-2.6.24.4.gz file from ftp.kernel.org. Copy the compressed patch file to the /usr/src directory. Move to that directory, and run a command similar to the following to make the upgrade:

```
$ sudo zcat patch-2.6.24.4.gz | patch -p0
```

If you're preparing a patch compressed in .bz2 format, substitute **bzcat** for the **zcat** command.

If there are problems with this part of the patch process, they'll appear as files with a .rej extension in the kernel source directories. If no such files appear, you should be able to proceed with the **make** and **make-kpkg** commands described later in this chapter, in the "Compile and Install the Kernel" section.

## Select a Baseline

If you're not patching a kernel, the next step is to select a baseline configuration. If you want to configure the current Ubuntu Server kernel as the baseline, the configuration is available from the /boot/config-`uname -r` file. This section assumes you've unpacked the source code for the current kernel in the /usr/src/linux directory. It takes two steps to set up the current kernel for customization:

1. Copy the current kernel configuration file:

   ```
   $ sudo cp /boot/config-`uname -r` /usr/src/linux/.config
   ```

2. Process the configuration file into an appropriate format:

   ```
   $ cd /usr/src/linux
   $ sudo make oldconfig
   ```

The **make oldconfig** command processes the content of the config-`uname -r` file, in a form used to automatically answer the questions as prompted by the **make config** command. The result is processed back into the /usr/src/linux/.config file, ready to use to compile the kernel—or for further customization.

If you're really familiar with kernel settings, you could just make a simple change to the .config file. For example, this file shows that IPv6 "mobility support" is not set:

```
# CONFIG_IPV6_MIP6 is not set
```

If you were configuring a kernel for a mobile device, you might enable the following option before recompiling the kernel. For more information on this option, see www.ietf .org/rfc/rfc3775.txt.

```
CONFIG_IPV6_MIP6=y
```

If you prefer to start from a baseline configuration for a specific CPU architecture, a group of configuration files are available in the arch/*architecture*/configs subdirectory. For example, there are two generic configuration files, i386_defconfig and x86_64_ defconfig, in the arch/x86/configs subdirectory. These files are associated with the standard Ubuntu architectures. If you're interested in other architectures, run the **ls /usr/src/linux/arch** command. You might be surprised at the number of architectures available for Linux. To review other baseline configurations, explore other arch/*architecture*/ configs subdirectories.

## Kernel Configuration Menus

As suggested, two kernel configuration menus are available. If you've installed the packages suggested so far in this chapter, you can start the ncurses-based tool. To do so, navigate to the /usr/src/linux directory (or whatever directory contains the Linux

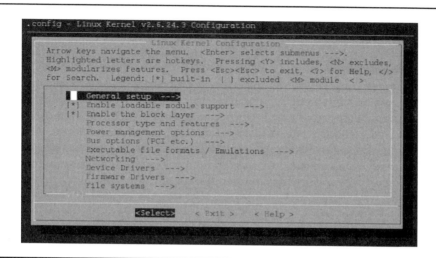

**Figure 19-2.** Linux Kernel Configuration menu

kernel source code) and run the **sudo make menuconfig** command. The standard ncurses menu is shown in Figure 19-2.

The Kernel Configuration menu as shown includes some clues. The top line indicates that it has imported settings from the .config file in the local directory. It also displays the generic kernel on which the Ubuntu Server kernel is based, version 2.6.24.3. It also includes several navigable menus, which you can use to explore the details of the kernel in the last major section of this chapter.

Once configuration and customization is complete, save the result with the following steps:

1. Select Exit and press ENTER.

2. Assuming changes have been made, the menu prompts you with the following question:

   ```
   Do you wish to save your new kernel configuration?
   <ESC><ESC> to continue.
   ```

   There are also Yes and No options available. To return to the main kernel menu shown in Figure 19-2, press the ESC key twice.

3. Select Yes.

4. Changes are saved to the .config file. The last configuration is backed up in the .config.old file.

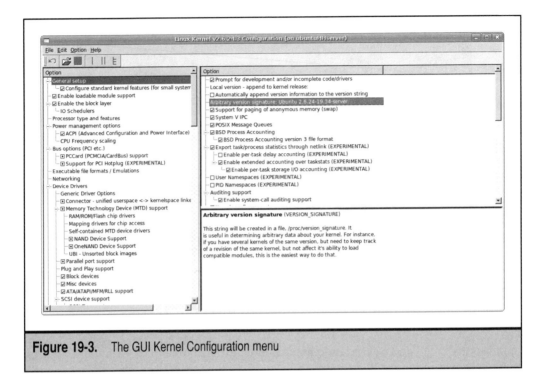

**Figure 19-3.** The GUI Kernel Configuration menu

Alternatively, if you prefer the GUI kernel configuration tool, navigate to the /usr/ src/linux directory (or whatever directory contains the Linux kernel source code) and run the **sudo make xconfig** command. The standard GUI kernel configuration menu is shown in Figure 19-3.

The GUI Kernel Configuration menu as shown includes similar clues. It assumes that you know the configuration is taken from the local .config file. However, the GUI screens, which include help screens, can help you visualize the settings in specific categories. While the same information is available in the ncurses-based menu, it's all on one screen in Figure 19-3. You can also use this menu to explore the details of the kernel in the last major section of this chapter.

Once configuration and customization is complete, you can save the result with the following steps:

1. Choose File | Save As.

2. In the Save As window that appears, you're prompted to save the new configuration in the .config file in the actual kernel source directory. For the Ubuntu kernel, that directory is /usr/src/linux-source-2.6.24/.

3. If you've created a soft link from /usr/src/linux to this directory, as described earlier in this chapter, that link does *not* appear in the Look In drop-down text box.

4. Click Save.

5. Choose File | Quit.

Changes are saved to the .config file. The last configuration is backed up in the .config.old file.

# Compile and Install the Kernel

This is one area where the Ubuntu kernel compilation process shines. It's a lot easier to compile and install a kernel. Some trial and error may be required; the original Hardy Heron Ubuntu Server kernel required a change to the Xen setting, as described shortly. That change is no longer required as of the Ubuntu kernel build for the first Hardy Heron update, version 2.6.24-19.

The following commands assume you've already customized the kernel as described in the previous section.

There was some work on configuring the Ubuntu Server kernel as a paravirtualized guest in a Xen-based virtual machine. But the associated setting led to an error during the kernel compilation process. The .config file based on the Ubuntu 2.6.24-16 version kernel required the following change, from

```
CONFIG_XEN=y
```

to

```
# CONFIG_XEN is not set
```

You can also change this setting in any of the kernel configuration tools, in the Processor Type And Features menu, Paravirtualized Guest Support submenu. (The Paravirtualized Guest Support option is not available for the 2.6.24-19-server kernel associated with the Hardy Heron 8.04.1 release.)

Make any other desired change using the desired kernel configuration menu of your choice. Once the change is saved, you're ready to compile the kernel. One way to do so is with the following command:

```
$ sudo make-kpkg buildpackage -rev=mike1 --initrd kernel_image \
 kernel_headers
```

In brief, it compiles the kernel, builds the kernel package in Debian format, adds *.mike1* as the revision level, and also builds an initial RAM disk image. It also builds a kernel headers package, which can be used to compile some specialty modules.

**TIP**   If you previously compiled modules under another kernel, you'll have to repeat the process after rebooting into the newly configured kernel.

Be aware that the process started by the **make-kpkg** command can take quite a bit of time; it took a couple of hours on one of the systems I set up on a virtual machine.

But when complete, it creates packages in the Debian format, with the .deb extension, in the /usr/src directory. These packages are suitable for installation. Based on the original Ubuntu Server kernel and the command shown above, that package is linux_image-2.6.24.3_mike1_i386.deb. Of course, the name would change on a different architecture.

 **NOTE** In some cases, the process for compiling a kernel appears to stop with an error. Fortunately, some errors are trivial; in that case, the kernel package is still created and written to the /usr/src directory.

Now you can install that Debian package with the following command:

```
$ sudo dpkg -i  linux_image-2.6.24.3_mike1_i386.deb
```

This command installs the Linux kernel in the /boot directory and creates appropriate menu entries in the GRUB configuration file, /boot/grub/menu.lst. The menu entries should be similar to the existing menu entries for booting Ubuntu. Review this file. You should see entries that correlate to appropriate files in the /boot directory, as the process of installing the new kernel runs the **update-grub** command to search this directory. The new kernel stanza should be the default stanza. Stanzas associated with existing kernels still should be there.

If everything goes as planned, you'll see vmlinuz, initrd.img, System.map, and config files in the /boot directory, with the new kernel version number (2.6.24.3) and **-rev** switch (mike1) as extensions. You should also see appropriate modules in the /lib/modules/2.6.24.3 directory.

Next, install the associated kernel headers with the following command:

```
$ sudo dpkg -i  linux_headers-2.6.24.3_mike1_i386.deb
```

Now reboot Linux. If everything works, the system should boot normally. The default GRUB stanza should correspond to the new kernel, which means it should now be loaded onto your system.

If a problem occurs, an error may appear during the boot process. Perhaps the most serious error is a "kernel panic." If you see that message, make a note of the line just before the panic. Someone may have already seen and solved the problem. But a system in a kernel panic stops responding to messages. In that event, reset the power on the local system and then boot into the original working kernel.

# KERNEL CONFIGURATION OPTIONS

Before customizing a kernel, you should examine some of the main kernel configuration options. Each of the aforementioned kernel configuration tools (**make config**, **make menuconfig, make xconfig**) includes help menus for most options. It's easier to follow along as these options are described with either the ncurses or GUI tool installed earlier in this chapter. To open the ncurses tool shown in Figure 19-2, run the following commands:

```
$ cd /usr/src/linux
$ sudo make menuconfig
```

Ncurses submenus are shown with a trailing arrow that looks like this: **--->**. To access these submenus, highlight the desired category and press ENTER. To return to a higher level menu, press TAB until the Exit key is highlighted and press ENTER.

In a number of sections, the option is not enabled. When some options are enabled, more kernel configuration options may be revealed.

If you prefer the GUI tool, substitute the **sudo make xconfig** command to open the graphical tool shown in Figure 19-3.

**NOTE** Only high-level options are described in this section. A full description of each Linux kernel configuration option would require a book-length work. For more in-depth information on the kernel, read *Linux Kernel in a Nutshell*, published by O'Reilly (2006). It's written by one of the main Linux kernel developers, Greg Kroah-Hartman.

## General Setup

Some General Setup kernel configuration options relate to hardware and the kernel. Despite the name, it is difficult to generalize the options in this category. For more information, consult the help text associated with each option.

Some General Setup settings are related to memory paging, including the System V IPC, POSIX Message Queues, and BSD Process Accounting settings. One subcategory configures standard features for small systems such as embedded devices.

## Enable Loadable Module Support

As suggested by the name, the Enable Loadable Module Support settings set conditions for how kernel modules are loaded and unloaded. By default, most modules are automatically loaded when new hardware is detected.

## Enable the Block Layer

The settings associated with the Block Layer allow Linux to mount partitions. Such settings should be disabled only for embedded devices. A couple of optional settings in this category provide support for files larger than 2TB as well as experimental support for SCSI generic version 4 devices. A subcategory is related to input/output (I/O) schedulers.

## Processor Type and Features

The settings associated with Processor Type and Features can provide support for a wide variety of CPUs, specialty timers, various levels of memory support, and more.

# Power Management Options

The settings associated with Power Management Options enable basic familiar power management features such as Suspend To RAM and Hibernation. It includes three subcategories: Advanced Configuration and Power Interface (ACPI), Advanced Power Management (APM), and CPU frequency scaling. As most modern systems use ACPI, most APM settings are disabled. CPU frequency scaling support different speeds and power modes on the main computer engine.

# Bus Options

The settings associated with Bus Options relate to attached hardware. The main settings enable access to PCI cards, PCI express cards, ISA cards, and more. Two subcategories exist that relate to PCMCIA (PC Card) devices, as well as the hotpluggable PCI devices often associated with removable storage devices.

# Executable File Formats / Emulations

The settings associated with the Executable File Formats / Emulations menu relate to binaries configured in the Executable and Linkable Format (ELF) as well as other miscellaneous formats such as the MS-DOS emulator.

# Networking

The settings associated with Networking are divided into eight categories. Take a few moments to explore the different categories, summarized in Table 19-1. You may gain respect for the amount of work kernel developers have done for all the different types of network cards, software settings, and more.

# Device Drivers

There are a substantial number of settings associated with Device Drivers, more than just the hardware drivers available for Linux. Some settings in this area are divided into different categories, entitled Memory Technology Devices, Parallel Port Support, Plug and Play Support, Block Devices, Misc Devices ATA/ATAPI/MFM/RLL Support, SCSI Device Support, and more. These categories are briefly explored here.

**Generic Driver Options**   These settings relate to firmware.

**Connector – Unified Userspace – Kernelspace Linker**   The Kernelspace Linker relates to kernel space, which includes the memory dedicated to the kernel, extensions, and related drivers. In addition, the Unified Userpace, relates to the user space, the memory allocated to other functions. The linker supports communication between kernel space and user space.

| Networking Category | Description |
| --- | --- |
| Networking Options | Software settings associated with different network protocols |
| Amateur Radio Support | Protocols associated with amateur and packet radio systems |
| IrDA (Infrared) Subsystem Support | Protocols, drivers, and options related to infrared devices |
| Bluetooth System Support | Protocols, drivers, and filters associated with Bluetooth devices |
| RxRPC Session Sockets | A session layer protocol for kernel communication |
| Wireless | Generic wireless protocols; does not include wireless network drivers |
| RF Switch Subsystem Support | For radio frequency switches associated with wireless and Bluetooth hardware |
| Plan 9 Resource Sharing | For the 9P2000 protocol |

**Table 19-1.**   Categories of Networking Settings in the Linux Kernel

In addition, the Unified Userpace, relates to the user space, the memory allocated to other functions. The linker supports communication between kernel space and user space.

**Memory Technology Devices**   The options shown in the Memory Technology Devices section support the wide variety of Flash memory devices.

**Parallel Port Support**   The options shown in the Parallel Port Support menu are based on hardware that can be connected via a parallel port. Parallel port devices range from printers to parallel port hard drives.

**Plug and Play Support**   The options shown under the Plug and Play Support section activate basic plug-and-play support.

**Block Devices**   The options available in the Block Devices section support drivers for floppy drives and nonstandard hard disks. For example, they may be configured to enable support for parallel port ATAPI CD-ROMs, tape drives, RAM disks, and even ATAPI floppy drives.

In addition, appropriate modules can enable loopback support and network block support for mounting ISO and remote network devices.

**Misc Devices**    The options available in the Misc Devices section relate to specialty situations. Included are specialty drivers for *some* portable systems from ASUS, Fujitsu, MSI, Sony, Texas Instruments, and Lenovo.

**ATA/IDE/MFM/RLL Support**    The ATA/IDE/MFM/RLL Support section is based on a bunch of acronyms. They all refer to PC hard disk and CD/DVD drive interfaces.

**SCSI Device Support**    The SCSI Device Support section includes drivers associated with SCSI hard disks, tape drivers, hardware RAID adapters, and more.

**Serial ATA (Prod) And Parallel ATA (Experimental) Drivers**    As one might expect, the kernel settings in the Serial ATA (Prod) And Parallel ATA (Experimental) Drivers section are related to SATA and PATA devices. Now that PC hard drives have been reclassified as Serial ATA (SATA) and Parallel ATA (PATA) devices, their drivers have been collected in this section. Be aware that several of the associated drivers are labeled as "Experimental" and even "Very Experimental" and therefore should not be used on production systems.

**Multiple Devices Driver Support (RAID and LVM)**    The Multiple Devices Driver Support (RAID and LVM) section relate to RAID (Redundant Array of Independent Disks) and LVM (Logical Volume Management) devices. RAID and LVM devices are generally enabled as modules. The list of RAID options in this section describe the versions of RAID supported by the Linux kernel.

**Fusion MPT Device Support**    High-speed SCSI adapters are part of the Fusion MPT Device Support section, associated with Message Passing Technology (MPT). This section includes drivers from a variety of manufacturers.

**IEEE 1394 (FireWire) Support**    The IEEE 1394 (FireWire) Support section includes drivers for these normally external devices connected through the noted high-speed plug-and-play connection. FireWire support is also known as iLink.

**I2O Device Support**    The I2O Device Support section relates to devices associated with the I2O specification. Also known as Intelligent I/O, such devices support split drivers that can optimize communication performance between a device and the rest of the local system.

**Macintosh Device Drivers**    Since Linux is now frequently installed on systems with Macintosh hardware, a separate section is included for related Macintosh Device Drivers. As of this writing, the only enabled device driver in this section enables two- and three-button emulation of the one-button Apple mouse.

**Network Device Support**    Linux supports a wide range of network cards. The Network Device Support section includes support for a wide variety of network adapters. Drivers for some newer adapters may still be "Experimental."

**ISDN Subsystem**   The ISDN Subsystem section includes drivers related to Integrated Services Digital Network (ISDN) cards. ISDN is still a fairly popular high-speed digital option for Internet connections through telephone networks outside of North America.

**Telephony Support**   The Telephony Support section describes special network cards to convert voice into the type of data that can be sent over a network. This section is not directly related to VoIP projects such as Asterisk.

**Input Device Support**   The Input Device Support section includes support for basic input devices: keyboards, mice, touchscreens, tablets, joysticks, and more. These devices are configured as modules by default, which allows Linux to recognize such devices with the help of plug-and-play detection.

**Character Devices**   The Character Devices section includes modules and settings for hardware that transmits data in byte streams. Examples include serial ports, virtual consoles, AGP video cards, and more.

**I2C Support**   The I2C Support section is associated with the slow serial bus protocol of the same name (I2C). This section includes support for algorithms, hardware buses, and related chips.

**SPI Support**   This SPI Support section specifies options that enable support for the Serial Peripheral Interface (SPI), mostly included with kernel modules.

**Dallas's 1-wire Bus**   The Dallas's 1-wire Bus section includes options that enable communication over single pin devices. Associated hardware is supported with modules.

**Power Supply Class Support**   The Power Supply Class Support section includes options associated with the control of Uninterruptable Power Supplies (UPS).

**Hardware Monitoring Support**   The Hardware Monitoring Support section includes modules that help monitor system health, such as temperature monitors, fans, and much more.

**Watchdog Timer Support**   The Watchdog Timer Support section includes modules that can reset or reboot a system in the event of specific software faults. A variety of hardware devices are included in this category.

**Sonics Silicon Backplane**   The Sonics Silicon Backplane section is associated with embedded systems, some of which include a bus of the same name. Some of these devices may be included on PCMCIA and PCI cards.

**Multifunction Device Drivers**   The Multifunction Device Drivers section includes a module that supports the Silicon Motion SM501 multimedia chip.

**Multimedia Devices**   The Multimedia Devices section includes options in several subsections, including Video for Linux, Video Capture Adapters, and Radio Adapters. It also includes support for Digital Video Broadcasting (DVB) and Digital Analog Broadcasting (DAB) hardware.

**Graphics Support** The Graphics Support section incorporates the wide variety of Linux support for Accelerated Graphics Protocol (AGP) hardware, a substantial number of framebuffer devices, LCD and flat panel displays, as well as devices that use the Direct Rendering Manager.

**Sound** The Sound section is much simplified from earlier kernels. Support is divided into two categories: the Advanced Linux Sound Architecture (ALSA) and the deprecated Open Sound System (OSS). It's assumed that all cards can be configured to one of these categories, with different types of support.

When support for ALSA devices is activated, it includes modules for ISA, PCI, SPI, USB, and PCMCIA sound devices, as well as the System On Chip Audio Support.

**HID Devices** The HID Devices section is associated with certain human interface devices (HIDs). As most actual HID devices are configured in the Input Device Support section, this section provides support for some Apple HID devices connected via a USB interface.

**USB Support** In the USB Support section, you can review the full range of support for USB devices available through the kernel. Specialty USB devices are available for serial converters, so-called DSL "modems," and various other "gadgets."

**MMC/SD/SDIO Support** The MMC/SD/SDIO Support section is associated with the ever-expanding variety of multimedia digital cards. MMC is short for multimedia cards. SD is associated with Secure Digital cards. SDIO is associated with specialized SD cards. While originally used on digital cameras and other small devices, the uses are expanding. Some systems even enable MMC/SD cards as boot devices or even hard drives.

**LED Support** The LED Support section is associated with control of light-emitting diode (LED) devices. Such devices are not related to keyboard LEDs.

**InfiniBand Support** The InfiniBand Support section relates to the InfiniBand and related protocols. It also includes modules for Host Channel Adapters (HCA) and the Remote Direct Memory Access (RDMA) protocol.

**EDAC – Error Detection and Correction (Experimental)** The EDAC - Error Detection and Correction (Experimental) section supports the reporting of hardware-related errors, especially those from RAM with error correction codes (ECCs) and PCI bus parity errors. Modules are available for several different chipsets.

**Real Time Clock** The Real Time Clock section helps the kernel work with the hardware clock. It incorporates support for a number of different hardware clock chips.

**DMA Engine Support** This DMA Engine Support section supports direct memory access (DMA) for certain hardware channels.

**Auxiliary Display Support** The Auxiliary Display Support section includes modules for certain LCD display drivers.

**Userspace I/O**  The Userspace I/O section enables access from userspace programs to kernel interrupts and memory locations.

# Firmware Drivers

The Firmware Drivers section is related to those nonvolatile systems. It includes various system calls such as those for BIOS-enhanced disk drives and the Extensible Firmware Interface (EFI).

# File Systems

The File Systems section includes support for a variety of different filesystems. (Remember that *file systems* is synonymous with *filesystems*.) Quotas, the *relatime* (not real time) /etc/fstab setting, and the automounter also fall in this category.

As Linux supports so many different hardware platforms, it includes support for a large number of filesystem types. However, because of the proprietary nature of some filesystems, the degree of support is variable. Support for a number of filesystems is experimental.

# Instrumentation Support

The Instrumentation Support section supports the use of the OProfile, Kprobes, and active markers to characterize system performance.

# Kernel Hacking

The Kernel Hacking section supports the options used to debug driver or related Linux kernel issues.

# Security Options

The Security Options section is focused on support for AppArmor and SELinux.

# Cryptographic API

The Cryptographic Options section includes a variety of algorithms that support strong encryption.

# Virtualization

The Virtualization section supports the configuration of the Linux system as a host for virtual machines. By default, modular support is configured for the Kernel-based Virtual Machine (KVM) and PCI drivers.

## Library Routines

The Library Routines section includes modules related to the detection of errors associated with the transmission of large files. This section includes modules associated with cyclic redundancy checks.

# SUMMARY

This chapter is focused on kernels. It's a lot easier to install kernels revised and packaged by Ubuntu in standard repositories. In fact, the process is essentially the same as installing new versions of other packages. You just need to make sure that all appropriate kernel packages, including those related to headers and restricted modules, are used.

The complexity comes with the process of recompiling the kernel. With the source code unpacked, you can apply patches as desired. The chapter described the process with the source code unpacked to a /usr/src subdirectory, linked to the /usr/src/linux directory. The current kernel configuration options from the /boot directory can be processed in the source code directory as the .config file. While you can customize this file directly, many, perhaps most, Linux gurus use configuration tools.

Two configuration tools available from the source code directory are available through the **make menuconfig** and **make xconfig** commands. Either tool allows you to navigate through and modify kernel settings. Once complete, the **make-kpkg** command can be used to create a binary kernel package in the /usr/src directory. When installed, that package installs the kernel, initial RAM disk, and more in the /boot directory. It also updates the GRUB configuration file with appropriate configuration stanzas.

# CHAPTER 20

## Virtual Machines
## and Terminal Servers

One key advantage of a virtual machine is that it turns a system into a small number of files. Such systems are easier to back up. Virtual machine systems are relatively easy to clone and customize as well. A lot of work has gone into virtualization in the past couple of years, and the Ubuntu Server Hardy Heron release is no exception. While this chapter can't cover all virtualization solutions by any means, it will show you how to set up VMware Server 2.0, VirtualBox Open Source Edition, and the Kernel-based Virtual Machine (KVM).

For the purpose of this chapter, I've downloaded the Ubuntu JeOS (pronounced "juice," short for Just enough Operating System) Hardy Heron ISO file. This file can be used for an installation CD with a custom version of Ubuntu Server, which includes a custom kernel optimized for running in a virtual machine. It does not include any network services or open TCP/IP ports. The installation of a desired network service opens just the needed port. The JeOS ISO file is relatively small at 100MB, and a basic installation works with as little as 128MB of RAM and a 500MB hard disk. Of course, more resources are required for any services subsequently installed. As of this writing, there is no separate ISO planned for the Intrepid Ibex JeOS release; it's available as a minimal installation from the Server ISO.

Ubuntu's implementation of the diskless client is based in part on the work of the Linux Terminal Server Project (LTSP). A diskless client supports multiple terminals running from the same computer, connected via a higher-speed network.

**NOTE**   Don't confuse the Kernel-based Virtual Machine with the Kernel, Video, Mouse switch, even though they share the same acronym (KVM).

# VIRTUAL MACHINE OPTIONS

Virtualization is a topic filled with choices. While VMware is the market leader, the open source edition of VirtualBox is the current third-party option available from Ubuntu repositories. Solutions native to and facilitated by the Linux kernel include the Xen virtual machine monitor and KVM. (KVM, and not Xen, was tested for this book.) On last count, about 50 different virtual machine managers were listed on Wikipedia.

This section is limited to a description on how to install VMware Server and VirtualBox on Ubuntu. Most virtual machine systems, including VMware Server, VirtualBox, and even KVM, support the Preboot Execution Environment (PXE) in their virtual network cards. This makes it possible to boot and install from a network-enabled installation source, as described in Chapter 2.

## VMware Server

This section describes one way to install VMware Server version 2.0 Release Candidate 2 on an Ubuntu Hardy Heron system. To download the required tarball package, navigate to www.vmware.com/products/server/. The final release of VMware Server 2.0 was made available just as this book goes to print. The version number listed in this section has already changed. While the "look and feel" of VMware Server version 1.0.x is quite different from version 2.0.x, the installation process on Linux systems is similar.

From the noted screen, click Download Now. Follow the instructions to register or login, if you already have a VMware account. You'll get a registration serial number in your e-mail to install VMware Server on Linux and links to the packages to install on 32- and 64-bit Linux (and Microsoft Windows) systems.

**NOTE** Through the Gutsy Gibbon release, VMware Server was freely and relatively easily available through the Ubuntu partner repository. It's possible that it will be available in the partner repository again in the future.

## Install VMware Server 2.0

This section assumes you're building VMware Server from the source code freely downloadable on the VMware website. While VMware Server is not itself open source, it is freely available under a non-exclusive license. In a moment, you'll see how to install VMware Server, step by step.

Before proceeding with the installation, be sure to install the latest kernel and source code or kernel development packages with kernel modules, as well as the GNU C Compiler (*gcc*), the binary utilities assembler (*binutils*), and the *make* package for the distribution. One way to install these prerequisite packages is with the following command:

```
$ sudo apt-get install build-essential linux-kernel-devel make \
linux-source xinetd
```

Once these tools are installed, proceed with the VMware Server installation. To install VMware Server on an Ubuntu Hardy Heron system, take the following steps:

1. Download the tarball. For this example, the tarball package available as of this writing is VMware-server-2.0.0-110949.x86_64.tar.gz. For the purpose of this exercise, download it to the /tmp directory.

2. Navigate to the /tmp directory with the **cd /tmp** command.

3. Make a copy of the registration serial number as provided possibly in a link from a confirmation e-mail.

4. Unpack the archive. As the tarball has a .tar.gz extension, that suggests the use of the **tar xzvf** command, to extract (**x**), unzip (**z**), verbosely (**v**) in case of errors, from the filename (**f**) that follows:

```
$ tar xzvf VMware-server-2.0.0-110949.x86_64.tar.gz
```

5. Navigate to the directory with the unpacked VMware server files:

```
$ cd /tmp/vmware-server-distrib
```

6. Run the **vmware-install.pl** script with super user privileges. The **./** in front of the script specifies the current directory:

```
$ sudo ./vmware-install.pl
```

7. Unless you really know what you're doing, accept the default to install binary files in the /usr/bin directory by pressing ENTER:

```
Creating a new VMware Server installer database using the tar4 format.
Installing VMware Server.
In which directory do you want to install the binary files?
[/usr/bin]
```

8. Generally, you should accept the default to set up the **vmware** configuration script in /etc/rc*x*.d/ directories, where *x* is between 0 and 6. To do so, press ENTER.

```
What is the directory that contains the init directories
(rc0.d/ to rc6.d/)?
[/etc]
```

9. The standard is to accept the default to set up the **vmware** service script in the /etc/init.d/ directory. To do so, press ENTER.

```
What is the directory that contains the init scripts
[/etc/init.d]
```

10. Unless you really know what you're doing, accept the default to set up the **vmware** daemon files in the /usr/sbin/ directory. To do so, press ENTER.

```
In which directory do you want to install the daemon files?
[/usr/sbin]
```

11. Unless you really know what you're doing, accept the default to set up the **vmware** library files in the /usr/lib/vmware/ directory. To do so, press ENTER.

```
In which directory do you want to install the library files?
[/usr/lib/vmware]
```

12. If the directory doesn't already exist, you'll be prompted to let the installation script create the /usr/lib/vmware directory.

13. Generally, you should accept the default to set up the **vmware** manual files in the /usr/share/man/ directory. To do so, press ENTER.

```
In which directory do you want to install the manual files?
[/usr/share/man]
```

14. Most users will accept the default to set up the **vmware** documentation files in the /usr/share/doc/vmware/ directory. To do so, press ENTER.

    ```
    In which directory do you want to install the documentation files?
    [/usr/share/doc/vmware]
    ```

15. Unless the directory already exists, you'll be prompted to let the installation script create the /usr/share/vmware/doc directory.

    There's also an uninstallation script available, as suggested by the following message:

    ```
    The installation of VMware Server 2.0.0 build-110949 for Linux completed
    successfully. You can decide to remove this software from your system
    at any time by invoking the following command:
    "/usr/bin/vmware-uninstall.pl".
    ```

16. Finally, you're prompted to configure the installed VMware system. Accept the default by pressing ENTER.

    ```
    Before running VMware Server for the first time, you need to configure
    it by invoking the following command: "/usr/bin/vmware-config.pl". Do
    you want this program to invoke the command for you now? [yes]
    ```

    VMware then stops any related running processes, with messages similar to this (as VMware is not yet installed, the "failed" messages for services being stopped are not a concern):

    ```
    Making sure services for VMware Server are stopped.
    Module vmmon not loaded
    Stopping VMware autostart virtual machines:
        Virtual machines                            failed
    Stopping VMware management services:
        VMware Virtual Infrastructure Web Access
        VMware Server Host Agent                    failed
    Stopping VMware services:
        VMware Authentication Daemon                done
        Virtual machine monitor                     done
    ```

17. Now you're told to read and accept the end user license agreement:

    ```
    You must read and accept the End User License Agreement to continue.
    Press Enter to display it.
    ```

18. If you want to read through the agreement more quickly, press ENTER and then the SPACEBAR until you see the following question, where you have to type **y** or **n** to accept or decline the agreement:

```
Do you accept? (yes/no) y
```

19. If appropriate VMware modules don't yet exist, accept the following offer to have them built. If all VMware modules currently exist, skip to step 23. It will work if the appropriate GCC compiler is installed, from the *gcc* package:

```
None of the pre-built vmmon modules for VMware Server is
suitable for your running kernel.  Do you want this program
to try to build the vmmon module for your system (you need
to have a C compiler installed on your system)? [yes]
```

20. The next message looks for C-language header files:

```
What is the location of the directory of C header files that match
your running kernel? [/lib/modules/2.6.24-19-server/build/include]
```

This cites the standard location for these files in an Ubuntu Hardy Heron system. If you don't see these specifics, the *linux-headers-`uname -r`* package might not be installed.

If everything goes well, a message similar to the following eventually appears:

```
The vmmon module loads perfectly in the running kernel.
```

21. Now you're prompted to let the installer create more modules, which should be accepted:

```
None of the pre-built vmci modules for VMware Server is suitable for
your running kernel.  Do you want this program to try to build the vmci
module for your system (you need to have a C compiler installed on your
system)? [yes]
```

22. After that success, you'll be prompted to let the installer create even more modules, which you should also accept:

```
None of the pre-built vsock modules for VMware Server is suitable for
your running kernel.  Do you want this program to try to build the vsock
module for your system (you need to have a C compiler installed on your
system)? [yes]
```

23.  After the vsock module success, you'll be prompted to configure networking. It's quite handy. It can be used to connect to VMware server virtual machines from remote locations. Accept the default to configure networking:

```
Do you want networking for your virtual machines? (yes/no/help) [yes]
```

24.  If this is the first time networking is configured for VMware, you'll see the following message for configuring a "bridged" network, which connects the virtual machine network card to a local physical network card.

```
Configuring a bridged network for vmnet0.
Please specify a name for this network.
[Bridged]
```

25.  Next, if there's more than one network interface, you're prompted to select one. As I'm testing this system on my laptop, I type the device for my wireless connection, **wlan0**:

```
Your computer has multiple ethernet network interfaces available: eth0,
wlan0.
Which one do you want to bridge to vmnet0? [eth0] wlan0
```

26.  The new interface is confirmed. Unless you want to configure connections to multiple networks, accept the default to avoid configuring another bridged network:

```
The following bridged networks have been defined:
. vmnet0 is bridged to wlan0
Do you wish to configure another bridged network? (yes/no) [no]
```

27.  The step which follows allows the configuration of Network Address Translation (NAT), which can support a private network for virtual machines. Avoid this option; type **no** and press ENTER:

```
Do you want to be able to use NAT networking in your virtual machines?
(yes/no) [yes] no
```

28.  The step which follows allows the configuration of Host-Only networing, which can support a private network with the VMware host system. Avoid this option; type **no** and press ENTER:

```
Do you want to be able to use host-only networking in your virtual
machines?
(yes/no) [yes] no
```

If you're rerunning the VMware Server installation program, as of this writing, you may see an option for a networking configuration wizard.

02
29. While the default port for remote connections to a VMware server is 902, it may already be in use. If so, the installation script suggests an alternative. If you're just using a VMware server locally, the port number does not matter. The associated message looks like this:

```
Please specify a port for remote console connections to use [902]
```

(Note that by using port 902, I'm able to connect to the virtual machines on my home desktop's VMware Server. Port 902 on my home hardware wireless router is forwarded to my desktop system, which allows me to connect from a remote VMware Server client.)

30. You're also prompted for a special port for HTTP and HTTPS connections, which is useful for the web-based administrative interface. Accept the suggested ports, to avoid interference with other web-based communication:

```
Please specify a port for standard http connections to use [8222]
Please specify a port for secure http (https) connections to use [8333]
```

31. The following prompts for a VMware administrative user. Type **yes**, and then type in a user previously configured for the current system.

```
The current administrative user for VMware Server  is ''.  Would
you like to specify a different administrator? [no] yes

Please specify the user whom you wish to be the VMware Server
administrator
michael
Using michael as the VMware Server administrator.
```

32. When the following message appears, it may help to set the directory to the virtual machine to a subdirectory of your home directory, or perhaps to a directory on a dedicated partition. Obviously, you could also accept the default.

```
In which directory do you want to keep your virtual machine files?
[/var/lib/vmware/Virtual Machines]
```

33. When you see a prompt for a serial number, type **yes**, and enter the registration serial number mentioned earlier.

```
Do you want to enter a serial number now? (yes/no/help) [no] yes
Please enter your 20-character serial number.
Type XXXXX-XXXXX-XXXXX-XXXXX or 'Enter' to cancel:
```

34. You're prompted to continue the installation process, with several steps associated with VMware VIX API that supports virtual machine scripts. Accept the defaults.

35. Review the following messages, which readies VMware for use:

```
Starting VMware services:
    Virtual machine monitor                             done
    Virtual machine communication interface             done
    Virtual ethernet                                    done
    Bridged networking on /dev/vmnet0                   done
    Host-only networking on /dev/vmnet1 (background)    done
    DHCP server on /dev/vmnet1                          done
    Host-only networking on /dev/vmnet8 (background)    done
    DHCP server on /dev/vmnet8                          done
    NAT service on /dev/vmnet8                          done
Starting VMware management services:
    VMware Server Host Agent (background)               done
    VMware Virtual Infrastructure Web Access
Starting VMware autostart virtual machines:
    Virtual machines                                    done

The configuration of VMware Server 2.0.0 build-110949 for Linux for this
running kernel completed successfully.
```

If you run into problems while the script is running, press CTRL-C. While this stops the script, it allows you to fix problems such as missing packages. You can then run the script again.

Older test versions of VMware Server 2.0 required the use of the root administrative account. That is no longer required.

To open VMware Server, open a command line in a GUI. Run the **vmware** command. It should open the default browser. If you haven't added a local security certificate before, you're shown an error page (Figure 20-1). (The display in browsers other than Mozilla Firefox will vary.)

1. Assuming the error page appears in the Firefox browser, as shown in Figure 20-1, click the Or You Can Add An Exception link.

2. In the additional information that appears in the browser, click Add Exception.

3. In the Add Security Exception window that appears, you should see https://127.0.0.1:8333/ in the Location text box. If you do, click Get Certificate.

4. When the Confirm Security Exception option is activated, click it.

5. You're prompted with a VMware Infrastructure Web Access screen; enter the credentials associated with the administrative user configured during the installation process. You should now have access to VMware Server 2.0, as shown in Figure 20-2.

You should now be able to create virtual machines using the GUI options as shown. Leave the Web Access screen open for now.

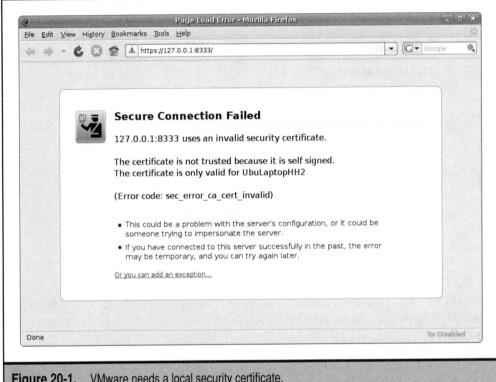

**Figure 20-1.** VMware needs a local security certificate.

## Configure a Datastore

Virtual machine hard disks are configured in files. As the files are used to simulate a hard disk, they are large. Therefore, the volume(s) you configure for datastores should have gigabytes of free space. To configure a datastore, take the following steps:

1.  Under the Commands pane in the upper-right section of the Web Access screen, click Add Datastore.

2.  In the Add Datastore window that appears, specify an arbitrary descriptive name for the datastore in the Name text box; for the purpose of this chapter, type **UbuntuVMs**.

3.  In the Directory Path text box, specify a directory path mounted on a partition or volume with a significant amount of free space. You can even specify a directory *that has been already mounted* from a remote system shared via NFS. Click OK.

4.  Review the Datastores section. You should see the new datastore listed.

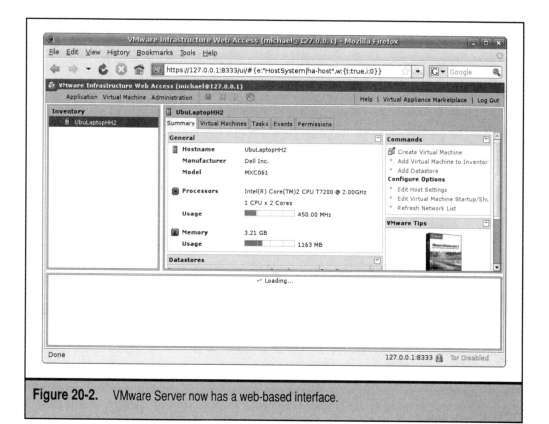

**Figure 20-2.**    VMware Server now has a web-based interface.

## Configure a Virtual Machine

Now you'll set up and configure a virtual machine. Once this section is complete, you'll be able to boot the virtual machine like any regular PC and install an operating system. One method to create a virtual machine uses the following steps:

1. From the toolbar, click Virtual Machine | Create Virtual Machine.

2. In the Create Virtual Machine window that appears, as shown in Figure 20-3, review the Pages pane on the left side. You're about to configure each of these items.

3. Specify a name and datastore for the virtual machine. Since we're creating an Ubuntu JeOS system, type **UbuntuJeOS1** in the Name text box. Select the datastore previously created, in this case, UbuntuVMs. This is the datastore created in the preceding section. Click Next to continue.

4. In the Guest Operating System screen, Select Linux Operating System. (Similar steps are associated with other categories of operating systems, such as Novell, Solaris, and Microsoft Windows.)

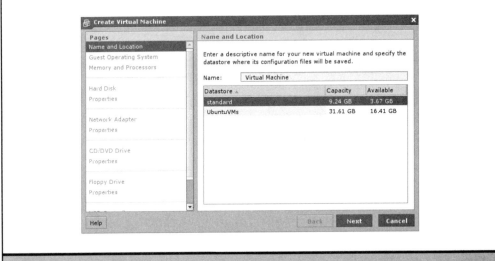

**Figure 20-3.** Create a virtual machine

5. Click the Version drop-down text box arrow and review the variety of Linux distributions that VMware Server can handle. Select the distribution that you're planning to install—or at least the latest available version thereof, in this case, Ubuntu Linux (32-bit), as that's the architecture associated with the Ubuntu JeOS release. Make your selection and click Next.

6. Set the RAM for the virtual machine; make sure not to take away too much from the host system. A good minimum for a GUI system is 256MB; a smaller number is usually practical for most text-based systems (including Ubuntu JeOS). In addition, if your system has multiple processors (or a multi-core CPU), you can assign one or more processors to the virtual machine. Select appropriate numbers and click Next.

7. You'll see a screen that describes three basic options for a virtual disk, as shown here:

| | |
|---|---|
| Create A New Virtual Disk | Add a file as a blank virtual disk |
| Use An Existing Virtual Disk | Use a previously created virtual disk. |
| Don't Add A Hard Disk | Suited for booting from a Live CD/DVD |

For the purpose of this exercise, select the Create A New Virtual Disk hyperlink.

8.  As shown in Figure 20-4 and in the following table, several properties are associated with virtual disks.

| | |
|---|---|
| Capacity | Size of the virtual disk; can be set to GB or MB; in my experience, a 4GB disk size is sufficient for a test system—smaller is adequate for a system based on Ubuntu JeOS. |
| Location | Default location or a configured datastore; should correspond to the datastore set in step 3. |
| File Options | Suboptions include Allocate All Disk Space Now and Split Disk into 2GB files. The 2GB limits are easier to defragment on a Microsoft Windows partition. |
| Disk Mode | Suboptions include Independent, Persistent, and Nonpersistent. The default (Persistent) enables snapshots. |
| Virtual Device Node | For configuration on one of two IDE adapters or one of four SCSI adapters. |
| Policies | For write policies to disk; the Optimize For Safety option is slower but saves data in the case of a problem such as a power failure. |

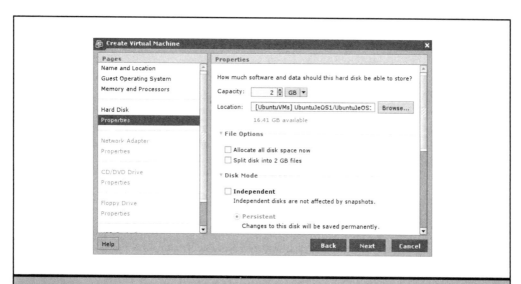

**Figure 20-4.**   Configure virtual disk properties

For the purpose of this exercise, I make several recommendations. Configure a 2GB system, using the UbuntuVMs datastore configured earlier. Split the disk into 2GB files, it can help you organize virtual machines. Retain the default Persistent disk mode and set up a device on the first available Virtual SCSI mode. For write caching, choose Optimize For Safety. But these are just recommendations; alternative selections usually work equally well. Make desired selections and click Next to continue.

9. Unless there is no networking on the host system (or you don't want to add networking on the virtual machine), click Add A Network Adapter.

10. You should see the following question: Which Network Will Your Virtual Machine Access? Generally, you should retain the defaults: Use Bridged Networking and Connect At Power On. Make appropriate choices and click Next to continue.

11. You should now see questions related to the CD/DVD drive, with three options:

| | |
|---|---|
| Use A Physical Drive | Appropriate for installations from a physical CD/DVD on the host system |
| Use An ISO Image | Best if you've just downloaded a Linux installation disk image, normally in ISO format |
| Don't Add A CD/DVD Drive | As the VMware network card supports network booting, can be used for network installations |

If you've downloaded the Ubuntu JeOS CD as an ISO image, as I have, select the Use An ISO Image option.

12. You're automatically taken to the Properties page for the ISO file. On this page, there are entries for Image File and whether to Connect At Power On. The Image File is associated with the ISO file location, relative to configured datastores. You can click Browse to search for an ISO file downloaded (or copied) to a datastore. For example, as I've configured an UbuntuVMs datastore, I've saved the Ubuntu JeOS ISO file to the corresponding directory, and the entry in the Image File text box for the Hardy Heron release would be

```
[UbuntuVMs]/jeos-8.04-jeos-i386.iso
```

Enter the datastore and the desired ISO file, and click Next to continue.

13. In the next step, you're asked whether a floppy drive, associated with a 1.44MB disk, is desired. For the purpose of this exercise, select Don't Add A Floppy Drive. One can be added later if desired.

14. In the step that follows, you're given the opportunity to add a USB controller. This would provide access to host physical USB controllers. For the purpose of this exercise, select Don't Add A USB Controller. One can be added later if desired.

15. Finally, the Ready To Complete window appears, as shown in Figure 20-5. It displays the virtual hardware configured so far. The More Hardware section of the window includes additional hardware components that can be configured. Not shown in the figure are options such as serial ports, parallel ports, and sound adapters.

    If you're ready, activate the Power On Your Virtual Machine Now check box, and click Finish to continue.

16. Click the Virtual Machines tab. In some cases, you may need to click Log Out and log back in before the new virtual machine appears.

17. You'll see the virtual machine just configured in the Inventory pane on the left side of the browser. Highlight it and click the Console tab that appears.

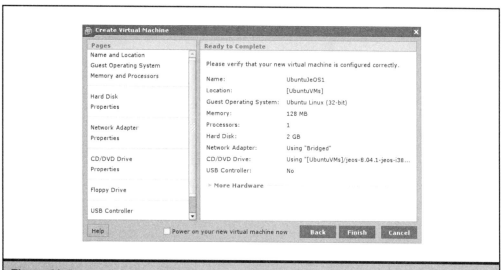

**Figure 20-5.** Ready to complete the configuration of a virtual machine

The following substeps need be run only once:

a. If you see The VMware Remote Console Plug-in Is Not Installed message, click the Install Plug-in link that appears. Normally, Firefox disables pop-ups; if so, click the Allow button in the upper-right corner of the browser.

b. In the Software Installation window that appears, click VMware Remote Console Plug-in, and click Install Now.

c. When the Add-ons window appears and installation of the new plug-in is complete, click Restart Firefox, click Restart to confirm, and log back into the VMware console.

18. If the system under the Console tab is labeled as Powered Off, click inside the console screen. Click in this area a second time to open the console in a new window, as shown in Figure 20-6. You're now ready to install an operating system in the virtual machine.

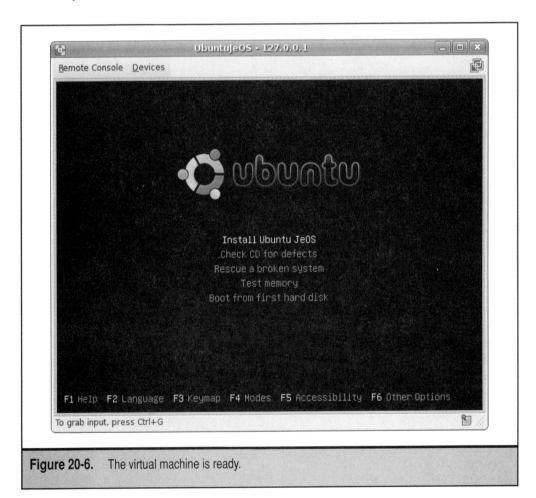

**Figure 20-6.** The virtual machine is ready.

# VirtualBox

The open source edition of VirtualBox is the virtual machine manager created by Sun Microsystems and released under the GPL. There is a more complete edition available for noncommercial use at www.virtualbox.org/wiki/VirtualBox_PUEL. This discussion is limited to the open source version.

Installation is as simple as that of any other package; one method is to use the following command:

```
$ sudo aptitude install virtualbox-ose virtualbox-ose-modules-`uname -r`
```

The installation process adds a vboxusers group to the /etc/group and /etc/gshadow configuration files. Regular users need to be added to this group to get privileges to use the VirtualBox system. You could run the Users Settings GUI tool, which can be started with the **users-admin** command. Alternatively, you could just add desired users to the vboxusers group in each file (the group ID number will vary):

```
vboxusers:x:124:michael
vboxusers:!::michael
```

The next time the noted account logs into the GUI, that user will be able to use the VirtualBox system. That user can now start VirtualBox from a command line in the GUI with the **virtualbox** command.

Then to create a new virtual machine, take the following steps:

1. Click New, or choose Machine | New, or press CTRL-N to start the Create New Virtual Machine wizard.

2. Read the introduction and click Next to continue.

3. In the VM Name and OS Type screen, enter a name for the new virtual machine and select an OS Type. Options are available for a variety of Microsoft, BSD (Berkeley Standard Distribution), and miscellaneous operating systems. The Linux options are associated with major kernel versions; any Linux distribution released in the past several years would correspond to the Linux 2.6 OS Type. Click Next to continue.

4. In the Memory screen, assign a Base Memory Size for the virtual machine. This value becomes the amount of RAM for the virtual machine. Be sure to leave enough RAM for other virtual machines as well as the localhost system. Make a selection and click Next to continue.

5. In the Virtual Hard Disk screen, unless a virtual hard disk already exists, you'll have to create one. Click New to start the Create New Virtual Disk wizard.

6. Read the introduction to the Create New Virtual Disk wizard and click Next to continue.

7. In the Virtual Disk Image Type screen, you'll see two options: Dynamically Expanding Image and Fixed-Size Image. What you select depends on your needs; both options create a file that is used as a hard disk image. The Dynamically Expanding Image starts as a small file. For more discussion, see www.virtualbox.org. Select one and click Next to continue.

8. In the Virtual Disk Location And Size screen, select an image filename and size. If you selected a Dynamically Expanding Image, the size will be a maximum for the file. Click Next to continue.

9. In the Summary screen, review the result. Note the image location; unless changed in the previous step, it will be created in your home directory, in a hidden .VirtualBox/ subdirectory. If you're satisfied with the result, click Finish to return to the Virtual Hard Disk screen described in step 5.

10. The new virtual hard disk, created in steps 6 through 9, is now shown as the default for the new virtual machine. Click Next to continue.

11. Review the summary for the virtual machine to be created, as shown in Figure 20-7. If you're satisfied with the settings, click Finish.

12. Back in the main VirtualBox OSE window, click the name of the virtual machine just created. When you're ready, click Start or choose Machine | Start.

13. The first time a virtual machine is created on VirtualBox, a First Run wizard appears. Read the introduction and click Next to continue. If the wizard does not appear, and you need to configure special settings, such as for an ISO file

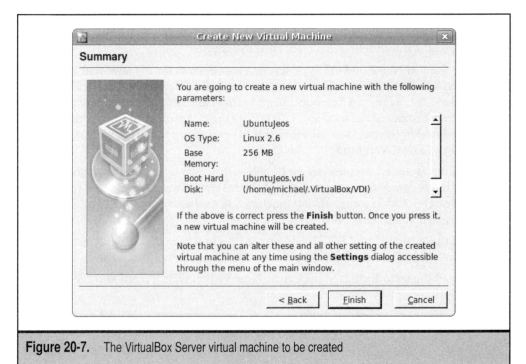

**Figure 20-7.**   The VirtualBox Server virtual machine to be created

mounted as a CD, click Settings. Then find and modify the options associated with the CD, and skip to step 17.

14. In the Select Installation Media window that appears, select appropriate installation media. The first choice is to select either a CD/DVD-ROM Device or Floppy Device. The second choice is for the Media Source, either an existing physical Host Drive or Image File.

    If you select Image File, and the desired image is not in the default VirtualBox directory, click Add and navigate to the location with the ISO file.

    Make the desired selection and click Select.

15. Confirm the configured installation media and click Next.

16. Read the configuration with respect to media. If satisfied, click Finish.

17. Click in the new window that appears, which is named after the virtual machine you just created. If you see a long message associated with Auto Capture Keyboard, be aware that keyboard control can be returned to the host with the right (not left) CTRL key.

18. If you want to configure a mouse in the virtual machine, choose Devices | Install Guest Additions. You're asked whether to download an associated CD image. Follow the instructions to download.

19. When the download is complete, click Mount. Click in the window; when the Auto Capture Keyboard message appears again, activate the Don't Show This Message Again check box and click Continue.

20. You can now install an operating system in the virtual machine, as shown in Figure 20-8. If that requires an installation CD/DVD, click Devices | Mount CD/DVD-ROM, and select the appropriate CD/DVD.

**NOTE** If you've installed the KVM software described later in this chapter, VirtualBox won't work, and will halt with an error message.

# Other Options

QEMU (Quick Emulator) is a *hypervisor*. It's also known as a virtual machine monitor that provides a framework in which multiple virtual machines can run on the same host system. Several virtualization solutions use the QEMU hypervisor, including Xen and KVM.

**NOTE** As of this writing, there are a variety of bugs associated with running Xen on the Hardy Heron release that affects its ability to connect via networks and more. But since the default Ubuntu solution is KVM, this chapter focuses on that virtualization method.

Another emerging option includes a minimal operating system on a server, sufficient to install a group of virtual machines, without the overhead of a full host version of Microsoft Windows Server or even Linux. It's available natively on a number of hardware servers.

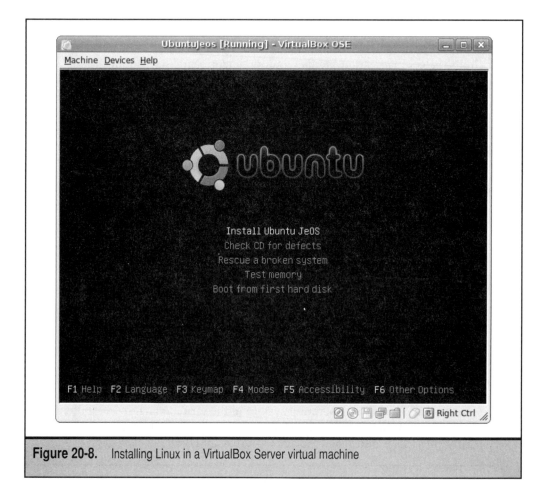

**Figure 20-8.** Installing Linux in a VirtualBox Server virtual machine

## Why Paravirtualization?

*Paravirtualization* supports a virtual machine with a limited amount of resources. Using paravirtualization, I can run several virtual machines on my desktop server, which has an older regular single-core CPU.

Paravirtualization requires a modified kernel, which is available for Linux systems that support Xen. But paravirtualization is limited: If you have a 64-bit system, paravirtualization allows only 64-bit clients; if you have a 32-bit system, paravirtualization supports only 32-bit clients. In addition, paravirtualization is not supported on Ubuntu Hardy Heron systems configured with KVM.

However, paravirtualization may no longer be limited to Linux clients. The work of KVM developers is documented at www.linux-kvm.com, which includes paravirtualized drivers suitable for a Microsoft Windows client.

# CONFIGURE KVM

As with Xen, KVM requires a CPU and BIOS where hardware virtualization is enabled. While Xen requires that you boot into a modified kernel, KVM requires only the installation of specialized modules. In hardware virtualized mode, KVM supports most operating systems, without modification, in a virtual machine. You can even run Microsoft Windows on KVM, which is one of the configurations demonstrated here.

## The Right Packages

To configure KVM on Ubuntu Server, you need the KVM modules and more. Additional useful packages can help configure and run virtual machines once KVM is installed. Some of the packages described in this section were originally created by Red Hat developers for their implementation of Xen. However, these packages work well for KVM-based virtual machines as well. One way to install these packages is with the following command:

```
$ sudo aptitude install kvm libvirt-bin ubuntu-vm-builder python-virtinst \
virt-manager virt-viewer
```

With dependencies, the command noted above also installs a number of other packages, which are listed in Table 20-1.

The installation process includes a couple of modules that depend on the hardware on the local system. For my laptop with an Intel dual-core CPU, it includes the following modules, as shown in the output to the **lsmod | grep kvm** command:

```
kvm_intel              36032  0
kvm                    115252 1 kvm_intel
```

There is a corresponding kvm_amd module for AMD multi-core systems. Systems without multiple cores (or multiple CPUs) won't be able to load the kvm_intel or kvm_amd modules.

The installation process also adds a kvm group to the /etc/group and /etc/gshadow configuration files. Regular users need to be added to this group to get privileges to create a virtual machine using KVM modules. You could run the Users Settings GUI tool, which can be started with the **users-admin** command. Alternatively, you could just add desired users to the kvm, libvirtd, and vde2-net groups in each file (the group ID numbers will vary):

```
kvm:x:126:michael
libvirtd:x:127:michael
vde2-net:x:128:michael

kvm:!::michael
libvirtd:!::michael
vde2-net:!::michael
```

The next time someone logs into the noted account, that user will be able to create virtual machines using KVM.

| Package | Description |
|---|---|
| bochsbios | Virtual BIOS from the Bochs project at http://bochs.sourceforge.net |
| bridge-utils | For an Ethernet bridge connecting the host to the virtual guests |
| daemon | Tool for the conversion of a process to a daemon |
| debootstrap | For bootstrapping a basic Debian system |
| dnsmasq-base | DNS caching proxy server |
| kpartx | Associated with virtual partition devices |
| kvm | Main KVM package |
| libvirt-bin | For interaction with virtualization, using the **virsh** command |
| libvirt0 | Virtualization library |
| python-gtk-vnc | VNC viewer for virtual machines |
| python-libvirt | Library that interacts with virtualization mechanisms, including KVM |
| python-urlgrabber | Tool for fetching files |
| python-virtinst | Tool that configures virtual guests in KVM and more |
| qemu | Processor emulator for KVM (and other virtualization tools) |
| sharutils | For shell archives |
| ubuntu-vm-builder | For the creation of a virtual machine |
| vde2 | A switch to link virtual machines |
| vgabios | For a video (VGA) BIOS |
| virt-manager | GUI application for configuring and managing virtual machines |
| virt-viewer | Graphical console viewer for virtual machines |

**Table 20-1.** Packages for the Kernel Virtual Machine

# Hardware Issues

Hardware virtualization doesn't work unless it's on a system with multiple CPUs (or a multi-core CPU). And then, if you want to run other unmodified operating systems such as Microsoft Windows on Linux with KVM (or Xen), you'll need a multi-core or multiple CPUs with hardware virtualization enabled. Some enterprises will want to run Windows on KVM (or Xen), such as those that continue to use a Microsoft authentication server while other services are converted to Linux.

If you want to configure KVM with hardware virtualization, you'll need hardware with the latest virtualization-enabled CPUs. Two examples are the Vanderpool- and Pacifica-enabled CPUs. The Vanderpool-enabled CPUs are also known as Intel Core Duo (and Core 2 Duo) chips. AMD has incorporated its Pacifica technologies into *some* of its latest CPUs.

Not all Core Duo/Core 2 Duo CPUs support hardware virtualization. For example, the Intel T2300E (and below) as well as the T5500 CPUs do not support it. If you have an AMD Turion 64-bit CPU, virtualization is supported only on TL-50 CPUs or above. There has been worldwide confusion on this matter: for example, one major laptop manufacturer has faced a class-action lawsuit in China for substituting T2300E CPUs for VT-capable T2300s.

A wiki of hardware virtual machine (HVM)–compatible CPUs is maintained on the XenSource website at http://wiki.xensource.com/xenwiki/HVM_Compatible_Processors. While the list is noted as "out of date" as of this writing, it's a sign of how the latest multi-core CPUs are HVM compatible.

But the right CPU is not enough. For example, as of this writing, several major laptop manufacturers disable virtualization on some or even all of their laptop systems, even those with VT-capable CPUs.

I'm writing this book on a laptop system with an Intel T7200 Core 2 Duo CPU. Before I could configure a KVM-based virtual machine, I enabled virtualization in the BIOS menu. While shopping for appropriate systems, I inspected the BIOS menu of each system, to make sure that I could enable virtualization. This may not be necessary with HVM compatible AMD CPUs, as AMD does not include the CPU option that allows manufacturers to disable virtualization.

If you have a system that disables virtualization, not all is lost. After a long series of public messages on its boards, HP included a BIOS update that allowed users to enable virtualization on at least some of its laptop systems. Perhaps you have an HP system. If HP is willing to allow virtualization, other vendors may be willing as well.

If you're not sure and can test the computer before buying it, ask for permission to boot a Live Linux CD. The Ubuntu Live CD/DVD is sufficient for this purpose. If it's an Intel system, make sure virtualization is enabled in the BIOS. Review the /proc/cpuinfo file. If that system is HVM capable, you'll see the **vmx** (Intel) or **svm** (AMD) flags in this file.

KVM networking reportedly can be troubled over a wireless network connection. A wireless connection is generally not recommended on any server system, much less a host with multiple virtual machines. I've tested the creation and operation of virtual machines on both a local physical Ethernet adapter, as well as a wireless adapter. For what it's worth, I think I just lucked out with a wireless adapter that is compatible with the KVM network bridge.

# KVM Network Configuration

To configure an appropriate bridge on a KVM host, a special bridge device is required. With that in mind, you'll also need to modify the /etc/network/interfaces configuration file to set up a bridge between the host system and any KVM virtual machines that are configured.

The following stanza is one way to configure a network bridge on a KVM host system. The bridge device is **br0**. This first example stanza is associated with a bridge between virtual machines and the first Ethernet adapter. For this configuration, I've disabled my wireless adapter.

```
auto br0
iface br0 inet dhcp
bridge_ports eth0
```

Alternatively, I've also configured a connection on my laptop system with a wireless adapter, configured on device **wlan0**. For this configuration, I've disabled the physical Ethernet network adapter.

```
auto br0
iface br0 inet dhcp
bridge_ports wlan0
```

# Create a Virtual Machine on KVM

This section illustrates two methods to create a virtual machine, using KVM modules and utilities. I've tested these methods on my laptop system with a dual-core CPU. I use the Ubuntu JeOS system and ISO file described earlier for this purpose. One advantage of JeOS is that it requires relatively few resources. I illustrate the configuration of a virtual machine from the command line using the **virt-install** command as well as the GUI Virtual Machine Manager, which can be started with the **virt-manager** command. Other tools are available, including the **ubuntu-vm-builder** command; however, the focus here is on the **virt-install** command as it is so closely related to the GUI Virtual Machine Manager.

## Configure a Virtual Machine from the Command Line

One command line script that can configure a KVM-based virtual machine from the command line is **virt-install**. You could specify all features, as specified in the associated man page, or you could let the **virt-install** command prompt for required information. When I run the **virt-install** command, I enter required information as follows, in boldface type:

```
$ virt-install
What is the name of your virtual machine? UbuntuJeOSHHvm2
 How much RAM should be allocated (in megabytes)? 256
 What would you like to use as the disk (file path)? /home/michael/UJvm2.img
 How large would you like the disk (/home/michael/UJvm2.img) to be
(in gigabytes)? 2
 Would you like to enable graphics support? (yes or no) yes
```

```
 What is the virtual CD image, CD device or install location? /home/michael/
jeos-8.04-jeos-i386.iso
Starting install...
libvir: QEMU error :
libvir: QEMU error :
libvir: QEMU error :
Creating storage file...   100% |====================|  2.0 GB     00:00
Creating domain...                                        0 B 00:00
```

The entries configure a 2GB file as a virtual disk in my home directory. It uses the Ubuntu JeOS ISO file, which was downloaded to the same directory. Graphics support enables automatic viewing of the virtual machine console, after the domain is created, in Figure 20-9.

The QEMU viewer facilitates the use of control keys under the Send Key menu. Available options include CTRL-ALT-DEL for rebooting, CTRL-ALT-BACKSPACE for exiting an X Window, PRINTSCREEN, and CTRL-ALT-FX, where $x$ can range between 1 and 9.

**Figure 20-9.**  A QEMU Viewer screen of a KVM virtual machine

## The Virtual Machine Manager

The Virtual Machine Manager also provides a GUI front end for the **virt-install** command. To start it, run **virt-manager** in the GUI. If you're familiar with the latest Red Hat distributions, you may recognize this tool, originally developed by Red Hat. However, not all of the features of the Virtual Machine Manager have been enabled for KVM on Ubuntu systems.

For the purpose of this chapter, I've installed the Ubuntu JeOS operating system on my laptop in fully virtualized mode. To do what I did, you'll need a system with a CPU (and for Intel-based systems, a BIOS) with virtualization enabled. If you do, you can create a KVM virtual machine with the following steps:

1. First, open the Virtual Machine Manager. Open a command line interface, and run the **virt-manager** command.

2. In the Virtual Machine Manager, highlight the localhost connection, and choose File | Open Connection. In the Open Connection window, review the options. The defaults are a QEMU hypervisor and a local connection (Xen may be an option if the appropriate kernel is installed and running). Remote connections tunneled through Secure Shell (SSH) connections are also possible. For the purpose of this exercise, accept the defaults and click Connect.

3. Back in the Virtual Machine Manager, highlight the localhost connection and click New. You'll see the Create A New Virtual System window, which specifies the information you'll need to add in the following steps. Read the descriptions and click Forward.

4. Specify a name for the KVM-based machine. Click Forward.

5. Select Fully Virtualized, a virtual CPU compatible with the local hardware CPU, and leave the Enable Kernel / Hardware Acceleration option selected. Click Forward.

6. If an error message appears, the current user account may not be confirmed a member of the kvm group, as described earlier. In that case, you'll have to log out and log back into the GUI, and then restart the process.

7. In the Locating Installation Media screen shown in Figure 20-10, you can select an installation source—from a local ISO file, a CD/DVD, or even from a remote system using a virtual network card.

   There are also several options for the guest operating system. Available options in the OS Type field are Windows, Linux, Unix, Generic, and Other. Options in the OS Variant field are based on the selected OS Type. KVM can accommodate Linux, Microsoft, and other operating system types, including Microsoft Windows Vista. Make desired selections and click Forward.

8. Now you'll see the Assigning Storage Space screen. In this case, you can set up a virtual disk on a file, as shown in Figure 20-11. The default is the current user's home directory, based on the name assigned in step 4. Assign an

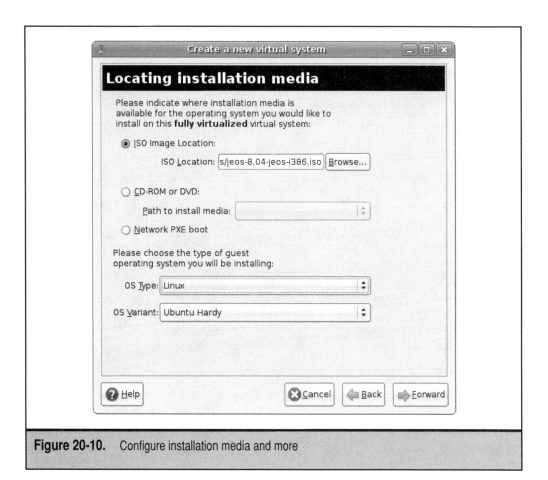

**Figure 20-10.** Configure installation media and more

appropriate size, and choose whether to Allocate Entire Virtual Disk Now. If you select this option, a file of the full size specified is immediately created. Make desired selections and click Forward.

9. In the Allocate Memory And CPU screen, you'll get to specify the amount of RAM and number of CPUs assigned to the virtual machine. Make sure to leave sufficient RAM for the host system. If you have a single CPU that happens to be dual-core, it's seen as two CPUs by KVM, and you can allocate some resources from both CPUs in this screen. Make desired selections and click Forward.

10. Finally, you get to review the prospective virtual machine as configured. Once you click Finish, a separate window is opened for the newly configured system, as shown in Figure 20-12.

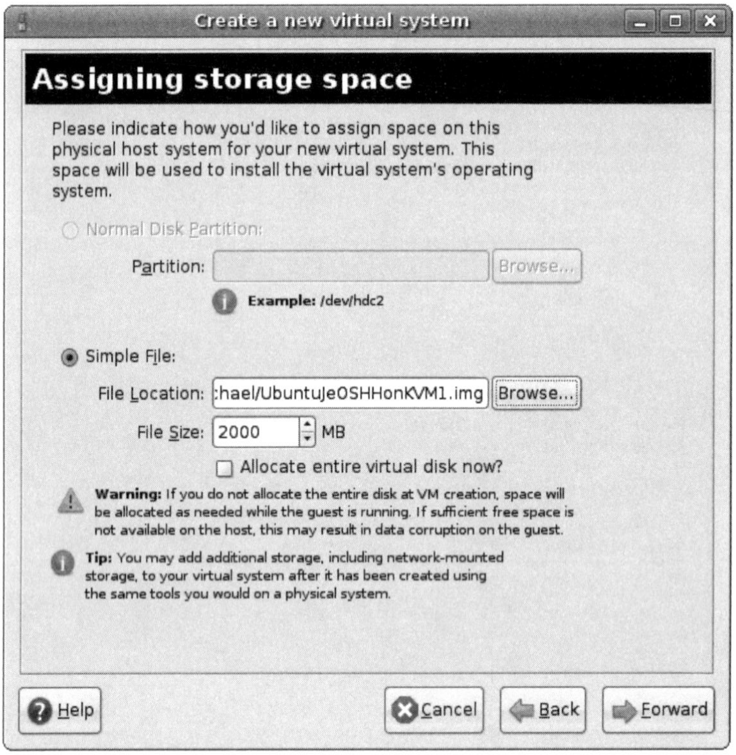

**Create a new virtual system**

# Assigning storage space

Please indicate how you'd like to assign space on this physical host system for your new virtual system. This space will be used to install the virtual system's operating system.

○ Normal Disk _Partition_:

Partition: [                    ] [ Browse... ]

ⓘ **Example:** /dev/hdc2

◉ Simple File:

File Location: [:hael/UbuntuJeOSHHonKVM1.img] [Browse...]

File Size: [2000] ▲▼ MB

☐ Allocate entire virtual disk now?

⚠ **Warning:** If you do not allocate the entire disk at VM creation, space will be allocated as needed while the guest is running. If sufficient free space is not available on the host, this may result in data corruption on the guest.

ⓘ **Tip:** You may add additional storage, including network-mounted storage, to your virtual system after it has been created using the same tools you would on a physical system.

[ⓗ _Help_]        [ⓧ _Cancel_] [⬅ _Back_] [➡ _Forward_]

**Figure 20-11.** Configure a virtual disk

If you want to return to one of these configured virtual machines with the Virtual Machine Manager, repeat steps 1 and 2. Configured virtual machines should appear in the Virtual Machine Manager window. Right-click the desired virtual machine and choose Open. A window should open for the desired virtual machine, with a Run button that can start the virtual system.

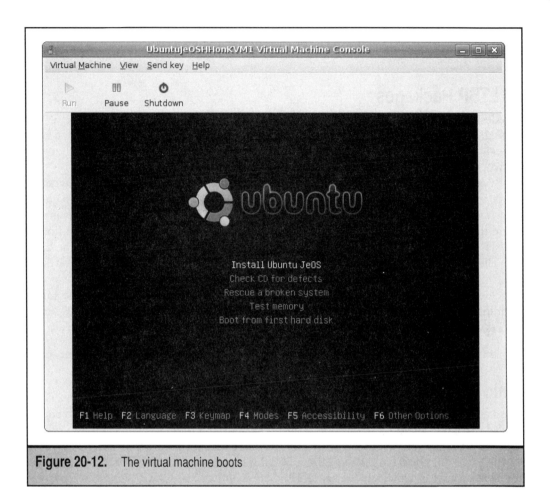

**Figure 20-12.**   The virtual machine boots

# SET UP THE LINUX TERMINAL SERVER PROJECT (LTSP)

Linux is a multiuser, multitasking system. The latest PCs and networks can handle the processing requirements for several GUI terminals simultaneously. With a diskless client, you can configure terminals with old hardware. Diskless clients on a network all run programs from the same system. Diskless clients can be a convenience for the administrator and a big cost saving for the organization.

If you're serious about terminal servers, consider the Edubuntu build of Ubuntu. It is preconfigured with the services required to set up terminal servers and includes several handy tools for managing terminal server clients. This section provides only the most basic outline to set up the LTSP infrastructure and won't be sufficient for most administrators. However, it should give you a basic understanding of the tools required to create a terminal server on Ubuntu.

*TIP* For instructions on the Edubuntu implementation of LTSP, see https://wiki.edubuntu.org/HardyClassroomServer.

## Install LTSP Packages

Diskless clients are not "dumb terminals"; they do require a bit of infrastructure. While local graphics hardware (video card, appropriate monitor) is required to display a GUI, a local hard drive isn't required. Diskless clients can be configured on systems where the network card and BIOS can be configured with the PXE.

There are three parts to the infrastructure for diskless clients: First, DHCP (Dynamic Host Configuration Protocol) services provide unique network addresses to each client, which was covered in Chapter 14. Second, TFTP (Trivial File Transfer Protocol) servers share the files required to boot the diskless client over a network; the configuration of a TFTP server is simpler than the FTP server configured in Chapter 17. Third, the basic thin client directory tree can be shared with an NFS server; for more information on NFS, see Chapter 16.

One Ubuntu implementation of diskless clients is based on the work of the Linux Terminal Server Project. In fact, the command that installs the appropriate LTSP server packages also installs the dhcp3-server and TFTP server packages by default:

```
$ sudo apt-get install ltsp-server ltsp-server-standalone ltsp-client-core
```

## Dynamic Host Configuration Protocol (DHCP) Services

The basic configuration of a DHCP server was covered in Chapter 14. This section covers special directives required to support a diskless client. Pointing PXE clients to the proper LTSP files depends on whether you already have an existing DHCP server for the local network. If you do, you'll need to add the following to the main DHCP server configuration file. Don't forget to substitute the actual IP address of the LTSP DHCP server for *ipaddress*:

```
next-server ipaddress;
```

Now for the DHCP server on the LTSP system, open up the DHCP configuration file, /etc/ltsp/dhcpd.conf. As suggested by the directive of the same name, the first directive suggests this configuration is authoritative for the configured range of network addresses:

```
authoritative;
```

The following directives are associated with a specific subnet; if you want to configure a different subnet, substitute appropriately:

```
subnet 192.168.0.0 netmask 255.255.255.0 {
    range 192.168.0.20 192.168.0.250;
```

On my own home local network, I use the same subnet, so I limit the **range** of available network addresses to those not assigned to other local systems.

As needed, I can specify the domain for the local network with the **domain-name** directive and the DNS servers for this client with the **domain-name-servers** directive. Substitute with a domain name and DNS server IP address suitable for your network:

```
option domain-name "example.com";
option domain-name-servers 192.168.0.1;
```

The **broadcast-address** directive, as suggested by its name, assigns a broadcast address. If you configure a different network address, remember to substitute an appropriate broadcast address for that network.

```
option broadcast-address 192.168.0.255
```

The **subnet-mask** directive can override the previous **netmask** directive, which may be useful for networks that are subdivided into more discrete networks. The default **subnet-mask** directive matches the default **netmask** directive. The **routers** directive specifies the gateway address for the network. Substitute as appropriate for the local network.

```
option routers 192.168.0.1
option subnet-mask 255.255.255.0
```

The directives that follow actually point the PXE network boot systems to the appropriate files and directories. The default is associated with the **--base** directory configured with the **ltsp-build-client** command.

```
option root-path "/opt/ltsp/i386";
```

But for the client configuration associated with a TFTP server, you'll need to change the path to

```
option root-path "/var/lib/tftpboot/ltsp/i386";
```

The following directive receives the string sent by a PXE client system, PXEClient. It also connects the PXE client to an initial image (nbi.img):

```
if substring( option vendor-class-identifier, 0, 9 ) = "PXEClient" {
    filename "/ltsp/i386/pxelinux.0";
} else {
    filename "/ltsp/i386/nbi.img";
}
}
```

Once you've configured this service as desired, don't forget to activate this service with the following command:

```
$ sudo /etc/init.d/dhcp3-server start
```

To confirm that it's reading the correct configuration file, I run the **ps aux | grep dhcp** command, which lists the following command line in the output:

```
/usr/sbin/dhcpd3 -q -pf /var/run/dhcp3-server/dhcpd.pid -cf
/etc/ltsp/dhcpd.conf
```

Pay attention to the last expression; if it points to a different configuration file, you might need to make sure the following directives are active in the /etc/init.d/dhcp3-server configuration file:

```
if [ -f /etc/ltsp/dhcpd.conf ]; then
      CONFIG_FILE=/etc/ltsp/dhcpd.conf
fi
```

## Trivial File Transfer Protocol

There are several available options for TFTP services for Ubuntu. The focus of this section is based on the *tftpd-hpa* package. It should be automatically configured. If you have a firewall on the local system, pay attention to the associated port number(s) listed in this file. Just remember that to test the TFTP service, you also need the *tftp-hpa* client package.

The simplest way to configure the TFTP service is through the /etc/default/tftpd-hpa configuration file. I use the following directives in my version of this file:

```
RUN_DAEMON="yes"
OPTIONS="-l -s /var/lib/tftpboot"
```

The directives are simple; the first is almost self-explanatory as it runs the /usr/sbin/in.tftpd daemon (the default is **no**). The second feeds command line options to the daemon. As can be verified with the in.tftpd man page, these default options run the server in standalone mode, using the /var/lib/tftpboot directory as the root directory for clients. The information from this file is fed to the associated start script, /etc/init.d/tftpd-hpa.

## NFS Sharing

Thin clients prior to Ubuntu Gutsy Gibbon rely on remote access with an NFS server. It's still an excellent option. While alternatives are available, the standard is the NFS kernel server. That and associated packages can be installed with the following command, which also installs other packages as required, such as portmap and nfs-common:

```
$ sudo apt-get install nfs-kernel-server
```

You'll need to create an NFS share of the top-level root directory that will be created for LTSP clients. Based on the information to this point, that directory is /var/lib/tftpboot/ltsp/i386; your configuration may be different. Refer to Chapter 16 for details on how to configure a shared directory via NFS.

# PXE Booting

Modern diskless clients require some sort of network boot card. Many modern systems configure access to the PXE environment through the boot menu. As there are a wide variety of options for the boot menu, they are not described here. If available, the PXE option should be listed in your computer's hardware documentation. If the PXE environment is selected, it should show messages similar to the following:

```
Network boot from some network card

CLIENT MAC ADDR: 00 0C 39 40 4E EA
GUID: 564DFD09-31C9-77F0-ED6C-CE86DA304EEA
DHCP:
```

If the LTSP client is properly configured on the server, the client PXE environment should automatically detect the DHCP server, along with the client files as configured. However, this may not work before related commands are run to create a diskless client template, as described in the next section.

If PXE booting is not available on the desired client's network card or BIOS, it's possible to create a boot CD or floppy that simulates the PXE boot process. For more information, see www.rom-o-matic.net.

# Security Issues for Diskless Client

Take care to avoid blockage by firewalls. One option for firewalls is created with the **iptables** command. To review a currently configured **iptables**-based firewall, run the **iptables -L** command. For now, you can enable access by flushing the firewall with the following command:

```
$ sudo iptables -F
```

> **NOTE**   Open ports are also required. For more information, see the discussion on the **netstat** command in Chapter 11.

The configuration of a firewall for an NFS server is a complex process. Chapter 16 includes a brief reference to fixing ports for this purpose. But many networks that include terminal servers and clients are already behind a firewall, so this section assumes that you do not configure one between those servers and clients.

Another source of security that may block terminal services is TCP wrappers. For more information, see Chapter 18.

# The Linux Terminal Server Project

Assuming you've run the command described earlier to install the LTSP server, you'll soon run the following command:

```
$ sudo ltsp-build-client
```

But don't run this command just yet, until you've read about all the command switches that will be used. If you want to create the client in the /var/lib/tftpboot directory, you'll need to add the **--base /var/lib/tftpboot** option:

```
$ sudo ltsp-build-client --base /var/lib/tftpboot/ltsp
```

If you're building clients for different architectures, pay attention to the **--arch** switch. For example, when I built i386 LTSP clients on my AMD 64-bit desktop system, I ran the following command. If you're running a system on an i386 architecture, the **--arch i386** switch will do no harm. You can even set up a server for a different distribution, based on the scripts in the /usr/share/debootstrap/scripts directory.

```
$ sudo ltsp-build-client --base /var/lib/tftpboot/ltsp --arch i386 \
--dist hardy --mirror http://mirrors.kernel.org
```

This command takes a few minutes or more (depending on hardware capabilities) to build a client system. After the first reboot of each terminal server, you may need to run the **ltsp-update-image** and possibly the **ltsp-update-sshkeys** commands. To update the appropriate base directory, update the image with the following command:

```
$ sudo ltsp-update-image --base /var/lib/tftpboot/ltsp --arch i386
```

# Boot the LTSP Client

If you use the PXE boot techniques described earlier, the client network card should boot the LTSP system automatically, assuming the DHCP and TFTP servers are running and are not blocked by any sort of firewall. When successful, you'll see a screen similar to that shown in Figure 20-13.

To troubleshoot problems with the LTSP client, open the default file in the /var/lib/tftpboot/ltsp/i386/boot/pxelinux.cfg directory. Delete the **quiet** and **splash** directives. The next time you boot the LTSP client, you'll see log messages associated with the boot process. In other words, it can help you identify where the LTSP client encounters a problem.

**Figure 20-13.**   A Hardy LTSP login screen

# SUMMARY

There are many options for virtual machines on Ubuntu. In general, a virtual machine includes a large file configured as a hard drive. It also includes virtual versions of the major components of the PC. As resources have to be shared with the host system, some planning is required to make sure that sufficient RAM is available for both the host and any virtual guest that you configure.

   Two popular third-party options are VMware Server and VirtualBox. While VMware Server is not open source, it is freely available and its creator is the market leader in virtualization. In contrast, Ubuntu includes the open source edition of VirtualBox, developed by Sun Microsystems. Both solutions can be customized for various Linux, Microsoft, and other operating systems.

Virtualization solutions native to Linux systems are KVM and Xen. While the Ubuntu Hardy Heron release is optimized for KVM, it requires a system either with multiple CPUs or a CPU with multiple cores, with hardware virtualization capabilities. Tools such as the **virt-install** command and the Virtual Machine Manager can be used to create virtual machines.

Diskless clients require the configuration of the same services, including DHCP, NFS, and TFTP. The Ubuntu implementation of diskless clients is based on the work of the Linux Terminal Server Project. If you're serious about LTSP, try the Edubuntu release of Ubuntu.

# GLOSSARY

| | |
|---|---|
| ~ | The tilde (~) represents the home directory of the currently active user. |
| **aa-audit** | The **aa-audit** command sets an AppArmor security profile to audit mode. |
| **aa-autodep** | The **aa-autodep** command suggests an AppArmor profile. |
| **aa-complain** | The **aa-complain** command sets an AppArmor security profile to complain mode. |
| **aa-genprof** | The **aa-genprof** command configures an AppArmor profile for a specified program or command. |
| **aa-status** | The **aa-status** command displays current AppArmor policies. |
| **aa-unconfined** | The **aa-unconfined** command displays processes without current AppArmor profiles. |
| **access control list (ACL)** | In Linux, an access control list (ACL) supports object-based permissions. ACLs can override standard octal permissions. ACLs assume the filesystem has been so configured and mounted. |

| | |
|---|---|
| **Address Resolution Protocol (ARP)** | The Address Resolution Protocol maps an IP address to the hardware address of a network card. |
| **Advanced Configuration and Power Interface (ACPI)** | The Advanced Configuration and Power Interface (ACPI) puts the operating system in control of power management. It needs no specialized settings in the BIOS. It supports fine-grained power management of just about every appropriate component. |
| **Alpha release** | For most software, the distribution of an Alpha release is limited to testers and developers within the company or organization. For Ubuntu, Alpha releases are publicly available. In fact, most developmental Ubuntu releases are Alpha releases and are intended for public developmental testing. |
| **Alternate CD** | The Ubuntu Alternate CD includes installation programs without a LiveCD boot option. |
| **apache2ctl** | The **apache2ctl** command can be used to start, stop, and gracefully restart the Apache service. It can also help Apache reread changes to the configuration file(s). |
| **AppArmor** | AppArmor is the mandatory access control (MAC) security system developed by Novell. It's the default MAC system for Ubuntu and is functionally similar to Red Hat's Security Enhanced Linux (SELinux). |
| **apt-cache** | The simplest way to review available repositories for package information is with the **apt-cache** command. For example, the **apt-cache search apache** command searches all repositories for packages that refer to the Apache web server. |
| **apt-file** | The **apt-file** command uses the repository databases to help search within uninstalled packages. |
| **apt-ftparchive** | The **apt-ftparchive** command can be used to configure a repository for client access. |
| **apt-get** | The **apt-get** commands can install and remove packages. Specifically, the **apt-get install** *package* and **apt-get remove** *package* commands are used to install and remove the package of your choice, with all dependencies. |
| **apt-mirror** | The **apt-mirror** command can be used to create a local mirror of part or all of the repository of your choice. |
| **aptitude** | The **aptitude** command can be used as a front end to many **apt-\*** commands. |

**arp** The **arp** command is used to view or modify the kernel's ARP table, and it can detect problems such as duplicate addresses on the network. Alternatively, the **arp** command can be used to add the required entries from your LAN.

**at** The **at** command is similar to **cron**, but it allows you to run a job on a one-time basis.

**auth** The **auth** directive in PAM establishes the identity of a user.

**bash** The current default shell for Ubuntu is the bash shell. The name *bash* is short for the Bourne Again Shell.

**Beta freeze** The Beta freeze is the development milestone after which package changes are further limited to minimize the risk of package dependency issues; comes before the Beta release.

**Beta release** A Beta release is software that has reached a point in the developmental process at which features and package changes are frozen and ready for testing on nonproduction systems in real-world situations.

**BIND (Berkeley Internet Name Domain)** BIND is the Unix/Linux software that is used to set up a Domain Name System (DNS) service. The associated daemon is **named**.

**/boot** The /boot directory is the directory that contains the main files required to boot Linux, including the Linux kernel and initial RAM disk. The /boot directory is often mounted on a separate partition.

**boot loader (or bootloader)** A Linux boot loader loads a configuration file that allows the user to select an operating system during the boot process. Available Linux boot loaders are GRUB and LILO.

**BOOTP** This TCP/IP protocol sends IP address information from a remote DHCP server.

**Breezy Badger** Breezy Badger is the code name for the third release of Ubuntu, version 5.10, released in October 2005.

**Bugsy Malone** The Ubuntu bug tracker, part of the Launchpad platform, is known as Bugsy Malone. It goes beyond standard user reports to collect information from the system with the bug.

**BulletProofX** The BulletProofX system is designed to create a graphical screen even when serious problems exist with the configuration of the X server. The files associated with the BulletProofX system were first implemented for Ubuntu Gutsy Gibbon.

| | |
|---|---|
| caching-only name server | A caching-only name server performs many of the functions of a DNS server. It stores the IP address associated with recent name searches for use by other computers on your LAN. |
| Canonical | Canonical, Ltd., is the commercial sponsor behind Ubuntu. Canonical also offers paid support subscriptions for Ubuntu Server. |
| chage | The **chage** command manages the expiration date of a password. |
| chattr | The **chattr** command allows you to change file attributes. |
| chgrp | The **chgrp** command changes the group that owns a file. |
| chmod | The **chmod** command changes the permissions on a file. |
| chown | The **chown** command changes ownership on a file. |
| CIFS (Common Internet File System) | CIFS is Microsoft's name for advances in its networking software. It's also covered by the latest version of Samba 3, which is included with Ubuntu. |
| CNAME (canonical name) | The CNAME is a way to assign several different names to a computer in a DNS database. For example, you can set up *www* as an alias for the computer with your web server. CNAME records cannot be assigned to a mail server (MX) or a Start of Authority (SOA) record. |
| cron | A cron is a service that runs jobs on a periodic basis. It's configured in /etc/crontab; by default, it executes jobs in the /etc/cron.hourly, /etc/cron.daily, /etc/cron.weekly, and /etc/cron.monthly directories. |
| crontab | Individual users can run the **crontab** command to configure jobs that are run periodically. |
| CUPS (Common Unix Printing System) | CUPS is the default print service for Ubuntu. |
| cupsaccept | The **cupsaccept** command enables a CUPS queue on a specified printer. |
| cupsdisable | The **cupsdisable** *printer* command disables the queue on the noted printer. |
| cupsenable | The **cupsenable** *printer* command enables the queue on the noted printer. |

| | |
|---|---|
| **cupsreject** | The **cupsreject** command disables a CUPS queue on a specified printer. |
| **cupstestppd** | The **cupstestppd** command can be used to make sure a PPD driver is formatted appropriately. |
| **daemon** | A process such as the web service (**apache2**) or DNS (**named**) that runs in the background and executes as required. |
| **Dapper Drake** | Dapper Drake is the code name for the first long term support (LTS) release of Ubuntu, version 6.06, released in June 2006. |
| **dash** | Ubuntu developers are working toward making the dash shell the default shell. The name *dash* is short for the Debian Almquist Shell. |
| **debconf** | The **debconf** command is a preconfiguration option associated with the Ubuntu installation process. It loads an associated preseed configuration file. |
| **Debian import freeze** | The Debian import freeze is the point at which new packages are no longer imported from the Debian Linux unstable (development) repository. |
| **Debian Linux** | Debian Linux is a distribution based on the work of volunteers. Ubuntu is based on the developmental testing packages of Debian Linux. |
| **depmod** | The **depmod** command scans available modules, finds dependencies for installed modules, and maps them out to a file (modules.dep). |
| **DHCP (Dynamic Host Configuration Protocol)** | DHCP clients lease IP addresses for a fixed period of time from a DHCP server on a local network. The BOOTP protocol allows DHCP clients to get IP address information from a remote DHCP server. The standard DHCP server daemon is **dhcpd3**. |
| **diskless client** | A diskless client is more than a "dumb terminal," as it requires a network card, and the BIOS on the terminal is enabled with the Preboot Execution Environment (PXE). Diskless clients are often implemented on Ubuntu systems via the Linux Terminal Server Project (LTSP). |
| **display manager** | A Linux display manager includes a dialog box for your username and password. The default display manager for Ubuntu is the GNOME display manager. |
| **displayconfig-gtk** | The **displayconfig-gtk** command starts the Screen and Graphics Preferences tool for configuring the X server. |

| | |
|---|---|
| **dmesg** | The **dmesg** command lists the kernel ring buffer and the initial boot messages. If your system boots successfully, /var/log/dmesg is one place to look for messages if you think you have boot problems. |
| **DNS (Domain Name System)** | The DNS service maintains a database of fully qualified domain names such as www.ubuntu.com and IP addresses such as 91.189.94.249. If the domain name is not in the local database, DNS is normally configured to look to other, more authoritative, DNS servers. The default DNS daemon is **named**. |
| **Domain Controller (DC)** | A DC is the governing server on Microsoft Windows networks, which includes authentication databases, including Active Directory (AD) networks. With Samba, Ubuntu can be configured as a PDC; with Samba 4.0, you should be able to configure Ubuntu as an AD DC. |
| **dpkg** | The **dpkg** command is the Debian package manager. It is analogous to the **rpm** command on Red Hat–based distributions. |
| **dpkg-reconfigure** | The **dpkg-reconfigure** command reconfigures the options for a currently installed package. |
| **Edgy Eft** | Edgy Eft is the code name for the second 2006 release of Ubuntu, version 6.10, released in October 2006. |
| **Edubuntu** | The Edubuntu release of Ubuntu is associated with educational applications. Edubuntu uses the GNOME desktop environment. |
| **Emacs** | The Emacs editor is a popular text editor that can be run from a text console. |
| **environment** | Each user's environment specifies default settings such as login prompts, terminals, the user's PATH, mail directories, and more. |
| **/etc/apt/sources.list** | The /etc/apt/sources.list configuration file includes connections to remote repositories for package management. |
| **/etc/bash.bashrc** | The /etc/bash.bashrc configuration file is used for aliases and functions, on a system-wide basis. |
| **/etc/bash_completion** | The /etc/bash_completion configuration file specifies default actions for certain commands. |
| **/etc/default/locale** | The /etc/default/locale configuration file specifies current language settings. |

| | |
|---|---|
| **/etc/default/nis** | The /etc/default/nis file is the main configuration file for an NIS server. |
| **/etc/exports** | The /etc/exports configuration file defines shared NFS directories. |
| **/etc/fstab** | The /etc/fstab configuration file defines default mounted directories. |
| **/etc/ftpusers** | The /etc/ftpusers file is commonly used by other FTP servers to configure users who are not allowed access through the server. |
| **/etc/gdm** | The /etc/gdm directory contains GNOME display manager configuration files. The main configuration file is gdm.conf; the customizable configuration file is gdm.conf-custom. |
| **/etc/group** | The /etc/group configuration file contains information for group accounts. |
| **/etc/gshadow** | The /etc/gshadow configuration file contains Shadow Password Suite information for group accounts. |
| **/etc/ldap.conf** | The /etc/ldap.conf configuration file specifies information for an LDAP client. |
| **/etc/lsb-release** | The /etc/lsb-release configuration file includes release information for the current distribution. |
| **/etc/network/interfaces** | The /etc/network/interfaces configuration file includes default network settings for the local system. |
| **/etc/nsswitch.conf** | The /etc/nsswitch.conf configuration file specifies a search order for domain names, usernames, and more. |
| **/etc/passwd** | The /etc/passwd configuration file contains information for user accounts. |
| **/etc/printcap** | The /etc/printcap configuration file contains a list of shared printers for the CUPS and LPRng print services, if so configured in the /etc/cups/cupsd.conf configuration file. |
| **/etc/profile** | The /etc/profile configuration file is used for system-wide environment and startup files. |
| **/etc/rcS.d** | The scripts in the /etc/rcS.d directory are started during the boot process, without reference to a runlevel. |
| **/etc/resolv.conf** | The /etc/resolv.conf configuration file specifies the IP address of DNS servers to search. |
| **/etc/samba/smb.conf** | The /etc/samba/smb.conf configuration file is used for the Samba server. |

**/etc/shadow**    The /etc/shadow configuration file contains information for user accounts, based on the Shadow Password Suite. Passwords in this file are encrypted and accessible only to the root user.

**/etc/sysctl.conf**    The /etc/sysctl.conf configuration file contains kernel configuration parameters.

**/etc/vsftpd.conf**    The /etc/vsftpd.conf configuration file is used for the vsFTP server.

**/etc/X11/xorg.conf**    The /etc/X11/xorg.conf configuration file defines the parameters for the X Window System.

**/etc/yp.conf**    The /etc/yp.conf configuration file specifies information for an NIS client.

**/etc/ypserv.conf**    The /etc/ypserv.conf configuration file specifies security information for an NIS server; it works with the /etc/default/nis configuration file.

**exportfs**    The **exportfs** command allows shared NFS directories to be shared with a network.

**fdisk**    The **fdisk** utility is a standard disk-partition command utility that allows you to modify the physical and logical disk partition layout.

**feature freeze**    A feature freeze is the point at which developers stop introducing new features and focus on bug fixes.

**Feisty Fawn**    The Feisty Fawn code name was used for the first 2007 release of Ubuntu, version 7.04, released in April 2007.

**filesystem (or file system)**    The word *filesystem* has multiple meanings in Linux. It refers to mounted directories; the root directory (/) filesystem is formatted on its own partition. It also refers to file formats; Linux partitions are typically formatted to the ext3 filesystem.

**Filesystem Hierarchy Standard (FHS)**    The Filesystem Hierarchy Standard (FHS) is the official way to organize files in Unix and Linux directories. The top-level directory is known as the root directory (/); users' home directories are configured in /home.

**find**    The **find** command searches for a desired file through a given directory and its subdirectories.

**firewall**    A firewall is a hardware or software system that prevents unauthorized access over a network. It is normally used to protect a private LAN from attacks through the Internet.

**Fluxbuntu**  An Ubuntu derivative that uses the Fluxbox window manager, Fluxbuntu limits itself to free software.

**fontconfig**  The **fontconfig** command is a now-obsolete tool cited in the UCP curriculum for font customization. Fonts can now be configured with the **dpkg-reconfigure fontconfig-config** command.

**forwarding name server**  A forwarding name server refers DNS requests to other DNS servers.

**Free Software Foundation (FSF)**  The Free Software Foundation is a nonprofit foundation. Per www.fsf.org, the FSF was formed to "promote computer user freedom and to defend the rights of all free software users." Much Linux software was cloned from Unix courtesy of the efforts of the FSF.

**Fridge**  Ubuntu's The Fridge provides "news, grassroots marketing, advocacy, team collaboration, and great original content." Available at http://fridge.ubuntu.com, it's essentially a community news site, detailing release announcements, conference events, hot new features, project reports, and more.

**fsck**  The **fsck** command checks the filesystem on a Linux partition for consistency. It should never be run on a mounted partition.

**FTP (File Transfer Protocol)**  The FTP protocol is a TCP/IP protocol designed to optimize file transfer between computers.

**gateway**  A gateway is a route from a computer to another network. A default gateway address is the IP address of a computer or router that connects a LAN with another network such as the Internet.

**gdmsetup**  The **gdmsetup** command opens the Login Window Preferences tool to configure the GNOME display manager login screen.

**GNOME**  GNOME is the default GUI desktop for Ubuntu, sometimes known by its acronym, GNU Network Object Model Environment; the acronym may be deprecated in the future.

**GNU (GNU's Not Unix)**  GNU is a recursive acronym, short for GNU's Not Unix. Recursive acronyms are a common jab in the open source community against conformity.

| | |
|---|---|
| **Gobuntu** | The Gobuntu release of Ubuntu is limited to open source software; it specifies GNOME as the default desktop environment. |
| **GPG (GNU Privacy Guard)** | GPG is an implementation of the OpenPGP standard included with Ubuntu. |
| **GPL (GNU General Public License)** | The GPL is an open source license developed by the FSF. For more information, see www.gnu.org/licenses/gpl.html. |
| **group ID** | Every Linux group has a group ID, as defined in /etc/group. |
| **groupadd** | The **groupadd** command adds local groups. |
| **groupdel** | The **groupdel** command deletes local groups. |
| **GRUB (Grand Unified Bootloader)** | GRUB is the default boot loader for Ubuntu; the main GRUB configuration file is /boot/grub/menu.lst. |
| **GTK+** | GTK+ is the acronym for the GIMP Toolkit, a cross-platform set of widgets used for creating graphical interface systems for the GNOME and Xfce desktop environments. |
| **Gutsy Gibbon** | Gutsy Gibbon is code name for the second 2007 release of Ubuntu, version 7.10, released in October 2007. |
| **hardware abstraction layer (HAL)** | Conceptually different from the Microsoft version, the Linux hardware abstraction layer (HAL) provides a constantly updated list of detected components. |
| **hardware virtualization** | Hardware virtualization is an abstraction of computer resources, for which many of the tasks are run by specially designed CPUs. Most multi-core CPUs from Intel and AMD can be configured for hardware virtualization through the BIOS. |
| **Hardy Heron** | Hardy Heron is the code name for the second LTS release of Ubuntu, version 8.04, released in April 2008. |
| **hdparm** | The **hdparm** command can help control a number of settings on CDs/DVDs and hard drives, including power consumption. |
| **Hoary Hedgehog** | Hoary Hedgehog is the code name for the second release of Ubuntu, version 5.04, released in April 2005. |
| **home directory** | The home directory is the login directory for Linux users. Normally, this is /home/*user*, where *user* is the user's login name. It's also represented by the tilde (~) in any Linux command. |
| **htpasswd** | The **htpasswd** command helps create passwords for accessing a website on a local web server. |

| | |
|---|---|
| **i386** | The i386 architecture in Ubuntu refers primarily to packages that can be installed on Intel 32-bit CPU systems and clones. |
| **ICMP (Internet Control Message Protocol)** | ICMP is the protocol used for sending online error control messages. It's associated with the **ping** command. |
| **ifconfig** | The **ifconfig** command is used to configure and display network devices. |
| **ifdown** | The **ifdown** command is used to activate a network device. |
| **ifup** | The **ifup** command is used to deactivate a network device. |
| **IMAP (Internet Message Access Protocol)** | IMAP is an e-mail protocol that works on port 143; connections to an IMAP server can be configured through the Evolution e-mail client. IMAP4 is the current standard for IMAP servers. IMAP connections can be encrypted with Evolution, if the server so supports it. |
| **init** | The **init** process is the first Linux process called by the kernel. This process starts other processes that compose a working Linux system, including the shell. |
| **initial RAM disk** | Many Linux distributions use an initial RAM disk in the boot process; it's stored as an initrd.img-`uname -r` file in the /boot directory. |
| **Internet Print Protocol (IPP)** | The Internet Print Protocol (IPP) is the evolving standard for printers shared over networks. It's being adapted by all major operating systems; the Linux implementation is CUPS. |
| **Intrepid Ibex** | Intrepid Ibex is the code name for the fall 2008 release of Ubuntu, version 8.10. |
| **IP forwarding** | IP forwarding occurs when data is forwarded between computers or networks through a computer; it's normally configured in the /etc/sysctl.conf file. |
| **iptables** | The **iptables** command is a packet filter that can regulate access using the ports or other information in packet headers. It is commonly used as a firewall. |
| **IPv4, IPv6** | IPv4 and IPv6 are different systems of IP addressing. Version 4 is what we use today and is based on 32-bit addresses; version 6 is coming online and is based on 128-bit addresses. |
| **iwconfig** | The **iwconfig** command can display current wireless settings and can configure a specific wireless card with network characteristics such as the ID, channel, encryption, transmitted power, and more. |

iwevent   The **iwevent** command monitors the system for other wireless events.

iwgetid   The **iwgetid** command identifies the wireless network ID; also known as the Extended Service Set ID (ESSID).

iwlist   The **iwlist** command lists wireless network interface data, such as channels, transmission power, and authorization keys.

iwpriv   The **iwpriv** command configures detailed parameters associated with a wireless network card.

iwspy   The **iwspy** command measures the quality of wireless link information.

Jaunty Jackalope   Jaunty Jackalope is the code name for the Spring 2009 release of Ubuntu, version 9.04.

JeOS   JeOS is the Ubuntu Server release designed for installation in virtual machines. It includes a specialized kernel as well as minimal memory requirements.

KDE   The K Desktop Environment is a GUI for Linux and Unix computers.

Kerberos 5   Kerberos 5 is a computer network authentication protocol that provides mutual authentication between client and server. It was developed at the Massachusetts Institute of Technology.

kernel   The kernel is the heart of any operating system. It loads device drivers. You can recompile a Linux kernel for additional drivers, for faster loading and to minimize the required memory.

Kernel-based Virtual Machine (KVM)   The Kernel-based Virtual Machine (KVM) is one virtualization technology native to Linux, similar to Xen.

kernel module   Kernel modules are pluggable drivers that can be loaded and unloaded into the kernel as needed. Some loaded kernel modules are shown with the **lsmod** command.

Kickstart   Kickstart is the automated installation system developed by Red Hat that allows you to supply the answers required during the installation process. When properly configured, a Kickstart file can allow you to start your computer and install Ubuntu automatically from a network source.

klogd   The kernel log daemon is **klogd**; it works with the system log daemon, **syslogd**.

Kubuntu   Kubuntu is a version of Ubuntu that installs KDE as the default GUI.

**LAMP**  LAMP is a stack of packages, which is also an Ubuntu Server installation option, that installs Linux, Apache, MySQL, and PHP. LAMP on other systems may substitute Perl or Python for PHP. It's sometimes also known as the LAMP stack.

**Landscape**  Landscape is Canonical's web-based system management service.

**Launchpad**  Launchpad is Canonical's proprietary platform for hosting open source projects, bug tracking, and more.

**lftp**  The **lftp** command starts a flexible FTP command line client.

**Lightweight Directory Access Protocol (LDAP)**  The Lightweight Directory Access Protocol supports a central database of authentication information on a networked server.

**LILO (Linux Loader)**  LILO is an older boot loader available for Ubuntu; it is an alternative to GRUB.

**Linux Documentation Project**  The Linux Documentation Project is a global effort to produce reliable documentation for all aspects of the Linux operating system. Its work is available online at www.tldp.org.

**Linux Terminal Server Project (LTSP)**  The Linux Terminal Server Project (LTSP) supports the creation of diskless clients that connect to an Ubuntu server.

**LiveCD**  A LiveCD is a computer operating system that boots directly from the CD/DVD drive, without being installed on the hard drive.

**locale**  The locale specifies the current localization settings for the system. The **locale -a** command returns available default language options.

**localization**  Localization is the way you customize Linux systems for language, dialect, custom, and country-specific formats such as currencies, character sets, and more.

**locate**  The **locate** command searches through a default database of files and directories. The database is refreshed daily with the **mlocate** or **slocate** script in the /etc/cron.daily/ directory.

**logical extent (LE)**  A logical extent (LE) is a chunk of disk space that corresponds to a physical extent (PE).

**logical volume (LV)**  A logical volume (LV) is composed of a group of logical extents (LEs).

**Logical Volume Management (LVM)**  Logical Volume Management (LVM) allows you to set up a filesystem on multiple partitions. Also known as the Logical Volume Manager.

**long term support (LTS)**   Regular releases of Ubuntu are supported for 18 months. long term support (LTS) releases are supported for three years on the desktop and five years on the server.

**lpadmin**   Members of the lpadmin group in /etc/group are configured by default as print administrators in the Ubuntu implementation of CUPS.

**lpc**   You can use the **lpc** command to scan all configured print devices and queues.

**lpinfo**   You can use the **lpinfo -v** command to display available print devices.

**lpq**   You can use the **lpq** command to view print jobs still in progress.

**lpr**   You can use the **lpr** command to send print requests.

**lprm**   You can use the **lprm** command to remove print jobs from the queue.

**lsattr**   The **lsattr** command lists file attributes.

**lsmod**   The **lsmod** command lists installed kernel modules.

**lspci**   The **lspci** command lists detected PCI devices and associated settings. The **lspci -v** and **lspci -vv** commands provide detailed data on each hardware device.

**lsusb**   The **lsusb** command lists detected USB buses and devices.

**ltsp-build-client**   The **ltsp-build-client** command builds the files required for an LTSP client system on an LTSP server.

**lvcreate**   The **lvcreate** command creates a logical volume (LV) from a specified number of available physical extents (PEs).

**lvdisplay**   The **lvdisplay** command specifies current configuration information for logical volumes (LVs).

**lvextend**   The **lvextend** command allows you to increase the physical volume (PV) area allocated to a logical volume (LV).

**lvremove**   The **lvremove** command is functionally the opposite of the **lvcreate** command.

**main repository**   The main repository includes open source packages supported by Canonical.

**masquerading**   Masquerading enables you to provide Internet access to all the computers on a LAN with a single public IP address.

**MBR (master boot record)** The MBR is the first sector of a bootable disk. Once the BIOS cycle is complete, it looks for a pointer on the boot disk's MBR, which then looks at a boot loader configuration file such as grub.conf to see how to start an operating system.

**MD** MD is an acronym, short for Multiple Devices. Often associated with software RAID devices and the **mdadm** command.

**MD5** MD5 is the acronym associated with the Message Digest 5 algorithm, a cryptographic hash function commonly used to encrypt Linux user passwords for the Shadow Password Suite.

**mdadm** The **mdadm** command manages MD devices for software RAID arrays.

**migrationtools** The migrationtools package includes scripts that can convert authentication databases to an LDAP format.

**mirror site** A mirror site is a server that stores the same information as the original server. Mirror sites are commonly used as alternative sites for Ubuntu repositories and CD/DVD ISO image files.

**mkfs** The **mkfs** command can help you format a newly configured partition. Variations are available including **mkfs.ext3**, which formats to the default ext3 filesystem.

**mksmbpasswd** The **mksmbpasswd** command helps prepare a Linux authentication database for use by Samba, for an NT 4–style database.

**modprobe** You can use the **modprobe** command to control device modules to be installed.

**mount** You can use the **mount** command to specify mounted partitions or attach local or network partitions to specified directories.

**mount.cifs and umount.cifs** The **mount.cifs** and **umount.cifs** commands, when properly configured, allow regular users to mount directories shared over a Microsoft Windows network through Samba. Ubuntu configures these commands with the SUID bit for regular users.

**multiverse repository** The multiverse repository includes packages not supported by Canonical and not open source.

**nano** The default text editor for Ubuntu Linux is nano. It's also another recursive acronym and stands for nano's another editor.

netstat — The **netstat** command displays connectivity information for your network cards. For example, the **netstat -r** command is used to display the routing tables as stored in your kernel. The **netstat -a** command lists open ports.

network-admin — The **network-admin** command starts the Network Settings tool in the GUI, which is the Ubuntu tool for administering network cards.

Network Time Protocol (NTP) — The Network Time Protocol allows you to synchronize your computer with a central timeserver. You can do this by editing /etc/ntpd.conf and activating the ntpd service.

NFS (Network File System) — NFS is a file-sharing protocol originally developed by Sun Microsystems; it is the networked filesystem most commonly used for networks of Linux and Unix computers. The default Ubuntu NFS server is the NFS kernel server.

NIC (network interface card) — An NIC connects your computer to a network. An NIC can be anything from a 10-Gigabit Ethernet adapter to a telephone modem.

NIS (Network Information Service) — NIS allows you to share one centrally managed authorization database for the Linux and Unix systems on your network.

nisdomainname — The **nisdomainname** command finds and can assign a domain name for the local system for an NIS network.

nmap — The **nmap** command is a port scanner that supports a review of open ports, which are potential security holes.

open source — *Open source* can refer to the software release technique or use license. Software released under an open source license can be copied and used on other distributions, as long as credit is given to the original author. The source code is included in the open source release, and it can be modified as long as the modified package is also released under the same open source license. (Disclaimer: this is not a legal analysis.)

PAM (Pluggable Authentication Modules) — PAM separates the authentication process from individual applications. PAM consists of a set of dynamically loadable library modules that configures how an application verifies its users before allowing access.

Parallel ATA (PATA) — Parallel ATA is the media standard associated with older IDE drives, also known as ATA (Advanced Technology Attachment).

**paravirtualization** Paravirtualization is a method for supporting virtual machines with a limited amount of resources. It requires an explicit port of an operating system to run, such as a specialized kernel. However, it does not require a multi-core CPU.

**parted** **parted** is a standard disk-partition command utility that allows you to modify the physical and logical disk partition layout. Be careful when using it, as changes are immediately written to the partition table.

**partprobe** You can use the **partprobe** command to reread a recently changed partition table without rebooting.

**passphrase** A passphrase enables a connection using encrypted keys on a server and client. The password is not transmitted over the network. A passphrase is commonly used to secure SSH connections.

**passwd** The **passwd** command changes the password of the specified user.

**PATH** PATH is a shell variable that specifies the directories (and in what order) the shell automatically searches for input commands and files.

**pdbedit** The **pdbedit** command can also be used to add or delete users; it's functionally similar to the **smbpasswd** command.

**PGP (Pretty Good Privacy)** PGP is a technique for encrypting messages, often used for e-mail. It includes a secure private- and public-key system. The Linux version of PGP is known as GPG (GNU Privacy Guard).

**PHP** PHP is a scripting language suited for website development. The acronym is recursive, short for PHP: Hypertext Preprocessor.

**physical extent (PE)** A PE is a chunk of disk space created from a physical volume (PV) for Logical Volume Management (LVM).

**physical volume (PV)** A PV is an area of space created for Logical Volume Management (LVM) that usually corresponds to a partition or a hard drive.

**PolicyKit** The PolicyKit is a tool that supports limited privileges to regular users for administrative processes.

**POP (Post Office Protocol)** POP is an e-mail protocol that works on port 110; connections to a POP server can be configured through the Evolution e-mail client. POP3 is the current standard for POP servers. POP3 connections can be encrypted, if the server supports it.

| | |
|---|---|
| **Postfix** | Postfix is the default e-mail server service for Ubuntu. |
| **Postscript Printer Definition (PPD)** | Postscript Printer Definition (PPD) files are drivers also available for Microsoft Windows systems that can be used for CUPS. |
| **Preboot Execution Environment (PXE)** | The Preboot Execution Environment boots computers over a network independent of local storage devices. |
| **Primary Domain Controller (PDC)** | A PDC is the governing server on a Microsoft Windows NT4 network. You can configure Ubuntu with Samba to function as a PDC or as a member server on more current Microsoft networks. |
| **public/private key** | Encryption standards such as PGP, GPG, and RSA are based on public/private key pairs. The private key is kept on the local computer; others can decrypt it with the public key. |
| **pvcreate** | The **pvcreate** command allows you to configure physical extents (PEs) from a properly configured partition. |
| **pvdisplay** | The **pvdisplay** command specifies current configuration information for physical volumes (PVs). |
| **QEMU** | QEMU, short for Quick Emulator, is a hypervisor. It's also known as a virtual machine monitor, and it provides a framework in which multiple virtual machines can run on the same host system. Several virtualization solutions use the QEMU hypervisor, including Xen and KVM. |
| **Qt** | Qt is nominally the acronym for the Q toolkit; the Q was included for trivial reasons. It's a cross-platform set of widgets for creating graphical interface systems for the KDE desktop environments. |
| **quota** | A quota is used to limit the ability of a user or group to consume disk space. Quotas can be configured by user or group and require configuration on filesystems in /etc/fstab. |
| **RAID (Redundant Array of Independent Disks)** | Ubuntu supports software RAID. You can use the installation program to set up software RAID 0, 1, 5, and 6 arrays. You can also set up RAID arrays using the **fdisk** or **parted** command with **mdadm**. Also known as Redundant Array of Inexpensive Disks. |

**RAID 0**    A RAID 0 array requires two or more partitions or hard drives. Reads and writes are done in parallel, increasing performance and filling up all partitions or hard drives equally. RAID 0 includes no redundancy; if any partition or hard drive in the array fails, all data in the array is lost.

**RAID 1**    A RAID 1 array requires two or more partitions or hard drives. RAID 1 is also known as mirroring, because the same information is written to both partitions. If one disk is damaged, all data will still be intact and accessible from the other disk.

**RAID 5**    A RAID 5 array requires three or more partitions. Parity information is striped across all partitions. If one disk fails, the data can be rebuilt. When a partition fails, parity information can be automatically written to a spare disk.

**RAID 6**    A RAID 6 array requires four or more partitions. Parity information is striped twice across all partitions. If one or two disks fail, the data can be rebuilt. When a partition fails, parity information can be automatically written to a spare disk.

**recovery mode**    When you boot Ubuntu in recovery mode, you're automatically logged in as the root user, without many services. If your Linux system has boot problems, recovery mode may provide a sufficient quantity of tools to fix the problem.

**refresh rate**    The refresh rate regulates the rate at which the image you see on your screen is redrawn, in hertz (Hz).

**release candidate**    A release candidate is the milestone in the development cycle where a production quality prerelease is made.

**reportbug-ng**    The **reportbug-ng** command is a search tool for Ubuntu bugs.

**repository**    A repository for Ubuntu is a dedicated part of a server with Ubuntu packages. Repositories available for Ubuntu include main, restricted, universe, multiverse, backports, updates, proposed, security, and partner.

**Rescue Mode**    Rescue Mode is an option available from the Ubuntu installation CD, which loads a fully functional version of Linux, with access to local hard disks.

**resize2fs**    The **resize2fs** command allows you to increase the size of a filesystem; often used after increasing the space associated with a LV.

**restricted repository**   The restricted repository includes packages supported by Canonical that are not open source.

**reverse (inverse) zone**   A DNS reverse (inverse) zone can be required by some servers, such as Apache and sendmail, to make sure an IP address points to a real computer. If the reverse zone hostname does not match the IP address, the server might not respond.

**rndc**   The **rndc** command can be used to start, stop, and restart the DNS service—as well as reread the configuration file.

**root**   This word has multiple meanings in Linux. The *root user* is the default administrative user. The *root directory* (/) is the top-level directory in Linux. The root user's home directory, /root, is a subdirectory of the root directory (/). In the GRUB configuration file, the first root directive specifies the partition with the /boot directory; the second root directive specifies the volume with the top-level root directory (/).

**route**   The **route** command is associated with routing tables. The command can be used with or without the **-n** switch and is equivalent to **netstat -r**.

**rpcinfo**   The **rpcinfo** command reports remote procedure call (RPC) information; commonly associated with NIS and NFS.

**rsync**   The **rsync** command is used to synchronize local and remote groups of files and is frequently used for backups or small changes to large repositories.

**runlevel**   A now obsolete construct for Linux, the runlevel was used to organize services with different functionality.

**Samba**   Samba is the Linux and Unix implementation of the Server Message Block protocol and the Common Internet File System (CIFS). It allows computers that run Linux and Unix to communicate with computers that run Microsoft Windows operating systems.

**Secure Shell (SSH)**   The Secure Shell service is a network protocol that enables secure communication over a network; it's implemented in Ubuntu with the openssh-server package.

**secure virtual hosts**   As with regular virtual hosts, you can configure multiple secure virtual hosts on a single Apache server.

**sendmail**   A standard e-mail server application used by most Internet e-mail. It's different from Sendmail, which is a commercial e-mail server application not installed on Ubuntu.

| | |
|---|---|
| sendmailconfig | The **sendmailconfig** command is a script that processes macro and database files in the /etc/mail directory for use by the sendmail e-mail server. |
| Serial ATA (SATA) | A newer standard on hard drives that facilitates faster communication and more reliable operation, SATA drives have device file labels similar to SCSI; for example, the first SATA drive is known as /dev/sda. |
| SGID | The SGID bit sets common group ID permissions on a file or directory. |
| Shadow Password Suite | The Shadow Password Suite creates an additional layer of protection for Linux users and groups in the /etc/shadow and /etc/gshadow files; passwords in these files are encrypted using the MD5 algorithm. |
| shadowconfig | The **shadowconfig** command can activate or deactivate the Shadow Password Suite. |
| shell | A shell provides a command line interface. |
| ShipIt | ShipIt is Ubuntu's free CD distribution and shipping service that allows anyone to request and receive physical copies of the Ubuntu distribution by postal mail. ShipIt is part of Ubuntu's technical infrastructure. |
| showmount | The **showmount** command lists the shared directories from an NFS server. |
| Shuttleworth, Mark | Mark Shuttleworth is the founder of Canonical, Ltd., which is dedicated to promoting certain free software projects, including Ubuntu. |
| slave (secondary master) name server | A slave name server performs many of the functions of a DNS server, relying on a master DNS server for data on the authoritative zone. |
| smbclient | The **smbclient** command can browse shared Samba directories. |
| smbpasswd | The **smbpasswd** command helps you create usernames and passwords for a Samba (Microsoft Windows) network. |
| SMTP (Simple Mail Transfer Protocol) | SMTP is a TCP/IP protocol for sending mail; used by sendmail and Postfix. SMTP connections can be encrypted. |

| | |
|---|---|
| **sticky bit** | The sticky bit on a directory allows files therein to be managed by the file owner. |
| **Structured Query Language (SQL)** | SQL is the basis for several database systems, including some that can be run on Linux, including MySQL and PostgreSQL. |
| **su** | The **su** command supports a move to a different user account from the command line. |
| **sudo** | The **sudo** command supports administrative access as configured in /etc/sudoers. It's the primary means for administering Ubuntu systems from the command line interface. |
| **sudoedit** | The **sudoedit** command edits a specified file based on administrative access rights as configured in /etc/sudoers; equivalent to **sudo -e**. |
| **SUID** | The SUID bit sets common user ID permissions on a file or directory. |
| **superuser (super user)** | The superuser represents a regular user who has taken root user privileges. Closely associated with the **su** and **sudo** commands. |
| **swap space** | Linux uses swap space for less frequently used data that would otherwise be stored in RAM. It is normally configured in Linux in a swap partition. |
| **Synaptic Package Manager** | The Synaptic Package Manager is a front end to several of the **apt-\*** commands, including **apt-get**, **apt-cdrom**, and **apt-cache**, which provide a visual overview of available packages. |
| **sysctl** | The **sysctl** command can be used to configure kernel parameters using the /etc/sysctl.conf configuration file; the **sysctl -p** rereads changes to that file. |
| **syslogd** | The system log daemon is **syslogd**; it works with the kernel log daemon, **klogd**. |
| **system-config-printer** | The **system-config-printer** command starts the Ubuntu printer configuration tool in a GUI desktop. |
| **tar** | The tape archive command, **tar**, can package or unpackage groups of files to or from a single compressible archive. |
| **Task Selector** | The Task Selector is a console-based tool that can be used to install or remove groups of packages. However, removing package groups with this tool is not recommended. It can be started with the **tasksel** command. |

| | |
|---|---|
| **TCP Wrappers** | TCP Wrappers is a security system that can regulate access to services that communicate with TCP packets. Such services are regulated in the /etc/hosts.allow and /etc/hosts.deny configuration files. |
| **Telnet** | A terminal emulation program associated with the **telnet** command, Telnet allows you to connect to remote computers. |
| **testparm** | The **testparm** command can be used as a syntax checker for the Samba configuration file, /etc/samba/smb.conf. |
| **Trivial File Transfer Protocol (TFTP)** | The Trivial File Transfer Protocol (TFTP) is a file-sharing service, similar to FTP. |
| **ubuntu** | Ubuntu is an old African word that roughly translates as "humanity toward others." |
| **Ubuntu Security Notices (USN)** | Ubuntu Security Notices (USN) are designed to help the administrator understand whether a security update is needed. The latest USN are available from www.ubuntu.com/usn. |
| **Ubuntu Server** | The release of Ubuntu focused on server applications. A GUI is not installed by default in Ubuntu Server. |
| **umask** | The **umask** command defines default permissions for newly created files. |
| **Universal Resource Identifier (URI)** | The Universal Resource Identifier (URI) is a superset of the well-known Universal Resource Locator (URL), commonly used for CUPS printer addresses and LDAP databases. |
| **universe repository** | The Ubuntu universe repository includes open source packages *not* supported by Canonical. |
| **update-alternatives** | The **update-alternatives** command configures files in the /etc/alternatives directory. For example, to configure the default editor on my system, I run the **sudo update-alternatives --config editor** command. |
| **Update Manager** | The Update Manager is a GUI tool that compares the current list of packages against the local database that lists available updates. |
| **Upstart** | Upstart is a series of scripts and configuration files that replace the init daemon and the /etc/inittab configuration file. |
| **user ID (UID)** | Every Linux user has a user ID, as defined in /etc/passwd. |
| **User Interface Freeze** | The User Interface Freeze is the development milestone when changes to the look, feel, and functionality of the GUI and related applications are frozen. |

| | |
|---|---|
| **useradd** | The **useradd** command adds local users. |
| **userdel** | The **userdel** command deletes local users. |
| **usermod** | The **usermod** command modifies different settings in /etc/passwd, such as expiration date and additional groups. |
| **users-admin** | The **users-admin** command starts the Users Settings tool in the GUI, which is the Ubuntu tool for administering users and groups. |
| **UTC** | For our purposes, UTC is the same as Greenwich Mean Time or US military Zulu time. The UTC acronym is based on a political compromise. |
| **UUID** | The UUID is the Universally Unique Identifier, associated with the partition, RAID device, or logical volume configured for a certain directory. It is often used to identify filesystems in the /etc/fstab configuration file. |
| **Very Secure FTP (vsFTP)** | The Very Secure FTP service is a commonly used FTP server. |
| **vgcreate** | The **vgcreate** command creates a volume group (VG) from one or more physical volumes (PVs) for Logical Volume Management (LVM). |
| **vgdisplay** | The **vgdisplay** command specifies current configuration information for volume groups (VGs). |
| **vgextend** | The **vgextend** command allows you to increase the extents or space allocated to a volume group (VG). |
| **vi** | The vi editor is a basic Linux text editor. While other editors are more popular, vi may be the only editor available in certain rescue environments. |
| **vigr** | The **vigr** command edits the /etc/group configuration file in the vi editor. |
| **vipw** | The **vipw** command edits the /etc/passwd configuration file in the vi editor. |
| **virtual hosts** | You can configure multiple websites as virtual hosts on a single Apache server in files located in the /etc/apache2/sites-enabled/ directory. |
| **virtual machine** | A virtual machine is a simulation of a physical computer. Programs and operating systems can be installed and run inside virtual machines, just as they are run on physical computers. Two virtual machines that can be installed on Ubuntu Server Edition are VMware Server and VirtualBox Open Source Edition. |

| | |
|---|---|
| **Virtual Network Computing (VNC)** | Virtual Network Computing (VNC) is a service that enables remote graphical connections. |
| **VirtualBox Open Source Edition** | The Open Source Edition of VirtualBox is the virtual machine manager created by Sun Microsystems, which is also released under the GPL. It's available from standard Ubuntu repositories. |
| **virtualization** | Virtualization is an abstraction of computer resources, most often associated with platform virtualization, in which you can include one or more virtual machines on a physical system. Options for virtualization on Ubuntu include KVM, VMware, and VirtualBox Open Source Edition. |
| **visudo** | The **visudo** command edits the /etc/sudoers configuration file in the vi editor. |
| **VMware** | VMware is a proprietary system with virtualization products freely available to all. |
| **volume group (VG)** | A volume group is a collection of physical volumes (PVs) in Logical Volume Management (LVM). |
| **Warty Warthog** | Warty Warthog is the code name for the first release of Ubuntu, version 4.10, released in October 2004. |
| **wildcard** | A wildcard is a special character used to substitute for others in an alphanumeric phrase; users and administrators can use wildcards in a single expression to specify multiple filenames and directives. |
| **window manager** | The window manager is a special type of X client that controls how other X clients appear on your display. |
| **WINS (Windows Internet Name Service)** | WINS provides name resolution on Microsoft networks; it can be activated on Samba. |
| **X client** | An X client is an application that uses the X server services to display output. |
| **X server** | The X server is the part of the X Window System that runs on a desktop. The X server draws images on a local screen, takes input from the local keyboard and mouse, and controls access to the local display. |
| **X Window System** | The X Window System is a GUI for Linux. Unlike other applications, the X Window System is a layered application. |
| **XDMCP** | XDMCP is short for the X Display Manager Control Protocol, which is designed for remote graphical logins. |

**Xfce Desktop**   Xfce is a GUI desktop environment that is the default for Xubuntu; Xfce is not currently an acronym.

**X.org**   The X.org server is the default X server for Ubuntu.

**Xubuntu**   Xubuntu is a version of Ubuntu that installs the Xfce desktop as the default GUI.

**ypbind**   The NIS client service is **ypbind**.

**ypserv**   The NIS server service is **ypserv**.

# INDEX

**G**

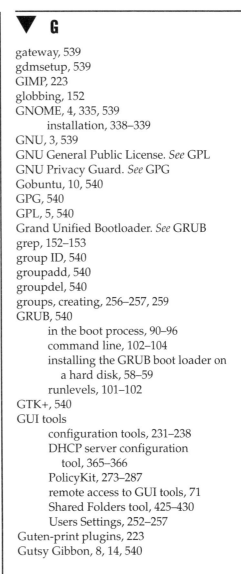 **H**

**I**

▼ **M**

## ▼ N

**O**

 **P**

**T**

**W**

**X**

 **Y**